Stan Lee
presents:

THE ESSENTIAL

IRON MAN

VOLUME 1

IRON MAN
STORIES
FROM
**TALES OF
SUSPENSE
#39-72**

ESSENTIAL IRON MAN® Vol. 1 No. 1, November, 2000. Contains material originally published in magazine form as TALES OF SUSPENSE #'s 39-72. Published by MARVEL COMICS., Bill Jemas, President; Bob Harras, Editor-in-Chief: Stan Lee, Chairman Emeritus. OFFICE OF PUBLICATION: 387 PARK AVENUE SOUTH, NEW YORK, N.Y. 10016. Copyright © 1962, 1963, 1964, 1965 and 2000. Marvel Characters, Inc. All rights reserved. ESSENTIAL IRON MAN (including all prominent characters featured in this issue and the distinctive likenesses thereof) is a registered trademark of MARVEL CHARACTERS, INC. No part of this book may be printed or reproduced in any manner without the written permission of the publisher. Printed in the U.S.A. First Printing, November, 2000. ISBN #0-7851-0759-2. GST. #R127032852. MARVEL COMICS is a division of MARVEL ENTERPRISES, INC. Peter Cuneo, Chief Executive Officer; Avi Arad, Chief Creative Officer.

10 9 8 7 6 5 4 3 2 1

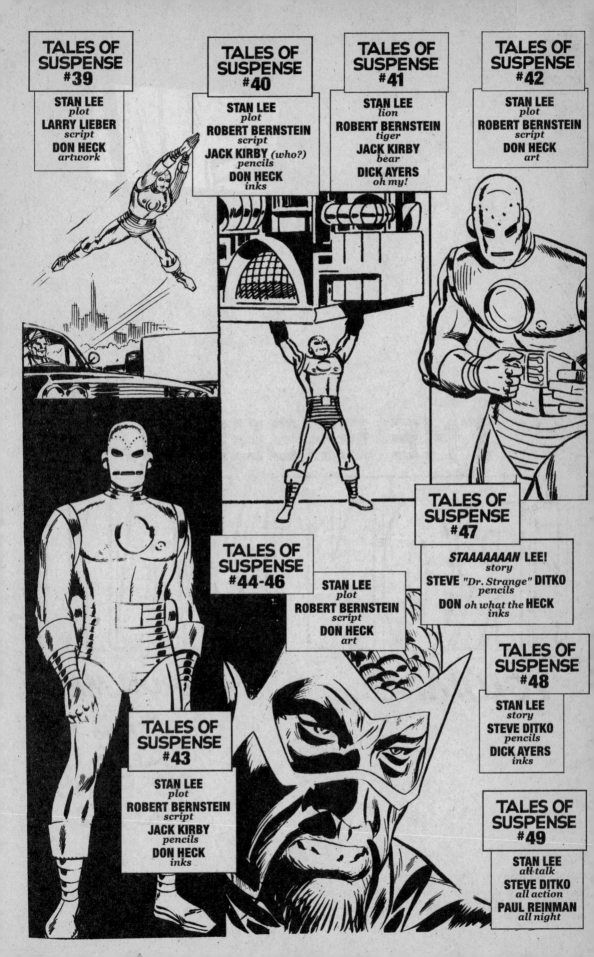

TALES OF SUSPENSE #39

STAN LEE
plot
LARRY LIEBER
script
DON HECK
artwork

TALES OF SUSPENSE #40

STAN LEE
plot
ROBERT BERNSTEIN
script
JACK KIRBY *(who?)*
pencils
DON HECK
inks

TALES OF SUSPENSE #41

STAN LEE
lion
ROBERT BERNSTEIN
tiger
JACK KIRBY
bear
DICK AYERS
oh my!

TALES OF SUSPENSE #42

STAN LEE
plot
ROBERT BERNSTEIN
script
DON HECK
art

TALES OF SUSPENSE #47

STAAAAAAAN LEE!
story
STEVE *"Dr. Strange"* DITKO
pencils
DON *oh what the* HECK
inks

TALES OF SUSPENSE #44-46

STAN LEE
plot
ROBERT BERNSTEIN
script
DON HECK
art

TALES OF SUSPENSE #48

STAN LEE
story
STEVE DITKO
pencils
DICK AYERS
inks

TALES OF SUSPENSE #43

STAN LEE
plot
ROBERT BERNSTEIN
script
JACK KIRBY
pencils
DON HECK
inks

TALES OF SUSPENSE #49

STAN LEE
all-talk
STEVE DITKO
all action
PAUL REINMAN
all night

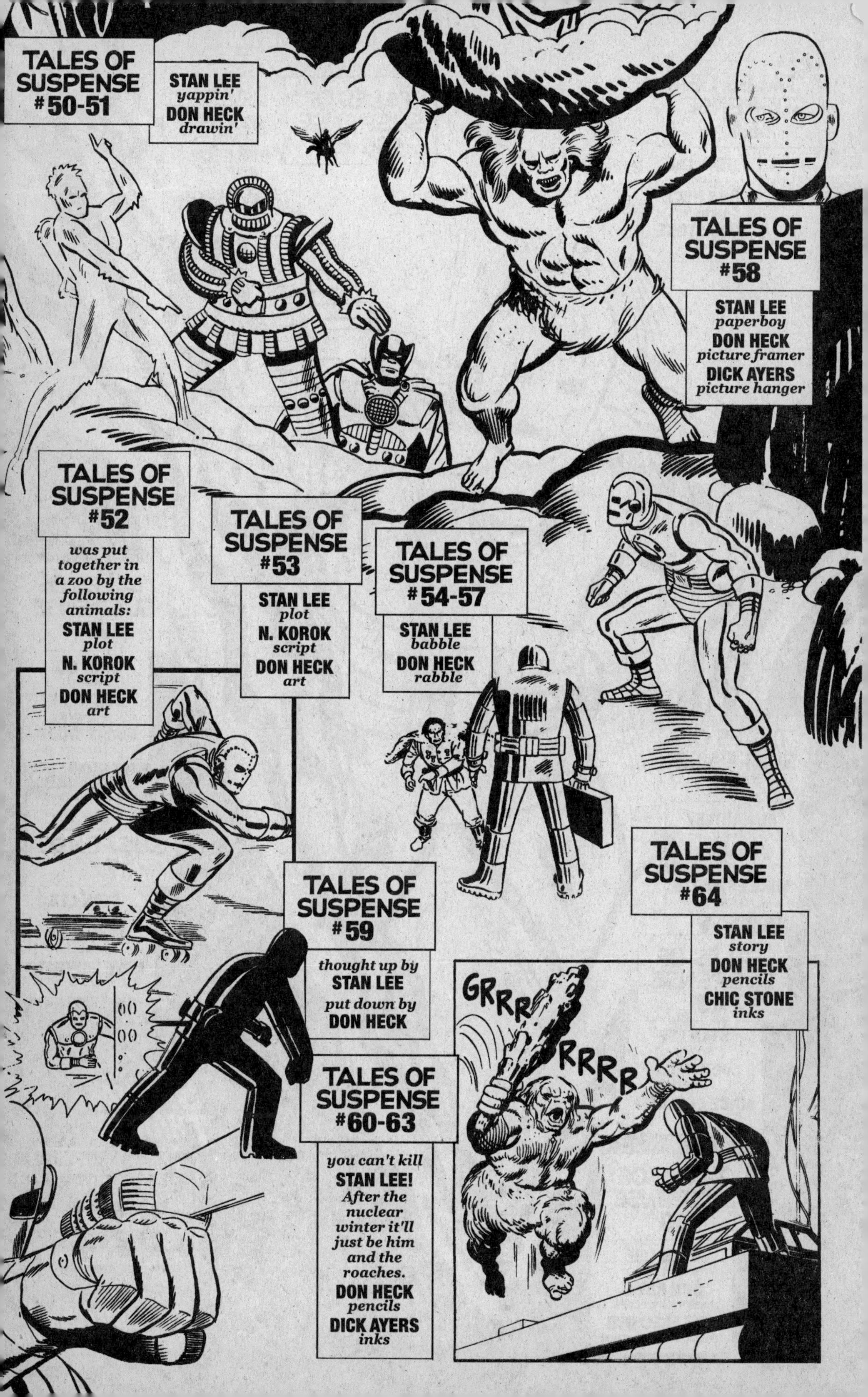
TALES OF SUSPENSE #50-51
STAN LEE yappin'
DON HECK drawin'
TALES OF SUSPENSE #58
STAN LEE paperboy
DON HECK picture framer
DICK AYERS picture hanger
TALES OF SUSPENSE #52
was put together in a zoo by the following animals:
STAN LEE plot
N. KOROK script
DON HECK art
TALES OF SUSPENSE #53
STAN LEE plot
N. KOROK script
DON HECK art
TALES OF SUSPENSE #54-57
STAN LEE babble
DON HECK rabble
TALES OF SUSPENSE #64
STAN LEE story
DON HECK pencils
CHIC STONE inks
TALES OF SUSPENSE #59
thought up by STAN LEE
put down by DON HECK
TALES OF SUSPENSE #60-63
you can't kill STAN LEE! After the nuclear winter it'll just be him and the roaches.
DON HECK pencils
DICK AYERS inks
GRRRRRRRR

TALES OF SUSPENSE #64

STAN LEE
story
DON HECK
pencils
CHIC STONE
inks

TALES OF SUSPENSE #65-67

STAN LEE
story
DON HECK
pencils
HEY! who let
MIKE ESPOSITO
in here?

TALES OF SUSPENSE #71

STAN LEE
story
DON HECK
pencils
WALLY WOOD
inks

TALES OF SUSPENSE #68

AL HARTLEY
story
DON HECK
pencils
MIKE ESPOSITO
inks

TALES OF SUSPENSE #72

STAN LEE
story
DON HECK
pencils
MIKE ESPOSITO
inks

TALES OF SUSPENSE #69

STAN LEE
story
DON HECK
pencils
VINCE COLLETTA
inks

TALES OF SUSPENSE #70

STAN LEE
makin' it up
DON HECK
makin' 'em talk
MIKE ESPOSITO
makin' it happen

SPECIAL THANKS:

ROGER BONAS *and*
ALL THE GUYS
at REPRO,
TOM BREVOORT,
editorial assistant
DOREEN MULRYAN,
and the helpful
staff of the
RALPH MACCHIO
PRIVATE COLLECTION

YEAH, BUT WHO LETTERED IT?

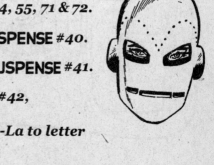

All right already!

ART SIMEK lettered TALES OF SUSPENSE #39, 43, 46, 51, 54, 55, 71 & 72.

JOHN DUFFI *put pen to paper on* TALES OF SUSPENSE #40.

MARTY EPP *is the guilty party on* TALES OF SUSPENSE #41.

E. THOMAS *whipped out* TALES OF SUSPENSE #42, *and*
SAM ROSEN *gave up his weekends in Shangri-La to letter* TALES OF SUSPENSE #44, 45, 47-49, 52 and 53; *the back-up story in* TALES OF SUSPENSE #55, 56-58, and 60-70.

RAY HOLLOWAY *lent his hand to* TALES OF SUSPENSE #50, *and*
NOBODY *took the credit for* TALES OF SUSPENSE #59, *which is a shame, because it looks terrific.*

AND THE REPRINT SPECIALISTS:

BRUCE TIMM
cover art

THE BUCCE
cover color

JONATHAN BABCOCK
interior design & touch-ups

SUZANNE GAFFNEY and **THOMAS VELAZQUEZ**
cover design

POLLY WATSON
reprint editor

BOB HARRAS
editor in chief

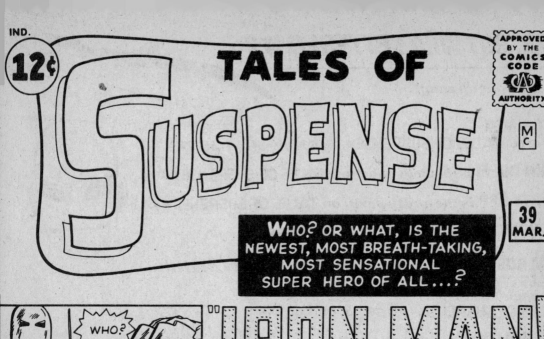

IND.

12¢

39 MAR.

APPROVED BY THE COMICS CODE AUTHORITY

TALES OF SUSPENSE

WHO? OR WHAT, IS THE NEWEST, MOST BREATH-TAKING, MOST SENSATIONAL SUPER HERO OF ALL...?

"IRON MAN!"

HE LIVES! HE WALKS! HE CONQUERS!

FROM THE TALENTED BULL-PEN WHERE THE FANTASTIC FOUR, SPIDER-MAN, THOR AND YOUR OTHER FAVORITE SUPER-HEROES WERE BORN!

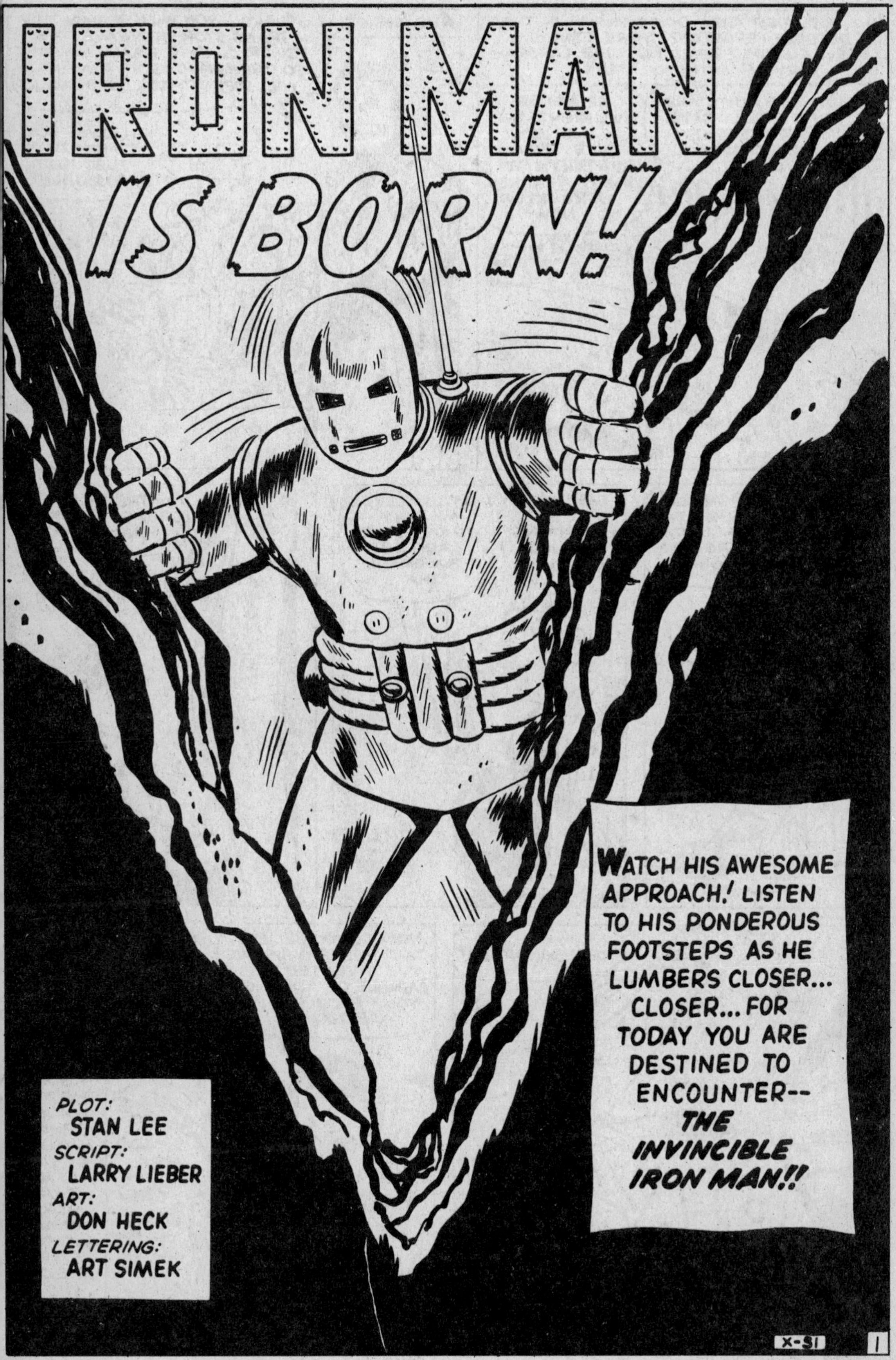
IRON MAN IS BORN!
WATCH HIS AWESOME APPROACH! LISTEN TO HIS PONDEROUS FOOTSTEPS AS HE LUMBERS CLOSER... CLOSER... FOR TODAY YOU ARE DESTINED TO ENCOUNTER-- THE INVINCIBLE IRON MAN!!
PLOT: STAN LEE
SCRIPT: LARRY LIEBER
ART: DON HECK
LETTERING: ART SIMEK
X-51
1

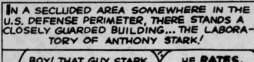

In a secluded area somewhere in the U.S. defense perimeter, there stands a closely guarded building... the laboratory of Anthony Stark!

BOY! THAT GUY STARK MUST REALLY RATE, TO GET A TWENTY-FOUR HOUR GUARD!

HE RATES, ALL RIGHT! THE COMMIES WOULD GIVE THEIR EYETEETH TO KNOW WHAT HE'S WORKING ON NOW!

And, inside...

GENERAL, YOU WILL SEE MY TINY TRANSISTOR INCREASE THE POWER OF THIS SMALL MAGNET SO TREMENDOUSLY THAT IT WILL OPEN THAT LOCKED VAULT!

OH, COME NOW, STARK! THAT JUST ISN'T POSSIBLE!

THINK SO? THERE! I'VE SWITCHED ON THE TRANSISTOR! IT'S ENERGIZING THE MAGNET!

CLICK

THE DOOR --IT'S BEGINNING TO BUDGE!

NATURALLY! MY TINY TRANSISTORS ARE SO POWERFUL THAT...

--THEY CAN INCREASE THE FORCE OF ANY DEVICE...

URRRRHHHHHH

URRRHHHHH

--A THOUSANDFOLD!

CRACK

NOW DO YOU BELIEVE THAT THE TRANSISTORS I'VE INVENTED ARE CAPABLE OF SOLVING YOUR PROBLEM IN VIETNAM?

STARK, AFTER WHAT I'VE JUST SEEN, I'M READY TO BELIEVE ANYTHING!

YES, IT WAS AN AMAZING DEMONSTRATION! BUT NOW, LET US LEARN MORE ABOUT THE MAN WHOSE GENIUS MADE IT POSSIBLE! LET US LEARN MORE ABOUT ANTHONY STARK, THE ONE WHO IS FATED TO BECOME... IRON MAN!

2

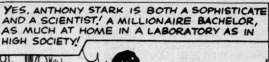

ANTHONY STARK... RICH, HANDSOME, KNOWN AS A GLAMOROUS PLAYBOY, CONSTANTLY IN THE COMPANY OF BEAUTIFUL, ADORING WOMEN...

LOOK! THERE'S TONY STARK!

UMMMNN... HE'S THE DREAMIEST THING THIS SIDE OF ROCK HUDSON!

THE RIVIERA WAS A REAL DRAG TILL **YOU** SHOWED UP, DARLING!

YES, ANTHONY STARK IS BOTH A SOPHISTICATE AND A SCIENTIST! A MILLIONAIRE BACHELOR, AS MUCH AT HOME IN A LABORATORY AS IN HIGH SOCIETY!

BUT, THIS MAN WHO SEEMS SO FORTUNATE, WHO'S ENVIED BY MILLIONS -- IS SOON DESTINED TO BECOME THE MOST TRAGIC FIGURE ON EARTH!

OUR TALE REALLY HAS ITS BEGINNING HALFWAY AROUND THE WORLD, IN A SOUTH VIETNAM JUNGLE, MENACED BY **WONG-CHU**, THE RED GUERRILLA TYRANT!

HAH! I HAVE BROUGHT **ANOTHER** VILLAGE TO ITS KNEES!

NOW FOR THE WRESTLING MATCH! IF ANY PRISONER CAN DEFEAT WONG-CHU, I FREE WHOLE VILLAGE!

DESPERATE TO SAVE THEIR VILLAGE, THE STRONGEST OF THE NATIVES ACCEPTS THE WAR LORD'S CHALLENGE...

AH, YOU ARE GOOD! BUT WONG-CHU **BETTER!**

ANOTHER, AND ANOTHER, TRIES IN VAIN...

I AM STRONGEST OF ALL! NEXT TO **WONG-CHU** OTHER MEN ARE BUT **FLEAS!**

IT IS OVER! NOW LET US PLUNDER THE TOWN! FOR **NONE** CAN STOP THE VICTORIOUS WONG-CHU!

3

MEANWHILE, ON THE OUTSKIRTS OF THE JUNGLE...

THE RED GUERRILLAS OUTNUMBER US! OUR HEAVY ARTILLERY COULD BEAT THEM, BUT WE CAN'T TRANSPORT SUCH BIG WEAPONS THROUGH THE DENSE JUNGLE!

SO, THAT'S WHERE MY MIDGET TRANSISTORS COME IN, EH?

RIGHT! THANKS TO YOUR INVENTIONS, OUR MORTARS ARE NO LARGER OR HEAVIER THAN FLASHLIGHTS! OUR MEN CAN CARRY THEM ANYWHERE!

TAKE COVER! THERE'S THE ENEMY! YOU'LL SEE YOUR GUNS IN ACTION NOW!

THAT'S WHY I WAS SENT HERE! TO MAKE SURE THEY WORK AS WELL AS PLANNED! IF NOT, I'LL FIX 'EM ON THE SPOT!

JUST LOOK AT THE REDS RETREAT!

STARK, YOUR WEAPONS ARE EVERYTHING WE HOPED FOR!

BATTLE-FILLED MINUTES LATER...

THE REDS NEVER KNEW WHAT HIT THEM!

BUT, THE JUNGLE HOLDS A THOUSAND PERILS! SOME NATURAL, OTHERS MAN-MADE...

AND, TRIPPING OVER A SMALL, CONCEALED STRING LEADS TO DISASTER...

BAROOM

A BOOBY-TRAP! OHHH...

MINUTES LATER...

YANKEE CIVILIAN STILL ALIVE! HIM MAYBE IMPORTANT OFFICIAL OF GOVERNMENT! I BRING HIM TO WONG-CHU! MAYBE GET REWARD!

OHHHH!

LATER, AT THE GUERRILLA CHIEF'S HEADQUARTERS...

HIS PAPERS REVEAL HE IS FAMOUS YANKEE WEAPONS INVENTOR! HOW IS HE?

BAD! MUCH SHRAPNEL NEAR HIS HEART! IMPOSSIBLE TO OPERATE! CANNOT LIVE LONGER THAN ONE WEEK!

IN A FEW DAYS SHRAPNEL WILL REACH HIS HEART-- THEN HE WILL DIE! NOTHING CAN SAVE HIM!

YES, HE CAN WORK TILL SHRAPNEL REACHES HEART!

BAH! WE CAN *USE* HIS GENIUS! WONG-CHU WILL *TRICK* HIM INTO SPENDING HIS LAST DAYS ON EARTH WORKING FOR *US!* IS HE STRONG ENOUGH NOW?

WE KNOW YOU ARE AMERICAN WEAPONS INVENTOR! IF YOU DESIGN POWERFUL NEW WEAPON FOR ME, AFTERWARDS I HAVE SURGEON SAVE YOUR LIFE!

HE'S LYING... IF THEY *COULD* THEY'D DO IT NOW, TO BE SURE I LIVE LONG ENOUGH TO DESIGN WEAPONS FOR THEM!

I KNOW I'VE ONLY DAYS TO LIVE, BUT MY LAST ACT WILL BE TO DEFEAT THIS GRINNING, SMIRKING, RED TERRORIST!

ALL RIGHT, WONG-CHU, I'LL DO IT!

I KNEW YOU WOULD NOT HESITATE TO BETRAY YOUR COUNTRY TO SAVE YOURSELF!

HERE ROOM WHERE YOU WORK! PLENTY OF SCRAP IRON! PLENTY TOOLS!

THIS I PROMISE YOU... I SHALL BUILD THE MOST FANTASTIC WEAPON OF ALL TIME!

I'LL *BUILD* IT, ALL RIGHT, BUT IT WILL BE MINE...

--MADE FOR ONLY ONE PURPOSE-- TO KEEP ME ALIVE!

CLICK!

EVERY TICK OF THE CLOCK BRINGS THE DEADLY PIECE OF SHRAPNEL CLOSER TO MY HEART! I'VE GOT TO WORK FASTER THAN I'VE EVER WORKED BEFORE! CAN'T AFFORD A SINGLE MISTAKE!

THEN, ON THE SECOND DAY OF TONY STARK'S RACE AGAINST TIME...

THIS OLD ONE, PROFESSOR YINSEN! ONCE GREAT SCIENTIST! NOW LOWLY MAN-SERVANT OF WONG-CHU... ...WILL *HELP* YOU BUILD WEAPON!

NO! I WILL *NEVER* HELP THE EVIL RED TYRANTS! NEVER!!

PROFESSOR YINSEN, IN COLLEGE I READ YOUR BOOKS! YOU WERE THE GREATEST PHYSICIST OF ALL! THEN, EVERYONE THOUGHT YOU HAD *DIED!*

I'D HAVE BEEN BETTER OFF IF I *HAD!* THEN, EVERYONE THOUGHT YOU HAD DIED! THEN, EVERY-ONE THOUGHT YOU HAD DIED! I WAS PRESSED INTO SLAVE LABOR BY THE REDS, AND WHEN I RESISTED, WONG-CHU TOOK ME PRISONER!

NO LONGER ABLE TO WORK IN SECRET, ANTHONY STARK MUST REVEAL HIS PLAN TO THE AGED SCHOLAR, THE ONLY HUMAN HE DARES TRUST!

AN IRON MAN! FANTASTIC! A MIGHTY, ELECTRONIC BODY, TO KEEP YOUR HEART BEATING AFTER THE SHRAPNEL REACHES IT! WE JUST MIGHT *SUCCEED!* THINK WHAT A CREATURE WE COULD CREATE! WHAT *WONDERS* HE SHALL PERFORM!

AND THE REDS THEMSELVES GAVE US ALL THE MATERIALS WE WILL NEED!

THUS, A DYING MAN'S DESPERATE RACE AGAINST TIME CONTINUES...

I'VE DONE EXTENSIVE WORK WITH TRANSISTORS! I CAN DESIGN THEM IN ANY SIZE TO PERFORM ANY FUNCTION!

WE SHALL USE THEM TO OPERATE THE MACHINE ELECTRONI-CALLY TO MOVE COUNTLESS GEARS AND CONTROL LEVERS!

ALL ACTIVITY MUST BE COORDINATED PERFECTLY! THE IRON FRAME MUST DUPLICATE EVERY ACTION OF THE HUMAN BODY!

IT SHALL, MY FRIEND! IT SHALL! THIS SHALL BE THE CROWNING ACHIEVEMENT OF MY LIFE!

HOURS PASS INTO DAYS, AS THE SHRAPNEL MOVES CLOSER AND CLOSER TO ANTHONY STARK'S HEART...

I CAN FEEL THE PRESSURE! MY TIME IS RUNNING OUT! WE MUST WORK *FASTER!*

THERE! THE SELF-LUBRICATION SYSTEM IS COMPLETED! JUST A LITTLE LONGER! YOU MUST HAVE COURAGE!

AND THEN, WHEN THE DOOMED AMERICAN'S CONDITION BE-COMES CRITICAL -- WHEN HE CAN NO LONGER STAND...

THE LIFE-GIVING HEART OF YOUR IRON BODY IS *READY!* QUICKLY... CLAMP IT AROUND YOUR CHEST!

6

THERE! IT IS DONE! WHEN I ACTIVATE THE MACHINE, YOUR OWN AMAZING TRANSISTORS WILL FURNISH THE POWER TO KEEP YOUR HEART BEATING! YOU SHOULD LIVE AS LONG AS THE IRON BODY OPERATES!

THIS GENERATOR WILL SOON BUILD UP ENOUGH ENERGY TO FURNISH ALL THE POWER YOU'LL NEED TO MOVE!

BUT SUDDENLY...

THE WARNING LIGHT WE INSTALLED-- IT FLASHES! SOMEONE IS APPROACHING!

IT MUST BE WONG-CHU! IF HE ENTERS NOW, ALL OUR WORK WILL HAVE BEEN IN VAIN!!

WONG-CHU MUST BE KEPT AWAY UNTIL THE MIGHTY ELECTRONIC BODY BEGINS TO POWER THE HEART OF ANTHONY STARK!

MY LIFE IS OF NO CONSEQUENCE! BUT I MUST GAIN TIME FOR IRON MAN TO LIVE!

THEN, BEFORE THE REDS CAN ENTER THE ROOM, THE BRAVE PROFESSOR YINSEN MAKES ONE DESPERATE LAST EFFORT...

DEATH TO WONG-CHU! DEATH TO THE EVIL TYRANT!

HE HAS GONE MAD! AFTER HIM! END HIS MISERABLE LIFE! HE IS OF NO FURTHER USE TO ME!

SLAM!

CLICK!

AND THUS THE GALLANT CHINESE SCIENTIST BUYS PRECIOUS SECONDS FOR ANTHONY STARK... WHILE THE LIFE-SUSTAINING MACHINE BUILDS UP MORE AND MORE POWER BEHIND THE LOCKED DOOR!!!

BANG!

IT IS DONE! DRAG HIM AWAY!

YOU WILL NOT HAVE DIED IN VAIN, MY FRIEND! I SWEAR IT! THE IRON MAN SWEARS IT!

7

THEN, EVEN AS PROFESSOR YINSEN BREATHES HIS LAST, THE ELECTRONIC MARVEL BEGINS TO STIR...

THE TRANSISTORS HAVE SUFFICIENT ENERGY NOW! MY HEART IS BEATING NORMALLY! THE MACHINE IS KEEPING ME ALIVE! *ALIVE!!*

AND THE TRANSISTOR-POWERED CIRCUITS ARE COORDINATED WITH MY BRAIN WAVES, JUST AS ANY LIVING HUMAN'S BRAIN CONTROLS HIS OWN BODY!

B-BUT I'M LOSING MY BALANCE!

THUD!

I'M LIKE A BABY LEARNING TO WALK! BUT I HAVEN'T TIME! I MUST LEARN QUICKLY! I MUST GET THE KNACK OF MANIPULATING THIS MASSIVE, UNBELIEVABLY POWERFUL IRON SHELL BEFORE THE REDS FIND ME -- OR ELSE I'LL BE AT THEIR MERCY!

BUT THE BRAIN WHICH HAS MASTERED THE SECRETS OF SCIENCE IS ALSO CAPABLE OF MASTERING ITS NEW BODY! AND SO...

I HAVE THE FEEL OF IT NOW! I CAN STAND-- MOVE-- EVEN *WALK* WITHOUT TOPPLING!

MEANWHILE, OUTSIDE THE LOCKED DOOR...

BREAK IT DOWN! SMASH IT! I MUST LEARN WHAT HAS HAPPENED IN THERE!

WHAM

WH

8

THEY'RE COMING! THIS IS MY GREATEST TEST! CAN THE THING I HAVE CREATED SURVIVE? THE THING WHICH IS LESS THAN HUMAN...YET, FAR MORE THAN MERELY HUMAN! THIS THING WHICH IS NOW-- ANTHONY STARK!!

WHAM

MY BRAIN STILL THINKS! MY HEART STILL BEATS! BUT, IN ORDER TO REMAIN ALIVE, I MUST SPEND THE REST OF MY LIFE IN THIS IRON PRISON!!

BUT, THIS BITTER REALIZATION IS SUDDENLY INTERRUPTED, AS THE IRON MAN SNAPS BACK TO REALITY...

THEY'LL SOON BE THRU THE DOOR... I MUST CONCEAL MYSELF UNTIL I CAN PLAN MY NEXT MOVE!

FORTUNATELY, YINSEN AND I EQUIPPED MY IRON BODY WITH MANY ATTACHMENTS, SUCH AS THESE!

I'LL FASTEN THESE SUCTION CUPS TO MY PALMS AND TURN ON MY TRANSISTOR- POWERED AIR- PRESSURE JETS!

THEY WORK! THEY GIVE ME THE POWER TO SOAR INTO THE AIR!

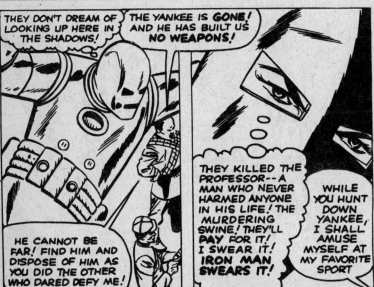

THEY DON'T DREAM OF LOOKING UP HERE IN THE SHADOWS!

THE YANKEE IS GONE! AND HE HAS BUILT US NO WEAPONS!

HE CANNOT BE FAR! FIND HIM AND DISPOSE OF HIM AS YOU DID THE OTHER WHO DARED DEFY ME!

THEY KILLED THE PROFESSOR--A MAN WHO NEVER HARMED ANYONE IN HIS LIFE! THE MURDERING SWINE! THEY'LL PAY FOR IT! I SWEAR IT! IRON MAN SWEARS IT!

WHILE YOU HUNT DOWN YANKEE, I SHALL AMUSE MYSELF AT MY FAVORITE SPORT

THEN, SECONDS AFTER THE REDS DEPART...

YES, WONG-CHU, AMUSE YOURSELF WHILE YOU STILL CAN! FOR OUR MOMENT OF RECKONING IS ALMOST AT HAND!

9

IN THE COURTYARD...
HAH! I WIN AGAIN! NONE CAN DEFEAT THE MIGHTY WAR LORD!

I SAY HE IS A COWARD! I CHALLENGE WONG-CHU!

WHO DARES SPEAK THUS TO WONG-CHU? SHOW YOURSELF! LET ME SEE THE FACE OF THE ONE I AM ABOUT TO DESTROY!

AS YOU WISH, TYRANT! FIRST, I SHALL REMOVE MY CLOTHES--

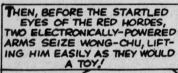

WHY DO YOU STARE, WONG-CHU? WHAT IS WRONG?

HAVE YOU NEVER SEEN AN IRON MAN BEFORE?!

YOU--YOU ARE NOT HUMAN! YOU ARE MACHINE!!

AND YOU ARE A HEARTLESS MAN OF EVIL WHO IS ABOUT TO PAY FOR HIS MISDEEDS!

THEN, BEFORE THE STARTLED EYES OF THE RED HORDES, TWO ELECTRONICALLY-POWERED ARMS SEIZE WONG-CHU, LIFTING HIM EASILY AS THEY WOULD A TOY!

YOU ARE NOT FACING A WOUNDED, DYING MAN NOW...

--OR AN AGED, GENTLE PROFESSOR!

THIS IS IRON MAN WHO OPPOSES YOU, AND ALL YOU STAND FOR!

10

YOU MAKE ME LOSE FACE! I DESTROY YOU!! EVEN YOU CAN BE SLAIN!

GUARDS-- OPEN FIRE!! DESTROY IRON MAN!

IT WILL TAKE MORE THAN SMALL ARMS FIRE TO PENETRATE MY CAST-IRON BODY!

PHANG

KAPOW!

KAPOW!

PAIING

GET GRENADES!! BRING BAZOOKAS!! QUICKLY, YOU FOOLS! QUICKLY!

BUT, BEFORE THE HEAVIER WEAPONS CAN BE BROUGHT INTO PLAY...

I'LL JUST REVERSE THE CHARGE ON THIS MAGNETIC TURBO-INSULATOR...

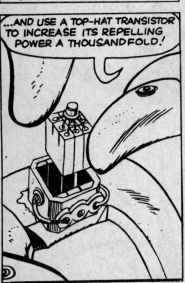

...AND USE A TOP-HAT TRANSISTOR TO INCREASE ITS REPELLING POWER A THOUSANDFOLD!

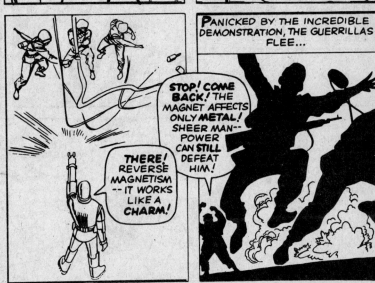

STOP! COME BACK! THE MAGNET AFFECTS ONLY METAL! SHEER MAN-- POWER CAN STILL DEFEAT HIM!

THERE! REVERSE MAGNETISM-- IT WORKS LIKE A CHARM!

PANICKED BY THE INCREDIBLE DEMONSTRATION, THE GUERRILLAS FLEE...

RUSHING INTO THE NEAREST BUILDING, WONG-CHU HEADS FOR THE STAIRS...

UPSTAIRS, THERE IS A LOUDSPEAKER! IN ALL THIS CONFUSION AND NOISE, THEY CAN-NOT HEAR ME! I MUST TALK OVER LOUD-SPEAKER!

LISTEN, MY WARRIORS! TEN THOUSAND YEN TO THE ONE WHO DESTROYS IRON MAN!

AWWKKK WWKKK BBBRRRK!

AN EASY MATTER FOR ME TO CREATE ELECTRICAL INTERFERENCE TO DROWN OUT HIS WORDS WITH STATIC!

11

AND THEN, TO FRUSTRATE THE WAR LORD'S EFFORTS EVEN FURTHER...

NOW I'LL SWITCH MY **OWN** VOICE ONTO THE LOUDSPEAKER!

DESERT WONG-CHU FLEE INTO THE JUNGLE!

WHA--WHAT IS **HAPPENING??** THOSE NOT **MY** WORDS!

NONE CAN DEFEAT **IRON MAN!** FLEE, BEFORE HE SLAYS YOU ALL!!

IN PANIC, AND WITHOUT LEADERSHIP, THEY'LL SOON BE CAPTURED BY SOUTH VIETNAM TROOPS!

HE'S LOCKED THE DOOR BUT THAT WON'T KEEP **ME** OUT!

AND NOW TO SETTLE WITH WONG-CHU!

MY POWERFUL TRANSISTOR MAKES THIS MINIATURE BUZZ SAW INSIDE MY INDEX FINGER-CONTAINER OUT-PERFORM ANYTHING A DOZEN TIMES ITS SIZE!

ZZZZZZZZ

ALL RIGHT, WAR LORD! YOU'RE **FINISHED!** COME DOWN HERE!

YOU MIGHT TERRIFY MY **TROOPS!** BUT NOT **WONG-CHU!**

TAKE **THIS,** MONSTER!

SMASH

NOW TO ORDER THE EXECUTION OF ALL MY PRISONERS!

--UGH!!-- HE WEIGHTED EACH DRAWER OF THIS CABINET WITH ROCKS!

12

BUT NO DRAWERS FILLED WITH ROCKS CAN HOLD BACK IRON LIMBS POWERED BY ELECTRONIC TRANSISTORS!

KNOWING HE'S DEFEATED, WONG-CHU IS TRYING TO MURDER ALL HIS PRISONERS BEFORE HE'S STOPPED! I CANNOT ALLOW THAT!

I'M FREE! BUT IT TOOK ALMOST ALL MY ELECTRICAL POWER! I'VE GOT TO RECHARGE! I'M TOO LOW ON ENERGY TO PURSUE WONG-CHU!

YET, I CAN'T LET HIM GET AWAY! WAIT! I HAVE IT!

UNFASTENING HIS LUBRICATING APPARATUS, THE IRON MAN SQUIRTS OUT A THIN STREAM OF OIL...

I ESTIMATED IT JUST RIGHT! THE PRESSURE'S GREAT ENOUGH FOR IT TO REACH THE AMMO DUMP!

GUARDS! GUARDS! SLAY THE PRISONERS! NOW!

AMM

BARROOM

SECONDS LATER, IRON MAN HAS RECHARGED HIS BATTERIES, AND THEN...

I HAVE SET THE PRISONERS FREE, AND THE REDS HAVE FLED IN BLIND PANIC!

IT'S ALL OVER! NOW, PROFESSOR YINSEN, REST EASY! YOU, WHO SACRIFICED YOUR LIFE TO SAVE MINE, HAVE BEEN AVENGED!

AS FOR THE IRON MAN, THAT METALLIC HULK WHO ONCE WAS ANTHONY STARK... WHO KNOWS WHAT DESTINY AWAITS HIM? TIME ALONE WILL PROVIDE THE ANSWER! TIME ALONE...

THE END

13

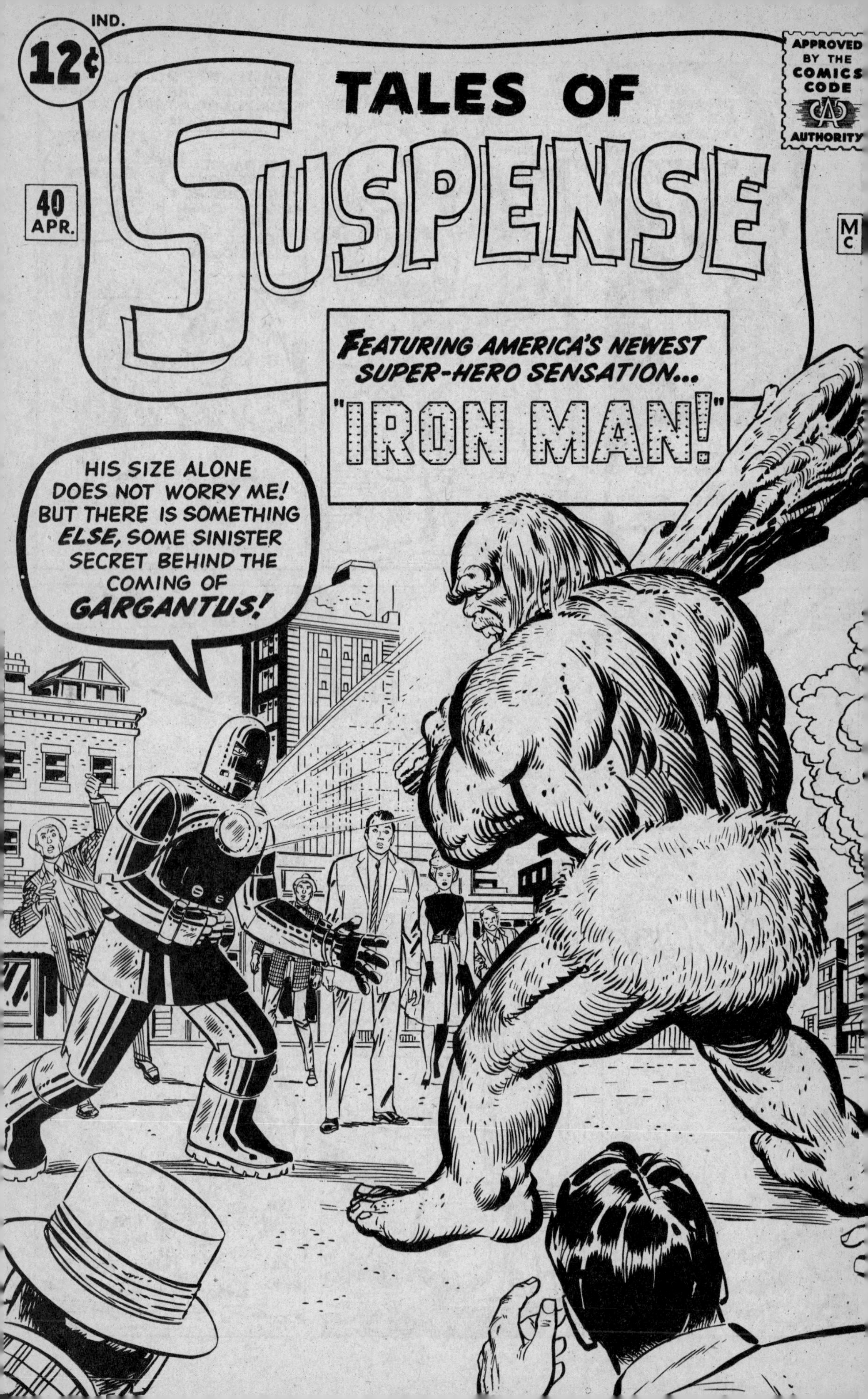
IND.
12¢
TALES OF SUSPENSE
APPROVED BY THE COMICS CODE AUTHORITY
40 APR.
MC
FEATURING AMERICA'S NEWEST SUPER-HERO SENSATION... "IRON MAN!"
HIS SIZE ALONE DOES NOT WORRY ME! BUT THERE IS SOMETHING ELSE, SOME SINISTER SECRET BEHIND THE COMING OF GARGANTUS!

IRON MAN
VERSUS
GARGANTUS!

HISTORY HAS RECORDED MANY A BITTER DUEL TO THE DEATH! BUT NEVER BEFORE HAS THE FUTURE OF ALL MANKIND DEPENDED ON THE GRIM OUTCOME OF ONE ENCOUNTER ...AS IN THE FANTASTIC SHOWDOWN BETWEEN TWO MIGHTY PHENOMENA OF THE PAST AND PRESENT... *IRON MAN* AND *GARGANTUS!*

PLOT: STAN LEE ··· SCRIPT: R. BERNS ··· ART: J. KIRBY ··· INKING: D. HECK ··· LETTERING: DUFFI

ANTHONY STARK IS A MAN WHO LEADS *THREE LIVES!* HE IS RECOGNIZED THROUGHOUT THE WORLD AS A MECHANICAL GENIUS! AT A SCIENTIFIC CONFERENCE IN GENEVA...

MR. STARK, IN THE NAME OF OUR INTERNATIONAL SOCIETY OF PHYSICISTS, I AWARD YOU OUR ANNUAL MEDAL OF HONOR FOR YOUR OUTSTANDING CONTRIBUTION TO MICRO-TRANSISTOR RESEARCH!

THANK YOU, PROFESSOR!

NOR DOES SCIENTIST ANTHONY STARK NEGLECT AMERICA'S COLD WAR STRUGGLE AGAINST THE COMMUNIST MENACE! AT A U.S. ARMY PROVING GROUNDS...

YOU MEAN THESE ROLLER SKATES WILL ENABLE AN ENTIRE INFANTRY DIVISION TO RACE DOWN A HIGHWAY AT 60 MILES AN HOUR?

PRECISELY, GENERAL! THE SKATES CAN EASILY BE CARRIED IN A PACK-- AND ARE COLLAPSIBLE!

THEY CAN BE CLAMPED ON THE SOLE OF A BOOT WITH AN ORDINARY SKATE KEY! BUT WHERE THESE SKATES DIFFER FROM TOYS LIES IN THE FACT THAT THEY HAVE *TINY, TRANSISTOR-POWERED ENGINES* TO *DRIVE THE SKATE WHEELS!*

MINUTES LATER, THE G.I.'s DEMONSTRATE...

INCREDIBLE! INFANTRY CAN NOW TRANSPORT ITSELF ON THE HIGHWAYS WITHOUT TRUCKS! THIS WILL REVOLUTIONIZE TROOP MOVEMENTS! YOU'RE A MILITARY *GENIUS*, STARK!

A GENIUS?

—WHOOSH-HH! WHOOSH-HH!

NO, GENERAL... JUST A SCIENTIST WHO REALIZES THAT THE BOUNDARIES OF SCIENCE ARE INFINITE...

NOBODY IN THE WORLD SUSPECTS HOW IT HAS HELPED *ME!* FOR I'D BE DEAD NOW IF NOT FOR MY SCIENTIFIC KNOWLEDGE!

THE "SECOND" ANTHONY STARK IS A SOPHISTICATED MILLIONAIRE PLAYBOY WHOM BEAUTIFUL WOMEN ADORE...

I'M MAD ABOUT YOU, TONY! WHY DON'T YOU COME TO MONTE CARLO MORE OFTEN SO I CAN SEE MORE OF YOU?

ER-- BUSINESS REASONS, MY SWEET! I'VE GOT INVESTMENTS ALL OVER THE WORLD THAT NEED LOOKING AFTER!

2

"I KNOW *YOU*, TONY STARK! YOUR INVESTMENTS" PROBABLY ALL WEAR SKIRTS AND ARE DYING TO MARRY YOU! YOUR NAME HAS BEEN LINKED WITH EVERY ACTRESS AND SOCIETY BEAUTY FROM HOLLYWOOD TO ROME!

TONY! JEANNE! I'VE BEEN LOOKING FOR YOU! WE'RE GOING SWIMMING!

A MOONLIGHT SWIM! THAT SHOULD BE GREAT FUN! LET'S GO, TONY!

OH...ER--COUNT ME *OUT*, JEANNE! I'VE HAD A HARD DAY, AND A SUDDEN TIREDNESS JUST CAME OVER ME! SO YOU RUN ALONG WITHOUT ME! I'M GOING BACK TO THE HOTEL!

HEY, JEANNE... YOU LOSING YOUR HOLD ON TONY?

WHAT GIRL *DOESN'T*, SOONER OR LATER? TONY PROBABLY HAS A MIDNIGHT DATE WITH SOME *OTHER* GAL! DARN HER LUCKY HIDE!

BUT LITTLE DOES JEANNE, OR ANY *OTHER* PERSON KNOW THAT TONY STARK HAS LEFT THE GAY PARTY FOR A MOST UNUSUAL DATE WITH...AN *ELECTRIC CORD!*

POOR JEANNE! SHE PROBABLY THOUGHT I WAS TRYING TO AVOID HER, BUT I *COULDN'T* GO SWIMMING! I CAN NEVER APPEAR ANYWHERE BARE-CHESTED BECAUSE I CONSTANTLY WEAR THIS *IRON CHEST PLATE!*

JUST AS OTHER MEN PLUG IN THEIR ELECTRIC SHAVERS FOR THEIR MORNING OR EVENING SHAVE, I MUST CONSTANTLY CHARGE UP THIS PLATE WHICH GIVES CONTINUED LIFE TO MY HEART!

MY TICKER WOULD STOP BEATING IF THE PLATE WERE REMOVED OR DIDN'T RECEIVE ITS REGULAR BOOSTER-SHOT! AH!...ELECTRICAL ENERGY IS POURING BACK! NOW I CAN CONTINUE LIVING...TO HELP HUMANITY AS *IRON MAN!*

IRON MAN... YES! *THIS* IS ANTHONY STARK'S THIRD AND MOST IMPORTANT IDENTITY...THE CREATURE IN THE UNBELIEVABLY POWERFUL IRON SHELL, EQUIPPED WITH MANY INGENIOUS ATTACHMENTS, BEFORE WHICH HIS ENEMIES COWER, WHETHER THEY BE GANGSTERS...

FOOL! YOU KNOW SMALL ARMS FIRE CANNOT PENETRATE MY IRON BODY!

HE'S RIGHT! WE *CAN'T* HURT *IRON MAN!*

3

...OR, IF *IRON MAN'S* ANTAGONIST IS SOME MADMAN OF SCIENCE WHO SEEKS TO RULE MANKIND...

GASP! MY SHRINKING RAY ISN'T WORKING!

NO, DOCTOR! I'M JAMMING ITS ELECTRONIC FIRING MECHANISM, WITH ELECTRICAL INTERFERENCE!

NOW, BEFORE I TURN YOU OVER TO THE POLICE, I'LL MAKE SURE THIS LAB NEVER SPAWNS ANOTHER INSTRUMENT OF DESTRUCTION!

AND SO IT IS THAT ANTHONY STARK LEADS A TRIPLE LIFE... IN THE SHADOW OF DEATH! ONE NIGHT, AS STARK TAKES A DATE TO A CIRCUS...

RUN FOR YOUR LIVES! THE *CATS* HAVE BROKEN LOOSE!

THIS IS A SITUATION *IRON MAN* HAD BETTER HANDLE BEFORE SOMEBODY'S *HURT!* BUT I MUST SLIP AWAY TO SWITCH TO MY METALLIC IDENTITY!

QUICK, MARION-- THIS WAY!

MOMENTS LATER...

TONY, WHERE ARE YOU *GOING?*

IS--IS HE ACTUALLY *AFRAID?*

TO A PHONE BOOTH TO CALL THE POLICE RIOT SQUAD! YOU KEEP HEADING FOR THE STREET WITH THE REST OF THE CROWD!

THEN, AS STARK FINDS A DESERTED CORNER UNDER THE GRANDSTAND...

NOBODY--NOT EVEN THE SHARPEST CUSTOMS OFFICER --KNOWS THAT IN MY ATTACHÉ CASE IS A *SECRET, X-RAY PROOF* COMPARTMENT CONTAINING ALL THE PARTS FOR MY *IRON MAN* UNIFORM IN *COLLAPSIBLE* FORM!

EVERYTHING--THANKS TO MY KNOWLEDGE OF MICROSCOPIC TRANSISTORS-- CAN BE UNFOLDED AND ELONGATED INTO MANY TIMES ITS ORIGINAL CARRYING SIZE!

4

... AND SO, IN A MATTER OF SECONDS, TONY IS ABLE TO DON THE COSTUME OF...

...IRON MAN!

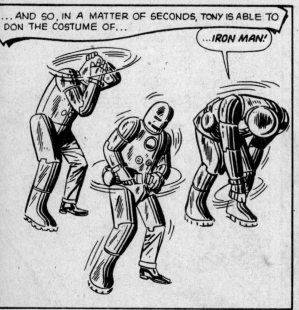

EXACTLY ONE MINUTE LATER...

WAIT! IRON MAN IS HERE! HE'LL TAKE CARE OF THE RAMPAGING ANIMALS!

OH! HOW-- HOW DREADFUL LOOKING HE IS!

UGH! HE LOOKS LIKE A CREATURE IN ONE OF THOSE SCIENCE FICTION FILMS!

MOMMA! MOMMA! ∴SOB∴... SAVE ME FROM THE UGLY MAN!

DAD...PLEASE... DON'T LET HIM COME NEAR ME!

GREAT SCOTT! I NEVER NOTICED IT BEFORE... BUT MY APPEARANCE TERRIFIES WOMEN AND CHILDREN AS IF I WERE A MONSTER!

WHY DIDN'T I REALIZE IT BEFORE? IN THIS DRAB IRON COSTUME, I'M A FRIGHTENING SIGHT TO THE VERY PEOPLE I WANT TO AID AND PROTECT! THEY KNOW I'LL FIGHT THEIR ENEMIES, YET THEY INSTINCTIVELY SHRINK AWAY FROM ME!

I MUST REMEMBER TO ALTER MY COSTUME SO I DON'T LOOK LIKE A WALKING NIGHTMARE! HMM... THAT LEOPARD IS COILED TO SPRING!

I'LL JUST SUBSTITUTE MYSELF FOR THE CAT'S INTENDED TARGET!

CRACK!!

NEXT MOMENT...

UH-OH! THERE ARE SOME OF HIS FRIENDS! SO I'LL TAKE TABBY BY THE TAIL AND...

...AND USE HIM TO KEEP THE *OTHERS* AT BAY!

NEXT MOMENT... *SURROUNDED!* THIS CALLS FOR ONE OF THE MANY *ATTACHMENTS* MY METAL BODY IS EQUIPPED WITH! I'LL JUST FASTEN THESE SUCTION CUPS TO MY PALMS AND TURN ON MY TRANSISTOR-POWERED AIR-PRESSURE JETS!

THEN, AS *IRON MAN* SOARS UPWARD...

NOW TO LAND RIGHT SMACK IN THE MIDDLE OF THE OTHER CATS!

I TIMED IT PERFECTLY! THAT'S RIGHT, KITTENS... HERE I AM! *LEAP* AT ME!

THEN, AS THE BEASTS CLAW ANGRILY AT *IRON MAN'S* BODY...

NOW I'LL TWIST A SMALL RHEO-STAT, STEPPING UP THE ELECTRICAL CURRENT IN MY METAL BODY! THAT SHOULD GIVE YOU THE SURPRISE OF YOUR TOOTHY LIVES!

THIS WON'T *INJURE* THEM, BUT IT'LL TAKE MOST OF THE *FIGHT OUT* OF THEM!

BR-RRTT!

YEOWWRR

THEN, AS THE BEASTS FLEE...

GREAT WORK, *IRON MAN!* THE MAN-EATERS ARE SCAMPERING BACK TO THEIR CAGES!

GOOD!

BUT THIS EXPERIENCE *TAUGHT* ME SOMETHING! I MUST RE-DESIGN MY COSTUME!!! IT'S SUPPOSED TO FRIGHTEN *FOES*-- NOT *FRIENDS!*

6

WE WON'T NEED THE POLICE, TONY! *IRON MAN* HANDLED THE EMERGENCY! BUT I CAN'T UNDERSTAND ONE THING... WHY DOES HE WEAR SUCH A *TERRIFYING* LOOKING COSTUME? HE ACTUALLY *FRIGHTENS* PEOPLE!

REALLY, MY DEAR? WHAT DO *YOU* THINK HE SHOULD WEAR?

WELL, HE BATTLES MENACES LIKE A HERO IN OLDEN TIMES! SO, IF HE'S A MODERN KNIGHT IN SHINING ARMOR, WHY DOESN'T HE WEAR *GOLDEN METAL* INSTEAD OF THAT AWFUL DULL GREY ARMOR?

HMM... WHY *NOT*, INDEED?

THEN, WHEN PEOPLE SEE HIS GOLDEN ARMOR, THEY WON'T PANIC! THEY'LL KNOW HE HAS A HEART OF GOLD AND AN APPEARANCE TO MATCH HIS GOLDEN DEEDS!

YOU KNOW, MARION, I WOULDN'T BE SURPRISED IF *IRON MAN* HIMSELF WERE TO GET THE SAME IDEA!

FINALLY, AT THE BUSTLING AIRPORT...

THEN I'LL SEE YOU NEXT SATURDAY NIGHT ...THAT IS, UNLESS YOU STAND ME UP!

ANY GIRL WHO'D STAND *YOU* UP, DARLING, WOULD HAVE TO BE STARK, RAVING *MA-A-AD!* I'LL TAKE THE 6:50 PLANE FROM GRANVILLE AND YOU'D BETTER BE WAITING!

THAT NIGHT, AT ANTHONY STARK'S LABORATORY...

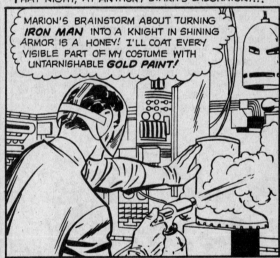

MARION'S BRAINSTORM ABOUT TURNING *IRON MAN* INTO A KNIGHT IN SHINING ARMOR IS A HONEY! I'LL COAT EVERY VISIBLE PART OF MY COSTUME WITH UNTARNISHABLE *GOLD PAINT!*

MOMENTS LATER, STARK SURVEYS HIS HANDIWORK...

WOW! WHAT A DIFFERENCE! LEAVE IT TO A WOMAN TO FIGURE OUT AN ATTRACTIVE APPEARANCE! THE ONLY ONES WHO NEED FEAR ME NOW ARE MY *FOES!*

THE FOLLOWING SATURDAY NIGHT, AT THE AIRPORT...

THAT'S STRANGE!... MARION ISN'T ON THAT PLANE!

SAY, PILOT... DIDN'T YOU PICK UP A FEMALE PASSENGER AT 6:50 TONIGHT IN GRANVILLE?

GRANVILLE?!! HAVEN'T YOU HEARD, MISTER? GRANVILLE SHUT DOWN ITS AIRPORT THREE DAYS AGO! *NO* PLANES ARE ALLOWED TO LAND OR LEAVE!

7

GOSH, I HAVEN'T SEEN AN AMERICAN PAPER IN A WEEK! I JUST GOT BACK FROM AFRICA AFTER COMPLETING A MISSION FOR *IRON MAN!* TELL ME... IS ANYTHING *WRONG* AT GRANVILLE?

WHO KNOWS? THERE *MIGHT* BE ...SINCE THE TOWN HAS COMPLETELY CUT ITSELF OFF FROM THE REST OF THE WORLD!

STARK QUICKLY BUYS A PAPER...

THAT PILOT WASN'T KIDDING! GRANVILLE'S *WALLED IN...* AND NOBODY CAN FIND OUT *WHO* BUILT THE WALL...OR *WHY!* NOBODY, THAT IS, EXCEPT A SPECIAL PAL OF MINE, NAMED *IRON MAN!*

□ GRANVILLE BEACON □
MYSTERIOUS WALL ENCIRCLES GRANVILLE
NO OUTSIDERS ALLOWED INTO TOWN! •••••••
LATEST BULLETIN
GRANVILLE CITY LIMITS

NEXT DAY, OUTSIDE GRANVILLE, AFTER IRON MAN EXPLAINS WHY HE HAS CHANGED THE COLOR OF HIS COSTUME...

THERE'S NOTHING WE CAN DO, *IRON MAN!* THE TOWN HAS THE LEGAL RIGHT TO PUT UP A WALL! NO TRAFFIC CAN GET IN OR OUT! WE'D BE BREAKING THE LAW IF WE BUSTED IN!

SO THE STATE'S HANDS ARE TIED, EH?

WELL, *MINE* AREN'T! I'LL DIG *UNDER* THAT WALL!

LATER, 20 FEET UNDERGROUND...

THIS TINY TRANSISTOR-POWERED DRILL WILL SOON BRING ME UNDER THE TOWN! BUT WHAT WILL I FIND THERE? WHY HAVE THE TOWNSPEOPLE PUT UP THAT WALL? WHY HAVE THEY BROKEN OFF ALL COMMUNICATION WITH THE OUTSIDE WORLD?

AND THEN, TO THE AMAZEMENT OF GRANVILLE'S CITIZENS...

DON'T BE UPSET, FOLKS! I'M *IRON MAN!* WHAT'S GOING ON? WHY DID YOU PUT UP *THAT WALL?*

WE CANNOT ANSWER YOU, BY ORDER OF *GARGANTUS!* IF WE DISOBEY, WE *DIE!*

GARGANTUS?

WE DARE NOT BE SEEN TALKING TO *IRON MAN!* HE'S AN INTRUDER! *ATTACK HIM!!* DRIVE HIM FROM OUR CITY!

YES! GARGANTUS WILL BE PLEASED IF WE GET RID OF *IRON MAN!*

STOP!! HAVE YOU GONE MAD? I'M HERE TO *HELP* YOU! WAIT--!!

BUT, AS THE CROWD'S FRENZY GETS WILDER...

AFTER HIM! DRIVE HIM AWAY!!

CROWD'S NOT NORMAL! THEY *KNOW* I'M NOT THEIR ENEMY...YET THEY'RE TREATING ME LIKE ONE! I *MUST* FIND OUT WHO THIS *GARGANTUS* IS!

THAT

8

WHAT'S *THIS?* THE TOWNSPEOPLE ARE ERECTING A HUGE STATUE...

SUDDENLY, THEY'RE *IGNORING* ME! THEY'RE ACTUALLY BOWING DOWN TO THAT STATUE! BUT *WHY?*

GALLOPING GEARS! IS *THAT* THE GARGANTUS THEY'RE ALL YELLING ABOUT? HE RESEMBLES A PREHISTORIC CREATURE WHO EXISTED 80,000 YEARS AGO -- THE *NEANDERTHAL MAN!*

BUT, WHEN THE CROWD AGAIN RISES TO ITS FEET...

LONG LIVE GARGANTUS!

THERE'S *IRON MAN!* GET *HIM!*

MIGHTY IS GARGANTUS!

THERE'S MORE TO THIS THAN MEETS THE EYES! THIS TOWN IS UNDER SOME SORT OF A *SPELL* -- AND ONE WAY TO BREAK A SPELL IS BY *SHOCK TREATMENT*... SO HERE GOES!

PUSHING A TEN-TON TRUCK IS A FAIRLY SIMPLE TASK FOR *IRON MAN!*

HEAR ME, PEOPLE OF GRANVILLE! THIS IS WHAT *IRON MAN* THINKS OF *GARGANTUS!*

CRASHH!

BUT, EVEN AS THE STATUE TOPPLES...

ALL HAIL *GARGANTUS*, RULER OF ALL MEN!

EVEN THOUGH THE STATUE IS *SMASHED* TO BITS, THEY'RE STILL PAYING HOMAGE TO IT AS IF *NOTHING* HAPPENED!... THEY'RE IN THE GRIP OF SOMETHING WHICH IS STRONGER THAN I THOUGHT!

EVERY CITIZEN SEEMS TO BE IN A DIFFERENT STATE OF *HYPNOSIS!* I'LL BET WHEN THEY ERECTED THAT WALL AROUND THE TOWN, THEY DIDN'T KNOW WHAT THEY WERE DOING THEN, EITHER!

THERE'S ONLY ONE WAY TO LEARN THE *ANSWER* TO ALL THIS! I MUST *FIND* GARGANTUS!

WHOOOSH-H-H!

THEN, AS IRON MAN SOARS THROUGH THE AIR...

EVEN THE TOWN POLICE ARE UNDER GARGANTUS'S SPELL! THEY MUST'VE RECEIVED ORDERS TO KILL ME, AND THEY'RE OBEYING THEM BLINDLY!

BANG!... BANG! BANG!

FINALLY, IRON MAN PERCHES ON A TALL BUILDING...

I'LL SEE IF I CAN GOAD GARGANTUS INTO APPEARING BY BROADCASTING A *CHALLENGE* TO HIM THROUGH THE TINY PUBLIC-ADDRESS SPEAKERS ATTACHED TO MY ACCESSORY BELT!

GARGANTUS! THIS IS IRON MAN! GARGANTUS! THIS IS IRON MAN! GARGANTUS! THIS IS IRON MAN!

I CHALLENGE YOU TO SHOW YOURSELF OR BE BRANDED A COWARD BEFORE THE PEOPLE OF GRANVILLE!

GRR-RR-RR!

AND THEN, AS IRON MAN'S STRIDENT VOICE ECHOES THROUGH THE TOWN, TWO MIGHTY, GIGANTIC HANDS BEND A SUPPLE FLAGPOLE BACK, BACK, BACK, UNTIL...

TWWANNGG!

10

GRRR RRRR

WOW! THAT'S HIM **NOW**...COMING AT ME! HE **IS** A NEANDERTHAL MAN...BUT BIGGER AND BROADER THAN ANY ANTHROPOLOGIST EVER DESCRIBED HIM!

NO **WONDER** THOSE TOWNSPEOPLE WERE MESMERIZED! HIS ENORMOUS EYES ARE LIKE MIRRORS REFLECTING THE SUN! AND NOW...HE'S TRYING TO HYPNOTIZE **ME**, TOO!

BUT, AS IRON MAN **TURNS** HIS GAZE SKYWARD...

WAIT A MINUTE! THERE'S NO SUN TO REFLECT! THAT DARK **CLOUD'S** BEEN HANGING OVER THIS TOWN EVER SINCE I ARRIVED!

THIS **FLAG** SHOULD TELL ME WHAT I WANT TO KNOW!

JUST AS I THOUGHT--IT'S RIPPLING IN THE BREEZE!

OKAY, GARGANTUS ...LET'S PLAY FOLLOW THE LEADER!

I'LL SLIDE DOWN TO THE STREET! BUT I'LL AVOID CRASHING INTO THE PAVEMENT BY REVERSING THE TRANSISTOR AIR-PRESSURE JETS IN MY PALM SUCTION CUPS!

THERE'S **MARION**, THE GIRL I HAD A DATE WITH! **SHE'S** BEEN MASS-HYPNOTIZED, TOO!!

AND HERE COMES **GARGANTUS**... CLIMBING DOWN THE SIDE OF THE BUILDING LIKE A NIMBLE GORILLA! I'LL STAY OUT OF HIS REACH FOR A WHILE!

11

AND SO...

GR-R-R

YOU'RE FURIOUS, EH, GARGANTUS, BECAUSE IT'S SHOWDOWN TIME! IF YOU CAN GET RID OF *ME*, YOU CAN KEEP MASS-HYPNOTIZING GRANVILLE'S POPULATION INTO DOING ANYTHING YOU COMMAND!

YOU CAN ORDER 'EM TO BUILD THAT WALL AROUND TOWN... PASS LAWS TO KEEP THE STATE AND FEDERAL GOVERNMENT OUT... MAKE SOME PEOPLE TURN INTO A SAVAGE MOB...

...WHILE OTHERS ARE COMMANDED TO BOW DOWN TO A STATUE BUILT TO GLORIFY YOUR POWER! WELL, THESE THREE TOP-HAT TRANSISTORS INSERTED INTO THREE MAGNETS WILL *DESTROY* ALL YOUR PLANS!

EACH MAGNET I'M THROWING TO EITHER SIDE OF YOU AND BEHIND YOU NOW HAS ITS ATTRACTING POWER MULTIPLIED BY A *THOUSAND-FOLD!*

YOU CAN'T MOVE ANY LONGER! YOU'RE BEGINNING TO FEEL THE TERRIBLE IRRESISTIBLE TUG OF THE MAGNETS, EACH OF WHICH IS PULLING YOUR BODY IN *DIFFERENT DIRECTIONS!*

SUDDENLY...

YES, GARGANTUS... YOU'RE FALLING APART LIKE THE HUGE *ROBOT* YOU ARE! YOUR TUBES, MOTORS AND GEARS WILL SOON LITTER THE STREETS!

AND THEN, AS THE GIANT ROBOT IS SHATTERED, THE STRANGE PARALYSIS FADES FROM THE TOWN!

¡GASP! WHAT HAPPENED? WHAT'S ALL THIS JUNK?

THE ELECTRONIC REMAINS OF A *ROBOT NEANDERTHAL MAN* NAMED *GARGANTUS!* LOOK SKYWARD WHERE MY SEARCHLIGHT IS PROBING!

MY POWERFUL BEAM CAN PENETRATE THE FAKE CLOUD TO REVEAL WHAT'S FLYING INSIDE IT... A *FLYING SAUCER* FROM *OUTER SPACE!*

I *REMEMBER* THAT DARK CLOUD! IT SUDDENLY PASSED OVER TOWN, AND FROM NOWHERE, GARGANTUS APPEARED...

"HE DROPPED OUT OF THE SKIES, WITH HIS ENORMOUS GLASSY EYES STARING AT THOSE WHO LOOKED UPWARD..."

I AM *GARGANTUS*, THE *MIGHTY ONE!* I HAVE COME TO RULE... FIRST YOU, THEN THE WORLD! HARKEN TO MY FIRST ORDER! BUILD A *WALL* AROUND YOUR TOWN!

WELL, I KNEW IT WAS NO ORDINARY CLOUD WHEN I NOTICED THAT THE HYPNOTIC BEAMS WERE POWERED FROM A MECHANISM *INSIDE* GARGANTUS, FOR THE DARK CLOUD HAD BLOCKED OUT ANY SUNLIGHT THAT COULD BE REFLECTED FROM *GARGANTUS'S* EYES!

ALSO, BY TESTING THE WIND WITH A FLAG, I REALIZED THAT THE CLOUD HAD REMAINED IN A STATIONARY POSITION FROM THE MOMENT I HAD ENTERED GRANVILLE! THEREFORE, IT WAS NOT A *DARK* CLOUD... OR IT WOULD'VE DRIFTED WITH THE WIND!

QUICK! START ALL ENGINES! THE INTRUDER IS TOSSING THE OBJECTS, WHICH RIPPED *GARGANTUS* APART, AT US!

WE'LL EXPLODE TOO, UNLESS I'VE GOTTEN BEYOND THEIR RANGE!

BAH! WE MUST REPORT TO OUR PLANET THAT OUR VISIT HERE WAS A *FAILURE!* THIS PLANET HAS CHANGED SINCE OUR ANCESTORS EXPLORED IT 80,000 YEARS AGO! IT IS NO LONGER PEOPLED BY CREATURES LIKE *GARGANTUS!*

WE COULD CONTROL THE ORDINARY INHABITANTS THROUGH MASS-HYPNOSIS, BUT THEY ALSO HAVE THOSE IRON MEN TO PROTECT THEM! THEY'RE TOO CLEVER FOR US TO CONQUER! SO OUR VESSELS MUST RETURN... LEST WE BE *DESTROYED!*

THERE GOES THE SAUCER! LET'S HOPE THEY'VE BEEN FRIGHTENED OFF-- *FOR GOOD!*

THEN, WHEN THE SAUCER HAS GONE...

YOU MAY ENTER NOW, GENTLEMEN! THINGS ARE NORMAL IN GRANVILLE AGAIN!

YOU BET-- THANKS TO *IRON MAN!*

AND, THE VERY NEXT DAY...

FORGIVE ME FOR STANDING YOU UP YESTERDAY, TONY, BUT A FANTASTIC THING HAPPENED IN GRANVILLE! DID YOU READ ABOUT IT IN THE PAPERS?

ER, NO! I DIDN'T HAVE TIME! I WAS RATHER BUSY *MYSELF* YESTERDAY!

I SURE WAS! I BET NOBODY EVER WORKED SO HARD TO FIND OUT WHAT HAPPENED TO HIS DATE!

15

THE END

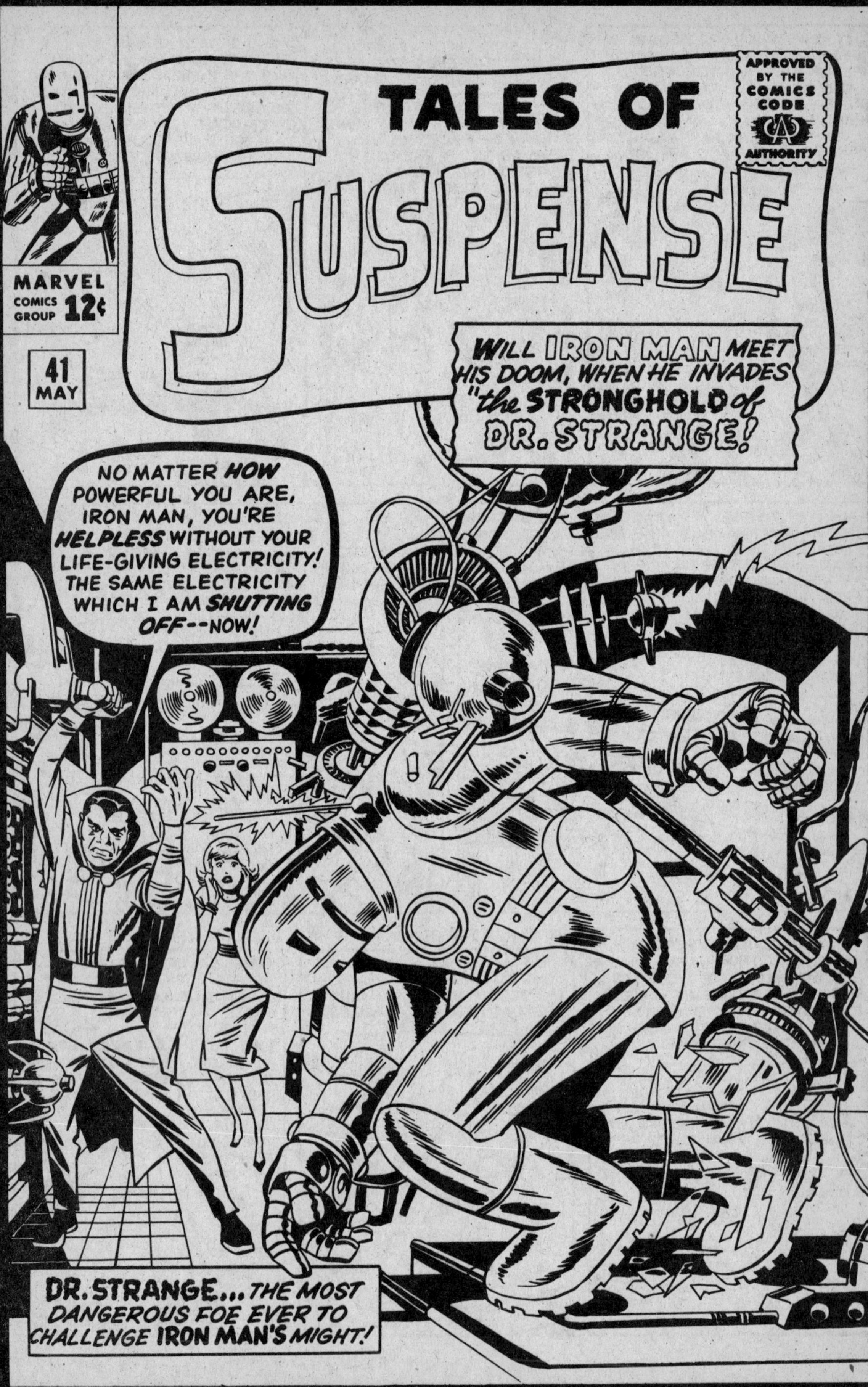

APPROVED BY THE COMICS CODE AUTHORITY
TALES OF SUSPENSE
MARVEL COMICS GROUP 12¢
41 MAY
WILL IRON MAN MEET HIS DOOM, WHEN HE INVADES "the STRONGHOLD of DR. STRANGE!
NO MATTER HOW POWERFUL YOU ARE, IRON MAN, YOU'RE HELPLESS WITHOUT YOUR LIFE-GIVING ELECTRICITY! THE SAME ELECTRICITY WHICH I AM SHUTTING OFF--NOW!
DR. STRANGE... THE MOST DANGEROUS FOE EVER TO CHALLENGE IRON MAN'S MIGHT!

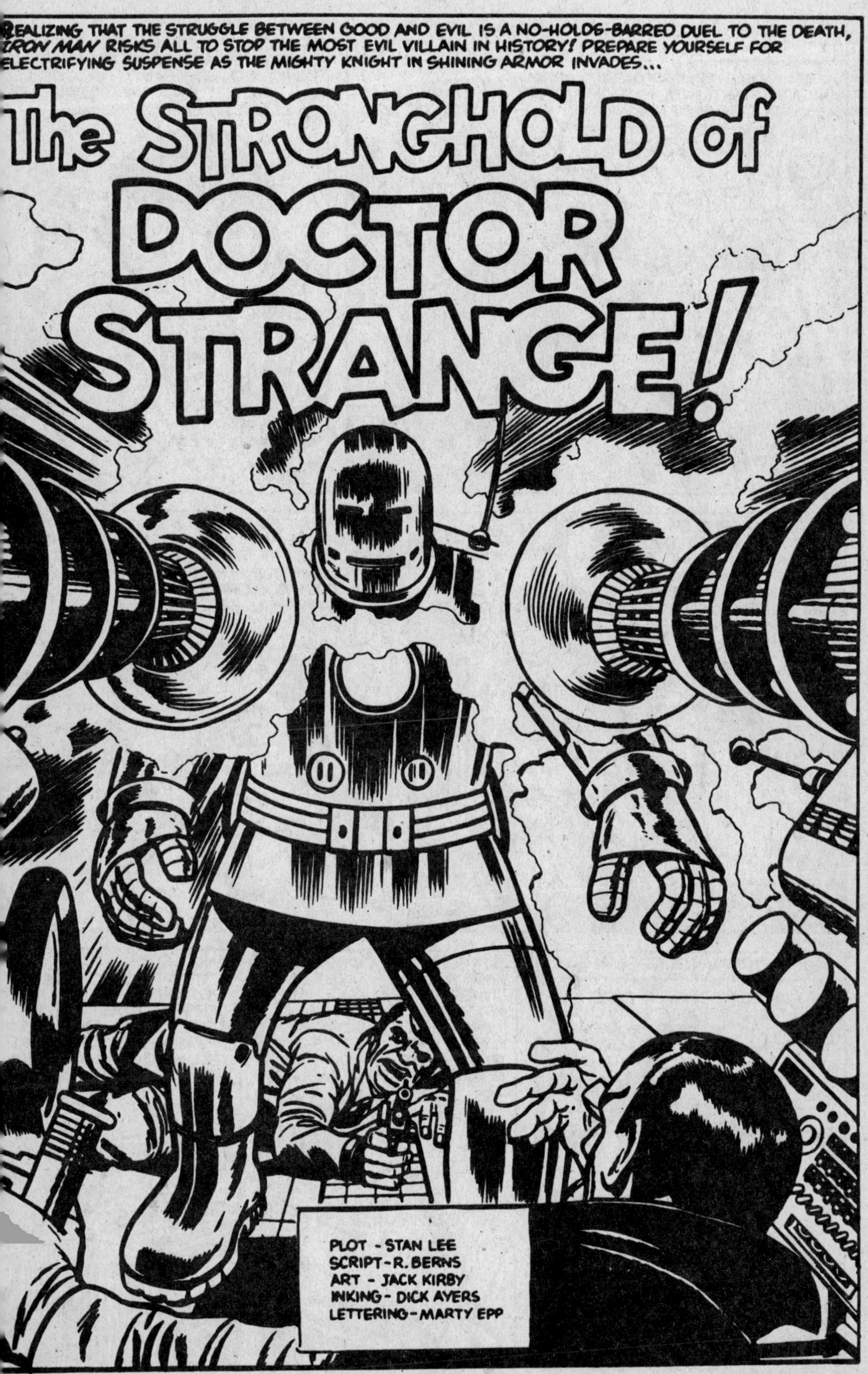

REALIZING THAT THE STRUGGLE BETWEEN GOOD AND EVIL IS A NO-HOLDS-BARRED DUEL TO THE DEATH, IRON MAN RISKS ALL TO STOP THE MOST EVIL VILLAIN IN HISTORY! PREPARE YOURSELF FOR ELECTRIFYING SUSPENSE AS THE MIGHTY KNIGHT IN SHINING ARMOR INVADES...
The STRONGHOLD of DOCTOR STRANGE!
PLOT - STAN LEE
SCRIPT - R. BERNS
ART - JACK KIRBY
INKING - DICK AYERS
LETTERING - MARTY EPP

ONE EVENING, AS MILLIONAIRE PLAYBOY ANTHONY STARK ATTENDS A HOSPITAL CHARITY DANCE...

ATTENTION, EVERYBODY! HERE'S A SPECIAL ANNOUNCEMENT! WILL *ANTHONY STARK* PLEASE STEP FORWARD?

ANTHONY STARK? WHY...THAT'S *YOU*, TONY!

CHILDREN'S HOSPITAL CHARITY

IF I'M *NOT*, THEN THE CHECK I GAVE THE HOSPITAL COMMITTEE WILL BOUNCE! DON'T GO AWAY, BABY! I'LL BE RIGHT BACK!

MMM DON'T KE ME WAITI TOO LON LOVER BO

AS FUND-RAISING CHAIRMAN, I WANT TO REPORT THAT OUR NEW HOSPITAL WING CAN NOW BE BUILT, THANKS TO ANTHONY STARK, WHO DONATED THIS CHECK FOR $100,000!

WOW!

THREE CHEERS FOR TONY STARK!

THANKS! NOW *I* HAVE AN ANNOUNCEMENT! I'VE...UH ...CONTACTED *IRON MAN* TO ENTERTAIN THE HOSPITAL CHILDREN TOMORROW AND THE SHOW WILL BE CARRIED LIVE ON TV!

WONDERFUL THE CHILDRE IDOLIZE *IRO MAN!*

THEN, AS THE DANCE RESUMES...

SO LADY-KILLER STARK IS JUST AN OLD SOFTIE AT HEART! HE SUPPORTS CHARITABLE CAUSES AND EVEN HAS TIME TO PLAN AMUSEMENTS FOR ORPHAN CHILDREN!

CAREFUL, DOLL! YOU'LL MAKE ME FLIP MY HALO!

BUT, TONY, I WISH YOUR OTHER ACTIVITIES DIDN'T KEEP YOU TOO BUSY TO THINK OF... ROMANCE!

HMM...I'M SURE I CAN SPARE A FEW MINUTES FOR SO WORTHY A CAUSE!

AND SO...

DO YOU MIND A PERSONAL QUESTION, TONY? DON'T YOU *EVER* INTEND TO FALL IN LOVE AND GET MARRIED?

HONE NO G WOU WANT MARRY ABSENTI HUSBAN

"THINK OF THE TIME I MUST SPEND MANAGING MY MUNITIONS PLANTS ALL OVER THE WORLD.."

THESE ATOMIC NAVAL CANNONS I DESIGNED ARE ABLE TO FIRE A NUCLEAR SALVO MORE THAN 500 MILES, THEREBY REVOLUTIONIZING BATTLESHIP FIRE-POWER!

"THEN, THERE'S MY *SCIENTIFIC* RESEARCH! SOMETIMES I WORK ON MEDICAL PROBLEMS..'"

'YOUR FLESH-HEALING SERUM WORKS PERFECTLY, STARK! IT CLOSES ANY OPEN WOUND IN TWO SECONDS WITH SYNTHETIC, LIQUID TISSUE!

"OTHER TIMES IT MIGHT BE A SPACE PROBLEM..."

EVERY RAY IS BOMBARDING THE CAPSULE, MR. STARK!

OKAY...NOW TO SEE IF THE ALLOY SHELL I INVENTED CAN RESIST PENETRATION OF ALL RADIATIONS A CAPSULE MIGHT ENCOUNTER IN OUTER SPACE!

"AND OF COURSE I'M ALWAYS TRYING TO HELP THE U.S. DEFENSE EFFORT..."

GREAT SCOTT, STARK! YOUR BURP-GUN IS OBLITERATING PILL BOXES AND BLOCK HOUSES AS IF THEY HAD BEEN STRUCK BY ARTILLERY SHELLS!

BAROOM

BRACKA BRAKKA BRAKKKA

EXACTLY WHAT MY NEW CARTRIDGES *ARE*, GENERAL! ARTILLERY SHELLS REDUCED TO THE SIZE OF .50 CALIBER MACHINE GUN BULLETS! AND THEY CAN BE FIRED AT THE RATE OF 1000 BULLETS A MINUTE!

INCREDIBLE!

ONLY ANTHONY STARK COULD HAVE CREATED THEM!

3

NOW I ASK YOU HONESTLY, WITH ALL THIS WORK, HOW CAN I FIND TIME TO SETTLE DOWN AND GET MARRIED?

TUSH, DARLING! WHEN THE RIGHT GIRL COMES ALONG ...WHICH I HOPE IS ME..YOU'LL *MAKE* TIME FOR MARRIAGE! NOW TAKE ME HOME!

LITTLE DOES SHE SUSPECT I DIDN'T TELL HER THE HALF OF IT! MY MOST IMPORTANT JOB.. MY BATTLE AGAINST INJUSTICE AND EVIL AS *IRON MAN!*

"IF *IRON MAN* ISN'T BATTLING GANGSTERS...

IT'S IRON MAN! HE'S CAUGHT US RED-HANDED CRACKIN' THIS SAFE!

CRASSSHHH

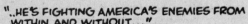

"..HE'S FIGHTING AMERICA'S ENEMIES FROM WITHIN AND WITHOUT..."

WE'RE TOO LATE, IRON MAN! THE COMMUNIST SPIES ARE ESCAPING IN THAT CHARTERED PLANE!

DON'T WORRY! THE PLANE WILL NEVER LEAVE THE GROUND!

THEY'RE SKIDDING AND CRASHING!

RIGHT! NOW YOU BOYS CAN RECOVER THE SECRET DOCUMENTS WHICH THEY TRIED TO STEAL!

" THEN THERE ARE THE MANY MENACES WHICH THREATEN MANKIND..."

LOOK! IRON MAN IS SHOVING THE PROW OF THE OTHER SHIP AWAY...AVOIDING A COLLISION!

BAM

WE CAN'T CONQUER THE EARTH! IT'S INHABITED BY METAL CREATURES WITH FANTASTIC STRENGTH, LIKE THAT ONE!

4

AND, IF *THAT* WEREN'T ENOUGH TO KEEP ME SINGLE FOREVER, THERE'S THE *METAL PLATE* I MUST WEAR CONSTANTLY AROUND MY CHEST...

"...IF THE PLATE ISN'T REGULARLY RE-CHARGED WITH BOOSTER-SHOTS OF ELECTRICITY, MY SHRAPNEL-PIERCED HEART WOULD SOON STOP BEATING!"

BZZZZ

BZZzzz

AND SO...

WHEN WILL I SEE YOU AGAIN, TONY!"?

NEXT TIME I'M IN TOWN, HONEY!

ACTUALLY, SHE COULD SEE ME *TOMORROW.* FOR I'LL BE ON COAST-TO-COAST TV, DEMON-STRATING MY POWERS AS *IRON MAN* TO THE HOSPITAL KIDS!

THE FOLLOWING DAY, NEAR THE NATIONAL HOSPITAL FOR ORPHANS...

NOBODY KNOWS I CARRY MY IRON MAN COSTUME IN THIS ATTACHE CASE! WHO'D DREAM THAT THE ARMOR I WEAR CAN BE UN-FOLDED AND STRETCHED TO MANY TIMES ITS ORIGINAL CARRYING SIZE!

PRESENTLY, AS *IRON MAN* ARRIVES AT THE HOSPITAL...

...TO BEGIN MY DEMONSTRATION, KIDS...I'LL DO A *JUGGLING* ACT! BUT NOT WITH ORANGES OR BASKETBALLS! NO...WITH *AUTOMOBILES!*

FIRST, I'LL SOAR INTO THE AIR WITH THE HELP OF MY TRANSISTOR-POWERED JETS!

WOW!

NOW, I'LL USE *MAGNETS* TO DRAW SEVERAL CARS TOWARD ME!

5

THIS IS *AMAZING!* BY ROTATING HIS TINY, TRANSISTOR-ENERGIZED MAGNETS, *IRON MAN* IS CAUSING *SEVEN CARS* TO REVOLVE AROUND HIM IN A FANTASTIC REMOTE-CONTROL JUGGLING ACT!

NOW HE'S MAKING THE CARS *TWIRL* IN ORBIT! THESE HOSPITAL KIDS ARE ABSOLUTELY *ENTRANCED!*

LATER, AS A CANNON FROM A NEARBY OLD FORT IS WHEELED INTO POSITION...

NOW FOR MY FINAL *STUNT!* FIRST, YOU'LL SEE WHAT THAT HEAVY CANNON WILL DO TO A TWO-FOOT THICK BRICK WALL!

BOOM

CRASHHH

NOW, THE ARTILLERYMEN WILL FIRE AN IDENTICAL CANNON BALL STRAIGHT AT ME! READY-*FIRE!*

BOOOM

H-HE *CAUGHT* IT!

BONNNG

WHOOOOSH

THIS IS INCREDIBLE! IRON MAN IS CRUSHING THE CANNON BALL INTO BITS IN HIS HANDS!

AS A SOUVENIR OF THE SHOW, I'LL GIVE EACH OF YOU A PIECE OF THE CANNON BALL!

WELL, YOU *SAW* IT, FOLKS! A DAZZLING EXHIBITION OF POWER WHICH ONLY ONE *OTHER* PERSON COULD POSSIBLY EQUAL... THE VILLAINOUS DR. STRANGE! BUT, OF COURSE, EVEN *STRANGE* HASN'T GOT IRON MAN'S ASTOUNDING PHYSICAL STRENGTH!

AND LUCKILY FOR MANKIND, THE EVIL GENIUS IS SAFELY LOCKED BEHIND BARS IN A MAXIMUM-SECURITY PRISON!

BUT, AT THAT MOMENT IN A PRISON RADIO REPAIR LAB...

THE FOOL! I'VE ONLY *ALLOWED* MYSELF TO STAY HERE TILL I COULD FORMULATE A NEW PLAN TO PLUNDER MY FELLOW HUMANS! AND NOW, I *HAVE* IT!

I *KNEW* IRON MAN WOULD APPEAR AT THAT CHILDREN'S HOSPITAL, LESS THAN A MILE FROM HERE! SO, I RIGGED UP THIS ELECTRONIC APPARATUS JUST FOR HIM!

YES, *IRON MAN HIMSELF* WILL RESCUE ME FROM THIS STEEL FORTRESS FROM WHICH NO CONVICT HAS EVER BEFORE ESCAPED! BUT, I AM NO *ORDINARY* CONVICT! I AM... *DOCTOR STRANGE!*

NOT FOR NOTHING HAVE I BEEN CALLED "THE MASTER OF EVIL"! I CREATED THIS TINY ELECTRONIC GADGET BY MODIFYING COMMON RADIO AND TV PARTS!

AND I WILL USE THE DEVICE TO CONTROL MY UNWITTING ALLY-- *IRON MAN!* BUT, TO DO THAT, I MUST RETURN TO MY CELL!

CLICK!

I'LL PRETEND I'M GETTING ANOTHER DIZZY ATTACK!

OHHHHH! TH-THIS ROOM IS SPINNING AROUND!

LOOK! DR. STRANGE IS GETTING ONE OF HIS FAINTING SPELLS!

7

WE MUST HELP HIM BACK TO HIS CELL BEFORE HE PASSES OUT! HE'S BEEN VERY SICK EVER SINCE HE WAS STRUCK BY LIGHTNING!

THE FOOLS! DID THEY THINK I'D REMAIN STUNNED FOREVER?

"I WAS STRUCK BY A LIGHTNING BOLT SIX MONTHS AGO WHEN U.S. PARATROOPS SURROUNDED AND ATTACKED MY MOUNTAIN LABORATORY..."

LIGHTNING HIT THAT RAY GUN DR. STRANGE WAS GOING TO FIRE AT US! CAPTURE HIM WHILE HE'S STILL STUNNED!

YEOOOWW!

SINCE THEN, I MADE EVERYONE BELIEVE I'M STILL SUFFERING FROM THE SHOCK! OTHERWISE, THEY'D HAVE PUT ME IN A MAXIMUM SECURITY CELL AND NEVER LET ME OUT OF IT!

BUT, LUCKILY, THAT LIGHTNING BLAST, AFTER THE FIRST PARALYZING EFFECTS, INCREASED THE ELECTRICAL ENERGY OF MY MIND! BUT THE FOOLS WILL ONLY DISCOVER THAT AFTER I LEAVE THIS RAT HOLE!

LATER, WHEN DR. STRANGE IS ALONE IN HIS CELL...

NOW TO MAKE THIS CONTRAPTION EMIT ULTRA-FREQUENCY WAVES THAT WILL FAN OUT TILL THEY HIT IRON MAN WHO MUST'VE ALREADY LEFT THE HOSPITAL!

SO, AS IRON MAN RETURNS TO HIS CAREFULLY CONCEALED CAR...

..MY HEAD! IT SUDDENLY FEELS SO HEAVY! AND MY BODY IS BECOMING NUMB!

I-I HEAR A VOICE COMING FROM FAR AWAY.. WHISPERING TO ME...

HEAR ME, IRON MAN! MY ULTRA-FREQUENCY WAVES HAVE AFFECTED THE ELECTRICITY IN YOUR BRAIN, HYPNOTIZING YOU! I AM YOUR MASTER AND YOU ARE MY SLAVE!

...ES, MASTER! I WAIT YOUR COMMANDS!

GOOD! BREAK INTO FEDERAL PRISON AND FREE ME!

THAT'S IT, IRON MAN! I'LL GUIDE YOUR EVERY STEP... TO THE CELL OF DR. STRANGE!

SOON, TO THE AMAZEMENT OF THE PRISON GUARDS...

IT'S IRON MAN! BUT WHY IS HE SMASHING DOWN OUR GATES?

SOMETHING'S WRONG! I CAN TELL BY THE WAY HE'S WALKING... AS IF HE'S IN A TRANCE!

CRRRASHH!

IRON MAN! WHAT'S THE MATTER WITH YOU! WHAT ARE YOU DOING HERE?

HE DOESN'T HEAR YOU! HE JUST KEEPS SHUFFLING TOWARD THE WALL! FOR PETE'S SAKE, GET OUT OF HIS WAY!

NICE WORK, IRON MAN! NOW CARRY ME OUT OF HERE!

CRRACK!

PWAAMM!

AS IRON MAN USES HIS AIR PRESSURE JET POWER...

HE CAME TO FREE DR. STRANGE! STOP HIM!

HOW? BULLETS BOUNCE OFF HIS ARMOR LIKE PEANUTS!

HA! WAIT 'TILL IRON MAN SNAPS OUT OF HIS SPELL AND REALIZES HE ENGINEERED MY ESCAPE!

BUT, BY THAT TIME I'LL BE EXECUTING MY MASTER PLAN TO DOMINATE THE WORLD! HOW PROUD MY DAUGHTER, CARLA WILL BE OF ME THEN! BECAUSE OF MY ABSOLUTE POWER, SHE'LL HAVE HER PICK OF KINGS AND BILLIONAIRES!

9

ABOVE ALL ELSE, I CRAVE MY DAUGHTER'S LOVE AND ADMIRATION! I MUST MAKE UP FOR ALL THE YEARS I'VE NEGLECTED HER WHILE I DEVOTED MYSELF TO A FANTASTIC LIFE OF CRIME!

THEREFORE, I'LL GIVE HER EVERYTHING... THE *EARTH* ITSELF! AND SHE'LL REIGN OVER IT LIKE A QUEEN, THANKS TO HER FATHER'S GENIUS!

WE'VE FLOWN FAR ENOUGH, IRON MAN! LAND AT ONCE!

HOURS LATER, THE STATE POLICE, COMBING THE AREA FOR IRON MAN AND DR. STRANGE, SEE A STUMBLING FIGURE...

WHERE AM I? I SEEM TO HAVE LOST ALL MEMORY OF MY ACTIONS SINCE I LEFT THE HOSPITAL!

LOOK! THERE'S IRON MAN! BUT DR. STRANGE IS NOT WITH HIM!

THEN, AS *IRON MAN* LISTENS IN HORROR TO WHAT HE HAS DONE...

DOCTOR STRANGE MUST'VE CAST AN HYPNOTIC SPELL OVER ME! BUT, IF IT'S THE LAST THING I DO, I'LL RECAPTURE HIM! I MUST REDEEM MYSELF!

POOR IRON MAN! HE FEELS LIKE A FOOL! HIS PRIDE WON'T LET HIM REST TILL HE GETS EVEN WITH DR. STRANGE!

WEEKS LATER ON A PRIVATE ISLAND OFF THE U.S. COAST...

THERE'S YOUR NEW HOME, CARLA! IT IS FROM *HERE* THAT I SHALL GIVE THE WORLD MY ULTIMATUM.. UNCONDITIONAL SURRENDER TO DR. STRANGE, OR EXTINCTION!

BUT, DAD I DON'T UNDER STAND! WHY MUS YOU DO ANYTHING SO DRASTI

FOOLISH CHILD! 'TIS BUT MY DUE! AS THE WORLD'S GREATEST SCIENTIFIC GENIUS I *SHOULD* RULE MANKIND! NOW I WILL INTRODUCE YOU TO MY ACCOMPLICES... THE MOST CUNNING SCIENTISTS AND POWER-MAD MILITARY MEN ON EARTH!

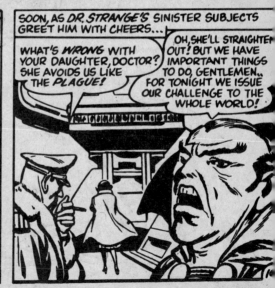

SOON, AS *DR. STRANGE'S* SINISTER SUBJECTS GREET HIM WITH CHEERS...

WHAT'S *WRONG* WITH YOUR DAUGHTER, DOCTOR? SHE AVOIDS US LIKE THE *PLAGUE*!

OH, SHE'LL STRAIGHTEN OUT! BUT WE HAVE IMPORTANT THINGS TO DO, GENTLEMEN.. FOR TONIGHT WE ISSUE OUR CHALLENGE TO THE WHOLE WORLD!

THAT EVENING, A 200 MEGATON BOMB EXPLODES IN OUTER SPACE!

BARROOOM!

ATTENTION, EARTH! THIS IS DR. STRANGE BROADCASTING FROM HIS IMPREGNABLE STRONGHOLD IN THE ATLANTIC OCEAN...

DOUBTLESS YOU'RE ALL NOW AWARE OF THE HUGE S-BOMB I EXPLODED IN OUTER SPACE...

WELL, I HAVE EVEN MORE OF THE SAME TYPE... ENOUGH TO DESTROY ALL LIFE ON EARTH!

UNLESS EVERY NATION SURRENDERS TO ME WITHIN 24 HOURS, I WILL BLOW THE WORLD TO SMITHEREENS! DISREGARD MY THREAT AND AS SURE AS MY NAME IS DR. STRANGE, I WILL BURY YOU ALL!

LATER, AFTER DR. STRANGE'S GHASTLY BROADCAST...

THE FOOLS HAVE LOCATED OUR STRONGHOLD AND ARE DROPPING A-BOMBS ON US! BUT, TO NO AVAIL, THANKS TO THE PROTECTIVE FORCE FIELD YOU INVENTED, DR. STRANGE!

YES, THE WORLD WILL SOON REALIZE IT HAS NO ALTERNATIVE BUT TO SURRENDER TO US!

NEXT MORNING, IN A SUBMARINE OFF DR. STRANGE'S ISLAND...

BUT IF THE WHOLE WORLD CAN'T FIGURE OUT A WAY TO STOP DR. STRANGE, HOW WILL YOU, SINGLE-HANDEDLY, DO THE JOB, IRON MAN?

I HAVE A PLAN! NOW DO AS I SAY! FIRE ME OUT OF TORPEDO-TUBE NUMBER ONE!

SOON, UNDERWATER...

JUST AS I THOUGHT! EVEN A SUPER-GENIUS LIKE DR. STRANGE CAN OMIT AN IMPORTANT DETAIL, LIKE EXTENDING HIS FORCE FIELD UNDERWATER! I'LL GET DR. STRANGE IF IT COSTS ME MY LIFE... BECAUSE IT WAS I WHO HELPED THE DEMONIAC MADMAN TO ESCAPE!

THEN, AS IRON MAN BURROWS SWIFTLY UNDER THE ISLE...

LUCKILY I DIDN'T REMAIN IN THE SEA WATER LONG ENOUGH TO RUST MY IRON SHELL! NOW TO LOCATE DR. STRANGE'S ELECTRICAL POWER PLANT!

MY BODY IS ATTUNED TO ELECTRICAL ENERGY AS A BLOODHOUND TO A SCENT! HMM.. I CAN FEEL MYSELF NEARING A MAJOR ELECTRICAL SOURCE NOW!

CARLA, WHAT *IS* IT? YOU HAVEN'T SPOKEN TO ME SINCE WE ARRIVED! TELL ME, CHILD!

IF YOU *MUST* KNOW, IT'S YOUR DESPOTIC ULTIMATUM AND YOUR WILLINGNESS TO DESTROY MANKIND IF THE EARTH DOESN'T SURRENDER TO YOU! I NEVER DREAMT YOU WERE SO EVIL!

BUT... YOU DON' KNOW WHAT YOU'RE *SAYING* I'VE DONE IT ALL FOR *YOU*.

IRON MAN!

WE MEET AGAIN, DR. STRANGE... BUT UNDER *DIFFERENT* CIRCUMSTANCES! YOU ARE NOT DEALING WITH A HYPNOTIZED AUTOMATON NOW!

CRRACKKKK!

THIS IS YOUR FINISH, STRANGE! I'M GOING TO SHORT-CIRCUIT ALL YOUR ELECTRICAL EQUIPMENT! YOU WILL BE LEFT *POWERLESS!*

BUT ANYTHING STRONG ENOUGH TO DESTROY MY DEVICES WILL ALSO DESTROY *YOU!* IT WILL MEAN THE END OF YOU TOO, IRON MAN!

WE'VE ALL GOT TO GO *SOME* TIME...AND I GUESS *THIS* IS AS GOOD A TIME AS *ANY!*

NO! NO! DON'T SMASH INTO THOSE GENERATORS!

HE *DID* IT! H-HE KNOCKED OUT MY MAIN POWER SOURCE!

RZZTT!

SSSTT!

SO, IRON MAN! NOW YOU'LL *PAY* FOR YOUR MEDDLING! I DON'T KNOW ALL YOUR SECRETS, BUT I *DO* KNOW YOU CAN'T EXIST WITHOUT ELECTRICAL ENERGY... AND NOW IT'S ALL DRAINING OUT OF YOU!

OHHH!

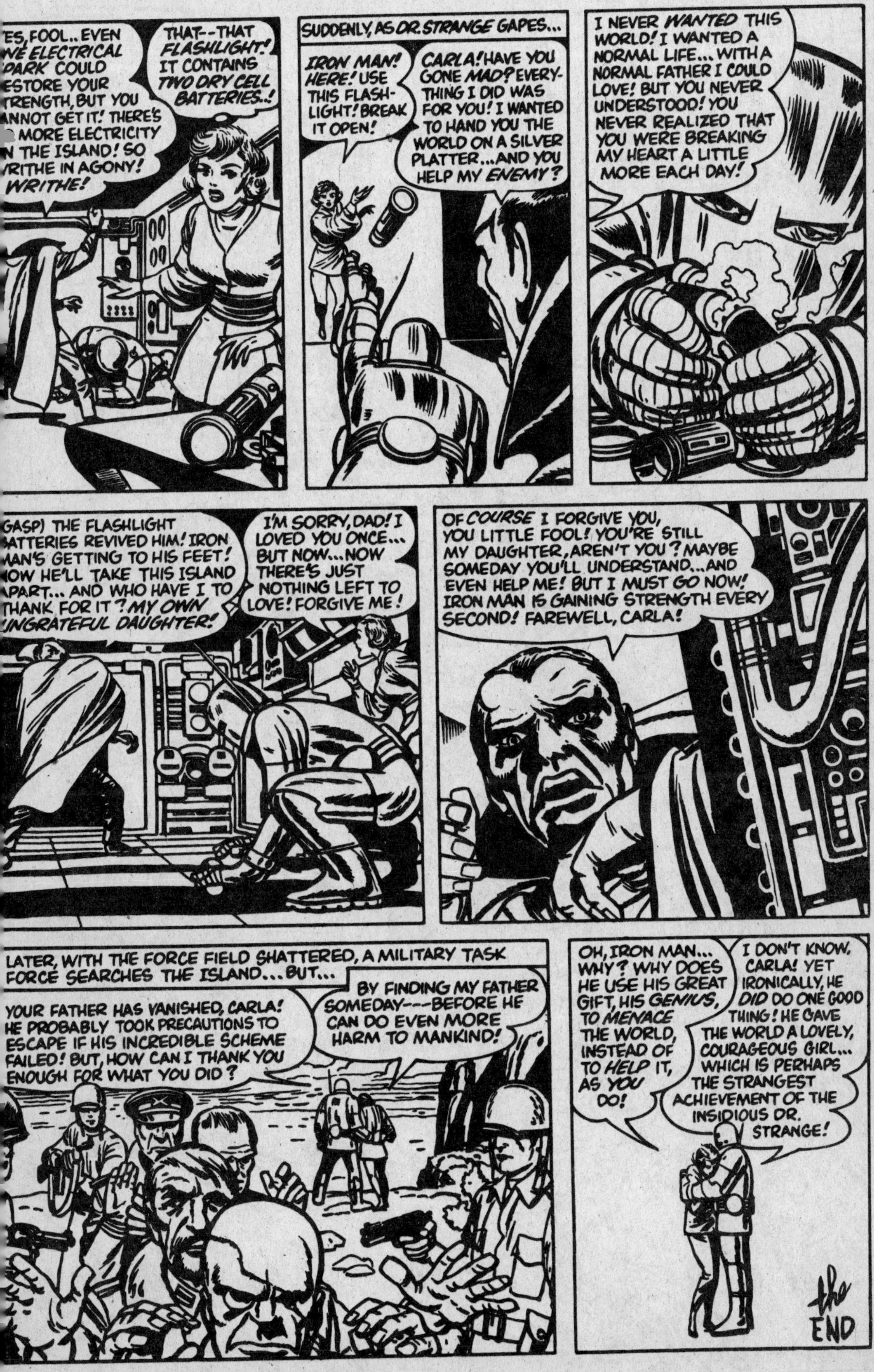

ES, FOOL.. EVEN HE ELECTRICAL PARK COULD ESTORE YOUR TRENGTH, BUT YOU ANNOT GET IT! THERE'S O MORE ELECTRICITY N THE ISLAND! SO RITHE IN AGONY! WRITHE!
THAT--THAT FLASHLIGHT! IT CONTAINS TWO DRY CELL BATTERIES..!
SUDDENLY, AS DR. STRANGE GAPES...
IRON MAN! HERE! USE THIS FLASHLIGHT! BREAK IT OPEN!
CARLA! HAVE YOU GONE MAD? EVERYTHING I DID WAS FOR YOU! I WANTED TO HAND YOU THE WORLD ON A SILVER PLATTER...AND YOU HELP MY ENEMY?
I NEVER WANTED THIS WORLD! I WANTED A NORMAL LIFE... WITH A NORMAL FATHER I COULD LOVE! BUT YOU NEVER UNDERSTOOD! YOU NEVER REALIZED THAT YOU WERE BREAKING MY HEART A LITTLE MORE EACH DAY!
GASP) THE FLASHLIGHT BATTERIES REVIVED HIM! IRON MAN'S GETTING TO HIS FEET! NOW HE'LL TAKE THIS ISLAND APART... AND WHO HAVE I TO THANK FOR IT? MY OWN UNGRATEFUL DAUGHTER!
I'M SORRY, DAD! I LOVED YOU ONCE... BUT NOW...NOW THERE'S JUST NOTHING LEFT TO LOVE! FORGIVE ME!
OF COURSE I FORGIVE YOU, YOU LITTLE FOOL! YOU'RE STILL MY DAUGHTER, AREN'T YOU? MAYBE SOMEDAY YOU'LL UNDERSTAND...AND EVEN HELP ME! BUT I MUST GO NOW! IRON MAN IS GAINING STRENGTH EVERY SECOND! FAREWELL, CARLA!
LATER, WITH THE FORCE FIELD SHATTERED, A MILITARY TASK FORCE SEARCHES THE ISLAND...BUT...
YOUR FATHER HAS VANISHED, CARLA! HE PROBABLY TOOK PRECAUTIONS TO ESCAPE IF HIS INCREDIBLE SCHEME FAILED! BUT, HOW CAN I THANK YOU ENOUGH FOR WHAT YOU DID?
BY FINDING MY FATHER SOMEDAY---BEFORE HE CAN DO EVEN MORE HARM TO MANKIND!
OH, IRON MAN... WHY? WHY DOES HE USE HIS GREAT GIFT, HIS GENIUS, TO MENACE THE WORLD, INSTEAD OF TO HELP IT, AS YOU DO!
I DON'T KNOW, CARLA! YET IRONICALLY, HE DID DO ONE GOOD THING! HE GAVE THE WORLD A LOVELY, COURAGEOUS GIRL... WHICH IS PERHAPS THE STRANGEST ACHIEVEMENT OF THE INSIDIOUS DR. STRANGE!
the END

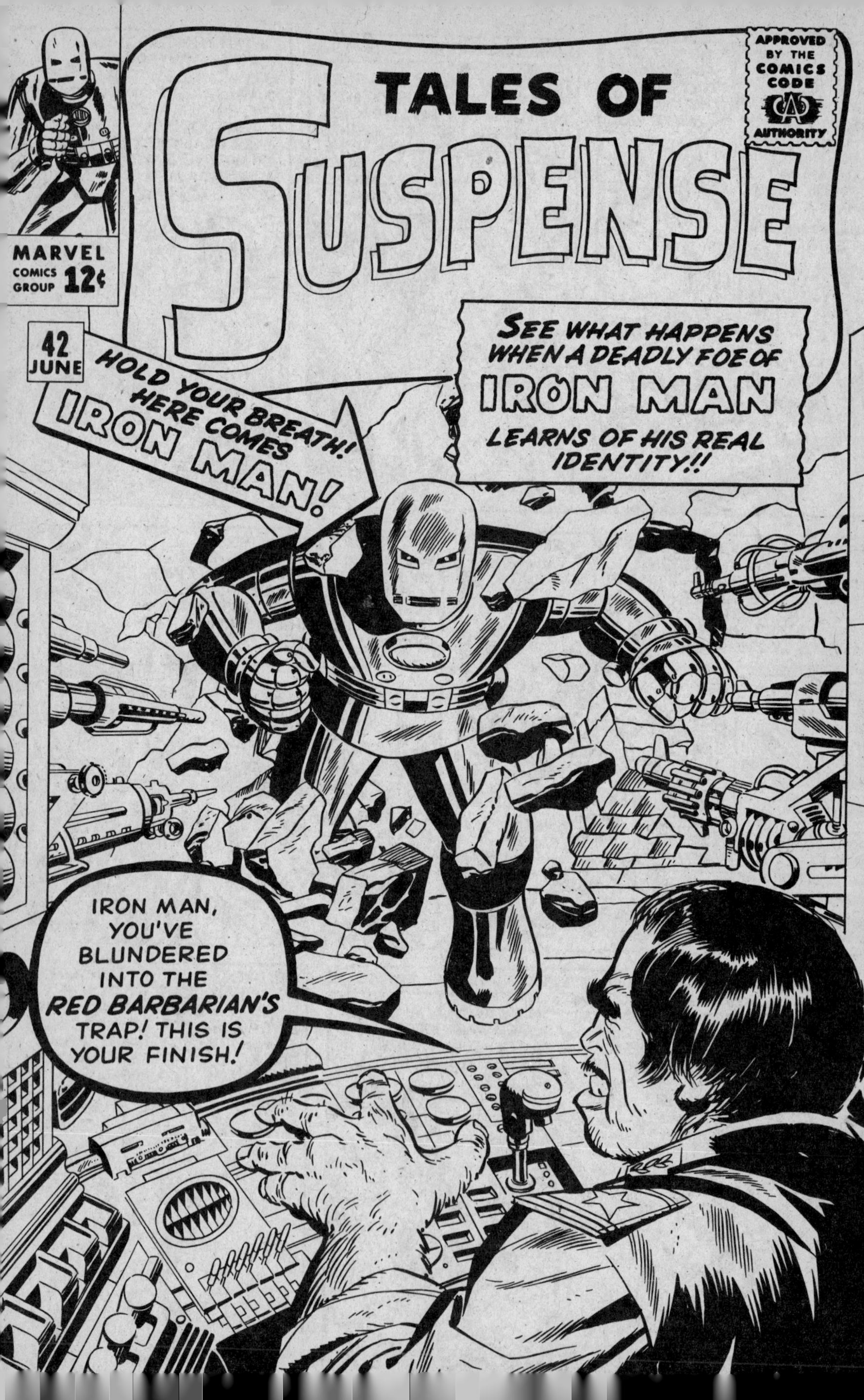

TALES OF SUSPENSE
APPROVED BY THE COMICS CODE AUTHORITY
MARVEL COMICS GROUP 12¢
42 JUNE
HOLD YOUR BREATH! HERE COMES IRON MAN!
SEE WHAT HAPPENS WHEN A DEADLY FOE OF IRON MAN LEARNS OF HIS REAL IDENTITY!!
IRON MAN, YOU'VE BLUNDERED INTO THE RED BARBARIAN'S TRAP! THIS IS YOUR FINISH!

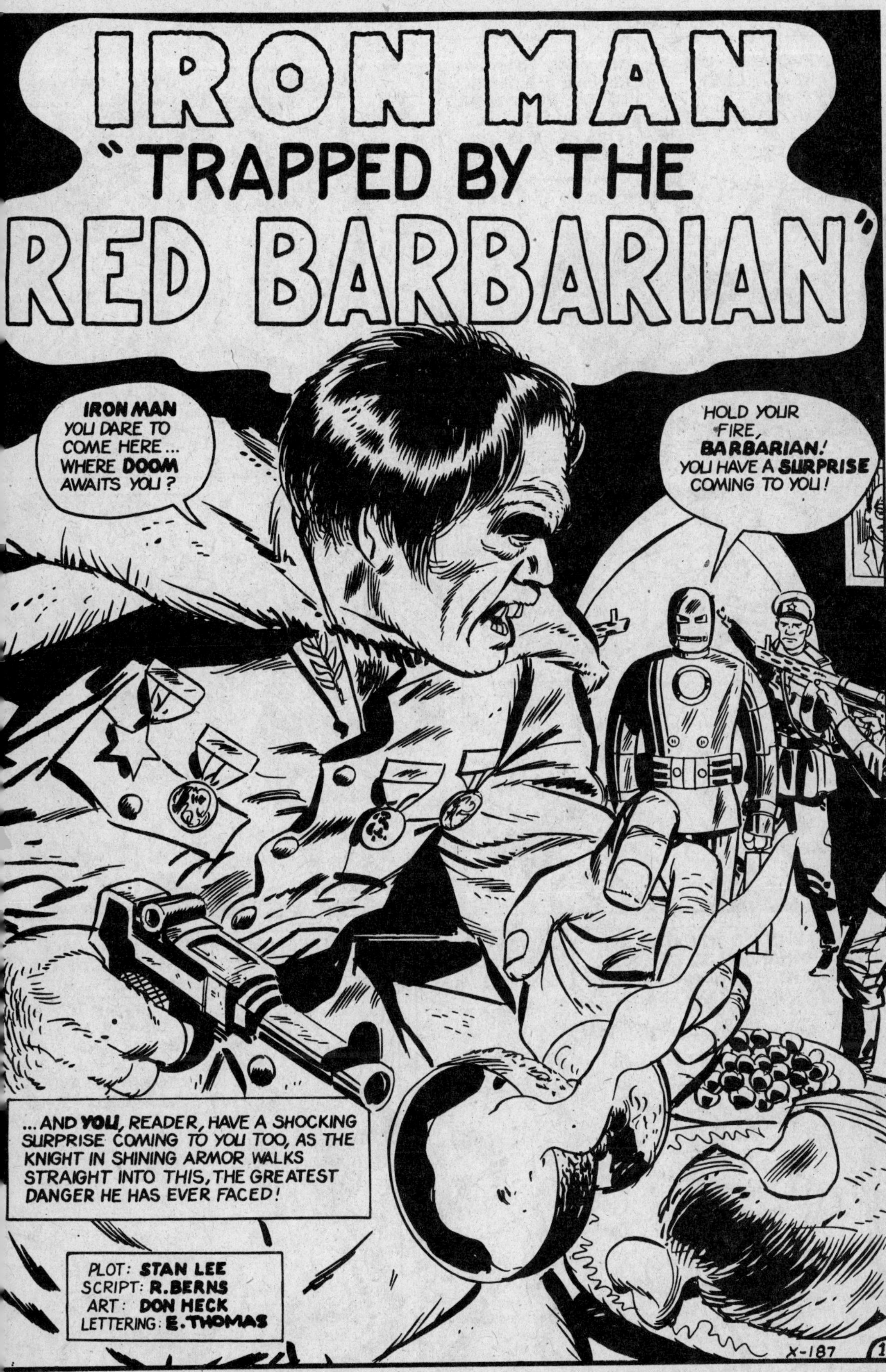
IRON MAN
"TRAPPED BY THE RED BARBARIAN"
IRON MAN YOU DARE TO COME HERE... WHERE DOOM AWAITS YOU?
HOLD YOUR FIRE, BARBARIAN! YOU HAVE A SURPRISE COMING TO YOU!
...AND YOU, READER, HAVE A SHOCKING SURPRISE COMING TO YOU TOO, AS THE KNIGHT IN SHINING ARMOR WALKS STRAIGHT INTO THIS, THE GREATEST DANGER HE HAS EVER FACED!
PLOT: STAN LEE
SCRIPT: R. BERNS
ART: DON HECK
LETTERING: E. THOMAS
X-187
1

ONE NIGHT, AT AN EAST COAST DOCK...

WELL, COMRADE...WE DID IT! WE NOT ONLY **LEARNED** ABOUT AMERICA'S NEWEST ATOM BOMB, BUT WE STOLE THE BOMB ITSELF!

YES, GREGORI! WE WILL RECEIVE THE THANKS OF THE **RED BARBARIAN** HIMSELF FOR THIS PIECE OF ESPIONAGE!

WAIT! BEFORE WE STORE THE CRATE IN THE HOLD, I'D LIKE TO TAKE ANOTHER LOOK AT THE WEAPON!

WHY NOT? IT IS EASILY OPENED WITH A CROWBAR!

THERE IT IS! I HEAR IT HAS REVOLUTIONARY NEW ELEMENTS OF DESIGN!

AND YOU HEAR **RIGHT!**

IRON MAN!

THE F.B.I WANTED TO CATCH YOU SPIES RED-HANDED, SO WE BAITED OUR TRAP WITH A PHONY, HOLLOW BOMB CONTAINING ONLY "YOURS TRULY"!

W-WE'VE BEEN TRICKED! SHOOT HIM!

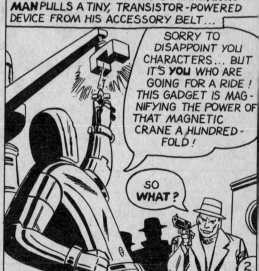

BUT BEFORE THE COMMIES CAN FIRE, **IRON MAN** PULLS A TINY, TRANSISTOR-POWERED DEVICE FROM HIS ACCESSORY BELT...

SORRY TO DISAPPOINT YOU CHARACTERS... BUT IT'S **YOU** WHO ARE GOING FOR A RIDE! THIS GADGET IS MAGNIFYING THE POWER OF THAT MAGNETIC CRANE A HUNDRED-FOLD!

SO WHAT?

2

SO **THIS!** ITS FIRST EFFECT WILL BE TO JERK YOUR GUNS UPWARDS SO THAT YOU FIRE HARMLESSLY INTO THE AIR!

THEN, THE WEAPONS **THEM-SELVES** WILL BE DRAWN TO THE MAGNET... AND **YOU** WITH THEM!

I'D ADVISE YOU NOT TO LET GO OF YOUR GUNS! IT'S QUITE A DROP TO THE DECK BELOW!

Y-YOU'RE WEARING AN IRON COSTUME! HOW COME **YOU'RE** NOT DRAWN UPWARD?

MY METAL CLOTHING CONTAINS ALLOYS WHICH REJECT MAGNETIC ATTRACTION! NOW DON'T GO AWAY, BECAUSE SOON YOU'LL HAVE AN ADMIRING AUDIENCE OF F.B.I AGENTS!

AND BRIEF MINUTES LATER...

GOOD WORK, **IRON MAN!** THANKS TO YOUR CLEVERNESS, ANOTHER COMMIE SPY RING HAS BEEN ROUNDED UP!

YES, BUT OUR JOB IS FAR FROM FINISHED! I'M SURE THE **RED BARBARIAN** MUST BE PLANNING NEW MISCHIEF

THE **RED BARBARIAN**?

THAT'S THE NAME OF A TOP RED GENERAL, NOTED FOR HIS BRUTALITY! HE CONTROLS THIS VAST COMMIE SPY NETWORK, AND HEAVEN HELP THE UNDER-COVER MAN WHO FLUBS AN ASSIGNMENT!

WHERE'S THE **RED BARBARIAN'S** HEADQUARTERS?

SOMEWHERE BEHIND THE IRON CURTAIN! BUT, I CAN'T TALK ANYMORE! MY TRANSISTORS ARE RUNNING DOWN --- I'VE GOT TO RECHARGE THEM! SO LONG FOR NOW, BOYS!

3

SOON, IN A DESERTED ALLEY NEAR THE WATERFRONT...:

THERE! ALL RECHARGED! NOW TO SWITCH TO MY SECRET IDENTITY AS ANTHONY STARK! SPEAKING OF THE **RED BARBARIAN**, I'LL BET HIS AGENTS ARE DYING TO FIND OUT WHAT'S GOING ON BEHIND THE WALLS OF MY LAB!

LITTLE DOES ANYONE SUSPECT THAT MY ENTIRE **IRON MAN** GARB IS COLLAPSED AND CONCEALED IN THIS ORDINARY ATTACHE CASE I'M CARRYING!

AND LITTLE DO THE COMMIES KNOW THAT I'M WORKING ON MY GREATEST WEAPON... A POCKET-SIZE DISINTEGRATOR RAY!

-OF COURSE, I HAVEN'T PERFECTED THE RAY YET! BUT EVEN SO, THE ENEMY SPY WHO LEARNS ITS SECRET WILL BECOME A NATIONAL HERO!

AN HOUR LATER, OUT OF TOWN...

BUT WHAT SPY CAN GET THROUGH THE HEAVY GUARD THE U.S. ARMY HAS THROWN AROUND MY PLANT TO MAKE SURE NOBODY BUT I ENTER OR LEAVE THE LAB?

NEXT DAY, ON THE LAB'S PROVING GROUNDS...

NOW, GENTLEMEN, YOU WILL SEE HOW MY DISINTEGRATOR RAY WORKS! NOTICE THAT IT CAN BE INSTALLED IN A COMMON FLASHLIGHT CASE...

...AIM IT AT A MONSTER TANK AND THE TANK INSTANTLY VANISHES!

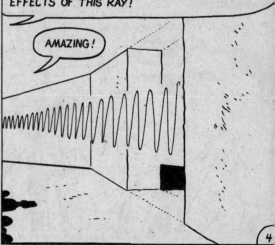

FOCUS ITS BEAM ON A TWO-FOOT THICK WALL AND... INSTANTANEOUS VAPORIZATION! NO EARTHLY SUBSTANCE CAN WITHSTAND THE EFFECTS OF THIS RAY!

AMAZING!

4

"YOU CAN EASILY SEE THAT, IF THE RAY WERE ENLARGED, IN A SPLIT-SECOND IT COULD WIPE OUT A FLEET OF ENEMY BATTLESHIPS OR EVEN A GREAT METROPOLIS"

OF COURSE, MY RAY STILL HAS A FEW BUGS IN IT--CONSISTENCY OF PERFORMANCE, ENLARGMENT PROBLEMS AND SO FORTH! BUT WHEN THE DEVICE IS PERFECTED...

PERFECTED? I STILL CAN'T BELIEVE WHAT I'VE ALREADY SEEN!

DO YOU KNOW THAT THE REDS WOULD PROBABLY GIVE UP HALF OF ASIA IF THEY COULD STEAL THE PLANS OF WHAT YOU'VE INVENTED SO FAR?

YOU KNOW SOMETHING, GENERAL? I BELIEVE THEY WOULD!

AND INDEED, AT THAT VERY MOMENT, IN A RED SATELLITE COUNTRY, AT THE HEADQUARTERS OF THE RED BARBARIAN....

EXCELLENCY, WE HAVE SENSATIONAL NEWS! OUR SPIES IN AMERICA REPORT THAT THE FAMOUS INVENTIVE GENIUS, ANTHONY STARK, IS WORKING ON AN ASTOUNDING NEW WEAPON TO MAKE AMERICA INVINCIBLE!

SO? WHERE ARE THE PLANS?

WELL, SIR,...UH...THE PLANS ARE NOT SO EASILY PROCURED! A HUGE SECURITY GUARD SURROUNDS STARK'S LABORATORY!

IDIOT! DID I ASK YOU WHAT THE OBSTACLES WERE?

BUT EXCELLENCY, VLIKOV SPOKE THE TRUTH! NOT EVEN A MOUSE CAN ENTER STARK'S PLANT WITHOUT BEING DETECTED BY THE SECURITY GUARDS!

ANOTHER APOLOGIST FOR FAILURE! COME HERE!

5

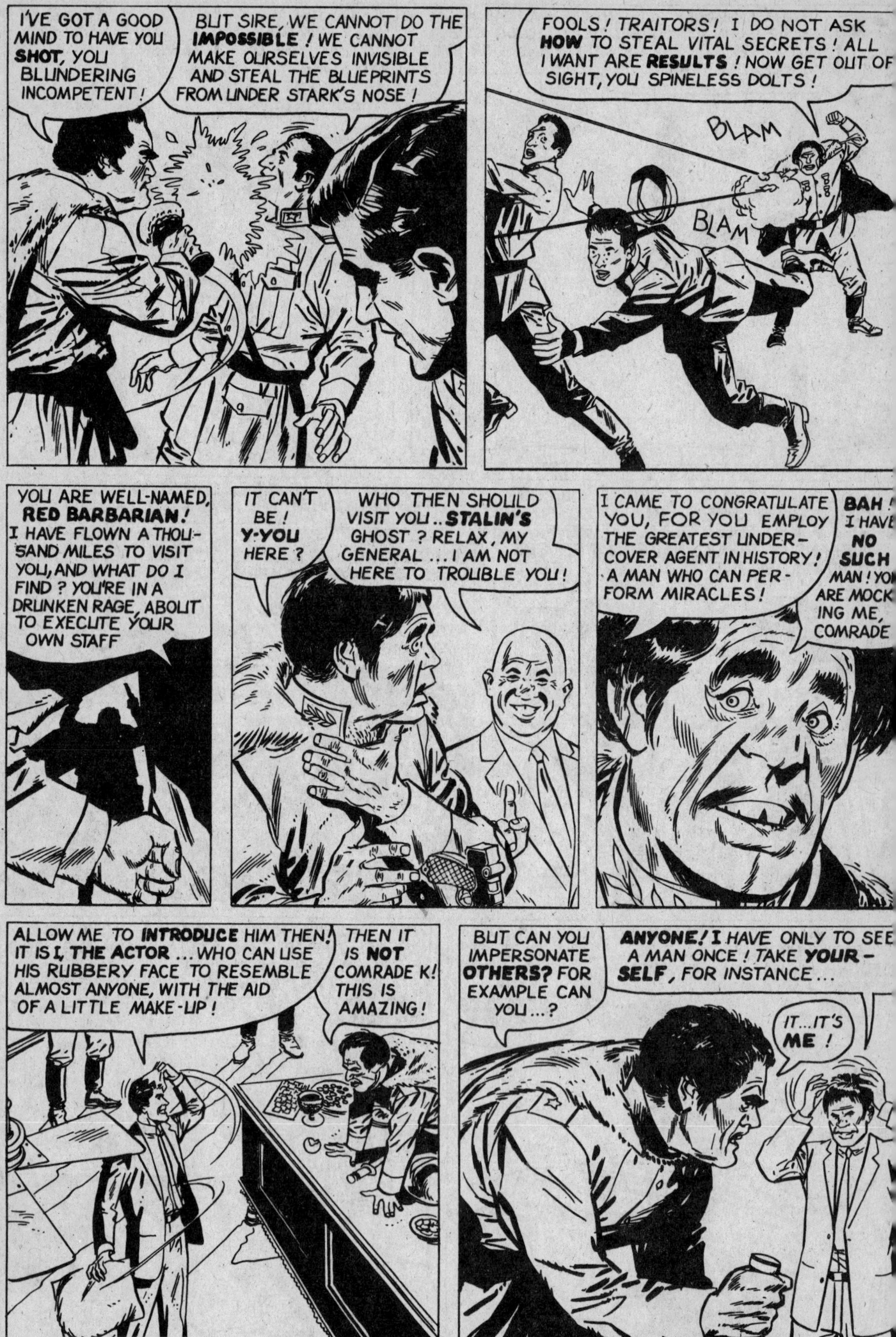
I'VE GOT A GOOD MIND TO HAVE YOU **SHOT**, YOU BLUNDERING INCOMPETENT!
BUT SIRE, WE CANNOT DO THE **IMPOSSIBLE**! WE CANNOT MAKE OURSELVES INVISIBLE AND STEAL THE BLUEPRINTS FROM UNDER STARK'S NOSE!
FOOLS! TRAITORS! I DO NOT ASK **HOW** TO STEAL VITAL SECRETS! ALL I WANT ARE **RESULTS**! NOW GET OUT OF SIGHT, YOU SPINELESS DOLTS!
BLAM
BLAM
YOU ARE WELL-NAMED, **RED BARBARIAN**! I HAVE FLOWN A THOUSAND MILES TO VISIT YOU, AND WHAT DO I FIND? YOU'RE IN A DRUNKEN RAGE, ABOUT TO EXECUTE YOUR OWN STAFF
IT CAN'T BE! **Y-YOU** HERE?
WHO THEN SHOULD VISIT YOU.. **STALIN'S** GHOST? RELAX, MY GENERAL ... I AM NOT HERE TO TROUBLE YOU!
I CAME TO CONGRATULATE YOU, FOR YOU EMPLOY THE GREATEST UNDER-COVER AGENT IN HISTORY! A MAN WHO CAN PERFORM MIRACLES!
BAH! I HAVE **NO SUCH** MAN! YOU ARE MOCKING ME, COMRADE
ALLOW ME TO **INTRODUCE** HIM THEN! IT IS I, **THE ACTOR** ... WHO CAN USE HIS RUBBERY FACE TO RESEMBLE ALMOST ANYONE, WITH THE AID OF A LITTLE MAKE-UP!
THEN IT IS **NOT** COMRADE K! THIS IS AMAZING!
BUT CAN YOU IMPERSONATE **OTHERS?** FOR EXAMPLE CAN YOU...?
ANYONE! I HAVE ONLY TO SEE A MAN ONCE! TAKE **YOURSELF**, FOR INSTANCE...
IT...IT'S **ME**!

ACTOR! EVEN IF THE JOKE IS ON ME, I MUST ADMIT YOU ARE A GENIUS AT IMPERSONATION! YOUR FACE IS WORTH A FORTUNE! SIT DOWN, ACTOR! HAVE SOME CAVIAR! I WANT TO TALK TO YOU!

I KNOW WHAT IT IS, GENERAL! I OVERHEARD EVERYTHING FROM THE DOORWAY!

YOU WOULD LIKE SOMEONE TO STEAL THE PLANS OF ANTHONY STARK'S NEW INVENTION! WELL, YOU CAME TO THE RIGHT MAN! OR RATHER, THE RIGHT MAN CAME TO YOU! DO YOU HAVE A PHOTO OF STARK?

OF COURSE!

MOMENTS LATER...

THIS IS CHILD'S PLAY FOR A MAN OF MY TALENTS!

BY LENIN'S BEARD... YOU ARE ANTHONY STARK! YOU COULD ENTER AND LEAVE HIS LABORATORY AT WILL! NO ONE WOULD CHALLENGE YOU!

CORRECT! AND WHAT WILL BE MY REWARD IF I RETURN HERE WITH ALL THE PLANS OF STARK'S NEW INVENTION?

ANYTHING YOU WISH! NAME IT AND IT SHALL BE YOURS!

HOWEVER, I WARN YOU, ACTOR...FAIL IN THIS MISSION, AND I WILL NAIL YOUR HIDE TO THE WALL!

NONSENSE, COMRADE GENERAL! HOW CAN I FAIL? I'LL BE GIVING THE PERFORMANCE OF MY LIFE!

WHAT ABOUT IRON MAN? I JUST RECEIVED NEWS HE BROKE UP ANOTHER SPY RING I ORGANIZED IN AMERICA!

IRON MAN DOESN'T WORRY ME! AS A MATTER OF FACT, I CAN EVEN IMPERSONATE HIM!

BAH! THAT IS NOT THE SAME AS DEFEATING IRON MAN! NOBODY IN MY ORGANIZATION HAS BEATEN HIM YET!

THEN I SHALL BE THE FIRST! A TOAST, GENERAL! TO THE DOUBLE DEFEAT OF ANTHONY STARK AND IRON MAN!

7

A FEW DAYS LATER, THE SPY ARRIVES IN THE U.S. BY POSING AS A FILM STAR...

BUT SIR REGINALD... WE THOUGHT YOU WERE IN ITALY, MAKING A PICTURE!

AS YOU SEE, THAT RUMOR WAS FALSE! I INTEND TO REMAIN IN AMERICA FOR A MONTH, TOURING AROUND, INCOGNITO!

INDEED, I'LL BE SEVERAL PEOPLE BEFORE I ARRIVE AT STARK'S LAB!

NEXT DAY, AT A TELEGRAPH OFFICE IN WASHINGTON, D.C....

SEND THIS TELEGRAM TO ANTHONY STARK, AT THE ADDRESS NOTED... AND MARK IT "RUSH"!

WHATEVER YOU SAY, SENATOR!

NOW TO CONTACT OUR SPIES HERE! THEY MUST HELP ME FAKE AN ENTRANCE INTO STARK'S LAB WHILE STARK FLIES TO WASHINGTON --- TO A NON-EXISTENT PENTAGON MEETING ARRANGED BY THE ACTOR!

PRESENTLY, AT AN UNDERGROUND HIDEOUT...

EXCELLENT DISGUISES, COMRADES! HOW LONG WILL IT TAKE OUR PRIVATE HELICOPTER TO TOUCH DOWN AT STARK'S LAB?

IN ABOUT TWO HOURS, ACTOR! STARK SHOULD BE ON A PLANE TO WASHINGTON BY THAT TIME!

TWO HOURS LATER, AT STARK'S LABORATORY...

MR. STARK! I-I THOUGHT YOU'D LEFT FOR WASHINGTON!

THE PENTAGON MEETING WAS CALLED OFF! ESCORT US TO MY PRIVATE OFFICE AT ONCE! I HAVE NO TIME TO WASTE!

BUT, MR. STARK... YOU GAVE ME STRICT ORDERS THAT NONE BUT YOU CAN ENTER YOUR SECRET QUARTERS!

WELL, TODAY IS AN EXCEPTION! THESE OFFICERS ARE TOP PENTAGON OFFICIALS! I HAVE NO SECRETS FROM THEM! OPEN THE DOOR, PLEASE!

MINUTES LATER...

GO TO WORK QUICKLY! THE GUARD WON'T BOTHER US! I TOLD HIM TO STAND OUTSIDE TILL I SUMMON HIM!

DA, ACTOR! WE'LL EACH TAKE A FILING CABINET, A DRAWER, A CLOSET... AND RANSACK THEM TILL WE FIND THE PLANS!

8

HELLO! WHAT'S **THIS**? VARIOUS METAL SPARE PARTS... GLEAMING LIKE **GOLD**!

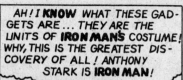

AH! **I KNOW** WHAT THESE GADGETS ARE... THEY ARE THE UNITS OF **IRON MAN'S** COSTUME! WHY, THIS IS THE GREATEST DISCOVERY OF ALL! ANTHONY STARK IS **IRON MAN**!

BUT I'LL TELL **NOBODY** ABOUT MY FIND! IT WILL BE MY ACE IN THE HOLE IF EVER I HAVE TO SAVE MY NECK TO REDEEM SOME BLUNDER!

ACTOR, LOOK! WE'VE FOUND THE BLUEPRINTS FOR STARK'S NEW INVENTION! IT'S A DISINTEGRATOR RAY!

GREAT! I'LL FLY THEM IMMEDIATELY TO THE **RED BARBARIAN**! MEANWHILE, YOU THREE HAVE A JOB! YOU WILL WAIT OUTSIDE! THEN, WHEN STARK RETURNS FROM HIS WILD GOOSE CHASE... ASSASSINATE HIM!

DA, **ACTOR**! BUT YOU MUST THINK OF SOME WAY TO GET RID OF HIS PERSONAL GUARD!

AND SO, OUTSIDE THE LAB...

TAKE THE REST OF THE NIGHT OFF! MY PENTAGON FRIENDS WILL REMAIN ON GUARD TILL I RETURN IN THE MORNING!

THANKS, MR. STARK!

AN HOUR LATER, ON A PRIVATE AIRLINER...

MY STARTLING DISCOVERY THAT STARK IS **IRON MAN** WILL REMAIN MY SECRET TILL THE RIGHT TIME ARRIVES TO REVEAL IT!

MEANWHILE, AS A BAFFLED GENIUS RETURNS TO HIS LAB...

I WONDER **WHO** COULD HAVE SENT ME THAT PHONY MESSAGE TO ATTEND AN EMERGENCY TOP LEVEL MEETING?

GET SET! HERE COMES THE **REAL** ANTHONY STARK!

9

GREETINGS, STARK... AND FAREWELL! NEVER AGAIN WILL YOUR GENIUS CONTRIBUTE TO OUR ENEMIES' CAUSE!

THE BULLETS ARE BOUNCING OFF HIM! HE MUST BE WEARING A BULLET-PROOF VEST!

ZING!

KAPOW!

THEY DON'T KNOW I'M WEARING IRON MAN'S CHEST APPARATUS UNDER MY SHIRT!

ZING

POW

HE'S DOUSED THE LIGHTS! QUICK! WE MUST GET HIM BEFORE HE ELUDES US.

TIME TO CHANGE TO IRON MAN!

AND SO, AS THE THREE HATCHET-MEN POKE AROUND IN THE DARK...

THAT BLACKOUT WAS STARK'S SIGNAL TO ME THAT HE WAS IN TROUBLE! AND I SEE HE WASN'T EXAGGERATING!

YEEOOWW! IT'S IRON MAN! HE'S A GUARD HERE, TOO!

NOW TO SCARE THE TRUTH OUT OF THEM!

TELL ME WHAT YOU'RE DOING HERE, OR SHALL I TRY TO MAKE YOU TALK?

NO... NO, DON'T... WE'LL TELL YOU EVERYTHING! IT WAS THE ACTOR! HE IMPERSONATED YOU! HE STOLE YOUR PLANS FOR THE DISINTEGRATOR RAY

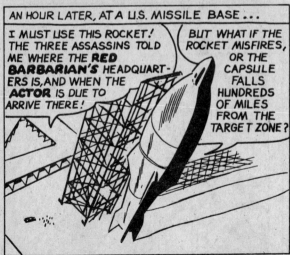

AN HOUR LATER, AT A U.S. MISSILE BASE...

I MUST USE THIS ROCKET! THE THREE ASSASSINS TOLD ME WHERE THE RED BARBARIAN'S HEADQUARTERS IS, AND WHEN THE ACTOR IS DUE TO ARRIVE THERE!

BUT WHAT IF THE ROCKET MISFIRES, OR THE CAPSULE FALLS HUNDREDS OF MILES FROM THE TARGET ZONE?

IT'S A CHANCE I'VE GOT TO TAKE! ROCKET-TRAVEL IS THE ONLY WAY I CAN BEAT THE ACTOR TO HIS DESTINATION SO I CAN INTERCEPT HIM AND RECAPTURE STARK'S BLUEPRINTS!

OKAY, IRON MAN GOOD LUCK!

10

MINUTES LATER...

BETTER PRAY, MEN! IF **IRON MAN** DOESN'T RETRIEVE STARK'S PLANS, THE IRON CURTAIN NATIONS WILL HAVE AN UNBEATABLE WEAPON!

PRESENTLY...

HMMM... I'M IN ORBIT NOW! MY ATTACHE CASE IS FLOATING WEIGHTLESSLY! BUT SOON A RADIO SIGNAL FROM A U.S. GUIDANCE-CONTROL CENTER WILL SEND THE CAPSULE EARTHWARD!

THEN, MINUTES LATER...

FATE'S WITH ME! I'M ONLY A FEW MILES FROM THE AIRPORT WHERE **THE ACTOR** IS DUE TO LAND... AND THIS TIME, I'LL BE WAITING FOR HIM!

AND SO...

YOUR CAR, **ACTOR!**

THANK YOU! I WILL DRIVE MYSELF TO THE GENERAL'S HEADQUARTERS

BUT EN ROUTE, THE ACTOR ENCOUNTERS A STRANGE ROAD BLOCK...

HOLD IT, **ACTOR!** WE'RE GOING TO HAVE A NICE CHAT IN THE WOODS!

IRON MAN! IT'S YOU!!

H-HOW DID YOU **GET** HERE?

DOES KHRUSHCHEV TELL KENNEDY? SORRY, PAL, BUT THAT'S **MY** SECRET! IN THE MEANTIME, I'LL MAKE A NICE COZY CELL FOR YOU OUT OF THIS CAR!

CRUNNCHH

SAY! THEY DON'T BUILD 'EM SO STRONG BEHIND THE IRON CURTAIN, **DO** THEY?

11

NOW I'LL GAG YOU WITH YOUR POCKET HANDKERCHIEF SO YOU'LL MAKE NO OUTCRY! AND..OH, YES...I'LL TAKE THOSE PLANS BACK FOR STARK!

HA...I WAS RIGHT TO KEEP THIS ACE IN THE HOLE! EVEN IRON MAN DOESN'T REALIZE I KNOW HE'S ANTHONY STARK!

SOON, AT THE RED BARBARIAN'S, HEADQUARTER[S]

LOOK! IT'S IRON MAN!

PUT DOWN YOUR WEAPONS, FOOL[S] AND TAKE ME TO YOUR COMMANDE[R] LET THE RED BARBARIAN DECI[DE] WHETHER YOU SHOULD DESTROY ME!

CRASH

IRON MAN! YOU DARE TO COME HERE... WHERE DEATH AWAITS YOU?

HA! SO I FOOLED YOU, TOO, EH, GENERAL? SORRY EXCELLENCY, BUT I'M THE ACTOR! THAT'S HOW I MANAGED TO STEAL STARK'S PLANS... BY IMPERSONATING IRON MAN!

ACTOR, YOU'RE A POSITIVE GENIUS! AND THE PLANS... WHERE ARE THEY?

INSIDE THIS ATTACHE CASE! UNFORTUNATELY, WE CANNOT OPEN IT FOR ANOTHER FOUR HOURS BECAUSE IT HAS A TIME LOCK!

YOU KNOW HOW INGENIOUS STARK IS WITH TINY THINGS! WELL, HE PLANTED A MINIATURE A-BOMB INSIDE THAT LOCK! IF WE OPEN IT NOW, WE'LL BE BLOWN TO BITS!

WE CAN[...] WHAT'S [...] HOURS [...] PARED T[...] THE VA[...] OF THE [...] PRINTS [...] SIDE TH[...] CASE [...]

GOOD! THAT'S WHAT I EXPECTED YOU TO SAY! WELL, I'LL GO HOME NOW, GENERAL... I'LL GET OUT OF THIS TIN CAN AND 4½ HOURS FROM NOW, WE'LL OPEN THE CASE TOGETHER!

WONDERFUL! YOU'VE DONE A BRILLIANT JOB, ACTOR! WE'LL BOTH GO DOWN IN HISTORY FOR THIS MASTERPIECE OF ESPIONAGE!

SOON AFTER, AS IRON MAN RETURNS TO HIS PRISONER...

OKAY, ACTOR! YOU CAN LEAVE NOW... WITHOUT THE PLANS, OF COURSE!

TOO BAD ABOUT T[...] PLANS, BUT RED [...] BARBARIAN W[...] FORGIVE ME WHEN [I] TELL HIM THAT IRO[N] MAN IS ANTHONY STARK!

BZZZ

THEN OUR SPIES CAN FINISH OFF IRON MAN, WHEN HE IS MORE VULNERABLE, AS STARK!

I MUST ESCAPE TO THE NEAREST WESTERN COUNTRY WHILE I STILL HAVE A CHANCE! SO I'LL USE MY TRANSISTOR-JET FLYING POWER...

SOON...

GENERAL, FORGIVE ME FOR LOSING THE PLANS! BUT YOU WON'T MIND SO MUCH IRON MAN OUTWITTING ME --- NOT WHEN YOU HEAR THE STILL MORE VALUABLE INFORMATION I HAVE TO GIVE YOU!

WHAT ARE YOU TALKING ABOUT?

IRON MAN! HE AMBUSHED ME AND TOOK THE DISINTEGRATOR RAY PLANS WITH HIM! BUT WAIT TILL YOU HEAR WHAT I KNOW ABOUT HIM!

IDIOT! WHERE IS THE ATTACHE CASE...THE ONE WITH THE TIME LOCK?

WHAT TIME LOCK? WHAT CASE? IRON MAN JUST RELEASED ME FROM A METAL PRISON...

YOU'RE LYING!! YOU WERE HERE AN HOUR AGO, IMPERSONATING IRON MAN!

BUT EXCELLENCY... I DON'T HAVE THE PLANS!

SO YOU TRY TO DECEIVE THE RED BARBARIAN, DO YOU?

YOU IMPERSONATED IRON MAN TO TRICK ME...TO STALL FOR TIME TILL YOU YOURSELF COULD DISPATCH THE BLUEPRINTS TO OUR LEADER AND TAKE THE CREDIT!

WAIT! GENERAL... IF YOU SAW IRON MAN IT MUST HAVE REALLY BEEN HIM --- NOT ME...OW-W

BAH! DO YOU THINK I'M INSANE TO FALL FOR SO FANTASTIC A STORY? GUARD, DISPATCH THIS TRAITOR!

GENERAL! (GASP) WAIT! I KNOW WHO THE IRON MAN IS!.. WAIT!

THE ACTOR IS GONE, EXCELLENCY!

HMMPPHH! SERVES HIM RIGHT FOR TRYING TO TRICK ME! IMAGINE! HE SAID THAT THE REAL IRON MAN CAME HERE TO RETRIEVE THE PLANS AND THAT HE KNEW IRON MAN'S SECRET IDENTITY! BY LENIN'S BEARD! WHAT A FAIRY TALE!

THE END

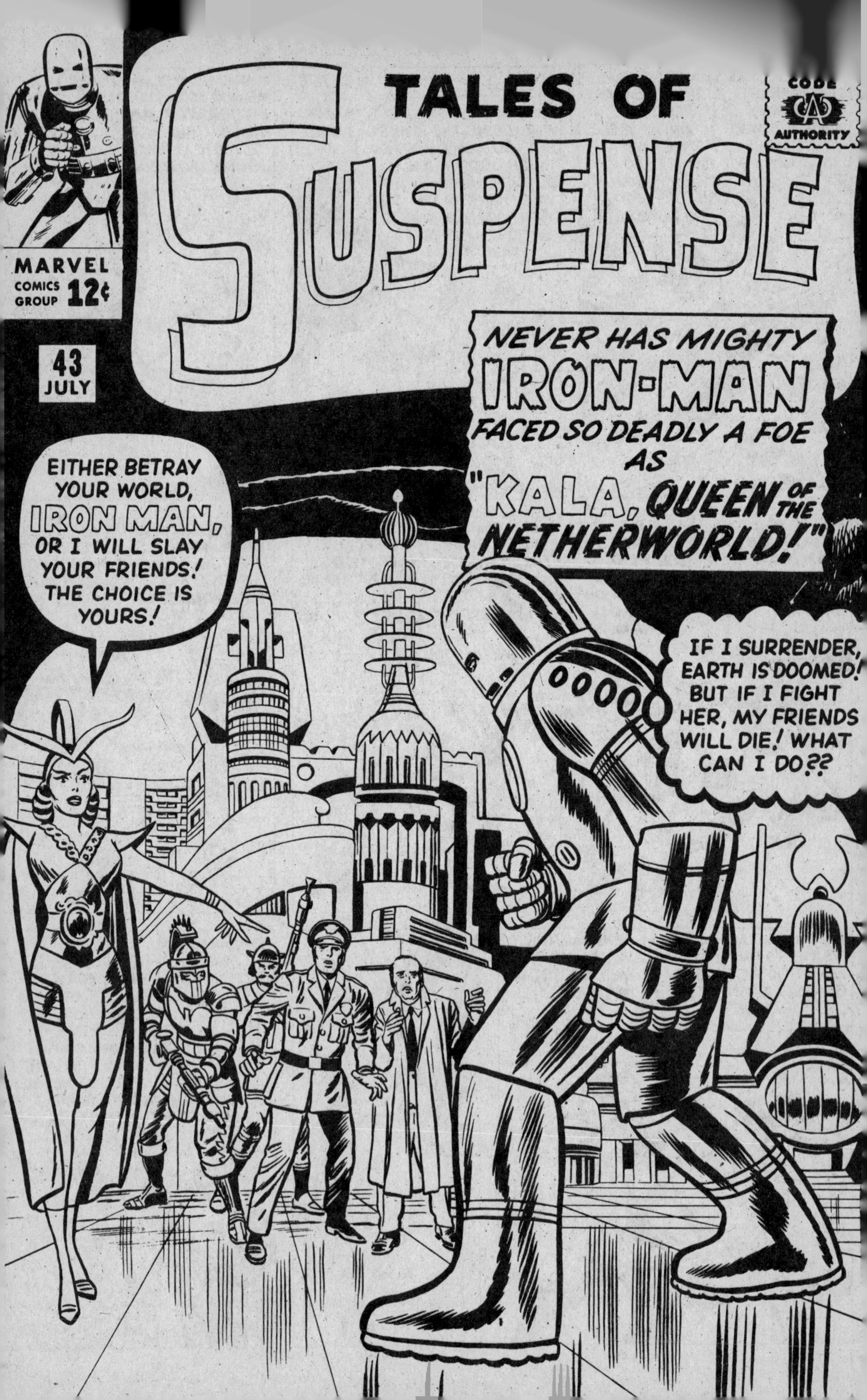
TALES OF SUSPENSE
CODE AUTHORITY
MARVEL COMICS GROUP 12¢
43 JULY
NEVER HAS MIGHTY IRON-MAN FACED SO DEADLY A FOE AS "KALA, QUEEN OF THE NETHERWORLD!"
EITHER BETRAY YOUR WORLD, IRON MAN, OR I WILL SLAY YOUR FRIENDS! THE CHOICE IS YOURS!
IF I SURRENDER, EARTH IS DOOMED! BUT IF I FIGHT HER, MY FRIENDS WILL DIE! WHAT CAN I DO??

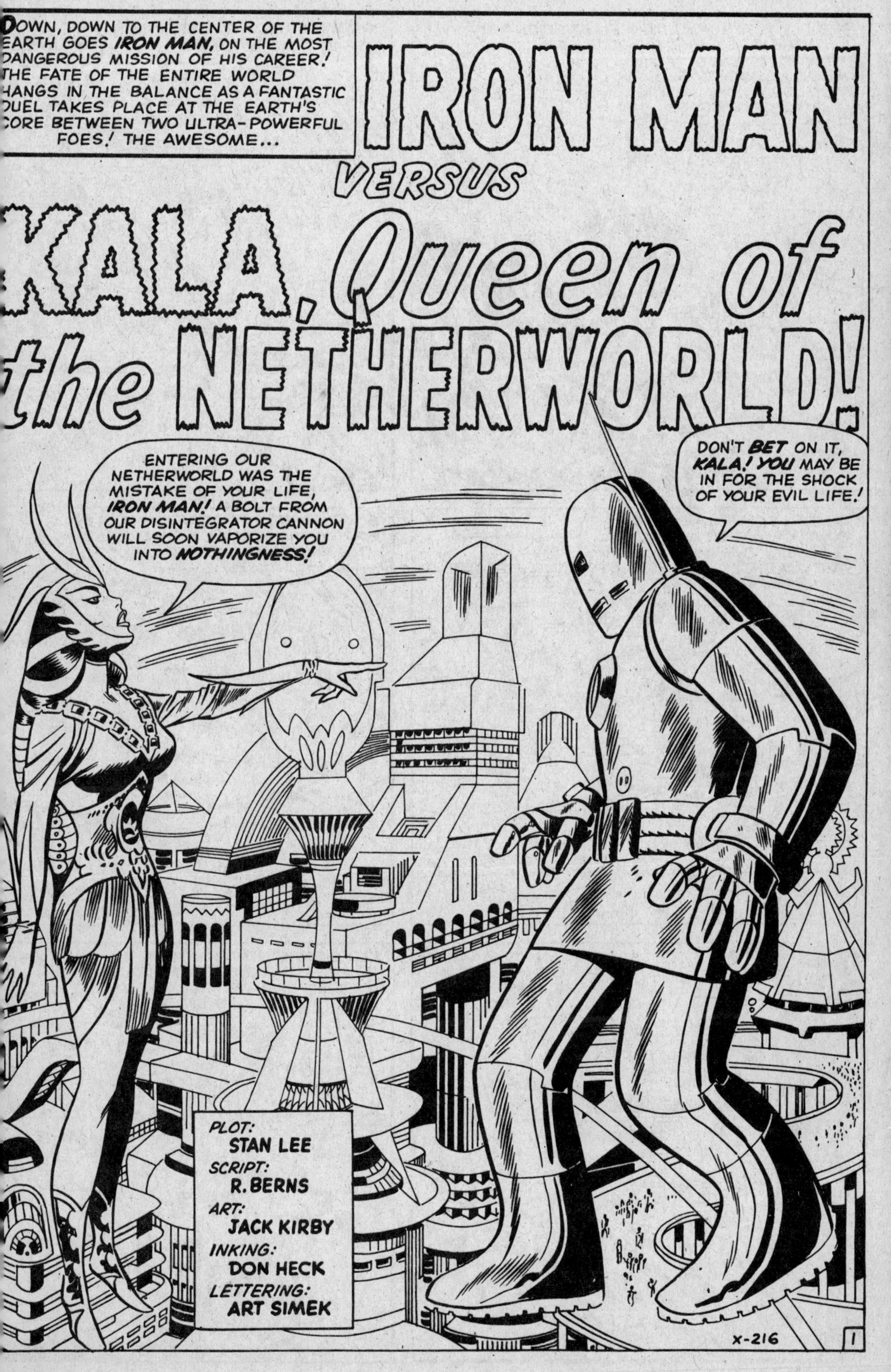
DOWN, DOWN TO THE CENTER OF THE EARTH GOES IRON MAN, ON THE MOST DANGEROUS MISSION OF HIS CAREER! THE FATE OF THE ENTIRE WORLD HANGS IN THE BALANCE AS A FANTASTIC DUEL TAKES PLACE AT THE EARTH'S CORE BETWEEN TWO ULTRA-POWERFUL FOES! THE AWESOME...
IRON MAN VERSUS KALA, Queen of the NETHERWORLD!
ENTERING OUR NETHERWORLD WAS THE MISTAKE OF YOUR LIFE, IRON MAN! A BOLT FROM OUR DISINTEGRATOR CANNON WILL SOON VAPORIZE YOU INTO NOTHINGNESS!
DON'T BET ON IT, KALA! YOU MAY BE IN FOR THE SHOCK OF YOUR EVIL LIFE!
PLOT: STAN LEE
SCRIPT: R.BERNS
ART: JACK KIRBY
INKING: DON HECK
LETTERING: ART SIMEK
X-216
1

ONE DAY, IN THE WIND TUNNEL AT SCIENTIST ANTHONY STARK'S PRIVATE LAB...

GOOD HEAVENS! THE WIND VELOCITY CONTROL PANEL EXPLODED!

WWHHHHRRRRR

BAAAAAM!

THE WIND'S GOING BERSERK! IT'S...OHHHHHH!

HELP!!

WHHHRRRRRR

GUARD! SOUND THE ALARM! CONTACT MISTER STARK! TELL HIM THE WIND MACHINES ARE GENERATING GUSTS OF TORNADO FORCE!

GOOD GRIEF! THE DRAFTS ARE RIPPING THE MISSILE WE WERE TESTING RIGHT OFF ITS MOUNTINGS!

RIPPP!

CRRASHHH

HEAVEN HELP ANYTHING THAT GETS IN THE WAY OF THAT THING!

I'LL SIGNAL MISTER STARK IN HIS PRIVATE OFFICE! BUT I DOUBT WHETHER EVEN HE CAN DO ANYTHING ABOUT THIS SITUATION!

BRAMMMMMM

SECONDS LATER...

TAKE IT EASY, GUARD! IT SO HAPPENS SOMEONE IS VISITING ME WHO CAN HANDLE THIS MENACE! IRON MAN WILL BE RIGHT THERE!

IRON MAN?! GOSH, WHAT A BREAK FOR US!

EMERGENCY PHONE

THEN, AS ANTHONY STARK QUICKLY OPENS HIS ATTACHÉ CASE...

LITTLE DOES ANYONE DREAM WHO IRON MAN REALLY IS! IN A MOMENT THIS COLLAPSIBLE ARMORED COSTUME WILL CONCEAL ANTHONY STARK'S BODY!

PRESENTLY, NEAR THE RUINED WIND TUNNEL...

LOOK! THERE'S IRON MAN! BUT WHAT CAN HE DO?

WELL, THOSE CYCLONIC WINDS SURE DON'T BOTHER HIM! IT'D TAKE AN EARTHQUAKE TO KNOCK HIM DOWN!

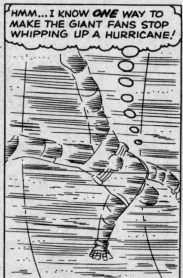

HMM...I KNOW ONE WAY TO MAKE THE GIANT FANS STOP WHIPPING UP A HURRICANE!

I'LL BLOW UP A STORM OF MY OWN...

...BY BECOMING A HUMAN FAN!

CRASH!

3

SOON AFTER, A MIGHTY METALLIC FIGURE LUMBERS OUT!

WOW! IT'S ALL JUST *SCRAP METAL* NOW!

DON'T WORRY! MISTER STARK CAN AFFORD TO ERECT *ANOTHER* SET OF BLOWERS THAT ARE FOOL-PROOF! NOW IT'S TIME I RETURNED TO HIM!

THEN, BACK IN STARK'S PRIVATE OFFICE...

I'D BETTER MAKE AN APPEARANCE AS ANTHONY STARK BEFORE MY STAFF STARTS WONDERING WHY *I* DIDN'T SHOW UP DURING THE EMERGENCY!

SINCE THERE'S LITTLE CHANCE OF ANOTHER CRISIS ARISING RIGHT AFTER THAT ONE, I'LL LEAVE MY COSTUME BEHIND!

GOSH, MISTER STARK, YOU SHOULD'VE SEEN *IRON MAN* IN ACTION! HE WAS SENSATIONAL!

YES, JIM...HE *IS* HANDY TO HAVE AROUND, ISN'T HE?

SUDDENLY...

YEEOWWWW!

≈GASP!≈ LOOK AT JIM!

WHAT TH...?!! H-HE'S DISINTE-GRATING!

HE-HE *VANISHED* RIGHT BEFORE OUR EYES! NOTHING'S LEFT BUT HIS *GUN!*

GREAT SCOTT! WHAT'S GOING ON? WE HEARD A TERRIBLE SCREAM!

IT'S JIM, THE GUARD! HE FADED AWAY INTO THIN AIR, LIKE A *GHOST!*

NEXT MOMENT...

YAAAAAA!

LOOK!! A MYSTERIOUS RAY OF LIGHT IS NOW ENVELOPING *EVANS!*

HE'S 'SAPPEARING 'UST AS JIM DID!

INCREDIBLE! IF WE DIDN'T **ALL** SEE THE SAME THING, I'D SAY ONE OF US **IMAGINED** IT!

MAYBE IT'S JUST SOME FORM OF MASS **HALLUCINATION!** ≈GASP!≈

MIGOSH! NOW SOMETHING IS SURROUNDING **MR. STARK!**

GET ME **OUT** OF HERE!

HE'S TRYING TO BREAK FREE, BUT HE **CAN'T!**

'HE THING IS SINKING INTO THE GROUND! 'VE MUST FREE HIM BEFORE IT'S TOO LATE!

WHACKKK

SOCKK

IT'S **IMPOSSIBLE!** IT DOESN'T SHATTER EVEN WITH **BULLETS!** THE SLUGS BOUNCE RIGHT **OFF** IT!

THEN STARK IS DOOMED... AND THE SAME FATE MIGHT OVERTAKE **ANY** OF US AT ANY MOMENT!

MEANWHILE, BELOW THE EARTH...

I'M DESCENDING AS IF I WERE ABOARD 'SOME SUPERNATURAL **ELEVATOR**, HEAD'ING FOR SOME UNBELIEVABLE **BASEMENT!** THIS CAN'T BE REAL! NOTHING OFFERS ANY **RESISTANCE** TO THIS GLASS CAGE! NO ROCK IMPEDES IT! BUT **HOW--??**

WAIT! I'M DROPPING INTO A STRANGE UNDERGROUND WORLD...

5

STARK HAS ARRIVED! *RELEASE HIM!*

YES, YOUR HIGHNESS!

BZZZZZ

BZZZZTTT

I AM *KALA,* QUEEN OF THE *NETHERWORLD!* WELCOME TO MY UNDERGROUND EMPIRE!

THIS IS FANTASTIC! NO ONE *SUSPECTED* THERE WAS ANY CIVILIZATION AT THE CORE OF THE EARTH!

WELL, NOW YOU KNOW *BETTER,* MR. STARK! SO WILL THE *WHOLE* WORLD, WHEN WE MAKE ITS ACQUAINTANCE! DO YOU RECOGNIZE ANY *FRIENDS?*

JIM! EVANS!

YES, MISTER STARK! *WE* JUST ARRIVED, TOO! WE'RE AT THE MERCY OF A BRILLIANT, RUTHLESS RACE!

YOUR FRIEND'S REMARK IS A *COMPLIMENT,* MR. STARK, FOR OUR CIVILIZATION *IS* SUPERIOR TO YOURS! WE NETHERWORLDERS POSSESS MANY SCIENTIFIC SECRETS UNKNOWN TO THE SURFACE WORLD!

NO DOUBT YOU CONSIDERED THE DISAPPEARANCE OF THESE TWO FOOLS AND YOURSELF AS SHEER MAGIC! BUT IT *WASN'T!* YOUR COMRADES WERE BROUGHT HERE IN ERROR, AS OUR ELECTRONIC RAYS PROBED THE SURFACE, LOOKING FOR *YOU!*

BUT WHAT DO YOU WANT *ME* FOR?

"I'LL EXPLAIN IN DUE TIME, MR. STARK! FIRST LET ME TELL YOU SOMETHING ABOUT *US!* WE NETHERWORLDERS ARE DESCENDANTS OF THE PEOPLE OF ATLANTIS, WHOSE EARTHLY CIVILIZATION WAS THE GLORY OF THE UNIVERSE!"

"THEN, AEONS AGO, ATLANTIS WAS MENACED BY GIGANTIC TIDAL WAVES, UNLEASHED BY A SERIES OF TERRIFYING LAND-AND-SEA QUAKES! BUT, OUR SCIENTIFIC GENIUSES WERE *PREPARED* FOR THE CATASTROPHE..."

QUICK! EVERYONE TO THE *DOME!*

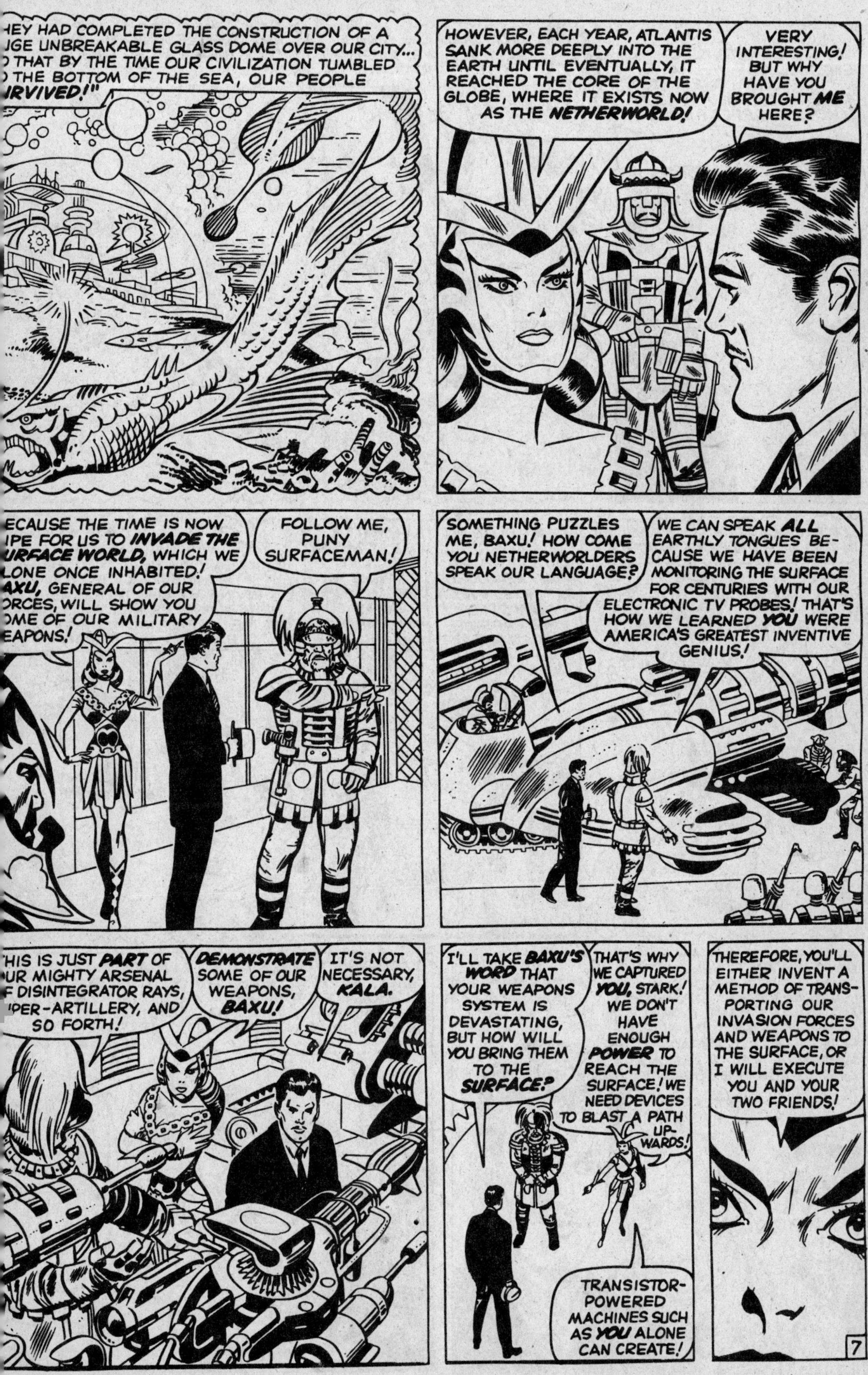

HEY HAD COMPLETED THE CONSTRUCTION OF A
UGE UNBREAKABLE GLASS DOME OVER OUR CITY...
O THAT BY THE TIME OUR CIVILIZATION TUMBLED
O THE BOTTOM OF THE SEA, OUR PEOPLE
URVIVED!"
HOWEVER, EACH YEAR, ATLANTIS SANK MORE DEEPLY INTO THE EARTH UNTIL EVENTUALLY, IT REACHED THE CORE OF THE GLOBE, WHERE IT EXISTS NOW AS THE NETHERWORLD!
VERY INTERESTING! BUT WHY HAVE YOU BROUGHT ME HERE?
ECAUSE THE TIME IS NOW IPE FOR US TO INVADE THE URFACE WORLD, WHICH WE LONE ONCE INHABITED! AXU, GENERAL OF OUR ORCES, WILL SHOW YOU OME OF OUR MILITARY EAPONS!
FOLLOW ME, PUNY SURFACEMAN!
SOMETHING PUZZLES ME, BAXU! HOW COME YOU NETHERWORLDERS SPEAK OUR LANGUAGE?
WE CAN SPEAK ALL EARTHLY TONGUES BECAUSE WE HAVE BEEN MONITORING THE SURFACE FOR CENTURIES WITH OUR ELECTRONIC TV PROBES! THAT'S HOW WE LEARNED YOU WERE AMERICA'S GREATEST INVENTIVE GENIUS!
THIS IS JUST PART OF UR MIGHTY ARSENAL F DISINTEGRATOR RAYS, UPER-ARTILLERY, AND SO FORTH!
DEMONSTRATE SOME OF OUR WEAPONS, BAXU!
IT'S NOT NECESSARY, KALA.
I'LL TAKE BAXU'S WORD THAT YOUR WEAPONS SYSTEM IS DEVASTATING, BUT HOW WILL YOU BRING THEM TO THE SURFACE?
THAT'S WHY WE CAPTURED YOU, STARK! WE DON'T HAVE ENOUGH POWER TO REACH THE SURFACE! WE NEED DEVICES TO BLAST A PATH UPWARDS!
TRANSISTOR-POWERED MACHINES SUCH AS YOU ALONE CAN CREATE!
THEREFORE, YOU'LL EITHER INVENT A METHOD OF TRANSPORTING OUR INVASION FORCES AND WEAPONS TO THE SURFACE, OR I WILL EXECUTE YOU AND YOUR TWO FRIENDS!
7

FOOLISH GIRL! DO YOU THINK OUR EARTH IS ENTIRELY DEFENSELESS? WE HAVE ONE PERSON ALONE... *IRON MAN*...WHO COULD SINGLE-HANDEDLY DEFEAT YOUR FORCES!

"*IRON MAN* CAN SINK A BATTLESHIP BY RIPPING OUT ITS BOTTOM..."

"...KNOCK SUPERSONIC-SPEED BOMBER OUT OF THE AIR WITH A SINGLE PUNCH,

POW!

"...OR BREAK A HUGE SPACE MISSILE IN TWO WITH HIS BARE HANDS...."

CRACK!

STARK DOES NOT LIE, *KALA!* I HAVE RECEIVED MANY MONITORED REPORTS OF *IRON MAN'S* DEEDS! PERHAPS WE SHOULD *DELAY* OUR INVASION PLANS, UNTIL....

BAH! YOU TALK LIKE A *TRAITOR*, BAXU! I *REPEAT* MY THREAT, STARK! DO AS I COMMAND OR YOU AND YOUR FRIENDS WILL DIE! AND NOT ONLY *THAT*...

"I WILL ACTIVATE A MACHINE WHICH CAN REVERSE THE EARTH'S AXIS CAUSING UPHEAVAL TO THE SURFACE WORLD, DE-STROYING ALL LIFE THERE, WHILE WE NETHERLANDERS WILL BE UNHARMED AT THE CORE OF THE PLANET! AND THIS IS NO IDLE THREAT!"

DON'T *LISTEN* TO HER, MISTER STARK! SHE'S PROBABLY LYING, AND *OUR* THREE LIVES ARE UNIMPORTANT COM-PARED WITH THE TERRIBLE FATE THAT WILL BEFALL MANKIND IF KALA'S LEGIONS EVER REACH THE SURFACE!

I *DISAGREE*, EVANS!

I'M GOING TO *HELP* KALA ALL I CAN! BUT I'LL REQUIRE A LABORATORY, TOTAL PRIVACY, CERTAIN MATERIALS, AND ABSOLUTELY NO INTERFERENCE!

I *KNEW* YOU'D CONSIDER YOUR OWN SKIN, BEFORE THAT OF YOUR FELLOW EARTHLINGS! BAXU, GIVE STARK EVERYTHIN[G] HE NEEDS TO AID OUR CAUSE!

...LAST YOU, STARK! WHEN THE CHIPS WERE DOWN, YOU TURNED **YELLOW**! YOU DON'T CARE **TWO PINS** FOR MANKIND!

WHY **SHOULD** I? ONE'S FIRST INSTINCT IS SELF-PRESERVATION! MY OWN LIFE IS ALL I CARE ABOUT! LET'S GO, **BAXU**! I'VE GOT WORK TO DO!

YOU DON'T APPROVE OF THIS EARTH INVASION, DO YOU, **BAXU?**

NO! FIRST, I'M NOT SURE WE **CAN** SUCCEED! WHO KNOWS WHAT UNKNOWN PROBLEMS WE MIGHT ENCOUNTER ON THE SURFACE? SECOND, I HATE TAKING ORDERS FROM A **WOMAN**!

THEN WHY **DO** YOU? AS GENERAL OF THE NETHER-WORLD ARMY, **YOU** COULD SEIZE POWER! BESIDES, I HAVE A FEELING YOU **LOVE** KALA, DESPITE HER ARROGANCE!

AYE! BUT I REFUSE TO KNUCKLE UNDER TO **ANY** FEMALE, BEAUTIFUL AS SHE MAY BE! BUT WE'RE NOT HERE TO DISCUSS **MY** PROBLEMS! I SHALL EQUIP YOUR LABORATORY!

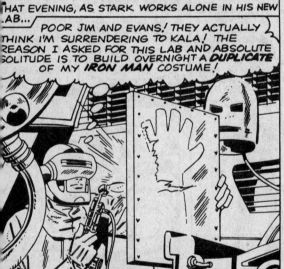

THAT EVENING, AS STARK WORKS ALONE IN HIS NEW LAB...

POOR JIM AND EVANS! THEY ACTUALLY THINK I'M SURRENDERING TO KALA! THE REASON I ASKED FOR THIS LAB AND ABSOLUTE SOLITUDE IS TO BUILD OVERNIGHT A **DUPLICATE** OF MY **IRON MAN** COSTUME!

NEXT MORNING...

STARK? THIS IS KALA! HOW ARE YOU PROGRESSING?

ADMIRABLY, YOUR HIGHNESS! IN FACT, YOU WILL SOON **SEE** THE FRUITS OF MY LABORS!

MOMENTS AFTER...

LOOK!!!

YES, **BAXU!** STARK **TRICKED** KALA! HE SPENT THE NIGHT MAKING HIS ESCAPE TO THE SURFACE, AND THEN SENT **ME** DOWN HERE TO FOIL YOUR INVASION PLOT!

DON'T BOTHER TRYING TO USE YOUR RAY PISTOL ON **ME**, BAXU! I'VE CRUMBLED IT TO POWDER!

=GASP!= THEN **YOU** MUST BE THE EARTH HERO STARK SPOKE ABOUT...

9

RIGHT, BAXU!...*IRON MAN!* I CAME TO GIVE YOU NETHER-WORLDERS A DEMONSTRATION OF WHAT WILL HAPPEN IF YOU SEND YOUR ARMY EARTHWARD!

YIIIIIIIII!

NOW YOU'RE GOING TO *SLAY* ME, IS *THAT* IT?

NO, BAXU! AS YOU KNO I HAVE ONLY TO STAM MY FOOT TO FLATTEN YOU INTO A PANCAKE. BUT I HAVE NO INTENTION OF HARMIN YOU!

STARK SPOKE WELL OF YOU AS A MAN OF COURAGE AND IN-TELLIGENCE, SO I WILL SPARE YOUR LIFE! I BELIEVE *YOU* SHOULD BE THE NATURAL RULER OF THE NETHERWORLD INSTEAD OF THAT BEAUTIFUL BUT VAIN CREATURE, *KALA!*

STILL, HER WEAPONS *ARE* TERRIFYING, *IRON MAN!* THEY MIGHT DESTROY YOU *DESPITE* YOUR AMAZING STRENGTH!

BUT IT'S NOT ONLY *BRUTE STRENGTH* I POSSESS, *BAXU!* STAND ASIDE AND WATCH WHAT I CAN DO WITH *ELECTRONIC POWERS!*

YOUR HIGHNESS! STARK FLED TO THE SURFACE AND SENT *IRON MAN* TO DO BATTLE WITH US! HE ALREADY SUBDUED *BAXU!*

THEN USE OU INVINCIBLE WEAPONS T DESTROY *IRON MAN* OBLITERAT HIM WITH OUR DISINTEGRATO CANNON!

FAREWELL, *IRON MAN!* SOON YOU WILL BE VAPORIZED INTO NOTHINGNESS!

ONLY IF I *LET* THAT DISINTEGRATOR BOLT HIT ME! BUT INSTEAD, I WILL AIM AN ELECTRONIC *REVERSE-ENERGY* BEAM AT THE BOLT!

SUDDENLY, THERE IS A LOUD *EXPLOSION* AS TH TWO BEAMS COLLIDE...

WHOOM!

AND THE RESULT? THE *DISINTEGRATOR* IS *DISINTEGRATED!* GOT ANY *OTHER* BRIGHT IDEAS, *KALA?*

YES! OUR IMPER-SONIC *FLAME THROWER!* IT WILL REDUCE YOUR IRON COSTUME TO *MOLTEN METAL!*

MERE FLAME, KALA? YOU LACK IMAGINATION! I HAVE MERELY TO TOSS A PELLET OF CONCENTRATED CHEMICAL CRYSTALS AT THE FLAME WHICH IS ABOUT TO ENGULF ME...

..AND *LO!* THE CRYSTALS TRANSFORM THE FLAME CHEMICALLY INTO *A BLOCK OF ICE...*

...WHICH, BY THE WAY SHATTERS TO BITS AGAINST MY BODY! *SNOW,* ANYONE?

DON'T GLOAT *YET,* IRON MAN! WE'LL GET YOU WITH OUR *MAGNETICALLY-DIRECTED MACHINE GUN* WHICH FIRES *ATOMIC BULLETS!*

BRACKA

BRACKA

BRACKA

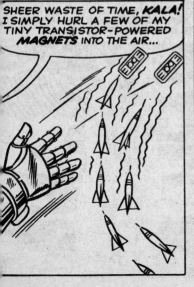

SHEER WASTE OF TIME, *KALA!* I SIMPLY HURL A FEW OF MY TINY TRANSISTOR-POWERED *MAGNETS* INTO THE AIR...

...AND YOUR ATOMIC BULLETS ALTER THEIR COURSE...*UPWARD!*

PWINNGG!

PWHNNGG!

PWINNG!

FOOLISH QUEEN! SO FAR I HAVE RESTRICTED MYSELF ONLY TO *DEFENSIVE* MEASURES AGAINST YOUR WEAPONS! *BUT...*

11

CAN YOU IMAGINE WHAT WOULD HAPPEN IF I PROTECTED *ALL EARTHMEN* BY *MULTIPLYING* THEM ELECTRONICALLY WITH COUNTLESS IMAGES?? *WATCH!!*

SEE, KALA? THE TINY MIRRORS I DISTRIBUTED...

...*CREATE MULTIPLE ILLUSIONS* OF ME...

...LIKE THE MANY VISIONS YOU MAY SEE IN A TRICK *MIRROR!*

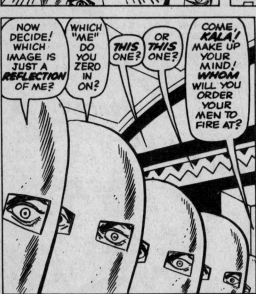

NOW *DECIDE!* WHICH IMAGE IS JUST A *REFLECTION* OF ME?

WHICH "*ME*" DO YOU *ZERO* IN ON?

THIS ONE?

OR *THIS* ONE?

COME, KALA! MAKE UP YOUR MIND! *WHOM* WILL YOU ORDER YOUR MEN TO FIRE AT?

SUDDENLY, IRON MAN DETACHES HIMSELF FROM THE MULTIPLE IMAGES, SEIZING *KALA* AS SHE SHRIEKS IN DISMAY...

WHILE YOU'RE MAKING UP YOUR MIND, I'LL TAKE YOU ON A LITTLE *JOURNEY!*

NO!!

YOU'RE MAD!! WE'LL CRASH INTO THE GLASS DOME AND BE *KILLED!*

NONSENSE. THE "*UNBREAKABLE*" GLASS WILL *YIELD* TO THE SPEED GENERATED BY MY ATTACHMENTS AND THE TRANSISTOR-POWERED CLIPPER IN MY HAND!

SEE? WE'RE PENETRATING THE GLASS AS IF IT WERE MADE OF *BUTTER!*

THE SAME GOES FOR THE LAYERS BETWEEN US AND THE SURFACE! MY NUCLEAR-POWERED CLIPPERS ARE GOUGING OUT A NICE, WIDE SHAFT.

BEHOLD, KALA! WE'RE ON EARTH'S SURFACE NOW... BUT *YOU* HAVEN'T SURVIVED THE JOURNEY AS WELL AS YOU MIGHT HAVE EXPECTED!

AS I FIGURED, THE ATMOSPHERE UP HERE IS VASTLY DIFFERENT FROM THAT IN THE NETHERWORLD... AND IT HAS CAUSED SOME HIDEOUS *CHANGES* IN YOU! LOOK INTO THAT POOL OF WATER!

BY THE GODS! I-I AM *HIDEOUS!* I'VE TURNED INTO AN OLD HAG!

EXACTLY! AND THE INSTANT YOUR NETHERWORLD ARMY HIT THE SURFACE, THEY WOULD *ALSO* AGE AND GROW WEAK AS OLD MEN! *NOW* DO YOU WANT TO INVADE EARTH? OR...

NO, *NO!* TAKE ME BACK! I *IMPLORE* YOU! I WANT TO BE YOUNG AND BEAUTIFUL AGAIN, EVEN IF IT MEANS REMAINING IN THE NETHERWORLD FOREVER!

A WISE DECISION, KALA! YOU MAY BE CRUEL AND AMBITIOUS, BUT YOU ARE *NOT* STUPID!

PRESENTLY, IN THE NETHERWORLD ONCE MORE...

I AM *MYSELF* AGAIN! THANK YOU, IRON MAN, FOR NOT DESTROYING MY BEAUTY! I WILL ALLOW STARK'S FRIENDS TO GO FREE!

IRON MAN! YOU HERE, TOO!??

YES... AND HE'S JUST WONDERFUL! WON'T YOU *STAY* HERE WITH ME, IRON MAN? TOGETHER, WE CAN RULE THE NETHERWORLD!

I'M FLATTERED BY YOUR INVITATION, KALA! BUT THERE ARE *OTHER* MEN MORE SUITABLE THAN *I* TO BECOME KING OF YOUR UNDER-GROUND EMPIRE! FOR EXAMPLE... *BAXU!*

MARRY *KALA,* BAXU... AND RULE WISELY! KALA WILL EXPLAIN TO YOU WHY ANY THOUGHT OF AN EARTH INVASION IS SHEER FOLLY!

I THOUGHT THAT LONG AGO! THANK YOU, *IRON MAN,* FOR TEACHING OUR RULER A WELL-DESERVED LESSON! NEVER FORGET THAT YOU'LL ALWAYS BE WELCOME HERE!

NEXT DAY ON EARTH, AT A COCKTAIL PARTY...

HMM... THERE'S TONY STARK, NEW YORK'S BIGGEST *WOLF!* AT LEAST HIS ADVENTURE UNDER THE EARTH KEPT HIM AWAY FROM THE *GIRLS* FOR A WHILE!!

THAT'S WHAT YOU THINK, BUB!

THE END

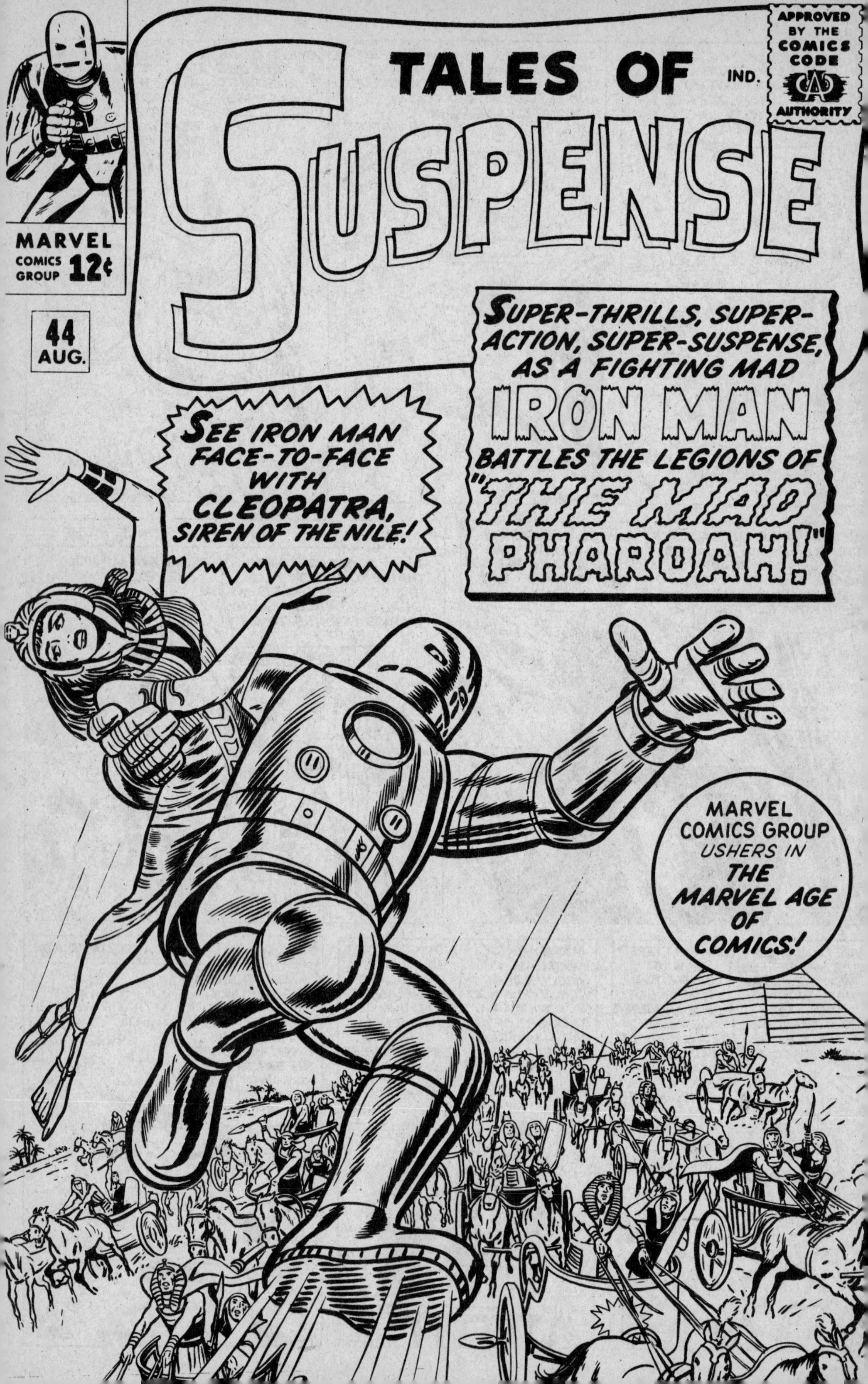
MARVEL COMICS GROUP 12¢
44 AUG.
TALES OF SUSPENSE
IND.
APPROVED BY THE COMICS CODE AUTHORITY
SUPER-THRILLS, SUPER-ACTION, SUPER-SUSPENSE, AS A FIGHTING MAD
IRON MAN
BATTLES THE LEGIONS OF "THE MAD PHAROAH!"
SEE IRON MAN FACE-TO-FACE WITH CLEOPATRA, SIREN OF THE NILE!
MARVEL COMICS GROUP USHERS IN THE MARVEL AGE OF COMICS!

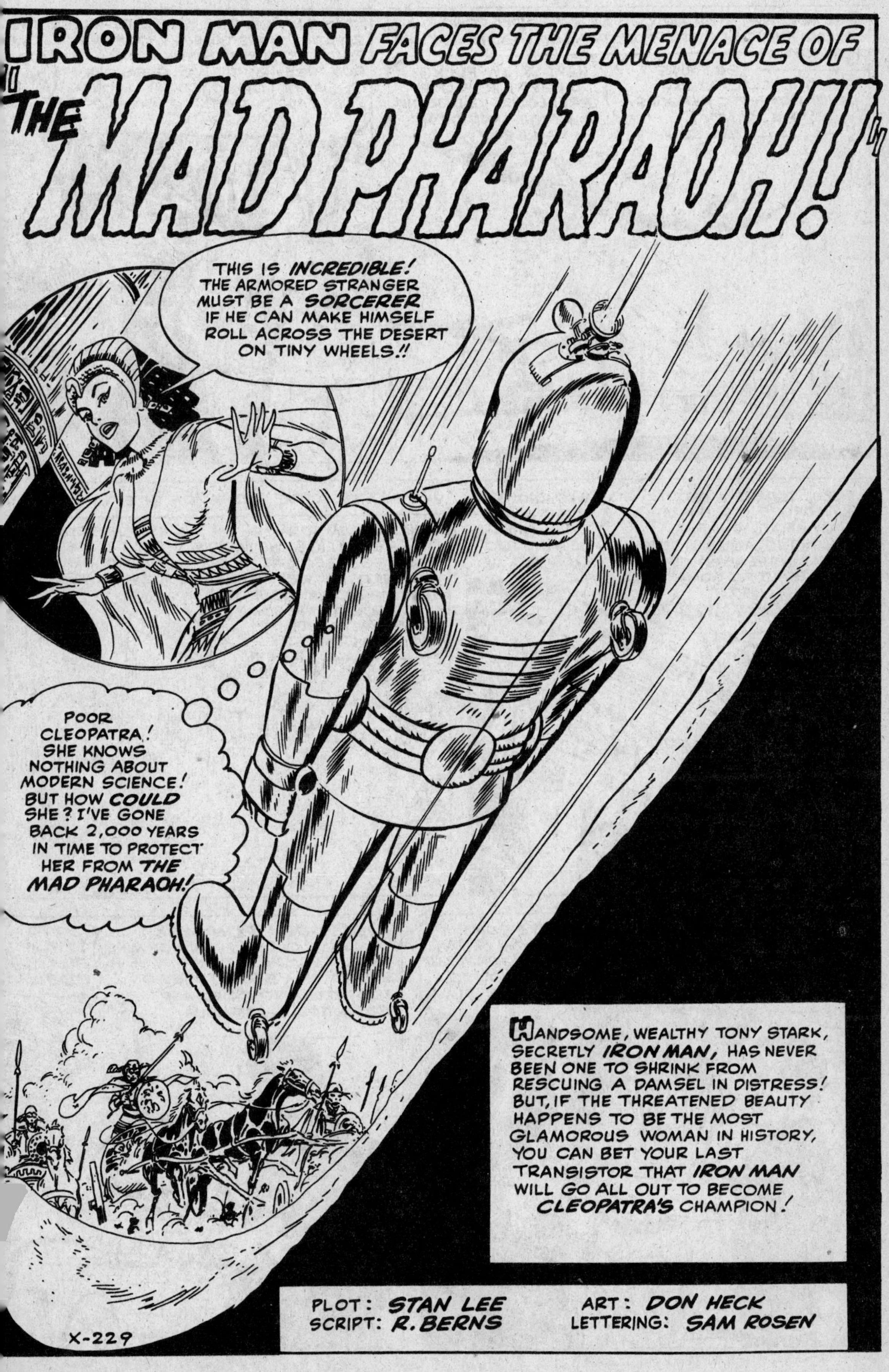
IRON MAN FACES THE MENACE OF
"THE MAD PHARAOH!"
THIS IS INCREDIBLE! THE ARMORED STRANGER MUST BE A SORCERER IF HE CAN MAKE HIMSELF ROLL ACROSS THE DESERT ON TINY WHEELS.!!
POOR CLEOPATRA! SHE KNOWS NOTHING ABOUT MODERN SCIENCE! BUT HOW COULD SHE? I'VE GONE BACK 2,000 YEARS IN TIME TO PROTECT HER FROM THE MAD PHARAOH!
HANDSOME, WEALTHY TONY STARK, SECRETLY IRON MAN, HAS NEVER BEEN ONE TO SHRINK FROM RESCUING A DAMSEL IN DISTRESS! BUT, IF THE THREATENED BEAUTY HAPPENS TO BE THE MOST GLAMOROUS WOMAN IN HISTORY, YOU CAN BET YOUR LAST TRANSISTOR THAT IRON MAN WILL GO ALL OUT TO BECOME CLEOPATRA'S CHAMPION!
PLOT: STAN LEE
SCRIPT: R. BERNS
ART: DON HECK
LETTERING: SAM ROSEN
X-229

ONE MORNING, AT AN AIRPORT, AS NEWSMEN CROWD AROUND ANTHONY STARK, WORLD-FAMOUS SCIENTIST AND PLAYBOY...

SO YOU'RE GOING TO CLEOPATRA-LAND! ROMANTIC REASONS, MR. STARK?

HARDLY! I'M FLYING TO EGYPT TO HELP AN ARCHEOLOGICAL FRIEND MAKE THE FIND OF HIS CAREER!

TOO BAD! KNOWING YOUR LADY-KILLER REPUTATION, WE THOUGHT YOU WERE EN ROUTE TO A NEW INTERNATIONAL ROMANCE! BY THE WAY, SPEAKING OF EGYPT, HOW DO YOU THINK YOU'D HAVE MADE OUT WITH THE "SIREN OF THE NILE"?

YOU MEA CLE PATR

RIGHT! TODAY'S MOST GLAMOROUS GIRLS ARE CRAZY ABOUT YOU! BUT WOULDN'T IT HAVE BEEN TOUGH-ER TO WIN THE HEART OF THE MOST BEAUTIFUL WOMAN WHO EVER LIVED... CLEOPATRA?

WHO KNOWS? RIGHT NOW, I THINK SHE'D BE A BIT TOO OLD FOR ME!

DAYS LATER, AT THE EXCAVATION SITE...

OUR PROBLEM TODAY IS WHERE TO DIG? KING HATAP'S TOMB MIGHT BE RIGHT UNDER OUR FEET! BUT WE'D SAVE A YEAR OF EXCAVATING IF YOU COULD LOCATE THE TOMB FOR US...YOU WITH YOUR INVENTIVE GENIUS!

I'M FLATTERED, PAUL! BUT THE ONE YOU SHOULD HAVE SENT FOR IS... IRON MAN

WITH HIS ELECTRONIC PROBING DEVICES, IRON MAN COULD SPOT THE TOMB IMMEDIATELY AND SAVE YOU MONTHS OF AIMLESS DIGGING!

BUT I DON'T KNOW IRON MAN! NOR WOULD I KNOW HOW TO CONTACT HIM!

WELL, I DO! IRON MAN IS A--ER..CLOSE FRIEND OF MINE, AND LUCKILY HE HAPPENS TO BE IN EGYPT ON A SECRET MISSION! I'LL RETURN TO CAIRO AND GET IN TOUCH WITH HIM!

GOSH, TONY..IF ONLY YOU COULD...

LITTLE DOES PAUL SUSPECT THAT HIS MILLIONAIRE INDUSTRIALIST PAL, TONY STARK, IS REALLY *IRON MAN!!* AND THAT MY COSTUME IS CONCEALED IN THIS ATTACHE CASE! I'LL AMUSE MYSELF IN CAIRO TONIGHT... THEN FLY BACK HERE TOMORROW AS *IRON MAN!*

THAT EVENING, AT A CAIRO NIGHT SPOT...

MORE CHAMPAGNE, MR. STARK?

UHH... NO, THANKS! I'M GETTING DIZZY! THE CHEST PLATE THAT KEEPS MY INJURED HEART BEATING NEEDS ELECTRICAL RE-CHARGING! I MUST RETURN TO MY HOTEL AT ONCE!

SOON AFTER, AT THE HOTEL...

BY JOVE! YOU LOOK PALE, STARK! ARE YOU ILL?

ER... PERHAPS THIS NIGHT CLUB WAS TOO STUFFY...

NIGHT CLUB... *BUNK!* I NEED RE-CHARGING... *FAST!!* IF THESE BELLHOPS DON'T GET ME TO MY ROOM SOON, I'LL PASS OUT!

MINUTES LATER...

=GASP!= SOCKET... GOT TO PLUG THIS CORD INTO A SOCKET!

...AHHH! HOW AMAZED THE WORLD WOULD BE TO SEE ME LYING ON THE FLOOR LIKE THIS... CLINGING TO LIFE BY AN ELECTRIC CURRENT...

BUT THEIR SHOCK WOULD BE EVEN *GREATER* IF THEY KNEW I WAS *IRON MAN.* BUT, ALAS, MANY SECRETS MUST LIVE AND DIE WITH ANTHONY STARK!

NEXT MORNING, BEFORE DAWN...

I'D BETTER SWITCH TO *IRON MAN* BEFORE THE CITY AWAKENS! WHEN I ARRIVE AT THE EXCAVATION, I'LL TELL PAUL THAT STARK REMAINED IN CAIRO FOR BUSINESS REASONS!

3.

LATER, AT THE ARCHEOLOGICAL DIGGINGS...

BEHOLD! *IRON MAN* APPROACHES!

ANTHONY STARK CONTACTED ME! HE SAID YOU WANTED ME TO LOCATE A TOMB FOR YOU!

YES, BUT IT WOULD TAKE SHEER *MAGIC* TO SEE THROUGH THESE WALLS!

NO! NOT MAGIC! MERELY A DEVICE LIKE THIS *TINY FLUOROSCOPE* ENERGIZED BY THE MOST POWERFUL TRANSISTORS IN EXISTENCE! IT CAN PENETRATE FOOT-THICK WALLS!

WE'RE IN LUCK! I'VE FOUND HATAP'S TOMB FIRST CRACK OUT OF THE BOX!

MARVEL-OUS! I'LL TELL THE WORKERS TO BEGIN DIGGING!

DON'T BOTHER! I'LL USE THESE DIAMOND DRILLS THAT CAN PENETRATE THE TOUGHEST ROCK! STAND BACK!

BZZZZZZZZ

BZZZZ

PRESTO! THE TOMB OF KING HATAP!

GASP! THERE'S HATAP'S ROYAL CREST, CARVED ON THE SARCOPHAGUS! THE POISON ASP!

DID YOU KNOW THAT BECAUSE OF HIS UNCANNY KNOWLEDGE OF BLACK ARTS AND HIS RUTHLESS CRIMES, HE WAS CALLED "*THE MAD PHARAOH*?

NO.. BUT IT'S LUCKY FOR MANKIND THAT HE'S NO MORE THAN A *MUMMY!*

4

MMM...I'VE NEVER **SEEN** SUCH MUMMY WRAPPINGS! HATAP MUST'VE HAD HIS OWN PECULIAR IDEAS ABOUT EMBALMING!

WELL, I'LL LEAVE **YOU** TO STUDY THEM! STARK SHOULD SHOW UP SOON TO EXPLORE THE TOMB WITH YOU!

PRESENTLY, A FEW MILES AWAY...

NOW FOR A QUICK CHANGE BACK TO STARK BEFORE THE GOOD PROFESSOR SUSPECTS WE ARE ONE AND THE SAME PERSON!

...ATER, AT THE EXCAVATION...

TONY, THE STRANGEST THING HAS HAPPENED! THE MUMMY HAS **VANISHED!!** ONE OF THE DIGGERS MUST HAVE **STOLEN** IT!

BUT WHAT WOULD A LABORER WANT WITH HATAP'S REMAINS?

I DON'T KNOW...BUT I MUST SEND OUT SEARCH PARTIES! THE THIEVES CAN'T HAVE GOTTEN FAR!

OKAY, PAUL...I'LL LOOK AFTER THINGS HERE!

GOOD, STARK! WE'RE WELL **RID** OF THAT ARCHEOLOGICAL FOOL!

WHO ARE **YOU**?! HOW DID YOU GET INTO MY TENT?

WAIT! THAT RING ON YOUR FINGER! IT'S THE **SACRED ASP!**

IS THAT **ALL** YOU CAN RECOGNIZE! LOOK AT MY FACE!

IT'S THE SAME AS...THE PAINTING OF **KING HATAP** ON THE SARCOPHAGUS!

CORRECT, STARK! **I AM HATAP,** THE "MUMMY" THEY ARE SEEKING! BUT NOBODY CARRIED ME OFF! I SIMPLY **WALKED** OUT OF THE SARCOPHAGUS!

5.

BUNK! THIS IS SOME KIND OF **HOAX!** **NOBODY** RETURNS FROM THE DEAD!

WHO SAID I **WAS** DEAD?! 2,000 YEARS AGO, ACCORDING TO HISTORY, I WAS KILLED BATTLING CLEOPATRA'S ARMY!

"BUT WHEN I STAGED MY REBELLION AGAINST CLEOPATRA, I TOOK CERTAIN **PRECAUTIONS** AGAINST DEFEAT..."

LOOK! HATAP KNOWS HIS CAUSE IS LOST! HE'S DRINKING POISON!

POISON, BAH! THE FOOLS DON'T **DREAM** WHAT I'M REALLY DOING!

"BY THE TIME CLEOPATRA'S SOLDIER REACHED ME, I LAY MOTIONLESS O. THE GROUND..."

HE IS RIGID! HIS HEART HAS STOPPED BEATING! HATAP IS DEAD!

THIS IS CAUSE FOR REJOICIN. LET US CARR. HIS CARCASS TO CLEOPATRA

"CLEOPATRA HAD ME EMBALMED AND ENTOMBED ACCORDING TO MY FINAL WILL AND INSTRUCTIONS..."

WITH HATAP GONE, GREAT CLEOPATRA, YOU NEED BATTLE NONE BUT THE ROMAN INVADERS!

TRUE! BUT FINISH THE BURIAL QUICKLY! HATAP'S TOMB GIVES ME A STRANGE, FEARFUL FEELING!

I DECEIVED **ALL** OFF THEM, STARK! I HAD SWALLOWED A SERUM THAT PUT ME IN A STATE OF **SUSPENDED ANIMATION** WHICH LASTED **2,000 YEARS!**

NOW I SHALL **RETURN** TO THE PAST, DEFEAT CLEOPATRA AND RULE EGYPT AS I HAD ORIGINALLY PLANNED! HOWEVER, **YOU**, STARK, WILL RETURN **WITH** ME! FOR I HAVE LEARNED WHO YOU ARE... AND HOW BRILLIANT YOU ARE!

AS ONE OF THE GREATEST SCIENTISTS OF THE 20TH CENTURY YOUR SKILLS WILL BE INVALUABLE TO ME! AND ONCE YOU SEE WHAT I HAVE DONE TO YOUR CAMP YOU WILL HAVE TO AGREE TO MY TERMS!

WITH MY SORCERY, I HAVE CAUSED A DISEASE TO AFFECT YOUR WORKERS! THE PLAGUE WILL SPREAD UNLESS YOU ENTER THE PAST! FOR ONLY *I* KNOW ITS CURE!

LOOKS LIKE I'VE NO CHOICE! OKAY, MISTER.. YOU WIN! I'LL GO WITH YOU!

MINUTES LATER...

I HAVE REVIVED YOUR MEN... ENDED THE PLAGUE! AND NOW, RUB THIS GOLDEN CHARM TWICE AND YOU SHALL BE TRANSPORTED INTO THE PAST WITH *ME!*

HE DOES NOT KNOW I'D BE BEGGING HIM TO TAKE ME, EVEN IF HE DIDN'T WANT TO!

A CHANCE TO TRAVEL TO THE PAST.!! IF HE CAN REALLY *DO* IT, IT WILL BE THE ADVENTURE OF A LIFETIME FOR ME ...AND FOR *IRON MAN!*

RUBBING THIS GOLDEN CHARM WILL SUMMON THE FORCES OF BLACK MAGIC...MYSTIC POWERS KNOWN ONLY TO ANCIENT EGYPTIAN SORCERY! IT WILL SUMMON THE *CHARIOT OF TIME!*

THEN I NEED ONLY RUB IT TWICE TO *RETURN* TO THE PRESENT?

AYE! BUT YOU SHALL *NOT* RETURN! NOT TILL YOU HAVE HELPED ME *DEFEAT CLEOPATRA!*

AND THEN, AFTER RUBBING THE CHARM...

AMAZING!! I KNOW I'M UNDER SOME OCCULT HYPNOTIC SPELL! WE ARE TRAVELING IN TIME... THROUGH HATAP'S POWERS OF MAGIC...AS HE CONJURES UP A VISION OF A NON-EXISTENT CHARIOT!

BUT, AS SUDDENLY AS IT BEGAN, THE ILLUSION ENDS AND ANTHONY STARK FINDS...

NO CAMP! NO MEN! I REALLY *AM* BACK IN ANCIENT EGYPT!

OF COURSE! NOW COME...YOU ARE MINE TO COMMAND!

THAT'S WHAT *YOU* THINK, MISTER! FROM HERE ON IN, IT'S EVERY MAN FOR HIMSELF!

IF I CAN JUST SLIDE DOWN THE BACK OF THIS SAND DUNE AND CHANGE TO *IRON MAN* BEFORE HE REACHES ME!

7.

FOOL! YOU CANNOT ESCAPE ME! HERE IN THIS LAND OF PHARAOHS, **I AM SUPREME!**

MADE IT! AND NOW, IF THERE'S GOING TO BE A BATTLE BETWEEN HATAP AND CLEOPATRA, **IRON MAN** WOULDN'T MISS IT FOR THE WORLD!

STARK! WHERE ARE YOU? **ANSWER ME!**

I'VE BURIED MY ATTACHE CASE! I WON'T NEED IT TILL I RETURN TO THE PRESENT!

BY ISIS! WHAT SORT OF **BIRD** IS THAT... ENCASED IN ARMOR, MAN-SHAPED! PERHAPS THAT IS WHY STARK DOESN'T REPLY! THAT FLYING MONSTER HAS **SLAIN** HIM!

I MUST FLEE, LEST HE ATTACK **ME,** TOO!

I SUSPECT THIS ISN'T THE LAST I'LL SEE OF HATAP! BUT MY FIRST CONCERN IS TO FIND THE COURT OF **CLEOPATRA!**

GOOD THING MY TRANSISTOR-POWERED AIR PRESSURE JETS ARE FULLY CHARGED! I WON'T BE ABLE TO RE-CHARGE THEM AGAIN TILL I RETURN TO THE PRESENT!

DOWN BELOW...A MIGHTY ROMAN LEGION... LAYING SIEGE TO AN EGYPTIAN PALACE! I GUESS A MAN HAS TO SIDE WITH THE UNDER-DOG, EVEN IN THE PAST! SO I'LL TRY TO HELP THE DEFENDING EGYPTIANS!

FIRST... I'LL KNOCK OUT THE ROMAN CATAPULTS!

BY THE GODS! A FLYING WARRIOR DESCENDS FROM THE SKY!

CR-R-RACK-K-K!

BEHOLD HOW HE PICKS UP OUR RED-HOT MISSILES IN HIS HANDS!

IF I DON'T HOLD THEM TOO LONG, THEY WON'T MELT THE SPECIAL ALLOY OF MY IRON GLOVES!

SWISHH-H-H!

8

SO I'LL GET RID OF THEM *FAST*, WHERE THEY'LL DO THE MOST GOOD!

SEE HOW HE HURLS THE FLAMING MISSILES AT OUR OWN DESERTED SHIPS, CUTTING OFF OUR RETREAT!

BY JUPITER! OUR SPEARS CANNOT PIERCE HIS ARMOR! HE IS NO ORDINARY HUMAN!

CLANG!

CLANG!

NO MATTER! WE CAN RUN HIM DOWN WITH OUR *CHARIOTS!*

HMM... HERE'S A CHANCE FOR ME TO THROW A *REAL* SCARE INTO THEM!

PLANTING HIS IRON FEET SOLIDLY ON THE GROUND, AND SETTING HIS "ANCHOR TRANSISTORS" TO HIGHEST INTENSITY, *IRON MAN* STANDS FIRM AS THE CHARIOTS APPROACH, AND...

IT IS LIKE CRASHING INTO THE SIDE OF A *MOUNTAIN!*

CRASH!

CRACK! SMAKK!

NEXT, I'LL GET RID OF THEIR ATTACK LADDERS!

CAN IT BE?! IS HE AN EGYPTIAN GOD COME TO EARTH TO *RESCUE* THEM??!

THEN, *IRON MAN* TAKES SOME MINIATURE, TRANSISTORIZED TEAR GAS BOMBS FROM HIS ACCESSORY BELT...

GASP! INDEED HE IS NO ORDINARY MORTAL! HE HURLS SMOKE WEAPONS THAT BLIND OUR EYES WITH TEARS!

QUICK! TAKE TO THE HILLS! ESCAPE WHILE WE STILL HAVE A CHANCE!

9

THE GODS BE THANKED! THEY HAVE SENT US A CHAMPION TO ROUT THE ROMAN LEGIONS!

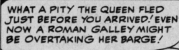

WHAT A PITY THE QUEEN FLED JUST BEFORE YOU ARRIVED! EVEN NOW A ROMAN GALLEY MIGHT BE OVERTAKING HER BARGE!

THE QUEEN? YOU MEAN CLEOPATRA?

THERE IS ONLY ONE QUEEN!

WOW! I'M IN FOR THE THRILL OF A LIFETIME...MEETING CLEOPATRA IN PERSON...THAT IS, IF THE ROMANS HAVEN'T CAPTURED HER FIRST!

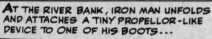

AT THE RIVER BANK, IRON MAN UNFOLDS AND ATTACHES A TINY PROPELLER-LIKE DEVICE TO ONE OF HIS BOOTS...

WITH THIS CLAMPED TO ONE BOOT, I CAN TURN MYSELF INTO A FLOATING SPEEDBOAT!

AND INDEED, MOMENTS LATER...

I'M JUST IN TIME! THERE'S A ROMAN GALLEY ABOUT TO ATTACK CLEOPATRA'S UNPROTECTED BARGE!

CRRRASHHHH!

ZIPPP!

ZIPPP!

...BUT NOT IF IRON MAN CAN HELP IT!

YOUR HIGHNESS! OBSERVE A GOLDEN-ARMORED STRANGER HAS SUNK THE ROMAN GALLEY. SAVING OUR VERY LIVES!

"...AND SO, FINALLY... IRON MAN MEETS THE SIREN OF THE NILE"...

MY PEOPLE SAY I OWE MY LIFE TO YOU, WHO SINGLE-HANDEDLY DEFEATED THE ROMANS!

GOOD GRIEF! SHE'S EVEN *MORE* BEAUTIFUL THAN HISTORY CLAIMS!

ER...I AM THE BEARER OF IMPORTANT TIDINGS, CLEOPATRA!

AFTER IRON MAN CONCLUDES HIS TALE...

SO *HATAP* THE EVIL SORCERER IS NOT DEAD! ALAS, I FEAR *HIM* MORE THAN THE ROMANS! EVEN NOW HE MUST BE GATHERING AN ARMY!

YES, BUT *I* CAN HANDLE HIM...

OH, NOBLE STRANGER, I WILL GRANT YOU *ANYTHING*... ANY WISH, IF YOU WOULD RID EGYPT OF THAT EVIL PRETENDER TO MY THRONE!

I ASK FOR NOTHING BUT TO SERVE YOUR HIGHNESS!

THERE IS SOMETHING VERY *DIFFERENT* ABOUT YOU! I SENSE THAT YOU ARE-- *NOT* A GOD WHO PROTECTS EGYPT! BUT...WHO *ARE* YOU?

SORRY, CLEOPATRA! I COULD NOT EVEN *BEGIN* TO EXPLAIN IT!

LATER, AT CLEOPATRA'S SUMMER PALACE...

MAY YOU RETURN VICTORIOUS OVER HATAP'S FORCES! I WILL OBSERVE THE BATTLE FROM A DISTANCE!

MY FIRST TASK WILL BE TO CAPTURE HATAP'S MAGICAL CHARM...

IF HE'S DESTROYED OR HIDDEN IT, I MAY BE STUCK IN THE PAST *FOREVER*!! CLEOPATRA'S BEAUTY IS *ALMOST* WORTH IT, BUT MY WORK IS IN THE 20TH CENTURY!

PRESENTLY, NEAR AN OASIS...

NOBLE *HATAP*! A SMALL FORCE OF CLEOPATRA'S SOLDIERS APPROACHES... LED BY A GOLDEN-ARMORED FIGURE!

IT IS *HE*! ...THE CREATURE WHO DESTROYED STARK! QUICKLY! TO THE CHARIOTS!

11

CAN YOU NOT WORK SOME MAGIC THAT WILL *CONQUER* THE ENEMY? YOU REMEMBER HOW THEY DEFEATED US ONCE BEFORE!

HOW CAN I *FORGET?* DID I NOT TAKE THE SERUM WHICH LEFT ME IN A STATE OF SUSPENDED ANIMATION FOR 2,000 YEARS!?

BUT NOW, I HAVE ANOTHER ESCAPE FROM DEATH! I NEED ONLY RUB THIS CHARM TWICE AND I'LL BE TRANSPORTED TO 1963... SAFE FROM MY ENEMIES' SWORDS!

OUR FORCE IS *LARGER* THAN THEIRS! *CHARGE!!* SCATTER THEM INTO THE SAND!

HERE THEY COME! AND HERE'S WHERE I USE MY LAST REMAINING TRANSISTOR CHARGE!

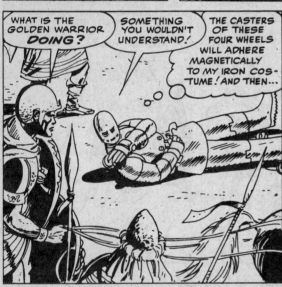

WHAT IS THE GOLDEN WARRIOR *DOING?*

SOMETHING YOU WOULDN'T UNDERSTAND!

THE CASTERS OF THESE FOUR WHEELS WILL ADHERE MAGNETICALLY TO MY IRON COSTUME! AND THEN...

...THIS TRANSISTOR-POWERED JET ENGINE WILL PROPEL ME FORWARD WITH THE THRUST OF A JUGGERNAUT!

RRRRRRRR

HATAP! SOMETHING APPROACHES WITH THE SPEED OF *LIGHTNING!*

IT IS THE *CREATURE!!* BUT *HOW? WHAT??!*

WHAMMMMM

WHISSSSSSSH

IRON MAN'S CHARGE SCATTERS HIS FOES LIKE TEN-PINS, UNTIL...

CURSE THE INTERFERING DEMON! MY MEN FLEE AS THEY DID BEFORE! MUST ESCAPE TO THE FUTURE... BEFORE CLEOPATRA'S ARMY DISPATCHES ME!

THE GOLDEN CHARM! HATAP'S GOING TO USE IT HIMSELF!

HOWEVER, AS IRON MAN SQUIRTS A BLOB OF OIL AT THE OBJECT...

IT SLIPPED OUT OF MY FINGERS! BEFORE I COULD RUB IT! I-I MUST GET IT BACK!

HATAP!! DON'T!! LOOK OUT FOR THAT UP-TURNED SWORD!

BUT HATAP DOESN'T HEAR IRON MAN'S WARNING, AND...

TRIPPED! I'M LOSING MY BALANCE!

HOW IRONIC! TO FALL ONTO ONE OF HIS OWN WEAPONS!

PRESENTLY, AS HATAP'S MEN FLEE FOR THE SECOND AND LAST TIME!

WELL, THIS TIME THE MAD PHARAOH REALLY GOT HIS JUST DESERTS! AND I HAVE THE MEANS TO RETURN TO THE PRESENT!

OH, WONDROUS STRANGER, WHOEVER YOU ARE, SAY YOU WILL REMAIN AND SHARE MY THRONE WITH ME!

FOR THOUGH I DO NOT KNOW YOUR REAL IDENTITY... I, CLEOPATRA, HAVE LOST MY HEART TO YOU!

I'LL REMEMBER, MY QUEEN ...FOR ALL TIME!

LOOK! HE'S VANISHING!

DAYS LATER, AS TONY STARK EXPLORE'S HATAP'S TOMB...

HERE'S ONE HIEROGLYPHIC DRAWING AS MYSTERIOUS AS THE MUMMY'S DISAPPEARANCE ITSELF! IT SHOWS CLEOPATRA EMBRACING A GOLDEN-ARMORED FIGURE!

I'LL BET THAT'S A TOUGH ONE TO FIGURE OUT!

A MONTH LATER, IN THE STATES, AS A MOVIE ABOUT CLEOPATRA IS PREMIERED...

WELL, STARK...DO YOU STILL THINK YOU COULD'VE MADE AN IMPRESSION ON CLEOPATRA, IF YOU HAD BOTH LIVED IN THE SAME TIME?

WHY NOT, OLD BOY! AFTER ALL, STRANGER THINGS HAVE HAPPENED!

AND THAT'S FOR SURE!

13

The END

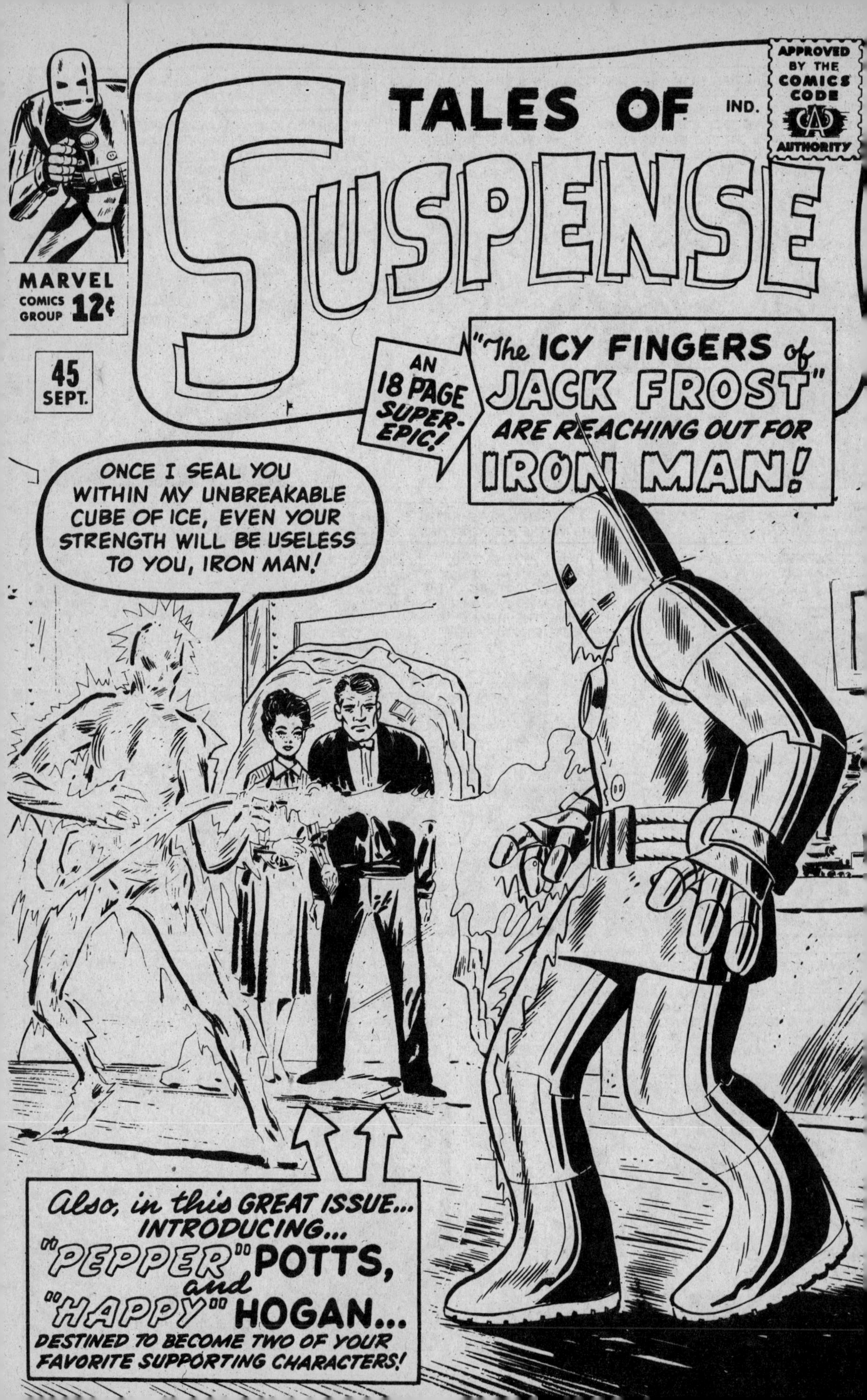

MARVEL COMICS GROUP 12¢
45 SEPT.
TALES OF SUSPENSE
IND.
APPROVED BY THE COMICS CODE AUTHORITY
AN 18 PAGE SUPER-EPIC!
"The ICY FINGERS of JACK FROST" ARE REACHING OUT FOR IRON MAN!
ONCE I SEAL YOU WITHIN MY UNBREAKABLE CUBE OF ICE, EVEN YOUR STRENGTH WILL BE USELESS TO YOU, IRON MAN!
Also, in this GREAT ISSUE... INTRODUCING... "PEPPER" POTTS, and "HAPPY" HOGAN... DESTINED TO BECOME TWO OF YOUR FAVORITE SUPPORTING CHARACTERS!

IRON MAN and "THE ICY FINGERS OF JACK FROST!"

STORY PLOT: STAN LEE
SCRIPT: R. BERNS
ART: DON HECK
LETTERING: S. ROSEN

X-347

1.

ONE DAY, NEAR INDIANAPOLIS...

HOLY SMOKE! WHAT'S *THAT*? IT'S GOING SO *FAST* I CAN'T TELL WHETHER IT'S A WHIRLWIND OR A STRIPPED-DOWN *ROD*!

IT'S PROBABLY SOME NUT DOING A TEST RUN ON THE PUBLIC HIGHWAY BEFORE ENTERING THE 500-MILE CLASSIC! LET'S *GET 'IM*!

WHOOSH

WE SHOULD HAVE *GUESSED*! LOOK WHO IT IS! *IRON MAN* USING HIS *JET SKATES*! THOSE TRANSISTOR-POWERED WHEELS OF HIS CAN DO *200 MILES AN HOUR*!

WELL, IF IRON MAN IS IN THAT KIND OF A HURRY IT MUST BE SOMETHING *IMPORTANT*.

WHOOSH

HE MUST BE ON THE TRAIL OF SOME SUPER-CRIMINAL, SO LET HIM ALONE! HE *KNOWS* WHAT HE'S DOING!

IT'S JUST AS WELL...WE'D NEVER BE ABLE TO *CATCH* HIM ANYWAY! Y'KNOW, I'M SURE GLAD THAT GUY IS ON *OUR* SIDE!

HMMM...THOSE OFFICERS STOPPED CHASING ME! THEY PROBABLY THINK I'M EN ROUTE TO SOME EMERGENCY! WELL, I *AM*, IN A WAY!

AS TONY STARK, I'M SCHEDULED TO DRIVE IN THE 500-MILE SPEEDWAY CLASSIC WHICH BEGINS SHORTLY! BUT HELPING THE F.B.I. CLAMP DOWN ON A SPY RING THIS MORNING MADE ME GOOD AND LATE!

NOW TO TAKE TO THE AIR.

THERE WAS NO DANGER OF MY SMASHING INTO A CAR ON THE HIGHWAY! I COULD'VE INSTANTLY SOARED INTO THE AIR WITH MY TRANSISTOR-POWERED JET DEVICES IF THE NEED AROSE!

HMM! *THERE'S* MY SPORTS CAR NOW!

I'LL MAKE A QUICK CHANGE FROM THIS COLLAPSIBLE "UNION SUIT" TO MY TONY STARK IDENTITY, THEN HEAD FOR THE RACE TRACK!

SOON AFTER, AT THE SPEEDWAY...

HEY, MR. STARK, WE WERE GETTING WORRIED! WHAT TOOK YOU SO LONG?

NOTHING THAT WOULD INTEREST YOU BOYS! HOW'S THE STARK SPECIAL?

PURRIN' LIKE A PERSIAN CAT, BOSS!

WITH THIS NEW ENGINE YOU OUGHTA PASS THEM OTHER CRATES LIKE THEY WAS STANDIN' STILL! POINT IS, HOW DO YOU FEEL ABOUT THE LONG GRIND AHEAD!?

I'LL PUT IT THIS WAY, MIKE. IRON MAN COULDN'T BE IN BETTER SHAPE.

MINUTES LATER, THE FAMED RACE BEGINS...

HMMM...IF I KEEP UP THIS PACE, I'LL NOT ONLY WIN EVERY LAP, BUT SET A NEW TRACK RECORD!

SUDDENLY, AS STARK ENTERS A TURN...

OHHH...I-I FEEL A TERRIBLE SQUEEZING PAIN IN MY CHEST! M-MUST BE MY HEART!

IN MY ANXIETY TO GET TO THE TRACK, I-I FORGOT TO RECHARGE MY METAL CHEST PLATE! =GASP= NOW THERE ISN'T ENOUGH ELECTRICAL ENERGY IN IT TO KEEP MY HEART PUMPING!

SOMETHING WRONG WITH THE STARK SPECIAL! STARK SEEMS TO BE WRITHING IN AGONY!

3

STARK'S LOSING CONTROL OF THE CAR! IT'S SKIDDING UP THE EMBANKMENT!

CRASH!

WHAMMM!

STARK'S A GONER! HE'S PINNED INSIDE THE CAR!

THE WHEEL'S BENT... CRUSHED AGAINST MY BODY! IF I WERE IRON MAN, I'D BE OUT OF HERE IN A SECOND! BUT NOW--

IRON MAN COULD SMASH OUT OF THIS CAR AS IF IT WERE MADE OF TISSUE PAPER! BUT I HAVEN'T THE STRENGTH EVEN TO MOVE MY HANDS!

DON'T GO NEAR THE WRECK! IT'S AFIRE! IT'LL BLOW UP ANY MOMENT!

BUT THERE'S SOMEONE INSIDE! CAN'T JUST LEAVE 'IM THERE! MEBBE I CAN PULL 'IM OUT!

NO!! GO BACK!! YOU CAN'T HELP ME! I'M PINNED BY THE WHEEL!

BIG DEAL! NOW YOU'RE UN-PINNED!

SNNAAAD

BUT WHEN THE...FLAMES HIT THE GAS TANK...

LOOK, BUB... I'M SCARED ENOUGH WITHOUT ANY HELP FROM YOU! SO CLAM UP AND LET'S GET OUT OF HERE, HUH?

TOO BAD NO *BOOKIE* AS AROUND! HE WOULD'VE GIVEN ME 10-TO-1 I'D BE TRUMMIN' A HARP NOW!

I'LL PAY YOU FIFTY TIMES AS MUCH IF YOU RUSH ME TO THE NEAREST MOTEL, LOCK ME ALONE IN A ROOM...AND NO QUESTIONS ASKED!

HEY! YOU'RE TURNIN' PALE AS MILK! SOMETHIN'S AILIN' YOU...AND IT AIN'T JUST FROM THE *CRACK-UP!*

I *TOLD* YOU... *UHHH* DON'T ASK QUESTIONS! CARRY ME TO YOUR CAR!

MAYBE I AIN'T NO LOUIS PASTEUR...BUT YOU DON'T LOOK LIKE YOU'RE GONNA *MAKE* IT! MAYBE WE OUGHTTA CALL A KILDARE!

NO! I-I CAN DOCTOR MY *SELF!* JUST GET ME TO THAT ROOM!!

GASP I'VE GOT TO HOLD OUT LONG ENOUGH TO CROSS ITS THRESHOLD, OTHERWISE IT'S THE END OF *IRON MAN* AND HIS *EXPLOITS*, TOO!

FINALLY...BEHIND A LOCKED MOTEL DOOR...

NOW! GOT TO MAKE IT TO THE WALL SOCKET...JUST A FEW INCHES MORE...

AHH...ELECTRIC CURRENT... IT'S LIKE ADRENALINE STIMULATING MY HEART BACK TO NORMAL ACTION!

HMM...SO I'VE CHEATED THE UNDERTAKER AGAIN, THANKS TO A GROUCHY STRANGER WHO PULLED ME OUT OF THE WRECK! I'VE GOT TO MAKE SURE I *REWARD* HIM HANDSOMELY!

5.

FIVE MINUTES LATER...

EXPLAIN SOMETHING TO ME, STARK! YOU CRAWLED INTO THAT ROOM LIKE YOU WERE OUT FOR THE COUNT! *NOW* YOU WALK OUT AS ALIVE AND STRONG AS *SONNY LISTON!* HOW COME?

IT'S A *MYSTERY*, CHUM! PLEASE STEP INTO THE LOBBY!

AND THEN, IN THE MOTEL COCKTAIL LOUNGE...

NAME?

HARRY HOGAN! DOWN AT STILLMAN'S GYM THEY NICKNAMED ME "HAPPY"...MOSTLY 'CAUSE NO ONE'S EVER CAUGHT ME WIT A SMILE!

HOW COME YOU GAVE UP YOUR RING CAREER?

BECAUSE I WAS TOO SUCCESSFUL... AT *LOSIN'*, THAT IS! AFTER I GOT A GUY AGAINST THE ROPES, I NEVER HAD THE HEART TO FINISH 'IM OFF! SO I GAVE IT UP!

HEY!! A CHECK FOR *FIFTY THOUSAND CLAMS!* IS *THAT* ALL YOU FIGGER YOUR LIFE IS WORTH, STARK?

WELL, IF YOU'RE DISSATISFIED, I'LL *DOUBLE* THE AMOUNT! AFTER ALL, I WOULDN'T *BE* HERE IF NOT FOR YOU!

ME...I'M *ALWAYS* DISSATISFIED! FORGET ABOUT PUTTIN' A PRICE ON YOURSELF...AND DON'T START THE "ETERNALLY GRATEFUL" BIT! I DIDN'T SAVE YOU FOR NO FEE! IT WAS JUST *REFLEX ACTION!*

BUT SURELY YO CAN *USE* SON MONEY!?

RIP!

MISTER, WHAT *I* CAN USE IS A NICE STEADY JOB WITH THREE WEEKS' VACATION WITH PAY, A GOOD PENSION PLAN, AN' ALL KINDS OF FRINGE BENEFITS!

HMM...IF I'M LIABLE TO BLACK OUT SUDDENLY, AS I ALMOST DID TODAY, IT WOULDN'T BE A BAD IDEA TO HIRE A COMBINATION *CHAUFFEUR- BODY- GUARD!*

ER...I COULD USE A *CHAUFFEUR*, HAPPY! IF YOU *WANT* IT, THE JOB'S YOURS!

NOW YOU'RE TALKIN A NICE, QUIET SAF JOB...NO BROKEN NOSES...NO KNOC OUT PUNCHES!! WHAT KIND OF CAR DO YOU HAVE...> DON'T LIKE JALOPIES!

WELL, I HAVE, AMONG OTHERS, A **ROLLS-ROYCE,** A **CADDY ELDORADO** AND A TWO-SEATER **JAGUAR CONVERTIBLE!** THEY MANAGE TO GET ME WHERE I'M GOING!

MMM...I HAD A **HUNCH** YOU WEREN'T EXACTLY STARVIN'!

WELL, THOSE CRATES ARE OKAY FOR A **START,** I GUESS!

I'M GLAD YOU'RE SATISFIED, HAPPY! NOW I'LL WRITE YOU A CHECK FOR TEN GRAND, SO YOU CAN GET A FEW ODDS AND ENDS TO PREPARE FOR THE JOB!

A FEW DAYS LATER, IN NEW YORK...

HOW DO I REACH YOUR **PLANT?** ALL I KNOW IS THAT IT'S IN FLUSHING, LONG ISLAND!

THAT'S MY **MAIN** RESEARCH CENTER, HAPPY! I HAVE **OTHER** PLANTS ALL OVER THE WORLD! ONE ON EACH CONTINENT!

THAT'S REAL IMPRESSIVE, BOSS, BUT IT **STILL** DON'T TELL ME WHERE TO HEAD FOR **NOW!**

PROCEED SOUTH ON GRAND CENTRAL PARKWAY! I'LL TELL YOU WHICH EXIT TO TURN OFF AT!

HEY! AIN'T THAT THE NEW BASEBALL STADIUM, AND THE SITE OF THE **WORLD'S FAIR?**

RIGHT! IT'LL BE EXCITING HAVING THE FAIR AS MY NEXT DOOR NEIGHBOR IN '64! TURN OFF AT THE NEXT EXIT, THEN MAKE A SHARP RIGHT TURN...

SOON... AS YOU'VE PROBABLY NOTICED, HAPPY, THE PLANT IS HEAVILY GUARDED! BOYS, MEET **HAPPY HOGAN,** MY NEW CHAUFFEUR!

HMM...IF HOGAN **DRIVES** LIKE I ONCE SEEN HIM **FIGHT,** YOU BETTER BE SURE YOU USE YOUR **SEAT BELT,** BOSS!

WHO ASKED **YOU,** BIG MOUTH? **YOU** I COULD FLATTEN WITH MY **PINKY!**

EASY, HAPPY! YOUR RING DAYS ARE OVER...EXCEPT AFTER I INTRODUCE YOU TO "PEPPER" POTTS, MY SECRETARY! YOU CAN FIGHT ALL YOU WANT TO WITH **HER!** I DO REGULARLY!

7

HEY! AIN'T THAT *IRON MAN?*

YES! HE...UH.. HAPPENS TO BE A GOOD *FRIEND* OF MINE! ALWAYS DROPS IN WHEN HE'S IN THE NEIGHBORHOOD!

MUST PLAY UP MY CLOSE "FRIENDSHIP" WITH IRON MAN.

IT ALIBIS IRON MAN'S SOMETIMES TOO COINCIDENTAL APPEARANCES WHENEVER I SWITCH IDENTITIES FOR SOME EMERGENCY!

WELL, THERE'S *ONE* GUY COULD HAVE BEEN HEAVYWEIGHT CHAMP *EASY!* HE COULD BEAT DEMPSEY, LOUIS, MARCIANO, LISTON, AND *ME* ALL TOGETHER, WITH ONE MITT STRAPPED BEHIND HIS BACK!

PEPPER, MEET *HAPPY HOGAN!* FROM NOW ON HE'LL BE MY PRIVATE CHAUFFEUR!

OH, *NO!* WITH ELIGIBLE BACHELORS AS SCARCE AROUND HERE AS DINOSAURS, YOU HIRE A BATTLE-SCARRED EX-PUG! IT COULDN'T BE A *ROCK HUDSON!* NO, HE HAS TO LOOK LIKE *BELA LUGOSI!*

DON'T PAY ANY ATTENTION TO MY KISSER, DOLL! BENEATH THIS ROUGH EXTERIOR BEATS A HEART FULLA LOVE AT FIRST SIGHT! Y'KNOW, YOU'RE *MY TYPE!*

INSULT WILL GET YOU NOWHERE MISTER HOGAN!

ARE YA BRUSHIN' ME OFF? *ME,* HAPPY HOGAN, WHO HAS FINALLY FOUND THE DAME OF HIS DREAMS?

MY DEAR MR. HOGAN, YOUR *DREAM* WOULD ONLY BE MY *NIGHTMARE!* IN SHORT... *YOU* WOULDN'T BE MY TYPE EVEN IF YOU *WERE* MY TYPE!

HMM, I GET THE PICTURE ...IT'S HIM... *STARK*... WHO MAKES YER TICKER GO THUMP, THUMP! RIGHT?

RIGHT! ONLY HE DOESN'T KNOW I'M ALIVE. BUT SOMEDAY HE WILL...AND THEN HE'LL GIVE UP ALL HIS ACTRESSES AND DEBUTANTES... AND *I'LL* BECOME *MRS. ANTHONY STARK!*

HOW D'YA LIKE *THAT?* I FLIP OVER A DOLL, AND WHAT HAPPENS? I GOT A *LOVE TRIANGLE* ON MY HANDS!

THE ONLY TRIANGLE IN THIS SITUATION IS YOUR *HEAD* MR. HOGAN... WHICH COMES TO A NICE SHARP *POINT!* NOW EXCUSE ME! I HAVE *WORK* TO DO!

MEANWHILE, IN STARK'S PRIVATE OFFICE...

WHILE I'VE GOT A MOMENT TO MYSELF, I'LL CHECK OUT MY *IRON MAN* COSTUME!

IF SOMETHING MALFUNCTIONS AT THE WRONG TIME, ANY ENEMY COULD REDUCE ME TO *JUNK!* HMM...ALL THE COMPRESSIBLE, COLLAPSIBLE COMPONENTS OF MY COSTUME EXPAND PERFECTLY!

MY CHAIN MAIL ARMOR NEEDS NO OILING!

THE AIR INTAKE VALVE IS OKAY!

SSSS!

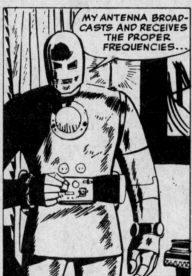

MY ANTENNA BROADCASTS AND RECEIVES THE PROPER FREQUENCIES...

MY ELECTRICAL SYSTEM IS ON THE BEAM!

CLICK!

EVERY DEVICE IN MY ACCESSORY BELT IS PRESENT AND ACCOUNTED FOR! LIKE A PILOT GIVES HIS PLANE A SHAKEDOWN CHECK BEFORE TAKE-OFF, I MUST MAKE SURE *MY* GEAR'S IN WORKING ORDER BEFORE I ZERO IN ON A MISSION! OH-OH! WHAT'S *THAT?!*

THE ALARM! SOMBODY'S TAMPERING WITH THE VAULT WHICH CONTAINS VITAL MATERIALS AND CASH RESERVES! WELL, I CAN REACH THE THIEF BEFORE THE *GUARDS* DO!

9.

ONLY *I* KNOW ABOUT THIS SECRET EXIT FROM MY OFFICE WHICH LEADS TO A LABYRINTH OF UNDERGROUND PASSAGEWAYS BENEATH EVERY SECTION OF THE PLANT!

ZZZITT

FUNNY! EVERY TIME I FEEL THAT *IRON MAN'S* JOB IS THANKLESS WORK...WEARING THIS CRAMPED, PAINFUL COSTUME AND RISKING MY NECK IN EVERY QUARTER OF THE GLOBE...

...SOMETHING ALWA[YS] HAPPENS WHICH N[O] ONE BUT *IRON MAN* CAN TACKL[E] PROPERLY!

CL[ANK]! CLANK!

I WONDER WHAT HUMAN RAT IS NIBBLING AT THE "CHEESE" LOCKED IN THE VAULT *THIS* TIME?

IT'S *PROFESSOR SHAPANKA*, ONE OF MY MOST TRUSTED SCIENTISTS!

WHIR!

IRON MAN! *GASP!* I WAS PREPARED FOR *ANYTHING* EXCEPT *YOU!*

SSSS!

STAY BACK! NOW... *NOW* I SEE ALL THE STORIES ABOUT YOU ARE *TRUE!* BULLETS ONLY BOUNCE HARMLESSLY OFF YOUR ARMOR!

BLAM!

BLAM BLAM!

BLAST YOU! I WOULD HAVE *DARED* TRY T[O] ROB STARK'S VAULT IF [I] KNEW *YOU* WERE A WATCHMAN HERE!

I'M *NOT!* I...UH.. JUST DROPPE[D] FOR A *VISIT*[!] HEARD THE AL[ARM] AND INVESTIGAT[ED] BEFORE STAR[K] DID! NOW GIV[E] ME YOUR GU[N!]

CRUNCH!

TALK, SHAPANKA! WHAT ARE YOU AFTER IN THIS VAULT?

THE FORMULA FOR STARK'S TINY TRANSISTORS! I COULD SELL IT FOR A *FORTUNE!*

CRUNCH!

LISTEN, IRON MAN! STARK'S FORMULAS ARE WORTH *MILLIONS!* HELP ME GET THEM AND I'LL MAKE YOU MY *PARTNER* IN THE MOST *FANTASTIC SCIENTIFIC DISCOVERY!*

YOU'RE WASTING YOUR BREATH, SHAPANKA! I'M LOCKING YOU IN THE VAULT TILL STARK ARRIVES!

RIP!

BUT I'VE FOUND THE SECRET OF *ETERNAL LIFE!* THINK OF IT! THE MONEY WOULD FINANCE MY RESEARCH INTO *HUMAN IMMORTALITY!*

YOU THINK ABOUT IT TILL STARK SHOWS UP!

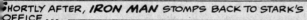

SHORTLY AFTER, *IRON MAN* STOMPS BACK TO STARK'S OFFICE...

BY THE TIME I RETURN TO THE VAULT AS TONY STARK, THE GUARDS WILL HAVE DISCOVERED SHAPANKA! SO I'LL HAVE TO COVER FOR *IRON MAN'S* BRIEF APPEARANCE AND DEPARTURE...

DID YA HEAR THAT *ALARM*, BOSS? SEEMS YOU GOT A *CROOK* IN YOUR ORGANIZATION! A PUNK NAMED SHAPANKA!

THAT'S *RIGHT,* MR. STARK! WE FOUND PROFESSOR SHAPANKA LOCKED IN THE VAULT! I'LL TAKE YOU TO HIM!

SHAP- ANKA?

YOU'VE GOT ME, STARK! OR RATHER, YOUR FRIEND *IRON MAN* GOT ME! I SUPPOSE YOU'LL CALL THE POLICE NOW, EH?

NO, SHAPANKA! PERHAPS THAT'S WHAT I *SHOULD* DO... BUT I WON'T! RELEASE THE PROFESSOR, BOYS!

I'M LETTING YOU *GO* BECAUSE OF THE BRILLIANT WORK YOU DID IN THE PAST! BUT YOU'RE NO LONG-ER A MAN WE CAN TRUST WITH THE VITAL SECRET PROJECTS I AM ENGAGED IN FOR THE GOVERNMENT! YOU'RE *WASHED UP,* PROFESSOR!

11.

SO PACK YOUR THINGS AND GET OUT, SHAPANKA, AND NEVER LET ME SEE YOU AGAIN!

HOW NOBLE OF YOU! BIG-HEARTED STARK TOSSING A CRUMB OF FREEDOM TO A LOWLY CROOK!

HOW ABOUT ADDING A FEW CRUMBS OF *SEVERANCE PAY*? YOU'VE GOT SO MUCH MONEY, STARK... YOU WOULDN'T MISS A FEW OF THOSE *GREENBACKS!*

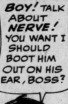

BOY! TALK ABOUT *NERVE!* YOU WANT I SHOULD BOOT HIM OUT ON HIS *EAR*, BOSS?

EASY, HAPPY! BETTER LEAVE WHILE I STILL FEEL SO GENEROUS, SHAPANKA! I MIGHT GET COLD FEET ABOUT RELEASING YOU!

COLD FEET! THAT'S *IT!* I WANTED MONEY... AND YOU JUS' HANDED ME A MILLION DOLLAR SOLUTION FOR *NOTHING!*

THANK YOU, STARK! AND ONE DAY, I'LL PERSONALLY DEMONSTRATE MY GRATITUDE TO YOU!

YOU'RE CRACKED, SHAPANKA! STOP OFF AT A GOOD PSYCHIATRIST ON YOUR WAY HOME!

COLD FEET! HA, HA! *COLD FEET!* THE WHOLE WORLD WILL SOMEDAY REMEMBER WHAT YOU SAID... AS I ACHIEVE *ETERNAL LIFE!*

SOMETHIN' TELLS ME *YOU'RE* NUTTY AS HIM FOR LETTIN' HIM GO!

YOU MAY BE RIGHT, HAPPY! HIS MAD RAVING ABOUT IMMORTALITY MAKES ME UNEASY!

WEEKS LATER, AT PROFESSOR SHAPANKA'S CELLAR LAB...

STARK DOESN'T REALIZE IT... BUT HE GAVE ME THE ONE CLUE I NEEDED TO PERFECT MY FORMULA FOR PROLONGING HUMAN LIFE... I FROZE AN ALLEY CAT IN THIS BLOCK OF ICE DAYS AGO...

MY HEAT RAY HAS NOW COMPLETELY MELTED THE ICE! LET'S SEE WHAT HAS HAPPENED TO THE CAT...

...S IN **PERFECT CONDITION!** IT LEAPS AWAY IN FRIGHT...AS ALIVE AS THE DAY I ENCASED IT IN THE LIFE-PRESERVING ICE! I'M A **GENIUS!**

MY THEORY IS PROVEN! FOR A LONG TIME SCIENTISTS HAVE KNOWN THAT FREEZING SOMETHING CAN STOP ITS AGING PROCESS INDEFINITELY... AS WITH FROZEN FOOD!

SURGEONS EVEN FREEZE PATIENTS ON THE OPERATING TABLE TO ENSURE THEIR SURVIVAL DURING DIFFICULT OPERATIONS! WHY NOT DO THE SAME FOR THE PURPOSE OF KEEPING A MAN YOUNG FOR-EVER?

I COULD LIVE FOREVER BY LYING IN AN ICE VAULT SOME-WHERE, ASLEEP, WHILE FROZEN! BUT WHAT GOOD WOULD **THAT** DO ME?

THAT'S WHERE STARK'S **COLD FEET** COMES IN! I WILL CREATE A SPECIAL FREEZING SUIT WHICH WILL KEEP MY BODY TEMPERATURE WAY, WAY DOWN! BUT I WILL **NOT** BE ASLEEP INSIDE AN ICE BLOCK!

OH, NO! MY SUIT WILL GIVE ME SPECIAL POWERS TO FREEZE WHATEVER IS NEAR ME...AND YET RENDER **ME** SAFE FROM ANYTHING! BEFORE I'M THROUGH THE SECRETS I TRIED TO STEAL FROM STARK WILL LOOK LIKE CHICKEN FEED!

AND SO, A WEEK LATER, AT A LONG ISLAND BANK...

HEY! LOOK WHAT'S WALKING IN...

WHY THE FANCY GET-UP, MISTER? WHAT DO YOU WANT?

WHAT DOES **ANYONE** WANT FROM A BANK? **MONEY** MY DEAR FELLOW! **COLD** CASH!

13.

F-FOR PETE'S SAKE...HE...HE'S TURNING HIMSELF INTO A WALKING *SNOWMAN!*

THAT CHANGE AFFECTS ONLY *ME!* ALL FURTHER CHANGES WILL AFFECT *YOU!*

BY SHOOTING FORTH COLD JETS OF OXYGEN, I CAN INSTANTLY FREEZE ANYTHING OR ANYONE ON CONTACT!

THERE'S ENOUGH AIR FOR YOU TO BREATHE...

...BUT YOU CAN'T MOVE TILL THE ICE MELTS!

I'M A ONE-MAN SPRINKLING SYSTEM...EXCEPT THAT WHATEVER I SPRINKLE TURNS IMMEDIATELY TO ICE! I LAUGH AT BURGLAR ALARMS, SINCE I CAN FREEZE THEIR ELECTRICAL SYSTEMS TO USELESSNE

THEN, AS THE WALKING SNOWMAN LEAVES THE MARBLE "IGLOO"...

ONE SIDE, *ALL* OF YOU!

FORTUNATELY, I HAVE A DEVICE THAT CAN DE-ICE ME INSTANTLY! SO, WITHIN SECONDS, I CAN AGAIN RESEMBLE A NORMAL HUMAN BEING!

I CAN'T WAIT TILL I MEET *STARK* AGAIN! I'LL GIVE HIM "COLD FEET" THAT HE'LL REMEMBER FOREVER!

"...AND *IRON MAN!* WHAT A FITTING REVENGE I'VE DREAMED UP FOR HIM! HE'LL BECOME UTTERLY HARMLESS WHEN I CONVERT HIM INTO A HUNK OF *COLD STEEL!!*"

THUS DAYS PASS, AS PROFESSOR SHAPANKA INSPIRES AWE IN THE HEARTS OF ALL NEW YORKERS!

THIS IS *AMAZING!* WE CAN'T STOP HIM! OUR BULLETS TURN INTO *SNOW FLAKES!*

HA! HA! MEANWHILE, I CAN ESCAPE WITH MY STOLEN *LOOT!*

BUT, JUST TO MAKE SURE I'M NOT PURSUED, I'LL PUT THAT POLICE CAR INTO A DEEP FREEZE!

GOSH, IT'S LUCKY I HAPPENED TO PASS WITH MY CAMERA! THIS'LL MAKE A TERRIFIC FRONT PAGE PICTURE FOR MY NEWSPAPER!

NEXT MORNING, AS SHAPANKA READS THE TABLOIDS...

WELL, THEY'VE EVEN GIVEN ME A *NAME* NOW! *"JACK FROST!"* HOW CORNY CAN YOU GET? YET, THE MONICKER *DOES* HAVE AN APPROPRIATE RING! *JACK FROST* I SHALL *REMAIN* TO MY TREMBLING PUBLIC!

NOW *JACK FROST* WILL PAY OFF ANTHONY STARK FOR FIRING PROFESSOR SHAPANKA! I'LL WALK RIGHT INTO HIS PLANT AND DESTROY IT, ALONG WITH EVERY ONE OF HIS PRECIOUS GOVERNMENTAL PROJECTS!

A HALF-HOUR LATER...

SOUND THE *ALARM!* IT'S THAT *JACK FROST* CHARACTER WE READ ABOUT IN THE PAPERS!

STAND *BACK,* *WHOEVER* YOU ARE, OR WE'LL *FIRE!*

FIRE, YOU FOOLS! MY *ICE* IS *MORE* THAN A MATCH FOR YOUR *USELESS* BULLETS!

GREAT GUNS! OUR SLUGS ARE TURNING INTO A SMALL BLIZZARD BEFORE THEY CAN HIT HIM!

MR. STARK! *MR. STARK!* IT'S *JACK FROST...* THE MENACE THE WHOLE *TOWN* IS BUZZING ABOUT! *HE'S AFTER YOU!* RUN FOR YOUR LIFE!

DON'T WORRY ABOUT *ME,* PEPPER! JUST STAY OUT OF THE WAY TILL HELP ARRIVES!

15.

I'LL CHANGE INSTANTLY TO *IRON MAN!* LATER, I'LL TELL MY STAFF I WAS HAVING A SECRET CONFERENCE WITH HIM...

MEANWHILE, OUTSIDE...

HEY... WHAT'S *THAT?* THE BELL SO SOON? I-I AIN'T HAD MY MINUTE'S SNOOZE BETWEEN ROUNDS!

IT'S *JACK FROST,* YOU IDIOT! HE'S HERE TO GET MR. STARK! *LOOK AT HIM!* HE'S BLOCKING THE ENTRANCE WITH *AN ICE WALL!*

CLANG! CLANG! CLA—

I ALWAYS HATED YOU, MISS POTTS! YOU ALWAYS TREATED ME SO COLDLY! NOW, IT'S *MY* TURN TO FREEZE *YOU* OUT!

I GOTTA WO FAST BEFO I GET THE COLD TREA MENT! I'LL SHOOT OFF THE LOCK OF STARK'S PRIVAT OFFICE SO MEB STARK CAN ESCA THAT NUT.

RAT TAT TAT TAT!

BUT THEN, AS HAPPY HOGAN BURSTS INTO STARK'S INNER SANCTUM...

JUMPIN' CATFISH! WHAT'S *IRON MAN* DOIN' HERE? HEY, WHERE'S MY EVER-LOVIN' *BOSS?*

WHEW! THAT WAS *CLOSE!* I TURNED MY BACK JUST IN TIME!

SUDDENLY

OUT OF MY WAY, FOO NOT THAT BEING KNOCKED "COLD" SHOULD BE ANY NOVELTY TO *YOU!*

IRON MAN! I DIDN'T EXPECT *YOU* TO BE HERE! BUT THIS GIVES ME THE CHANCE I'VE BEEN *WAITING* FOR!

DON'T COME ANY CLOSER!

WAIT! I RECOGNIZE THAT VOICE!

OF COURSE! I AM **PROFESSOR SHAPANKA**! AND I NOTICE THAT THE BRAVE **IRON MAN** FINALLY COWERS BEFORE A FORCE STRONGER THAN HIMSELF!

NOT REALLY, SHAPANKA! YOU'LL SOON SEE...

I... I'M **FALLING**...!

GOT HIM... TEMPORARILY! NOW TO SHUT THE TRAP DOOR AND LEAVE HIM TO WANDER IN THE UNDERGROUND LABYRINTH!

BUT, AS THE SLIDING FLOOR STARTS TO ROLL BACK...

A NEAT TRICK, **IRON MAN**, BUT IT WON'T WORK! I'M FREEZING THE MOTOR THAT MAKES THAT DOOR SLIDE BACK AND FORTH!

NOW IT'S **STUCK**! AND IN A MOMENT I'LL HAVE CLIMBED BACK INTO THE ROOM WITH YOU!

THE ICY FINGERS OF JACK FROST, GRIPPING THE OPEN TRAP-DOOR!

WELL, IT WON'T BE HARD FOR **IRON MAN** TO MAKE YOU LOSE YOUR GRIP!!

SMACK!

FOOL! I'VE GOT AS MANY FINGERS... OR HANDS... AS I CARE TO CREATE WITH MY ICE-MAKING MECHANISM!

HE'S RIGHT! ALREADY I'M BEGINNING TO FEEL AN ICY NUMBNESS SPREAD THROUGH MY BODY! ...RIGHT THROUGH MY IRON UNIFORM!!

THERE'S ONLY ONE CHANCE IN A MILLION FOR ME TO DEFEAT HIM AS LONG AS HE DOESN'T KNOW I'M ALSO **TONY STARK**! FIRST, I'LL TURN ON MY SEARCHLIGHT BEAM **FULL POWER**!

AND **NOW**, IRON MAN...

17.

BY HOOKING IT UP WITH CERTAIN MINIATURIZED GENERATORS, I CAN TURN IT INTO A *HEAT RAY!* THAT'LL STALL YOU UNTIL I'VE FASHIONED THE ONLY WEAPON THAT CAN *COMPLETELY* DEFEAT YOU!

A...*MINIATURE FURNACE!*

LUCKILY I HAD THE RIGHT COMPONENT PARTS IN MY ACCESSORY BELT!

ALL RIGHT, *JACK FROST...* WE'VE DANCED TO YOUR TUN AND NOW IT'S TIME TO PAY THE FIDDLER! HERE, *THIS* WILL WARM YOU UP!

TURN IT OFF! *GASP* *TURN IT OFF!!*

CAN'T MOVE! I-I FEEL AS THOUGH I'M IN THE MIDDLE OF A *BLAST FURNACE!* OH NO! MY ICE IS *MELTING!*

I MUST GET HAPPY AND ANYBODY *ELSE* JACK FROST HAS FROZEN OUT OF THE OFFICE!

I SHOULD BE GRATEFUL TO *JACK FROST* FOR *ONE* THING... I NEVER HEARD PEPPER OR HAPPY SO *QUIET* BEFORE!

LOOK! IT'S *IRON MAN!* JACK FROST HAS MET HIS WATERLOO

PRESENTLY, A SCORCHED FIGURE STAGGERS OUT...

NO MORE! NO MORE, PLEASE! I-I GIVE UP!

GRAB HIM, BOYS, WHILE I ADJUST THE AUTOMATIC SPRINKLER SYSTEM!

BOY! MR. STARK WILL SURE BE GRATEFUL TO *IRON MAN* FOR THIS! SAY, WHERE *IS* THE BOSS, ANYWAY?

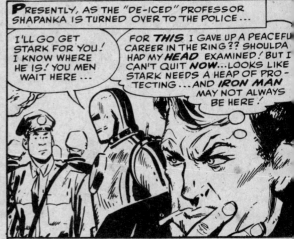

PRESENTLY, AS THE "DE-ICED" PROFESSOR SHAPANKA IS TURNED OVER TO THE POLICE...

I'LL GO GET STARK FOR YOU! I KNOW WHERE HE IS! YOU MEN WAIT HERE...

FOR *THIS* I GAVE UP A PEACEFUL CAREER IN THE RING?? SHOULDA HAD MY *HEAD* EXAMINED! BUT I CAN'T QUIT *NOW*...LOOKS LIKE STARK NEEDS A HEAP OF PROTECTING...AND *IRON MAN* MAY NOT ALWAYS BE HERE!

THEY SAY THAT IGNORANCE IS BLISS...SO HAPPY HOGAN SHOULD BE THE MOST BLISSFUL GUY IN TOWN! MORE OF THE SAME NEXT ISSUE! DON'T MISS IT!

The End

18.

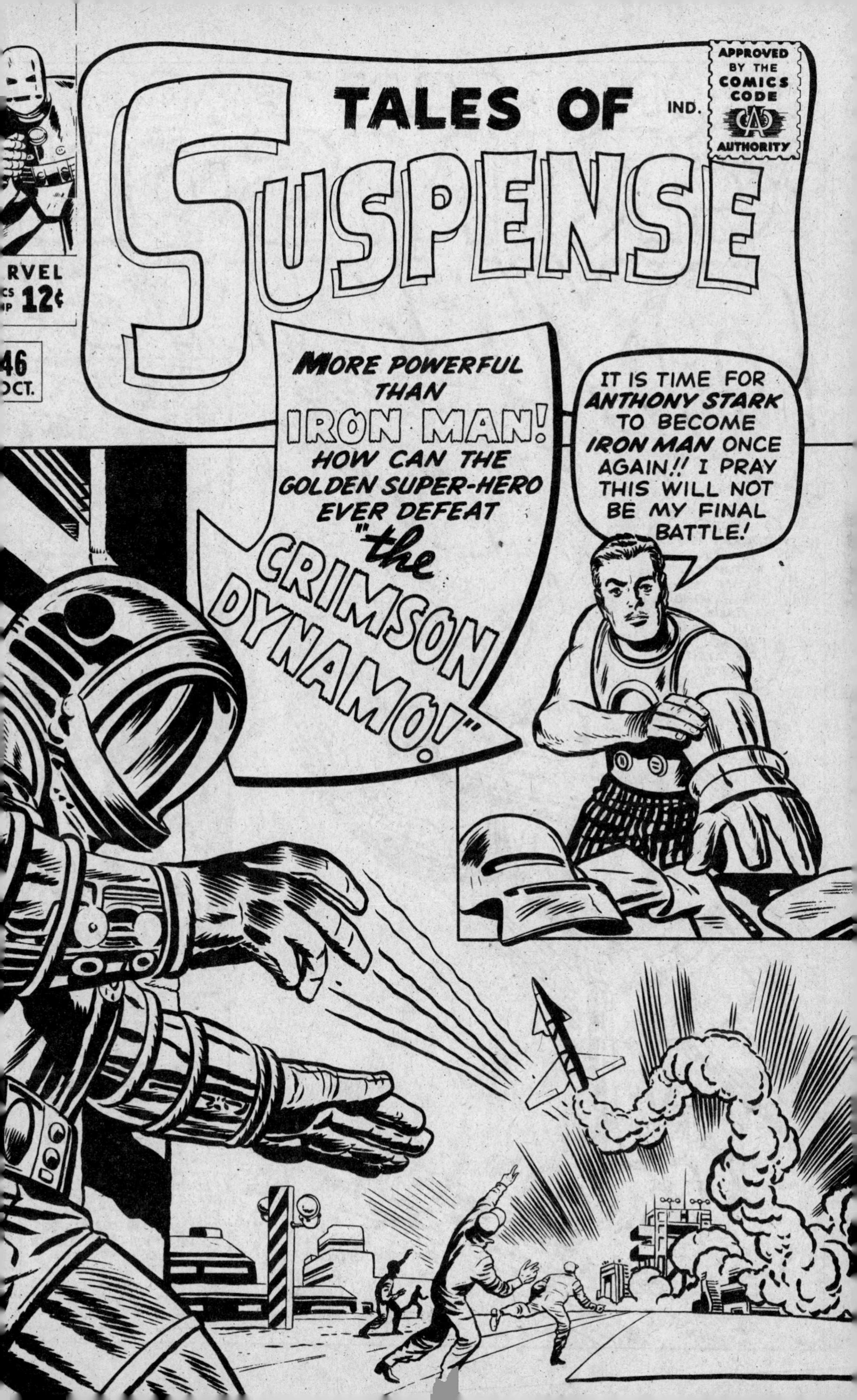

TALES OF SUSPENSE
IND.
APPROVED BY THE COMICS CODE AUTHORITY
RVEL
12¢
46
OCT.
MORE POWERFUL THAN IRON MAN! HOW CAN THE GOLDEN SUPER-HERO EVER DEFEAT "the CRIMSON DYNAMO!"
IT IS TIME FOR ANTHONY STARK TO BECOME IRON MAN ONCE AGAIN!! I PRAY THIS WILL NOT BE MY FINAL BATTLE!

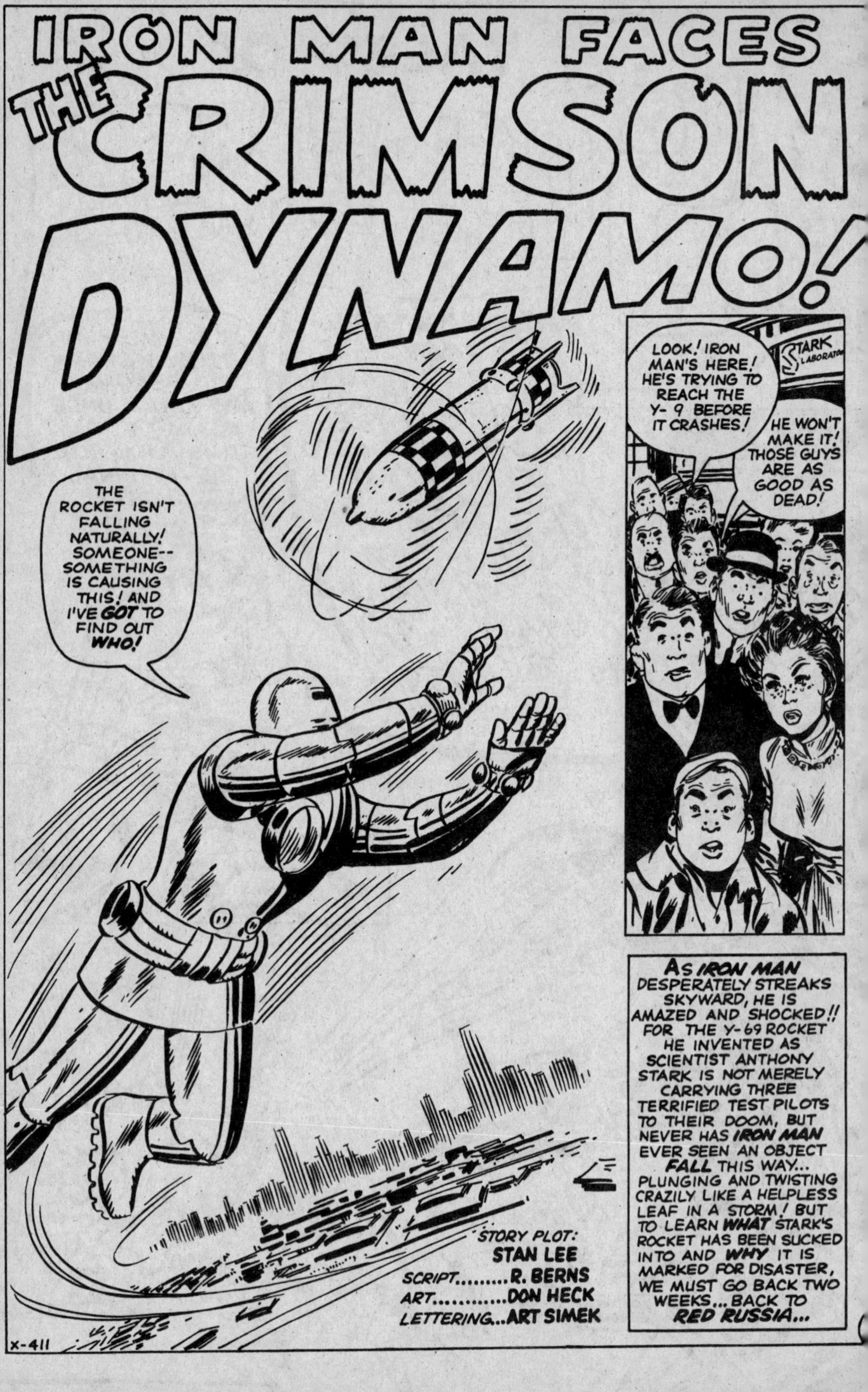
IRON MAN FACES
THE CRIMSON DYNAMO!
THE ROCKET ISN'T FALLING NATURALLY! SOMEONE-- SOMETHING IS CAUSING THIS! AND I'VE GOT TO FIND OUT WHO!
STARK
LOOK! IRON MAN'S HERE! HE'S TRYING TO REACH THE Y-9 BEFORE IT CRASHES!
HE WON'T MAKE IT! THOSE GUYS ARE AS GOOD AS DEAD!
AS IRON MAN DESPERATELY STREAKS SKYWARD, HE IS AMAZED AND SHOCKED!! FOR THE Y-69 ROCKET HE INVENTED AS SCIENTIST ANTHONY STARK IS NOT MERELY CARRYING THREE TERRIFIED TEST PILOTS TO THEIR DOOM, BUT NEVER HAS IRON MAN EVER SEEN AN OBJECT FALL THIS WAY... PLUNGING AND TWISTING CRAZILY LIKE A HELPLESS LEAF IN A STORM! BUT TO LEARN WHAT STARK'S ROCKET HAS BEEN SUCKED INTO AND WHY IT IS MARKED FOR DISASTER, WE MUST GO BACK TWO WEEKS... BACK TO RED RUSSIA...
STORY PLOT: STAN LEE
SCRIPT........R. BERNS
ART...........DON HECK
LETTERING...ART SIMEK
X-411

CAN YOU RECOGNIZE THE PUDGY, SCOWLING FIGURE ENTERING A STRANGE LABORATORY JUST OUTSIDE MOSCOW?

GUARDS! FOLLOW ME!

IF YOU DON'T, THEN YOU KNOW NOTHING ABOUT THE COLD WAR! FOR THIS STOCKY FELLOW IS THE "MR. BIG" OF THE IRON CURTAIN!

HERE WE ARE, EXCELLENCY! THE LABORATORY OF THE CRIMSON DYNAMO!

HOW I HATE THIS PROFESSOR VANKO... AND FEAR HIM!

BUT VANKO IS THE WORLD'S GREATEST EXPERT ON ELECTRICITY! SO I MUST REGRETFULLY USE HIM, AND NOT LIQUIDATE HIM!

AH! COMRADE LEADER! I AM HONORED BY YOUR PRESENCE!

STOP LYING, VANKO! I AM AWARE OF YOUR ARROGANCE! YOU THINK YOU'RE THE CLEVEREST MAN IN THE NATION, EVEN MORE INGENIOUS AND IMPORTANT THAN I!

I, MORE IMPORTANT THAN OUR GLORIOUS LEADER? SURELY YOU JEST!

I NEVER JOKE, VANKO! BUT I'M NOT HERE TO MATCH WITS! YOU'RE SUPPOSED TO GIVE ME A PRIVATE DEMONSTRATION OF SOME NEW SCIENTIFIC DISCOVERY! GET ON WITH IT!

AT ONCE, YOUR EXCELLENCY! FIRST, I MUST DON A PECULIAR COSTUME!

"PECULIAR"? YOU LOOK RIDICULOUS, VANKO... LIKE A HUMAN DYNAMO!

PRECISELY WHAT I AM COMRADE! I'M ALL WIRED UP TO PERFORM ELECTRIC MIRACLES! YOU'LL BE... UH... SHOCKED AT MY POWERS!

2.

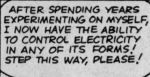

AFTER SPENDING YEARS EXPERIMENTING ON MYSELF, I NOW HAVE THE ABILITY TO CONTROL ELECTRICITY IN ANY OF ITS FORMS! STEP THIS WAY, PLEASE!

IRON MAN!... BY LENIN'S BEARD! YOU HAVE LURED ME INTO A TRAP, VANKO! GET HIM!

NONSENSE! TELL YOUR GUARDS TO LOWER THEIR WEAPONS! THAT FIGURE IS A MERE ROBOT, OPERATING UNDER MY REMOTE CONTROL!

I SIMPLY PRESS A BUTTON AND HE SHUFFLES FORWARD!

BUT WHY TOWARD ME, YOU IDIOT? IRON MAN WILL DESTROY ME... OR IS THAT WHAT YOU WANT? TO ASSASSINATE ME!

CLANK! CLANK! CLA

WELL! WE ARE NERVOUS AND SUSPICIOUS TODAY! NO, COMRADE, I AM MERELY DEMONSTRATING WHAT I CAN DO TO IRON MAN!

TNT

THE ROBOT EXPLODED!

EXACTLY! AT THE PUSH OF A TINY BUTTON, MY RHEOSTAT EMITTED ENOUGH VOLTS OF ELECTRICITY TO SHORT-CIRCUIT EVERY ELECTRONIC CONTRAPTION IRON MAN POSSESSES!

VAROOM

THEN COULD YOU BLOW THE REAL IRON MAN TO BITS?

YES... PROVIDED I'VE LINED UP THE PROPER FREQUENCIES AND OTHER TECHNICAL MATTERS YOU WOULDN'T UNDERSTAND! NOW OBSERVE THAT TANK!

CLANK! CLANK! CLANK!

RRRRRRRRRR!

IT'S ADVANCING TOWARD ME!

WE'LL GO GET SOME HELP, YOUR EXCELLENCY!

CORRECT! YET THERE IS NO ONE INSIDE! I ALONE CONTROL IT!

GUARDS! COME BACK! IT'S FOLLOWING ME! THE TANK IS *AFTER* ME!

CLANK! CLANK! CLANK!

I'M TRAPPED!!

AND THE TANK! IT'S COMING CLOSER AND CLOSER! VANKO, YOU DIABOLICAL COUNTER-REVOLUTIONIST!

SUCH PANIC FROM THE MIGHTIEST MAN IN THE COMMUNIST BLOC? VERY UNSEEMLY, COMRADE!...

BUT THE TANK! *THE TANK!*

I'LL TAKE CARE OF THE TANK! IT WILL STOP EXACTLY TWO INCHES IN FRONT OF YOU!

SEE? NOW STEP THIS WAY, YOUR EXCELLENCY!

YOU *DID* IT! IT OBEYED YOU AS IF IT'S *ALIVE!*

YOU'VE SEEN *NOTHING* YET! WATCH... I'M FIRING AN ELECTRIC BOLT FROM MY FINGERTIPS WHICH WILL COMPLETELY *DESTROY* THE STEEL MONSTER!

IMPRESSED?

-GULP- TOTALLY!

IN FACT, VANKO IS *SO* POWERFUL, HE MAY ONE DAY TURN AGAINST *ME!* HOWEVER, HIS ELECTRIC GENIUS SHALL SERVE ME WELL BEFORE I... ELIMINATE HIM!

4

HAVE YOU HEARD OF **ANTHONY STARK?**

WHO HAS NOT? STARK IS AMERICA'S GREATEST WEAPONRY SCIENTIST! WITHOUT HIM, THE AMERICAN DEFENSE EFFORT WOULD BE FAR WEAKER!

DA! THUS, BY STOPPING STARK'S OPERATIONS, THE U.S. WOULD LAG BEHIND US IN THE ARMS RACE! HOWEVER, NONE OF OUR AGENTS HAVE BEEN ABLE TO SABOTAGE STARK BECAUSE HE IS ALWAYS GUARDED BY **IRON MAN!** CAN YOU DEFEAT THE **REAL** IRON MAN AS YOU DID THAT **ROBOT** OF IRON MAN?

WHAT DO **YOU** THINK COM-RADE?

I THINK YOU CAN DO MOST **ANY-THING,** MY FRIEND! GO TO AMERICA, WRECK STARK'S PROJECTS AND GET RID OF IRON MAN!

THIS HAS BEEN WHAT I'VE BEEN SLAVING FOR, COMRADE LEADER! A CHANCE TO **PROVE** I'M THE MOST POWERFUL MAN ON EARTH! YOU SHALL SOON HAVE IRON MAN'S **REAL** HEAD!

EXCELLENT! AND I SHALL REWARD YOU HANDSOMELY FOR IT!

...BY REMOVING **YOURS!**

AND SO, TWO WEEKS LATER, AT ANTHONY STARK'S MAIN TESTING GROUND IN THE U.S....

ME...I WOULDN'T GO UP IN ONE OF THOSE THINGS IF THEY GAVE ME FORT KNOX!

NATURALLY NOT, HAPPY! IF YOU HAD ANY REAL COURAGE, YOU'D BE HEAVYWEIGHT CHAMP NOW INSTEAD OF MR. STARK'S CHAUFFEUR!

BOY! WITH FRIENDS LIKE **YOU,** PEPPER, I DON'T NEED **ENEMIES!** FOR YOUR INFO, FRECKLE-FACE, I GAVE UP THE RING BECAUSE I DIDN'T WANNA **HURT** ANYBODY!

ANYBODY NAMED HAPPY HOGAN, YOU MEAN!

5

AW, **YOU'D** PROBABLY EVEN FIND FAULT WITH *IRON MAN!* AND SPEAKIN' OF IRON MAN, I'D FEEL A LOT BETTER IF HE WAS HERE **NOW**, JUST IN CASE SOMETHING GOES WRONG WITH THAT *MISSILE* THE BOSS IS LAUNCHIN'!

HMM... HAPPY MAY *HAVE* SOMETHING THERE!

I'LL HEAD FOR MY OFFICE AND CHANGE TO *IRON MAN!* BUT I NEED A PRETEXT TO LEAVE...

ER... I HAVE TO PHONE THE PENTAGON! MEANTIME, CONDUCT THE LAUNCH ACCORDING TO PLAN!

YES, SIR, MR. STARK!

MOMENTS LATER, IN HIS OFFICE...

I'LL BE DRESSED BY THE TIME THE MISSILE IS FIRED! THIS COLLAPSIBLE EXTENSIBLE ARMOR IS A SNAP TO GET IN AND OUT OF!

AT THE SAME TIME, NEARBY, A WEIRD FIGURE PREPARES TO DESTROY BOTH THE MISSILE...AND IRON MAN HIMSELF!

AH! THERE GOES STARK'S MULTI-MILLION DOLLAR INVESTMENT! NOW TO USE MY ELECTRICAL POWERS TO AFFECT THE PLANE'S CIRCUITS AND CAUSE A DISASTER!

THEN, AS MANY ANXIOUS EYES WATCH THE VAULTING MISSILE...

HOLY CATS! LOOK AT THOSE DIALS REVOLVE! EVERY ELECTRIC CIRCUIT IS OUT OF WHACK! WE'RE DIVING BACK TO EARTH!

NO! IT'S *NOT* A DIVE! WE'RE SPINNING, TWISTING, FALLING... ALL AT THE SAME TIME!

IT ISN'T *POSSIBLE!* STARK TRIPLE-CHECKED ALL SYSTEMS!

STARK!! HE-- HE *FAILED!* AND WE'LL PAY WITH OUR *LIVES!*

GOT TO SAVE THOSE MEN-- THAT MISSILE-- NO MATTER WHAT!

LOOK! IRON MAN'S UP THERE! BUT CAN HE REACH THE FALLING SHIP *IN TIME?*

6

ONLY **ONE** THING TO DO... MEET THE CRAFT IN MID-AIR AND LESSEN THE SPEED OF ITS DESCENT! THIS WAY I CAN BUFFER THE FALL SO THE **MEN** AREN'T INJURED!

IRON MAN MANAGED TO SLOW THE SHIP DOWN!! BUT...HE TOOK THE FULL BRUNT OF THE IMPACT **HIMSELF!**

I...I **DID** IT! THEY'RE **SAFE!**

WHAM!

LOOK AT THE WAY HE'S **STAGGERING!** IT ALMOST KNOCKED HIM OUT!

IT WOULD HAVE **KILLED** ANY OTHER LIVING BEING! WE OWE OUR **LIVES** TO THAT GUY... **WHATEVER** HE IS!

THE LEADER WAS **RIGHT**!! IRON MAN HOVERS AROUND AND PROTECTS STARK'S INVENTIONS LIKE A ONE-MAN ARMY! HE JUST FRUSTRATED A PERFECT JOB OF SABOTAGE! BUT HE CAN'T BE AT **ALL** OF STARK'S PLANTS AT ONCE!

PRESENTLY, AFTER IRON MAN LEAVES AND STARK RE-APPEARS...

I'VE NEVER SEEN ANYTHING **LIKE** IT, MR. STARK! EVERY ELECTRICAL CONNECTION... EVERY PIECE OF ELECTRICAL MACHINERY IS BURNED TO A **CINDER!**

BUT **HOW? WHY? WHAT** COULD'VE AFFECTED ALL OUR ELECTRICAL APPARATUS??

THEN, AS THE DAYS AND WEEKS PASS, THE **CRIMSON DYNAMO** SECRETLY **ADDS** TO THE MYSTERY AT STARK'S PLANTS AROUND THE COUNTRY...

KABOOM!

GREAT GUNS! THE ROCKET EXPLODED SECONDS AFTER IT LEFT THE PAD! IT'S A GOOD THING WE HAD ONLY **ROBOTS** ABOARD!

7.

ANOTHER DAY...

I'VE NEVER SEEN ANYTHING *LIKE* THIS BEFORE! ALL OUR ELECTRICAL EQUIPMENT HAS BURST TO *FLAME!*

ZZZZTT!

ZZZZTT!

KABOOM!

WE'D BETTER GET *OUT* OF HERE BEFORE WE'RE *TRAPPED!*

ELSEWHERE...

KABOOM!

STARK

HA! THIS IS THE *TENTH PLANT* I'VE RUINED! YET NOBODY...NOT EVEN THE BRILLIANT *STARK* HIMSELF... CAN FIGURE OUT WHAT'S *CAUSING* THESE MYSTERIOUS FIRES!

THAT WEEKEND, AS A STUNNED TONY STARK SURVEYS THE DAMAGE OF YET ANOTHER PLANT IN HIS INDUSTRIAL COMPLEX...

THIS IS *INCREDIBLE!* EVERY ENEMY AGENT IN THE NATION MUST HAVE PICKED *ME* AS THEIR EXCLUSIVE TARGET FOR SABOTAGE!

COULD BE, STARK! BUT IF THEY *HAVE*...AND YOU CAN'T STOP THEM...YOU WON'T BE ABLE TO DELIVER VITAL EQUIPMENT TO THE GOVERNMENT ANYMORE! YOU'LL BE *RUINED!*

ARE YOU HINTING THAT MY *CONTRACTS* MAY BE TAKEN *AWAY* FROM ME?

THE PENTAGON HAS *NO* ALTERNATIVE, STARK! THE COUNTRY'S *DEFENSE* IS AT STAKE! IF YOU GET FOULED UP, WE MUST TURN TO *OTHER* COMPANIES!

AS STILL MORE FACTORIES ARE RAZED, STRANGE WHISPERS BEGIN TO CIRCULATE IN WASHINGTON, D.C....

A FUNNY IDEA HAS OCCURRED TO ME, SENATOR! ISN'T IT A LITTLE *TOO* COINCIDENTAL THAT ONLY *STARK'S* PLANTS ARE BEING SABOTAGED?

ARE YOU SAYING THAT STARK MAY BE DELIBERATELY SABOTAGING HIS *OWN* PLANTS?!

IF STARK *IS* A COMMUNIST AGENT, LOOK AT THE SWEET SPOT HE'S IN! FIRST, HE GRABS UP DOZENS OF GOVERNMENT CONTRACTS! THIS MAKES THE U.S. HEAVILY DEPENDENT ON HIS INDUSTRIAL EMPIRE FOR STRATEGIC WEAPONS AND RESEARCH!

THEN HE WRECKS HIS OWN PLANTS! *RESULT?* NO DELIVERIES! WASTED RESEARCH AND EXPERIMENTS! WE FALL BEHIND THE COMMUNISTS...

BY GEORGE! IF YOU'RE *RIGHT*...! WE HAVE TO INVESTIGATE STARK *THOROUGHLY!!*

8

DAYS LATER, AT STARK'S MAIN OFFICE IN FLUSHING, NEW YORK...

WELL, LITTLE FRIENDS, WE MADE ALL THE HEADLINES! THE GOVERNMENT IS LOSING CONFIDENCE IN US! ALL OUR CONTRACTS MAY BE WITHDRAWN!!

IN WHICH CASE YOU LOSE EVERY NICKEL YOU'VE GOT AND WIND UP BANKRUPT, HUH?

RIGHT, HAPPY! FROM PARK AVENUE TYCOON TO BOWERY BUM IN THREE SHORT WEEKS! AND, THE WORST OF IT IS... I DON'T KNOW WHO'S RUINING ME AND MY WORK!

BOY! IF I HAD ANY BRAINS I'D TAKE MY WALKIN' PAPERS RIGHT NOW!

BUT, I'M TOO HANDSOME TO HAVE BRAINS ALSO! SO I GUESS I'LL STICK WITH YA TILL THE END, BOSS!

ME TOO, MR. STARK! SOMEBODY HAS TO KEEP HAPPY FROM DRIVING YOU NUTS!

THANKS, KIDS! I... I'LL NEVER FORGET THIS!

SOMEONE IS GUNNING FOR ME... THAT'S FOR SURE! BUT WHO? IF HE'D ONLY SHOW HIMSELF OR MAKE SOME TELL-TALE SLIP-UP, I COULD GO AFTER HIM, AS IRON MAN!

BUT, AS STARK HELPLESSLY TRIES TO FATHOM THE UNKNOWN, THE "UNKNOWN" HAS IRON MAN VERY MUCH ON HIS MIND...

I'VE DAMAGED STARK'S PLANTS, BUT I'M STILL NOT SATISFIED! NOT ONCE, AT ANY OF THE OTHER FACTORIES, DID IRON MAN COME FORTH TO PROTECT STARK'S PROPERTY!

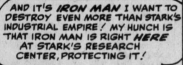

AND IT'S IRON MAN I WANT TO DESTROY EVEN MORE THAN STARK'S INDUSTRIAL EMPIRE! MY HUNCH IS THAT IRON MAN IS RIGHT HERE AT STARK'S RESEARCH CENTER, PROTECTING IT!

ANYWAY, I'LL SOON FIND OUT! I'LL HEAD STRAIGHT FOR THE PLANT AND CHALLENGE IRON MAN! IF I DEFEAT HIM, I'LL RETURN HOME A NATIONAL HERO, POWERFUL ENOUGH TO REPLACE EVEN THE LEADER HIMSELF!

KRACK!

DANGER FENCE ELECTRIFIED HIGH VOLTAGE

THE ELECTRICAL LINES! THEY'RE SHORT-CIRCUITING AND CAUSING FIRES AS THEY DID IN MY OTHER PLANTS! THAT MEANS THE SABOTEUR IS ATTACKING US HERE! HAPPY! PEPPER! ALERT THE GUARDS!

RIGHT, BOSS!

MEANWHILE, I'LL SWITCH TO IRON MAN! THIS IS MY CHANCE TO PAY OFF A FEW "DEBTS"!

AS STARK, I'D BE TRAPPED IN THIS FLAMING ROOM! BUT AS IRON MAN, I CAN SMASH RIGHT THROUGH THE WALL TO THE OUTSIDE!

NEXT MOMENT...

THERE HE IS! THAT MUST BE THE MYSTERIOUS SABOTEUR! HE MUST BE AWFULLY SURE OF HIS POWERS TO COME KNOCKING AT MY FRONT DOOR!

IRON MAN! AT LAST! NOW TO LINE UP YOUR FREQUENCY!

CRASH!

HMM...JUDGING BY HIS ACTS OF SABOTAGE, THAT CHARACTER POSSESSES VAST ELECTRICAL POWERS! HE MIGHT DO TO ME WHAT HE DID TO MY PLANTS...IF I LET HIM!

THERE! NOW TO EMIT THE ELECTRICAL VOLTAGE THAT WILL DESTROY IRON MAN INSIDE HIS METAL SHELL!

(GASP!) SOMETHING'S WRONG! MY ELECTRICAL BOLTS ARE NOT AFFECTING IRON MAN!

NO, CHUM...BECAUSE I USED MY TRANSISTOR POWER TO SET UP AN ELECTRICAL FORCE FIELD...TO SHIELD ME FROM YOUR ELECTRICAL ONSLAUGHT!

CRACK!

THEN I WILL ELECTRIFY THE GROUND UNDER YOUR METAL BOOTS! THAT WILL FINISH YOU!

WRONG AGAIN! NOT WHEN I'M AIR-BORNE! EVEN YOU CAN'T DEFY SCIENTIFIC LAW!

CRACKLE!

10.

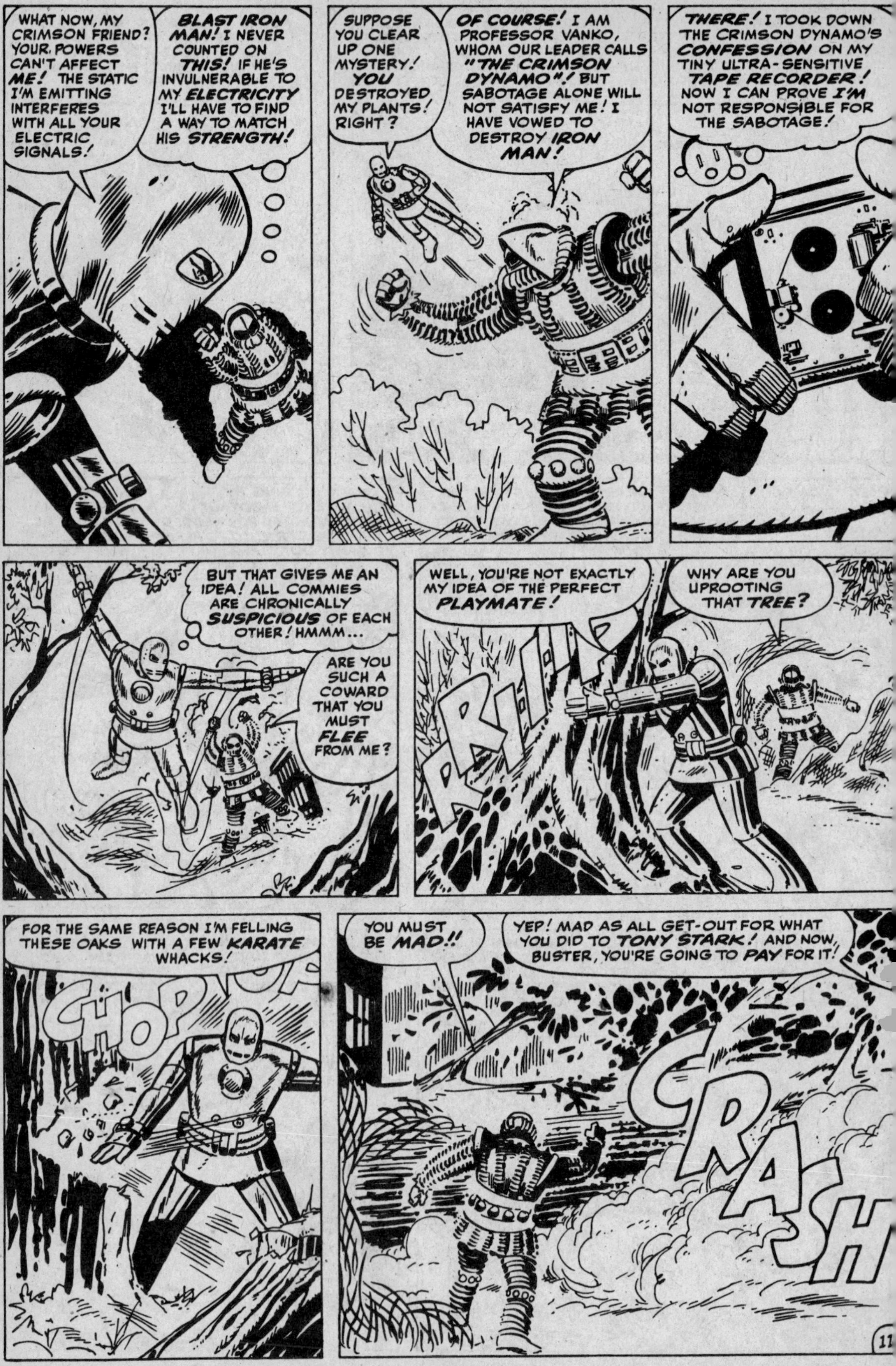

WHAT NOW, MY CRIMSON FRIEND? YOUR POWERS CAN'T AFFECT ME! THE STATIC I'M EMITTING INTERFERES WITH ALL YOUR ELECTRIC SIGNALS!
BLAST IRON MAN! I NEVER COUNTED ON THIS! IF HE'S INVULNERABLE TO MY ELECTRICITY I'LL HAVE TO FIND A WAY TO MATCH HIS STRENGTH!
SUPPOSE YOU CLEAR UP ONE MYSTERY! YOU DESTROYED MY PLANTS! RIGHT?
OF COURSE! I AM PROFESSOR VANKO, WHOM OUR LEADER CALLS "THE CRIMSON DYNAMO"! BUT SABOTAGE ALONE WILL NOT SATISFY ME! I HAVE VOWED TO DESTROY IRON MAN!
THERE! I TOOK DOWN THE CRIMSON DYNAMO'S CONFESSION ON MY TINY ULTRA-SENSITIVE TAPE RECORDER! NOW I CAN PROVE I'M NOT RESPONSIBLE FOR THE SABOTAGE!
BUT THAT GIVES ME AN IDEA! ALL COMMIES ARE CHRONICALLY SUSPICIOUS OF EACH OTHER! HMMM...
ARE YOU SUCH A COWARD THAT YOU MUST FLEE FROM ME?
WELL, YOU'RE NOT EXACTLY MY IDEA OF THE PERFECT PLAYMATE!
WHY ARE YOU UPROOTING THAT TREE?
RRIIIP
FOR THE SAME REASON I'M FELLING THESE OAKS WITH A FEW KARATE WHACKS!
CHOP
YOU MUST BE MAD!!
YEP! MAD AS ALL GET-OUT FOR WHAT YOU DID TO TONY STARK! AND NOW, BUSTER, YOU'RE GOING TO PAY FOR IT!
CRASH

HAVE YOU EVER BEEN IMPRISONED INSIDE OF A SQUARE OF FALLEN TREES?

WAIT! DON'T...

I--I'M TRAPPED!

BLAST YOU, IRON MAN! WHERE ARE YOU GOING NOW?

DOES KENNEDY TELL KHRUSHCHEV? YOU'LL FIND OUT SOON ENOUGH!

MINUTES LATER, AS IRON MAN REAPPEARS...

W-WHERE ARE YOU TAKING ME?

TO FLUSHING BAY, WHERE WE'RE GOING FOR A LITTLE SWIM!

BUT IF WE HIT THE WATER, THE SHOCK WILL ELECTRO-CUTE BOTH OF US!

WHO CARES, AS LONG AS I MAKE SURE YOU NEVER MENACE US AGAIN? SINCE WE CANNOT DEFEAT ONE ANOTHER, WE'LL BOTH PAY THE PRICE FOR FAILURE...

NO! NO! WAIT! I DON'T WANT TO DIE... STOP! I SURRENDER!! YOU WIN!!

NOW YOU'RE BEGINNING TO MAKE SENSE! BY THE WAY, I'M INTERCEPTING A RADIO MESSAGE FROM BEHIND THE IRON CURTAIN RIGHT NOW ON MY BUILT-IN RECEIVER...

IT MIGHT INTEREST YOU TO EAVESDROP WITH ME! HERE'S A TINY PAIR OF EAR-PLUGS! TUNE IN AND LEARN YOUR REWARD FOR TRYING TO DESTROY ME! IT WILL SHOW YOU HOW TRUSTWORTHY YOUR LEADER IS!

REMEMBER, COMRADES! SEIZE VANKO THE INSTANT HE RETURNS, AND MACHINE-GUN HIM! I CANNOT TAKE ANY CHANCES OF THE CRIMSON DYNAMO BEING MORE POPULAR THAN I! SO VANKO MUST BE LIQUIDATED!

12

THE UNSCRUPULOUS SCOUNDREL! SO! *DEATH* WAS TO BE MY REWARD FOR SERVING HIM!

POOR VANKO! HE DOESN'T KNOW HE REALLY HEARD *MY* VOICE, NOT HIS LEADER'S!

"WHEN I LEFT VANKO MOMENTARILY... I QUICKLY RECORDED THE SPEECH HE JUST HEARD ON MY *TAPE MACHINE!* I WAS CERTAIN THAT HE'D *BELIEVE* IT... BECAUSE HE KNOWS HOW TREACHEROUS ALL COMMUNISTS ARE!"

THANK YOU, IRON MAN! YOU HAVE SAVED MY LIFE! I REALIZE NOW THAT MY SCIENTIFIC GENIUS HAS BEEN AT THE SERVICE OF A SAVAGE, DOUBLE-DEALING SYSTEM!

MY RUSE WORKED! NOW FOR A *REAL* TWIST!

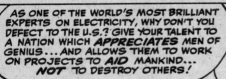

AS ONE OF THE WORLD'S MOST BRILLIANT EXPERTS ON ELECTRICITY, WHY DON'T YOU DEFECT TO THE U.S.? GIVE YOUR TALENT TO A NATION WHICH *APPRECIATES* MEN OF GENIUS... AND ALLOWS THEM TO WORK ON PROJECTS TO *AID* MANKIND... *NOT* TO DESTROY OTHERS!

I ACCEPT YOUR OFFER, IRON MAN! AND TO SHOW MY GOOD FAITH...

... A RED SPY NETWORK IS HOLDING A FORTUNE IN GOLD FOR SABOTAGE PURPOSES! I'LL LEAD THE F.B.I. TO THE RING AND USE THAT GOLD TO REBUILD WHAT I'VE DESTROYED!

AND I'LL GUARANTEE YOU A TOP JOB WITH STARK'S COMPANY... RUNNING YOUR OWN ELECTRICAL RESEARCH DEPARTMENT!

FINALLY, AT STARK'S PLANT...

GET ME AN EYE DOCTOR! I'M *SEEING* THINGS! IRON MAN ACTIN' BUDDY-BUDDY WITH THAT RED SABOTEUR!

YOU'RE *WRONG*, HAPPY! HE'S BEEN PROMOTED FROM ENEMY SABOTEUR TO TOP RESEARCH MAN FOR ANTHONY STARK!

AND, HALF-WAY AROUND THE WORLD...

IDIOTS! TRAITORS! THERE IS *NO ONE* I CAN TRUST! VANKO IS NOW SHARING HIS GREAT KNOWLEDGE WITH THE ACCURSED *ANTHONY STARK!*

BUT IT IS ALL *IRON MAN'S* FAULT! ONCE AGAIN THE HATED AMERICAN DEFENDER HAS FOILED MY PLANS! BUT *NEXT TIME* SHALL BE DIFFERENT! NEXT TIME I SHALL *BURY* IRON MAN!

WRONG, COMRADE! "NEXT TIME" IRON MAN HAS AN ENTIRELY *DIFFERENT* EXTRA-LONG EIGHTEEN PAGE EPIC ADVENTURE AS HE BATTLES THE *MYSTERIOUS MELTER!* DON'T MISS IT!!

-THE END-

13.

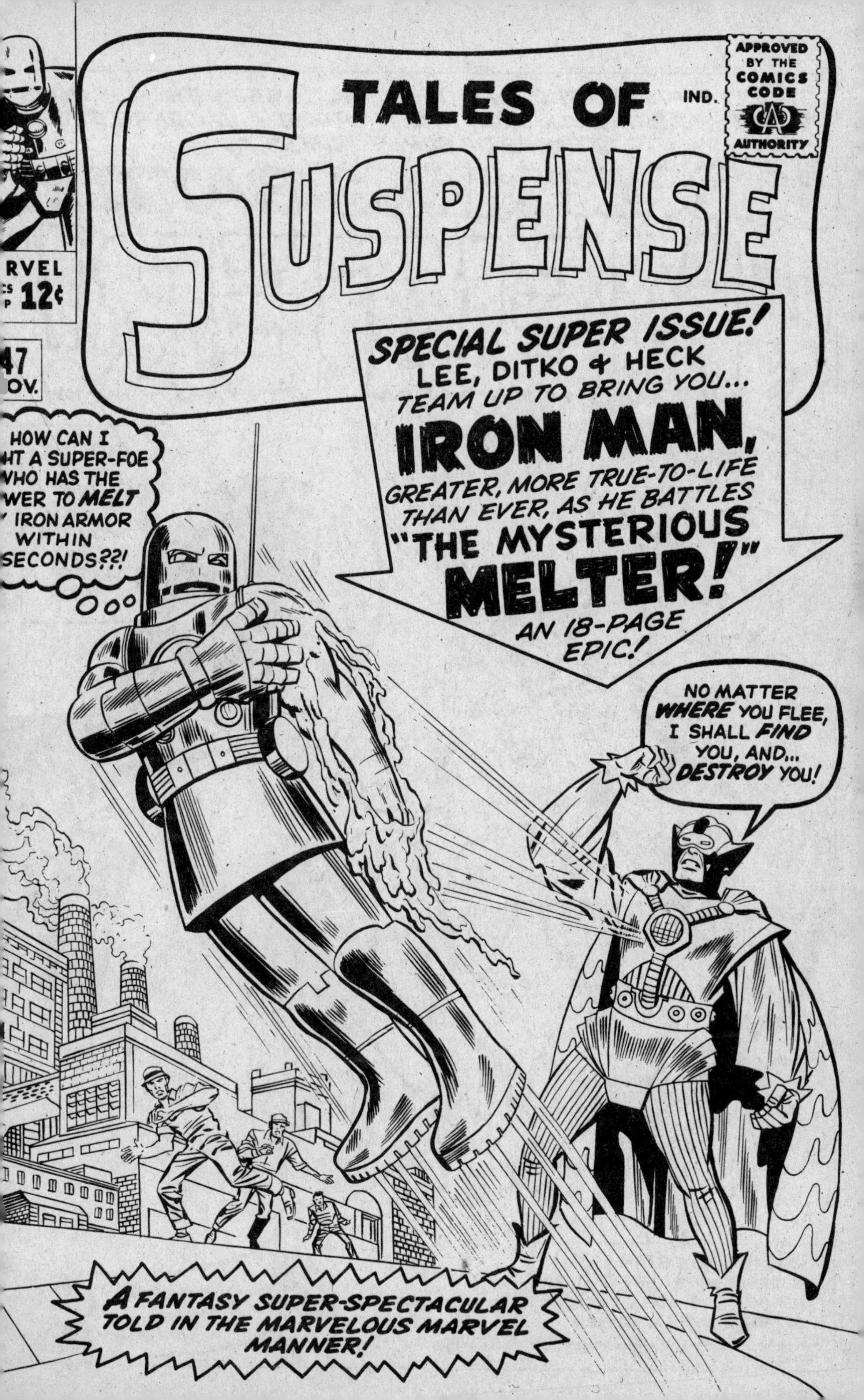
TALES OF SUSPENSE
IND.
APPROVED BY THE COMICS CODE AUTHORITY
RVEL
12¢
47
OV.
SPECIAL SUPER ISSUE!
LEE, DITKO & HECK TEAM UP TO BRING YOU...
IRON MAN,
GREATER, MORE TRUE-TO-LIFE THAN EVER, AS HE BATTLES
"THE MYSTERIOUS MELTER!"
AN 18-PAGE EPIC!
HOW CAN I HT A SUPER-FOE VHO HAS THE WER TO MELT IRON ARMOR WITHIN SECONDS??!
NO MATTER WHERE YOU FLEE, I SHALL FIND YOU, AND... DESTROY YOU!
A FANTASY SUPER-SPECTACULAR TOLD IN THE MARVELOUS MARVEL MANNER!

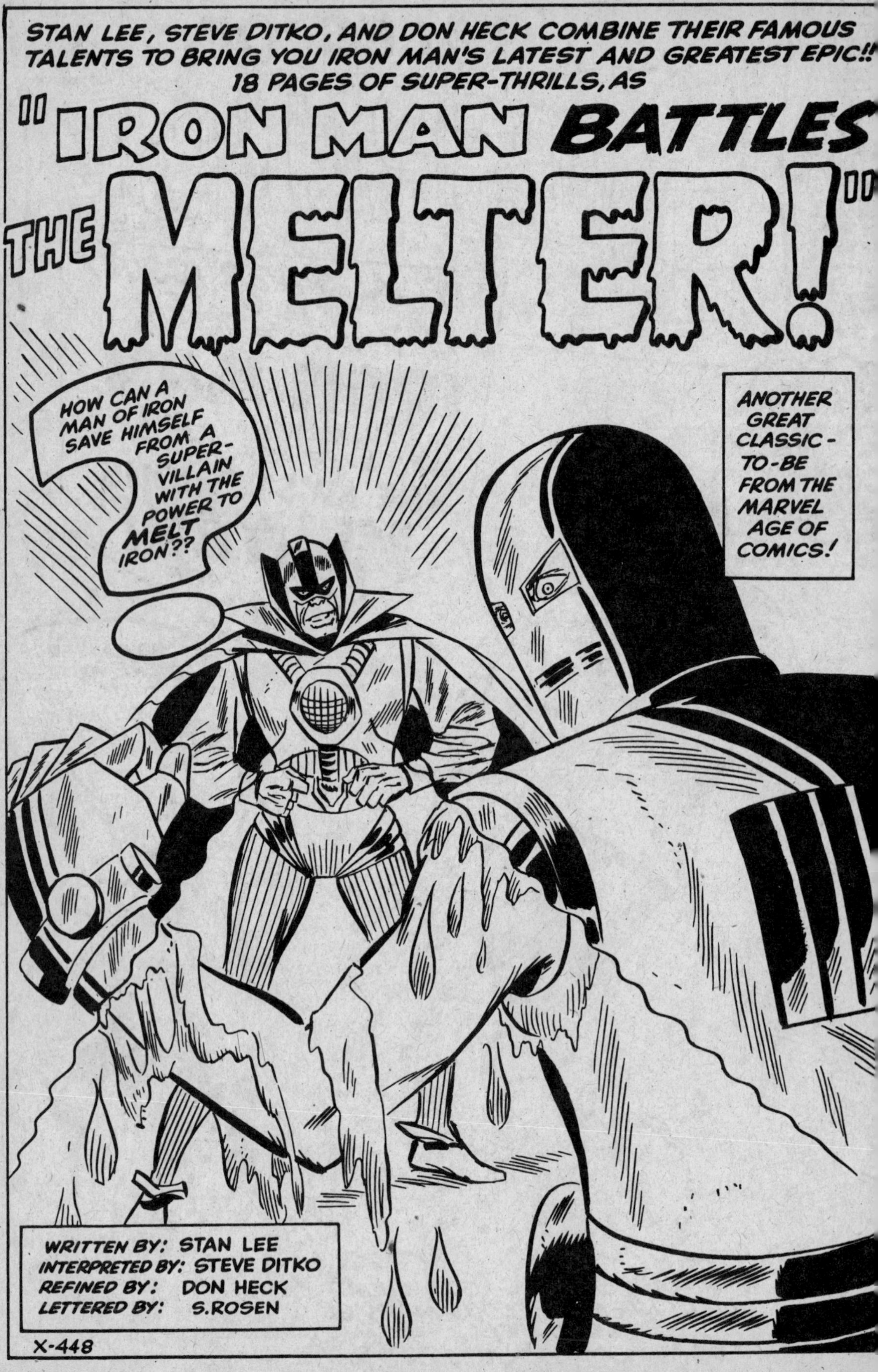
STAN LEE, STEVE DITKO, AND DON HECK COMBINE THEIR FAMOUS TALENTS TO BRING YOU IRON MAN'S LATEST AND GREATEST EPIC!! 18 PAGES OF SUPER-THRILLS, AS
"IRON MAN BATTLES THE MELTER!"
HOW CAN A MAN OF IRON SAVE HIMSELF FROM A SUPER-VILLAIN WITH THE POWER TO MELT IRON??
ANOTHER GREAT CLASSIC-TO-BE FROM THE MARVEL AGE OF COMICS!
WRITTEN BY: STAN LEE
INTERPRETED BY: STEVE DITKO
REFINED BY: DON HECK
LETTERED BY: S.ROSEN
X-448

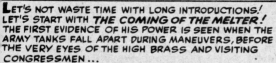

LET'S NOT WASTE TIME WITH LONG INTRODUCTIONS! LET'S START WITH *THE COMING OF THE MELTER!* THE FIRST EVIDENCE OF HIS POWER IS SEEN WHEN THE ARMY TANKS FALL APART DURING MANEUVERS, BEFORE THE VERY EYES OF THE HIGH BRASS AND VISITING CONGRESSMEN...

OUR TANKS!! WHAT'S *HAPPENING* TO THEM??!

GENERAL!! *LOOK!*

THE POINTS OF STRESS OF BOTH TANKS HAVE BEEN *WEAKENED* TO THE BREAKING POINT!

INCREDIBLE! IT'S ALMOST AS THOUGH EVERY VITAL JOINT HAS BEEN... *MELTED!*

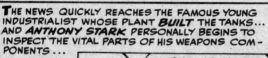

THE NEWS QUICKLY REACHES THE FAMOUS YOUNG INDUSTRIALIST WHOSE PLANT *BUILT* THE TANKS... AND *ANTHONY STARK* PERSONALLY BEGINS TO INSPECT THE VITAL PARTS OF HIS WEAPONS COMPONENTS...

THE IRON IN THOSE TANKS *COULDN'T* HAVE BEEN DEFECTIVE! I BUY THE BEST QUALITY, PAY THE HIGHEST PRICES! AND YET...

EVERYTHING *HERE* SEEMS A-OKAY!

SUDDENLY...

OHHHH...

I *KNEW* YOU'D SHOW UP SOONER OR LATER, STARK!

NOW TO APPLY MY SHORT-RANGE *MELTING RAY* TO THIS NEW SHIPMENT OF STARK'S WAR MATERIALS!

THIS WILL SLOW UP THE ARMY'S DEFENSE EFFORT... AND COST STARK *A FORTUNE!*

THUS I ACCOMPLISH MY TWO OBJECTIVES! I STRIKE BACK AT THE U.S. ARMED FORCES... AND GET REVENGE ON MY OLD RIVAL, TONY STARK!

BY THE TIME HE WAKES UP, I'LL BE *GONE!* TOO BAD HE'LL NEVER KNOW WHO I REALLY *AM!* HE'LL NEVER SUSPECT THAT THE *MELTER* IS REALLY HIS FORMER *COMPETITOR,* BRUNO HORGAN!

BRUNO HORGAN, ALIAS *THE MELTER,* SMUGLY THINKS BACK TO THE TIME OF HIS LAST MEETING WITH TONY STARK...

HORGAN, STARK'S REPORT SHOWS THAT YOUR FACTORY HAS BEEN USING INFERIOR MATERIALS! THEREFORE, WE ARE REVOKING YOUR ARMY CONTRACT AND ORDERING *STARK'S* COMPANY TO BUILD OUR TANKS!

I'LL GET MY REVENGE! STARK WILL *PAY* FOR THIS!

THEN, THE *MELTER* REMEMBERS HOW HE ACCIDENTALLY DISCOVERED HIS SECRET OF DISSOLVING IRON! ONE OF THE ELECTRONIC TESTING DEVICES IN HIS LABORATORY, BUILT OF INFERIOR PARTS, HAD GONE HAYWIRE AND...

THAT INSPECTION BEAM IS AFFECTING THE IRON UNITS IT'S SHINING ON! IT'S MAKING THEM *MELT!* BUT HOW...

STUDYING THIS DEVICE ALONE IN HIS LAB, HORGAN FINDS THE SOURCE OF ITS POWER, AND MANAGES TO FIT IT INTO A SMALL, COMPACT UNIT!

THIS IS SENSATIONAL! MY MELTING BEAM WILL DISSOLVE IRON LIKE FLAME MELTS BUTTER! WHAT A *DISCOVERY!!*

IRON IS THE MOST IMPORTANT METAL ON EARTH! BY BEING ABLE TO MELT IT AT WILL, I BECOME THE MOST POWERFUL *MAN* IN THE WORLD!!

I MUST PLAN *CAREFULLY!* I MUST *USE* MY POWER TO DESTROY MY ENEMIES...AND TO MAKE *ME* SUPREME!

AFTER DAYS OF SECRET WORK...

THIS PORTABLE BEAM MAKES ME *INVINCIBLE!* *NO ONE* CAN DEFY ME!

3.

WITH A MASK, TO CONCEAL MY IDENTITY, I CAN PLUNDER AT WILL! THE VERY *SIGHT* OF ME WILL STRIKE FEAR INTO THE HEARTS OF MEN! NO WEAPON CAN MENACE ME, FOR I CAN MELT THEM *ALL!*

IN FACT, THE WORLD WILL SOON COME TO KNOW ME AS *THE MELTER!!*

AND NOW, WE AGAIN PICK UP THE THREADS OF OUR GRIPPING TALE, AS *THE MELTER* PREPARES HIS NEXT MOVE ...

I WILL NOT FINISH YOU OFF NOW, STARK! THAT WOULD BE TOO MERCIFUL! I PREFER YOU TO *LIVE* SO THAT I CAN TOY WITH YOU SOME MORE ... SO THAT I CAN STEADILY DEFEAT YOU AT EVERY TURN!

MEANWHILE, INSIDE ANTHONY STARK'S SUITE OF EXECUTIVE OFFICES ...

HAPPY, WOULD YOU FIND MR. STARK AND TELL HIM I HAVE SOME REPORTS FOR HIM TO SIGN?

LOOK, DOLL! I'M HIS EVER-LOVIN' *CHAUFFEUR*, NOT A BLOODHOUND! BUT IF YOU CAN BEAR TO HAVE ME TAKE MY LOVEABLE SELF AWAY FOR A MINUTE, I GUESS I CAN DO IT!

WHAT A GAL! I *KNOW* SHE'S NUTS ABOUT ME! IF ONLY *SHE* KNEW IT! HEY! MR. STARK! WHAT *HAPPENED,* BOSS?

BLOW WEAKENED ME! PAIN IN CHEST... MUST RECHARGE... FAST!

I, EH, TRIPPED AND FELL! HELP ME TO MY OFFICE, HAPPY!

YOU LOOK *PALE,* MR. STARK! SOMETHING'S WRONG, I *KNOW* IT! PLEASE LET ME CALL A *DOCTOR!*

NO, PEPPER! I'LL BE ALL RIGHT! I ... JUST WANT TO BE ALONE IN HERE ... TO REST! NO DOCTOR! THAT'S AN *ORDER!*

4

IF A DOCTOR EVER DISCOVERED THIS LIFE-GIVING CHEST PLATE I WEAR, MY SECRET WOULD BE OUT! HOW COULD I EXPLAIN TO PEPPER AND HAPPY THAT ALL I NEED TO DO IS RECHARGE MY TRANSISTOR BATTERIES TO REGAIN MY STAMINA?

AHH...I CAN FEEL THE STRENGTH SURGING BACK... ANOTHER FEW MINUTES MIGHT HAVE BEEN...TOO LATE!

MEANWHILE, IN ANOTHER PART OF STARK'S VAST MUNITIONS FACTORY...

HOW EASY IT IS FOR ME TO MELT ANY LOCK! NOW THAT I'VE GAINED ACCESS TO STARK'S POWER PLANT, I CAN PUT HIS ENTIRE FACTORY OUT OF OPERATION WITH ONE STROKE!

BUT THE MELTER OVERLOOKS ANTHONY STARK'S PROTECTIVE ALARMS, AND AN URGENT SIGNAL FLASHES ON THE MUNITIONS MAKER'S WALL...

SOMEONE HAS BROKEN INTO THE POWER PLANT!

WITHOUT A SECOND'S HESITATION, STARK OPENS A LOCKED ATTACHE CASE AND TAKES OUT THE COMPONENT PARTS OF HIS FLEXIBLE IRON MAN COSTUME...

WHATEVER MUST BE DONE CAN BE DONE BETTER BY... IRON MAN!

THUNDERING DOWN HIS SECRET UNDERGROUND PASSAGEWAY, THE GREAT GOLDEN GLADIATOR RACES FOR THE POWER PLANT...

GOOD THING I MADE THIS TUNNEL SOUND-PROOF! THE THUMPING OF MY IRON BOOTS WOULD BE A DEAD GIVEAWAY IF ANYONE SHOULD HEAR THEM!

NOW TO BEGIN MELTING STARK'S MAIN GENERATORS! WITHOUT THE POWER HE NEEDS, HIS WHOLE FACTORY WILL COME TO A STANDSTILL!

CHARLIE... LOOK!!

WHO IS IT? HOW DID HE GET UP THERE

HE'S USING SOME KIND OF *ENERGY BEAM*... PLAYING IT ON OUR GENERATORS! HOLY COW... THEY'RE STARTING TO..TO *MELT!*

ANOTHER FEW SECONDS AND STARK WILL BE *RUINED!*

[L]ET'S GO! [W]E'VE GOT TO [A]LERT THE [G]UARDS... [W]ARN MR. STARK!!

TOO LATE! NOTHING CAN STOP HIM *NOW!*

[B]UT AT THAT INSTANT, THE MOST IMPRESSIVE FIGURE OF ALL COMES HURTLING TOWARDS THE MASKED MELTER...

DROP THAT, MISTER... OR YOU'LL *WISH* YOU *HAD!*

IRON MAN! I HAD *HEARD* YOU WORKED FOR STARK, BUT THOUGHT IT WAS JUST A RUMOR TO FRIGHTEN AWAY SABOTEURS!

WELL, WELL! THIS IS MORE THAN I DARED *HOPE* FOR!

ONCE THE WORLD LEARNS THAT *THE MELTER* HAS DEFEATED *IRON MAN, NONE* WILL DARE TO OPPOSE ME! AND SO... I SHALL TURN MY DESTRUCTIVE BEAM ON *YOU!*

GOOD! HE SWUNG HIS BEAM AWAY FROM THE GENERATORS! BUT... WHAT IF IT HAS THE SAME EFFECT ON MY *ARMORED SUIT!???*

6.

IRON MAN! THE PRIDE OF DEMOCRACY! GUARDIAN OF STARK'S WEAPONS WORKS! DEFENDER OF THE WEAK AND HELPLESS! HAH! HOW *EASILY* THE MIGHTY CAN BE DEFEATED!

HIS BEAM WORKS!! IF...IF HE MELTS ANY *MORE* OF MY ARMOR, MY *IDENTITY* WILL BE REVEALED...AND WORSE...MY *CHEST PLATE* WILL BE DESTROYED!

BEFORE THE SLOWER-MOVING *MELTER* CAN RE DIRECT HIS POTENT BEAM UPWARD, *IRON MAN* APPLIES HIS EMERGENCY JETS AND STREAKS OVER THE HEAD OF HIS STARTLED FOE!

GOT TO GET OUT OF RANGE!

THEN, WITH HIS TRANSISTOR ENERGY ACTIVATORS TURNED TO "FULL-POWER", THE MIGHTY MYSTERY MAN CRASHES DESPERATELY THROUGH THE THICKLY INSULATED POWER PLANT WALL!

HE'S FASTER THAN I *THOUGHT!*

JUST IN TIME!!

I'VE NEVER FACED SUCH AN ENEMY BEFORE! WHO *IS* HE? WHERE DID HE GET HIS *POWER*? AND, MOST IMPORTANT, HOW CAN I *FIGHT* HIM WHEN I DARE NOT *FACE* HIM?!!

USED UP TOO MUCH POWER BREAKING THROUGH THE WALL! HAVE TO SLOW DOWN... TILL BATTERIES RECHARGE! THESE *TRANSISTOR MAGNETS* SHOULD KEEP THE MELTER FROM REACHING ME NOW!

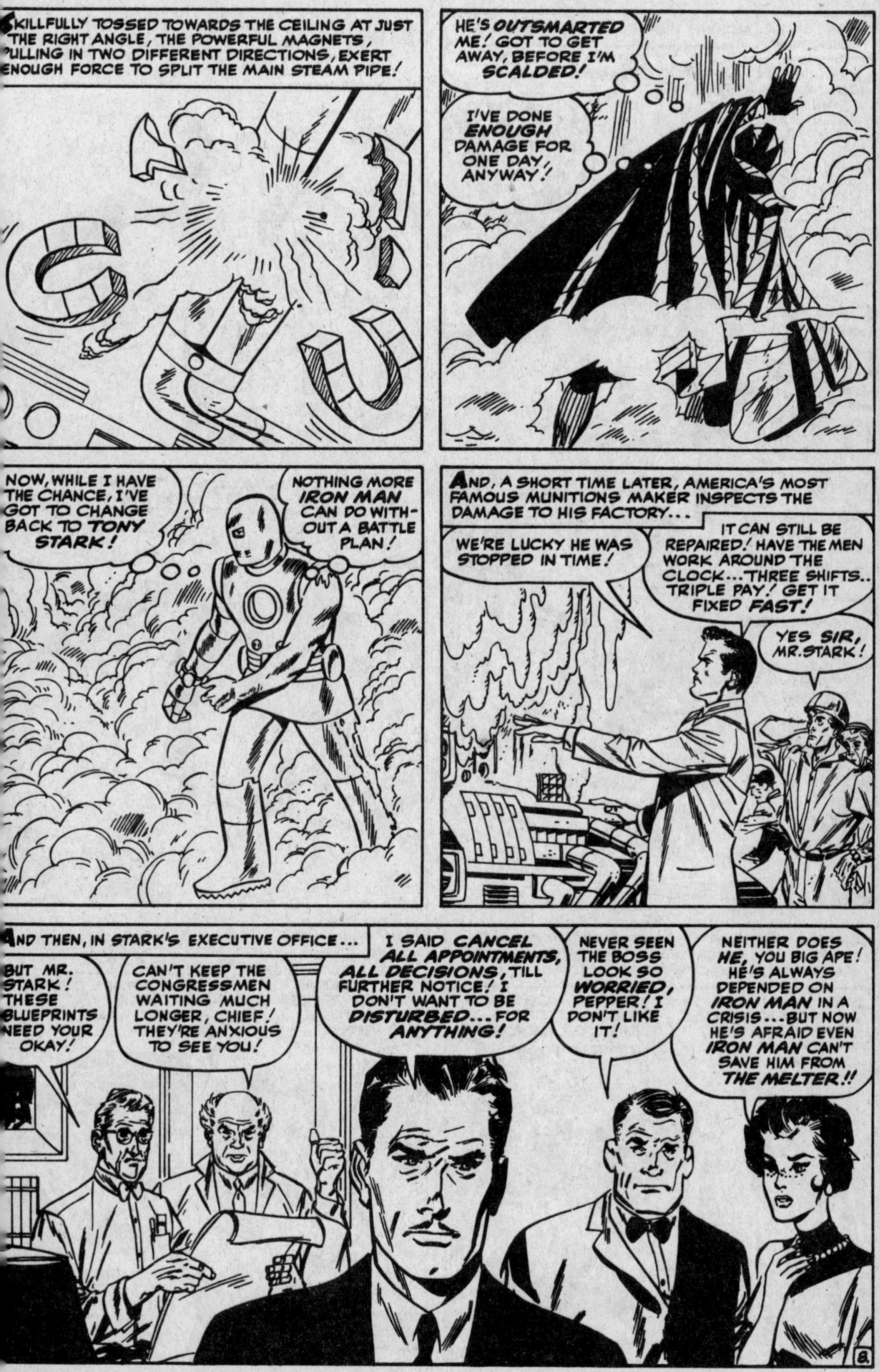
SKILLFULLY TOSSED TOWARDS THE CEILING AT JUST THE RIGHT ANGLE, THE POWERFUL MAGNETS, PULLING IN TWO DIFFERENT DIRECTIONS, EXERT ENOUGH FORCE TO SPLIT THE MAIN STEAM PIPE!
HE'S OUTSMARTED ME! GOT TO GET AWAY, BEFORE I'M SCALDED!
I'VE DONE ENOUGH DAMAGE FOR ONE DAY, ANYWAY!
NOW, WHILE I HAVE THE CHANCE, I'VE GOT TO CHANGE BACK TO TONY STARK!
NOTHING MORE IRON MAN CAN DO WITHOUT A BATTLE PLAN!
AND, A SHORT TIME LATER, AMERICA'S MOST FAMOUS MUNITIONS MAKER INSPECTS THE DAMAGE TO HIS FACTORY...
WE'RE LUCKY HE WAS STOPPED IN TIME!
IT CAN STILL BE REPAIRED! HAVE THE MEN WORK AROUND THE CLOCK...THREE SHIFTS.. TRIPLE PAY! GET IT FIXED FAST!
YES SIR, MR. STARK!
AND THEN, IN STARK'S EXECUTIVE OFFICE...
BUT MR. STARK! THESE BLUEPRINTS NEED YOUR OKAY!
CAN'T KEEP THE CONGRESSMEN WAITING MUCH LONGER, CHIEF! THEY'RE ANXIOUS TO SEE YOU!
I SAID CANCEL ALL APPOINTMENTS, ALL DECISIONS, TILL FURTHER NOTICE! I DON'T WANT TO BE DISTURBED... FOR ANYTHING!
NEVER SEEN THE BOSS LOOK SO WORRIED, PEPPER! I DON'T LIKE IT!
NEITHER DOES HE, YOU BIG APE! HE'S ALWAYS DEPENDED ON IRON MAN IN A CRISIS...BUT NOW HE'S AFRAID EVEN IRON MAN CAN'T SAVE HIM FROM THE MELTER!!
8

THEN, AFTER LOCKING HIMSELF IN HIS PRIVATE WORKSHOP...

WHAT DO I DO *NOW?* IRON MAN IS HELPLESS AGAINST AN ENEMY WITH THE ABILITY TO *MELT* IRON! AND YET, WITHOUT MY OTHER IDENTITY, I'M JUST AN ORDINARY HUMAN ... MORE VULNERABLE THAN MOST BECAUSE MY HEART WOULD STOP WITHOUT MY CHEST PLATE!

FACE IT, STARK...YOU'RE RUNNING SCARED!

I DON'T *DARE* CONFRONT THE MELTER AGAIN AS *IRON MAN!* IF HE SHOULD DESTROY MY IRON HELMET REVEALING MY IDENTITY, TONY STARK WOULD BE PREY FOR EVERY CRIMINAL WHO WANTS REVENGE ON IRON MAN!

WHAT'S THE *MATTER* WITH ME? I'M *STILL* NOT HELPLESS! I'VE STILL GOT THE GREATEST WEAPON IN THE WORLD...A HUMAN *BRAIN!*

THE BRAIN THAT CREATED *IRON MAN* SHOULD BE ABLE TO INVENT A DEFENSE AGAINST *THE MELTER!*

I'VE GOT TO *THINK* ... GOT TO FIND THE ANSWER...NO MATTER *HOW LONG* IT TAKES! FOR IF THE MELTER ISN'T STOPPED, NO PERSON NO COMMUNITY, NO *NATION* ON EARTH WILL BE SAFE!

AND SO, THE MANY-TALENTED ANTHONY STARK LOCKS HIMSELF AWAY FROM THE OUTSIDE WORLD, AS NORMAL LIFE GOES ON WITHOUT HIM ...

BUT I HAD A DATE WITH TONY STARK! *NO ONE* STANDS UP THE MOST FAMOUS NAME IN HOLLYWOOD!

SORRY, MISS GLITTER! MR. STARK CAN'T BE DISTURBED FOR *ANYONE!*

MAN! WOULDN'T I LIKE TO PINCH-HIT IN *THAT* LEAGUE!

PUT YOUR EYES BACK IN YOUR HEAD, HAPPY! I THOUGHT YOU WEREN'T *INTERESTED* IN BEAUTIFUL GIRLS!

I'M *NOT!* I JUST LIKE *YOU!*

WELL!! LOOK WHO'S *TALKING!* THE POOR MAN'S BELA LUGOSI!

FOR THE LUVVA PETE! *NOW* WHAT DID I SAY TO MAKE THOSE LITTLE PINK EYES OF YOURS FLASH?

9

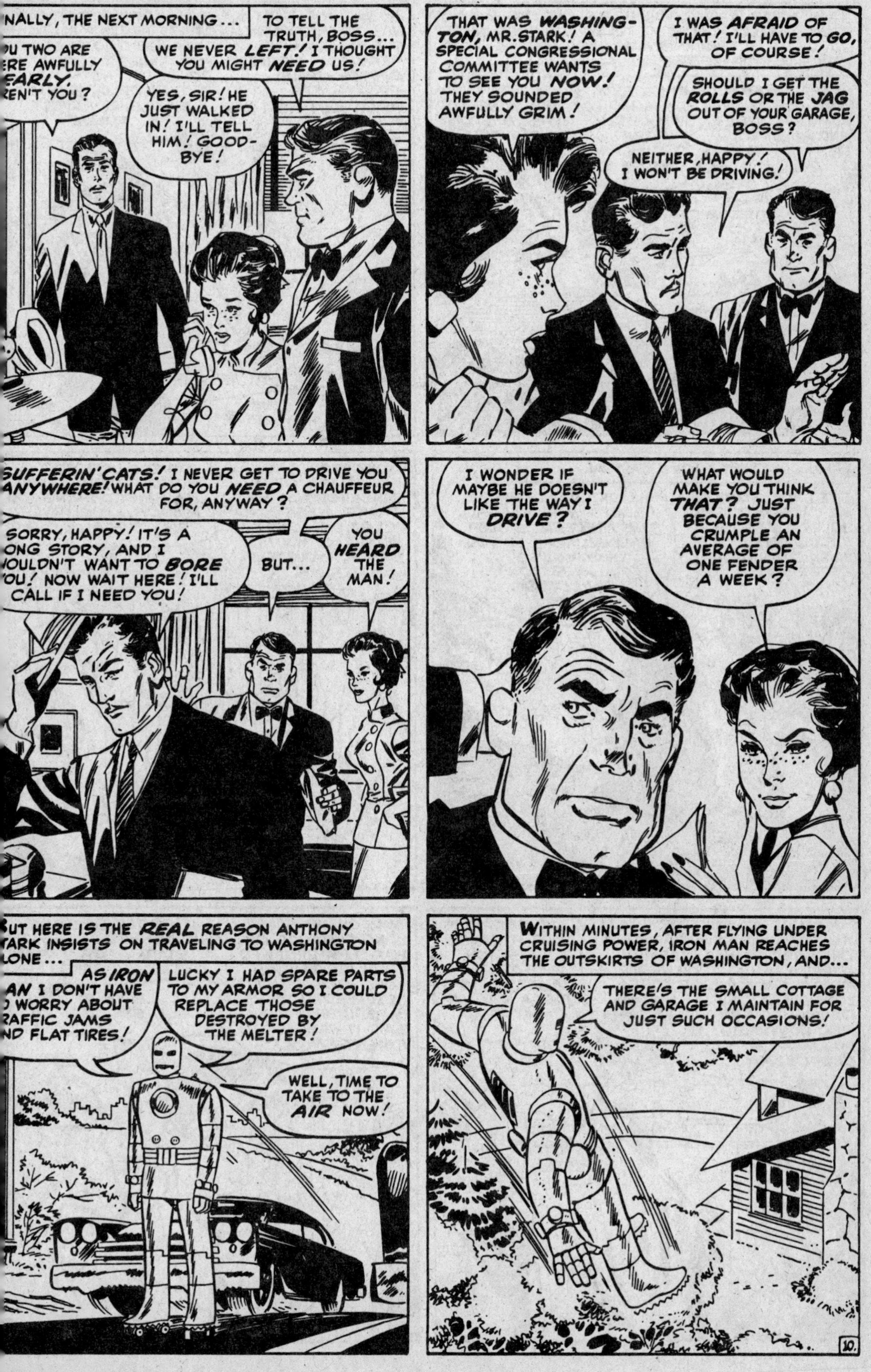
NALLY, THE NEXT MORNING...
TO TELL THE TRUTH, BOSS... WE NEVER LEFT! I THOUGHT YOU MIGHT NEED US!
U TWO ARE ERE AWFULLY EARLY, REN'T YOU?
YES, SIR! HE JUST WALKED IN! I'LL TELL HIM! GOOD-BYE!
THAT WAS WASHINGTON, MR. STARK! A SPECIAL CONGRESSIONAL COMMITTEE WANTS TO SEE YOU NOW! THEY SOUNDED AWFULLY GRIM!
I WAS AFRAID OF THAT! I'LL HAVE TO GO, OF COURSE!
SHOULD I GET THE ROLLS OR THE JAG OUT OF YOUR GARAGE, BOSS?
NEITHER, HAPPY! I WON'T BE DRIVING!
SUFFERIN' CATS! I NEVER GET TO DRIVE YOU ANYWHERE! WHAT DO YOU NEED A CHAUFFEUR FOR, ANYWAY?
SORRY, HAPPY! IT'S A ONG STORY, AND I OULDN'T WANT TO BORE OU! NOW WAIT HERE! I'LL CALL IF I NEED YOU!
BUT...
YOU HEARD THE MAN!
I WONDER IF MAYBE HE DOESN'T LIKE THE WAY I DRIVE?
WHAT WOULD MAKE YOU THINK THAT? JUST BECAUSE YOU CRUMPLE AN AVERAGE OF ONE FENDER A WEEK?
UT HERE IS THE REAL REASON ANTHONY TARK INSISTS ON TRAVELING TO WASHINGTON LONE...
AS IRON AN I DON'T HAVE O WORRY ABOUT RAFFIC JAMS ND FLAT TIRES!
LUCKY I HAD SPARE PARTS TO MY ARMOR SO I COULD REPLACE THOSE DESTROYED BY THE MELTER!
WELL, TIME TO TAKE TO THE AIR NOW!
WITHIN MINUTES, AFTER FLYING UNDER CRUISING POWER, IRON MAN REACHES THE OUTSKIRTS OF WASHINGTON, AND...
THERE'S THE SMALL COTTAGE AND GARAGE I MAINTAIN FOR JUST SUCH OCCASIONS!
10.

THEN, AFTER A QUICK CHANGE IN ONE OF HIS MANY STRATEGICALLY-LOCATED, FULLY-EQUIPPED SECRET COTTAGES, ANTHONY STARK RESUMES THE LAST FEW MILES OF HIS TRIP...

WHAT A *MESS!* THE *MELTER* RUNNING LOOSE AND ABLE TO DESTROY IRON MAN...

...MY FACTORY DAMAGED... WITH STILL MORE TROUBLE IN STORE...

...AND NOW, AN URGENT SUMMONS TO *WASHINGTON!* IT CAN ONLY MEAN A *NEW* SERIOUS PROBLEM!

LOOK, JOE! THAT WAS *TONY STARK,* THE MILLIONAIRE *PLAYBOY,* IN THAT CUSTOM-BUILT SPORTS CAR WHICH JUST WENT BY!

YEAH! NOTHIN' TO DO BUT CRUISE AROUND ALL DAY IN THAT $10,000 TOY, LOOKIN' FOR THINGS TO SPEND HIS DOUGH ON! NOT A WORRY IN THE WORLD! BOY, SOME GUYS SURE HAVE IT *MADE!*

FINALLY, IN THE NATION'S CAPITAL...

I TELL YOU, STARK, WE CAN NO LONGER TOLERATE THESE "ACCIDENTS"! NOT WHEN OUR NATIONAL DEFENSE IS INVOLVED!

ALL OF THIS NONSENSE ABOUT A MAN YOU CALL *THE MELTER* IS JUST *BALDERDASH!* DO YOU THINK YOU'RE TALKING TO *CHILDREN,* STARK?!

YOUR PRODUCTION HAS FALLEN OFF DANGEROUSLY! YOUR TANKS WERE FOUND TO BE DEFECTIVE! WHAT HAVE YOU TO *SAY* FOR YOURSELF, MAN?

IT'S TOO LATE FOR *WORDS,* GENTLEMEN! I'LL HAVE TO BRING YOU *PROOF*... I'LL HAVE TO TRAP *THE MELTER!*

BECAUSE OF YOUR EXCELLENT PAST RECORD WE ARE GIVING YOU ONE MORE CHANCE! EITHER STRAIGHTEN OUT THE TROUBLE AT YOUR FACTORY, OR YOU'LL LOSE EVERY ONE OF YOUR GOVERNMENT CONTRACTS! DO I MAKE MYSELF *CLEAR?*

AND GET RID OF YOUR STRANGE OBSESSION WITH *THE MELTER!* HE'S JUST A *HALLUCINATION!*

PARDON ME, SIR! A LONG DISTANCE CALL WAS JUST RECEIVED FROM MR. STARK'S LONG ISLAND FACTORY! HE'S NEEDED THERE IMMEDIATELY! THEY SAID IT WAS AN *EMERGENCY!*

IT BETTER BE SOMETHING YOU CAN REMEDY STARK! FOR *YOUR* SAKE!

I'LL LEAVE AT ONCE, SENATOR!

WE CAN'T *DO* ANYTHING WITH THIS MELTED IRON, SIR! IT'S ALL FUSED TOGETHER! IT'LL TAKE A WEEK JUST TO *REMOVE* IT! 'TILL THEN, WE CAN'T PRODUCE A *THING!*

IT'S EVEN WORSE THAN I *THOUGHT!*

STAY WITH IT, CHUCK! DO THE BEST YOU CAN! I'LL SEE IF I CAN CONTACT *IRON MAN!* PERHAPS *HE* CAN HELP!

YES, SIR, MR. STARK!

IRON MAN! A FAT LOT OF GOOD HE'LL DO IF *THE MELTER* SHOWS UP AGAIN!

FAR AS *I* CAN SEE, IRON MAN HAS *HAD* IT!

ONCE AGAIN, ONE OF THE WORLD'S MOST DRAMATIC TRANSFORMATIONS TAKES PLACE BEHIND THE LOCKED DOORS OF STARK'S INNER OFFICE...

IT'S NOW OR NEVER! I'VE GOT TO FIND THE MELTER, AND *DEFEAT* HIM SOMEHOW, OR ELSE WATCH MY *LIFE'S WORK* GO DOWN THE DRAIN!

BUT FIRST I'LL TACKLE THAT FUSED POWER PLANT!

BUT EVEN AS IRON MAN COMES TO LIFE, TWO MERCILESS EYES SURVEY STARK'S FACTORY FROM A PLACE OF CONCEALMENT...

I'VE *SUCCEEDED!*

STARK IS PRACTICALLY OUT OF BUSINESS! NOW I CAN TACKLE EVEN *BIGGER* PROJECTS!

BUT THEN HE SEES ...

IRON MAN! I NEVER DREAMED HE WOULD *DARE* TO RETURN!

HE'S USING HIS OWN TRANSISTOR-POWERED STRENGTH AND SKILL TO REPAIR THE DAMAGE! HE CAN MOVE HIS IRON LIMBS MORE SKILLFULLY THAN ANY DERRICK TO CLEAR AWAY THE RUBBLE!

12.

I'LL REACH HIM BEFORE HE CAN DO STARK ANY *GOOD!* AND *THIS* TIME I'LL MAKE SURE I STOP HIM... *PERMANENTLY!!*

CLEAR THE *PLANT!* IT'S A RED ALERT! THE MELTER'S BEEN SIGHTED AGAIN!

HEAD FOR COVER, PEPPER! I'LL TRY TO FIND THE BOSS!

YOU? YOU COULDN'T FIND A *TREE* IN A *FOREST!* I'LL GET MR. STARK!

NO TELLING *WHERE* HE IS NOW! IF THE MELTER FINDS HIM... TRAPS HIM...

COME *BACK* HERE, YOU DIZZY DAME! AT A TIME LIKE *THIS* YOU'D BE AS MUCH HELP AS A *WATER GUN* DURING THE *CHICAGO FIRE!*

ULP! IRON MAN... *LOOK!!*

WHAT *IS* IT, MEN?

ALLOW *ME* TO ANSWER THAT, MY *DOOMED FOE!* IT IS *THE MELTER...* THE ONE YOU SHALL NOT ESCAPE FROM AGAIN!

IT *HAD* TO HAPPEN SOONER OR LATER! THIS IS THE *SHOWDOWN,* MISTER!

NOW WE'RE IN FOR IT! IF THE MELTER BEATS IRON MAN, WE'D BETTER *ALL* HEAD FOR THE HILLS!

NO *WONDE—* THEY CALL YOU "HAPPY!" YOU'RE JUS A BORN *OPTIMIST.*

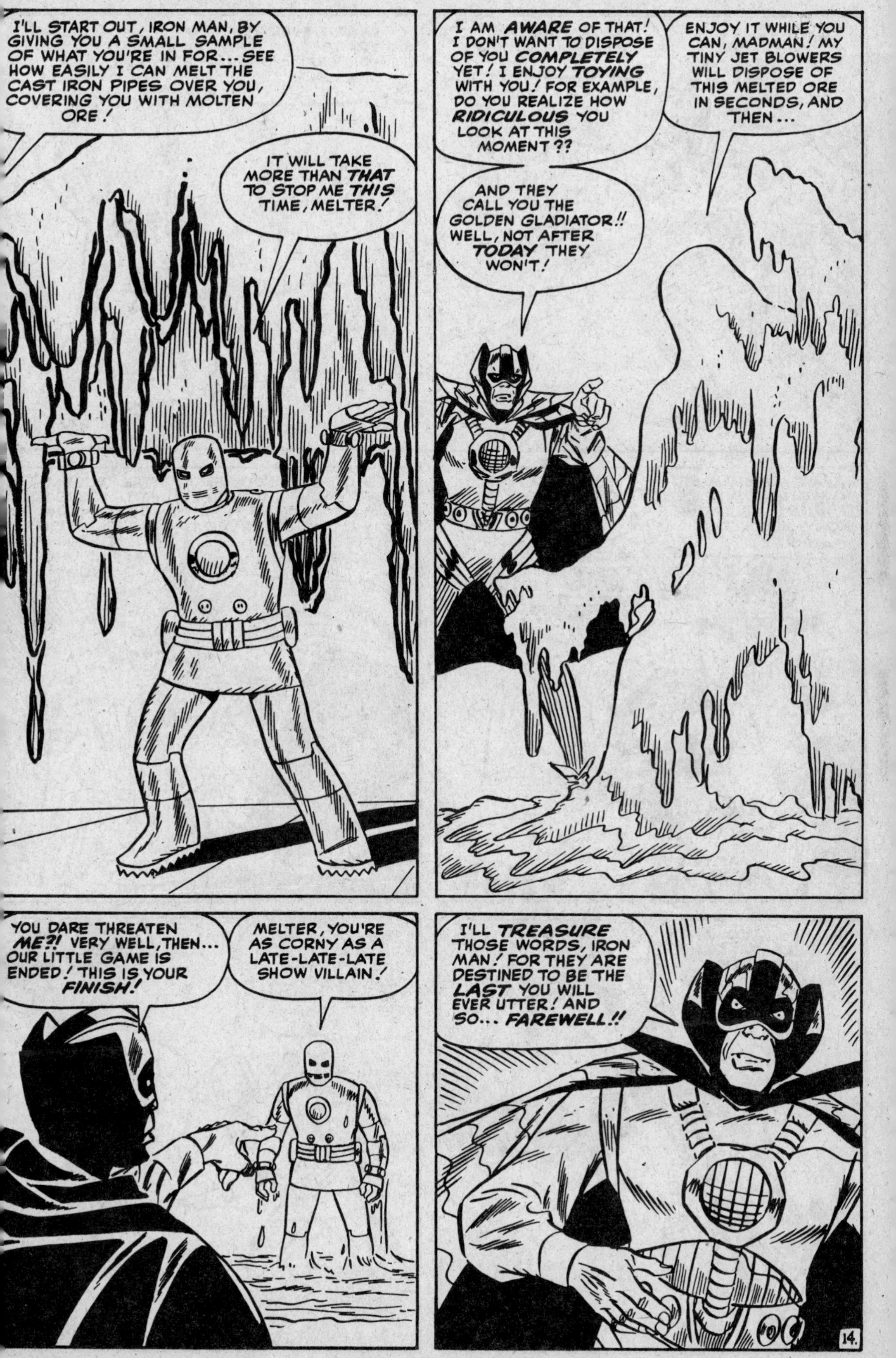

I'LL START OUT, IRON MAN, BY GIVING YOU A SMALL SAMPLE OF WHAT YOU'RE IN FOR... SEE HOW EASILY I CAN MELT THE CAST IRON PIPES OVER YOU, COVERING YOU WITH MOLTEN ORE!
IT WILL TAKE MORE THAN THAT TO STOP ME THIS TIME, MELTER!
I AM AWARE OF THAT! I DON'T WANT TO DISPOSE OF YOU COMPLETELY YET! I ENJOY TOYING WITH YOU! FOR EXAMPLE, DO YOU REALIZE HOW RIDICULOUS YOU LOOK AT THIS MOMENT??
AND THEY CALL YOU THE GOLDEN GLADIATOR!! WELL, NOT AFTER TODAY THEY WON'T!
ENJOY IT WHILE YOU CAN, MADMAN! MY TINY JET BLOWERS WILL DISPOSE OF THIS MELTED ORE IN SECONDS, AND THEN...
MELTER, YOU'RE AS CORNY AS A LATE-LATE-LATE SHOW VILLAIN!
YOU DARE THREATEN ME?! VERY WELL, THEN... OUR LITTLE GAME IS ENDED! THIS IS YOUR FINISH!
I'LL TREASURE THOSE WORDS, IRON MAN! FOR THEY ARE DESTINED TO BE THE LAST YOU WILL EVER UTTER! AND SO... FAREWELL!!

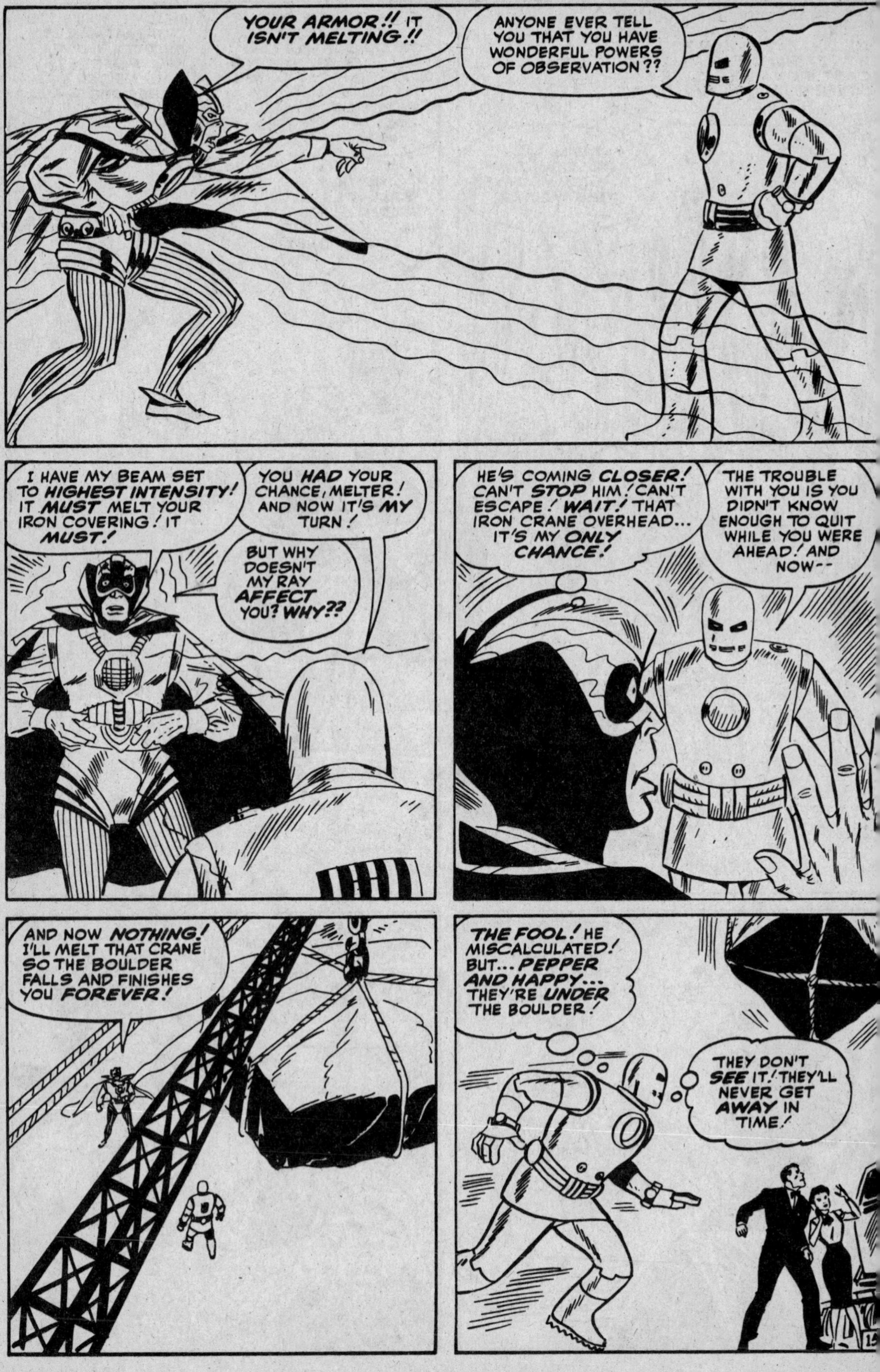
YOUR ARMOR!! IT ISN'T MELTING!!
ANYONE EVER TELL YOU THAT YOU HAVE WONDERFUL POWERS OF OBSERVATION??
I HAVE MY BEAM SET TO HIGHEST INTENSITY! IT MUST MELT YOUR IRON COVERING! IT MUST!
YOU HAD YOUR CHANCE, MELTER! AND NOW IT'S MY TURN!
BUT WHY DOESN'T MY RAY AFFECT YOU? WHY??
HE'S COMING CLOSER! CAN'T STOP HIM! CAN'T ESCAPE! WAIT! THAT IRON CRANE OVERHEAD... IT'S MY ONLY CHANCE!
THE TROUBLE WITH YOU IS YOU DIDN'T KNOW ENOUGH TO QUIT WHILE YOU WERE AHEAD! AND NOW--
AND NOW NOTHING! I'LL MELT THAT CRANE SO THE BOULDER FALLS AND FINISHES YOU FOREVER!
THE FOOL! HE MISCALCULATED! BUT... PEPPER AND HAPPY... THEY'RE UNDER THE BOULDER!
THEY DON'T SEE IT! THEY'LL NEVER GET AWAY IN TIME!

MOVING WITH THE SPEED OF THOUGHT, IRON MAN ACTIVATES HIS TRANSISTOR POWER JETS AT THE HIGHEST INTENSITY, AND THEN, WITH LESS THAN A MICROSECOND TO SPARE...

IT'S FALLING! IF ONLY I CAN BE IN TIME! IF ONLY... AHH... GOT IT!!

LOOK OUT!

OH!

YOU TWO STAY OUT OF HARM'S WAY WHILE I GO AFTER THE MELTER! I SAW HIM DUCK BACK INTO THE PLANT!

≷WHEW≶ NOW THERE'S ONE HANDY GENT TO HAVE AROUND, EH, PEPPER?

ALL OF A SUDDEN, HAPPY, THAT WALKING TIN CAN IS THE HANDSOMEST MALE I'VE EVER SEEN!

AND A SCANT FEW FEET AWAY, INSIDE THE HUGE FACTORY...

I'VE GOT TO STAY OUT OF IRON MAN'S REACH TILL I CAN FIGURE OUT WHY MY MELTING BEAM HAD NO EFFECT ON HIM!

BUT DESPITE THE MELTER'S HEAD START, IRON MAN KNOWS EVERY INCH OF THE SPRAWLING PLANT BETTER THAN ANYONE, AND SO... MINUTES LATER...

FLIGHT IS USELESS! WE'RE ON MY HOME GROUND NOW!

YOU!!

HE DOESN'T KNOW THAT I CAN CONTROL EVERY AUTOMATIC FIRE-DOOR IN THE FACTORY BY MY TRANSISTORIZED BELT PANEL!

I.. I'M TRAPPED!

16.

I'M NOT BEATEN YET! IF I CAN'T DESTROY *YOU*, I'LL MELT THE IRON STRUCTURE OF THE REINFORCED FLOOR *UNDER* YOU!

YOU'RE CRACKING UP, MY FRIEND! HAVE YOU FORGOTTEN ABOUT MY TRANSISTOR-POWERED JETS, WHICH ENABLE ME TO COUNTERACT THE FORCE OF GRAVITY?

BLAST YOU! IS THERE *NO* WAY TO STOP YOU?

PERHAPS THERE *IS*, BUT *YOU* HAVEN'T DISCOVERED IT! AND NOW, LET'S PUT AN *END* TO THIS LITTLE FARCE, ONCE AND FOR ALL!

HE RIPPED OUT A STRIP OF IRON FLOORING... AS IF IT WERE *PAPER*!

I'VE GOT TO ESCAPE! HE'S UNBEATABLE!

I'LL MELT THROUGH THIS IRON DRAIN COVER BELOW ME... AND THEN...

...WITH LUCK, I CAN LOSE MYSELF IN THE UNDERGROUND DISPOSAL SYSTEM!

I'D RATHER CHANCE *DROWNING* THAN BEING CAUGHT BY *IRON MAN!*

THEN, BEFORE IRON MAN, WHOSE POWER-JETS ARE NOW ALMOST DRAINED OF ENERGY, CAN REACH THE SPOT, ALL IS SILENT... AND DARK... AND STILL...

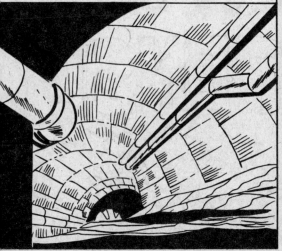

IT'S MIGHTY FRUSTRATING! I CAN'T BE SURE WHETHER THE MELTER *DROWNED*, OR *ESCAPED* TO MENACE ME ANOTHER TIME!

FOR, IF HE EVER *SHOULD* RETURN, I MAY NOT BE ABLE TO *TRICK HIM* THIS WAY A SECOND TIME!

HE NEVER SUSPECTED THAT HIS MELTING RAY *DID* WORK AGAINST IRON MAN... BUT I WASN'T *REALLY* IRON MAN THIS TIME!

UNKNOWN TO ANYONE, I *REDESIGNED* MY ARMOR, MAKING IT ENTIRELY OUT OF TOUGH EXTRUDED *ALUMINUM!*

WELL, I HAVEN'T TIME TO DWELL ON THE *PAST!* I'VE STILL GOT A BIG *FACTORY* TO RUN... AND *WEAPONS* TO PRODUCE FOR OUR DEFENSE!

IT'S TIME FOR *IRON MAN* TO FADE AWAY AGAIN WHILE *TONY STARK* TAKES OVER!

WHAT'S EVERYONE *STANDING AROUND* FOR? THE MELTER IS *DEFEATED* FOR NOW, AND WE'VE STILL GOT A *MESS* TO CLEAN UP! CHUCK, GET THE *WORK CREW* GOING! HOP *TO* IT, MEN!

PEPPER, REPORT TO MY OFFICE! WE'VE A LOT OF DICTATION TO CATCH UP ON!

I DON'T KNOW WHEN THINGS ARE *WORSE* 'ROUND HERE, WHEN WE'RE IN BIG TROUBLE, OR WHEN EVERYTHING'S BACK TO ≡UGH≡ *NORMAL!*

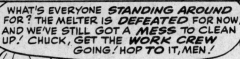

YES SIR, MR. STARK!

18.

NEXT ISSUE: ONE OF THE GREATEST ARTIST AND WRITER TEAMS IN COMICS *AGAIN* JOIN TALENTS TO BRING YOU AN ALL-NEW, FEATURE-LENGTH IRON MAN EPIC! *DON'T MISS IT!!*

The End

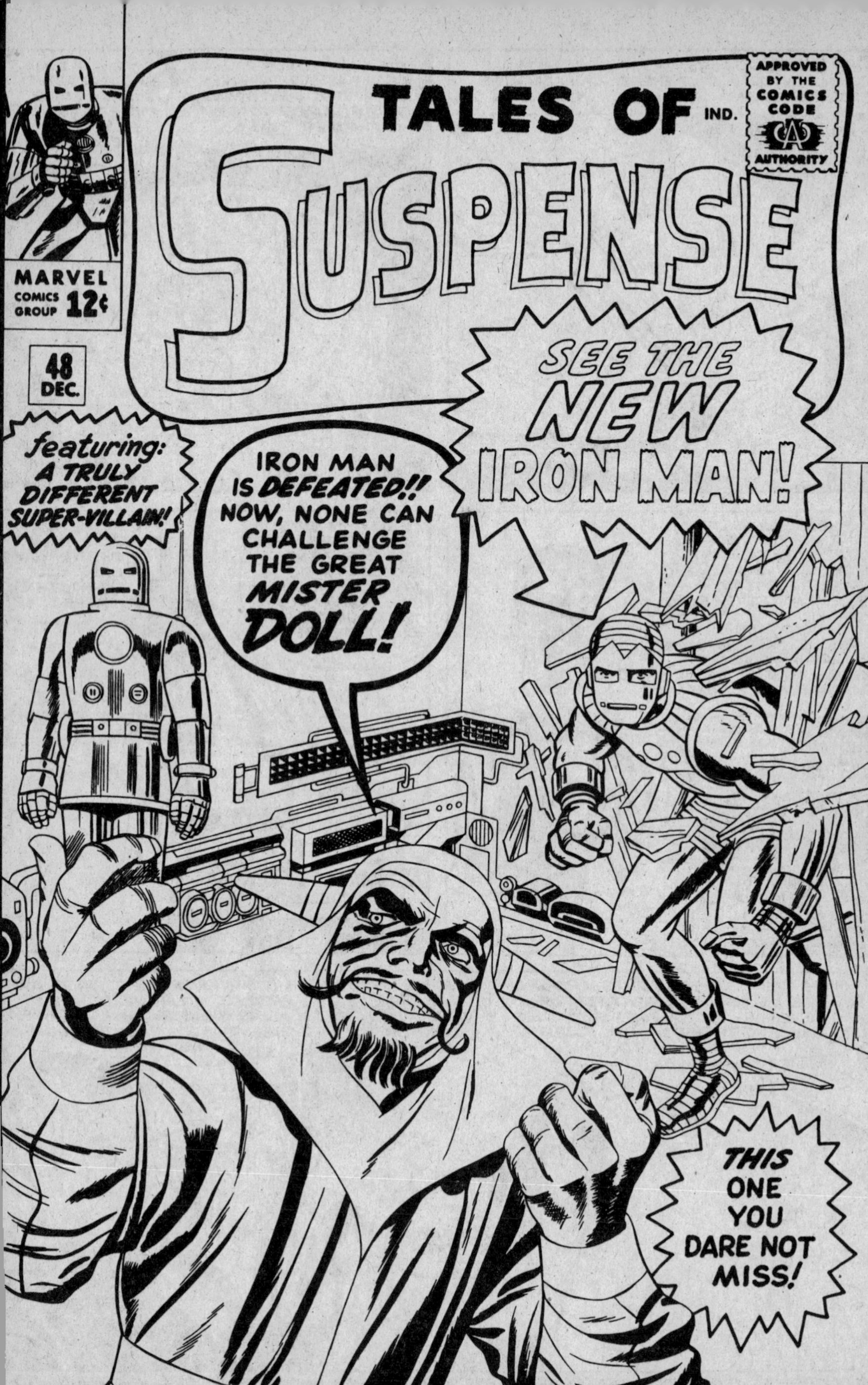

TALES OF
IND.
SUSPENSE
APPROVED BY THE COMICS CODE AUTHORITY
MARVEL COMICS GROUP 12¢
48 DEC.
featuring: A TRULY DIFFERENT SUPER-VILLAIN!
SEE THE NEW IRON MAN!
IRON MAN IS DEFEATED!! NOW, NONE CAN CHALLENGE THE GREAT MISTER DOLL!
THIS ONE YOU DARE NOT MISS!

THE *NEW* IRON MAN BATTLES...
"the *MYSTERIOUS* MR. DOLL!"

A SPECIAL BOOK-LENGTH MARVEL MASTERWORK!

I *WARNED* YOU, IRON MAN!! MERE STRENGTH IS *USELESS* AGAINST THE POWERS OF *MR. DOLL!*

*T*HIS IS THE TYPE OF TALE WHICH WE HONESTLY BELIEVE WILL BECOME A CLASSIC IN THE YEARS THAT FOLLOW!

IT HAS *EVERYTHING!*

• A POWERFUL, SEEMINGLY UNBEATABLE VILLAIN!
• A SUPER HERO WHO REACHES NEW HEIGHTS OF GREATNESS, AS YOU SHALL SEE!
• PRODUCED BY A COMBO OF COMICDOM'S BRIGHTEST STARS!

•

OKAY, WE WENT OUT ON A LIMB WITH OUR OPINION! NOW, HERE'S THE ACID TEST! READ ON...

WRITTEN BY: *STAN LEE*
ART: *STEVE DITKO* AND *DICK AYERS*
LETTERING: *S. ROSEN*

EVER NOTICE HOW SOME TALES SEEM TO START SLOWLY, THEN PICK UP SPEED UNTIL THE EXCITEMENT BECOMES ALMOST UNBEARABLE? WELL, JUST *WATCH!* WE'LL START IN THE EXECUTIVE OFFICES OF MILLIONAIRE MANUFACTURER, *TONY STARK!*

MR. CARTER SAYS THE DEAL IS *OFF*, MR. STARK!

HE *CAN'T!* I WAS COUNTING ON HIM SUPPLYING ME WITH THE *STEEL* I NEED! I'LL HAVE TO GO *SEE* HIM, PEPPER!

WANT ME TO DRIVE YOUR JAG, OR THE CADDIE, BOSS?

NEITHER, HAPPY! YOU WAIT HERE! I'LL DRIVE ONE OF THE SPORTS CARS MYSELF!

PHOOEY! HE NEEDS A CHAUFFEUR LIKE A HOLE IN THE HEAD! WHAT DOES HE KEEP ME AROUND FOR, ANYWAY?

WELL, IT CERTAINLY ISN'T BECAUSE OF YOUR SUNNY PERSONALITY! RELAX, SUNBEAM THE BOSS KNOWS WHAT HE'S DOING!

LATER, AT THE IMPOSING RESIDENCE OF WEALTHY STEEL TYCOON, CHARLETON CARTER...

CARTER HAS NEVER BACKED DOWN ON A DEAL BEFORE! I KNOW HE'S *RICH* ENOUGH TO SUPPLY ME WITH THE MATERIAL I NEED! WHAT CAN BE *WRONG?*

THEN, AS TONY STARK ENTERS THE IMPOSING GATES, HE SEES...

THERE'S NO MASQUERADE PARTY GOING ON! THAT MEANS ANY GUY SLINKING AROUND IN THE SHADOWS WEARING A GET-UP LIKE *THAT* MUST BE UP TO NO GOOD!

SILENTLY, THE AMAZING TONY STARK STOPS HIS CAR AND TAKES A GOLDEN SUIT OF FLEXIBLE IRON FROM HIS EVER-PRESENT ATTACHE CASE...

AND IF THERE'S ANY *TROUBLE* BREWING, I CAN FACE IT A LOT BETTER IN THE POWERFUL GUISE OF... *IRON MAN!*

THAT CHARACTER IN HALLOWEEN DUDS WALKED THROUGH THE FRONT DOOR LIKE HE *OWNED* THE PLACE! I DON'T LIKE THE LOOKS OF IT!

A CRY OF PAIN FROM THE LOWER WINDOW!

NO TIME FOR THE FRONT DOOR *NOW!* LITTLE LOYAL POWER-JETS, DO YOUR STUFF!

NO!!.! DON'T....! HELP!!

PLEASE...DON'T KEEP ME ANYMORE! I'LL SIGN EVERY-THING OVER TO YOU! I'VE ALREADY CANCELED MY CONTRACT WITH TONY STARK! YOU CAN HAVE MY ENTIRE BUSINESS...BUT LET ME GO!!

CERTAINLY! *MR. DOLL* WOULD NOT *DREAM* OF KEEPING YOU! ALL I DO IS KEEP THIS LITTLE DOLL WHICH I HOLD! IF THAT KEEPS *YOU,* TOO, IT IS JUST AN UNFORTUNATE CO-INCIDENCE! NOW...

..SIGN THOSE PAPERS, OR I'LL *NEVER* RELEASE THE DOLL!

HOLD IT, MR. DOLL! I DON'T KNOW WHO YOU ARE, OR WHAT YOU'RE UP TO, BUT I'M PUTTING A *STOP* TO IT RIGHT *NOW!*

IRON MAN!

HAVE TO WORK *FAST*...CHANGE FACE ON MY DOLL...

ALL RIGHT, MISTER... *TALK!* HOW DO YOU MANAGE TO SUBDUE YOUR VICTIMS BY HURT-ING THAT LIFELESS LITTLE DOLL YOU'RE HOLDING?

I SAID *TALK!* THIS ISN'T SOME FRIGHTENED, ELDERLY BUSINESS-MAN YOU'RE UP AGAINST! THIS IS *IRON MAN* ...AND I'M NOT HERE TO PLAY GAMES!

YOU WAITED TOO LONG, YOU FOOL! NOW *YOU* WILL BE AS HELPLESS AS ALL THE OTHERS!

SEE? I HAVE ALTERED THE FACE OF MY DOLL TO RESEMBLE *YOU!*

NOW, ALL I NEED DO IS GIVE IT ONE LITTLE SQUEEZE... JUST LIKE THIS... DO YOU *SEE?* ...AND WAIT FOR YOUR REACTION!

MY BONES! THEY'RE BEGINNING TO THROB...TO ACHE!

MY IRON ARMOR GIVES ME NO PRO-TECTION! I FEEL A SENSATION WITHIN MY OWN BODY! IT'S... IT'S GROWING TIGHTER... I'VE GOT TO ESCAPE!

3

HAD TO LET HIM DOWN! CAN'T FIGHT HIM! CAN'T THINK OF ANYTHING...ANYTHING EXCEPT GETTING AWAY FROM THAT DOLL!

HAH! IF ONLY THE UNKNOWING *PUBLIC* COULD SEE THEIR MIGHTY IDOL NOW! YOUR MUCH-VAUNTED STRENGTH IS *USELESS* AGAINST THE MYSTIC POWERS OF *MR. DOLL!*

EVERYTHING'S GETTING *WORSE.* CAN'T STAND IT! I'LL MOVE BACK...FURTHER AWAY FROM HIM...PERHAPS I CAN ESCAPE HIS...*WHA...??* THE BALCONY! I..I'M LOSING MY BALANCE!

IRON MAN, LET YOUR LAST THOUGHTS BE OF HOW *EASILY* MR. DOLL DEFEATED YOU!

HELPLESSLY, THE PAIN-WRACKED *IRON MAN* FALLS TO THE WATER BELOW...

AND LONG MINUTES LATER, HIS BARELY-CONSCIOUS FORM IS WASHED ASHORE, OUT OF SIGHT OF HIS TRIUMPHANT FOE!

NO SIGN OF HIM! HE'LL NEVER TROUBLE ME AGAIN! NOW TO RETURN TO MY TASK AT HAND!

THERE! I HAVE RESHAPED THE FEATURES OF MY LITTLE PLAY-THING AGAIN! YOUR BRIEF RESPITE IS OVER! AND NOW, WILL YOU SIGN THOSE PAPERS?

YES! ANY-THING!...*ANYTHING!* HOW CAN I RESIST THE PERSON WHO DEFEAT-ED *IRON MAN?!*

BUT, SOME DISTANCE AWAY, IRON MAN CRAWLS TO THE SHORE AS THE ACHE LEAVES HIS BODY... FOR THE DOLL WHICH *MR. DOLL* HOLDS IS NO LONGER IN HIS OWN IMAGE!

LUCKY THE PAIN ENDED! COULDN'T HAVE STOOD MUCH MORE!

4

...EAKLY, IRON MAN LIMPS BACK O CARTER'S MANSION, BUT WHEN HE REACHES HIS GOAL...

HARD TO MOVE...MY CHEST DEVICE NEEDS RECHARGING! IT WAS SUBJECTED TO TOO GREAT A STRAIN!

AND SO...

MR. DOLL WINS THE *FIRST* ROUND HANDS DOWN!

MUST REACH MY OFFICE FAST! BEGINNING TO FEEL GROGGY! IF I DON'T CHARGE MY HEART REACTOR TRANSISTORS SOON, I'M DONE FOR!

FIRST TIME THE BOSS EVER CHARGED IN WITHOUT WAVING HELLO! WONDER WHAT'S WRONG?

CAN'T BLACK OUT...NOT WHEN I'M SO CLOSE...GOT TO KEEP GOING...

...AND THEN, AFTER REACHING HIS SECRET TUNNEL WHICH LEADS TO IS PRIVATE SANCTUM...

JUST ANOTHER FEW STEPS...EVERYTHING'S GOING DARK...KEEP GOING...MUST KEEP GOING...

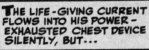

REACHED IT! NOW TO PLUG IN THE CORD... HARD TO HOLD IT!

...CAN'T FIGHT ANYMORE!

CAN'T... OHHHH...

THE LONG MOMENTS TICK BY AS THE UNCONSCIOUS TONY STARK LIES MOTIONLESS ON THE FLOOR...

THE LIFE-GIVING CURRENT FLOWS INTO HIS POWER-EXHAUSTED CHEST DEVICE SILENTLY, BUT...

...IS IT *TOO LATE*??

5.

THE NEXT DAY...

HAPPY, I'M WORRIED! I CAN'T LOCATE MR. STARK ANYWHERE! IT'S NOT LIKE HIM TO VANISH THIS WAY!

RELAX, PEPPER! NOTHING CAN HAPPEN TO A GUY WITH ALL HIS DOUGH! BESIDES, IRON MAN'S USUALLY AROUND, KEEPIN' AN EYE ON HIM!

TELL ME, BABY, WOULD YOU WORRY THAT WAY IF I WAS EVER MISSING?

SURE, HAPPY! AFTER I GOT THROUGH CELEBRATING!

OH, I JUST REMEMBERED ANOTHER PLACE I CAN CALL!

SECONDS LATER, THE BELL IN ANTHONY STARK'S PRIVATE EXTENSION RINGS SHRILLY THROUGH THE SILENT ROOM...

RRING!

AS THE FAINT FLICKER OF AN EYELID SEEMS TO APPEAR...

AND THEN...

I- I'M ALIVE! THE CHARGE SAVED ME... JUST IN TIME!

HELLO, PEPPER? OF COURSE I'M ALL RIGHT! I, EH, HAD SOME THINGS TO ATTEND TO LAST NIGHT AND SLEPT IN MY LAB!

I DON'T WANT TO BE DISTURBED FOR THE NEXT FEW HOURS...FOR ANYTHING!!

AND THEN, AFTER PUTTING DOWN THE PHONE...

I NEVER REALIZED HOW VULNERABLE IRON MAN IS! I SEEM TO NEED RECHARGING MORE AND MORE OFTEN!

IT'S THIS IRON SUIT OF MINE! IT'S TOO HEAVY! WEIGHS ME DOWN TOO MUCH! SAPS TOO MUCH OF MY ENERGY MERELY TO SUPPORT THE WEIGHT!

PERHAPS... I SHOULD GIVE UP THE ROLE OF IRON MAN... FOREVER....!!

IT'S ONLY A MATTER OF TIME BEFORE MY HEART FAILS ME IF I CONTINUE MY DANGEROUS GAME!

AND YET...

CAN'T GIVE UP! I'D PREFER DEATH, TO ADMITTING DEFEAT AT THE HANDS OF A MENACE LIKE MR. DOLL!

THE ONLY THING TO DO IS TO DESIGN A *NEW* IRON MAN COSTUME...ONE WHICH WILL BE LIGHTER IN WEIGHT.. LESS BULKY...SO THAT IT WILL NOT BE SO GREAT A STRAIN ON MY HEART!

AND SO THE BRILLIANT ANTHONY STARK WORKS...WORKS...AS FEW MEN HAVE EVER WORKED BEFORE!

I'M *GETTING IT!* IT'S FAR LIGHTER...BUT JUST AS STRONG!

MEANWHILE, AT A NEIGHBORHOOD POLICE PRECINCT..

MR. CARTER, WE *KNOW* YOU WOULDN'T HAVE SIGNED AWAY YOUR ENTIRE BUSINESS, YOUR ENTIRE FORTUNE, TO A STRANGER WITH THE WHACKY NAME OF *MR. DOLL* UNLESS YOU WERE *FORCED* TO! BUT WE CAN'T HELP YOU UNLESS YOU COOPERATE! YOU'VE *GOT* TO SWEAR OUT A *COMPLAINT!*

NO! *NO!* I WOULDN'T *DARE!*

POLICE

MONEY ISN'T... EVERYTHING! AT LEAST I AM FREE... OF.. *HIM!*

NEVER SAW A MAN SO FRIGHTENED IN MY LIFE! WHAT KIND OF *HOLD* CAN THAT DOLL CHARACTER HAVE ON HIM?

BEATS ME! CARTER IS THE THIRD MILLIONAIRE TO SIGN HIS FORTUNE OVER TO MR. DOLL! WE'VE GOT TO FIGURE OUT HIS NEXT VICTIM IN *ADVANCE*...AND BEAT HIM TO IT!

AND, IN A GLOOMY ROOM NOT FAR AWAY, MR. DOLL IS *ALSO* LAYING HIS PLANS...

SO LONG AS I HAVE THE MYSTIC POWER OF MY LITTLE DOLL, NO FORCE ON EARTH CAN RESIST ME!

I HAVE ALREADY OBTAINED THE FORTUNES OF THE THREE RICHEST MEN IN THE CITY... AND NOW FOR MY *FOURTH* VICTIM...THE WEALTHY WEAPONS MANUFACTURER... *ANTHONY STARK!*

7.

BUT PERHAPS THE EVIL **MR. DOLL** WOULD NOT GRIN SO CONFIDENTLY IF HE COULD SEE WHAT ANTHONY STARK IS DOING AT THAT MOMENT...

IT'S FINISHED! I NOW HAVE A COMPLETE **IRON MAN** OUTFIT... ALL NEW, ALL LIGHTWEIGHT AND FAR MORE FLEXIBLE THAN MY FORMER GARB!

AND YET, THIS NEW IRON ARMOR IS EVERY BIT AS POWERFUL! IN FACT, IN SOME WAYS, IT'S **MORE** POWERFUL, FOR, DUE TO ITS LIGHTER WEIGHT, I'LL BE ABLE TO CARRY STILL MORE PROTECTIVE DEVICES!

THE "HEART" OF MY APPARATUS IS THIS SMOOTH-FITTING CENTER SECTION! ALTHOUGH IT SEEMS WAFER-THIN, IT CONTAINS MORE THAN MEETS THE EYE!

ALL I NEED DO IS RELEASE A SPRING CATCH, AND THE PANEL SECTIONS HINGE OPEN TO ALLOW ME QUICK ACCESS TO MY MINIATURE TRANSISTOR BATTERIES, WHICH ARE CLIPPED TO THE INSIDE OF EACH PANEL!

EACH INTERCHANGEABLE ARM-LEG ADAPTOR CONTAINS ITS OWN BUILT-IN POWER UNITS, IN CASE THE MAIN TRANSISTOR BATTERY SHOULD FAIL!

I SIMPLY SLIP THE ADAPTOR OVER MY WRIST, AND THEN...

...A POWERFUL MAGNETIC PULL FROM MY BUILT-IN SHOULDER MAGNETS DOES THE REST!

CLICK!

ALL DONE IN LESS THAN TWO SECONDS!

8

MY NEW TYPE GLOVES ALSO WORK ON THE SAME PRINCIPLE.

STRONG... FLEXIBLE... EASILY – ATTACHED...

...AND HELD SECURELY IN PLACE BY MAGNETIC ATTRACTION!

CLICK!

SLIM AS THEY ARE, THESE FISTS PACK *TWICE* THE WALLOP OF MY PREVIOUS ONES!

NOW FOR MY LEG UNITS...

I CAN STAND UPRIGHT AND LET MY MAGNETS DO THE WORK!

CLICK!

PERFECT! SMOOTH, SUPPLE, FORM-FITTING, AND WITH THE STRENGTH OF DUCTILE IRON!

MY SHOES ARE A REAL TRIUMPH OF COMPACT, MINIATURIZED POWER! THESE JET UNITS ARE LESS THAN ONE INCH THICK!

WHEN EVERY SECOND COUNTS, I'VE ONLY TO STEP DOWN HARD...

...AND LET THE MAGNETIC FORCE DO THE REST!

CLICK!

CLICK!

9.

FINALLY, INSTEAD OF THE BULKY, CUMBERSOME HEAD-GEAR I *USED* TO WEAR, I'VE COMPLETELY REDESIGNED MY HEAD-MASK! IT'S SO LIGHT, I'LL HARDLY KNOW I'M WEARING IT!

I SIMPLY ATTACH THE NECK UNIT FIRST, THEN SLIP THE FACE SHIELD DOWN OVER MY FEATURES.

THIS NEW MASK SERVES TWO PURPOSES...ONE, IT PREVENTS MY TRUE IDENTITY FROM BEING DISCOVERED, AND TWO...

...IT ENABLES MY *EXPRESSION* TO SHOW...WHICH WILL PSYCHOLOGICALLY AID IN INSTILLING *FEAR* IN THE HEARTS OF MY ENEMIES!

AND *NOW*, THOUGH *MR. DOLL* WON THE FIRST ROUND IN HIS BATTLE WITH THE *OLD* IRON MAN...

...HE'S LIABLE TO FIND THE *NEW* IRON MAN A FAR MORE DIFFICULT FOE TO BEAT!

AND SO, THE NEW *IRON MAN*, CHAMPION OF CHAMPIONS, IS BORN!

JUST THEN, VIA HIS CLOSED-CIRCUIT INTERCOM SYSTEM, TONY STARK RECEIVES AN URGENT MESSAGE FROM PEPPER POTTS...

CALLING MR. STARK! CALLING MR. STARK! PLEASE REPORT TO FRONT OFFICE IMMEDIATELY! CALLING MR... STARK...

WONDER WHAT KINDA TROUBLE THE BOSS IS IN *NOW?* THAT COP DIDN'T LOOK LIKE HE WAS *KIDDIN'* WHEN HE SAID HE WANTED TO SEE HIM!

TONY STARK SPEAKING, PEPPER! I'LL BE RIGHT THERE! TAKE YOUR FINGER OFF THE PANIC BUTTON, KID!

MY NEW COSTUME'S WORKING PERFECTLY! IT'S SLIPPING OFF AS EASILY AS IT SLIPPED ON!

MINUTES LATER, IN ANTHONY STARK'S MAIN OFFICE...

...AND THAT'S THE STORY, MR. STARK! THIS GUY DOLL HAS VICTIMIZED THE RICHEST MEN IN TOWN, SO THE CHIEF FIGURED *YOU'D* BE HIS NEXT TARGET, BECAUSE YOU'RE THE WEALTHIEST GUY ON THE LIST OF THOSE HE HASN'T YET TACKLED!

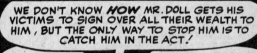

WE DON'T KNOW *HOW* MR. DOLL GETS HIS VICTIMS TO SIGN OVER ALL THEIR WEALTH TO HIM, BUT THE ONLY WAY TO STOP HIM IS TO CATCH HIM IN THE ACT!

SO, YOU WANT *ME* TO BE A DECOY, EH? WELL, WHY NOT?

HAPPY, I'M SCARED! WHAT IF MR. STARK GETS *HURT?*

RELAX, BABY! YOU'VE ALWAYS GOT *ME!*

THAT'S *ONE* OF THE THINGS I'M SCARED OF!!

NOW, THEN, MR. STARK! I'LL REMAIN ON DUTY HERE JUST IN CASE YOU NEED ME!

OH, NO...EH, THAT WON'T BE NECESSARY! I'VE PLENTY OF PRIVATE GUARDS TO GIVE ME PROTECTION!

CAN'T LET A POLICEMAN STAY AT MY SIDE... WOULDN'T BE ABLE TO CHANGE TO IRON MAN IF I DO!

VERY WELL, THEN! BUT BE SURE YOU DON'T LET MR. STARK OUT OF YOUR SIGHT FOR A MINUTE... UNDERSTAND?

DON'T WORRY, OFFICER! WE WON'T LET ANYTHING HAPPEN TO THE BOSS!

HMM! I'LL HAVE TO FIND A WAY TO SHAKE MY OWN GUARD AND TURN BACK TO IRON MAN!

11.

As soon as the police officer leaves, Stark gets an idea...

LOOK, BILL, HOW ABOUT GETTING LOST FOR A WHILE? I WANT TO BE ALONE WITH PEPPER! I'VE BEEN WAITING TO ASK HER FOR A DATE!

SORRY, CHIEF! YOU HEARD THAT OFFICER'S ORDERS! I CAN'T LET YOU OUT OF MY SIGHT!

HAPPY! DID YOU HEAR THAT??!

MR. STARK WANTS TO BE ALONE WITH ME...HE WANTS TO ASK ME FOR A DATE! I..I NEVER SUSPECTED!

DID YOU LOSE YOUR MARBLES, RED? WHY WOULD A GUY WHO HAS EVERY GLAMOR GIRL IN HOLLYWOOD CHASIN' HIM KNOCK HIMSELF OUT TO MAKE TIME WITH YOU??!

SEE THIS ROOM, BILL? THERE'S NO WAY OUT EXCEPT THROUGH THAT DOOR! IF YOU STAND OUTSIDE THE DOOR, NOBODY CAN GET TO ME! IS IT A DEAL?

WELL, OKAY! I GUESS THERE'S NO HARM IN LEAVING YOU IN HERE, CHIEF!

TO THINK THAT HE'S BEEN MAAAD ABOUT ME ALL THESE MONTHS AND I NEVER SUSPECTED!

MISTER STARK! TONY! SWEETHEART! WHY DIDN'T YOU TELL ME YOU CARED, YOU BASHFUL DREAMBOAT YOU!

PEPPER! THAT'S GREAT! KEEP IT UP! LET BILL THINK WE'RE CRAZY ABOUT EACH OTHER! LET HIM KEEP HEARING YOU...

...WHILE I SLIP OUT THIS SECRET EXIT AND TRY TO FIND IRON MAN! YOU KEEP TALKING TO YOURSELF FOR BILL'S BENEFIT, KID! YOU'RE A GREAT LITTLE ACTRESS!

ACTRESS!?? B-BUT I MEANT.. THAT IS...I.. :SOB:

SECONDS LATER, IN HIS HIDDEN LAB, TONY STARK CHANGES HIS IDENTITY ONCE MORE, PREPARING FOR WHAT MAY BE THE MOST DIFFICULT BATTLE OF HIS LIFE!

POOR PEPPER! I HATED TO TREAT HER THAT WAY, BUT I HAD NO OTHER CHOICE!

AND THUS, THE **NEW** IRON MAN MAKES HIS FIRST [P]UBLIC APPEARANCE...

[Y]OU MAY [R]ETURN TO YOUR [N]ORMAL [D]UTIES! [I']LL GUARD [A]NTHONY [S]TARK NOW!

IRON MAN! YOU'VE **CHANGED**!

I SAID YOU'RE **DISMISSED**!

IF NOT FOR HIS **VOICE**, I'D NEVER BELIEVE HE WAS THE REAL IRON MAN!

AND THEN, AS A DETERMINED **IRON MAN** TAKES OVER, HIS DREADED FOE APPEARS OUTSIDE OF STARK'S FACTORY ENTRANCE, EASILY CAUSING THE GUARDS TO FALL INTO A FAINT MERELY BY PRESSING VARIOUS NERVES ON HIS AWESOME DOLL!

NOTHING HUMAN CAN STOP MR. DOLL!

[S]UDDENLY...

HELP! SOME STRANGELY DRESSED MENACE HAS INVADED THE FACTORY! HE CAN'T BE STOPPED!

IT'S **HIM**...AT **LAST**!!

I'VE BEEN **WAITING** FOR YOU, MR. DOLL!

IRON MAN! YOU'VE **CHANGED**!! BUT NO MATTER! EVEN **NOW** I AM CHANGING THE FEATURES OF MY LITTLE DOLL TO RESEMBLE YOU! **THERE**! IT'S DONE!

HE'S TWISTING THE DOLL'S ARM... AND I FEEL IT IN MY **OWN** ARM! NO WONDER HE'S SO SURE OF HIMSELF!

BUT SINCE CHANGING MY UNIFORM AND LIGHTENING THE LOAD ON MY HEART, I CAN BETTER **RESIST** THE PAIN! BUT I MUSTN'T LET HIM KNOW! I'VE GOT TO **OUT-BLUFF** HIM SOMEHOW!

13.

OBEY ME, IRON MAN, OR I'LL INCREASE THE PRESSURE! DRIVE EVERYONE OUT OF THIS FACTORY! *NOW!*

AN EASY MATTER FOR ONE WITH TRANSISTOR-POWERED MUSCLES!

OUT... ALL OF YOU! OUT!!

GANGWAY! YOU DON'T HAVETA TELL ME TWICE!

I'VE DECIDED THAT THIS FACTORY WILL MAKE A PERFECT HEADQUARTERS FOR ME! AND WITH *YOU* UNDER MY CONTROL, *NO ONE* CAN DRIVE ME FROM IT!

GOOD! HE THINKS HE'S WON! NOW TO KEEP HIM TALKING!

HOW DID YOU GET YOUR GREAT POWER, MR. DOLL?

IN *AFRICA!* I STOLE THE SECRET OF THIS MAGICAL LITTLE FIGURINE FROM A WITCH DOCTOR WHO WAS FOOLISH ENOUGH TO BEFRIEND ME!

BUT ENOUGH OF THAT! NOW I MUST MAKE MR. ANTHONY STARK SIGN HIS FACTORY AND HIS GREAT FORTUNE OVER TO ME! SO LONG AS I HAVE EVERYTHING IN WRITING, NICE AND LEGAL, THE LAW CAN'T TOUCH ME!

IT WILL BE A SIMPLE MATTER TO MAKE STARK COME CRAWLING TO ME! NO MATTER *WHERE* HE IS, HE WILL *FEEL* IT WHEN I PINCH THIS DOLL!

HE DOESN'T SUSPECT THAT *I* AM TONY STARK! *I'M* THE ONE WHO WILL FEEL THE PAIN!

IF I *SHOW* THAT I'M HURT, HE'LL DISCOVER MY SECRET!! I MUSTN'T LET HIM KNOW... NO MATTER WHAT... HE MUST NEVER SUSPECT!!

AND SO BEGINS THE TOUGHEST BATTLE OF IRON MAN'S CAREER...

THERE! STARK WON'T BE ABLE TO STAND THIS FOR LONG!

SILENTLY, SUMMONING UP EVERY OUNCE OF RAW COURAGE, OF FIGHTING NERVE, OF IRON-WILLED DETERMINATION, TONY STARK TURNS AWAY, FIGHTING DESPERATELY TO HIDE THE ANGUISH HE IS FEELING!

LOOK AT YOU, TURNING AWAY FROM MY LITTLE PET! WHO WOULD EVER HAVE THOUGHT THAT THE MIGHTY *IRON MAN* IS SO *SQUEAMISH*

...OUT, YOU WEAKLING! I'LL SUMMON YOU WHEN I WANT YOU AGAIN! AND DON'T TRY TO ESCAPE... I CAN ALTER MY DOLL TO RESEMBLE YOU SECONDS, AND BRING YOU BACK ON YOUR KNEES!

IT WORKED! JUST WHAT I WANTED HIM TO SAY!

WITHIN HIS CONCEALING IRON MAN ARMOR, TONY STARK RESISTS THE INTENSE PAIN HE FEELS UNTIL HE FINALLY FLINGS HIMSELF ACROSS THE THRESHOLD OF HIS PRIVATE LAB...

NOW... IF I CAN ONLY HOLD OUT A FEW MINUTES LONGER... I... I KNOW THE WAY TO BEAT MR. DOLL!

I'LL SET THE TIME LOCK... THE DOOR WON'T OPEN FOR A HALF HOUR!... NO MATTER WHAT HAPPENS! SO I'M LOCKED IN... WON'T BE ABLE TO WEAKEN AND GO TO MR. DOLL EVEN IF I WANT TO!

NOW FOR THE MOST DANGEROUS GAMBLE I'VE EVER TAKEN!

THERE'S ONLY ONE WAY TO STOP THE PAIN HE'S MAKING ME FEEL...

I'VE GOT TO REMOVE MY HEART-ACTIVATOR UNIT! AS MY HEARTBEAT SLOWS DOWN, IT DEADENS MY NERVES... I FEEL NOTHING...

BUT IF I DON'T CONNECT IT AGAIN WITHIN MINUTES... I'M DOOMED!

AND SO, AS HE FEELS THE LIFE BEGIN TO EBB FROM HIS BODY, TONY STARK WORKS AS NO MAN HAS EVER WORKED BEFORE... KNOWING HE HAS TO FINISH HIS TASK IN TIME... IF HE IS TO SAVE HIMSELF... AND THE HUMAN RACE... FROM THE MENACE OF MR. DOLL!

GETTING DIZZY... THINGS ARE SPINNING AROUND... BUT CAN'T STOP NOW...

AND FINALLY, WITH HIS LAST REMAINING BIT OF ENERGY, WITH ONLY MOMENTS TO SPARE...

I COMPLETED IT!! MUST CONNECT CHEST DEVICE... START HEART PUMPING AGAIN!

15.

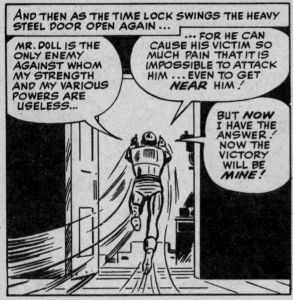

AND THEN AS THE TIME LOCK SWINGS THE HEAVY STEEL DOOR OPEN AGAIN...

MR. DOLL IS THE ONLY ENEMY AGAINST WHOM MY STRENGTH AND MY VARIOUS POWERS ARE USELESS...

...FOR HE CAN CAUSE HIS VICTIM SO MUCH PAIN THAT IT IS IMPOSSIBLE TO ATTACK HIM ...EVEN TO GET NEAR HIM!

BUT NOW I HAVE THE ANSWER! NOW THE VICTORY WILL BE MINE!

IRON MAN! YOU DARE BREAK IN THIS WAY!

WELL, NO MATTER! BEFORE YOU TAKE ANOTHER STEP, I SHALL HAVE MY DOLL MOLDED TO RESEMBLE YOU AGAIN, AND STOP YOU IN YOUR TRACKS WITH A BOLT OF PAIN!

I HAVE TRAINED MYSELF TO ALTER MY DOLL'S FEATURES IN A SPLIT SECOND! ONCE AGAIN YOU ARE POWERLESS BEFORE ME, IRON MAN ...AND THIS TIME I SHALL DESTROY YOU ...FOR I HAVE NO FURTHER NEED OF YOU!

FAREWELL, IRON MAN! ALL I NEED DO IS DROP MY DOLL FROM THIS HEIGHT AND YOU ARE DOOMED!!

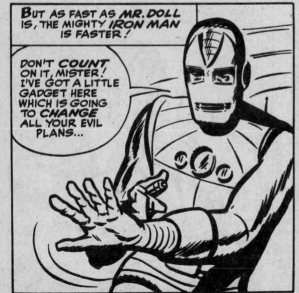

BUT AS FAST AS MR. DOLL IS, THE MIGHTY IRON MAN IS FASTER!

DON'T COUNT ON IT, MISTER! I'VE GOT A LITTLE GADGET HERE WHICH IS GOING TO CHANGE ALL YOUR EVIL PLANS...

THEN, BEFORE MR. DOLL CAN DROP HIS SINISTER DOLL TO THE FLOOR, IRON MAN AIMS THE DEVICE HE HAS HASTILY CONSTRUCTED, AND...

...AND THIS IS IT!!

AT THE SPLIT SECOND THAT MR. DOLL IS ABOUT TO DROP THE FATAL DOLL, *IRON MAN'S* STRANGE BEAM STRIKES IT, BATHING IT IN AN EERIE GLOW!

AND THEN, ALMOST FASTER THAN THE EYE CAN FOLLOW, IRON MAN'S FINGERS, AIDED BY HIS POWERFUL MINIATURE TRANSISTORS, MOVE THE BEAM SLIGHTLY, CAUSING IT TO CHANGE THE APPEARANCE OF THE DOLL'S FACE...

...UNTIL, MUCH FASTER THAN IT TAKES TO READ THIS LINE, THE SILHOUETTE OF THE DOLL WHICH MR. DOLL IS ABOUT TO DROP RESEMBLES THE ARCH-VILLAIN *HIMSELF!*

BUT BEFORE HE REALIZES FULLY WHAT HE IS DOING... BEFORE HE CAN STOP HIMSELF... MR. DOLL DROPS THE TINY FIGURINE, AND...:

NO!! I..I DIDN'T MEAN TO....!!

AS THE MAGICAL OBJECT STRIKES THE FLOOR, SO DOES MR. DOLL SEEM TO CRUMBLE, AND FALL TO THE GROUND, HELPLESS...UNCONSCIOUS... THOROUGHLY DEFEATED!!

I'VE WON!!

MINUTES LATER, STILL SOMEWHAT SHAKEN BY HIS GRUELING EXPERIENCE, IRON MAN QUICKLY SUMMONS THE FACTORY GUARDS...

WHAT *HAPPENED,* IRON MAN? WHERE IS MR. DOLL?

YOU'LL FIND HIM IN THE HALLWAY OF THE SUB-BASEMENT! TAKE HIM AWAY!

HEY! DON'T GO BARKIN' OUT ORDERS AT *ME,* BUB! DON'T FORGET, *I'M* MR. STARK'S PERSONAL CHAUFFEUR!

SURE, SURE! I'LL BET YOU'D BE A SENSATION ON "WHAT'S MY LINE?" NOW WAIT HERE WHILE I FIND STARK FOR YOU!

WHEW! I SURE WOULDN'T WANT TO BE ON THE WRONG SIDE OF *THAT* GUY!

17.

ONCE AGAIN, IRON MAN BECOMES ANTHONY STARK IN THE PRIVACY OF HIS LOCKED LAB...

HARD TO BELIEVE THAT ALL IT TOOK TO DEFEAT MR. DOLL WAS A TRANSISTOR-POWERED *FORCE BEAM*...

...WITH ENOUGH ENERGY TO ALTER THE SHAPE OF HIS OWN DOLL!

And THEN... HI, BOSS! SAY, DID *YOU* MISS A HEAP OF EXCITEMENT!! IRON MAN PUT THE KIBOSH ON MR. DOLL...WITH AN ASSIST BY *ME*, OF COURSE! YOU SHOULDA SEEN ME IN ACTION!!

SAY, WHERE'S *PEPPER?* I THOUGHT SHE WAS WITH *YOU!*

PEPPER!? GOOD LORD! I CLEAN FORGOT....

HEY, WAIT! WHAT'S WRONG? IS SHE IN SOME KINDA *TROUBLE?* BECAUSE IF YOU NEED SOME MORE HELP...

...I'LL BE GLAD TO GO AND FETCH THE COPS!

FORGET IT, *HAPPY! SHE'S* IN NO TROUBLE... BUT I HAVE A HUNCH *I'M* GOING TO BE!

SAY, BLUE EYES!.. WHAT ARE YOU DOIN' ALONE IN *HERE?*

I'M AFRAID IT'S *MY* FAULT! I ASKED PEPPER TO *WAIT* HERE, AND THEN...

AND THEN YOU FORGOT ALL *ABOUT* ME!!

AW, DON'T BE MAD, GORGEOUS! HOW'DJA LIKE OL' HAPPY TO TAKE YA TO A MOVIE TONIGHT?

IT'S THE MOST REPREHENSIBLE, REPULSIVE, RIDICULOUS IDEA I'VE EVER HEARD!

YEAH! BUT WHAT'S YOUR *ANSWER?*

HOLY MACKEREL! MR. DOLL IS ON HIS WAY TO THE POKEY...EVERYTHING'S BACK TO NORMAL HERE... NOBODY WAS HURT IN THE FIGHT...AND *SHE'S* ANGRY! HOW DO YOU FIGGER WOMEN?

WOMEN I CAN FIGURE, HAPPY! BUT *PEPPER...* SHE'S IN A CLASS BY HERSELF!

The End

NEXT ISSUE: THE *NEW* IRON MAN STARS IN A FAST-MOVING THRILLER WITH THE ACCENT ON *ACTION!* SEE YOU THEN!

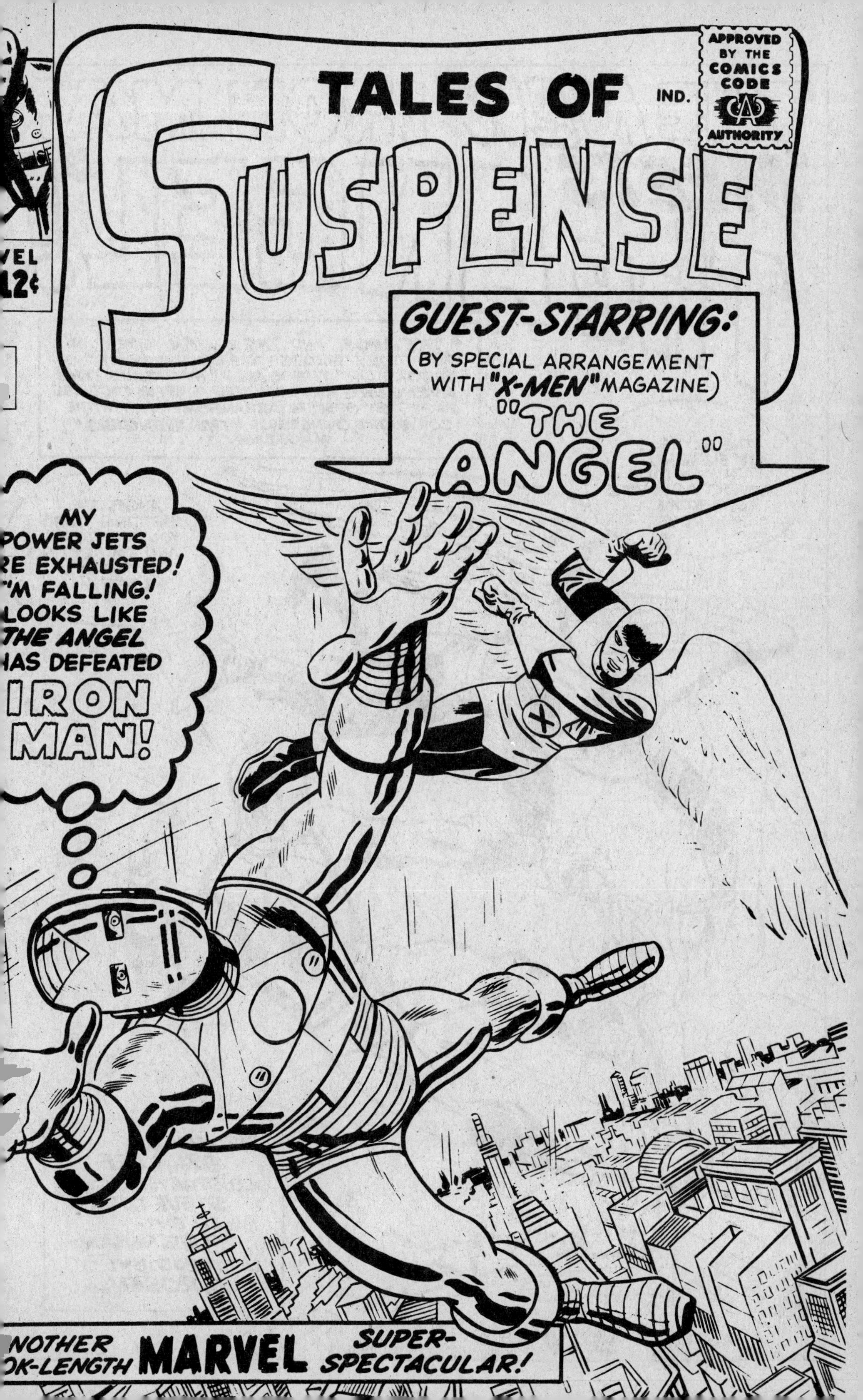

APPROVED BY THE COMICS CODE AUTHORITY
TALES OF SUSPENSE
IND.
VEL
12¢
GUEST-STARRING:
(BY SPECIAL ARRANGEMENT WITH "X-MEN" MAGAZINE)
"THE ANGEL"
MY POWER JETS RE EXHAUSTED! 'M FALLING! LOOKS LIKE THE ANGEL HAS DEFEATED IRON MAN!
NOTHER OK-LENGTH MARVEL SUPER-SPECTACULAR!

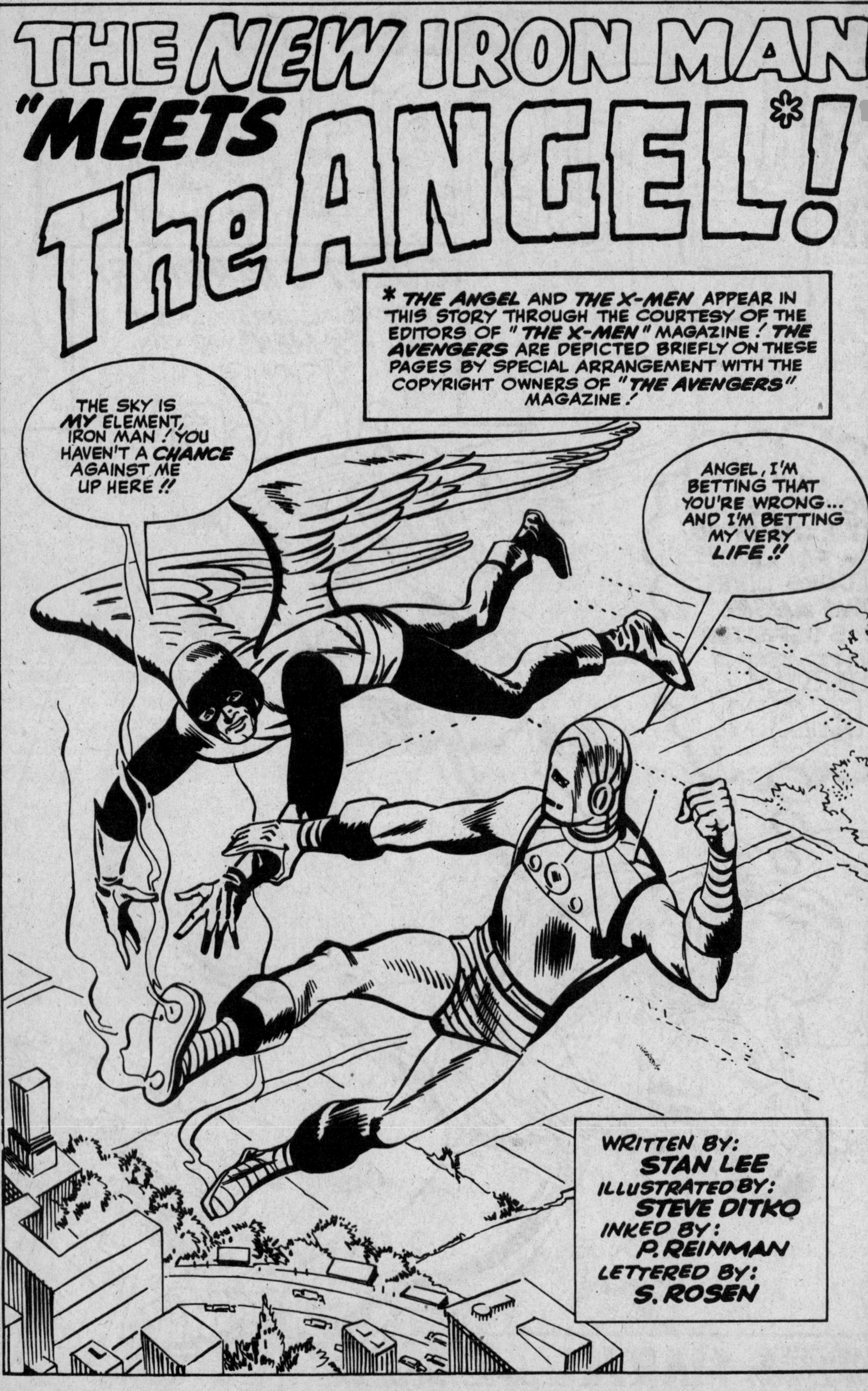
THE NEW IRON MAN "MEETS The ANGEL*!
* THE ANGEL AND THE X-MEN APPEAR IN THIS STORY THROUGH THE COURTESY OF THE EDITORS OF "THE X-MEN" MAGAZINE! THE AVENGERS ARE DEPICTED BRIEFLY ON THESE PAGES BY SPECIAL ARRANGEMENT WITH THE COPYRIGHT OWNERS OF "THE AVENGERS" MAGAZINE!
THE SKY IS MY ELEMENT, IRON MAN! YOU HAVEN'T A CHANCE AGAINST ME UP HERE!!
ANGEL, I'M BETTING THAT YOU'RE WRONG... AND I'M BETTING MY VERY LIFE!!
WRITTEN BY: STAN LEE
ILLUSTRATED BY: STEVE DITKO
INKED BY: P. REINMAN
LETTERED BY: S. ROSEN

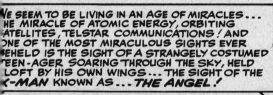

WE SEEM TO BE LIVING IN AN AGE OF MIRACLES...THE MIRACLE OF ATOMIC ENERGY, ORBITING SATELLITES, TELSTAR COMMUNICATIONS! AND ONE OF THE MOST MIRACULOUS SIGHTS EVER BEHELD IS THE SIGHT OF A STRANGELY COSTUMED TEEN-AGER SOARING THROUGH THE SKY, HELD ALOFT BY HIS OWN WINGS...THE SIGHT OF THE X-MAN KNOWN AS...*THE ANGEL!*

I CAN REACH THE PROFESSOR'S SCHOOL IN WESTCHESTER FASTER IF I TAKE A SHORT CUT OVER THE FACTORY BELOW!

STARK

BUT THE "FACTORY BELOW" HAPPENS TO BE THE WEAPONS PLANT OF ANTHONY STARK, WHERE A VITAL ATOMIC TEST IS ABOUT TO TAKE PLACE!

SOMEONE IS WAVING TO ME BELOW! GOSH...IT'S *IRON MAN!* I NEVER THOUGHT I'D ACTUALLY *SEE* HIM IN THE FLESH...IF THAT *IS* FLESH!

BACK, YOU YOUNG FOOL...*GET BACK!* A DEADLY ATOMIC EXPLOSION IS ABOUT TO BE DETONATED HERE!!

IT'S NO USE! HE DOESN'T *HEAR* ME! ONLY ONE THING TO DO!

I'LL HAVE TO USE MY POWER JETS TO FLY *UP* TO HIM...GOT TO WARN HIM *AWAY!!*

HE'S ZOOMING UP TO ME! PROBABLY JUST AS ANXIOUS TO SEE *ME!* BOY, WAIT'LL I TELL THE GANG AT PROFESSOR X'S ABOUT *THIS!!*

HE'S SHOUTING SOMETHING!...TRYING TO MAKE ME LEAVE...!! BUT..WHY..??

THE EXPLOSION WILL GO OFF AT ANY MOMENT! TURN BACK... CAN'T YOU HEAR?? *TURN BACK!!*

AND THEN, IN THE NEXT SPLIT-SECOND, IT IS TOO LATE FOR TURNING BACK! TOO LATE FOR WORDS, FOR ACTIONS, FOR ANYTHING! IN THAT FATEFUL SPLIT-SECOND, A HIGHLY-REFINED NUCLEAR EXPLOSION TAKES PLACE, DANGEROUSLY CLOSE TO *IRON MAN* AND *THE ANGEL!!*

2.

PROTECTED BY HIS HEAVILY-INSULATED FLEXIBLE METAL COSTUME, *IRON MAN* IS ABLE TO WITHSTAND THE TREMENDOUS SHOCK OF THE EXPLOSION WITHOUT SUFFERING ANY LASTING ILL EFFECTS!

UGH!! TOO LATE... TOO LATE TO SAVE THE ANGEL!

BUT THE ANGEL, WEARING NO SUCH PROTECTIVE CLOTHING, RECEIVES THE BRUNT OF THE RADIOACTIVITY...

THAT'S WHY HE TRIED TO SIGNAL ME AWAY!! AN ATOMIC EXPLOSION! AND I CAUGHT WHATEVER RADIOACTIVITY THERE *WAS*!!

LUCKY MY WINGS WERE POWERFUL ENOUGH TO KEEP ME FROM BEING BLOWN CLEAR OUT OF THE SKY!

AND THEN, BEFORE ANOTHER INSTANT PASSES, IT HAPPENS! THE SUBTLE, DANGEROUS *CHANGE* COMES OVER THE ANGEL!!

I FEEL DIFFERENT! AS THOUGH I'M A NEW PERSON.!!

A SMARTER, CRAFTIER, SLYER PERSON!

AND YES... I ADMIT IT! A FAR MORE *EVIL* PERSON!

MEANTIME, HAVING FULLY RECOVERED FROM THE IMPACT OF THE DETONATION, IRON MAN HEADS FOR THE ANGEL AGAIN!

I'VE *GOT* TO REACH HIM! ...SEE IF HE NEEDS ANY HELP!

I DON'T KNOW WHAT THAT CLUMSY FOOL IS FOLLOWING ME FOR...BUT I'LL SHOW HIM THAT *NOBODY* CAN CATCH THE *ANGEL*!

MY JETS ARE LOSING POWER!! I'VE OVER-TAXED THEM...FLOWN TOO HIGH, TOO FAST!!

HE KNOWS I'M IN TROUBLE... BUT HE'S TAUNTING ME! HE'S STAYING JUST OUT OF REACH!

IT'S JUST AS I FEARED! THE EXPLOSION CHANGED HIS PERSONALITY MADE HIM CRUEL... MERCILESS.

O MORE TIME TO ORRY ABOUT *HIM* OW...HAVE TO AVE MYSELF! MY OWER-JETS ARE OMPLETELY XHAUSTED! I.. M ABOUT TO LUMMET TO EARTH!

MUSTN'T PANIC!! GOT ONE SLIM CHANCE....!

MY AGNETIC EPELLER!! F ONLY HE POWER *STRONG* NOUGH!

IT'S *WORKING!* I AIMED IT AT THE GROUND BELOW!

I CAN FEEL IT *REPELLING* THE GROUND.. PUSHING AGAINST IT.. BREAK- ING MY FALL!

STARK

IT'S ACTING LIKE A BRAKE...REALLY CUTTING MY SPEED! IF ONLY IT CUTS IT *ENOUGH!* GOING TO HIT NOW! THIS IS *IT!!*

MADE IT!! SOME LIGHT DAMAGE TO MY ROTECTIVE CHEST LATE, BUT IT WON'T E DIFFICULT TO REPAIR!

MMM, *BOY!* I JUST LOVE YOU LITTLE MAGNETIC REPELLERS!

MINUTES LATER, IN HIS PRIVATE LAB, IRON MAN BECOMES MILLIONAIRE MANUFACTURER ANTHONY STARK AGAIN, AS HE BROADCASTS A CALL TO HIS SECRETARY, PEPPER POTTS...

PEPPER, I'LL BE IN MY LAB FOR THE NEXT HOUR OR TWO! I DON'T WANT TO BE DISTURBED!

I READ YOU LOUD AND CLEAR, BOSS!

4.

A SHORT TIME LATER, A STARTLING ANNOUNCEMENT IS MADE IN *PROFESSOR XAVIER'S SCHOOL FOR GIFTED YOUNGSTERS!*..

THAT'S RIGHT... YOU HEARD ME! I'M *QUITTING*... AND THERE'S *NOTHING* YOU CAN DO ABOUT IT!

INSIDE THE VAST MAIN CHAMBER, *CYCLOPS, THE BEAST, ICE MAN,* AND *MARVEL GIRL* ALL REGISTER STUNNED DISBELIEF AT THE NEWS!

ANGEL, YOU *CAN'T!*

YOU WERE ONE OF THE *FIRST* X-MEN! WE STARTED TOGETHER!

AW, DON'T LET 'IM RIB YOU! HE'S JUST *KIDDIN'*

NO, HE'S *NOT!* I CAN *TELL!* HE *MEANS* IT!

YOU'RE BLAMED *RIGHT* I MEAN IT! WHY SHOULD I WASTE MY TALENTS ON *YOU* LIGHTWEIGHTS??

WE'RE THE *GOOD* MUTANTS! HAW... BIG DEAL! I'M GONNA FIND THE *BAD* ONES...THE ONES THAT WANNA RULE THE EARTH! THE ONES WE'RE SUPPOSED TO *FIGHT...!*

...AND I'M GONNA JOIN UP WITH *THEM!* THAT'S WHERE THE *ACTION* IS!

OH NO YOU *DON'T,* PAL! YOU DON'T BREAK UP *THIS* COMBO SO EASILY!

I DON' KNOW WHAT THE GAG IS, BU PROFESSO X AIN'T GONNA *LIKE* IT!

WE MUS *STOP* HIM UNTI THE PRO FESSO GET HERE

STOP ME?? HAH! YOU EARTH-BOUND CLODS HAVEN'T A *CHANCE* AGAINST THE *ANGEL!* SEE?

HEY! LEGGO, YOU OVERSIZED PARAKEET!

STAND BACK, LADIES AND GENTS! OL' *CYCLOPS* WILL STOP HIM WITH A LOW-INTENSITY ENERGY BLAST!

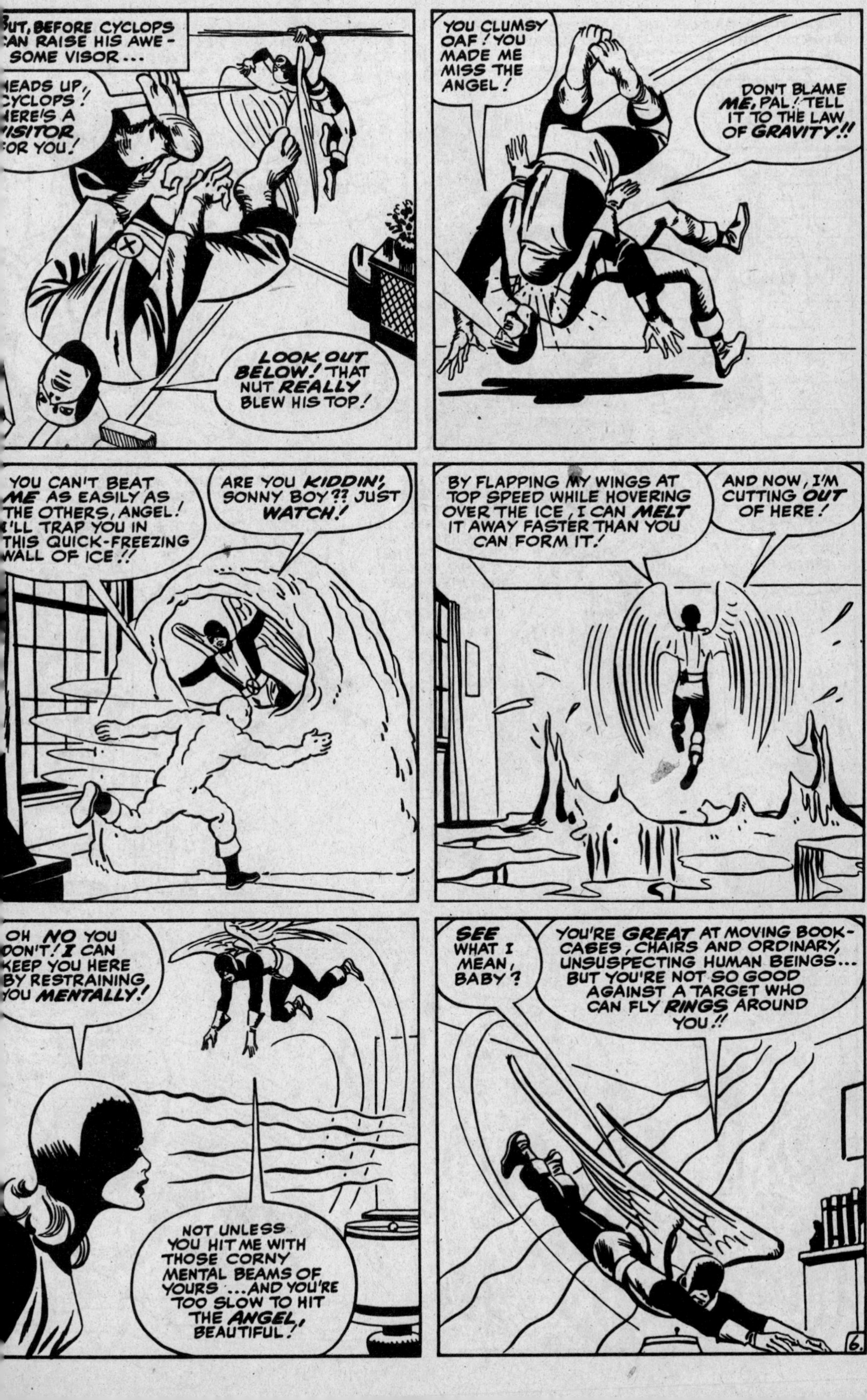
BUT, BEFORE CYCLOPS CAN RAISE HIS AWE-SOME VISOR...
HEADS UP, CYCLOPS! HERE'S A VISITOR FOR YOU!
LOOK OUT BELOW! THAT NUT REALLY BLEW HIS TOP!
YOU CLUMSY OAF! YOU MADE ME MISS THE ANGEL!
DON'T BLAME ME, PAL! TELL IT TO THE LAW OF GRAVITY!!
YOU CAN'T BEAT ME AS EASILY AS THE OTHERS, ANGEL! I'LL TRAP YOU IN THIS QUICK-FREEZING WALL OF ICE!!
ARE YOU KIDDIN', SONNY BOY?? JUST WATCH!
BY FLAPPING MY WINGS AT TOP SPEED WHILE HOVERING OVER THE ICE, I CAN MELT IT AWAY FASTER THAN YOU CAN FORM IT!
AND NOW, I'M CUTTING OUT OF HERE!
OH NO YOU DON'T! I CAN KEEP YOU HERE BY RESTRAINING YOU MENTALLY!
NOT UNLESS YOU HIT ME WITH THOSE CORNY MENTAL BEAMS OF YOURS ...AND YOU'RE TOO SLOW TO HIT THE ANGEL, BEAUTIFUL!
SEE WHAT I MEAN, BABY?
YOU'RE GREAT AT MOVING BOOK-CASES, CHAIRS AND ORDINARY, UNSUSPECTING HUMAN BEINGS... BUT YOU'RE NOT SO GOOD AGAINST A TARGET WHO CAN FLY RINGS AROUND YOU!!
6.

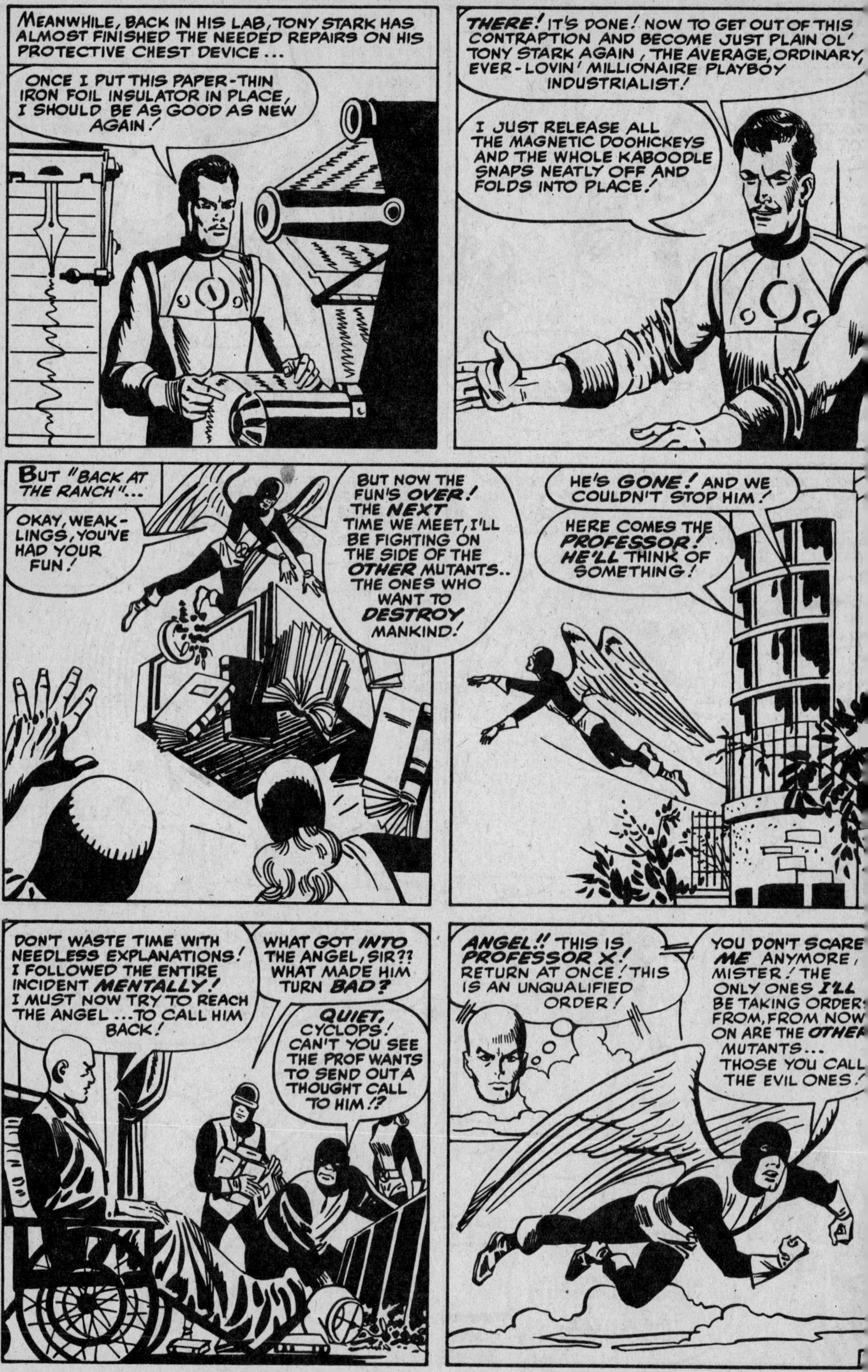
MEANWHILE, BACK IN HIS LAB, TONY STARK HAS ALMOST FINISHED THE NEEDED REPAIRS ON HIS PROTECTIVE CHEST DEVICE ...
ONCE I PUT THIS PAPER-THIN IRON FOIL INSULATOR IN PLACE, I SHOULD BE AS GOOD AS NEW AGAIN!
THERE! IT'S DONE! NOW TO GET OUT OF THIS CONTRAPTION AND BECOME JUST PLAIN OL' TONY STARK AGAIN, THE AVERAGE, ORDINARY, EVER-LOVIN' MILLIONAIRE PLAYBOY INDUSTRIALIST!
I JUST RELEASE ALL THE MAGNETIC DOOHICKEYS AND THE WHOLE KABOODLE SNAPS NEATLY OFF AND FOLDS INTO PLACE!
BUT "BACK AT THE RANCH"...
OKAY, WEAKLINGS, YOU'VE HAD YOUR FUN!
BUT NOW THE FUN'S OVER! THE NEXT TIME WE MEET, I'LL BE FIGHTING ON THE SIDE OF THE OTHER MUTANTS.. THE ONES WHO WANT TO DESTROY MANKIND!
HE'S GONE! AND WE COULDN'T STOP HIM!
HERE COMES THE PROFESSOR! HE'LL THINK OF SOMETHING!
DON'T WASTE TIME WITH NEEDLESS EXPLANATIONS! I FOLLOWED THE ENTIRE INCIDENT MENTALLY! I MUST NOW TRY TO REACH THE ANGEL ...TO CALL HIM BACK!
WHAT GOT INTO THE ANGEL, SIR?? WHAT MADE HIM TURN BAD?
QUIET, CYCLOPS! CAN'T YOU SEE THE PROF WANTS TO SEND OUT A THOUGHT CALL TO HIM!?
ANGEL!! THIS IS PROFESSOR X! RETURN AT ONCE! THIS IS AN UNQUALIFIED ORDER!
YOU DON'T SCARE ME ANYMORE, MISTER! THE ONLY ONES I'LL BE TAKING ORDERS FROM, FROM NOW ON ARE THE OTHER MUTANTS... THOSE YOU CALL THE EVIL ONES!

BACK IN HIS CHAMBER, PROFESSOR X BROODS, NOT SUSPECTING THE *REAL* REASON FOR THE ANGEL'S CHANGE OF CHARACTER!

THIS IS MY MOST *SERIOUS* FAILURE!

IF I COULD FAIL WITH THE ANGEL, HOW DO I KNOW *WHO* WILL BE *NEXT*? AM I TRAINING A GROUP OF POWERFUL X-MEN WHO WILL ONE DAY TURN *AGAINST* MANKIND??

PERHAPS WE SHOULD STOP OUR PROGRAM! PERHAPS... IT WAS WRONG FROM THE START!

BUT BEFORE WE MAKE ANY SUCH DECISION, WE MUST FINISH THE JOB AT HAND! WE MUST *STOP* THE ANGEL! FOR IF HE JOINS THE EVIL MUTANTS, BRINGING WITH HIM HIS *X-MEN* TRAINING, WE MAY FIND THEY ARE TOO POWERFUL EVEN FOR *US* TO CHALLENGE!

WE MUST TAKE NO CHANCES! WE MUST REQUEST *HELP*....CYCLOPS, CONTACT THE *AVENGERS*!

YES, *SIR*, PROFESSOR!

MINUTES LATER, CYCLOPS BROADCASTS AN URGENT APPEAL OVER A SECRET WAVE LENGTH USED ONLY BY THE X-MEN AND OTHER SPECIALLY LICENSED CRIME-FIGHTING ORGANIZATIONS!

THIS IS THE *X-MEN* CALLING THE *AVENGERS*! COME IN, *AVENGERS*! DO YOU READ ME? DO YOU READ ME?

KEEP TRYIN', CYCLOPS!

THE *AVENGERS*!! A DEDICATED GROUP OF EARTH'S MIGHTIEST SUPER HEROES...CONSISTING OF *THE HULK, MIGHTY THOR, GIANT-MAN*, THE WONDERFUL *WASP*, AND... *IRON MAN*!! THE CALL HAS GONE OUT TO THEM... BUT WILL THEY RESPOND???

FAR TO THE WEST, IN A NEW MEXICO PROVING GROUND, BRUCE BANNER IS AT WORK IN A LAB... WHICH MEANS THERE IS NO *HULK* AT THAT MOMENT TO RECEIVE THE X-MEN'S MESSAGE!!

WHILE MIGHTY *THOR* IN HIS OTHER IDENTITY AS DR. DON BLAKE, IS MAKING HIS ROUNDS AT MUNICIPAL HOSPITAL, FAR FROM HIS SHORT WAVE RECEIVING SET....!

AND *GIANT MAN* AND THE WONDERFUL *WASP* ARE ENJOYING A RARE SOCIAL EVENING TOGETHER AS HENRY PYM AND JANET VAN DYNE... AND ONLY HAVE EYES AND THOUGHTS FOR EACH OTHER!

8.

OF ALL THE *AVENGERS*, ONLY *IRON MAN* RECEIVES THE X-MEN'S CALL ... AS IT IS TRANSMITTED TO HIM THROUGH HIS CONCEALED SHOULDER RECEIVER WHICH IS ALWAYS IN POSITION ON HIS HIDDEN CHEST DEVICE!

SAY, BOSS, DID I JUST HEAR SOMEONE ELSE'S VOICE??

NO, HAPPY! YOU'RE ONLY IMAGINING THINGS! NOW EXCUSE ME... I'D LIKE TO BE ALONE!

DID YOU HEAR *THAT*?? DID YOU HEAR HOW HE SPOKE TO ME?? TO *ME*... HIS PERSONAL CHAUFFEUR, HIS TRUSTED PAL! I'VE GOT A GOOD MIND TO *QUIT*!

QUIT *WHAT*, HAPPY?? YOU HAVEN'T DONE A BIT OF WORK SINCE YOU *CAME* HERE!

OH, *HO*! *YOU* TOO!... I THINK IT'S A CON-SPIRACY!!

POOR PEPPER! YOU TRY TO HIDE THE FACT THAT YOU'RE *NUTS* ABOUT ME BY MAKING INSULTING REMARKS! BUT YOU DON'T FOOL ME, BABY! I KNOW HOW YOU FEEL ABOUT ME!

IF YOU REALLY *DID* KNOW, MR. HOGAN, YOU'D JOIN THE FOREIGN LEGION! THAT IS, IF THEY'D LOWER THEIR STANDARDS AND *TAKE* YOU!

MEANTIME, INSIDE STARK'S PRIVATE OFFICE...

IT MUST BE PRETTY SERIOUS IF PROFESSOR X WANTS THE *AVENGERS* TO HELP HIS X-MEN STOP THE ANGEL!

BUT *I'M* THE ONLY ONE WHO RECEIVED THE CALL! NONE OF THE OTHER AVENGERS RESPONDED!

WELL, I WON'T *TELL* THE OTHERS! I'LL HANDLE *THIS* LITTLE JOB BY *MYSELF*!

AFTER ALL, IN A WAY IT'S MY FAULT THAT THE ANGEL WAS TRANSFORMED INTO A POTENTIAL MENACE.

AND SO, ANTHONY STARK... IN THE PERSON OF *IRON MAN*..WILL UNDO THE HARM THAT'S BEEN DONE ... OR DIE TRYING!!

MEANWHILE, THE *ANGEL* FLIES OVER NEW YORK WITH JUST ONE THOUGHT IN MIND...

I'VE GOT TO CONTACT THE EVIL MUTANTS AND JOIN UP WITH THEM...BUT IT'S EASIER SAID THAN DONE! HOW DO I *FIND* THEM?

WELL, THERE'S ONLY ONE THING TO DO... I'LL LET *THEM* FIND *ME!*

HEY, CHARLIE! SOME GUY WITH *WINGS* JUST STOLE SOME *T.N.T.* FROM US AND FLEW AWAY WITH IT!

YOU KNOW IT AND *I* KNOW IT, ROCCO! BUT DON'T TELL ANY-ONE *ELSE* OR THEY'LL SEND US OFF TO THE "HAPPY FARM"!

DYNAMITE

THERE! THAT EXPLOSION, HIGH OVER THE CITY, OUGHT TO MAKE *EVERYBODY* SIT UP AND TAKE NOTICE!

AND IF *THAT* DIDN'T DO THE TRICK, I'LL DROP SOME *MORE* OVER THE HARBOR...

JUST IN CASE SOME OF THE "BAD GUYS" ARE LEAVING FOR A CRUISE!

WELL, THAT'S THE *LAST* OF IT! I DIDN'T DO ANY DAMAGE, BUT SURE MADE A WING-DING OF A RACKET!

NOW I'LL JUST WAIT AROUND FOR THE X-MEN'S MUTANT ENEMIES TO CONTACT ME!

AND WHEN THEY *DO*... AND WHEN I *JOIN* THEM...*THAT'S* WHEN THE DAMAGE *WILL* START! THAT'S WHEN ORDINARY HUMANS BETTER HEAD FOR THE HILLS!

10

BUT THE WARY EVIL MUTANTS, RECOGNIZING THE ANGEL, SUSPECT A *TRAP* AND DO *NOT* SHOW THEMSELVES! INSTEAD, A POWERFUL, MASKED FIGURE APPEARS ON THE SCENE, PROPELLED BY HIS ASTONISHING POWER JETS!

HOLD IT, OFFICERS! *DON'T SHOOT!*

IT'S *IRON MAN!*

NO TIME TO EXPLAIN NOW! BUT THE ANGEL ISN'T REALLY RESPONSIBLE FOR WHAT HE'S DOING! GIVE *ME* A CHANCE TO STOP HIM BEFORE YOU ATTACK, CHIEF!

WELL, I DON'T KNOW WHAT THE *REGULATIONS* WOULD SAY ABOUT THIS! ...BUT SEEING IT'S *YOU*...ALL RIGHT! YOU HAVE *TEN MINUTES.*

DON'T KNOW WHAT I CAN ACCOMPLISH IN A SCANT TEN MINUTES, BUT I'VE GOT TO *TRY!*

ANGEL... STOP. *WAIT!* I'VE GOT TO *TALK* TO YOU!

YOU AGAIN?? LOOKS LIKE I'LL HAVE TO POLISH YOU OFF FOR *GOOD* NOW!

DIDN'T EXPECT THIS LITTLE MANEUVER, DID YOU?!

MY JETS *CAN'T* MAKE ME AS NIMBLE AS HIS *WINGS* MAKE *HIM!* HE CAN FLY *RINGS* AROUND ME!

BUT WHAT'S HE TRYING TO...? OHHHH!

HAH! GOT YOU!!

BY HOLDING MY LEGS, HE'S FORCING ME TO *TURN* AGAINST MY WILL!

HOPE YOUR PASSPORT IS IN ORDER, PAL...

BECAUSE YOU'RE ABOUT TO TAKE A LITTLE *TRIP!*

HE'S AIMING ME TOWARD THE *GROUND!* IF I DON'T STOP MYSELF I'LL CRASH LIKE A BURNED-OUT ROCKET!

OKAY, SONNY-BOY! *NOW* YOU'LL LEARN THAT *IRON MAN* KNOWS A FEW TRICKS, TOO!

HE CUT OFF HIS JETS! BUT *WHY??*

IN CASE YOU WERE WONDERING, I *FIGURED* THAT SURPRISE MOVE OF MINE WOULD CATCH YOU OFF GUARD LONG ENOUGH FOR ME TO *GRAB* YOU...LIKE *THIS!*

HOLDING THE ANGEL'S SLIM WRISTS IN A VISE-LIKE GRIP, IRON MAN APPLIES HIS JETS AT HALF-POWER AND BRINGS HIS STRUGGLING QUARRY DOWN TO EARTH AT LA GUARDIA AIRPORT!

OKAY, THE COFFEE BREAK'S *OVER*, SON! NOW I WANT TO TELL YOU *WHY* YOU'RE ACTING AS YOU ARE...AND WHAT WE HAVE TO *DO* ABOUT IT!

BUT NOT REALIZING THE EXTENT OF THE ANGEL'S PERSONALITY CHANGE, IRON MAN CARELESSLY RELAXES HIS GRIP FOR AN INSTANT AND...

HE BROKE *AWAY* FROM ME!

CAN'T BE THAT UNTHINKING WHEN YOU'RE DEALING WITH AN X-MAN, CHUM! OR SHOULD I SAY... AN *EX-X-MAN??!*

HEY! HOW COME I DON'T HEAR YOU *LAUGHING?* THAT WAS A GAS!

HE'S TRYING TO GET OUT THE OTHER SIDE OF THE HANGAR! BUT *I* KNOW HOW TO *STOP* HIM!

WITHOUT A SECOND'S HESITATION, *IRON MAN* HURLS THREE POWERFUL TRANSISTOR MAGNETS IN THE DIRECTION OF THE ANGEL!

FLY STRAIGHT AND TRUE, LITTLE FRIENDS!

THAT WALKING HULK OF TIN IS *CRACKING UP!* WHAT DOES HE EXPECT TO GAIN BY TOSSING THOSE TOYS PAST ME??

12.

BUT IRON MAN'S FLYING FOE SOON LEARNS THAT THOSE LITTLE "TOYS", POWERED BY THEIR MIGHTY TRANSISTORS, HAVE A PULL WHICH CANNOT BE BROKEN BY MERE FLESH AND BLOOD!

CAN'T *BUDGE* THOSE *BLAMED* THINGS! SO *THAT'S* IT! HE THINKS HE CAN LOCK ME IN!

YOU'VE GOT *ANOTHER* THINK COMING, IRON MAN! THIS HANGAR HAS MORE THAN *ONE* DOOR!

BLAST IT! NO MORE MAGNETS LEFT! COULDN'T MANAGE TO CLAMP THAT DOOR SHUT IN TIME!

DESPERATELY, IRON MAN RACE FROM HANGAR TO HANGAR, SEEKING HIS AIRBORNE FOE UNTIL...

NO SIGN OF HIM IN THE SKY! HE MUST STILL B IN ...*HEY!* WHA...?

I WAS *WAITING* FOR YOU TO STEP IN THERE, TIN HEAD!

THIS TIME *I'LL* DO THE LOCKING, AND *YOU'LL* BE THE ONE WHO CAN'T GET OUT! SO LONG, SUCKER!

CLICK!

SLAM!

SWITCHING ON HIS EMERGENCY LIGHT BEAM, IRON MAN TAKES QUICK STOCK OF HIS SITUATION ...

A FINE THING! THE DREADED *IRON MAN*, LOCKED UP IN A *STORAGE* BUILDING!

WELL, THERE'S ONLY *ONE* WAY TO OPEN A LOCK WHEN YOU HAVEN'T GOT THE KEY...ONE WAY, THAT IS, IF YOU'RE *IRON MAN*....!

...AND *THAT* IS TO ACTIVATE YOUR ARM POWER-PACK TO ITS HIGHEST INTENSITY...GIVING YOUR MUSCLES ENOUGH STRENGTH TO *FORCE* THE LOCK AS THOUGH IT'S MADE OF CARDBOARD!

(CUT-AWAY) VIEW

WHEW...THAT WAS A *STRAIN* EVEN FOR *ME!* NOW I'VE GOT TO START HUNTING FOR THE ANGEL ALL OVER AG--OH, NO... *THERE* HE IS ...ATOP THAT WATER TOWER ...

WHAT'S *KEEPING* THE EVIL MUTANTS ?? WHY DON'T THEY JOIN ME ??

I STILL FEEL HE HASN'T TURNED COMPLETELY BAD... THERE'S STILL A CHANCE OF SHOCKING HIM BACK TO HIS NORMAL SELF! AND I'D BETTER BE RIGHT. !

...FOR THE ONLY WAY I CAN THINK OF DOING IT IS BY LETTING MY OWN LIFE HANG IN THE BALANCE!

WELL, NOBODY'S GETTING ANY YOUNGER... AND THE ONLY WAY TO FIND OUT IF A STUNT WILL WORK IS BY TRYING IT! SO HERE GOES!

POWER JETS TURNED TO MAXIMUM... FULL SPEED AHEAD!!

AT THAT SPLIT-SECOND, THE ANGEL HEARS THE SOUND OF IRON MAN'S JETS, AND TURNS...

YOU AGAIN?? ARE YOU SURE THERE'S ONLY ONE OF YOU?

ONE OF ME IS MORE THAN ENOUGH... AS YOU'RE ABOUT TO FIND OUT!

GOT YOU!!

I KNEW THAT EVEN YOUR UNCANNY MANEUVERABILITY WOULDN'T HELP YOU TO DODGE A HEAD-ON THRUST, USING THE FULL POWER OF MY JETS!!

IRON MAN, YOU'RE A FOOL! THOSE JET GIZMOS OF YOURS CAN'T HAVE MUCH MORE LIFE IN THEM THE WAY YOU'VE BEEN USING THEM ALL DAY...!

... AND THE HIGHER YOU TAKE ME, THE MORE STRAIN YOU PUT ON THEM, AND THE QUICKER YOUR TRANSISTORS WILL BURN OUT!! AND WHEN THAT HAPPENS, BROTHER... YOU'RE COOKED!!

IN FACT, IT SOUNDS TO ME AS THOUGH THEY'RE STARTING TO SPUTTER NOW... AND IT COULDN'T HAVE HAPPENED AT A BETTER TIME!

HE'S RIGHT! I'VE OVER-TAXED MY TRANSISTORS! C-CAN'T REMAIN ALOFT ANY LONGER!

14.

As IRON MAN'S MAIN POWER SOURCE BEGINS TO FAIL, THE PERFECTLY BALANCED *ANGEL* EASILY BREAKS FREE FROM HIS HEAVIER FOE... A FOE WHO BEGINS TO QUIVER IN THE AIR... AND THEN...

I-I'M STARTING TO *FALL!*

DON'T GIVE UP, BUDDY! MAYBE YOU'LL BE LUCKY AND GROW A PAIR OF WINGS... LIKE *ME!*

THIS IS YOUR *FINISH,* IRON MAN... AND GOOD RIDDANCE!

I *WARNE* YOU TO STO HOUNDING M BUT YOU WOULDN'T LISTEN! TH IT OVER, RU POT, ON YO WAY DOW

LOOKS LIKE I GUESSED *WRONG* THIS TIME!

AND THIS IS *ONE* GAME IN WHICH THERE'S NO SECOND CHANCE!

EVEN MY *MAGNETIC REPELLER* WON'T BE ABLE TO SAVE ME... NOT AT THE SPEED I'M FALLING AT *NOW!!*

IT'S TOO BAD I WASN'T ABLE TO HELP THE *ANGEL!* THE POLICE ARE SURE TO SHOOT HIM DOWN AS SOON AS HE FLIES WITHIN RANGE!

WISH I COU THINK OF A IMMORTAL LAST SENTE TO SAY... BUT ALL I FEEL LIKE SHOUTING IS... *HELP!*

AND STILL HOVERING ABOVE, WE FIND...

WHY DID HE TRY TO BUTT INTO MY AFFAIRS? HE SAID HE WANTED TO HELP! THE *FOOL! HE* NEEDS HELP NOW... BUT HE HASN'T A CHANCE!

WHILE, ON THE GROUND BELOW, AS THE POLICE WAIT TENSELY, LONG-RANGE T.V. CAMERAS COVER EVERY INCH OF IRON MAN'S EARTHWA PLUNGE, AS A SHOCKED NATION SEEMS TO HOLD ITS BREATH... STARING IN STUNNED D! BELIEF!

YOU CAN ALMOST SEE HIM WITH THE NAKED EYE NOW!

IT *CAN'T* THE END O IRON MAN IT JUST *CAN'T* BE!

JUST ANOTHER FEW SECONDS AND IT'LL BE ALL OVER! I KINDA WISH I COULD HAVE SAID GOOD-BYE TO PEPPER AND HAPPY!

AND DIRECTLY ABOVE THE PLUMMETING FIGURE...

WHAT'S THE MATTER WITH ME? WHY DO I FEEL SO SHOCKED?

HE WAS MY ENEMY... AS ALL CRIME FIGHTERS ARE! WHY CAN'T I BE GLAD OF HIS FATE?

IT'S NOT MY FAULT! I DIDN'T ASK HIM TO TRY TO BATTLE ME!

ALL I HAVE TO DO IS CLOSE MY EYES AND WAIT ANOTHER FEW SECONDS... THEN IT'LL BE OVER FOR HIM... FOREVER!

NO! I CAN'T! I CAN'T!

SUDDENLY, THE STRANGE TEEN-AGE MUTANT BEGINS A POWER-DIVE... STREAKING TOWARDS THE FALLING IRON MAN...

I'VE GOT TO SAVE HIM!

THE ANGEL! HE'S COMING AFTER ME! BUT HE'LL NEVER MAKE IT!...

UNLESS I CAN SLOW MY FALL... JUST ENOUGH TO GIVE HIM THE TIME HE NEEDS!

GOT TO TRY MY MAG-NETIC REPELLERS AGAIN... IF THEY CAN EVEN SLOW ME DOWN FOR A FEW SECONDS...

THE GROUND IS COMING SO CLOSE! AND THE REPELLERS ARE SO WEAK!

IT'S NO USE! I'M BOUND TO CRASH!

16.

AND THEN, JUST A FEW FATAL FEET ABOVE THE GROUND...THE GROUND WHICH SEEMS TO BE CAREENING MADLY UP TOWARDS IRON MAN TO SEIZE HIM IN A DEADLY EMBRACE!

IT'S GOT TO BE *NOW*...I MUSTN'T MISS!!

GOT YOU!!

ANGEL! YOU *DID* IT! YOU JUSTIFIED MY FAITH IN YOU!!

YOUR *FAITH* IN ME??? WHAT ARE YOU *TALKIN'* ABOUT??

I *KNEW* MY POWER-JETS WOULD FAIL WHEN I REACHED A CERTAIN HEIGHT...BUT I *HAD* TO DO IT!!...TO MAKE YOU SAVE ME!

TO PROVE TO THE POLICE...AND TO *YOURSELF*...THAT YOU'RE *NOT* EVIL!!

WE SAW THE WHOLE THING, IRON MAN! LUCKY THING WE HELD OUR FIRE!

WHAT GIVES WITH THAT *ANGEL* CHARACTER? IS HE *FOR* US, OR *AGIN'* US?

I THINK YOU'LL FIND HE'S *FOR* US FROM NOW ON! THIS LITTLE INCIDENT BROUGHT HIM BACK TO NORMAL!

HE WASN'T REALLY TO BLAME FOR HIS ACTIONS, CHIEF! HE WAS AFFECTED BY SOME ATOMIC RAYS AT A TEST CONDUCTED BY ANTHONY STARK AT HIS WEAPONS PLANT! THE RAYS AFFECTED HIS BRAIN FOR A TIME...UNTIL *NOW*!

SO *THAT'S* THE ANSWER! I SHOULD HAVE GUESSED!

17.

THEN YOU RISKED YOUR LIFE TO SHOCK ME BACK TO MYSELF!! YOU DID A THING LIKE THAT FOR SOMEONE YOU DON'T EVEN REALLY KNOW!

I HAD HEARD OF YOU... AND OF THE ASTOUNDING X-MEN... THAT WAS ENOUGH JUSTIFICATION FOR ME! AND SPEAKING OF THE X-MEN... LOOK!!

ANGEL! WE SAW THE WHOLE THING IN THE PROFESSOR'S VIEWSCOPE!

YOU'RE NORMAL AGAIN! I'M SO HAPPY I COULD CRY!

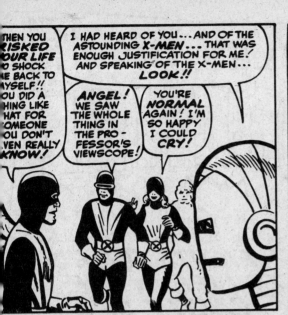

AND, BACK IN WESTCHESTER, IN A QUIET CHAMBER, A QUIET MAN SITS, FOLLOWING THE ENTIRE SCENE BY MENTAL PROJECTION...

SO I DID NOT FAIL! MY X-MEN TRAINING PROGRAM IS SUCCESSFUL!

EVEN UNDER THE INFLUENCE OF ATOMIC RADIATION, ANGEL COULD NOT PERMIT A FELLOW MORTAL TO DIE!

AND THEN, UNHEARD, UNNOTICED, UNSENSED BY ANYONE ELSE, THE X-MEN PICK UP A SHARP, COMMANDING THOUGHT... THE SILENT EMISSARY OF PROFESSOR X!

YOUR TASK IS FINISHED, MY X-MEN! RETURN TO THE SCHOOL AT ONCE! THERE IS STILL A VAST AMOUNT OF NEW TRAINING FOR YOU TO UNDERGO! CLASS STARTS IN ONE HOUR! ANY TARDINESS WILL NOT BE TOLERATED!

WE'VE GOT TO GO NOW, IRON MAN! BUT I MUST TELL YOU THIS... IF YOU EVER NEED HELP... NO MATTER HOW DEADLY THE TROUBLE... CALL ON ME... CALL ON THE X-MEN!

I'LL REMEMBER, MY YOUNG FRIEND! PERHAPS ONE DAY WE MIGHT FIGHT SIDE-BY-SIDE RATHER THAN AS ENEMIES! AND WHAT A FIGHT THAT WOULD BE!

FINALLY, AFTER IRON MAN HAS RECHARGED HIS TRANSISTORS, SO STRONG IS THE MENTAL POWER OF PROFESSOR X THAT ONE FINAL THOUGHT, BEAMED AT IRON MAN, ACTUALLY PENETRATES HIS BRAIN!

YOU RISKED YOUR LIFE FOR ONE OF MY X-MEN! NO MATTER WHO YOU REALLY ARE, I SHALL REPAY YOU SOME DAY! I PROMISE YOU THAT!

THAT THOUGHT..! LIKE SOMEONE INVISIBLE, WHISPERING INTO MY EAR!

18.

BUT NOW I MUST RETURN TO MY OTHER IDENTITY AS TONY STARK! PEPPER AND HAPPY, BLESS THEIR HEARTS, WERE PROBABLY LOOKING AFTER THINGS FOR ME AT THE PLANT DURING MY ABSENCE...

...AND KNOWING THEM, SOMEONE COULD HAVE STOLEN THE WHOLE FACTORY FROM UNDER THEIR NOSES WHILE THEY ARGUE ABOUT WHICH OF THEM IS MY MOST ALERT ASSISTANT!

MORE SURPRISES, DRAMA, AND THRILLS WITH IRON MAN NEXT ISSUE, AS THE GOLDEN GLADIATOR CONTINUES TO CLIMB HIGHER AND HIGHER ON POPULARITY POLLS THROUGHOUT THE NATION! SO, FOR SUPER-THRILLS IN THE MARVELOUS MARVEL MANNER, DON'T DARE MISS SUSPENSE #50!! SEE YOU THEN!

The END.

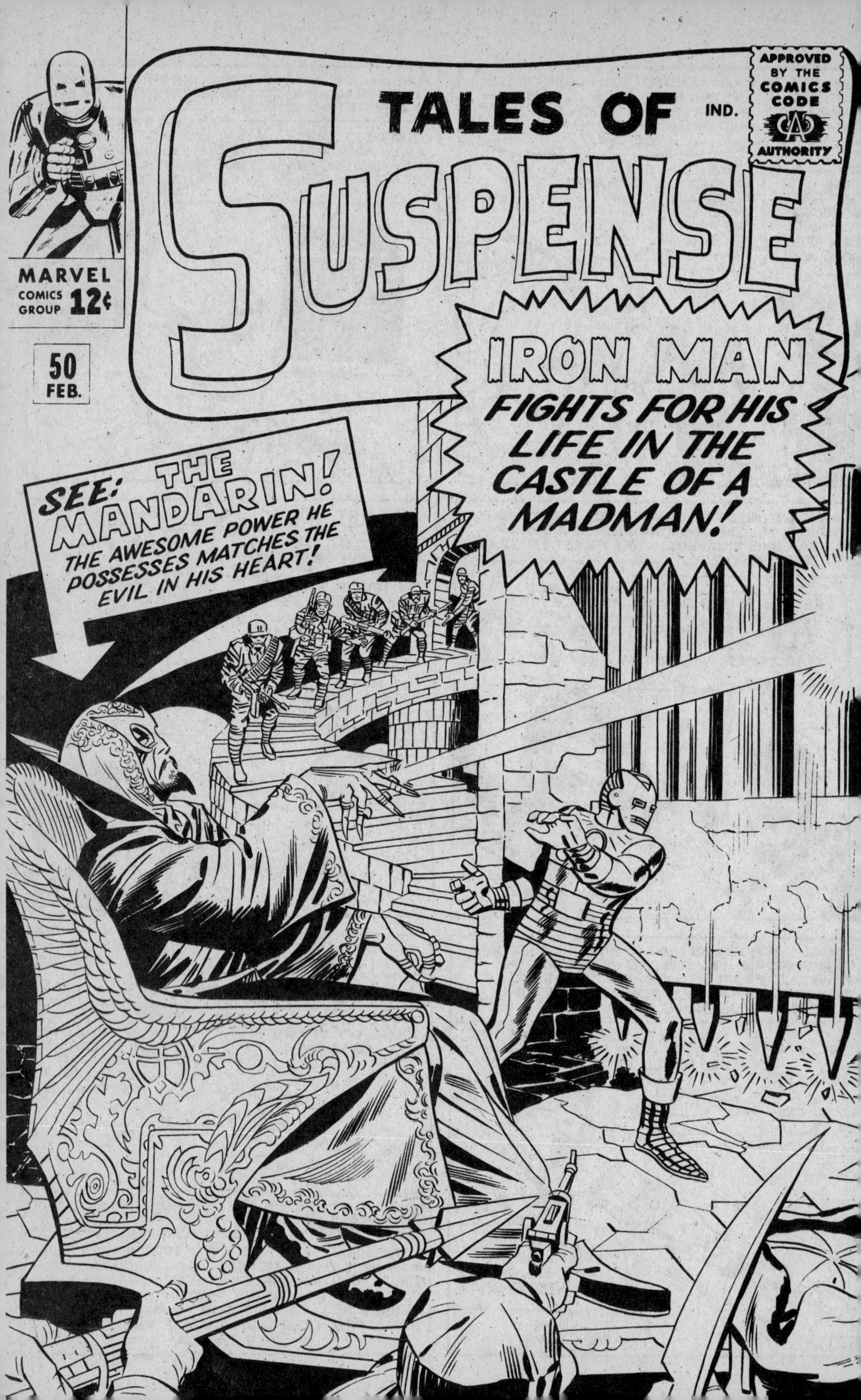

MARVEL COMICS GROUP 12¢
50 FEB.
TALES OF SUSPENSE
IND.
APPROVED BY THE COMICS CODE AUTHORITY
IRON MAN FIGHTS FOR HIS LIFE IN THE CASTLE OF A MADMAN!
SEE: THE MANDARIN! THE AWESOME POWER HE POSSESSES MATCHES THE EVIL IN HIS HEART!

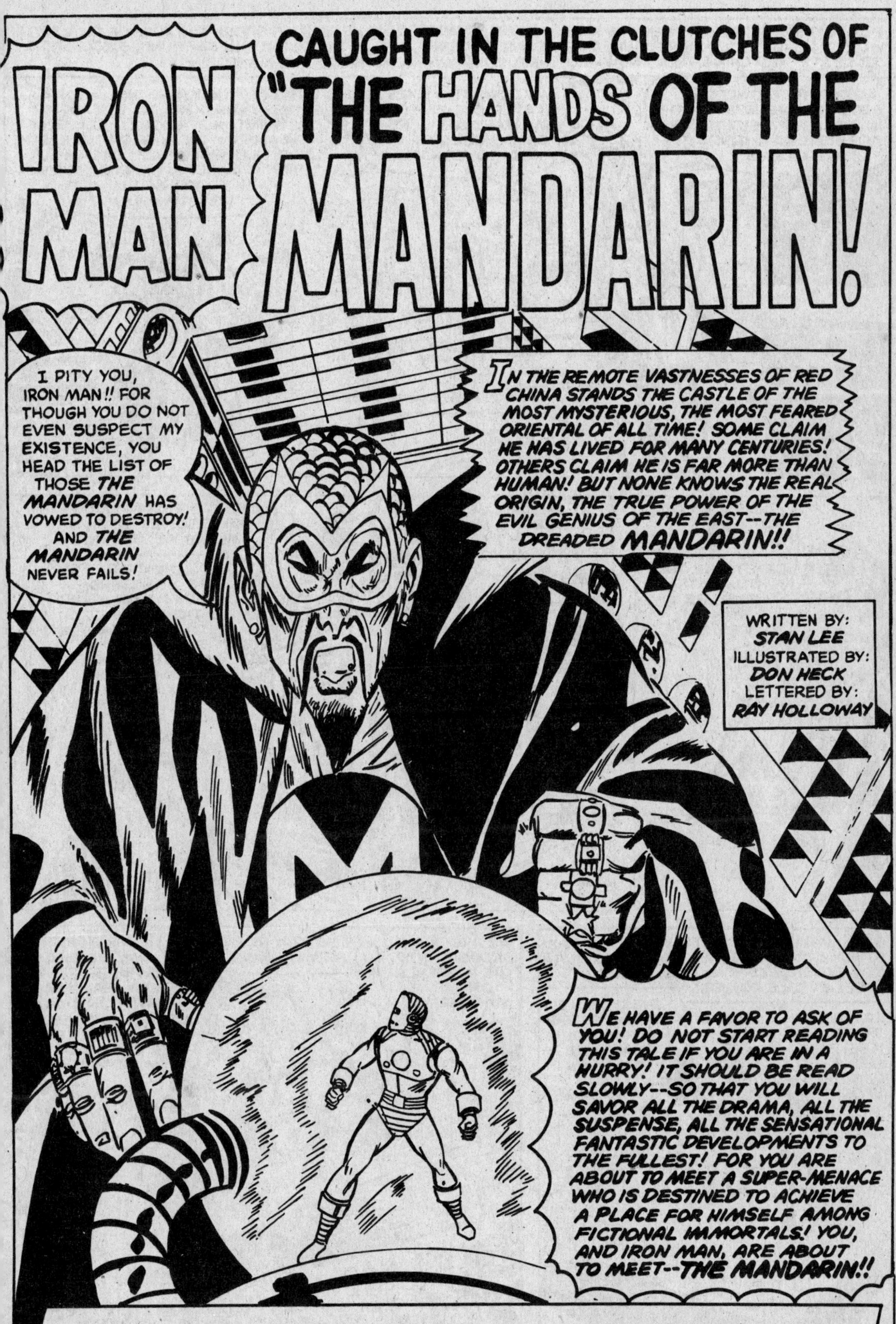
IRON MAN
CAUGHT IN THE CLUTCHES OF
"THE HANDS OF THE MANDARIN!
I PITY YOU, IRON MAN!! FOR THOUGH YOU DO NOT EVEN SUSPECT MY EXISTENCE, YOU HEAD THE LIST OF THOSE THE MANDARIN HAS VOWED TO DESTROY! AND THE MANDARIN NEVER FAILS!
IN THE REMOTE VASTNESSES OF RED CHINA STANDS THE CASTLE OF THE MOST MYSTERIOUS, THE MOST FEARED ORIENTAL OF ALL TIME! SOME CLAIM HE HAS LIVED FOR MANY CENTURIES! OTHERS CLAIM HE IS FAR MORE THAN HUMAN! BUT NONE KNOWS THE REAL ORIGIN, THE TRUE POWER OF THE EVIL GENIUS OF THE EAST--THE DREADED MANDARIN!!
WRITTEN BY: STAN LEE ILLUSTRATED BY: DON HECK LETTERED BY: RAY HOLLOWAY
WE HAVE A FAVOR TO ASK OF YOU! DO NOT START READING THIS TALE IF YOU ARE IN A HURRY! IT SHOULD BE READ SLOWLY--SO THAT YOU WILL SAVOR ALL THE DRAMA, ALL THE SUSPENSE, ALL THE SENSATIONAL FANTASTIC DEVELOPMENTS TO THE FULLEST! FOR YOU ARE ABOUT TO MEET A SUPER-MENACE WHO IS DESTINED TO ACHIEVE A PLACE FOR HIMSELF AMONG FICTIONAL IMMORTALS! YOU, AND IRON MAN, ARE ABOUT TO MEET--THE MANDARIN!!

FOR YEARS MEN HAVE SPOKEN THE NAME OF *THE MANDARIN* IN HUSHED WHISPERS! TO THOSE OF THE WESTERN WORLD, HE IS LITTLE MORE THAN A FEARSOME LEGEND! BUT IN THE ORIENT--IN SEETHING, SMOLDERING, SECRETIVE RED CHINA, MEN KNOW--TO THEIR SORROW--HOW *REAL* THE MANDARIN IS!

MASTER, THIS LOWLY ONE BEGS FORGIVENESS FOR THIS INTERRUPTION! BUT THERE ARE VISITORS OUTSIDE THE CASTLE!

MY UNWORTHY EYES REVEAL THAT THEY ARE FOUR HIGH MILITARY OFFICERS-- EMISSARIES OF THE RED GOVERNMENT!

WHAT!! THEY DARE DISTURB *ME??* THEY DARE COME TO MY CASTLE WITHOUT INVITATION?!! I'LL ERASE THEM FROM THE FACE OF THE EARTH FOR THAT INSOLENCE! I'LL--*NO!* FIRST I'LL HEAR THEIR BLABBING NEWS--*THEN* I'LL ACT ACCORDINGLY!!

THEIR EYES ARE NOT WORTHY OF GAZING UPON MY ALL-SEEING CRYSTAL GLOBE! SO, WITH A GESTURE, I MAKE IT *VANISH!*

AT ANOTHER GESTURE, I LOWER THE DRAWBRIDGE OVER MY IMPASSABLE MOAT!

SEE? THE DRAWBRIDGE IS BEING LOWERED! THAT MEANS WE MAY ENTER!

I WOULD RATHER FACE FIRE-BREATHING DRAGONS THAN STAND IN THE PRESENCE OF THE MANDARIN!

WE HAVE NO CHOICE! OUR COMMUNIST OVERLORDS WILL SLAY US IF WE FAIL IN OUR MISSION!

ONCE WITHIN THE CASTLE'S WALLS, THE AWE-STRICKEN VISITORS ARE CONFRONTED WITH NEW EVIDENCE OF THE MANDARIN'S UNBELIEVABLE POWER...

A PORTION OF THE FLOOR ITSELF IS RISING-- WITH US UPON IT!

THERE IS NO LIMIT TO THE MIRACULOUS FEATS THE MANDARIN CAN PERFORM!!!!

WE ARE BEING BROUGHT INTO THE PRESENCE OF THE MANDARIN!

LET US PRAY HE RECEIVES US WITH FAVOR!

IF WE DISPLEASE HIM, WE SHALL NEVER BE HEARD FROM AGAIN! WHAT POWER ON EARTH COULD EVER RESCUE A PRISONER FROM THE CASTLE OF THE MANDARIN??

2

SECONDS LATER, THE FEARFUL UNIFORMED VISITORS DESCEND, TO FIND THEY ARE FACE TO FACE WITH THE MOST FEARED POTENTATE OF THE EAST...

I HAVE ALLOWED YOU TO DISTURB MY MEDITATIONS! LET ME HEAR THE PURPOSE OF YOUR ERRAND! WHO AMONG YOU IS THE SPOKESMAN?

I AM! I AM GENERAL HO LEE, YOUR EXCELLENCY! AND THESE ARE---

SPARE ME SUCH TRIVIA! YOUR PETTY IDENTITIES DO NOT INTEREST ME! SPEAK!

WE HAVE COME TO ASK YOU TO SHARE YOUR ATOMIC KNOWLEDGE WITH OUR GOVERNMENT! WITH YOUR HELP, WE COULD MENACE THE WORLD WITH NUCLEAR DESTRUCTION!

IF YOU WOULD EVEN CONSENT TO GIVE US THE SECRET OF YOUR POWER RINGS, WE WOULD BE MOST GRATEFUL TO YOU!

WHAT??! YOU DARE ASK ME TO REVEAL MY SECRETS TO YOU??! DO YOU THINK THE MANDARIN CARES TO HELP YOU OR YOUR RED MASTERS? THE MANDARIN HELPS NOBODY! SOON, THE ENTIRE WORLD WILL GROVEL AT MY FEET!

YOU HAVE SIXTY SECONDS TO LEAVE! THE AUDIENCE IS ENDED! GO!

CAN IT BE THAT ONE LONE MAN CAN INSTILL SUCH FEAR IN THE HEARTS OF HIGH OFFICERS OF THE RED CHINESE ARMY?!!

WE CAN DISCUSS THAT LATER--AFTER WE ARE SAFE!! RIGHT NOW BE SILENT--AND RUN!!

MEANWHILE, HALF-A-WORLD AWAY, OTHERS ARE ALSO DISCUSSING THE MYSTERIOUS MANDARIN! AT A HIGH LEVEL MEETING IN THE PENTAGON...

NO, I HAVE NEVER HEARD OF THE MANDARIN! BUT, IF IT IS IMPORTANT TO YOU TO GAIN INFORMATION ABOUT HIM, I'LL BE HAPPY TO DO WHAT I CAN, GENERAL!

WE KNEW WE COULD COUNT ON YOU, IRON MAN! RUMORS FROM OUT OF RED CHINA INDICATE THAT HE IS THE GREATEST SINGLE POWER IN THAT NATION...AND FOR OUR OWN SECURITY, WE MUST LEARN MORE ABOUT HIM!

A SHORT TIME LATER, THE IMPRESSIVE FORM OF IRON MAN, KEPT ALOFT BY HIS TRANSISTOR-POWERED JETS, APPROACHES THE WEAPONS FACTORY OF ANTHONY STARK, IRON MAN'S ALTER EGO!

IF THE MILITARY HIGH COMMAND WANTS ME TO LEAVE FOR RED CHINA IMMEDIATELY, I'D BETTER PUT MY HOUSE IN ORDER AS TONY STARK!

3

THEN, SECRETLY ENTERING HIS PRIVATE SANCTUM BY MEANS OF AN UNDERGROUND PASSAGE, IRON MAN QUICKLY CHANGES INTO HIS OTHER IDENTITY!

I JUST REMEMBERED--I WAS SUPPOSED TO ATTEND AN EMPLOYEES' DINNER TONIGHT, AND MAKE A SPEECH! BUT I'LL HAVE TO BEG OFF!

HOPE THEY WON'T MIND THE BOSS SAYING HE CAN'T ATTEND THEIR DINNER!

ABOUT OUR DINNER TONIGHT, MR. STARK--WE'RE REALLY LOOKING FORWARD TO HAVING YOU AS GUEST OF HONOR, SIR!

I-I'M SORRY, BILL! I'M AFRAID I WON'T BE ABLE TO MAKE IT AFTER ALL! SOMETHING RATHER IMPORTANT HAS COME UP!

THEN, STARK MEETS HIS PRIVATE CHAUFFEUR, HAPPY HOGAN, OUTSIDE OF HIS OFFICE, AS HIS SECRETARY, PEPPER POTTS, EAGERLY APPROACHES...

--SO I'D LIKE YOU TO ATTEND THE DINNER IN MY PLACE, HAPPY!

CAN'T WAIT TILL THE BOSS SEES ME IN MY NEW MAKEUP AND MY NEW HAIRDO!

SURE, THE BOSS CAN'T BE BOTHERED WASTING TIME WITH US POOR STOOGES--SO HE SENDS HIS FLUNKY INSTEAD! THE MEN SURE AIN'T GONNA LIKE THIS!!

JUST MY LUCK! MR. STARK HASN'T EVEN GLANCED MY WAY YET!

NOW HOLD ON, BILL! YOU'RE NOT BEING FAIR TO ME! I WISH I COULD EXPLAIN!!

WHAT'S TO EXPLAIN?? WE GET THE MESSAGE! A BIG SHOT LIKE YOU CAN'T ASSOCIATE WITH THE HIRED HANDS! ALL YOU CARE ABOUT IS DAMES AND DOUGH--

UGH!

WHO DO YOU THINK YOU'RE TALKIN' TO, MISTER?! MR. STARK IS THE BEST BOSS YOU'LL EVER HAVE! TROUBLE IS, HE AIN'T TOUGH ENOUGH WITH GRIPERS LIKE YOU! THIS IS THE ONLY LANGUAGE YOU UNDERSTAND!

HAPPY!!

YOU EVER PULL A STUNT LIKE THAT AGAIN, AND YOU'RE THROUGH HERE--UNDERSTAND? ANY EMPLOYEE CAN TALK TO ME ANY WAY HE WANTS TO--AND IF HE GETS OUT OF LINE, I'LL HANDLE IT...MY OWN WAY!

I APPRECIATE YOUR LOYALTY, YOU BIG CLOWN, BUT WE DON'T SETTLE THINGS WITH OUR FISTS AT MY FACTORY!!

MEN! A GIRL SPENDS ALL DAY AT THE BEAUTY PARLOR GETTING A NEW HAIRDO, AND COVERING HER FRECKLES--BUT DO YOU NOTICE?? NO! I COULD LOOK LIKE AN OLD DISHRAG FOR ALL YOU'D CARE!

PEPPER! FOR HEAVEN'S SAKE!! I DIDN'T EVEN KNOW IT WAS YOU! Y-YOU'RE BEAUTIFUL!

I KINDA LIKED YOU THE OTHER WAY!

4

HOURS LATER, AN UNMARKED JET FLIES A HAZARDOUS ROUTE DEEP INTO THE INTERIOR OF RED CHINA WITH ONE OF THE WORLD'S MOST COLORFUL ADVENTURERS ABOARD...

THIS IS *IT*, IRON MAN! GOOD LUCK, FELLA!

I DON'T KNOW WHO HE REALLY IS, BUT HE SURE HAS *GUTS* TO SPARE!

YEAH! IF I EVER SAW A SUICIDE MISSION--THIS IS *IT*!

SOME RED OBSERVERS ARE SURE TO SEE ME FALL!

I'VE GOT TO SEE TO IT THAT THEY DON'T SEARCH FOR ME WHEN I LAND!

AHHH--A YANKEE-TYPE JET HAS DROPPED A SPY OVER OUR TERRITORY! ARE THEY NAIVE ENOUGH TO THINK WE WOULD NOT *OBSERVE* THAT?!!

SEE WHERE HE FALLS AND WE WILL CAPTURE HIM BEFORE HE CAN BURY HIS CHUTE!

NO! THERE IS NO NEED TO BOTHER! HIS PARACHUTE DID NOT OPEN! HE PLUNGED TO HIS DEATH FROM SO GREAT A HEIGHT!

THE BUNGLING DEMOCRACIES CANNOT EVEN MAKE *CHUTES* THAT WORK CORRECTLY!

BUT THE SMUG OFFICER WOULD SOON CHANGE HIS MIND IF HE COULD SEE THE NEWCOMER WHO HAD FALLEN ON HIS SOIL *NOW*!

THERE! I WAITED TILL THE LAST POSSIBLE SECOND BEFORE APPLYING MY POWER JETS! ANYONE WHO *SAW* ME IS CERTAIN TO THINK I FELL TO MY DEATH HERE IN THE HILLS!

AND THEN, AFTER LONG HOURS OF WALKING THROUGH THE DENSE UNDERBRUSH OF THE WINDING MOUNTAIN TRAILS....

THERE IT IS, JUST WHERE THE C.I.A. SAID IT WOULD BE! THE CASTLE OF THE *MANDARIN*!

5

THEN, BEFORE IRON MAN CAN MAKE ANOTHER MOVE, AN ADVANCE PATROL OF THE MANDARIN'S PRIVATE GUARD ATTACKS HIM FROM BEHIND! BUT THIS IS NO *ORDINARY* FOE THEY HAVE CHALLENGED!

DEATH TO THE ENEMY INTRUDER! UGH!!

QUICKLY! STOP THE IRON-GARBED STRANGER! IF HE GETS PAST US, THE MANDARIN WILL HAVE OUR LIVES!

BUT HOW DO YOU STOP A MAN WITH IRON FISTS, TRAN-SISTOR-POWERED MUSCLES, AND JET-SWIFT SPEED?

I MIGHT HAVE *KNOWN* THE MANDARIN WOULD HAVE SOME OF HIS *OWN* GUARDS STATIONED AROUND HIS CASTLE!

THE ANSWER IS--YOU *DON'T*--UNLESS YOU HAVE FAR MORE POWER AND SKILL THAN THE FIVE SIMPLE SOLDIERS WHO HAVE DARED TO TACKLE ONE OF THE MIGHTIEST HUMAN FIGHTING MACHINES OF ALL TIME!

SWEET DREAMS, LITTLE FRIENDS!

AND NOW FOR THE MANDARIN!

BETTER CHECK MY ENERGY GAUGE AND SEE--UH-OH! THE RESERVE POWER LEVEL IS FALLING! MUST BE A SHORT-CIRCUIT SOMEWHERE!

BUT I'VE NO TIME TO STOP AND FIDDLE WITH IT *NOW*!

IT JUST MEANS I'LL HAVE TO FINISH MY TASK WITHOUT WASTING A MINUTE, AND MAKE MY WAY BACK BEFORE THE POWER RUNS OUT!

BUT, WITHIN A SECRET VIEWING CHAMBER INSIDE THE MIGHTY CASTLE, THE *MANDARIN* HAS OBSERVED EVERY-THING THAT HAS TRANSPIRED...AND HE CHUCKLES SOFTLY AS HE TOUCHES A SENSITIVE DIAL...

SO! IRON MAN HIM-SELF HAS DARED INVADE MY DOMAIN! HOW CONVENIENT OF HIM TO PLACE HIMSELF WITHIN MY GRASP!

ZZZTT!

WHA--?? A RAY-- SHOOTING OUT FROM THE CASTLE WALL!!!

I'M BEING IRRESISTIBLY DRAWN TOWARDS THE FORTRESS BY A FORM OF MAGNETIC ATTRACTION!

6

MINUTES LATER, THE STRANGE RAY DEPOSITS IRON MAN IN A GLOOMY CHAMBER WITHIN THE MYSTERIOUS CASTLE! AND THEN...

THE WALLS-- THEY'RE CLOSING IN!!!

WHATEVER I DO WILL HAVE TO BE DONE FAST!! BUT-- *WHAT??*

THE WALLS ARE SHEER *GRANITE!!* I-I CAN'T MAKE A *DENT!*

WAIT! THAT AIR VENT ABOVE ME-- IF I CAN JUST REACH IT IN TIME--!!

WELCOME, IRON MAN, TO THE STRONGHOLD OF THE *MANDARIN!* I HOPE YOU WILL ENJOY YOUR STAY HERE--OR YOU SHALL NEVER LEAVE ALIVE!

YOU PASSED YOUR FIRST TEST-- MY CLOSING WALLS-- WITH ADMIRABLE SKILL! IT WILL BE A PLEASURE TO DEFEAT A WORTHY ADVERSARY!

NOW, LET ME SEE HOW YOU WITHSTAND THE CHALLENGE OF MY *PARALYSIS RAY!*

LOOK, YOU WEAK APOLOGY FOR GENGHIS KHAN-- IRON MAN CAN TAKE ANYTHING *YOU* CAN DISH OUT, AND LOTS *MORE* BESIDES! MY ULTRA-BEAM CHEST LIGHT CAN DISPEL *ANY* RAY OF LESS THAN COSMIC INTENSITY!

ZZZ ZZZ

I CAN SEE NOW THAT THE WORLD WILL NEVER BE SAFE SO LONG AS A POWER-MAD DESPOT LIKE *YOU* REMAINS FREE! SO I'M GOING TO MAKE SURE THAT YOU CAN NEVER MENACE ANYONE AGAIN--OR I'LL DIE TRYING!

7

THOSE ARE BRAVE WORDS, MAN OF IRON! ESPECIALLY BRAVE FROM ONE WHOSE LIFE IS NEARING ITS FINAL MOMENTS!

TALK IS CHEAP, MISTER! ONCE I GET MY HANDS ON YOU, I'LL--*WHA*--??

HE'S VANISHED! HOW--?? HE MUST HAVE DONE IT WITH *MIRRORS*!

CRASH!

WERE YOU NAIVE ENOUGH TO THINK THAT MERE SPEED AND BRUTE FORCE COULD CATCH THE *MANDARIN*??

WHATEVER IT TAKES, FELLA--YOU CAN BE SURE I'LL FIND A WAY TO *DO* IT!

AND IF YOU'RE TOO TRICKY FOR ME TO GET MY HANDS ON, THEN I'LL CATCH YOU WITH A BLAST OF HIGH-FREQUENCY WAVES! *NOTHING* CAN ESCAPE THEM!

NOTHING PERHAPS-- SAVE THE *HANDS OF THE MANDARIN*!!

CLICK

ZZZZTT

HAVE YOU EVER STOPPED TO THINK WHAT HAPPENS WHEN A HIGH-FREQUENCY WAVE ENCOUNTERS *ANOTHER* SUCH WAVE??

ZZZZ-T

THEY *NULLIFY* EACH OTHER--LIKE *THIS*!

HIS HANDS--RINGS ON EACH FINGER-- THEY MUST EACH REPRESENT A *DIFFERENT* WEAPON-- A DIFFERENT POWER! HE'S EVEN MORE DANGEROUS THAN I THOUGHT!

POW!

8

I'VE GOT TO TURN THE VOLUME DOWN! HE MANAGED TO *AMPLIFY* THE SOUND AND TURN IT BACK AGAINST *ME*!

JUST IN TIME! IT ALMOST *DEAFENED* ME!

AND NOW I'LL--WHA--?? I CAN'T *MOVE*! I'M FROZEN IN MY TRACKS!!

A SIMPLE MATTER TO ACCOMPLISH.... FOR ONE WITH A *PARALYZER* RAY!

THE HANDS OF THE MANDARIN HAVE *TEN FINGERS*-- AND EACH ONE IS A MIGHTY WEAPON IN ITSELF!!

BUT THE MIGHTIEST WEAPON OF *ALL* IS YET TO BE REVEALED! I SHALL *TOY* WITH YOU A WHILE LONGER FIRST!

MEANWHILE, BACK IN THE STATES, PEPPER POTTS DECIDES TO MAKE A PHONE CALL...

IF TONY STARK ISN'T GOING TO TAKE ME TO THE EMPLOYEES' DINNER, I'LL GET ANOTHER ESCORT!

ANYTHING'S BETTER THAN SITTING HOME ALONE!

AND SPEAKING OF "ANYTHING"---

HELLO HAPPY! WHO ARE YOU TAKING TO THE DINNER TONIGHT?

IS IT REALLY *YOU*! YOU'RE FINALLY CALLIN' OLD *HAPPY*??! I *KNEW* MY IRRESISTIBLE CHARM WOULD GETCHA SOONER OR LATER, DOLLFACE! I'LL PICK YOU UP RIGHT AWAY!

THE BIG OX! HE'S GOT ALL THE CHARM OF A RUSTY DOORKNOB! BUT HE'S BETTER THAN NO DATE AT *ALL*-- I THINK!

WHEREVER THE BOSS IS NOW, I HOPE HE *STAYS* THERE A WHILE! WITHOUT *HIM* TO CRAMP MY STYLE, I'M GONNA REALLY *OPERATE*!

9

BUT HAPPY HOGAN'S FRIVOLOUS WORDS WOULD TURN TO ASHES IN HIS MOUTH IF HE COULD SUSPECT THE TRUE PLIGHT OF HIS MISSING BOSS RIGHT NOW---

YOU ARE A POWERFUL FOE, IRON MAN! NEVER HAS AN ENEMY SHAKEN OFF THE EFFECTS OF MY PARALYSIS RAY IN SO SHORT A TIME!

SKIP THE COMPLIMENTS, CHUM! I KNOW I'M NOT WINNING ANY POPULARITY CONTESTS IN YOUR LEAGUE!

IF YOU DIDN'T TRY TO FINISH ME OFF WHILE I COULDN'T MOVE, IT'S ONLY BECAUSE YOU HAVE SOMETHING WORSE IN STORE FOR ME NOW! SO SKIP THE SWEET-TALK AND LET'S GET ON WITH IT!

YOU DO NOT FOOL ME! YOUR SHARP TONGUE CANNOT HIDE THE FEAR WHICH MUST BE GNAWING AT YOUR HEART! THERE! WITH ONE GESTURE I ELECTRIFY THE WALLS OF THIS CHAMBER, SO THAT YOU CANNOT ESCAPE! AND NOW--

NOW YOU WILL LEARN WHAT I HAVE BEEN SAVING YOU FOR!! IT IS MY FAVORITE PASTIME-- AND A MOST DEADLY PASTIME!

AND SO, IRON MAN, PREPARE TO MEET YOUR FINISH AT THE HANDS OF THE GREATEST KARATE MASTER THE WORLD HAS EVER KNOWN!

HE'S SPLINTERED THAT IRON BAR LIKE A TOOTHPICK-- WITH A SINGLE KARATE BLOW!

10

I SHALL ENJOY THE LUXURY OF PUMMELING YOU WITH MY MIGHTY FISTS--TO SOFTEN YOU UP FOR THE FINAL DEFEAT!

GOT TO KEEP OUT OF THE REACH OF HIS HANDS! MY IRON SUIT WILL FURNISH ALMOST NO PROTECTION AGAINST KARATE BLOWS LIKE *HIS!*

WHERE IS THE MUCH-VAUNTED POWER OF IRON MAN ?? SEE HOW EASILY I CAN COUNTER YOUR HARM-LESS BLOW, AND THEN PUSH YOUR FIST AWAY!

ALSO, MY TRANSISTOR POWER IS GETTING WEAKER EACH SECOND! I'VE GOT TO SAVE IT! CAN'T USE IT UP IN NEEDLESS FENCING-- OWWW!

MY TRANSISTORS SHOULDN'T BE *SO* WEAK--UNLESS--*AHH--THAT'S* IT! WHILE I WAS PARALYZED, *HE* TAMPERED WITH THEM, SO THAT I'D THINK HIM STRONGER THAN HE REALLY IS!!

HAH! I SEE YOU TURN-- LOOKING FOR A PLACE TO RUN! BUT THERE IS NO ESCAPE!

ESCAPE MY *FOOT!* I'M JUST TRYIN' TO THINK OF A *PLAN!*

NOT ONLY DOES THE MANDARIN POSSESS SUPERHUMAN STRENGTH, BUT HE'S THE *BRAINIEST* ENEMY I'VE EVER FACED! TONY, OLD BOY, MAYBE YOU SHOULD HAVE STUCK TO YOUR FACTORY IN THE STATES!

HE'S GETTING READY TO FINISH ME OFF WITH A FINAL KARATE BLOW! WELL, ONE THING'S SURE--IF I CASH IN MY CHIPS, THERE'LL BE NO CHRISTMAS BONUS THIS YEAR FOR POOR PEPPER AND HAPPY!

I'VE TOYED WITH YOU LONG ENOUGH, IRON MAN! NOW THE MANDARIN SHALL STRIKE !!

11

SUDDENLY, THE COSTUMED CRUSADER SEEMS TO HAVE LOST HIS REASON, AS HE FRANTICALLY STUDIES THE BUILT-IN SLIDE-RULE CALCULATOR IN HIS ARM...

--AT AN ANGLE OF 38 DEGREES, THE VELOCITY DECREASES BY FIFTY-TWO PERCENT...

IT'S MY ONLY CHANCE! I'VE GOT TO TRY IT! MY TRANSISTORS ARE TOO WEAK FOR ANYTHING ELSE!

THE MANDARIN IS SO AMUSED BY IRON MAN'S APPARENT MOOD OF MADNESS THAT HE DELAYS HIS BLOW LONG ENOUGH TO MOCK THE AMERICAN, BUT THEN...

WEAK AMERICAN! SO GREAT IS YOUR FEAR THAT IT DROVE YOU MAD!

BUT EVEN MADNESS CANNOT SAVE YOU NOW!

HERE COMES THE BLOW! I'D BETTER BE RIGHT!

THWUP!

ARGGHHH!

WHO'S LAUGHING NOW, SUNNY JIM?

HE'S OUT! THE PAIN WAS TOO MUCH FOR HIM!

I CAN TURN OFF THE JUICE FROM THE WALLS NOW!

IT WAS A LONG CHANCE, BUT IT WORKED! HE THOUGHT I HAD FLIPPED MY WIG WHEN I USED MY CALCULATOR, BUT ACTUALLY I WAS FIGURING EXACTLY WHAT WAY TO TURN MY BODY, INSURING THAT HIS HAND WOULD STRIKE IT AT THE WRONG ANGLE!

TOO BAD I CAN'T STAY AROUND LONG ENOUGH TO FINISH OFF THIS CASTLE AND END THE MANDARIN'S POWER-- BUT MY PICKUP PLANE SHOULD BE OVERHEAD RIGHT NOW-- AND IF I'M NOT THERE, HE WON'T WAIT!

12

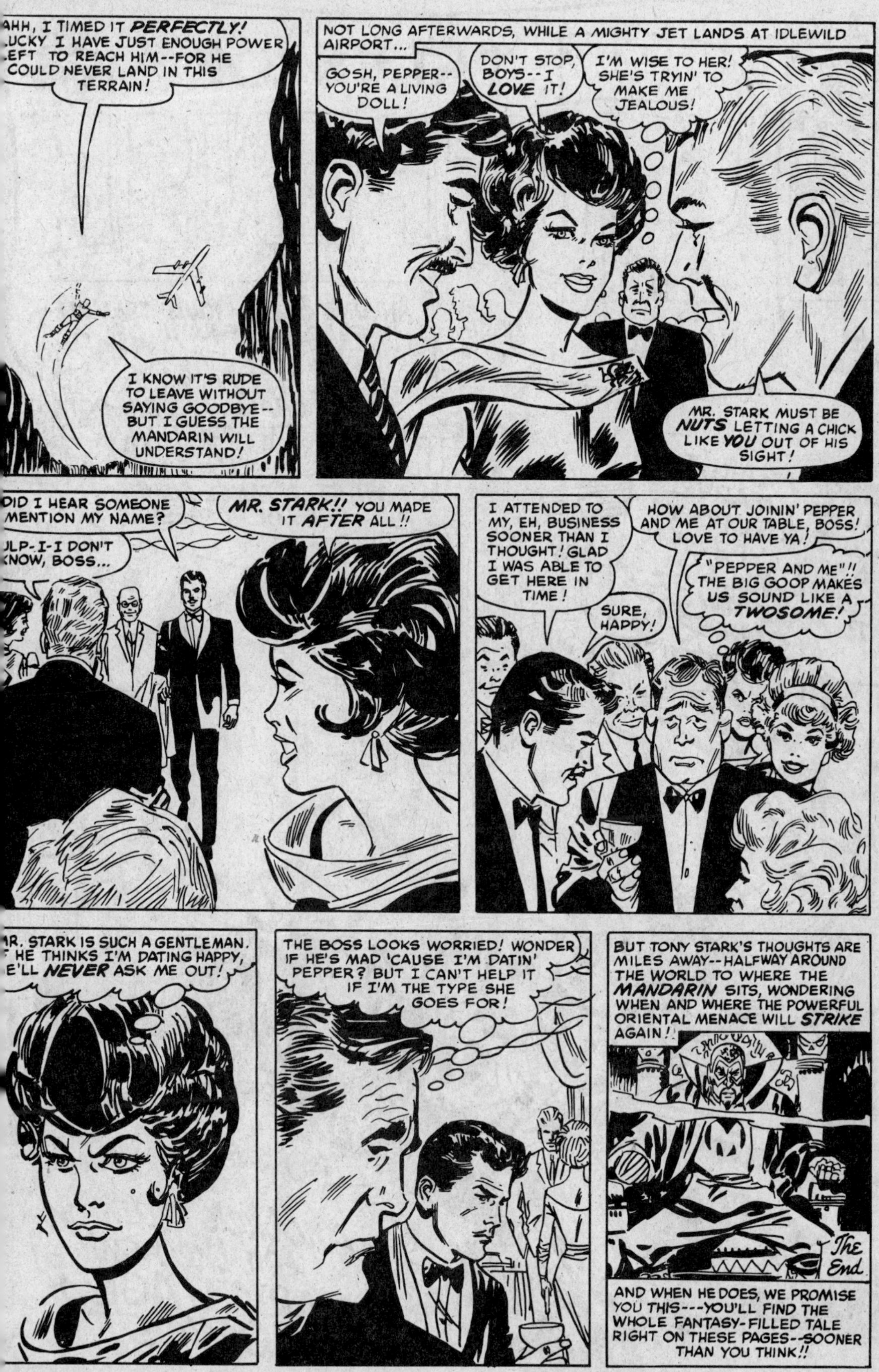
AHH, I TIMED IT PERFECTLY! LUCKY I HAVE JUST ENOUGH POWER LEFT TO REACH HIM--FOR HE COULD NEVER LAND IN THIS TERRAIN!
I KNOW IT'S RUDE TO LEAVE WITHOUT SAYING GOODBYE--BUT I GUESS THE MANDARIN WILL UNDERSTAND!
NOT LONG AFTERWARDS, WHILE A MIGHTY JET LANDS AT IDLEWILD AIRPORT...
GOSH, PEPPER--YOU'RE A LIVING DOLL!
DON'T STOP, BOYS--I LOVE IT!
I'M WISE TO HER! SHE'S TRYIN' TO MAKE ME JEALOUS!
MR. STARK MUST BE NUTS LETTING A CHICK LIKE YOU OUT OF HIS SIGHT!
DID I HEAR SOMEONE MENTION MY NAME?
GULP-I-I DON'T KNOW, BOSS...
MR. STARK!! YOU MADE IT AFTER ALL!!
I ATTENDED TO MY, EH, BUSINESS SOONER THAN I THOUGHT! GLAD I WAS ABLE TO GET HERE IN TIME!
HOW ABOUT JOININ' PEPPER AND ME AT OUR TABLE, BOSS! LOVE TO HAVE YA!
SURE, HAPPY!
"PEPPER AND ME"!! THE BIG GOOP MAKES US SOUND LIKE A TWOSOME!
MR. STARK IS SUCH A GENTLEMAN. IF HE THINKS I'M DATING HAPPY, HE'LL NEVER ASK ME OUT!
THE BOSS LOOKS WORRIED! WONDER IF HE'S MAD 'CAUSE I'M DATIN' PEPPER? BUT I CAN'T HELP IT IF I'M THE TYPE SHE GOES FOR!
BUT TONY STARK'S THOUGHTS ARE MILES AWAY--HALFWAY AROUND THE WORLD TO WHERE THE MANDARIN SITS, WONDERING WHEN AND WHERE THE POWERFUL ORIENTAL MENACE WILL STRIKE AGAIN!
The End
AND WHEN HE DOES, WE PROMISE YOU THIS---YOU'LL FIND THE WHOLE FANTASY-FILLED TALE RIGHT ON THESE PAGES--SOONER THAN YOU THINK!!

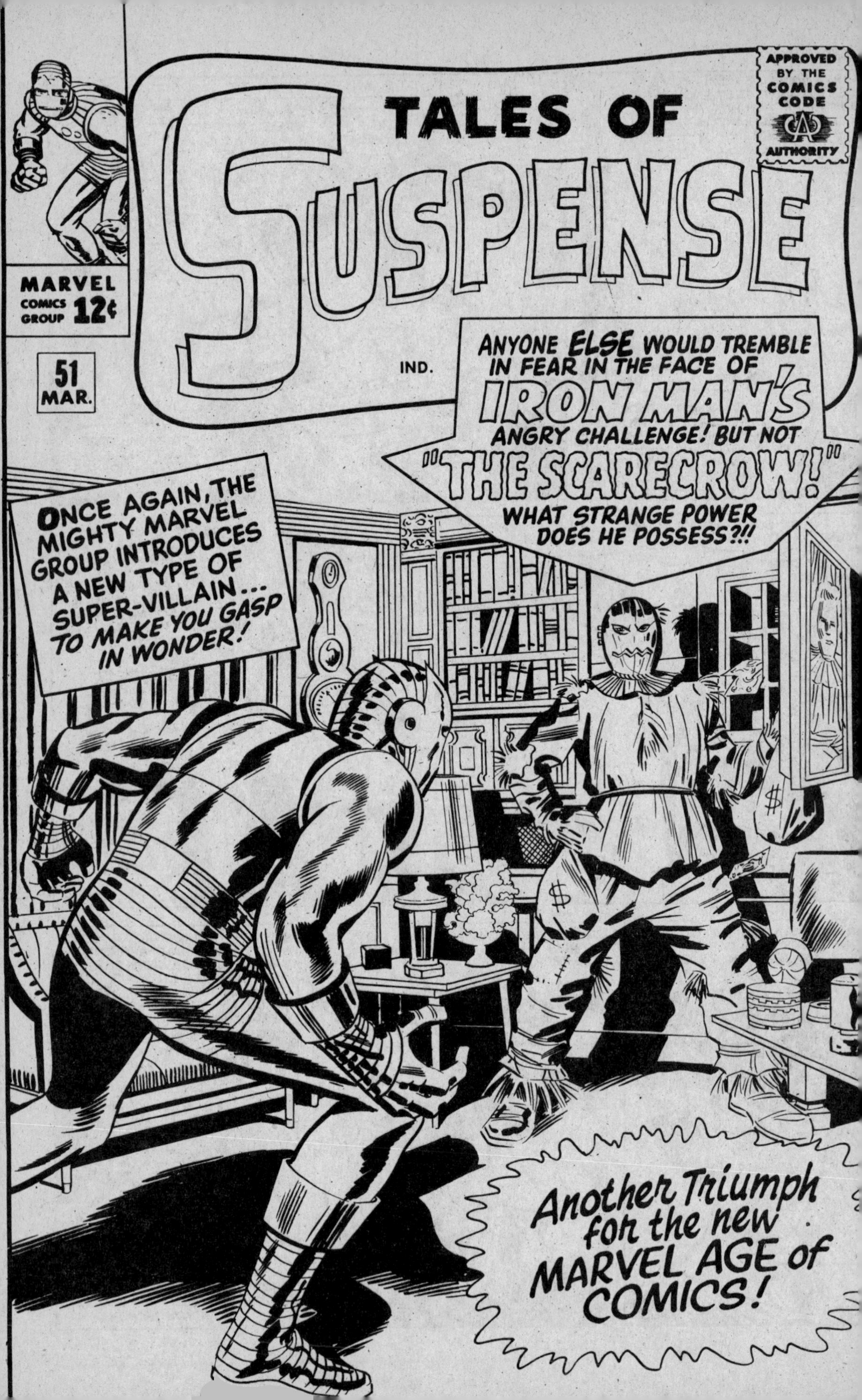
APPROVED BY THE COMICS CODE AUTHORITY
TALES OF SUSPENSE
MARVEL COMICS GROUP 12¢
51 MAR.
IND.
ANYONE ELSE WOULD TREMBLE IN FEAR IN THE FACE OF IRON MAN'S ANGRY CHALLENGE! BUT NOT "THE SCARECROW!" WHAT STRANGE POWER DOES HE POSSESS?!!
ONCE AGAIN, THE MIGHTY MARVEL GROUP INTRODUCES A NEW TYPE OF SUPER-VILLAIN... SUPER-VILLAIN... TO MAKE YOU GASP IN WONDER!
Another Triumph for the new MARVEL AGE of COMICS!

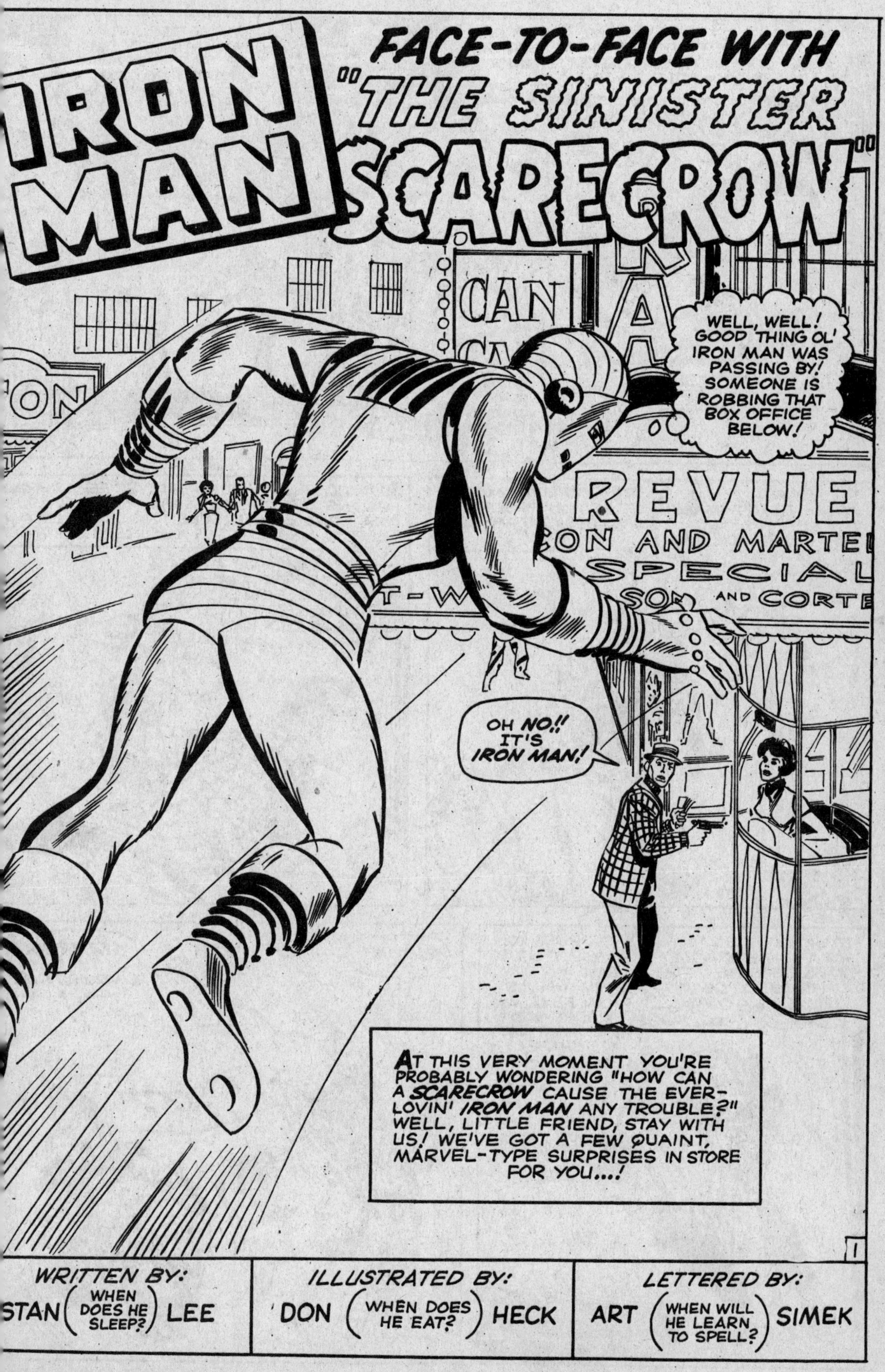

IRON MAN
FACE-TO-FACE WITH "THE SINISTER SCARECROW"
WELL, WELL! GOOD THING OL' IRON MAN WAS PASSING BY! SOMEONE IS ROBBING THAT BOX OFFICE BELOW!
REVUE
OH NO!! IT'S IRON MAN!
AT THIS VERY MOMENT YOU'RE PROBABLY WONDERING "HOW CAN A SCARECROW CAUSE THE EVER-LOVIN' IRON MAN ANY TROUBLE?" WELL, LITTLE FRIEND, STAY WITH US! WE'VE GOT A FEW QUAINT, MARVEL-TYPE SURPRISES IN STORE FOR YOU...!
1
WRITTEN BY: STAN (WHEN DOES HE SLEEP?) LEE
ILLUSTRATED BY: DON (WHEN DOES HE EAT?) HECK
LETTERED BY: ART (WHEN WILL HE LEARN TO SPELL?) SIMEK

YOU WON'T GET AWAY FROM ME BY RUNNING INTO THE *THEATER*, FELLA! WHERE *YOU* GO, *I* CAN GO--AND A *LOT FASTER*, THANKS TO MY LITTLE OL' JETS!

BUT I BETTER HOLD DOWN MY SPEED! THAT JOKER CAN'T GET AWAY --AND IF I GO *TOO* FAST, I MAY BOWL AN INNOCENT BYSTANDER OVER!

I'LL FLY *ABOVE* HIM, WHERE I CAN'T SMASH INTO ANYBODY, AND THEN I'LL POUNCE DOWN ON HIM!

TRYING TO RUN UP ON THE STAGE WON'T HELP YOU, PAL! THIS ISN'T AMATEUR NIGHT!

*S*UDDENLY, THE FRANTIC FUGITIVE VEERS SHARPLY RUNNING PAST THE ORCHESTRA PIT! AND, AS HE DOES SO, THE ENTERTAINER NAMED THE UNCANN' UMBERTO, WHOSE ACT HE HAS INTERRUPTED, GET AN IDEA!

SAY! WHAT A GREAT *PUBLICITY* BREAK IT WOULD BE FOR ME IF *I* CAN CATCH THAT PUNK BEFORE *IRON MAN* GETS HIM!

IT SHOULDN'T BE TOUGH FOR A TRAINED *CONTORTIONIST* LIKE ME! AFTER SLIPPIN' OUT OF *CHAINS*, THIS'LL BE A *CINCH*!

I'LL JUST ROLL MYSELF INTO A BALL AND BOWL HIM OVER! I CAN BEND MY BODY INTO ALMOST *ANY* SHAPE!

OOOF!

STRRRRIKE THREE! YOU'RE *OUT!*

A FEW SECONDS LATER...

YOU CAN FINISH YOUR ACT, UMBERTO! I'LL HAUL HIM OFF TO JAIL NOW! THAT WAS A PRETTY TRICKY MANEUVER OF YOURS!

SEEING HOW YOU OPERATE, I'M MIGHTY GLAD YOU'RE ON THE SIDE OF THE *LAW*, PAL!

YEAH, I GUESS A GUY LIKE ME *WOULD* MAKE A MIGHTY TOUGH OPPONENT!

AS A MATTER OF FACT, I SUDDENLY REALIZE I GAINED A LOT *MORE* OUT OF THIS THAN JUST SOME FAST PUBLICITY!! YOU JUST HANDED ME THE *INSPIRATION* OF A LIFETIME!

WHY SHOULD A GUY LIKE *ME* KNOCK MYSELF OUT ENTERTAINING RUBES IN CRUMMY VAUDEVILLE SHOWS WHEN I COULD MAKE A FORTUNE BY USING MY TALENT IN *OTHER* WAYS?

I COULD BECOME THE WORLD'S BEST *BURGLAR*! WITH MY RUBBERY BODY AND MY KNOWLEDGE OF HOW TO BREAK LOCKS AND CHAINS, NOTHING COULD STOP ME!

INSTEAD OF BEING THE EXTRA ADDED ATTRACTION ON A VAUDEVILLE BILL, I'LL BE THE *STAR* OF THE UNDERWORLD!

MIGHT AS WELL GET MYSELF SOME SORT OF *DISGUISE*, TOO! IN CASE ANYONE *SEES* ME, THEY WON'T KNOW WHO I REALLY *AM*!

SAY! THERE'S JUST THE THING! MY BODY IS ALMOST AS FLEXIBLE AS A SCARECROW'S ANYWAY!

GOOD THING THE STREET'S DARK AND LONELY AT THIS HOUR! NOW, I'VE JUST GOT ONE *MORE* LITTLE THING TO DO!

"THORNTON AND HIS TRAINED CROWS" HAVE BEEN ON THE SAME BILL WITH ME FOR MONTHS...

...BUT THE TIME HAS COME WHEN THOSE CROWS WILL *DO* ME A LOT MORE GOOD THAN THORNTON!

NO SIMPLE DOOR LOCK CAN STOP THE GREATEST ESCAPE ARTIST OF OUR TIME! LUCKY THE BIRDS HAVE SEEN ME BEFORE-- THEY *TRUST* ME!

THORNTON'S AN OLD MAN! HE WAS GONNA RETIRE AFTER THIS BOOKING ANYWAY! SO HE WON'T MISS THE BIRDS!

NOW TO GET OUT OF HERE BEFORE HE WAKES UP!

3

REACHING HIS OWN APARTMENT, THE UNCANNY UMBERTO PUTS HIS NEW-FOUND "PARTNERS" THROUGH THEIR PACES!

PERFECT! YOU LITTLE CRITTERS ARE JUST WHAT I **NEED!** YOU UNDERSTAND MY HAND MOTIONS AND MY TONE OF VOICE-- AND YOU CAN GO PLACES WHERE I CAN'T!

NOW LET'S FIND US A GOOD JOB TO PULL! SOMETHING WORTHY OF OUR LITTLE TEAM!

HEY! LOOK, HERE'S A PICTURE OF **ANTHONY STARK**, THE MILLIONAIRE PLAYBOY, OUT WITH A COUPLE OF FILM STARS!

A SWINGER LIKE **HIM** HAS A DATE ALMOST EVERY NIGHT-- WHICH MEANS HIS APARTMENT IS **EMPTY** MOST OF THE TIME! HMMM...

AND, SPEAKING OF TONY STARK, LET'S TURN OUR ATTENTION NOW TO HIS MAIN RECEPTION ROOM IN HIS FLUSHING, LONG ISLAND FACTORY WHERE WE FIND...

YOU MAY TELL MR. STARK THAT VERONICA VOGUE IS HERE TO SEE HIM, MY GOOD WOMAN!

SORRY, MISS VOGUE, HE'S OUT OF TOWN FOR THE WEEK!

WHAT? THAT'S **IMPOSSIBLE!** WE HAD A **DATE** TONIGHT!

NOBODY STANDS UP VERONICA VOGUE!! ARE YOU SURE YOU'RE TELLING THE **TRUTH**, YOU LITTLE **SNIP**??!

OH, YES INDEED! I'M AFRAID MR STARK FORGOT ALL **ABOUT** YOUR DATE! TSK TSK-- I'M **SO** SORRY.

WELL! IT'LL BE A COLD DAY IN JUNE BEFORE HE GETS ANOTHER DATE WITH **ME!** GOOD**BYE!**

IT **WORKED!** DON'T SLAM THE DOOR ON YOUR WAY OUT, "MY GOOD WOMAN"!!

A FEW MINUTES LATER...

PEPPER, DID A CERTAIN GORGEOUS, WILLOWY BLONDE CALL TO SEE ME YET?

OH, NO SIR! THERE HAVE BEEN NO BLONDES HERE ALL AFTERNOON!

THAT SERVES THAT SNOOTY VERONICA VOGUE RIGHT!

ANYWAY, I DIDN'T REALLY TELL A LIE! I COULD TELL BY THE DARK PARTING IN HER HAIR THAT SHE REALLY **ISN'T** A BLONDE!

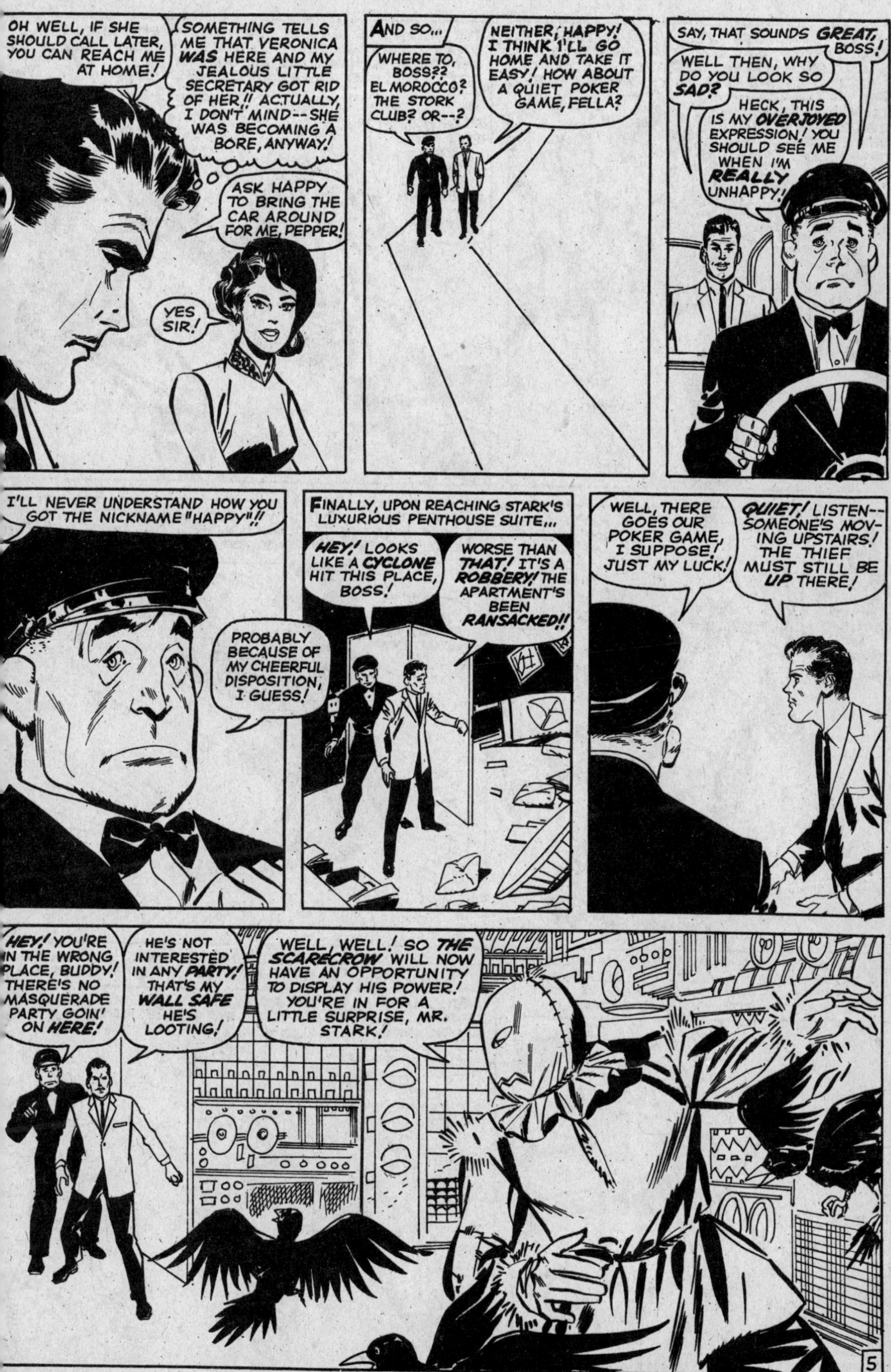
OH WELL, IF SHE SHOULD CALL LATER, YOU CAN REACH ME AT HOME!
SOMETHING TELLS ME THAT VERONICA WAS HERE AND MY JEALOUS LITTLE SECRETARY GOT RID OF HER!! ACTUALLY, I DON'T MIND--SHE WAS BECOMING A BORE, ANYWAY!
ASK HAPPY TO BRING THE CAR AROUND FOR ME, PEPPER!
YES SIR!
AND SO...
WHERE TO, BOSS?? EL MOROCCO? THE STORK CLUB? OR--?
NEITHER, HAPPY! I THINK I'LL GO HOME AND TAKE IT EASY! HOW ABOUT A QUIET POKER GAME, FELLA?
SAY, THAT SOUNDS GREAT, BOSS!
WELL THEN, WHY DO YOU LOOK SO SAD?
HECK, THIS IS MY OVERJOYED EXPRESSION! YOU SHOULD SEE ME WHEN I'M REALLY UNHAPPY!
I'LL NEVER UNDERSTAND HOW YOU GOT THE NICKNAME "HAPPY"!!
PROBABLY BECAUSE OF MY CHEERFUL DISPOSITION, I GUESS!
FINALLY, UPON REACHING STARK'S LUXURIOUS PENTHOUSE SUITE...
HEY! LOOKS LIKE A CYCLONE HIT THIS PLACE, BOSS!
WORSE THAN THAT! IT'S A ROBBERY! THE APARTMENT'S BEEN RANSACKED!!
WELL, THERE GOES OUR POKER GAME, I SUPPOSE! JUST MY LUCK!
QUIET! LISTEN--SOMEONE'S MOVING UPSTAIRS! THE THIEF MUST STILL BE UP THERE!
HEY! YOU'RE IN THE WRONG PLACE, BUDDY! THERE'S NO MASQUERADE PARTY GOIN' ON HERE!
HE'S NOT INTERESTED IN ANY PARTY! THAT'S MY WALL SAFE HE'S LOOTING!
WELL, WELL! SO THE SCARECROW WILL NOW HAVE AN OPPORTUNITY TO DISPLAY HIS POWER! YOU'RE IN FOR A LITTLE SURPRISE, MR. STARK!
5

STAND ASIDE, BOSS! I'LL TAKE CARE OF THAT RUNT! I'LL SHOW HIM HOW I USED TO DO IT IN THE RING!

CAREFUL, HAPPY! REMEMBER, YOU LOST MORE FIGHTS THAN YOU WON!

SO YOU CALL ME A RUNT, DO YOU?? YOU'LL LIVE TO REGRET THAT!

THE ONLY REASON I LOST SO MANY FIGHTS WHEN I WAS A BOXER IS BECAUSE I WAS TOO SOFT-HEARTED TO WANNA HURT ANYONE! BUT I DON'T FEEL THAT WAY ABOUT CROOKS--SEE?

AH, BUT THE SCARECROW IS NO MERE CROOK! YOU'RE ABOUT TO BE BEATEN BY A MASTER!

HEY! HOLD STILL! STOP SQUIRMIN'! WHA--?? HOW'D YOU GET UP THERE??

YOU'VE SEEN NOTHING YET, MY MUSCLE-BOUND FRIEND! NOW WATCH CLOSELY...

I'VE SPENT MOST OF MY ADULT LIFE KEEPING MY BODY IN PERFECT CONDITION FOR THE WORK I USED TO DO! IT'S CHILD'S PLAY FOR ONE AS AGILE AS THE SCARECROW TO TOSS YOU AROUND LIKE A SACK OF POTATOES!

THIS IS EXTREMELY MORTIFYIN'!!

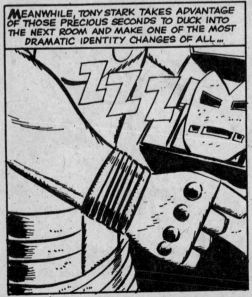

MEANWHILE, TONY STARK TAKES ADVANTAGE OF THOSE PRECIOUS SECONDS TO DUCK INTO THE NEXT ROOM AND MAKE ONE OF THE MOST DRAMATIC IDENTITY CHANGES OF ALL...

ALL RIGHT, SCARECROW! FUN TIME'S OVER! DO YOU GIVE UP NOW, OR DO YOU WANT TO BE STOPPED THE HARD WAY??

IRON MAN! I HEARD THAT STARK KEPT YOU AROUND AS A BODYGUARD!

BUT YOU DON'T SCARE ME EITHER! THE SCARECROW IS FAR MORE DANGEROUS THAN YOU SUSPECT!

DANGEROUS, EH? THEN WHY DON'T YOU STAND STILL AND PROVE IT?

JUST FOLLOW ME, MY OVERCONFIDENT OPPONENT -- I'LL PROVE IT IN MY OWN INCOMPARABLE WAY!

BIG DEAL! YOU DON'T THINK A LOCKED DOOR WILL STOP IRON MAN, DO YOU?

SLAM!

AND I HOPE YOU'LL FORGIVE ME IF I DON'T STAY THERE AND WAIT FOR YOUR REPLY!

CRASH!

SUDDENLY, AS IRON MAN SMASHES INTO THE OTHER ROOM, A THICK, ENTANGLING DRAPERY IS DROPPED OVER HIS HEAD...

WHA--??

YOU SEE? YOU FAILED TO TAKE MY TRAINED CROWS INTO ACCOUNT! SEE HOW OBEDIENTLY THEY FOLLOW MY WHISPERED ORDERS!

I CAN FEEL THEM WRAPPING THE DRAPERY SASH CORD AROUND ME!

IT'S INCREDIBLE! THEY'RE PULLING IT TAUT!

TEMPORARILY OFF-BALANCE -- UNABLE TO SEE -- THE POWERFUL IRON MAN LOSES HIS FOOTING AND...

STILL THINK YOU CAN BEAT THE SCARECROW???

THUMP!

BUT MERE CLOTH DRAPERIES AND A CORD SASH CANNOT HOLD THE MIGHTY MAN OF IRON FOR LONG...

AND NOW, SCARECROW -- YOU'LL START LAUGHING OUT OF THE OTHER SIDE OF YOUR MOUTH!

7

HE'S *GONE!* WAIT-- THE CROWS ARE FLYING OUT THE WINDOW!

THAT MUST BE WHERE HE WENT!

BUT WHEREVER *HE* CAN GO-- *IRON MAN* CAN FOLLOW! HE CAN'T HAVE GOTTEN FAR!

BUT, OUR HERO IS MORE CORRECT THAN HE SUSPECTS-- THE SCARECROW DIDN'T GO FAR AT *ALL!* IN FACT, HE DIDN'T EVEN LEAVE!

IT WAS *CHILD'S PLAY* TO OUT-WIT THAT OVERRATED FOOL!

NOW I CAN RIFLE TONY STARK'S SAFE AT MY LEISURE, WHILE HIS WITLESS BODYGUARD WASTES HIS TIME SEARCHING THE CITY FOR ME!

BUT, IN HIS EXUBERENCE, THE SCARECROW HAS FORGOTTEN ABOUT HAPPY HOGAN WHO RE-GAINS CONSCIOUSNESS WITH AN ACHING HEAD AND AN ANGRY HEART!

OHHH, MY ACHIN' DOME!

HEY! THAT RAT FINK IS STILL *HERE!*

HOLD IT, PUNK! YOU TOOK ME BY SURPRISE THE FIRST TIME, BUT *NOW* I'VE GOT YA!

BAH! I'VE GOT WHAT I WANT NOW-- I CANNOT WASTE MY SKILL ON EVERY LOUD-MOUTHED BUFFOON I MEET!

WOW! I NEVER SAW ANY-ONE MOVE SO *FAST!* ALL I GOT FOR MY TROUBLE IS A HUNK OF *CLOTH!*

HOLY SMOKE! I DON'T KNOW HOW HE GOT DOWN THERE-- BUT I SURE AIN'T GONNA TRY IT!

HE DOESN'T SUSPECT THAT SOME OF MY CROWS WERE ABLE TO SUPPORT MY WEIGHT JUST ENOUGH TO BREAK MY FALL!

MEANWHILE, THE OTHER THREE CROWS WHICH IRON MAN HAS BEEN FOLLOWING, SUDDENLY SEPARATE, AS THOUGH AT A PREARRANGED SIGNAL...

LOOKS LIKE I'M REALLY STYMIED NOW! I CAN'T FOLLOW IN THREE DIFFERENT DIRECTIONS!

AND, AS IRON MAN RETURNS TO STARK'S APARTMENT IN DEFEAT...

MMMM, I GOT A BETTER HAUL THAN EXPECTED! HERE ARE THE PLANS FOR SOME NEW, TRANSISTORIZED WEAPONS STARK IS DESIGNING FOR THE DEFENSE DEPART- MENT!

A MILLIONAIRE LIKE STARK WILL PAY A *FORTUNE* TO KEEP THESE FROM FALLING INTO THE HANDS OF THE COMMIES! AND *I'M* JUST THE GUY TO *TAKE* THAT FORTUNE FROM HIM!

AT MY COMMAND, LITTLE SLAVES -- BRING ME THE TELEPHONE! *NOW!*

WHILE BACK AT STARK'S APART- MENT...

TOO BAD THE SCARECROW GOT AWAY FROM IRON MAN, HAPPY! I IMAGINE MY ARMORED FRIEND IS STILL SEARCH- ING FOR HIM, EH?

YEAH, BOSS! OH, THERE'S THE PHONE!

RINNNG!

YES, THIS IS ANTHONY STARK! WHO--? THE *SCARECROW?!!* YOU WANT ME TO MEET YOU? TO BUY BACK MY STOLEN PLANS ?!!

YOU CAN'T *GO,* BOSS! YOUR LIFE WON'T BE WORTH A PLUGGED NICKLE IF HE GETS A HOLD OF YOU AGAIN!

I'M NO HERO, HAPPY! YOU REPORT BACK TO THE OFFICE! I'LL ALERT *IRON MAN* -- IF I CAN FIND HIM!

AND THEN...

NOW THAT HAPPY'S GONE, I CAN *REALLY* GO INTO ACTION! THE FIRST THING TO DO IS PUT A LITTLE GADGET OF MINE INTO THIS BRIEFCASE! I'LL PROVE TO THE SCARECROW THAT HE'S NOT AS CLEVER AS HE THINKS!

...FOR THIS SIMPLE LITTLE TRANSISTOR- IZED GADGET WILL BRING ABOUT HIS DOWNFALL!

WHAT *IS* THIS ODD- LOOKING DEVICE? WE'LL LEARN IN DUE TIME...

A SHORT TIME LATER...

THIS IS WHERE HE TOLD ME TO MEET HIM! I DARE NOT ARRIVE AS *IRON MAN,* FOR IT MIGHT FRIGHTEN HIM AWAY! SO TONY STARK HIMSELF WILL HAVE TO PLAY THIS HAND -- FOR BETTER OR WORSE!

9

SECONDS LATER, THE STARTLING FIGURE OF THE **SCARECROW** DARTS OUT OF THE SHADOWS, AND...

GIVE ME THAT BRIEF-CASE, YOU UNSUSPECTING FOOL!

THIS IS ONLY THE *FIRST* PAYMENT I'LL DEMAND BEFORE YOU GET YOUR PLANS BACK!!

AND NOW, MY LITTLE PETS WILL ENTERTAIN YOU WHILE I RELUCTANTLY TAKE MY LEAVE!

THE CROWS--THEY'RE ATTACKING ME! HAVE TO BEAT THEM OFF.

I'D BE INSANE TO REMAIN IN AMERICA AFTER STEALING THESE PLANS!

INSTEAD, I'LL GO SOME-WHERE WHERE I'LL BE SAFE!

LEAPING ONTO A WAITING MOTOR-BOAT, THE SCARECROW CALLS HIS CROWS TO HIM, AND THEN...

AT LAST! NOW IT'S TIME FOR *IRON MAN* TO APPEAR--AND DO WHAT TONY STARK CAN'T HOPE TO DO ALONE!

OF ALL THE FOES I'VE EVER FACED, THERE HAVE BEEN *NONE* WHO I'VE BEEN SO *ANXIOUS* TO MEET UP WITH AGAIN--TO GET MY HANDS ON!

SOON I'LL BE SAFE FOREVER--IN A LAND WHERE ALL ENEMIES OF AMERICA ARE WELCOMED--A LAND WHERE THEY WILL RESPECT A MAN OF MY UNUSUAL TALENTS...

BEFORE NIGHT FALLS I'LL BE AN HONORED VISITOR ON THE ISLAND OF *CUBA!*

AND THERE'S THE CUBAN GUNBOAT *NOW* WHICH I PLANNED TO RENDEZVOUS WITH! IT WILL PROTECT ME FROM ANY PURSUIT.

AND SO, THE COSTUMED TRAITOR BOARDS THE CUBAN GUNBOAT, AND...

THESE ARE THE PLANS FOR THE NEW AMERICAN WEAPONS WHICH I PROMISED YOU!

GOOD! THE BEARDED ONE WILL PAY HANDSOMELY FOR THEM! AND NOW, WE MUST LEAVE THESE WATERS!

IT WILL GO HARD WITH US IF ANY YANKEE DESTROYERS FIND US VIOLATING THEIR WATERS! LET US HURRY!

BUT THEN, A STARTLING THING OCCURS...

WHAT MADNESS IS THIS?? THE CASE IS FLYING OUT OF MY HANDS!!

AND WHY SHOULDN'T IT?? YOU HAVE NO RIGHT TO IT! IT BELONGS TO AMERICA!

MY DEVICE WORKED PERFECTLY! I KNEW MY TRANSISTOR MAGNET WOULD ATTRACT IT AT THE PROPER TIME!

IRON MAN!

ATTACK HIM, MY COMRADES! NO REWARD WILL BE TOO GREAT FOR THE MAN WHO DESTROYS ONE OF THE YANKEES' MOST POWERFUL DEFENDERS!

BUT OUR BULLETS BOUNCE HARMLESSLY OFF HIS ARMOR!

LUCKY FOR ME THEY'RE USING ONLY SMALL ARMS FIRE! I WOULDN'T WANT TO BE FACING A MACHINE GUN LIKE THIS!

AND NOW THAT YOU'VE ALL GOTTEN THAT OUT OF YOUR SYSTEMS...

TO MY SIDE, COMRADES! DEATH TO IRON MAN!

WHY WAIT FOR THEM TO JOIN YOU?? HERE, I'LL GET YOU ALL TOGETHER IN A MUCH FASTER WAY!

HELLLLLPPP!

11

AND NOW, *SCARECROW*, DON'T THINK I'VE FORGOTTEN YOU! I WAS JUST SAVING *YOU* FOR LAST!

NO--*NO! DON'T!* YOU'VE GOT ME ALL *WRONG!* I-I'M REALLY ON *YOUR* SIDE! I WAS JUST TRYING TO *TRICK* THE REDS--THAT'S ALL!

OF *COURSE* YOU WERE, PAL! I WOULDN'T DOUBT YOU FOR A *MINUTE!*

TO SHOW HOW I BELIEVE YOU, I'LL JUST TOSS YOU IN FOR A SWIM, SO YOU WON'T GET TOO BORED WHILE I TAKE CARE OF A LITTLE UNFINISHED BUSINESS!

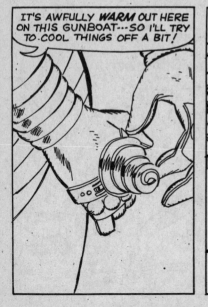

IT'S AWFULLY *WARM* OUT HERE ON THIS GUNBOAT---SO I'LL TRY TO COOL THINGS OFF A BIT!

THERE! I'LL DRILL A FEW AIR HOLES-- FOR VENTILATION!

BZZZZ

OH, HOW *CARELESS* OF ME! I DRILLED THEM TOO DEEP! I STRUCK *WATER!*

WELL, ALL THE SAILORS HAVE NICE, SNUG LIFE-JACKETS ON, AND A LITTLE REFRESHING SWIM SHOULD DO THEM A LOT OF GOOD!

TOO BAD ABOUT THE BOAT, THOUGH,! TSK TSK-- THEY JUST DON'T BUILD 'EM LIKE THEY USED TO

4

MEANWHILE, THE SCARECROW STILL HAS ONE LAST ESCAPE-ACE UP HIS SLEEVE--

THAT'S IT, MY PETS! *FASTER!* WE MUST REACH CUBA BEFORE IRON MAN CAN CATCH ME AGAIN!

AND, IRON MAN, SAFELY ABOARD THE SCARECROW'S BOAT, IS FORCED TO WATCH HIS QUARRY FADE FROM SIGHT...

BLAST THE LUCK! MY JET TRANSISTORS ARE ALMOST DRAINED OF POWER! I CAN'T FLY AFTER HIM!

AND IN THIS BOAT, THE CUBAN SHORE BATTERIES COULD PICK ME OFF LIKE A CLAY PIGEON IF I GET ANY CLOSER!

WELL, I RECOVERED THE PLANS-- CHASED THE SCARECROW OUT OF THE COUNTRY, AND PUT ONE ENEMY GUNBOAT OUT OF ACTION! I GUESS THAT WASN'T *TOO* BAD FOR AN AFTERNOON'S WORK!

NOW I'D BETTER HEAD BACK TO THE STATES AND TO MY OTHER IDENTITY AS TONY STARK!

...ATER... HI, BOSS! DID YOU SEND IRON MAN AFTER THE SCARECROW??

NATURALLY! I DON'T THINK OL' STRAWHEAD WILL BE BOTHERING US AGAIN FOR A WHILE!

BY THE WAY, PEPPER, I HAVE SOMETHING FOR YOU...

YOU *DO*??

I WAS SUPPOSED TO TAKE VERONICA VOGUE TO A BROADWAY SHOW, BUT SHE NEVER SHOWED UP! AND I HATE TO WASTE THESE TICKETS!

THIS IS MY LUCKY DAY! NOW THAT I GOT RID OF THAT BLONDE BANDIT, MR. WONDERFUL WILL DATE *ME!*

...BUT, BEING YOU AND HAPPY HAVE BEEN WORKING SO HARD LATELY, I THOUGHT YOU'D BOTH ENJOY THE SHOW! SO HERE, HAPPY-- BE SURE YOU GET PEPPER THERE IN TIME FOR THE OPENING CURTAIN!

MUCH OBLIGED, BOSS!

OH NO!

STARK *KNOWS* ABOUT VERONICA VOGUE! *THAT'S* WHY HE'S DOING THIS! BUT JUST *WAIT!* HE'LL BE SORRY! I MIGHT EVEN GROW TO *LIKE* HAPPY!

ECCCH! WHAT AM I *THINKING??* I'D BETTER BITE MY TONGUE!

SEE YOU LATER, LOVER GIRL!

MEANWHILE, A SCANT NINETY MILES FROM AMERICA, A BITTER MAN BROODS--AND BIDES HIS TIME-- EXILED! A MAN WITHOUT A COUNTRY!!

I UNDERESTIMATED IRON MAN ONCE--BUT I WON'T DO IT A SECOND TIME!

AND SO WE TAKE LEAVE OF OUR LITTLE GROUP OF CHARACTERS UNTIL NEXT ISSUE WHEN IRON MAN RETURNS WITH NEW THRILLS AND SURPRISES! SEE YOU THEN!

The END

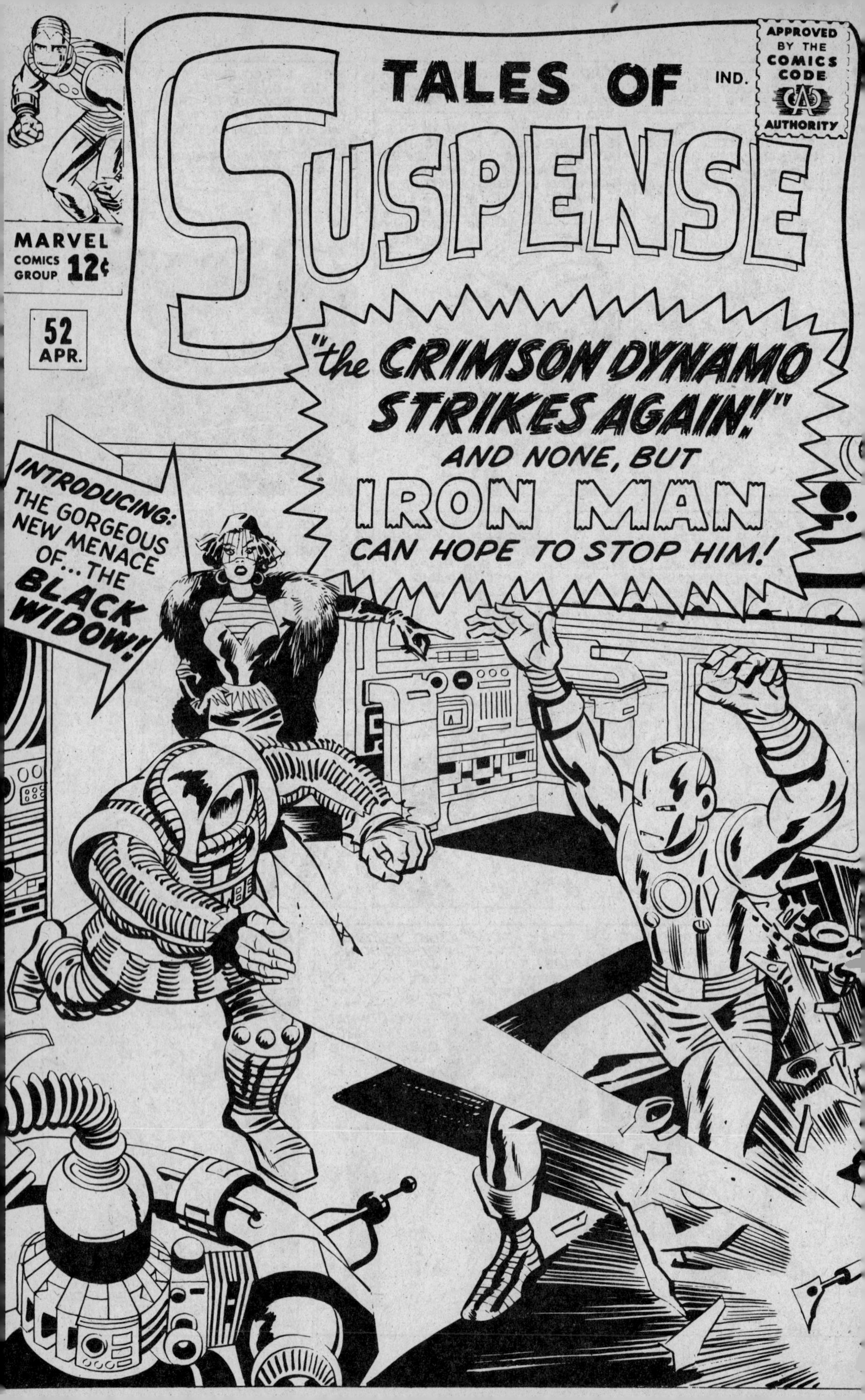

APPROVED BY THE COMICS CODE AUTHORITY
TALES OF
IND.
SUSPENSE
MARVEL COMICS GROUP 12¢
52 APR.
"the CRIMSON DYNAMO STRIKES AGAIN!"
AND NONE, BUT
IRON MAN
CAN HOPE TO STOP HIM!
INTRODUCING: THE GORGEOUS NEW MENACE OF... THE BLACK WIDOW!

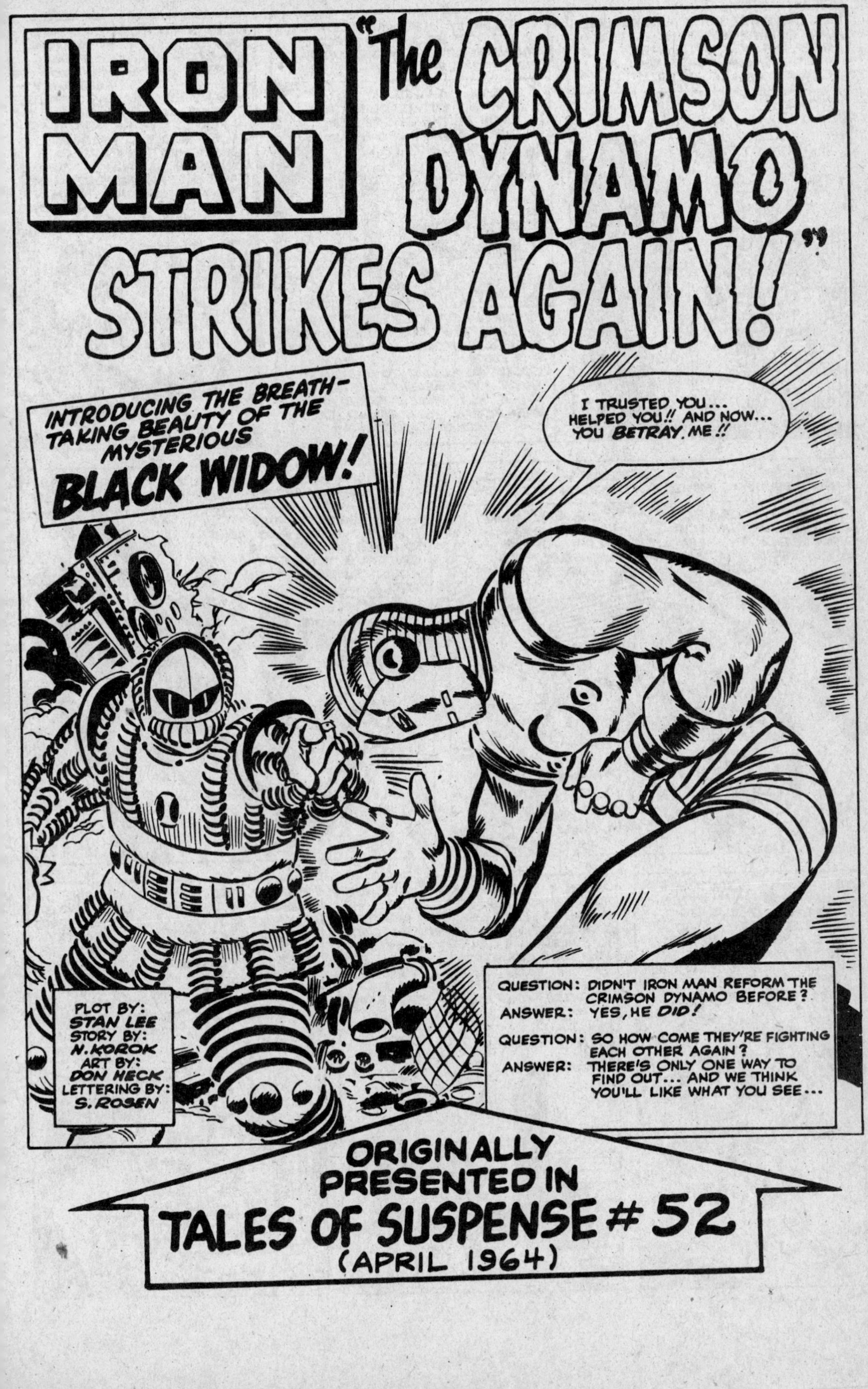
IRON MAN
"The CRIMSON DYNAMO STRIKES AGAIN!"
INTRODUCING THE BREATH-TAKING BEAUTY OF THE MYSTERIOUS BLACK WIDOW!
I TRUSTED YOU... HELPED YOU!! AND NOW... YOU BETRAY ME!!
PLOT BY: STAN LEE STORY BY: N. KOROK ART BY: DON HECK LETTERING BY: S. ROSEN
QUESTION: DIDN'T IRON MAN REFORM THE CRIMSON DYNAMO BEFORE?
ANSWER: YES, HE DID!
QUESTION: SO HOW COME THEY'RE FIGHTING EACH OTHER AGAIN?
ANSWER: THERE'S ONLY ONE WAY TO FIND OUT... AND WE THINK YOU'LL LIKE WHAT YOU SEE...

ORIGINALLY PRESENTED IN
TALES OF SUSPENSE #52
(APRIL 1964)

LATE ONE NIGHT, IN THE MAIN RESEARCH PLANT OF ANTHONY STARK, MILLIONAIRE PLAYBOY AND TALENTED MUNITIONS MANUFACTURER, A STRANGE FIGURE APPEARS...

HE SILENTLY, MECHANICALLY MOVES TO THE TOP SECRET PROJECT OF THE VAST STARK EXPERIMENTAL ENTERPRISES...

I'VE PLEDGED MY BRAIN AND MY ENTIRE BEING TO FATHOM THE SECRET OF THE *LASER LIGHT*... I WILL NOT FAIL!

EDITOR'S NOTE: THE "LASER LIGHT" APPEARS IN PARALLEL PHOTON RAYS OF EQUAL FORCE, NOT DIFFUSED LIKE ORDINARY LIGHT! IF A WAY COULD BE FOUND TO HANDLE SUCH A DANGEROUS LIGHT SAFELY, IT WOULD BE THE PERFECT WEAPON... AS IT COULD BURN THROUGH ANYTHING!

WHILE IN HIS PRIVATE OFFICE, TONY STARK, CHECKING OVER HIS *IRON MAN* COSTUME, SEES...

I CAN REST EASY NOW! EVERY TRANSISTORIZED PART OF MY IRON MAN SUIT IS IN PERFECT WORKING ORDER! HMM... TOO BAD THOSE WHO QUESTIONED THE CRIMSON DYNAMO'S LOYALTY TO ME CAN'T SEE PROFESSOR VANKO *NOW*... WORKING DOWN THERE LONG AFTER EVERYONE ELSE HAS GONE!

THE MACHINE VIBRATES, AND SUDDENLY THE CRIMSON FIGURE BELOW IS BATHED IN A DEADLY, EERIE GLOW!

NOW, WITH MY CRIMSON DYNAMO COSTUME FOR PROTECTION, I'LL FIND OUT IF MY LASER RAY GUN IS SAFE TO USE!

OH, *NO*!! VANKO IS RISKING HIS LIFE... USING *HIMSELF* AS A *GUINEA PIG*!!

WITH SCANT SECONDS TO SPARE, STARK HURLS HIMSELF DOWN TOWARDS THE DANGEROUS LASER LIGHT RAY...

GOOD THING THERE'S NO ONE AROUND TO QUESTION WHY THE CAUTIOUS TONY STARK WOULD SUDDENLY TURN INTO A MAN OF *ACTION*!

THOSE RAYS ALMOST *DISINTEGRATED* YOU, PROFESSOR VANKO!! YOU MUSTN'T TAKE CHANCES LIKE *THAT*!

I'VE *FAILED*! I *STILL* HAVEN'T FOUND A WAY TO MAKE THE LASER LIGHT SAFE TO USE!

WHEN I VOLUNTEERED TO HELP YOU PERFECT A LASER LIGHT WEAPON, I THOUGHT, WITH MY VAST KNOWLEDGE, I COULD AID YOUR COUNTRY... PAY YOU BACK... PAY *AMERICA* BACK... FOR TREATING ME SO FAIR!

SURE YOU *DID*... AND WHAT'S MORE, YOU *WILL*, TOO... BUT WE'RE NOT SO DESPERATE THAT YOU MUST GIVE UP YOUR LIFE TO HELP!

EVEN MY SPECIALLY DESIGNED CRIMSON DYNAMO SUIT AFFORDED NO PROTECTION AGAINST THE DEADLY *LASER BEAMS*... I'LL HAVE TO START AGAIN... SOME *NEW* WAY...

THAT'S THE STORY OF OUR LIVES IN SCIENCE, VANKO... TRY AND TRY AGAIN! BUT MEANWHILE, I SUGGEST YOU ADD SOME ADDITIONAL LEAD COATING FOR PROTECTION... JUST IN CASE...

2.

LEAVING PROFESSOR VANKO, TONY STARK THINKS BACK...BACK TO THE TIME WHEN VANKO, AS *THE CRIMSON DYNAMO*, WAS IN THE EMPLOY OF THE REDS...BEFORE IRON MAN DEFEATED HIM AND ENABLED HIM TO DEFECT AND WORK FOR AMERICA!

YOU'VE *BEATEN* ME, IRON MAN, BUT I SHALL DIE LIKE A *MAN*!

NO *NEED* FOR YOU TO DIE! AMERICANS ARE NOT MURDERERS! I HAVE AN OFFER TO MAKE TO YOU...

BUT, THOUSANDS OF MILES AWAY, IN A PRIVATE SCREENING ROOM, A SHORT PUDGY FIGURE IS FILLED WITH UNCONTROLLABLE RAGE!

THERE, EXCELLENCY! FROM THESE SECRET FILMS YOU SEE ABSOLUTE PROOF OF VANKO'S TREASON!

THE TRAITOR!! HE HAS JOINED THE AMERICANS! HE MUST BE *ELIMINATED!* STOP THE FILM!

THIS IS A JOB FOR *THE BLACK WIDOW*... AND THE MAN KNOWN AS... *BORIS!*

AND, A SHORT TIME LATER!

YOU SENT FOR ME, COMRADE LEADER?

AND YOU, TOO, BORIS! *COME HERE!* WALK AROUND THE DESK... I WANT TO *SHOW* YOU SOMETHING...

WALK AROUND??

BORIS DOES NOT *WALK AROUND* PUNY OBSTACLES...

...IT IS EASIER TO HURL THEM ASIDE... *SO!!*

THERE ARE YOUR *TARGETS!* THE AMERICAN MUNITIONS-MAKER, *STARK*, AND THE TRAITOR *VANKO!* BUT IT WILL ALSO BE NECESSARY TO DISPOSE OF STARK'S MIGHTY BODYGUARD... *IRON MAN!*

HMM...THAT ANTHONY STARK IS *HANDSOME* AS WELL AS WEALTHY! HE WILL MAKE AN INTERESTING ASSIGNMENT FOR THE BLACK WIDOW!

3.

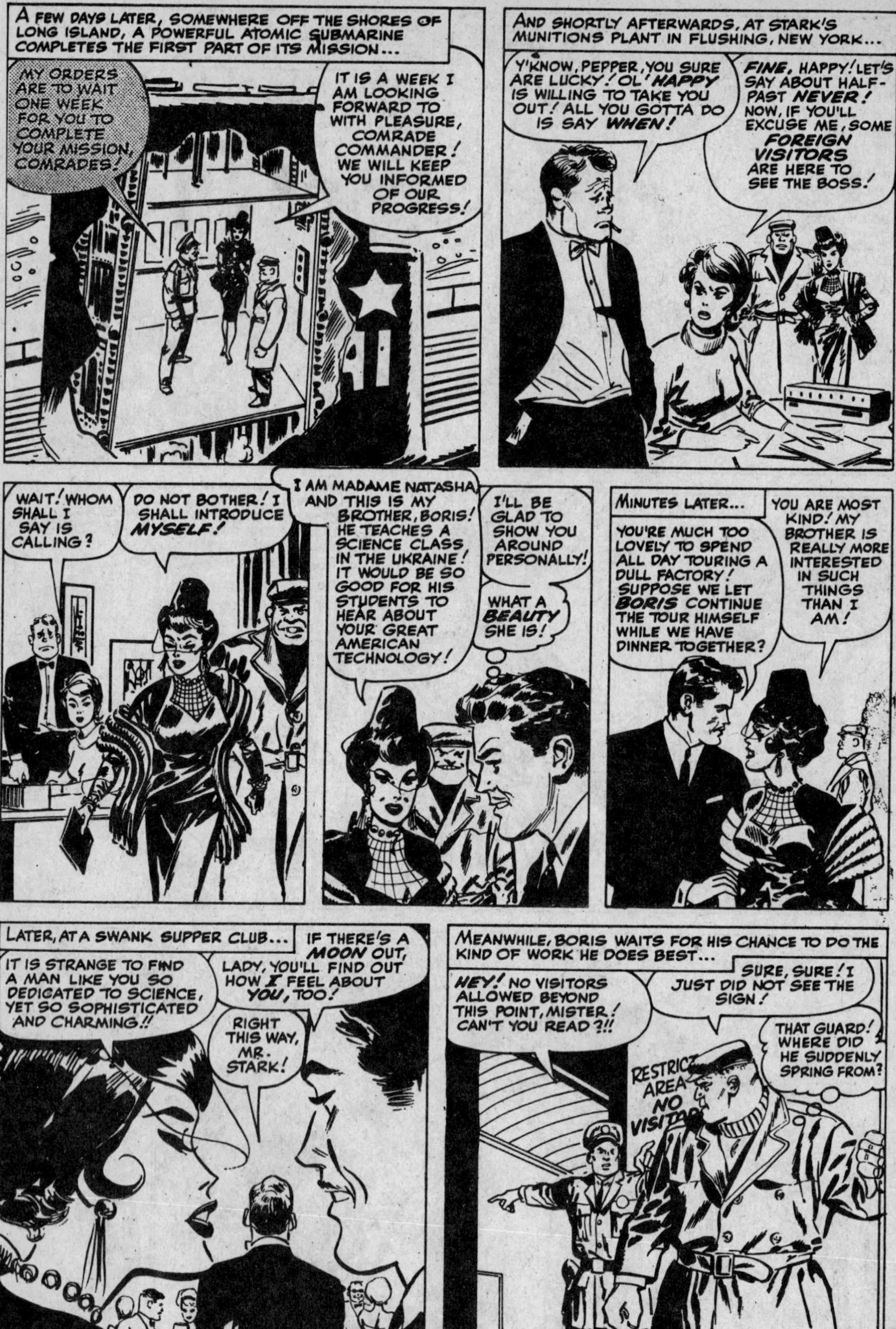
A FEW DAYS LATER, SOMEWHERE OFF THE SHORES OF LONG ISLAND, A POWERFUL ATOMIC SUBMARINE COMPLETES THE FIRST PART OF ITS MISSION...
MY ORDERS ARE TO WAIT ONE WEEK FOR YOU TO COMPLETE YOUR MISSION, COMRADES!
IT IS A WEEK I AM LOOKING FORWARD TO WITH PLEASURE, COMRADE COMMANDER! WE WILL KEEP YOU INFORMED OF OUR PROGRESS!
AND SHORTLY AFTERWARDS, AT STARK'S MUNITIONS PLANT IN FLUSHING, NEW YORK...
Y'KNOW, PEPPER, YOU SURE ARE LUCKY! OL' HAPPY IS WILLING TO TAKE YOU OUT! ALL YOU GOTTA DO IS SAY WHEN!
FINE, HAPPY! LET'S SAY ABOUT HALF-PAST NEVER! NOW, IF YOU'LL EXCUSE ME, SOME FOREIGN VISITORS ARE HERE TO SEE THE BOSS!
WAIT! WHOM SHALL I SAY IS CALLING?
DO NOT BOTHER! I SHALL INTRODUCE MYSELF!
I AM MADAME NATASHA AND THIS IS MY BROTHER, BORIS! HE TEACHES A SCIENCE CLASS IN THE UKRAINE! IT WOULD BE SO GOOD FOR HIS STUDENTS TO HEAR ABOUT YOUR GREAT AMERICAN TECHNOLOGY!
I'LL BE GLAD TO SHOW YOU AROUND PERSONALLY!
WHAT A BEAUTY SHE IS!
MINUTES LATER...
YOU'RE MUCH TOO LOVELY TO SPEND ALL DAY TOURING A DULL FACTORY! SUPPOSE WE LET BORIS CONTINUE THE TOUR HIMSELF WHILE WE HAVE DINNER TOGETHER?
YOU ARE MOST KIND! MY BROTHER IS REALLY MORE INTERESTED IN SUCH THINGS THAN I AM!
LATER, AT A SWANK SUPPER CLUB...
IT IS STRANGE TO FIND A MAN LIKE YOU SO DEDICATED TO SCIENCE, YET SO SOPHISTICATED AND CHARMING!!
IF THERE'S A MOON OUT, LADY, YOU'LL FIND OUT HOW I FEEL ABOUT YOU, TOO!
RIGHT THIS WAY, MR. STARK!
MEANWHILE, BORIS WAITS FOR HIS CHANCE TO DO THE KIND OF WORK HE DOES BEST...
HEY! NO VISITORS ALLOWED BEYOND THIS POINT, MISTER! CAN'T YOU READ?!!
SURE, SURE! I JUST DID NOT SEE THE SIGN!
THAT GUARD! WHERE DID HE SUDDENLY SPRING FROM?
4

HE IS NOW GOING ON HIS ROUNDS, SO I SHALL GET ON WITH MY JOB! I KNOW VANKO MUST BE WORKING HERE... IN THIS RESTRICTED AREA!

FROM A SMALL CONTAINER, A MYSTERIOUS FLUID IS EJECTED... AND EATS ITS WAY THROUGH THE METAL DOOR...

AH! NOW IT HAS CREATED AN OPENING LARGE ENOUGH...

...FOR BORIS TO USE H.S STRENGTH!

CRUNC

GREETINGS, PROFESSOR VANKO, FROM THE PAST!

BORIS!! YOU HERE? YOU ARE WASTING YOUR TIME! I AM FINISHED WITH THE KREMLIN! STAY AWAY FROM ME!

RIP!

I BRING YOU A MESSAGE FROM OUR GLORIOUS LEADER! YOU MUST HELP ME SABOTAGE STARK'S PLANT AND HIS NEW SECRET PROJECT! IF YOU DO, YOUR LIFE WILL BE SPARED!

NEVER! THE AMERICANS HAVE BEEN GOOD TO ME! I SHALL NEVER BETRAY THEM! I..I'LL CALL THE GUARDS!

THERE WON'T BE TIME FOR YOUR GUARDS TO HELP YOU, VANKO! REMEMBER THIS LITTLE TOY? YOU INVENTED IT...FOR US! SO YOU KNOW WHAT IT CAN DO!

THE JET PARALYZER... I HAD FORGOTTEN ALL ABOUT IT! I DESIGNED IT YEARS AGO...

AH! THE MAGNETIC ARTIFICIAL FIBERS ARE FORMING... A VERY USEFUL INVENTION!!

OHHH...THE SPRAY!! I CANNOT RESIST...THE TENTACLES ARE SPREADING ...HOLDING ME...I'M HELPLESS!!

5.

AND, AS THE POWERFUL RAY GUN TAKES EFFECT...

SO! NOW YOU ARE WRAPPED IN THE UNBREAKABLE NET! IT WAS A BRILLIANT INVENTION, VANKO! TOO BAD *YOU* HAD TO BE ONE OF ITS VICTIMS!

ONLY ONE MORE THING... I'LL START THIS LONG-PLAYING TAPE-RECORDING OF YOUR VOICE, TAKEN AT YOUR LAST LECTURE IN MOSCOW!

THEN, OUTSIDE THE LAB...

HEY! WHERE ARE YOU GOING WITH THAT *PACKAGE*?

DELIVERING IT FOR PROFESSOR VANKO...

YOU CAN CHECK WITH *HIM*, IF YOU WANT... ALTHOUGH HE MAY NOT LIKE BEING INTERRUPTED IN THE MIDDLE OF A LECTURE...

HUH? OH, YEAH... I CAN *HEAR* HIM... AND I KNOW THAT GUY'S TEMPER WHEN HE'S DISTURBED... OKAY, PAL... TAKE OFF!

AS SOON AS WE FIND THE PROPER WAY OF DEALING WITH...

LATER... AT A MIDNIGHT RENDEZVOUS...

WE RECEIVED YOUR SIGNAL! WHAT HAVE YOU *THERE*?

ONLY THE FIRST INSTALLMENT! TAKE GOOD CARE OF HIM AND KEEP HIM UNDER GUARD WHEN HE RECOVERS! I'LL BE BACK SOON WITH *ANOTHER*!

OUR LEADER SAID TO EXTERMINATE VANKO... NEVER DREAMING I COULD BRING HIM BACK *ALIVE*! I'LL BE A GREATER HERO NOW... AND MORE SO WHEN I'VE BEATEN STARK, AS WELL AS THE OVER-RATED *IRON MAN*! THE BLACK WIDOW AND BORIS CAN DEFEAT *ANYONE*!!

RETURNING SECRETLY TO THE PLANT, BORIS AGAIN SLIPS INTO VANKO'S LAB AND CAREFULLY DONS THE AWESOME SUIT OF THE CRIMSON DYNAMO...

THIS ELECTRIFIED SUIT WILL BE THE PERFECT DISGUISE FOR ME! NONE WILL SUSPECT THAT I AM NOT VANKO! AND NOW FOR *IRON MAN*... WHOSE DEFEAT WILL BE MY GREATEST TRIUMPH!

6.

WITHOUT A MOMENT'S HESITATION, USING THE STARTLING POWER OF THE CRIMSON DYNAMO, BORIS BEGINS A ONE-MAN CAMPAIGN OF SABOTAGE FROM WITHIN STARK'S FACTORY...

THIS WILL SERVE A DOUBLE PURPOSE! IT WILL SLOW DOWN AMERICA'S DEFENSE PRODUCTION, AND MORE IMPORTANT, IT WILL BRING *IRON MAN* INTO THE OPEN WHERE I CAN *DESTROY* HIM, SO THAT HE CAN NEVER FRUSTRATE OUR PLANS FOR WORLD CONQUEST AGAIN!

CRACK!

MOMENTS LATER...

IT'S TOO BAD YOUR VISIT HERE HAS TO END IN A FEW DAYS, MADAME NATASHA!

I FIND MYSELF REGRETTING IT, TOO! I SHALL *MISS* YOU!

AN URGENT MESSAGE, MR. STARK! I'M SORRY TO INTERRUPT...

AND SO...

IT WAS HAPPY! HE SAID I WAS *NEEDED!* THERE WAS A MYSTERIOUS EXPLOSION AT THE PLANT...AND NO SIGN OF VANKO...

STARK CANNOT FOOL ME! HE IS *WORRIED!* BORIS MUST HAVE STRUCK A TELLING BLOW!

DON'T COME ANY CLOSER! IT COULD BE *DANGEROUS!* I'LL HAVE TO *LEAVE* YOU HERE!

WHAT A GLORIOUS SIGHT! STARK'S PLANT IS AN INFERNO!

WHAT A COLD WOMAN SHE IS! SO *UNMOVED* BY ALL THIS EXCITEMENT!

GLAD YOU'RE BACK, BOSS! MAYBE *YOU* CAN GET THINGS UNDER CONTROL NOW! THE FIRE STARTED IN THE AREA OF VANKO'S LAB! BUT *HE'S GONE!*

KEEP *AT* IT, HAPPY! I'LL BE WITH YOU AS SOON AS I ATTEND TO SOMETHING!

MUST CHANGE INTO MY OTHER GUISE... THAT OF *IRON MAN!*

AND, SPLIT SECONDS LATER...

AND NOW TO FIND OUT WHAT'S *BEHIND* ALL THIS! AS ARMOR-PLATED *IRON MAN*, I CAN PLUNGE INTO THIS BLAZING INFERNO WITHOUT BURNING ALIVE!

7.

LOOK! IT'S IRON MAN! HE'S TOO LATE TO STOP THE DAMAGE... BUT HE STILL MAY BE ABLE TO SAVE THE *REST* OF THE FACTORY!

I'VE GOT TO FIND VANKO! HIS WORK WITH THE LASER LIGHT RAY MIGHT HAVE STARTED THIS!

SECONDS LATER...

THE CRIMSON DYNAMO! VANKO! THANK HEAVEN YOU'RE ALL RIGHT! FOLLOW ME! I'LL GET YOU *OUT* OF HERE!

CRASH!

IRON MAN, AT LAST! THE FOOL THINKS I'M VANKO!

WHAT'S *WRONG?* OH, YOU DON'T WANT TO LEAVE THE LASER RAY MACHINE, EH? OKAY, I'LL HELP YOU GET IT *OUT* OF HERE!

I'LL WAIT TILL HE *LIFTS* THE MACHINE! THEN BORIS SHALL *STRIKE!*

LET'S HOPE WE CAN SAVE IT IN TIME! IT WOULD TAKE *YEARS* TO REBUILD IF IT'S DESTROYED!

NOW'S MY CHANCE!... WHILE HE'S COMPLETELY *OFF-GUARD!*

OHH!

A PERFECT OPPORTUNITY TO USE THE ELECTRICAL CHARGE VANKO PROVIDED IN THIS SUIT!

I'M BEING DRAINED OF MY TRANSISTOR POWER... *VANKO!* CAN IT *BE!?* HAVE YOU REALLY TURNED ON ME? WAS I MISTAKEN *AFTER* ALL?! UHH... GROWING WEAKER... B-BLACKING OUT...

HAH! THE MUCH-VAUNTED IRON MAN, HELPLESS ONCE HIS ELECTRICAL TRANSISTOR CIRCUITS ARE DAMAGED! WITHIN SECONDS HE'LL BE UNCONSCIOUS, AND THEN...

UNDER COVER OF THE THICK BLANKET OF SMOKE, I'LL ESCAPE WITH MY GREATEST PRIZE! AND IF I'M SEEN, THE FOOLS WILL THINK I'M *RESCUING IRON MAN!*

8.

YOU SUBDUED *IRON MAN*, COMRADE? INCREDIBLE! ARE YOU SURE HE'S *TOTALLY HARMLESS?*

COMPLETELY, COMRADE COMMANDER! HE HAS RECEIVED ENOUGH ELECTRIC CURRENT TO DESTROY *TWENTY* MEN!

NOW IRON MAN IS HELPLESS AND LOCKED BEHIND DOORS OF PLATE STEEL! YOU NEED WORRY ABOUT HIM NO LONGER!

SO YOU SAY! BUT I HAVE HEARD *TOO MUCH* OF THIS MAN! I SHALL NOT RELAX UNTIL HE IS OFF MY SHIP AND SAFELY IMPRISONED IN THE HOMELAND!

CL**ANK!**

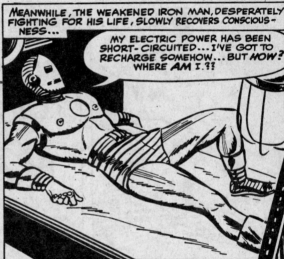

MOMENTS LATER...

WHAT A *HERO'S WELCOME* I SHALL RECEIVE WHEN I RETURN! NOW, THE FINAL DETAIL.... THE BLACK WIDOW AND I WILL EASILY FINISH OFF ANTHONY STARK...NOW THAT HIS IRON BODY GUARD CANNOT HELP HIM!

MEANWHILE, THE WEAKENED IRON MAN, DESPERATELY FIGHTING FOR HIS LIFE, SLOWLY RECOVERS CONSCIOUSNESS...

MY ELECTRIC POWER HAS BEEN SHORT-CIRCUITED...I'VE GOT TO RECHARGE SOMEHOW...BUT *HOW?* WHERE AM I.??

CAN'T WAIT MUCH LONGER... MUST FIND SOME ELECTRIC CURRENT TO REACTIVATE MY CIRCUITS!! WAIT...THAT LIGHT BULB...OVERHEAD...

SUMMONING ALL HIS REMAINING STRENGTH, IRON MAN SMASHES THE GLASS BULB, AND...

LUCKY I CARRY THIS SPARE EXTENSION CORD FOR ANY EMERGENCIES...AH...I CAN FEEL MY ENERGY...MY VERY LIFE FORCE...FEEDING BACK...

NOW, WITH THE FULL POWER OF IRON MAN, I CAN TEAR THIS PLACE APART, AND...*VANKO!!* WHAT HAVE THEY *DONE* TO YOU? SO IT WAS SOMEONE *ELSE* WHO STRUCK ME DOWN...I SHOULD HAVE *GUESSED!*

9.

IN SECONDS, IRON MAN RIPS OFF THE SYNTHETIC WIRE MESH NET, FREEING VANKO! THEN, SLEDGE-HAMMER FISTS, AIDED BY POWERFUL TRANSISTOR FORCE, BATTER AN ESCAPE ROUTE RIGHT THROUGH THE STEEL SHELL OF THE SUB...

SMASH!

UNTIL...

YOU *DID* IT, IRON MAN!! YOU *FREED* US! BUT...ARE YOUR SMALL FLYING JETS POWERFUL ENOUGH TO CARRY *MY* WEIGHT, TOO?

THEY'RE *ULTRA-TURBO JETS*, VANKO! THEY COULD LIFT AN *ELEPHANT*, IF NEED BE! *THERE*... WE'RE SAFELY OUT OF RANGE NOW!

THEY'VE *ESCAPED!* WE'LL PAY WITH OUR *LIVES* FOR THIS!

IT'S ALL *MY* FAULT FOR INVOLVING YOU IN MY PAST, IRON MAN! MY ENEMIES DO NOT GIVE UP EASILY!

THAT'S WHAT MAKES THEM *DANGEROUS*, VANKO, BUT WE'LL SHOW THEM *WE* CAN BE EQUALLY *DANGEROUS!*

THINKING HE'S DEFEATED YOU, BORIS WILL RETURN TO THE FACTORY TO DESTROY OUR LASER RAY WEAPON!!

BORIS! SO HE'S THE ONE!

IRON MAN... *LOOK!* MY CRIMSON DYNAMO COSTUME! IT MUST BE *HIM!*

YOU MUST BE *CAREFUL!* HE, TOO, IS A SCIENTIST...A MAN OF GREAT ABILITY...AND GREATER *STRENGTH!!*

NO, VANKO! THIS IS NO TIME FOR CAUTION!! I'VE *RETURNED*,

IRON MAN! NOW??

WE'LL PLAY TWENTY QUESTIONS LATER, YOU TREACHEROUS SPY!! RIGHT NOW, WE'LL FIND OUT HOW GOOD YOU ARE WHEN I'VE GOT *BOTH HANDS FREE!*

CRASH

10.

WHA..? SOMETHING'S WRONG! THE SAME ELECTRICAL THRUST I USED BEFORE ... IT HAS NO EFFECT!

NATURALLY! I'VE ALTERED MY FREQUENCY WAVE LENGTH! YOU CAN'T BEAT ME TWICE WITH THE SAME STUNT!

CRACKLE!

IT DOES NOT MATTER! I AM STILL POWERFUL ENOUGH TO DESTROY YOU WITH MY BARE HAN...OOOF!!

POW!

GUESS AGAIN, BORIS! I'M NO WEAKLING MYSELF!

FINISH HIM, IRON MAN, WHILE YOU CAN! YOU MUST... HE WILL NEVER GIVE UP!

CAN'T, VANKO! WE DON'T PLAY THAT WAY! HE'S HAD ENOUGH! WELL SEND FOR THE POLICE NOW!

BUT, DURING THOSE FEW SECONDS OF INDECISION, THE CRAFTY BORIS SECRETLY READJUSTS HIS OWN ELECTRIC WAVE LENGTH ... AND THEN ...

THAT'S WHY WE WILL BURY YOU... WE'RE NOT AS TRUSTING AS YOU!

HIS ELECTRIC CHARGE CAN AFFECT ME NOW! I WAS ASLEEP AT THE SWITCH!

AS IRON MAN, MOMENTARILY WEAKENED, REELS BACK, BORIS FOLLOWS UP HIS ADVANTAGE BY RESORTING TO HIS OWN BRUTE STRENGTH WHICH IS GREATLY INCREASED BY THE ELECTRIC POWER OF THE CRIMSON DYNAMO ARMOR...

NOW TO DESTROY YOU AS EASILY AS I WOULD A FLEA!

LITTLE OL' TRANSISTORS, IF I EVER NEEDED YOU... I NEED YOU NOW!

DESPERATELY APPLYING HIS OWN FULL-FREQUENCY POWER, IRON MAN ALSO GOES INTO ACTION AGAIN ...

I'LL BE BACK AS SOON AS I PUT THIS TOY OUT OF HARM'S WAY...THE INSTRUMENTS IN IT ARE TOO VALUABLE TO RISK IN OUR LITTLE GAME!

HE FLEW UP TO THE MACHINE!! TOOK IT FROM ME EFFORTLESSLY! NOW I REALIZE HOW TREMENDOUS HIS POWER IS!!

11.

PLACING THE INVALUABLE DEVICE OUT OF HARM'S WAY, IRON MAN SPEEDILY *RETURNS* TO THE BATTLE!

ALL RIGHT, PLAYMATE! LET'S WRAP THIS UP FOR *KEEPS* NOW!

BUT, UNEXPECTEDLY, THE *BLACK WIDOW* REAPPEARS!

IT LOOKS LIKE THE END FOR BORIS! MUCH AS I DISLIKE THAT BRUTISH OAF, I'LL HAVE TO AID HIM *SOMEHOW*...SOME RUSE TO TRICK THE AMERICAN...

MADAM NATASHA! I MUST HAVE UNWITTINGLY PINNED HER UNDER THE MACHINE WHEN I SET IT DOWN!!

IRON MAN! HELP ME!!

GULLIBLE FOOL! IT *WORKED!*

I'LL GET IT OFF! *OHH!* A..A JET OF WATER ON MY BACK!! *BORIS*...HE'S SHORT-CIRCUITING ME!

I SHOULD HAVE *GUESSED!* THE TWO OF YOU.....YOU'RE WORKING TOGETHER!!

IT WILL TAKE JUST A SECOND TO GENERATE ENOUGH FORCE TO ELECTROCUTE YOU..TO FINISH YOU FOREVER!

BUT *VANKO*, AWARE OF IRON MAN'S DANGER, CATCHES THE ASSASSIN OFF GUARD...

I CAN'T DO MUCH...BUT IF I CAN JUST GIVE IRON MAN THE FEW SECONDS HE NEEDS....!

FOOL! IT'S LIKE A MOUSE ATTACKING A TIGER! YOU CAN ACCOMPLISH *NOTHING!*

SO! YOU FLEE! YOU ARE TOO SQUEAMISH TO WATCH AS I FINISH OFF IRON MAN, EH?

I HAVE *ONE* CHANCE LEFT...THE PROJECT THAT WAS TO HAVE BEEN MY SUPREME SCIENTIFIC ACHIEVEMENT...IT MAY *YET* SAVE IRON MAN!

YOU'VE WAITED *TOO LONG*, BORIS! THIS *LASER LIGHT PISTOL* WILL STOP YOU NOW...

YOUR BLUFF WON'T WORK, VANKO! I KNOW THE WEAPON IS NOT YET PERFECTED! IT WILL DESTROY THE ONE WHO *USES* IT AS WELL AS THE VICTIM! YOU WOULD NOT *DARE!*

ANOTHER SECOND... ALL I NEED...

12.

NOW STAND ASIDE, VANKO! I SHALL ATTEND TO YOU ONCE IRON MAN IS DESTROYED!

NO, BORIS! YOU HAVE GONE TOO FAR! YOU THINK NO MAN WOULD GIVE UP HIS LIFE FOR AN IDEAL, DO YOU? YOU ARE WRONG!

I WOULD DARE ANYTHING FOR THIS COUNTRY... WHICH HAS BEEN SO GOOD TO ME!

NO! VANKO.. DON'T!

WORDS! WORDS! NOW OUT OF MY WAY, OLD MAN!

NOT JUST WORDS, BORIS... BUT DEEDS! IS THERE ANY MORE FITTING WAY TO GLORIFY MY GREATEST PROJECT THAN TO DESTROY AN ENEMY OF FREEDOM WITH IT?!!

NO.!! YOU ARE MAD! YOU WILL DIE ALSO... STOP!!

I MUST ESCAPE IN THE CONFUSION! WE HAVE FAILED!

BOOM!

LATER... POOR VANKO! HE SACRIFICED HIS LIFE TO PROVE HIS LOYALTY TO OUR NATION! HE SHALL NEVER BE FORGOTTEN!

THEN, AFTER RESUMING HIS TRUE IDENTITY AS ANTHONY STARK...

HEY, BOSS! WE JUST GOT SOME HOT REPORTS ON THAT PHONY SISTER OF BORIS! SHE'S A REAL MATA HARI, CALLED THE BLACK WIDOW! WHY DON'T WE GO AFTER HER??

WHY BOTHER, HAPPY? SHE'S FAILED IN HER MISSION! WHERE CAN SHE GO? WHERE CAN SHE HIDE? IN A WAY, I PITY HER! ALL THAT BEAUTY OUTSIDE... BUT INSIDE... NOTHING!!

YET, WHAT OF THE BEAUTIFUL, DANGEROUSLY IRRESISTIBLE BLACK WIDOW? SHE IS STILL AT LARGE, ON SOME FOG-FILLED STREET IN SOME CROWDED CITY... LONELY... ABANDONED... ALWAYS HIDING! HER CONSTANT COMPANION... FEAR!

I MUST KEEP MOVING... I KNOW TOO WELL THE PENALTY FOR FAILURE!!

BUT, TIME IS LONG, AND UNENDING... AND FATE WORKS IN MYSTERIOUS WAYS! NEXT ISSUE THE BLACK WIDOW RETURNS, MORE DEADLY THAN EVER! SO DON'T MISS THE GREAT TALES OF SUSPENSE #53, WHERE ANOTHER THRILLING IRON MAN ADVENTURE AWAITS YOU!

The End

13.

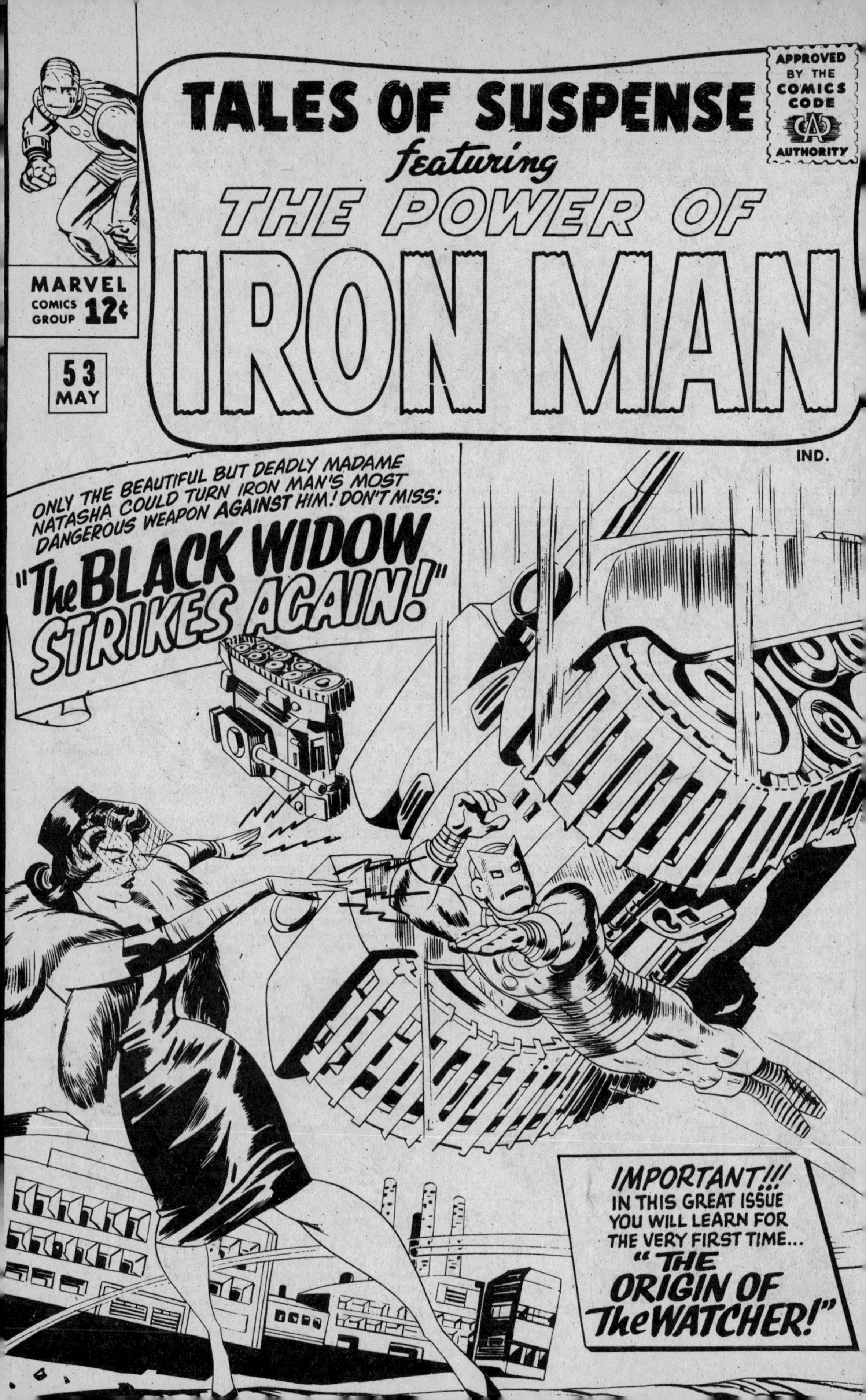

TALES OF SUSPENSE
featuring
THE POWER OF
IRON MAN
APPROVED BY THE COMICS CODE AUTHORITY
MARVEL COMICS GROUP 12¢
53 MAY
IND.
ONLY THE BEAUTIFUL BUT DEADLY MADAME NATASHA COULD TURN IRON MAN'S MOST DANGEROUS WEAPON AGAINST HIM! DON'T MISS:
"The BLACK WIDOW STRIKES AGAIN!"
IMPORTANT!!! IN THIS GREAT ISSUE YOU WILL LEARN FOR THE VERY FIRST TIME... "THE ORIGIN OF The WATCHER!"

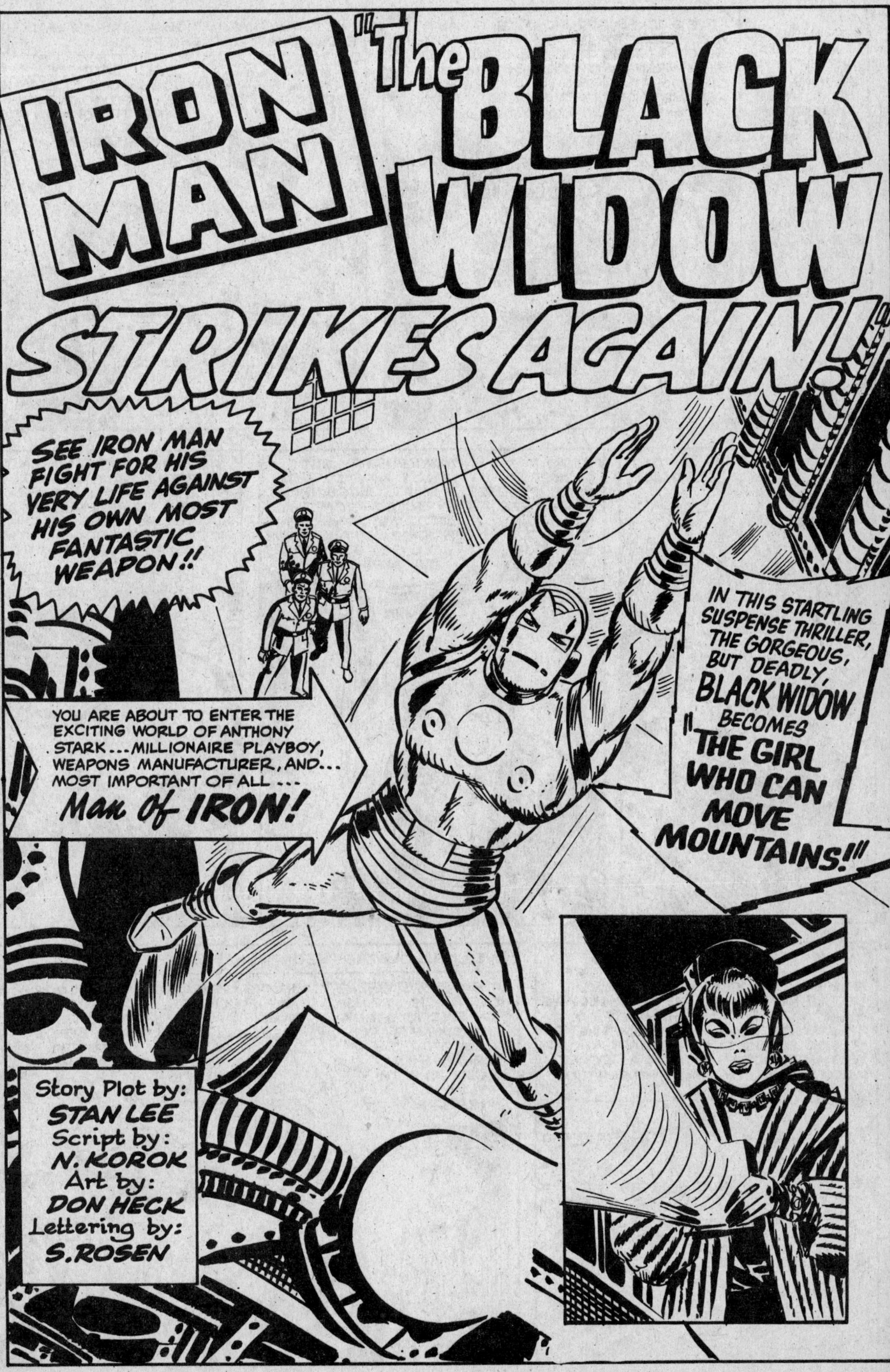
IRON MAN
"The BLACK WIDOW STRIKES AGAIN!"
SEE IRON MAN FIGHT FOR HIS VERY LIFE AGAINST HIS OWN MOST FANTASTIC WEAPON!!
YOU ARE ABOUT TO ENTER THE EXCITING WORLD OF ANTHONY STARK... MILLIONAIRE PLAYBOY, WEAPONS MANUFACTURER, AND... MOST IMPORTANT OF ALL... Man of IRON!
IN THIS STARTLING SUSPENSE THRILLER, THE GORGEOUS, BUT DEADLY, BLACK WIDOW BECOMES "THE GIRL WHO CAN MOVE MOUNTAINS!"
Story Plot by: STAN LEE
Script by: N. KOROK
Art by: DON HECK
Lettering by: S. ROSEN

ONE EVENING, IN THE PRIVATE LABORATORY OF HANDSOME TONY STARK, AN EXPERIMENT BEGINS ...ONE WHICH WILL HAVE BIZARRE AND FAR-REACHING CONSEQUENCES...

I'VE WORKED FOR *MONTHS* ON AN *ANTI-GRAVITY DEVICE* WITHOUT SUCCESS! *THIS* TIME, I'LL LEAVE IT TO BLIND CHANCE! I ARRANGED THE CIRCUITS AT RANDOM...DON'T EVEN REMEMBER THE FORMULA! BUT I MAY AS WELL TEST IT, ANYWAY...

SUDDENLY, "HAPPY" HOGAN, STARK'S SAD-FACED CHAUFFEUR ENTERS, AND...

IT'S WORKING! A ONE IN A MILLION SHOT...AND IT'S *WORKING!*

HOLY MACKEREL! THE BOSS DOESN'T SEE THAT HEAVY GIZMO OVER HIS HEAD! IT'S GONNA DROP ON HIM...UNLESS I CAN MOVE *FAST!!*

WHA...?!!

GOTCHA!!

CRASH

LUCKY I DECIDED TO POKE MY NOSE IN AND SEE IF YOU WERE READY TO GET YOUR LIFT HOME, BOSS! WHAT *GIVES* HERE?

THANKS, HAPPY, BUT I THINK I ALREADY *GOT* MY LIFT...MORE THAN I EXPECTED FROM THAT LITTLE MACHINE! DON'T BOTHER WAITING...I'VE STILL GOT SOME THINGS TO FINISH UP!

THE WIRES *FUSED* WHEN I DROPPED IT! ALTHOUGH IT STILL WORKS, I'LL *NEVER* BE ABLE TO ANALYZE ITS MAKEUP NOW! WELL, I'D BETTER GET IN TOUCH WITH THE DEFENSE DEPARTMENT...

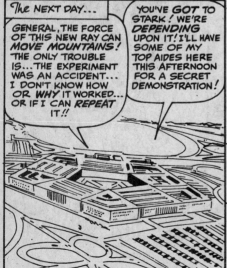

The NEXT DAY...

GENERAL, THE FORCE OF THIS NEW RAY CAN *MOVE MOUNTAINS!* THE ONLY TROUBLE IS...THE EXPERIMENT WAS AN ACCIDENT... I DON'T KNOW HOW OR *WHY* IT WORKED... OR IF I CAN *REPEAT* IT!!

YOU'VE *GOT* TO STARK! WE'RE *DEPENDING* UPON IT! I'LL HAVE SOME OF MY *TOP* AIDES HERE THIS AFTERNOON FOR A SECRET DEMONSTRATION!

BUT SOMEHOW THE "SECRET" HAS LEAKED OUT, AND...

IT'S BEYOND BELIEF! YOUR RAY IS LIFTING THAT FIVE TON TANK LIKE CONFETTI! THINK WHAT ONE OF OUR *DIVISIONS* COULD DO WITH SUCH A WEAPON!!

THANKS, GENERAL! NOW IF I ONLY *KNEW* HOW...

HOW DID THAT PRESS PHOTOGRAPHER GET WIND OF THIS? IT'S TOO SOON TO ANNOUNCE THE RAY!

THIS SCOOP OUGHTTA BE WORTH A FIFTY BUCK BONUS FROM THE PAPER!

2

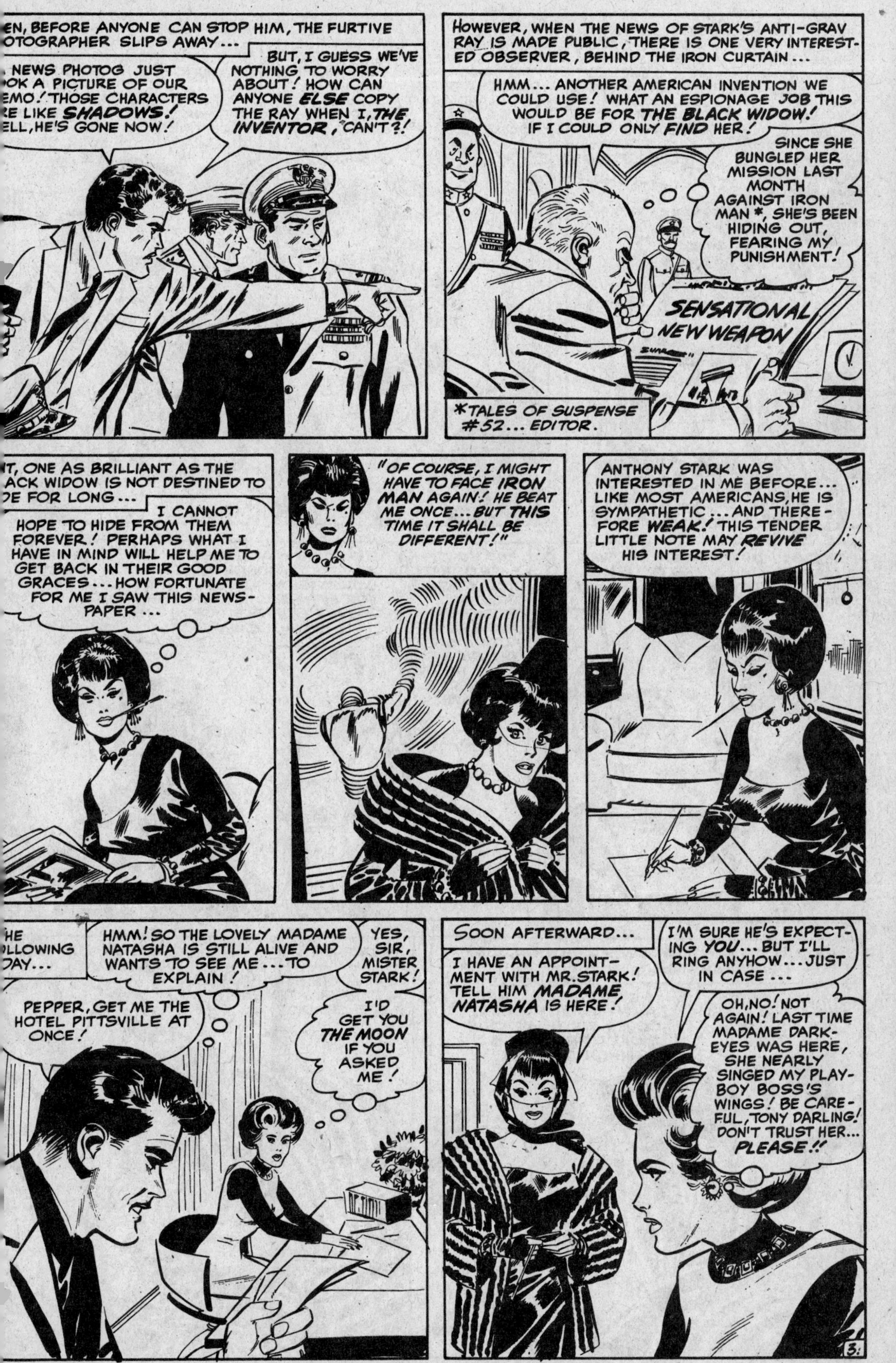
EN, BEFORE ANYONE CAN STOP HIM, THE FURTIVE OTOGRAPHER SLIPS AWAY...
NEWS PHOTOG JUST OK A PICTURE OF OUR EMO! THOSE CHARACTERS E LIKE SHADOWS! ELL, HE'S GONE NOW!
BUT, I GUESS WE'VE NOTHING TO WORRY ABOUT! HOW CAN ANYONE ELSE COPY THE RAY WHEN I, THE INVENTOR, CAN'T?!
HOWEVER, WHEN THE NEWS OF STARK'S ANTI-GRAV RAY IS MADE PUBLIC, THERE IS ONE VERY INTEREST-ED OBSERVER, BEHIND THE IRON CURTAIN...
HMM... ANOTHER AMERICAN INVENTION WE COULD USE! WHAT AN ESPIONAGE JOB THIS WOULD BE FOR THE BLACK WIDOW! IF I COULD ONLY FIND HER!
SINCE SHE BUNGLED HER MISSION LAST MONTH AGAINST IRON MAN *, SHE'S BEEN HIDING OUT, FEARING MY PUNISHMENT!
SENSATIONAL NEW WEAPON
*TALES OF SUSPENSE #52... EDITOR.
T, ONE AS BRILLIANT AS THE ACK WIDOW IS NOT DESTINED TO DE FOR LONG...
I CANNOT HOPE TO HIDE FROM THEM FOREVER! PERHAPS WHAT I HAVE IN MIND WILL HELP ME TO GET BACK IN THEIR GOOD GRACES... HOW FORTUNATE FOR ME I SAW THIS NEWS-PAPER...
"OF COURSE, I MIGHT HAVE TO FACE IRON MAN AGAIN! HE BEAT ME ONCE... BUT THIS TIME IT SHALL BE DIFFERENT!"
ANTHONY STARK WAS INTERESTED IN ME BEFORE... LIKE MOST AMERICANS, HE IS SYMPATHETIC... AND THERE-FORE WEAK! THIS TENDER LITTLE NOTE MAY REVIVE HIS INTEREST!
HE LLOWING DAY...
HMM! SO THE LOVELY MADAME NATASHA IS STILL ALIVE AND WANTS TO SEE ME... TO EXPLAIN!
YES, SIR, MISTER STARK!
PEPPER, GET ME THE HOTEL PITTSVILLE AT ONCE!
I'D GET YOU THE MOON IF YOU ASKED ME!
SOON AFTERWARD...
I HAVE AN APPOINT-MENT WITH MR. STARK! TELL HIM MADAME NATASHA IS HERE!
I'M SURE HE'S EXPECT-ING YOU... BUT I'LL RING ANYHOW... JUST IN CASE...
OH, NO! NOT AGAIN! LAST TIME MADAME DARK-EYES WAS HERE, SHE NEARLY SINGED MY PLAY-BOY BOSS'S WINGS! BE CARE-FUL, TONY DARLING! DON'T TRUST HER... PLEASE!!
3

HEY, GORGEOUS! ISN'T THAT THE SAME DAME WHO...WHO...

STOP STUTTERING AND PUSH YOUR EYEBALLS BACK, HAPPY! SHE'S OUT OF YOUR LEAGUE!

AND HOW I WISH SHE WAS OUT OF TONY'S LEAGUE, TOO!

AW, BABY! YOU KNOW I ONLY GOT EYES FOR YOU! WHY DONTCHA BREAK DOWN AND ADMIT YOU'RE CRAZY ABOUT ME.!?

THAT WOULDN'T BE A BREAK-DOWN...IT WOULD BE A COMPLETE NERVOUS COLLAPSE, YOU BIG GORILLA!

WHILE INSIDE...

IT IS SO GOOD OF YOU TO SEE ME.!...I FEEL SO ASHAMED... TO THINK I ONCE TRIED TO HARM YOU...

THERE, THERE! I DON'T MAKE A PRACTICE OF HARBORING GRUDGES! THE IMPORTANT THING IS THAT YOU REALIZE YOUR MISTAKE. WE ALL MAKE THEM!

SPEAKING OF MISTAKES, I MADE A LULU MYSELF, THE OTHER DAY! PERHAPS YOU READ OF IT?

WHY, NO... WHAT?

AND SO IT SEEMS THAT TONY STARK, BRILLIANT SCIENTIST AND MAN OF ACTION, ISN'T THE FIRST TO BE TAKEN IN BY A PAIR OF LIMPID EYES...

IT'S MY NEW ANTI-GRAVITY RAY! I WAS FOOL ENOUGH TO LET THE WORLD KNOW ABOUT IT TOO SOON! FOR EVEN I CAN'T MAKE ANOTHER ONE... I STUMBLED UPON THIS BY ACCIDENT!

THAT LITTLE BOX? IT LOOKS SO SIMPLE YOU MUS[T] BE JOKIN[G]

STUNG BY THE BLACK WIDOW'S REACTION, TONY STARK DEMONSTRATES...

JOKING? WATCH THIS! THAT STEEL SAFE WEIGHS A TON!

INCREDIBLE! IF I COULD STEAL THAT ANTI-GRAVITY RAY, I COULD WRITE MY OWN TICKET BEHIND THE IRON CURTAIN!

SUDDENLY...

OHH...THE STRAIN... ALL THE EXCITEMENT... I FEEL SO DIZZY...

SHE'S FAINTED!

6

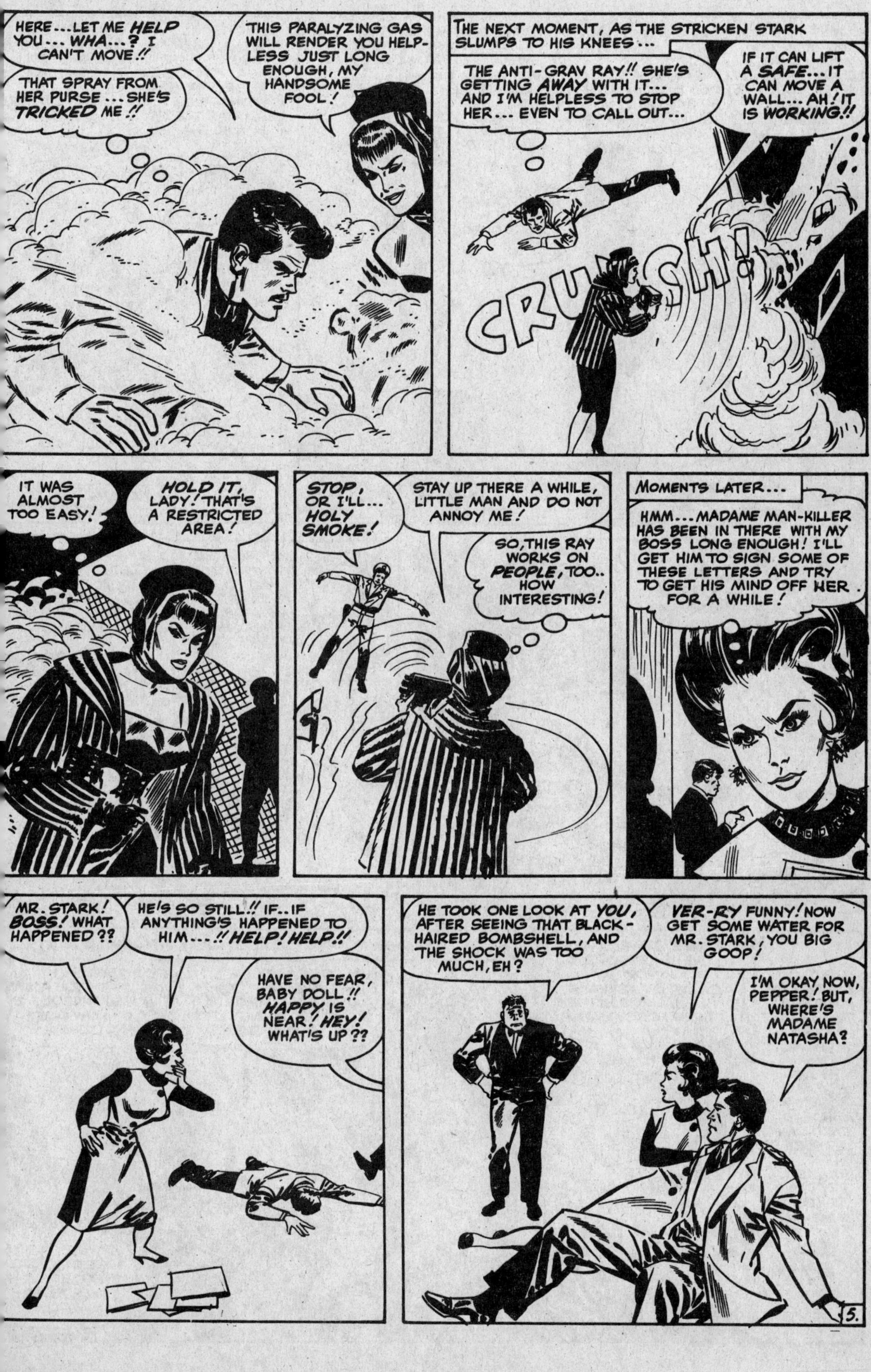
HERE...LET ME HELP YOU... WHA...? I CAN'T MOVE!!
THAT SPRAY FROM HER PURSE... SHE'S TRICKED ME!!
THIS PARALYZING GAS WILL RENDER YOU HELPLESS JUST LONG ENOUGH, MY HANDSOME FOOL!
THE NEXT MOMENT, AS THE STRICKEN STARK SLUMPS TO HIS KNEES...
THE ANTI-GRAV RAY!! SHE'S GETTING AWAY WITH IT... AND I'M HELPLESS TO STOP HER... EVEN TO CALL OUT...
IF IT CAN LIFT A SAFE... IT CAN MOVE A WALL... AH! IT IS WORKING!!
CRUNCH!
IT WAS ALMOST TOO EASY!
HOLD IT, LADY! THAT'S A RESTRICTED AREA!
STOP, OR I'LL... HOLY SMOKE!
STAY UP THERE A WHILE, LITTLE MAN AND DO NOT ANNOY ME!
SO, THIS RAY WORKS ON PEOPLE, TOO.. HOW INTERESTING!
MOMENTS LATER...
HMM... MADAME MAN-KILLER HAS BEEN IN THERE WITH MY BOSS LONG ENOUGH! I'LL GET HIM TO SIGN SOME OF THESE LETTERS AND TRY TO GET HIS MIND OFF HER FOR A WHILE!
MR. STARK! BOSS! WHAT HAPPENED??
HE'S SO STILL!! IF.. IF ANYTHING'S HAPPENED TO HIM...!! HELP! HELP!!
HAVE NO FEAR, BABY DOLL!! HAPPY IS NEAR! HEY! WHAT'S UP??
HE TOOK ONE LOOK AT YOU, AFTER SEEING THAT BLACK-HAIRED BOMBSHELL, AND THE SHOCK WAS TOO MUCH, EH?
VER-RY FUNNY! NOW GET SOME WATER FOR MR. STARK, YOU BIG GOOP!
I'M OKAY NOW, PEPPER! BUT, WHERE'S MADAME NATASHA?
5.

GONE WITH THE WIND, BOSS! AND GOOD RIDDANCE! SAY! WHAT'S *HE* DOING UP THERE?

I'LL EXPLAIN LATER! HE'LL DRIFT DOWN AGAIN IN A FEW SECONDS! AS FOR *ME*... I'VE GOT A *JOB* TO DO!

I UNDERESTIMATED THE *BLACK WIDOW*! I *KNEW* SHE WAS UP TO NO GOOD, BUT I HAD TO PRETEND I TRUSTED HER...TO LEARN WHAT SHE WAS AFTER! I NEVER THOUGHT SHE'D MOVE SO FAST...SO UNEXPECTEDLY!

WELL, SHE *WON* ROUND ONE FROM TONY STARK...

BUT SHE'LL FIND *IRON MAN* A *TOUGHER* FOE TO BEAT! I'LL GIVE MYSELF A SHAKE-DOWN FLIGHT NOW, TO BE SURE I'M IN TOP SHAPE!

AFTER ALL, AS IRON MAN I WAS ABLE TO DEFEAT BOTH HER AND HER PARTNER BORIS...*

*ED. NOTE: TALES OF SUSPENSE #52

"PERHAPS I WAS JUST *LUCKY* THEN, WHEN THEY SEEMED TO HAVE THE UPPER HAND! BUT, I'M STILL *GAME* TO TRY AGAIN!"

"AND *THIS* TIME I WON'T ALLOW HER TO *ESCAPE*, TO MENACE ME AT SOME FUTURE TIME!"

BORIS IS FINISHED! I'LL LET THE BLACK WIDOW GO...AFTER ALL, SHE *IS* JUST A WOMAN...AND SUCH A LOVELY ONE!

BUT, CUNNING AND RUTHLESS THOUGH SHE MAY BE, MADAME NATASHA *IS* A WOMAN, AS *IRON MAN* HAS SAID...AND, AS SUCH, SHE *LOVES* PRETTY THINGS! SO...

THOSE JEWELS ARE LOVELY! BEFORE I WORK FOR MY *COUNTRY* PERHAPS I SHALL DO SOME-THING FOR *MYSELF*!

LATER, A TRANS-ATLANTIC CALL TO A VERY INTERESTED PARTY...

YES, COMRADE LEADER! I HAVE THE NEW "TOY" YOU'VE READ ABOUT! BUT FIRST I MUST KNOW.. AM I *FORGIVEN*?

FORGIVEN? OF COURSE! YOU KNOW HOW GENEROUS I AM! HOW SOFT-HEARTED I AM!

QUICK!! IGOR HAVE THIS CALL *TRACED*! IT'S THE BLACK WIDOW!!

NOW LISTEN CLOSELY, MY LITTLE PIGEON! HERE IS WHAT I WANT YOU TO DO...

YES, *OF COURSE,* COMRADE LEADER! *THIS* TIME I WILL DEFINITELY ELIMINATE BOTH STARK AND IRON MAN! THE BLACK WIDOW NEVER FAILS *TWICE!*

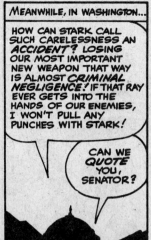

MEANWHILE, IN WASHINGTON...

HOW CAN STARK CALL SUCH CARELESSNESS AN *ACCIDENT?* LOSING OUR MOST IMPORTANT NEW WEAPON THAT WAY IS ALMOST *CRIMINAL NEGLIGENCE!* IF THAT RAY EVER GETS INTO THE HANDS OF OUR ENEMIES, I WON'T PULL ANY PUNCHES WITH STARK!

CAN WE *QUOTE* YOU, SENATOR?

AS FOR TONY STARK, HE TRIES DESPERATELY TO RECREATE THE RAY GUN...

IT'S NO USE... I *CAN'T* DUPLICATE IT!! RIGHT NOW, THE DANGEROUS BLACK WIDOW HAS THE ONLY WORKING MODEL!

LOOK AT THIS STORY... "STARK'S LOYALTY IN DOUBT... ??" OF ALL THE...

THE *NERVE* OF THAT PAPER, *WRITING* SUCH A THING! AFTER ALL MR. STARK CONTRIBUTED TO OUR NATION'S *DEFENSE!!*

HEY, TAKE IT EASY, PEP! I DIDN'T *PRINT* IT... I ONLY *BOUGHT* IT!

FINALLY, STARK REALIZES WHATEVER IS TO BE DONE MUST BE DONE AS IRON MAN... THE BLACK WIDOW MUST BE FOUND!

CAN'T WASTE ANY MORE TIME IN THE LAB, NOT WHILE MADAME NATASHA IS STILL FREE!

I'LL GIVE MYSELF A FULL, HIGH-INTENSITY ELECTRIC CHARGE! FOR, IF NATASHA EVER TURNS MY OWN ANTI-GRAV WEAPON *AGAINST* ME, I'LL NEED EVERY OUNCE OF POWER I CAN MUSTER!

STRANGE HOW MUCH I OWE TO MY LIFE-GIVING TRANSISTORS! THEY NOT ONLY POWER MY *IRON MAN* ARMOR, BUT THEY KEEP MY INJURED HEART BEATING SO THAT TONY STARK CAN REMAIN ALIVE! MY VERY EXISTENCE IS HANGING BY AN ELECTRIC CORD!

WELL, ENOUGH PHILOSOPHY FOR NOW! IF I KNOW MY WOMEN, AND NOBODY KNOWS THEM BETTER THAN TONY STARK, *THE BLACK WIDOW* MUST BE IMPATIENT TO *STRIKE* BY NOW! AND WHATEVER SHE DOES... SHE'LL FIND *IRON MAN* READY FOR HER THIS TIME!

7.

BUT NO SOONER HAS THE POWERFUL FIGURE LEFT HIS HOME BASE THAN DISASTER STRIKES ELSEWHERE!

NOW FOR MY FIRST STRIKE AGAINST DEMOCRACY!!

AH! IT IS WORKING PERFECTLY!!

RUN FOR YOUR LIVES!! THE WHOLE PLACE HAS GONE MAD!!

MOVING THE SIMPLE CONTROL LEVER, THE BLACK WIDOW IS ABLE TO PERFORM THE SEEMINGLY IMPOSSIBLE!

HOLY COW!! LOOK AT THAT HUGE TANK, FLOATING RIGHT OUT OF THE PLANT! IT'S BLACK MAGIC!

WITHIN SECONDS, IRON MAN LEARNS THE SHOCKING NEWS ON HIS BUILT-IN RADIO RECEIVER, AS HE RETURNS TO HIS FACTORY AT TOP SPEED...

SO IT'S BEGUN! THE BLACK WIDOW HAS STRUCK!!

MOVING LIKE A ONE-MAN DERRICK, HARNESSING HIS TRANSISTOR ENERGY OUTPUT TO THE FULLEST, IRON MAN QUICKLY REPAIRS THE DAMAGE...

AT LEAST I'M ABLE TO SET THINGS RIGHT... BUT I CAN'T COVER ALL MY FACTORIES AT ONCE...

WILL YOU LOOK AT THAT GUY? LIFTING A WHOLE STEEL SECTION!

YEAH! TOO BAD HE WASN'T HERE A HALF-HOUR AGO!

BUT, AS IRON MAN FEVERISHLY WORKS AT ONE OF THE FACTORIES IN HIS VAST SPRAWLING, INDUSTRIAL COMPLEX, THE BLACK WIDOW, AIDED BY THE AWESOME WEAPON WHICH HE HIMSELF CREATED, IS MILES AWAY, ATTACKING ANOTHER OF HIS VITAL PRODUCTION PLANT

IT IS UNCANNY!! THE POWER OF ANTHONY STARK'S INVENTION SEEMS TO BE VIRTUALLY UNLIMITED! AND, IT ALLOWS ME TO REMAIN AT A SAFE DISTANCE WHILE I PERFORM MY MISSION OF SABOTAGE!

RRRIP!

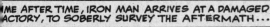

LATE AGAIN! HOW CAN I EVER CATCH UP WITH HER? SHE HAS THE CUNNING OF A FOX, AND THE STOLEN POWER OF ONE OF THE WORLD'S MOST AWESOME WEAPONS!!

BUT, LATER THAT NIGHT, AN UNEXPECTED MEETING TAKES PLACE...

WHAT'S THIS? IGOR! STANSKY! HOW DARE YOU COME HERE, YOU FOOLS!

A THOUSAND APOLOGIES, DEAR LADY, BUT WE ARE ONLY SOLDIERS...LIKE YOU! WE HAVE OUR ORDERS...WE ARE HERE TO HELP YOU...

WHEN OUR COMRADE LEADER INSTRUCTS, WE LISTEN...AS YOU SHALL, TOO!

THE ORDERS ARE BRIEF...AND BOLD...

FIRST ANTHONY STARK, THEN IRON MAN, THEN FORT KNOX? THAT'S QUITE AN ORDER!

PERHAPS, FOR ANYONE BUT YOU, MADAME NATASHA! WITH THE WEAPON YOU HAVE STOLEN FROM STARK, ANYTHING IS POSSIBLE!

ONE MORE THING...BEFORE WE LEAVE, WE WANT A PERSONAL DEMONSTRATION OF THE WEAPON'S POWER!

LET ME HAVE IT! NOW...I SHALL POINT IT AT THAT CAR AND PUSH THE CONTROL LEVER!

STANSKY! YOU FOOL! GIVE IT BACK TO ME! YOU HAVE NEITHER THE SKILL, NOR THE INTELLIGENCE!! NO!!

SILENCE, WOMAN!

AND THUS, THE SPIES MAKE THEIR FIRST BIG MISTAKE!! FOR, A VENGEFUL FLYING FIGURE IS IN THE VICINITY!

THAT CAR! FLOATING IN THE AIR! IT MEANS I'VE FOUND HER AT LAST!

I MUST ATTACK QUICKLY... TAKE HER BY SURPRISE... KEEP HER OFF BALANCE!

THE RAY IS COMING FROM THAT WINDOW! THIS IS THE MOMENT!!

9

BEFORE THE REDS KNOW WHAT HAS HAPPENED, THE FULL FIGHTING FURY OF *IRON MAN* SCATTERS THEM LIKE TEN-PINS!

MUST GET THE RAY BACK WHILE I CAN!

IT'S IRON MAN!! =UGHH!=

SHE STILL HAS THE ANTI-GRAV WEAPON! PERHAPS I CAN OUT-BLUFF HER...

THAT RAY WON'T WORK AGAINST *ME*! HAND IT OVER!!

NICE TRY, IRON MAN...

BUT THE BLACK WIDOW IS NOT AS GULLIBLE AS *THAT*!

TOO LATE! SHE'S AIMED IT AT ME!

ZZZZ!

I WON'T RESIST! I'LL BIDE MY TIME... SAVE MY ENERGY... LET HER THINK I'M HELPLESS! THEN, I'LL STRIKE WHEN THEY LEAST EXPECT IT!!

IGOR! STANSKY! QUICK... SEIZE HIM WHILE HE'S HELPLESS!

DA!

GOOD! I KNEW YOU'D GROW TOO CARELESS! WHEN THEY PASSED BETWEEN THE RAY AND ME, IT BROKE THE BEAM'S ENERGY! AND *NOW*...

HE'S ATTACKING!! WE HAVEN'T A CHANCE! RUN!!

COME BACK, YOU COWARDS! WAIT!

10.

VERY WELL, THEN! I'LL DEFEAT YOU ALONE! THIS ANTI-GRAV MACHINE MAKES ME COMPLETELY UNBEATABLE!

SHE'S AIMING THE WEAPON AT ME AGAIN... WITH THE CONTROL SET AT "REVERSE"! I'M PINNED DOWN... CAN'T MOVE!!

WHIRRRMMMMM

FAREWELL, IRON MAN! *THIS* TIME MY VICTORY IS COMPLETE!

RACING OUTSIDE, THE BLACK WIDOW FINDS HER COWARDLY CO-SPIES, AND THEN...

YOU ARE *RAISING* THE BUILDING! WHY??

BRRR

WHY? YOU BLIND FOOLS!! WHEN I SHUT *OFF* THE RAY, THE STRUCTURE WILL *FALL*, TRAPPING IRON MAN *FOREVER*!

THEN, THE BLACK WIDOW SUITS THE ACTION TO HER WORDS! BUT LITTLE DOES SHE DREAM THAT THE GENIUS OF TONY STARK, WHO CREATED THE ANTI-GRAV WEAPON, *ALSO* CREATED MINIATURE TRANSISTORS IN IRON MAN'S COSTUME WHICH ARE POWERFUL ENOUGH TO COUNTERACT THE FORCE OF THE FALLING BUILDING!

THE RAY IS *OFF* ME AGAIN! I'M FREE TO TAKE THE INITIATIVE ONCE MORE!

MINUTES LATER...

THEY'VE GONE!! BUT I ADJUSTED MY RADAR CIRCUIT TO THE FREQUENCY OF THE ANTI-GRAV DEVICE! I CAN FIND HER AGAIN WITH EASE... AS SOON AS I RECHARGE MY LIFE-SAVING TRANSISTORS!

AND SO, NOT SUSPECTING THAT IRON MAN STILL LIVES, WE FIND THE BLACK WIDOW SURVEYING THE HIDDEN GOLD VAULTS OF *FORT KNOX*...

DO NOTHING RASH, MADAME NATASHA! EVEN IF WE CAN GET PAST THOSE ARMY TANKS, WE STILL HAVE A MUCH BIGGER PROBLEM! THE FORT KNOX GOLD IS HIDDEN DEEP IN THAT MOUNTAIN! HOW WILL WE GET AT IT?

YOU HAVE NO IMAGINATION, IGOR!... WATCH!!

WE WILL *MOVE THE MOUNTAIN*...

BRRR!

INCREDIBLE! THE RAY CAN DO *ANYTHING*!!

11.

THE *TANKS* HAVE SEEN US! THEY'RE ATTACKING! SHOOT!!

IDIOTS! ONLY *ONE* THING CAN STOP THEM!

Then, with the awesome anti-grav ray trained on them, the tanks dangle above the ground...

SEE? NOTHING CAN STOP ME! THE TANKS ARE HELPLESS!

BUT, MADAME NATASHA...

SILENCE! I MUST PLAN OUR *NEXT MOVE!*

But, that "next move" is destined never to be made! For, at that instant...

WOW!! IF EVER A GUY ARRIVED IN THE NICK OF TIME! I'VE GOT TO SAVE THOSE TANKS... *SOMEHOW!!*

Without a second's hesitation, Iron Man hurls himself into the dangerous ray...

AH! THAT *DOES* IT! MY PASSING THROUGH THE RAY BEAM COUNTERACTS ITS ANTI-GRAVITY POWER...

IRON MAN!! STILL ALIVE?? IT CAN'T BE!

Even the man of iron isn't strong enough to catch two forty-ton tanks! But, moving with split-second timing, he strikes each as it falls, slowing their descent, thus allowing them to right themselves and land safely on their resilient steel treads!

NOW THAT THE TANKS ARE OKAY, I'LL FIND A WAY TO GET MY ANTI-GRAV DEVICE BACK... OR DIE TRYING!

17

'THE BLACK WIDOW IS AIMING THE RAY AT ME AGAIN! BUT THIS TIME I'VE A SURPRISE IN STORE FOR HER!'

AFTER ALL, IT'S ONLY FITTING THAT THE MAN WHO CREATED THE WEAPON SHOULD FINALLY FIND A WAY TO NULLIFY IT!

HEN, WITH LIGHTNING SPEED, A TINY BEAM OF LIGHT FROM TRANSISTORIZED FINGERS FINDS TS MARK...

OH NO!! THE RAY IS LOSING ITS POWER!!

EXACTLY AS I PLANNED, BEAUTIFUL! THIS PROTON ELECTRIC CHARGE WILL DESTROY THE OUTPUT OF THE RAY FOREVER!!

BUT WITH THE RAY OUT OF ACTION, THE MOUNTAIN'S FALLING AGAIN!! GOT TO SAVE THOSE TWO RED AGENTS FROM BEING CRUSHED!

WHAT MANNER OF MEN ARE THESE AMERICANS, WHO RISK THEIR LIVES FOR THEIR ENEMIES??

WE WERE ALMOST KILLED!

YOU SAVED US!! I...I DO NOT UNDERSTAND!

THAT'S THE TROUBLE WITH YOU COMMIES! YOU JUST DON'T DIG US!

CRASH

MINUTES LATER...

WE'LL TAKE CARE OF THESE TWO SPIES NOW, IRON MAN!

BUT WHAT ABOUT THE ANTI-GRAV WEAPON? THE BLACK WIDOW DISAPPEARED WITH IT!

IT WON'T DO HER ANY GOOD, MAJOR! MY PROTON BEAM DESTROYED ITS POWER COMPLETELY!

IMAGINE STARK ALLOWING THAT WEAPON TO BE STOLEN! IF YOU ASK ME, HE'S JUST AN OVER-RATED PLAY-BOY...OR WORSE!

IT'S A GOOD THING HE HAS YOU AROUND TO CORRECT HIS BUMBLING MISTAKES!!

YES, IT IS, MAJOR!...A FAR BETTER THING THAN ANYONE SUSPECTS!

NEXT ISH: IRON MAN FACES A NEW, SENSATIONAL SUPER-VILLAIN, WITH THE USUAL LEE-HECK BRAND OF DRAMA, ACTION, AND SURPRISES! SEE YOU THEN! The END.

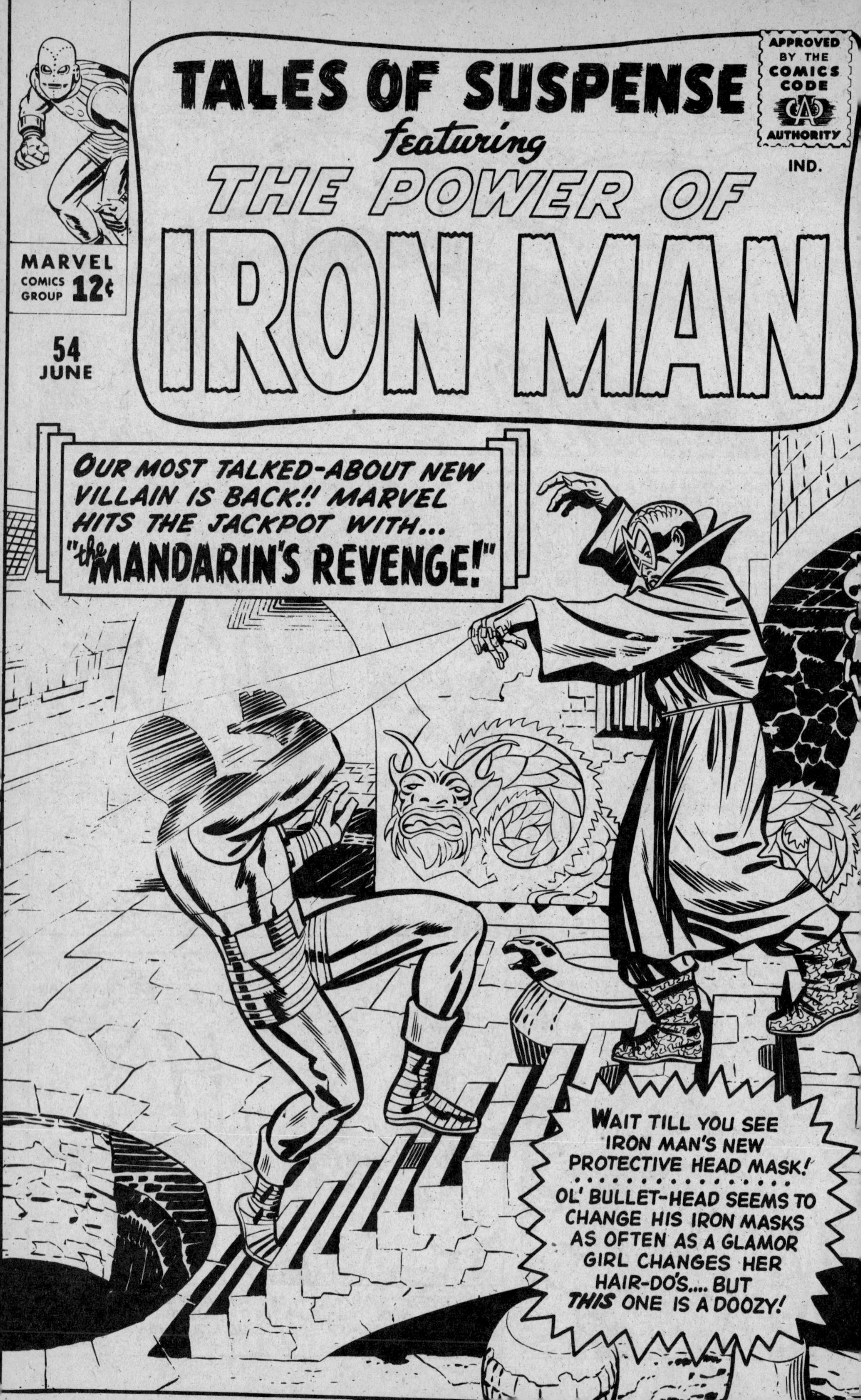
TALES OF SUSPENSE
featuring
THE POWER OF
IRON MAN
APPROVED BY THE COMICS CODE AUTHORITY
IND.
MARVEL COMICS GROUP 12¢
54
JUNE
OUR MOST TALKED-ABOUT NEW VILLAIN IS BACK!! MARVEL HITS THE JACKPOT WITH... "the MANDARIN'S REVENGE!"
WAIT TILL YOU SEE IRON MAN'S NEW PROTECTIVE HEAD MASK!
OL' BULLET-HEAD SEEMS TO CHANGE HIS IRON MASKS AS OFTEN AS A GLAMOR GIRL CHANGES HER HAIR-DO'S.... BUT THIS ONE IS A DOOZY!

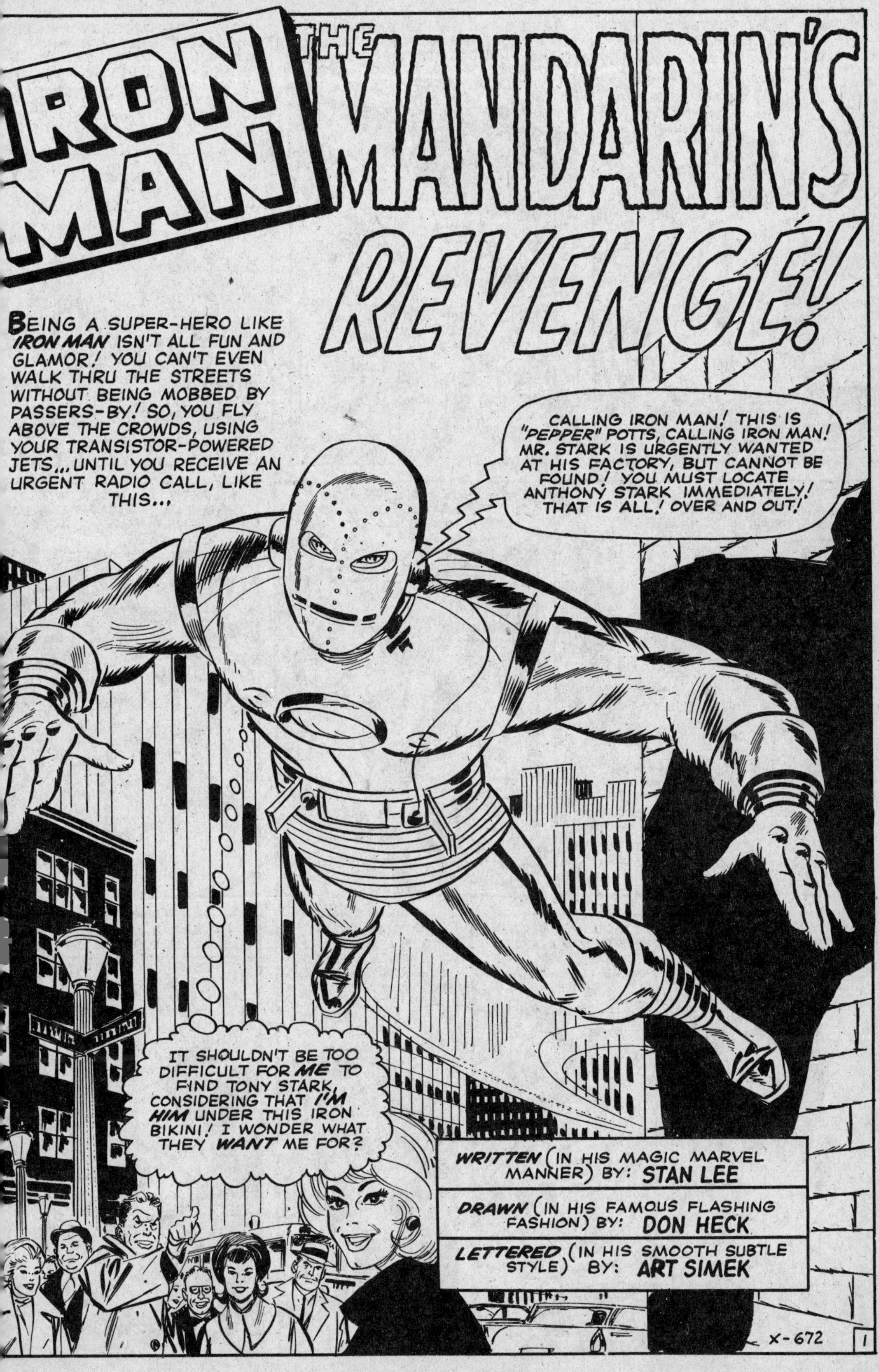
IRON MAN
THE MANDARIN'S REVENGE!
BEING A SUPER-HERO LIKE IRON MAN ISN'T ALL FUN AND GLAMOR! YOU CAN'T EVEN WALK THRU THE STREETS WITHOUT BEING MOBBED BY PASSERS-BY! SO, YOU FLY ABOVE THE CROWDS, USING YOUR TRANSISTOR-POWERED JETS... UNTIL YOU RECEIVE AN URGENT RADIO CALL, LIKE THIS...
CALLING IRON MAN! THIS IS "PEPPER" POTTS, CALLING IRON MAN! MR. STARK IS URGENTLY WANTED AT HIS FACTORY, BUT CANNOT BE FOUND! YOU MUST LOCATE ANTHONY STARK IMMEDIATELY! THAT IS ALL! OVER AND OUT!
IT SHOULDN'T BE TOO DIFFICULT FOR ME TO FIND TONY STARK, CONSIDERING THAT I'M HIM UNDER THIS IRON BIKINI! I WONDER WHAT THEY WANT ME FOR?
WRITTEN (IN HIS MAGIC MARVEL MANNER) BY: STAN LEE
DRAWN (IN HIS FAMOUS FLASHING FASHION) BY: DON HECK
LETTERED (IN HIS SMOOTH SUBTLE STYLE) BY: ART SIMEK
X-672
1

I WONDER IF PEPPER EVER SUSPECTS THAT HER BOSS, TONY STARK, AND HIS MYSTERIOUS BODY-GUARD, IRON MAN, ARE ONE AND THE SAME?

HERE'S THE SECRET ENTRANCE TO MY HIDDEN TUNNEL UNDER THE FACTORY! IT COST A SMALL FORTUNE TO CONSTRUCT, BUT IT WAS WORTH IT!

LEAVING AND ENTERING UNSEEN IS THE ONLY WAY TO GUARD MY DOUBLE IDENTITY!

NOW, AT THE PRESS OF A BUTTON MY ROLLER WHEELS EMERGE! WHEN I USED TO GO SKATING YEARS AGO, I NEVER DREAMED I'D BE DOING IT AS AN *ADULT* LATER ON! BUT IT'S A GOOD WAY TO SAVE MY TRANSISTOR POWER OVER SHORT DISTANCES!

I'M GLAD I HAD A CHANCE TO CHECK OUT THE NEW HELMET I DESIGNED! IT'S STRONGER AND LIGHTER THAN MY OTHER ONE, AND MORE COMFORTABLE!

SO FAR SO GOOD! ALL'S CLEAR IN MY PRIVATE OFFICE! NOW FOR A QUICK CHANGE...

I'M GLAD I MADE MY ARMOR OUT OF *FLEXIBLE* IRON, SO THAT IT'S EASY TO MANIPULATE!

THE PARTS ALL FOLD INTO THEMSELVES AND FIT SNUGLY WITHIN MY DUMMY ATTACHE CASE!

=WHEW!= IT'S A *RELIEF* TO GET OUT OF THIS STUFFY IRON MASK!

ALTHOUGH I SHOULDN'T *KNOCK* MY ARMOR! IT'S SAVED MY LIFE MORE TIMES THAN I CAN REMEMBER!!

AND THAT'S THAT! OL' BULLET-HEAD IS SAFELY TUCKED AWAY IN HIS CASE, AND NOW MR. MONEY-BAGS STARK WILL MAKE HIS APPEARANCE!

THEN, EMERGING FROM HIS LUXURIOUS PRIVATE OFFICE...

IRON MAN SAID I WAS WANTED HERE, PEPPER! IS ANYTHING WRONG?

WE DON'T *KNOW!* YOU'RE WANTED AT THE *PENTAGON* --AT ONCE!

IT MUST B SERIOU BOSS!

...AND OF COURSE YOU WOULDN'T DREAM OF GOING TO WASHINGTON WITHOUT TAKING YOUR GAL FRIDAY, WOULD YOU?

I'D LIKE TO BE WITH PEPPER *ALWAYS*... BUT, DARE NOT EXPOSE HER TO THE DANGERS THAT *IRON MAN* MUST FACE!

SORRY, PEPPER! YOU AND HAPPY WILL HAVE TO STAY HERE TO MIND THE STORE!

BUT, MR. STARK-- WON'T YOU NEED ME TO TAKE NOTES?? TO KEEP YOUR RECORDS! *OTHER* EXECS ALWAYS TAKE THEIR STAFF TO IMPORTANT MEETINGS! BESIDES, I JUST GOT THE MOST *DARLING* NEW TRAVELING CASE!

YOU'LL HAVE TO SAVE IT FOR YOUR VACATION, RED! ALL THE NOTES I NEED CAN BE TAKEN BY THE MINIATURE *RECORDER* I CARRY IN MY ATTACHE CASE! BESIDES, I SUSPECT THIS WON'T BE A *PLEASURE* TRIP!

WHAT ABOUT *ME*, BOSS? WHICH CAR DO YOU WANT ME TO DRIVE YOU IN? THE XK-E, OR THE JAG?

NEITHER, HAPPY! I'LL HAVE *IRON MAN* DRIVE ME THERE-- I MAY *NEED* HIM!

OKAY BY ME! I'LL STAY AND KEEP *PEPPER* COMPANY!

WELL-- THANKS FOR *NOTHING*!!

LOOK, SUNNY JIM-- WHEN I WANT ANY COMPANY, I'LL PICK MY *OWN*!

AWW, YOU'RE JUST ANGRY BECAUSE I ALWAYS PLAY SO HARD-TO-GET!

HMMPH! YOU'RE ABOUT AS HARD-TO-GET AS THE *COMMON COLD*!

YOU WON'T HAVE MUCH TIME TO KEEP *ANYONE* COMPANY, HAPPY! I'M SENDING YOU ON AN INSPECTION TOUR OF MY OTHER STARK FACTORIES!

BUT, BOSS-- I DON'T KNOW ANYTHING ABOUT THAT KINDA JAZZ! I'M JUST A *CHAUFFEUR*!

WELL, IT'S TIME THAT YOU *LEARNED*! MY ORDERS *STAND*! I'LL CONTACT YOU WHEN I RETURN!

HOW CAN SUCH A WALKING DREAMBOAT BE SUCH A HARD-HEADED *BOSS*??

EASY! EVERYONE KNOWS BOSSES AIN'T REALLY HUMAN!

3

THEN, IN STARK'S PRIVATE OFFICE... WHAT'S GOTTEN *INTO* ME?? WHY WAS I SO ROUGH ON HAPPY? I DON'T *REALLY* NEED HIM TO MAKE A TOUR OF MY FACTORIES!! I MIGHT AS WELL ADMIT THE *TRUTH* TO MYSELF--

I'M *JEALOUS!* JEALOUS OF HIS ATTENTIONS TOWARDS PEPPER! THAT'S THE *REAL* ANSWER!

SHE *SAYS* SHE'S NOT INTERESTED IN HIM--BUT I SOMETIMES THINK IT'S A LITTLE GAME THEY PLAY! BENEATH THE BICKERING, A ROMANCE MAY BE GROWING!

BUT WHAT RIGHT DO *I* HAVE TO OBJECT?? ME, A MAN WHO LIVES AT THE EDGE OF DEATH! A MAN WHOSE EVERY MOMENT MAY BE HIS LAST!

BUT, TONY STARK IS FORCED TO END HIS MUSINGS AS HE AGAIN BECOMES THE POWERFUL *IRON MAN,* STREAKING OVER THE CITY LIKE A GOLDEN GLADIATOR!

AT TOP SPEED, MY TRANSISTORS HAVE ENOUGH THRUST TO GET ME ACROSS THE HUDSON AND INTO NEW JERSEY--

THEN, ON THE TURNPIKE, I CAN RECHARGE THEM BY RESORTING TO MY ROLLER WHEELS! WITH THEIR OWN JET MOTORS, THEY CAN KEEP ME GOING EASILY AT NORMAL HIGHWAY SPEED...

...UNTIL I CAN PUT MY FLYING JETS INTO ACTION AGAIN! THIS SURE BEATS GETTING STUCK TRAFFIC JAMS

NOT BAD! LESS THAN AN HOUR, AND THERE'S THE CAPITOL *NOW!*

MINUTES LATER, SECRETLY CHANGING BACK TO TONY STARK, THE HANDSOME AVENGER ENTERS A PENTAGON BRIEFING ROOM, WHERE HE LEARNS...

LET'S GET RIGHT TO THE POINT, STARK! WE'VE BEEN USING YOUR NEW OBSERVER MISSILES IN VIET NAM--BUT THE RESULTS HAVE BEEN *DISASTEROUS!!*

YOUR MISSILES, WORKING BY REMOTE CONTROL, WERE SUPPOSED TO TAKE PICTURES FOR US BEHIND ENEMY LINES--BUT AFTER TAKING THE FIRST FEW PICTURES, WHICH YOU SEE THERE-- EVERY ONE OF THEM HAS EITHER *CRASHED* OR *DISAPPEARED!*

I DON'T UNDERSTAND! I CHECKED THEM OUT *MYSELF!* THEY WERE ALL A-OKAY! AND THEY'RE FASTER THAN *ANYTHING* THE REDS CAN PUT IN THE AIR TO SHOOT THEM DOWN!

MAYBE THEY'RE NOT AS FAST AS YOU CLAIM! MAYBE YOU SOLD US A BUM PRODUCT, MISTER!

NEGATIVE, COLONEL! I'LL GO TO VIET NAM MYSELF IMMEDIATELY AND GET TO THE BOTTOM OF THIS!

OUR SCENE NOW CHANGES TO A ROCKET TEST AREA WHERE A LONG RANGE I.C.B.M. IS BEING READIED FOR A SHOT OVER THE PACIFIC...

TWELVE MINUTES TO COUNTDOWN...

UNDER THE MISSILE'S "BELLY," WE FIND A STRANGE HITCH-HIKER!

MY BUILT-IN OXYGEN MASK AND MY FLEXIBLE ARMOR SHOULD ENABLE ME TO ENDURE THE SHOCK OF BLAST-OFF!

AND, THIS WAY I'LL SAVE MY PRECIOUS TRANSISTOR POWER FOR THE ORIENT, WHERE I'LL REALLY NEED IT!

LATER, AFTER A BREATH-TAKING RIDE OVER THE PACIFIC AT INCREDIBLE ROCKET SPEED...

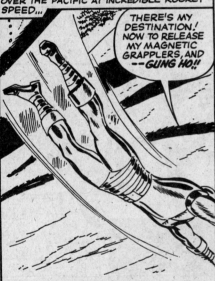

THERE'S MY DESTINATION! NOW TO RELEASE MY MAGNETIC GRAPPLERS, AND --GUNG HO!!

LANDING SAFELY BY MEANS OF HIS BUILT-IN JETS, IRON MAN AGAIN CHANGES IDENTITIES -- AND WITHIN MINUTES, TONY STARK, INVENTOR AND WEAPONS MANUFACTURER IS AT A HEAVILY-GUARDED MISSILE BASE IN THE FAR EAST...

I KNOW THERE'S NOTHING FUNCTIONALLY WRONG WITH MY OBSERVER MISSILES, GENERAL! SOME EXTERNAL FORCE MUST BE AFFECTING THEM!

WE HAVE ONE IN THE AIR RIGHT AT THIS MOMENT! YOU CAN FOLLOW ITS PROGRESS THRU OUR RADIO TELESCOPE! PERHAPS IT WILL GIVE YOU A CLUE TO WHAT'S WRONG!

THE MISSILE IS SLOWING DOWN--CHANGING COURSE-- AS THOUGH BEING PULLED BY AN UNSEEN FORCE BEAM!!

IF WHAT I SUSPECT IS TRUE, THE ENEMY HAS A WEAPON WHICH POSES A GRAVE THREAT TO OUR DEFENSES! BUT WHO COULD HAVE INVENTED SUCH A CLEVER DEVICE, UNLESS--

OF COURSE! I SHOULD HAVE GUESSED BY THE SPOT WHERE IT HAPPENED! IT'S THE STRONGHOLD OF THE MANDARIN-- THE MOST BRILLIANT EVIL GENIUS IN THE ORIENT!!

5

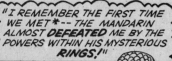

"I REMEMBER THE FIRST TIME WE MET*-- THE MANDARIN ALMOST *DEFEATED* ME BY THE POWERS WITHIN HIS MYSTERIOUS *RINGS!*"

*TALES OF SUSPENSE #50 "THE HANDS OF THE MANDARIN" --EDITOR

"HE WORE A DIFFERENT RING ON EVERY FINGER, AND EACH HAD A DEADLY, UNEXPECTED POWER WHICH HE CONTROLLED AT WILL!"

"NOT ONLY IS THE MANDARIN AN *UNDENIABLE* MASTER OF *SCIENCE*, HE'S ALSO A SAVAGE, SUPER-STRONG *FIGHTER* WHOSE STRENGTH CAN ALMOST MATCH MY *OWN!*"

"AND, IN A FIGHT, HIS GREATEST WEAPON IS HIS MASTERY OF *KARATE*, WHICH MIGHT HAVE SHATTERED MY ARMOR IF I MADE ONE WRONG *MOVE!*"

IT *MUST* BE THE MANDARIN WHO IS ATTACKING MY MISSILES-- WHICH MEANS I *HAVE* TO FACE HIM AGAIN!

EXCUSING HIMSELF FROM THE MILITARY STAFF ON THE GROUNDS THAT HE WANTS TO DO SOME BASIC RESEARCH, TONY STARK AGAIN PREPARES TO BATTLE AGAINST ALMOST HOPELESS ODDS!

IF I ATTACK HIM AS *IRON MAN*, HIS ELECTRONIC DEFENSES WILL DESTROY ME ON SIGHT! MY ONLY CHANCE IS TO REMAIN IN THE IDENTITY OF TONY STARK AND ALLOW MYSELF TO BE CAPTURED AND BROUGHT BEFORE THE MANDARIN FOR QUESTION-ING!

IT'S LIKE WALKING INTO A DRAGON'S MOUTH-- BUT THERE'S NO OTHER WAY! I'VE GOT TO PROTECT OUR MISSILES -- IF IT COSTS ME MY *LIFE!*

I KNOW THE MANDARIN HAS NO MORE LOVE FOR THE REDS THAN HE HAS FOR *US!* HIS OBJECTIVE IS TO DESTROY *ALL* MILITARY MIGHT, SO THAT *HIS* POWER WILL BE SUPREME!

HERE'S THE TUNNEL LEADING TO HIS MOUNTAINTOP CASTLE NOW! THIS IS *IT!!*

SUDDENLY, AS THE SPEEDING JEEP APPROACHES, A HEAVY IRON GATE CLANGS DOWN, AND...

CAN'T *STOP* IN TIME!! GONNA *HIT!--UGHH!!--*

SCREECH!

CLANK!

6

AND, IN HIS PLUSH, HEAVILY-GUARDED THRONE ROOM, THE MASTER OF ALL HE SURVEYS GIVES A SATISFIED CHUCKLE!

WHO CAN THAT WITLESS FOOL BE WHO DARES ATTEMPT TO ENTER THE CASTLE OF THE *MANDARIN!* THRU MY WIDE-ANGLE VIEWSCREEN NOT THE SMALLEST *INSECT* CAN APPROACH ME WITHOUT BEING DETECTED!

BY ACTIVATING THE SMALLEST POWER OF ONE OF MY MYSTIC RINGS, I CAN EASILY BLOCK THE OCCIDENTAL'S ENTRANCE WHILE MY GUARDS TAKE HIM PRISONER!

NOW, I *PERSONALLY* SHALL VISIT THE INTERROGATION AREA AND LEARN THE REASON FOR HIS BEING HERE-- BEFORE I HAVE HIM PUT TO DEATH!

MEANWHILE...

THERE MUST BE A GREAT *TREASURE* LOCKED WITHIN!

I *KNEW* THEY'D TRY TO OPEN MY ATTACHE CASE! GOOD THING I TOOK A FEW SIMPLE PRECAUTIONS!

AS THE LOCK SPRINGS OPEN, TONY STARK QUICKLY COVERS HIS NOSE WITH A CHEMICALLY-TREATED CLOTH --BUT THE OTHERS ARE NOT SO LUCKY!

WE'VE BEEN *TRICKED!!* SLEEP GAS!! DON'T BREATHE-- DON'T-- OHHH...

THEY'LL BE OUT FOR A GOOD HALF HOUR! NOW TO CHANGE TO *IRON MAN,* CRASH THRU THE WALL, AND THEN-- UH OH.!! HERE'S MY PIGEON.!!

IRON MAN!! YOU *DARE* ATTACK ME AGAIN ??!! *THIS* TIME I'LL SHOW YOU NO MERCY!

YOU WEREN'T EXACTLY A KIND-HEARTED CHERUB *LAST* TIME EITHER, MANDARIN!

7

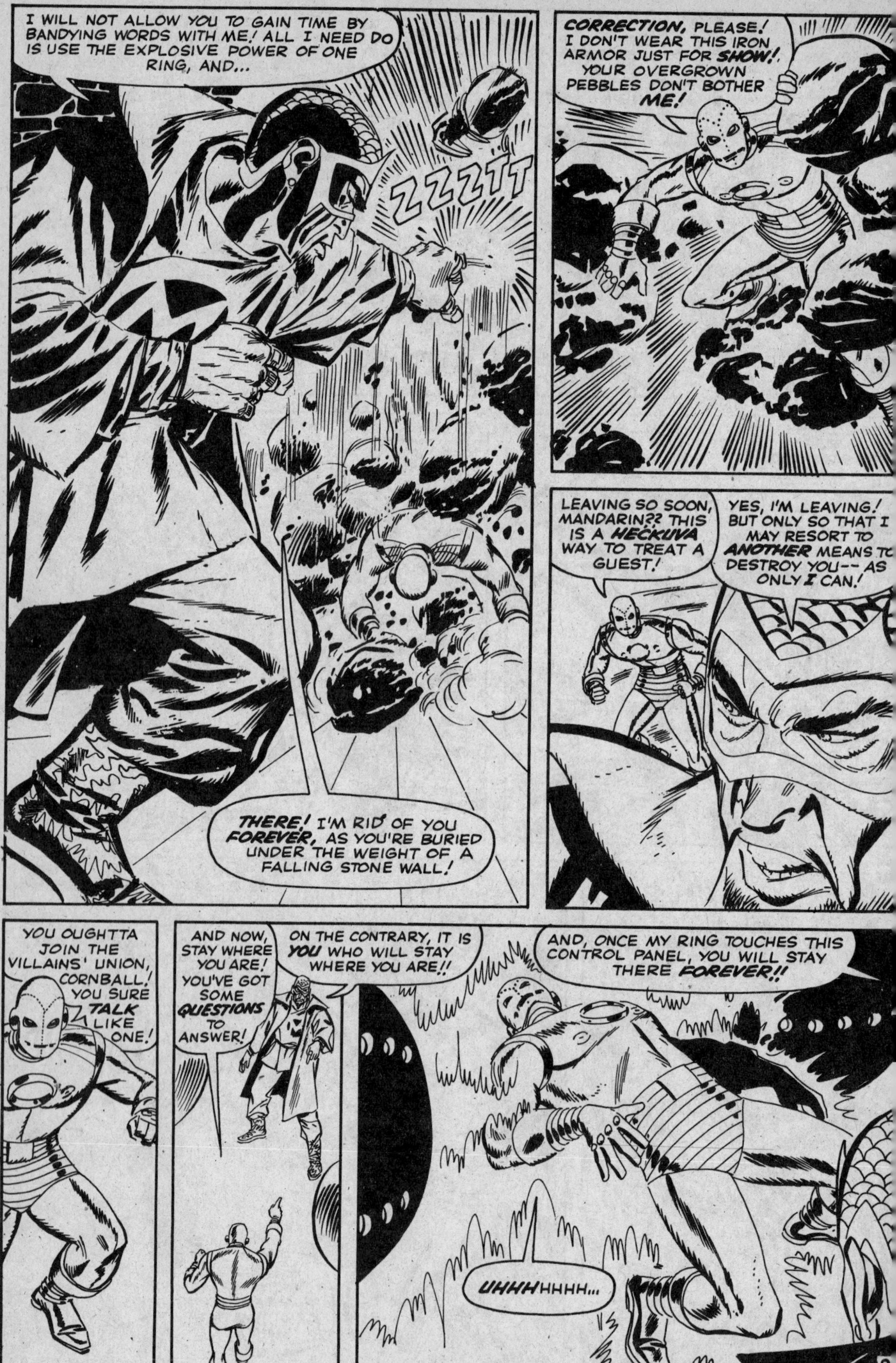
I WILL NOT ALLOW YOU TO GAIN TIME BY BANDYING WORDS WITH ME! ALL I NEED DO IS USE THE EXPLOSIVE POWER OF ONE RING, AND...
ZZZTT
THERE! I'M RID OF YOU FOREVER, AS YOU'RE BURIED UNDER THE WEIGHT OF A FALLING STONE WALL!
CORRECTION, PLEASE! I DON'T WEAR THIS IRON ARMOR JUST FOR SHOW! YOUR OVERGROWN PEBBLES DON'T BOTHER ME!
LEAVING SO SOON, MANDARIN?? THIS IS A HECKUVA WAY TO TREAT A GUEST!
YES, I'M LEAVING! BUT ONLY SO THAT I MAY RESORT TO ANOTHER MEANS TO DESTROY YOU-- AS ONLY I CAN!
YOU OUGHTTA JOIN THE VILLAINS' UNION, CORNBALL! YOU SURE TALK LIKE ONE!
AND NOW, STAY WHERE YOU ARE! YOU'VE GOT SOME QUESTIONS TO ANSWER!
ON THE CONTRARY, IT IS YOU WHO WILL STAY WHERE YOU ARE!!
AND, ONCE MY RING TOUCHES THIS CONTROL PANEL, YOU WILL STAY THERE FOREVER!!
UHHHHHHH...
8

WHAT??!! YOU STILL **MOVE!!** YOU STILL **LIVE!!** YOUR ARMOR MUST BE **MORE** THAN MERE IRON!! I HAVE **UNDER-ESTIMATED** YOU!

THAT'S WHAT I'VE BEEN TRYIN' TO **TELL** YOU, BIG MOUTH! MY ARMOR IS JUST A HOUSING FOR THE CUTEST LITTLE SUPER-POWERED **JETS** YOU EVER SAW!

SHRUGGING OFF THE EFFECTS OF THE ELECTRICAL CHARGE HE RECEIVED, WHICH HIS TRANSISTORIZED GROUNDING WIRES DISPELLED, IRON MAN DUCKS JUST IN TIME TO SAVE HIMSELF FROM A BLOW WHICH SHATTERS A STONE SLAB AS THOUGH IT'S CARDBOARD!!!

NO MATTER **HOW** INGENIOUS YOUR PROTECTIVE DEVICES ARE, THERE IS **STILL** NO PROTECTION AGAINST A LETHAL **KARATE BLOW!**

YOU'RE WRONG **AGAIN**, CHUCKLES!! DID YOU EVER HEAR OF **SPEED** AND **AGILITY??**

OTHERS TREMBLE BEFORE ME, BUT **YOU** MERELY **MOCK** ME!! OTHERS ARE PARALYZED WITH FEAR IN MY PRESENCE, BUT **YOU** DEFY ME!! WHAT MANNER OF BEING **ARE** YOU?

BEFORE I DESTROY YOU COMPLETELY, I MAKE YOU AN **OFFER!** AGREE TO BECOME MY **ALLY**-- SERVE ME-- AND TOGETHER WE CAN RULE THE WORLD! FOR YOUR POWER IS SECOND ONLY TO **MINE!**

I'M DEEPLY TOUCHED BY YOUR GENEROSITY, MANDARIN, BUT I'D RATHER TEAM UP WITH A **RATTLESNAKE!** I'LL NEVER REST TILL YOU, AND EVERYTHING YOU STAND FOR, ARE ERASED FROM THE FACE OF THE EARTH!! DO I MAKE MYSELF CLEAR??

FOOL!! YOU COULD HAVE SHARED THE WORLD'S GREATEST EMPIRE WITH ME!! BUT INSTEAD, YOU HAVE CHOSEN **ANNIHILATION!!** FROM THIS MOMENT ON, YOU ARE **DOOMED!**

CRUNCH

9

HE **SOUNDS** LIKE A HOLD-OVER FROM THE LATE LATE SHOW-- BUT HE'S GOT THE MOXIE TO BACK UP HIS WORDS! AS FOR ME, MY TRANSISTORS ARE BEGINNING TO WEAKEN! I'VE GOT TO STAY CLEAR TILL I FIND A WAY TO RECHARGE THEM.!!

HAH! I SEE THAT MY WORDS HAVE BROUGHT **FEAR** TO YOUR HEART! YOU TRY TO ESCAPE ME! BUT YOU SHALL LEARN THERE **IS** NO ESCAPE FROM THE MANDARIN!

IN RESPECT TO YOUR VALOR AS A FOE, I SHALL GIVE YOU GREAT HONOR!! I SHALL LET YOU BE SLAIN BY A WARRIOR'S SWORD!!

THAT'S REAL **KIND** OF YOU! I'M ALL CHOKED UP!!

SWISH!

AND **STILL** YOU HURL FLIPPANT REMARKS AT ME!! WELL, **THIS** SHALL PUT A STOP TO THEM! **NO** SWORDSMAN IS MY EQUAL.!!

BOY, YOU'RE A REAL MODEST MARVIN! IS THERE ANYTHING YOU **CAN'T** DO?? HOW'S YOUR **KNITTING**, FOR INSTANCE??

YOU ARE BACKED AGAINST A STONE WALL! YOU CAN RUN NO FURTHER! AND NOW, I SHALL ALWAYS **REMEMBER** YOU THIS WAY-- WITH A TAUNT ON YOUR LIPS, AND COURAGE IN YOUR EYES.!!

I HATE TO USE UP SO MUCH OF MY REMAINING JET-POWER, BUT ONLY THRU THE AID OF MY TRANSISTORS CAN I DODGE HIS FATAL SWORD THRUST !! -WHEW!- JUST **MADE** IT!

THUD!!

10

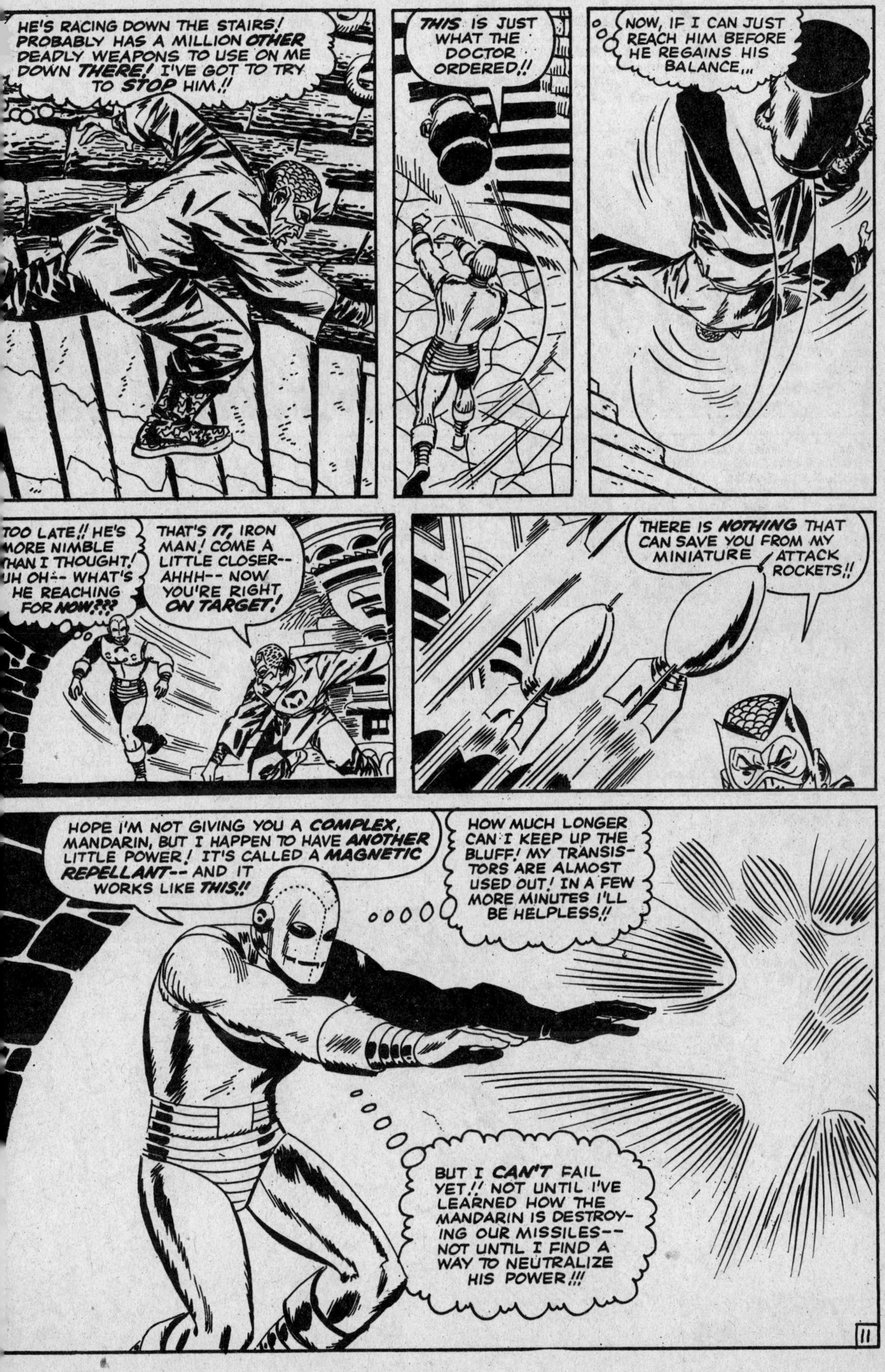
HE'S RACING DOWN THE STAIRS! PROBABLY HAS A MILLION OTHER DEADLY WEAPONS TO USE ON ME DOWN THERE! I'VE GOT TO TRY TO STOP HIM!!
THIS IS JUST WHAT THE DOCTOR ORDERED!!
NOW, IF I CAN JUST REACH HIM BEFORE HE REGAINS HIS BALANCE...
TOO LATE!! HE'S MORE NIMBLE THAN I THOUGHT! UH OH-- WHAT'S HE REACHING FOR NOW???
THAT'S IT, IRON MAN! COME A LITTLE CLOSER-- AHHH-- NOW YOU'RE RIGHT ON TARGET!
THERE IS NOTHING THAT CAN SAVE YOU FROM MY MINIATURE ATTACK ROCKETS!!
HOPE I'M NOT GIVING YOU A COMPLEX, MANDARIN, BUT I HAPPEN TO HAVE ANOTHER LITTLE POWER! IT'S CALLED A MAGNETIC REPELLANT-- AND IT WORKS LIKE THIS!!
HOW MUCH LONGER CAN I KEEP UP THE BLUFF! MY TRANSISTORS ARE ALMOST USED OUT! IN A FEW MORE MINUTES I'LL BE HELPLESS!!
BUT I CAN'T FAIL YET!! NOT UNTIL I'VE LEARNED HOW THE MANDARIN IS DESTROYING OUR MISSILES-- NOT UNTIL I FIND A WAY TO NEUTRALIZE HIS POWER!!!
11

I *COMPLIMENT* YOU, IRON MAN! YOU HAVE GIVEN ME THE MOST STIMULATING BATTLE OF MY CAREER! BUT ALL THINGS MUST END--AND MY *BLACK LIGHT* RING BEAM WILL END THIS HERE AND NOW!

I KNEW I COULDN'T PREPARE AGAINST THE POWERS OF *ALL* HIS RINGS! MY HIGH INTENSITY CHEST BEACON CAN'T EVEN *BEGIN* TO PENETRATE THIS WALL OF BLACKNESS! I CAN'T SEE A *THING*!!

RAW COURAGE ALONE CANNOT FOREVER SAVE YOU FROM MY BRILLIANT ATTACK! NOW, ALL I NEED DO IS COVER THAT PATCH OF BLACK LIGHT WITH UNBREAKABLE STEEL BANDS...

...AND WHEREEVER YOU ARE WITHIN THE DARKNESS, YOU WILL BE HOPELESSLY TRAPPED!

HE'S *RIGHT*! THE MAGNETIC TIPS OF THE STEEL CABLES WERE ATTRACTED TO MY IRON SUIT! THEY'RE GETTING TIGHTER...

AND SO THE BATTLE ENDS, IN THE ONLY WAY IT *CAN*-- WITH TOTAL VICTORY FOR THE MANDARIN--AND COMPLETE DEFEAT FOR MY LUCKLESS FOE!!

IF MY TRANSISTORS WERE CHARGED AT FULL POWER, I COULD SNAP THESE CABLES WITHOUT HALF TRYING!! BUT NOW, I CAN'T EVEN MOVE A MUSCLE!! AND YET-- I *DARE NOT* GIVE UP! THERE'S TOO MUCH AT STAKE!!

WITH A SMUG, SELF-SATISFIED CHORTLE, THE EVIL **MANDARIN** POINTS HIS FINGER LAZILY AT HIS CONTROL PANEL, AND THE ENERGY FROM ONE OF HIS RINGS ACTIVATES A GLEAMING BUTTON...

THEN, SLOWLY, PONDEROUSLY, A GROUP OF THROBBING **DYNAMOS** DESCEND FROM THE CEILING, SURROUNDING IRON MAN...

EVEN IF YOU **COULD** SNAP THOSE CABLES, IT WOULD NOT HELP YOU NOW!

THE TIME HAS **COME**, IRON MAN!! IF YOU KNOW ANY PRAYERS, SAY THEM NOW, WHILE YOU STILL **CAN!**

I-I ALWAYS **WONDERED** HOW THE END WOULD BE!! I **KNEW** IT HAD TO COME SOMETIME! BUT, IF ONLY I HADN'T BEEN SO COLD TO PEPPER AND HAPPY THE LAST TIME I SAW THEM!

MY TRANSISTORS ARE OF NO USE TO ME NOW! I'M AT THE MERCY OF MY MOST DANGEROUS ENEMY! MY SECONDS ARE NUMBERED! AND YET-- I WON'T GIVE UP WHILE THERE'S A BREATH OF LIFE IN ME! I'LL BEG FOR NO MERCY-- I WON'T WEAKEN!

IF THIS **IS** TO BE MY FINISH, I'LL SHOW HOW AN **AMERICAN** FACES DEATH! I'LL SHOW THAT **NOTHING** CAN SHATTER THE FAITH OF A MAN WHO FIGHTS FOR FREEDOM! SOMEHOW, EVEN IN DEFEAT, I'LL BE **VICTORIOUS!!**

The END

YES, WE **COULD** HAVE ENDED OUR TALE AT THIS POINT-- BUT THERE IS JUST TOO MUCH ACTION, TOO MUCH DRAMA, TOO MUCH EXCITEMENT FOR US TO RUSH IT! AND SO, **NEXT** ISSUE IN **IRON MAN #55**, YOU WILL READ THE STARTLING CONCLUSION OF THIS GREAT ADVENTURE-- TOLD, AS ALWAYS, IN THE MAGNIFICENT **MARVEL MANNER!!!** RESERVE YOUR COPY AT YOUR DEALER'S **NOW**-- IT'S SURE TO BE A SELL-OUT!

3

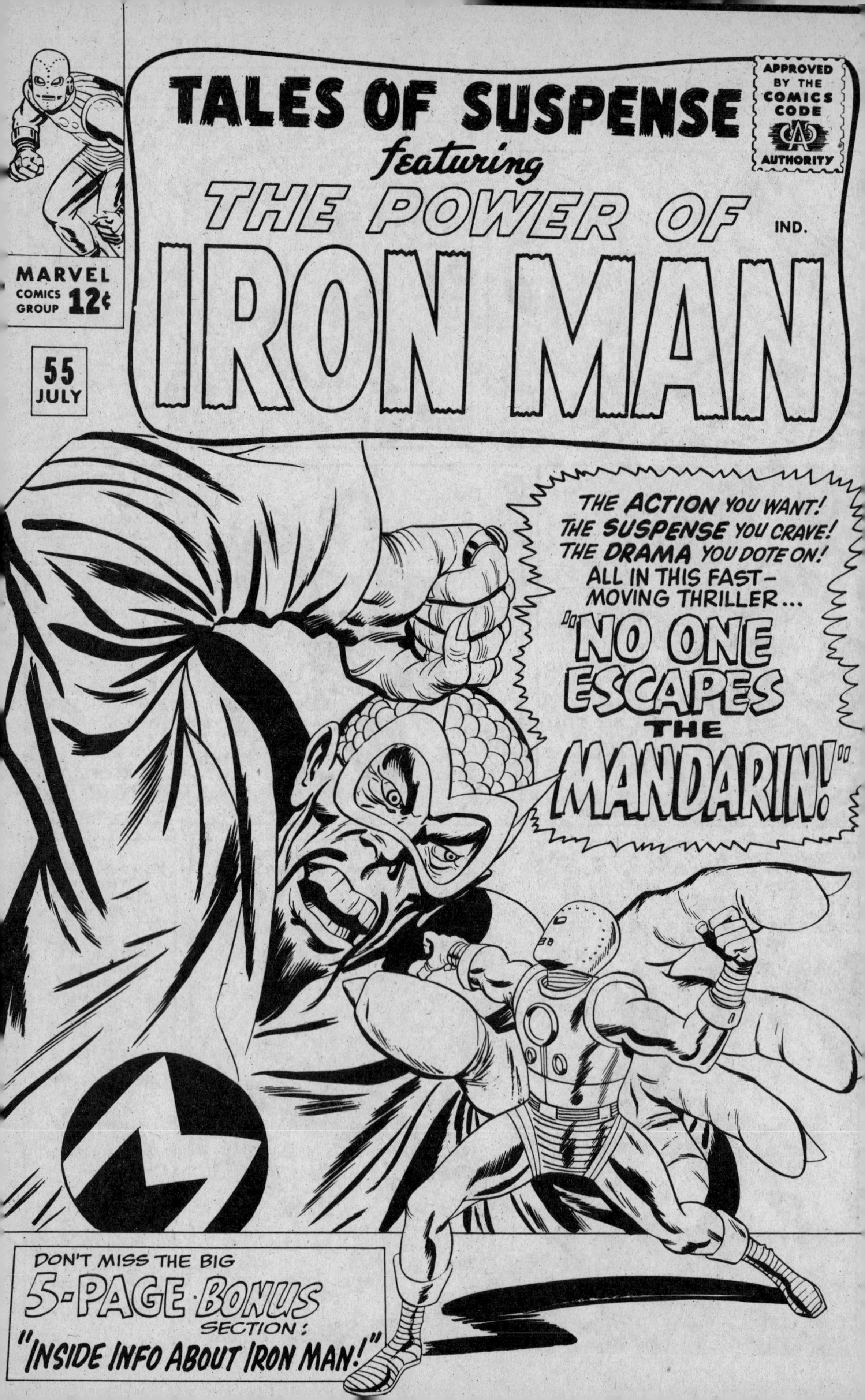
APPROVED BY THE COMICS CODE AUTHORITY
TALES OF SUSPENSE
featuring
THE POWER OF
IRON MAN
IND.
MARVEL COMICS GROUP 12¢
55 JULY
THE ACTION YOU WANT!
THE SUSPENSE YOU CRAVE!
THE DRAMA YOU DOTE ON!
ALL IN THIS FAST-MOVING THRILLER...
"NO ONE ESCAPES THE MANDARIN!"
DON'T MISS THE BIG
5-PAGE BONUS SECTION:
"INSIDE INFO ABOUT IRON MAN!"

IRON MAN
"NO ONE ESCAPES THE MANDARIN!"

LAST ISSUE WE LEFT IRON MAN TRAPPED BY THE MOST POWERFUL ARCH-VILLAIN OF THE ORIENT... THE MYSTERIOUS *MANDARIN!* HIS TRANSISTORS DRAINED OF THEIR POWER, THE GOLDEN AVENGER WAITS FOR HIS DOOM WITH QUIET COURAGE UNTIL AMAZINGLY, A *SMILE* APPEARS ON THE IRON COUNTENANCE OF THE TRAPPED MAN...

IRON MAN! ARE YOU *MAD?* YOU DARE SMILE IN THE FACE OF DEATH?!! IF YOU THINK I WILL NOT DESTROY YOU NOW, YOU ARE *WRONG!*

I'VE ONLY ONE SLIM CHANCE... A *BLUFF*... BUT IF I PLAY IT RIGHT, IT MAY WORK! THE MANDARIN DOESN'T KNOW *ONE* THING...

...HE DOESN'T KNOW THAT ANTHONY STARK AND IRON MAN ARE ONE AND THE SAME! HE THINKS STARK IS STILL RUNNING LOOSE IN THE CASTLE!

THIS MAY POSSIBLY BE THE *GREATEST* IRON MAN EPIC YET PRODUCED BY THE MIGHTY MARVEL GROUP!

WRITTEN BY FRIENDLY **STAN LEE**
ILLUSTRATED BY FAITHFUL **DON HECK**
LETTERED BY FEARLESS **ART SIMEK**

X-673

1

WHY *SHOULDN'T* I SMILE? WHILE YOU WASTE TIME WITH *ME,* ANTHONY STARK HAS PROBABLY FOUND OUT WHERE YOU KEEP YOUR ANTI-MISSILE MISSILES --AND HE COULD BE *DESTROYING* THEM THIS VERY MINUTE!

STARK! I FORGOT ABOUT HIM!

YOU. WERE A *FOOL* TO REMIND ME! I'LL STOP STARK BEFORE HE CAN DO ANY HARM, THEN I'LL RETURN AND CONTINUE WHERE WE LEFT OFF!!

AS FOR *YOU,* I'LL SET MY CABLE CONTROL TO "HOLD STEADY"!

IT *WORKED!!* NOW IF HE'LL ONLY STAY AWAY LONG ENOUGH--!!

ACTIVATED BY THE POWER IN MY MIRACULOUS RINGS, THOSE CABLES WILL HOLD YOU FAST. YOU'LL LEARN THAT YOU CAN'T ESCAPE *THE MANDARIN!*

EVEN *HIS* DIABOLICAL BRAIN DOESN'T REALIZE THE POWER BUILT INTO MY ARMOR! MY MINIATURE *GENERATOR* IS WORKING FULL BLAST TO BRING MY BUILT-IN TRANSISTORS UP TO PEAK STRENGTH! ALL I NEED IS *TIME*--

A FEW SECONDS LATER...

--TIME TO RECHARGE ALL MY POWER UNITS! TIME TO LET MY TRANSISTORS GIVE ME THE STRENGTH TO DO-- *THIS!!*

SNAP

SNAP

SNAP

2

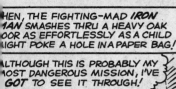

THEN, THE FIGHTING-MAD *IRON MAN* SMASHES THRU A HEAVY OAK DOOR AS EFFORTLESSLY AS A CHILD MIGHT POKE A HOLE IN A PAPER BAG!

ALTHOUGH THIS IS PROBABLY MY MOST DANGEROUS MISSION, I'VE GOT TO SEE IT THROUGH!

I'VE *GOT* TO FIND OUT HOW THE MANDARIN HAS BEEN ABLE TO DESTROY THE MISSILES I MADE FOR THE U.S. FORCES IN THE FAR EAST!

AS TONY STARK, I CAME HERE TO GET THAT INFO--AND I'M NOT LEAVING IT WITHOUT IT!

STARK, THE REDS HAVE *NOTHING* FAST ENOUGH TO SHOOT DOWN YOUR MISSILES -- SO YOUR *DESIGN* MUST BE TO BLAME!

MY DESIGN WAS *PERFECT!* ONLY THE *MANDARIN* COULD BE BEHIND THIS! I'VE GOT TO FIND OUT!

"IF I'D APPEARED AS *IRON MAN*, THE MANDARIN WOULD HAVE *DESTROYED* ME ON SIGHT! BUT HE WAS CONTENT TO MERELY *CAPTURE* MR. TONY STARK!"

I'LL ESCAPE FROM THE GUARDS BY USING *SLEEP GAS!*

"ESCAPING THE MANDARIN'S TROOPS, I CHANGED TO *IRON MAN*, AND OUR FIGHT BEGAN IN ERNEST!"

CRASH!

"BUT, ON HIS HOME GROUNDS, THE MANDARIN HAD TOO MANY WEAPONS I WASN'T PREPARED FOR, AND FINALLY..."

"HE CAPTURED ME! BUT, LUCKY FOR OL' TONY STARK, *IRON MAN* ISN'T THE TYPE TO *STAY* CAPTURED FOR LONG!"

BREAKING THESE CABLES ISN'T ENOUGH! I'VE GOT TO FIND A WAY TO DEFEAT THE MANDARIN, ONCE AND FOR ALL!

LUCKILY, MY POWER JETS ARE COMPLETELY NOISELESS WHEN OPERATING ON LOW POWER! I CAN FOLLOW HIM WITHOUT BEING HEARD!

BUT I'VE GOT TO BE ON GUARD EVERY SECOND! HIS SENSES ARE SHARP, AND HIS REFLEXES ARE ALMOST INHUMANLY FAST!

I SEEM TO SENSE ANOTHER PRESENCE NEAR ME!

THE MISSILES MUST BE INSIDE THAT ROOM HE'S ENTERING!

3

BUT, THE AREA INTO WHICH THE MANDARIN ENTERS IS FAR MORE THAN A "ROOM"! IT IS A HUGE, HIGH-DOMED CHAMBER, CONTAINING THE MISSILES WHICH THE EVIL GENIUS HAS CAPTURED IN THE PAST WEEKS...

EVERYTHING IS IN ORDER HERE! NOTHING HAS BEEN DISTURBED! AND THERE IS NO SIGN OF STARK!

STARK! IF YOU'RE HIDING, SHOW YOURSELF! THE LONGER I HAVE TO SEARCH FOR YOU, THE WORSE YOUR FATE WILL BE!!

BAH! I'LL WASTE NO MORE TIME ON THE HELPLESS AMERICAN! I'LL GO BACK AND FINISH OFF IRON MAN NOW!

BUT, AT THAT MOMENT, A WARNING LIGHT FLASHES, AND...

THE SIGNAL! ANOTHER MISSILE IS ABOUT TO BE LAUNCHED!!

AND, MANY MILES AWAY, AT AN ALLIED BASE...

EVEN THOUGH WE HAVEN'T HEARD FROM STARK YET, WE CAN'T DELAY THE LAUNCHING ANY LONGER! BEGIN THE COUNTDOWN...

YES, SIR...

AND LET'S HOPE THIS ONE DOES ITS JOB AND RETURNS SAFELY! I CAN'T BELIEVE STARK MADE THEM ALL DEFECTIVE AT HIS FACTORY IN THE STATES!

AND SO, THE BLAST-OFF OCCURS, THOUGH NONE OF THOSE PRESENT SUSPECT THAT HOSTILE EYES, MANY MILES AWAY, ARE ALSO WITNESSING THE SIGHT!

A PERFECT LAUNCHING! SOON THE MANDARIN WILL HAVE ANOTHER EGG FOR HIS LITTLE NEST!

4

MY INTERCEPTOR RAY CAN CATCH ANYTHING THAT MOVES, REGARDLESS OF SPEED...

...AND CAN *RETURN* THAT OBJECT TO MY CASTLE WITHIN THE HOUR!!

I'VE SEEN *ENOUGH!* SO *THAT'S* HOW YOU DO IT,!! WITH A *RAY!!*

IRON MAN! HOW--??

SORRY, CHUM-- I HAVEN'T TIME FOR A BIG GABFEST NOW!!

NO MATTER *HOW* POWERFUL YOU ARE, I'LL SHOW YOU WHAT A MAN OF *IRON* CAN DO WHEN HE GETS HIS TEMPER UP!!

ZZZTT

BUT *FIRST*, I'LL MAKE SURE THAT THIS RAY OF YOURS NEVER DAMAGES ANOTHER OF OUR MISSILES!

R'IP

YOU *FOOL!* YOU'VE BEEN WASTING YOUR TIME! ONCE I START THE RAY! AUTOMATIC RELAYS TAKE OVER! *NOTHING* CAN STOP IT NOW!

BUT *YOU* ARE FAR LESS FORTUNATE! YOU *CAN* BE STOPPED, AS I PROVED BEFORE, AND SHALL PROVE *AGAIN!*

SO! YOU'RE FLEEING IN PANIC! THE MIGHTY *IRON MAN* HAS FINALLY TURNED COWARD, EH?

NOT A CHANCE, PLAYMATE! I'VE GOT TO PAY A LITTLE *VISIT* RIGHT NOW-- TO A FLYING *MISSILE!*

5

I TIMED IT JUST RIGHT! THE MISSILE'S ABOVE ME *NOW!*

BY *HITTING* IT AT THE RIGHT ANGLE AND SPEED, I CAN MAKE IT VEER FROM ITS COURSE, THEREBY MISSING THE MANDARIN'S RAY!!

I *DID* IT! BUT, IN SAVING THE MISSILE, I *MYSELF* AM NOW TRAPPED BY THE STRANGE RAY! IT'S PULLING ME BACK TO THE CASTLE!!

THE RAY IS SO POWERFUL THAT MY TRANSISTOR JETS CAN'T RESIST IT!!

HE THWARTED ME AGAIN, BY SAVING THE MISSILE! FOR THAT, I'LL SEE THAT HIS FINISH IS A *SLOW* ONE!!!

I'VE GOT TO MOVE *FAST!* IN ANOTHER FEW SECONDS, I'LL BE HELPLESS IN THE MANDARIN'S CASTLE AGAIN! BUT, IF I CAN BREAK OFF A PIECE OF THE STONE MASONRY AS I'M DRAWN THRU THE WINDOW--

--AND THEN HURL IT AT THE RAY'S POWER PLANT-- IT MAY HELP TO ACCOMPLISH THE NEARLY *IMPOSSIBLE!*

DON'T THROW THAT, YOU *FOOL!* THE MACHINE IS POWERED BY NITRO-FISSION!!! IT WILL *EXPLODE!!*

6

I'VE GOT *NEWS* FOR YOU, MANDARIN!! THAT'S THE *IDEA*!!

VAROOM!

NOTHING CAN SAVE YOU NOW, IRON MAN! YOU HAVE GONE *TOO FAR*! I NO LONGER CARE ABOUT MISSILES, ABOUT WORLD CONQUEST, ABOUT *ANYTHING*!

I HAVE BUT ONE THOUGHT IN MIND-- BUT ONE BURNING AMBITION...

...AND IT IS TO SEE YOU COMPLETELY DESTROYED BEFORE MY EYES! NOW, WHILE YOU ARE ALONE IN MY CASTLE, WITH NO WAY TO ESCAPE, WITH NO PLACE TO TURN...

...YOU SHALL FEEL THE THE POWER OF MY RINGS AS NO VICTIM BEFORE YOU HAS EVER FELT THEM!!!

SO! AGAIN YOU TRY TO FLEE ME! BUT *THIS* TIME YOU SHALL NOT SUCCEED! REMEMBER-- NO ONE *ESCAPES THE MANDARIN!!!*

-: *WHEW!* :- HE WASN'T *KIDDIN'*! WHO'D HAVE SUSPECTED THAT HIS PINKY RING CONTAINED A *DISINTEGRATOR RAY!!*

7

MAYBE NOT--BUT HERE'S *ONE* GUY WHO'S GONNA *TRY,* I *SAY!!* THE FLOOR'S OPENING BENEATH MY FEET!!

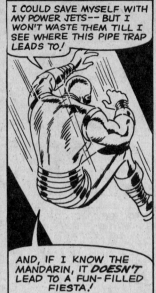

I COULD SAVE MYSELF WITH MY POWER JETS-- BUT I WON'T WASTE THEM TILL I SEE WHERE THIS PIPE TRAP LEADS TO!

AND, IF I KNOW THE MANDARIN, IT *DOESN'T* LEAD TO A FUN-FILLED FIESTA!

MEANWHILE, HALFWAY AROUND THE WORLD IN TONY STARK'S LONG ISLAND MUNITIONS FACTORY, HAPPY HOGAN IS TRYING TO MANAGE THINGS FOR HIS ABSENT BOSS...

HOW DO *I* KNOW WHAT TO DO IF THE MAIN COAXIAL CIRCUITS ARE BEGINNING TO BACK-FIRE??! TRY TURNING THE *PLUG* UPSIDE DOWN, OR SOMETHIN'??!

NO, I DON'T KNOW *WHERE* MR. STARK IS! CAN'T ANYONE HERE THINK FOR HIMSELF?

HERE'S SOME MORE FORMS TO BE SIGNED, HAPPY! HOW DO YOU *LIKE* BEING AN EXECUTIVE?

I SHOULDA HAD MY *HEAD* EXAMINED, PEPPER!

IF YOU ASK *ME,* THAT WOULDN'T TAKE VERY LONG! NOT WITH *YOUR* HEAD!

HEY, *WAIT!* YOU CAN'T *LEAVE* ME WITH ALL THIS PAPER WORK!!

WANNA BET?

AND I USEDTA THINK IT WAS *EASY* TO BE MR. BIG! STARK OUGHTTA GET A *MEDAL!*

NO *WONDER* HE'S ALWAYS RUNNIN' OFF ON *TRIPS!*

RI-ING

THERE'S ONLY ONE THING FOR ME TO DO-- I'LL HEAD FOR THE HILLS TILL THE BOSS GETS BACK!

HAPPY HOGAN!! COME *BACK* HERE!!

UH OH! THE VOICE OF DOOM!

YOU'RE WANTED IN THE NEW WEAPONS DEVELOPMENT SECTION, ON THE DOUBLE!!

I JUST *TOLD* 'EM WHAT TO DO THERE AN *HOUR* AGO!! DIDN'T THEY *LISTEN* TO ME?

THAT'S THE *TROUBLE*-- THEY *DID!* THEY BUILT THE NEW TRANSISTOR-POWERED HOWITZER TO YOUR SPECIFICATIONS-- NOW THEY WANT TO KNOW-- ARE YOU *KIDDING?*

WELL-- *NOBODY'S* PERFECT!

HOGAN, I THINK WE'D BETTER WAIT TILL MR. STARK GETS BACK--AND WITH *YOU* IN CHARGE THAT BETTER BE *SOON.*

...BUT IT MAY BE LATER THAN THEY THINK-- *MUCH* LATER--

THERE'S THE *BOTTOM* NOW--!

UNLESS I MISS MY GUESS, THAT'S A DEADLY POOL OF *ACID* BELOW ME!!

WHICH MEANS IT'S TIME TO MAKE A *BREAK* FOR IT-- *FAST!*

*B*EFORE REACHING THE FATAL LIQUID BELOW, THE POWERFUL AVENGER LASHES OUT WITH TWO IRON FISTS, SMASHING HIS WAY THRU THE SIDE OF THE SMOOTH, SLIPPERY PIPE...

CRASH!

...THAT LITTLE TOBOGGAN RIDE GAVE ME THE TIME I NEEDED FOR ANOTHER QUICK *RECHARGE!*

AND NOW, I'M READY FOR ANYTHING ELSE THE MANDARIN MAY TOSS AT ME!

*B*UT, THE MANDARIN'S NEXT ASSAULT COMES MORE SWIFTLY--MORE *UNEXPECTEDLY*--THAN IRON MAN COULD POSSIBLY SUSPECT...

LITTLE DOES HE DREAM THAT I CAN OBSERVE HIS EVERY MOVE, ANYWHERE IN MY CASTLE FORTRESS! IT IS AMUSING TO TOY WITH HIM THIS WAY--TO ATTACK HIM AGAIN AND AGAIN UNTIL HE CAN BEAR NO MORE!

ZZZZZZT...

WHIRRR

...MY BUILT-IN EAR PHONES JUST PICKED UP A FAINT, HIGH-PITCHED SOUND--LIKE A STEEL *SPRING* BEING COILED! BUT, WHAT CAN IT *MEAN?*

AWHAMMM!

A SPLIT-SECOND LATER, THE GOLDEN GLADIATOR GETS HIS *ANSWER*--WITH SHATTERING IMPACT!!

CRASH

*N*OTHING HUMAN COULD SURVIVE SUCH A BLOW-- UNLESS PROTECTED BY THE STRONGEST TRANSISTOR-POWERED GAUGE STEEL ON EARTH--THE ARMOR OF IRON MAN!!

*A*ND SO...

EVEN MY ARMOR CAN'T TAKE MANY *MORE* SUCH ATTACKS! I'VE BEEN FORCED *CLEAN* THRU THE *FLOOR!!*

9

THEN, WHIRLING ABOUT SUDDENLY, IRON MAN SEES...

AND NOW, MY DIMINUTIVE FOE, I'LL CRUSH YOU LIKE THE PUNY FLEA YOU ARE!!

GUESS *AGAIN*, MISTER! *SIZE* DOESN'T IMPRESS ME! I'VE GOT A PARTNER NAMED *GIANT-MAN* WHO CAN BE *JUST* AS BIG --AND A LOT LESS CORNY!

EVEN IF YOU WERE THE SIZE OF A *HOUSE*, WITH THE AID OF MY POWER JETS I CAN HIT YOU LIKE A *MISSILE*, AND BOWL YOU OVER BEFORE YOU--!!!

MY APOLOGIES TO GIANT-MAN!! *YOU'RE* JUST A *PHONY!* YOU'RE *FADING AWAY!*

IT WAS JUST AN ELABORATE COMPLEX OF *MIRRORS*, ARRANGED TO ENLARGE THE ORIGINAL IMAGE OF THE MANDARIN!!

CRASH

THIS IRON BIKINI OF MINE SURE COMES IN HANDY! THESE GIGANTIC PIECES OF BROKEN GLASS COULD FINISH ME IN SECONDS IF I WEREN'T SO PROTECTED!

THEN, GLIDING DOWN TO THE FLOOR AGAIN, THE MILLIONAIRE AVENGER SLOWLY TURNS TO LOOK BEHIND HIM... I WAS *AFRAID* OF THIS! THERE'S NO *LIMIT* TO HIS DEADLY BAG OF TRICKS!!

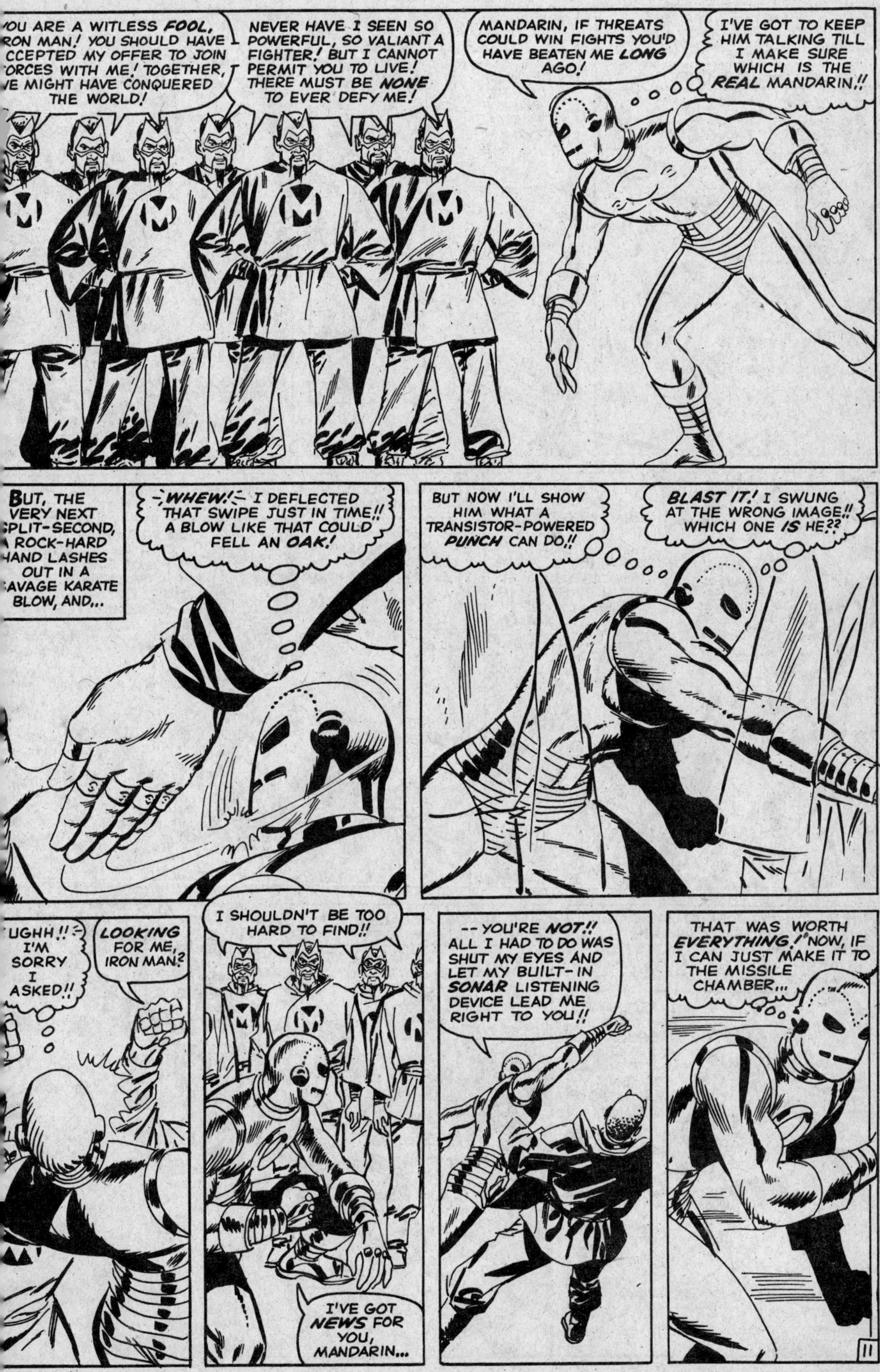
YOU ARE A WITLESS FOOL, IRON MAN! YOU SHOULD HAVE ACCEPTED MY OFFER TO JOIN FORCES WITH ME! TOGETHER, WE MIGHT HAVE CONQUERED THE WORLD!
NEVER HAVE I SEEN SO POWERFUL, SO VALIANT A FIGHTER! BUT I CANNOT PERMIT YOU TO LIVE! THERE MUST BE NONE TO EVER DEFY ME!
MANDARIN, IF THREATS COULD WIN FIGHTS YOU'D HAVE BEATEN ME LONG AGO!
I'VE GOT TO KEEP HIM TALKING TILL I MAKE SURE WHICH IS THE REAL MANDARIN!!
BUT, THE VERY NEXT SPLIT-SECOND, A ROCK-HARD HAND LASHES OUT IN A SAVAGE KARATE BLOW, AND...
-WHEW!- I DEFLECTED THAT SWIPE JUST IN TIME!! A BLOW LIKE THAT COULD FELL AN OAK!
BUT NOW I'LL SHOW HIM WHAT A TRANSISTOR-POWERED PUNCH CAN DO!!
BLAST IT! I SWUNG AT THE WRONG IMAGE!! WHICH ONE IS HE??
UGHH!! I'M SORRY I ASKED!!
LOOKING FOR ME, IRON MAN?
I SHOULDN'T BE TOO HARD TO FIND!!
I'VE GOT NEWS FOR YOU, MANDARIN...
--YOU'RE NOT!! ALL I HAD TO DO WAS SHUT MY EYES AND LET MY BUILT-IN SONAR LISTENING DEVICE LEAD ME RIGHT TO YOU!!
THAT WAS WORTH EVERYTHING! NOW, IF I CAN JUST MAKE IT TO THE MISSILE CHAMBER...
11

SECONDS LATER, LIVID WITH UNCONTROLLABLE FURY, THE MANDARIN RACES THRU HIS CASTLE HALL LIKE A RAGING HUMAN ENGINE OF DESTRUCTION!!

I'LL GET HIM!! IF IT TAKES THE REST OF MY LIFE-- IF IT'S THE LAST THING I DO-- I'LL GET HIM!!!

THE CORRIDOR IS EMPTY! IT'S THOSE ACCURSED JETS OF HIS! HE MUST HAVE FLOWN THRU THE HALL!!

THE CAPTURED MISSILES HE MANAGED TO SEND THEM BACK ON THEIR WAY! BUT THAT WAS HIS BIGGEST MISTAKE!

HE FORGOT MY INTERCEPT RAY!! I CAN STILL STOP THEM!!

I'LL REACH THE CONTROL PANEL IN PLENTY OF TIME! THEN, AFTER I'VE REGAINED THE MISSILES, I'LL TEAR THIS CASTLE APART STONE BY STONE IF I MUST, UNTIL I FIND IRON MAN!

BUT, UPON REACHING HIS MASTER CONTROL PANEL, THE ORIENTAL MASTER OF MENACE FINDS...

HE OUT-SMARTED ME!! HE SMASHED THE CONTROLS! MY RAY IS DESTROYED!!

IT WOULD TAKE YEARS TO ASSEMBLE THE MATERIALS TO BUILD ANOTHER! FOR THIS HE'LL PAY A THOUSAND TIMES OVER! I'LL NEVER STOP SEARCHING FOR HIM!!

BETTER LUCK NEXT TIME, MANDY! IRON M

BUT, AS THE MADDENED MANDARIN RANTS AND RAVES WITHIN HIS SINISTER CASTLE, THE OBJECT OF HIS WRATH HURTLES SAFELY AWAY AT ROCKET SPEED--!

I'M GLAD I BUILT THESE BABIES NICE AND ROOMY! NOW TO CHANGE TO TONY STARK BEFORE I LAND!

AND, NEAR THE ALERTED U.S. BASE A FEW MINUTES LATER...

HANG ON, SOLDIER! A MISSILE JUST LANDED IN THAT CLEARING!

LOOKED LIKE ONE OF OURS!!

LOOK! IT'S STARK! HE BROUGHT THE BIRDS HOME TO ROOST!

HOW ABOUT A LIFT, BOYS? THAT BOUNCIN' JEEP LOOKS LIKE A CADILLAC TO ME RIGHT NOW!

THEN, AFTER A FAST ARMY JET RIDE HALFWAY 'ROUND THE GLOBE, A TRIUMPHANT TONY STARK ADDRESSES A TOP BRASS MEETING IN THE PENTAGON...

GENTLEMEN, THERE WILL BE NO FURTHER TROUBLE WITH OUR MISSILES IN THAT SECTOR!

DON'T KNOW OR CARE HOW YOU DID IT, STARK! BUT WELL DONE, MY BOY!

BY THE TIME THE MANDARIN COMES UP WITH ANOTHER INTERCEPT RAY, I'LL HAVE INVENTED A COUNTER-RAY TO NULLIFY IT! HE WON'T CATCH ME NAPPING AGAIN!

AND THEN, AT KENNEDY AIRPORT IN NEW YORK...

HOPE ALL WENT WELL AT THE FACTORY IN MY ABSENCE!

LOOK, HAPPY! THERE HE IS! IT'S THE BOSS!

SO? WHO WERE YOU EXPECTIN'-- PETER PAN???

I KNEW THEY'D BE HERE! PEPPER LOOKS MORE GORGEOUS THAN EVER.!!

OH, BOSS-- BOSS,!! WE WERE SO WORRIED ABOUT YOU!!

REALLY?? I'LL HAVE TO WORRY YOU MORE OFTEN!

HOW DID THINGS GO AT THE PLANT WHILE I WAS GONE, HAPPY?

SMOOTH AS SILK, BOSS! YOU KNOW ME-- I WATCHED EVERYTHING LIKE A HAWK!

THE NEWS OVER THE RADIO SAID YOU MANAGED TO GET ALL OUR MISSILES BACK, MR. STARK! HOW ON EARTH DID YOU DO IT???

IT WASN'T TOO HARD, PEPPER! I DIDN'T DO IT ALONE-- I HAD SOME, EH, VERY POWERFUL HELP!

NO NEED TO DRIVE SO FAST, HAPPY! WE'VE GOT ALL THE TIME IN THE WORLD NOW!

NUTS! I CAN'T STAND SEEIN' HIM SIT SO CLOSE TO HER! I'LL FIND A REAL BUMPY ROAD FOR 'EM!

BUT THEN...

POW!

CALL US WHEN IT'S FIXED, HAPPY! PEPPER AND I WILL LOOK AT THE MOON FOR A WHILE!

SOME GUYS ARE BORN LUCKY! I DO ALL THE WORK, WHILE HE LIVES IT UP! WHAT I WOULDN'T GIVE FOR A SOFT LIFE LIKE TONY STARK'S!!

BECAUSE YOU DEMANDED IT---

STARTING NEXT ISH: EVERY IRON-MAN STORY WILL BE A FULL EIGHTEEN PAGES LONG!

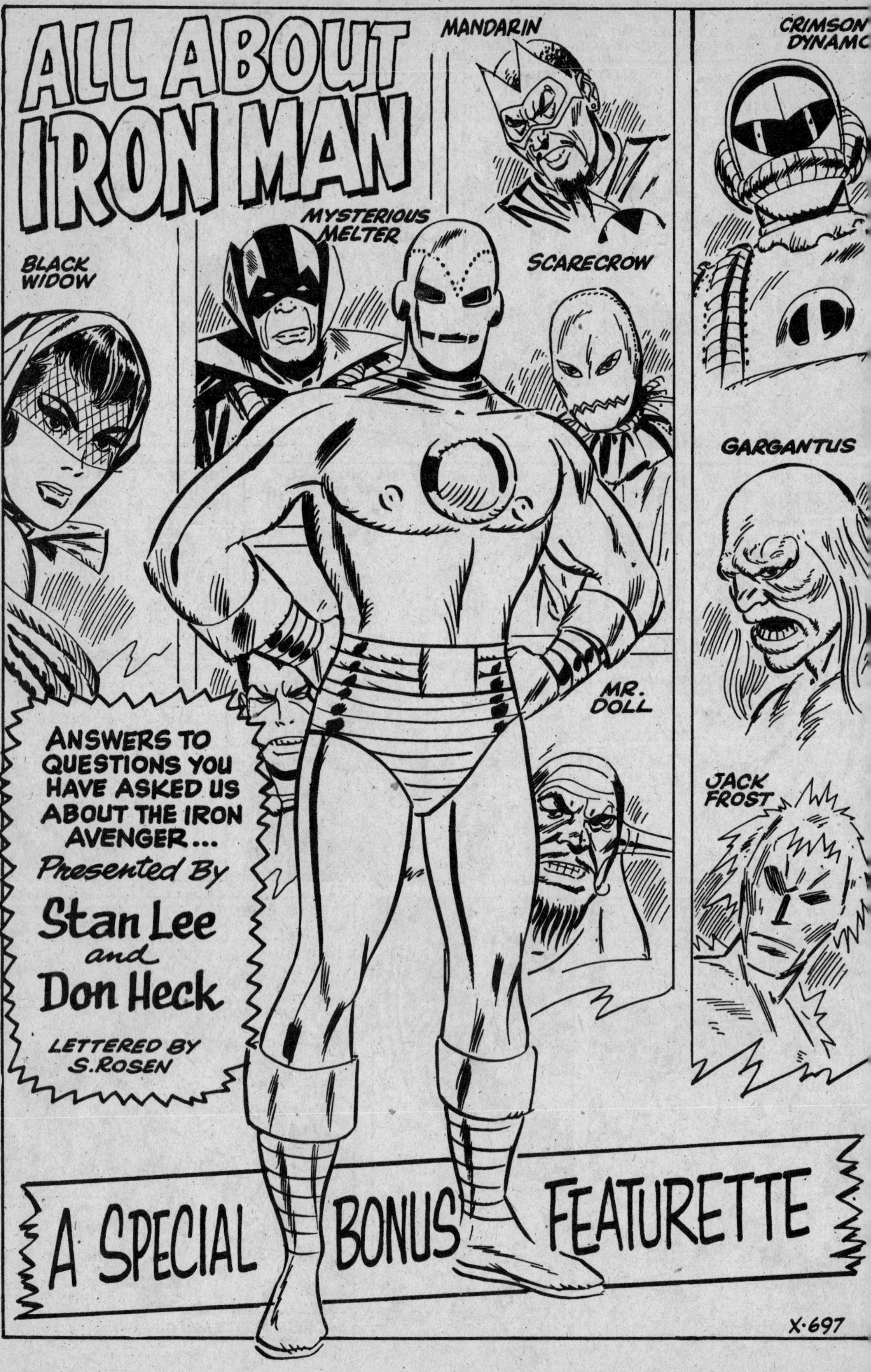

ALL ABOUT IRON MAN
MANDARIN
CRIMSON DYNAMO
MYSTERIOUS MELTER
BLACK WIDOW
SCARECROW
GARGANTUS
MR. DOLL
JACK FROST
ANSWERS TO QUESTIONS YOU HAVE ASKED US ABOUT THE IRON AVENGER... Presented By Stan Lee and Don Heck
LETTERED BY S.ROSEN
A SPECIAL BONUS FEATURETTE
X-697

Panel 1: ONE QUESTION MOST FREQUENTLY ASKED IS: "HOW DOES TONY STARK CHANGE INTO IRON MAN?" AND NOW, WE'LL LET THE HANDSOME ADVENTURER HIMSELF TELL YOU...

Panel 2: THOUGH IT SEEMS HARD TO BELIEVE, I CARRY MY ENTIRE IRON MAN APPARATUS IN THIS SLIM ATTACHE CASE!

IT HAS AN ELECTRONIC LOCK WHICH ONLY I CAN OPEN!

Panel 3: THEN, WHEN I'M CERTAIN I'M SAFE FROM PRYING EYES, I LIFT THE LID...

Panel 4: ...AND REMOVE THE ONE DUMMY SHIRT WHICH IS ALWAYS ON TOP!

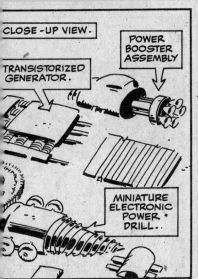

Panel 5: CLOSE-UP VIEW.

TRANSISTORIZED GENERATOR.

POWER BOOSTER ASSEMBLY

MINIATURE ELECTRONIC POWER DRILL..

Panel 6: REMOVING MY JACKET AND SHIRT, I CHECK MY LIFE-GIVING CHEST DEVICE, WHICH KEEPS MY INJURED HEART BEATING!

ZZZzzt.!

Panel 7: THEN, SATISFIED THAT ALL IS IN PERFECT WORKING ORDER, I TAKE MY ARM ARMOR FROM THE CASE...

CUT-AWAY VIEW

Panel 8: IT SNAPS INTO PLACE IN SECONDS, HELD FAST BY MAGNETIC POWER!

Panel 9: NEXT, MY IRON GLOVES...

Panel 10: ...FOLLOWED BY MY LEG ARMOR...

Panel 11: ...AFTER WHICH MY BOOTS SNAP FIRMLY INTO PLACE!

CLICK!

CUT-AWAY VIEW

2.

THEN COMES ONE OF MY MOST IMPORTANT PIECES OF EQUIPMENT... MY FLEXIBLE BELT!

IT HOUSES MOST OF MY POWERFUL SUB-MINIATURE DEVICES!

DO NOT BE DECEIVED BY THE FACT THAT MY COSTUME IS LIGHTWEIGHT! IT IS THE STRONGEST ARMOR KNOWN TO MAN!

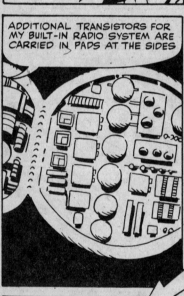

ADDITIONAL TRANSISTORS FOR MY BUILT-IN RADIO SYSTEM ARE CARRIED IN PADS AT THE SIDES

DUE TO LONG HOURS OF PRACTICE, I CAN DON MY ARMOR IN SECONDS!

CLICK!

...AND NOW, *IRON MAN* IS READY FOR WHATEVER MAY BEFALL!

AND FINALLY, MY NEW, LIGHTWEIGHT HELMET SLIPS FIRMLY INTO PLACE!

THEN, BY ACTIVATING MY BUILT-IN GENERATOR, I GIVE MYSELF A FULL POWER CHARGE...

MORE INFO *about* IRON-MAN!

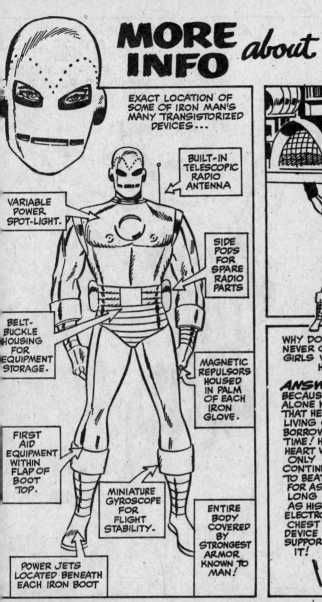

EXACT LOCATION OF SOME OF IRON MAN'S MANY TRANSISTORIZED DEVICES...

BUILT-IN TELESCOPIC RADIO ANTENNA

VARIABLE POWER SPOT-LIGHT.

SIDE PODS FOR SPARE RADIO PARTS

BELT-BUCKLE HOUSING FOR EQUIPMENT STORAGE.

MAGNETIC REPULSORS HOUSED IN PALM OF EACH IRON GLOVE.

FIRST AID EQUIPMENT WITHIN FLAP OF BOOT TOP.

MINIATURE GYROSCOPE FOR FLIGHT STABILITY.

ENTIRE BODY COVERED BY STRONGEST ARMOR KNOWN TO MAN!

POWER JETS LOCATED BENEATH EACH IRON BOOT

IRON MAN ACCOMPLISHES HIS AMAZING FEATS OF STRENGTH BECAUSE OF THE TINY TRANSISTORS WITHIN HIS ARMOR WHICH INCREASE HIS POWER TREMENDOUSLY!

THE MORE STRAIN PLACED UPON THESE SUB-MINIATURE TRANSISTORS, THE SHORTER THEIR LIFE-SPAN IS BETWEEN CHARGES!

THIS APPLIES TO IRON MAN'S FLYING SPEED AS WELL! THE SLOWER HE FLIES, THE LONGER HIS TRANSISTORS WILL FUNCTION BEFORE NEEDING A RECHARGE!

WHY DOES ANTHONY STARK...RICH, HANDSOME, ELIGIBLE... NEVER GET SERIOUS WITH ANY OF THE GLAMOROUS GIRLS WHO ARE MAD ABOUT HIM?

ANSWER: BECAUSE HE ALONE KNOWS THAT HE IS LIVING ON BORROWED TIME! HIS HEART WILL ONLY CONTINUE TO BEAT FOR AS LONG AS HIS ELECTRONIC CHEST DEVICE SUPPORTS IT!

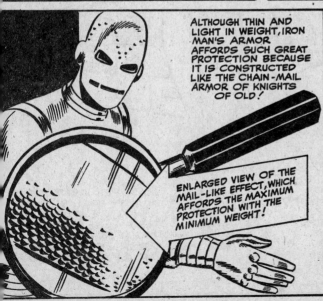

ALTHOUGH THIN AND LIGHT IN WEIGHT, IRON MAN'S ARMOR AFFORDS SUCH GREAT PROTECTION BECAUSE IT IS CONSTRUCTED LIKE THE CHAIN-MAIL ARMOR OF KNIGHTS OF OLD!

ENLARGED VIEW OF THE MAIL-LIKE EFFECT, WHICH AFFORDS THE MAXIMUM PROTECTION WITH THE MINIMUM WEIGHT!

MANY READERS HAVE ASKED WHY HAPPY HOGAN NEVER SMILES!? WHEN WE PUT THAT QUESTION TO HIM, THIS IS THE ANSWER WE RECEIVED...

ARE YOU KIDDIN'? I'M SMILIN' RIGHT NOW!

SO HAPPY'S FORLORN EXPRESSION MAY WELL BE ONE OF THE GREAT UNEXPLAINED MYSTERIES OF OUR TIME!

4.

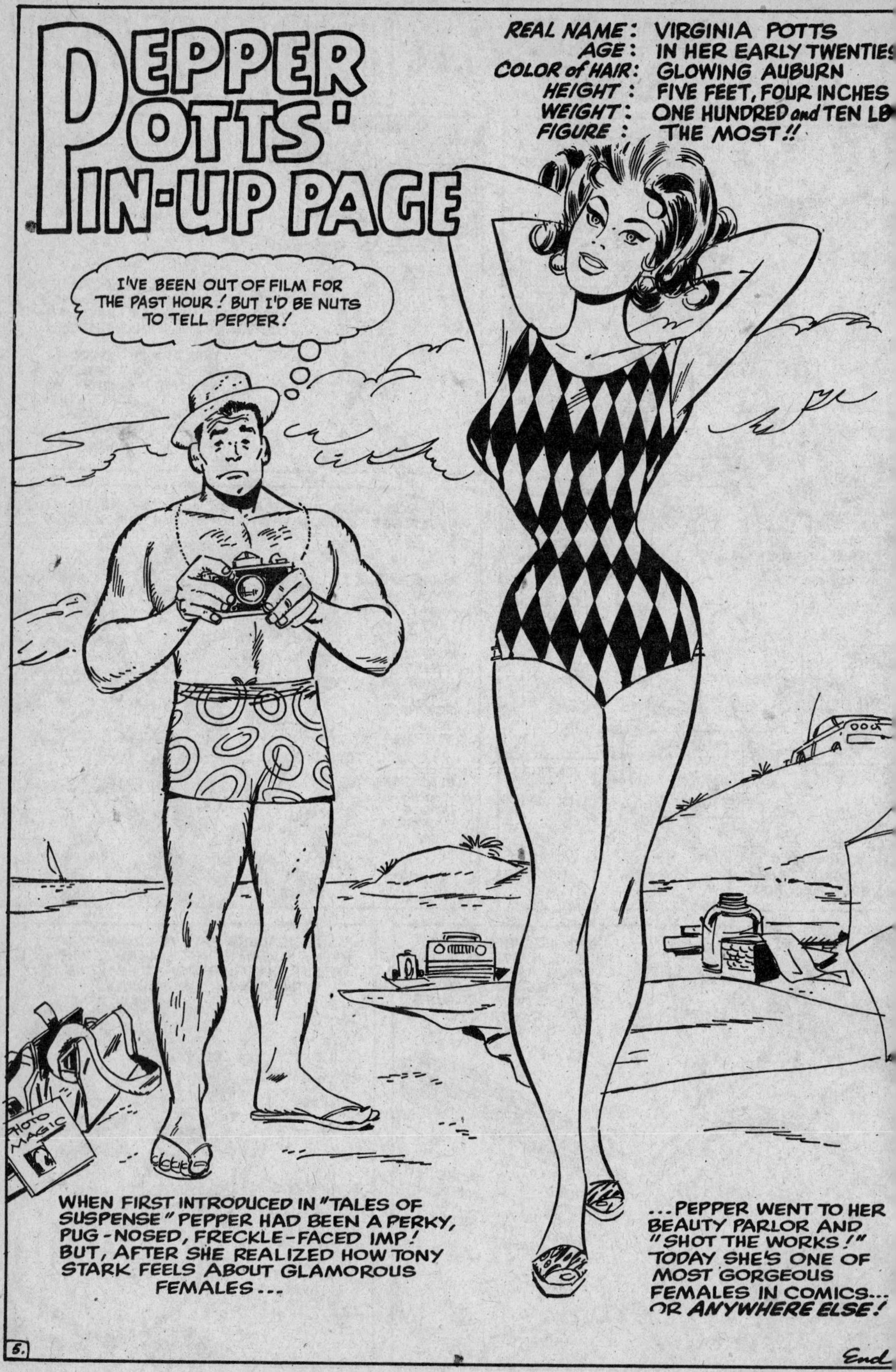
PEPPER POTTS' PIN-UP PAGE
REAL NAME: VIRGINIA POTTS
AGE: IN HER EARLY TWENTIES
COLOR of HAIR: GLOWING AUBURN
HEIGHT: FIVE FEET, FOUR INCHES
WEIGHT: ONE HUNDRED and TEN LB
FIGURE: THE MOST!!
I'VE BEEN OUT OF FILM FOR THE PAST HOUR! BUT I'D BE NUTS TO TELL PEPPER!
PHOTO MAGIC
WHEN FIRST INTRODUCED IN "TALES OF SUSPENSE" PEPPER HAD BEEN A PERKY, PUG-NOSED, FRECKLE-FACED IMP! BUT, AFTER SHE REALIZED HOW TONY STARK FEELS ABOUT GLAMOROUS FEMALES...
...PEPPER WENT TO HER BEAUTY PARLOR AND "SHOT THE WORKS!" TODAY SHE'S ONE OF MOST GORGEOUS FEMALES IN COMICS... OR ANYWHERE ELSE!
5.
End

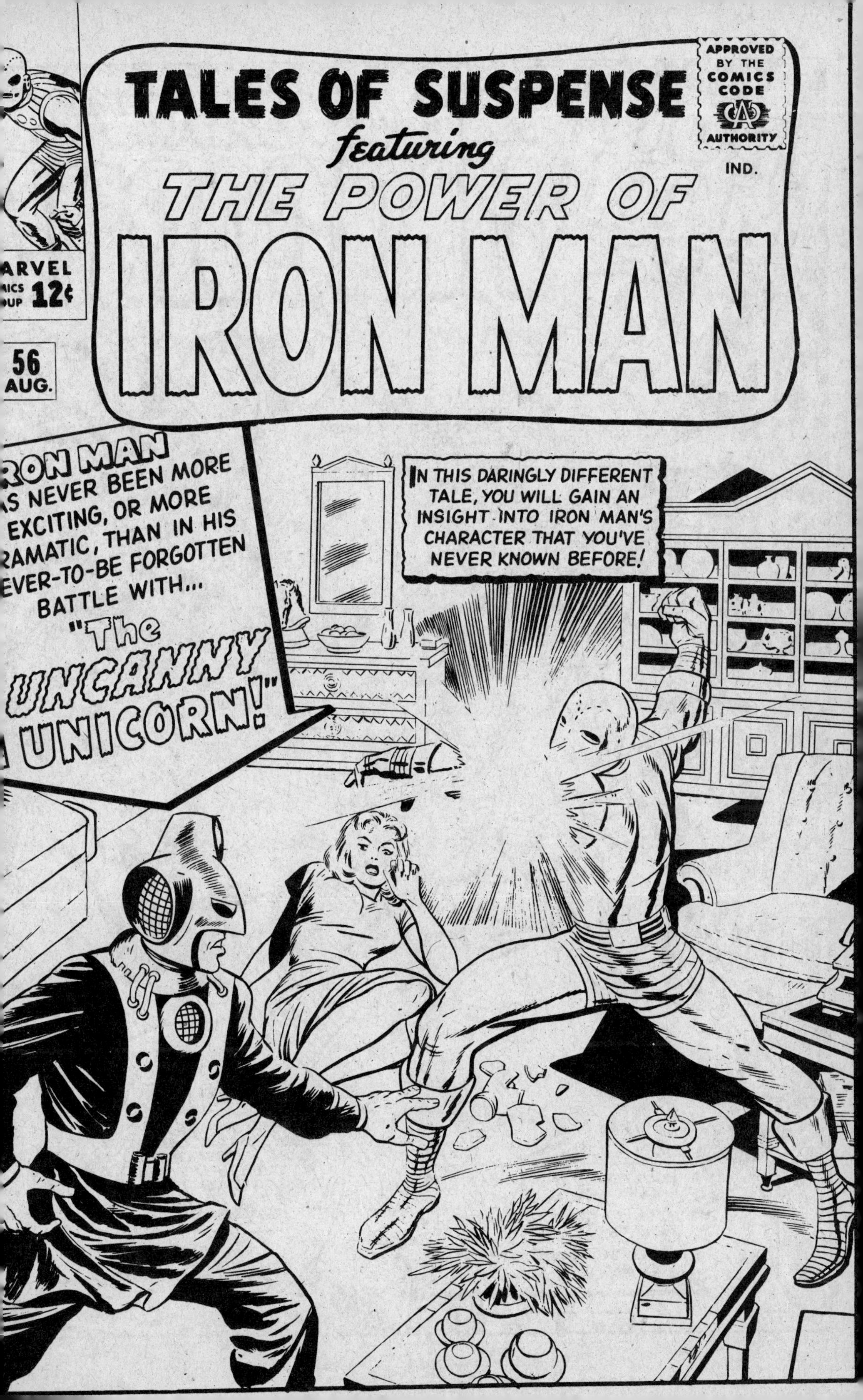

TALES OF SUSPENSE
featuring
THE POWER OF
IRON MAN
APPROVED BY THE COMICS CODE AUTHORITY
IND.
ARVEL
ICS
UP 12¢
56
AUG.
RON MAN
S NEVER BEEN MORE EXCITING, OR MORE RAMATIC, THAN IN HIS EVER-TO-BE FORGOTTEN BATTLE WITH...
"The UNCANNY UNICORN!"
IN THIS DARINGLY DIFFERENT TALE, YOU WILL GAIN AN INSIGHT INTO IRON MAN'S CHARACTER THAT YOU'VE NEVER KNOWN BEFORE!

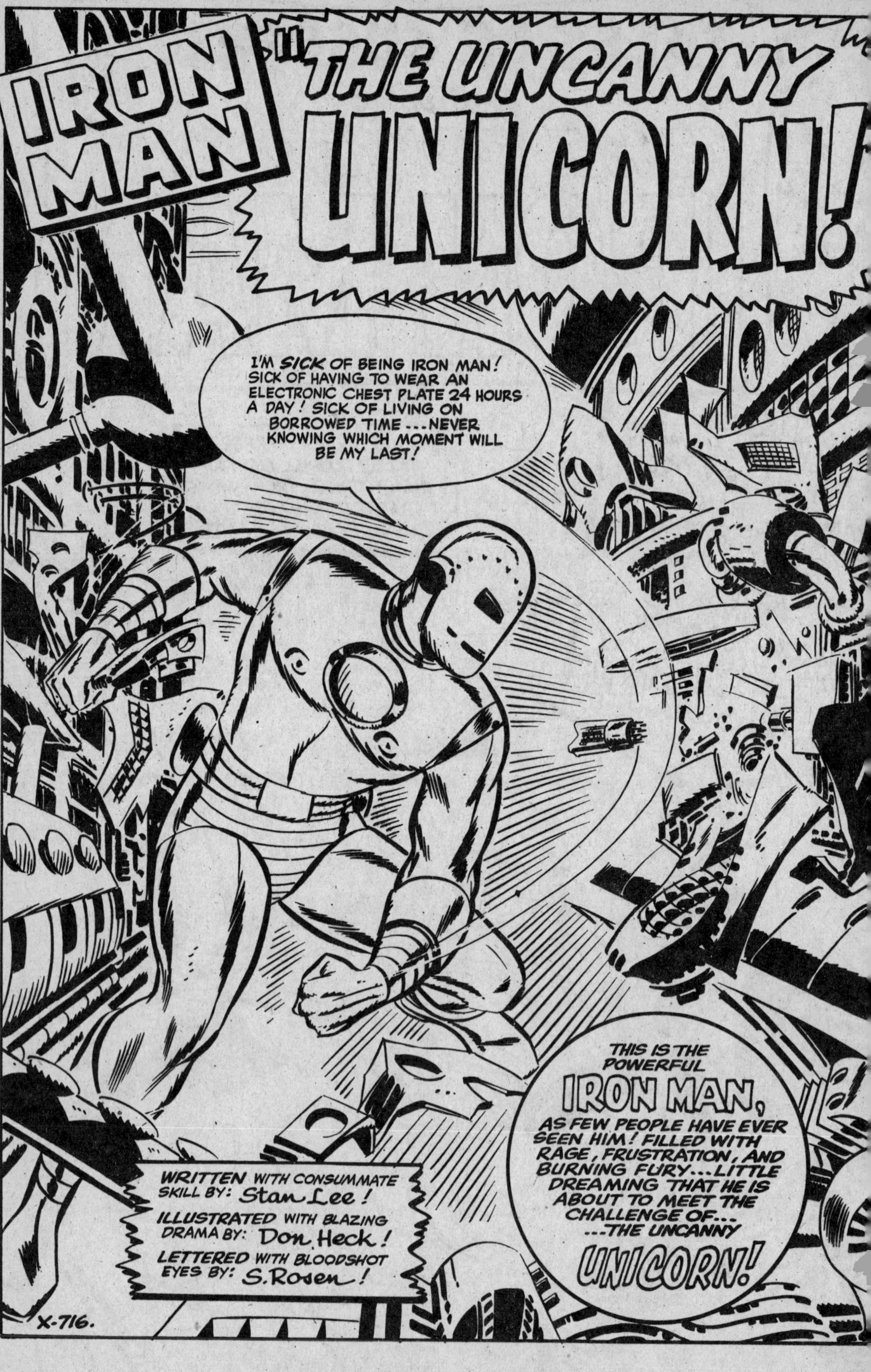
IRON MAN
"THE UNCANNY UNICORN!"
I'M SICK OF BEING IRON MAN! SICK OF HAVING TO WEAR AN ELECTRONIC CHEST PLATE 24 HOURS A DAY! SICK OF LIVING ON BORROWED TIME ... NEVER KNOWING WHICH MOMENT WILL BE MY LAST!
THIS IS THE POWERFUL IRON MAN, AS FEW PEOPLE HAVE EVER SEEN HIM! FILLED WITH RAGE, FRUSTRATION, AND BURNING FURY... LITTLE DREAMING THAT HE IS ABOUT TO MEET THE CHALLENGE OF... ...THE UNCANNY UNICORN!
WRITTEN WITH CONSUMMATE SKILL BY: Stan Lee!
ILLUSTRATED WITH BLAZING DRAMA BY: Don Heck!
LETTERED WITH BLOODSHOT EYES BY: S. Rosen!
X-716.

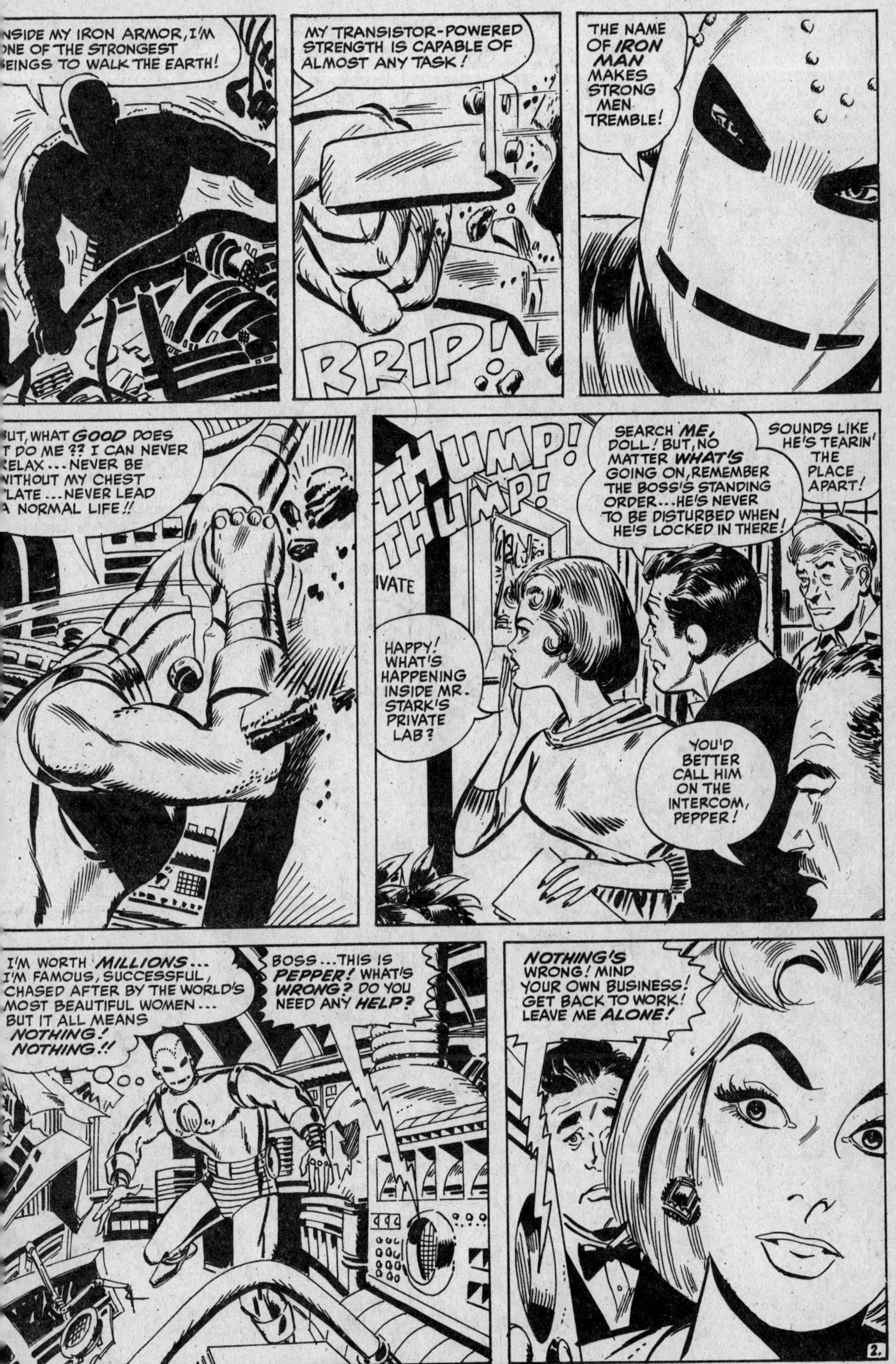
NSIDE MY IRON ARMOR, I'M ONE OF THE STRONGEST BEINGS TO WALK THE EARTH!
MY TRANSISTOR-POWERED STRENGTH IS CAPABLE OF ALMOST ANY TASK!
RRIP!
THE NAME OF IRON MAN MAKES STRONG MEN TREMBLE!
BUT, WHAT GOOD DOES IT DO ME?? I CAN NEVER RELAX... NEVER BE WITHOUT MY CHEST PLATE... NEVER LEAD A NORMAL LIFE!!
THUMP! THUMP!
IVATE
SEARCH ME, DOLL! BUT, NO MATTER WHAT'S GOING ON, REMEMBER THE BOSS'S STANDING ORDER... HE'S NEVER TO BE DISTURBED WHEN HE'S LOCKED IN THERE!
SOUNDS LIKE HE'S TEARIN' THE PLACE APART!
HAPPY! WHAT'S HAPPENING INSIDE MR. STARK'S PRIVATE LAB?
YOU'D BETTER CALL HIM ON THE INTERCOM, PEPPER!
I'M WORTH MILLIONS... I'M FAMOUS, SUCCESSFUL, CHASED AFTER BY THE WORLD'S MOST BEAUTIFUL WOMEN... BUT IT ALL MEANS NOTHING! NOTHING!!
BOSS... THIS IS PEPPER! WHAT'S WRONG? DO YOU NEED ANY HELP?
NOTHING'S WRONG! MIND YOUR OWN BUSINESS! GET BACK TO WORK! LEAVE ME ALONE!
2.

NOBODY CAN HELP ME! NOBODY CAN REPAIR MY DAMAGED HEART! NOBODY CAN GUARANTEE HOW MUCH LONGER IT WILL KEEP BEATING! NOBODY CAN EVER KNOW THE TORMENT FELT BY IRON MAN!

NO! I MUST CONTINUE TO LIVE IN A SHADOW WORLD...SPENDING HALF MY DAYS AS THE GOLDEN AVENGER, AND THE OTHER HALF AS ANTHONY STARK, THE ENVY OF A MILLION MEN...BUT ONE OF THE UNHAPPIEST HUMANS ALIVE!!

BUT THERE STILL IS TIME TO CHANGE! STILL TIME TO ENJOY WHATEVER YEARS MAY BE LEFT TO ME! I'VE GOT THE MONEY...THE LOOKS... WHY NOT??

I'M THROUGH BEING IRON MAN! THIS IS THE LAST TIME I'LL EVER WEAR THIS CUMBERSOME OUTFIT! FROM NOW ON I'LL REMAIN AS TONY STARK, MILLIONAIRE PLAYBOY!!

LET THE AVENGERS STICK TO CRIME-FIGHTING! I'LL HAVE A BALL!

MINUTES LATER....

MR. STARK! YOU'RE ALL RIGHT!

I'D BE ALL RIGHT, TOO IF SHE'D LOOK AT ME LIKE THAT!!

PEPPER, GET ME MY LITTLE BLACK BOOK! YOU KNOW THE ONE!

3.

ATTA GIRL, PEP! LET'S SEE NOW... AHH, YES! *THIS* IS THE ONE! YES *INDEED!*

HAPPY! ROLL OUT MY NEW JAG...THE SPORTY TWO-SEATER!

SURE, BOSS! WHERE AM I DRIVIN' YOU TO ?? THE STORK CLUB, OR...?

YOU??

WHO SAID ANYTHING ABOUT *YOU?* WHEN I'M ON A DATE, I DON'T NEED A *CHAPERONE!*

NOW WARM UP THE COUPE! AND IF THERE'S A SPECK OF DUST ON 'ER, YOU'D BETTER START *PACKING!!*

SURE, BOSS! RIGHT AWAY!!

WHAT'S COME *OVER* HIM? HE'S NEVER ACTED THIS WAY... SPOKEN TO US THIS WAY BEFORE!

AND ⹀SOB⹀ IF HE WANTED A *DATE...* DOESN'T HE REALIZE HOW *I* FEEL ABOUT HIM? WON'T HE EVER NOTICE...?

OH, THE PHONE!

RINNG!

MISS POTTS! THIS IS THE *AVENGERS!* IT IS IMPORTANT THAT WE CONTACT *IRON MAN!* DO YOU KNOW HIS WHERE-ABOUTS?

HE'S MR. STARK'S PERSONAL BODYGUARD! PERHAPS MR. STARK KNOWS! JUST A MOMENT...!

I *HEARD* THAT, PEPPER! TELL THEM I SENT IRON MAN AWAY FOR A VACATION! A *LONG* VACATION!!

BUT, MR. STARK... WHAT IF HE'S *NEEDED?*

SORRY, GIRL! *EVERYONE* NEEDS A VACATION... EVEN OL' SHELL HEAD!

4.

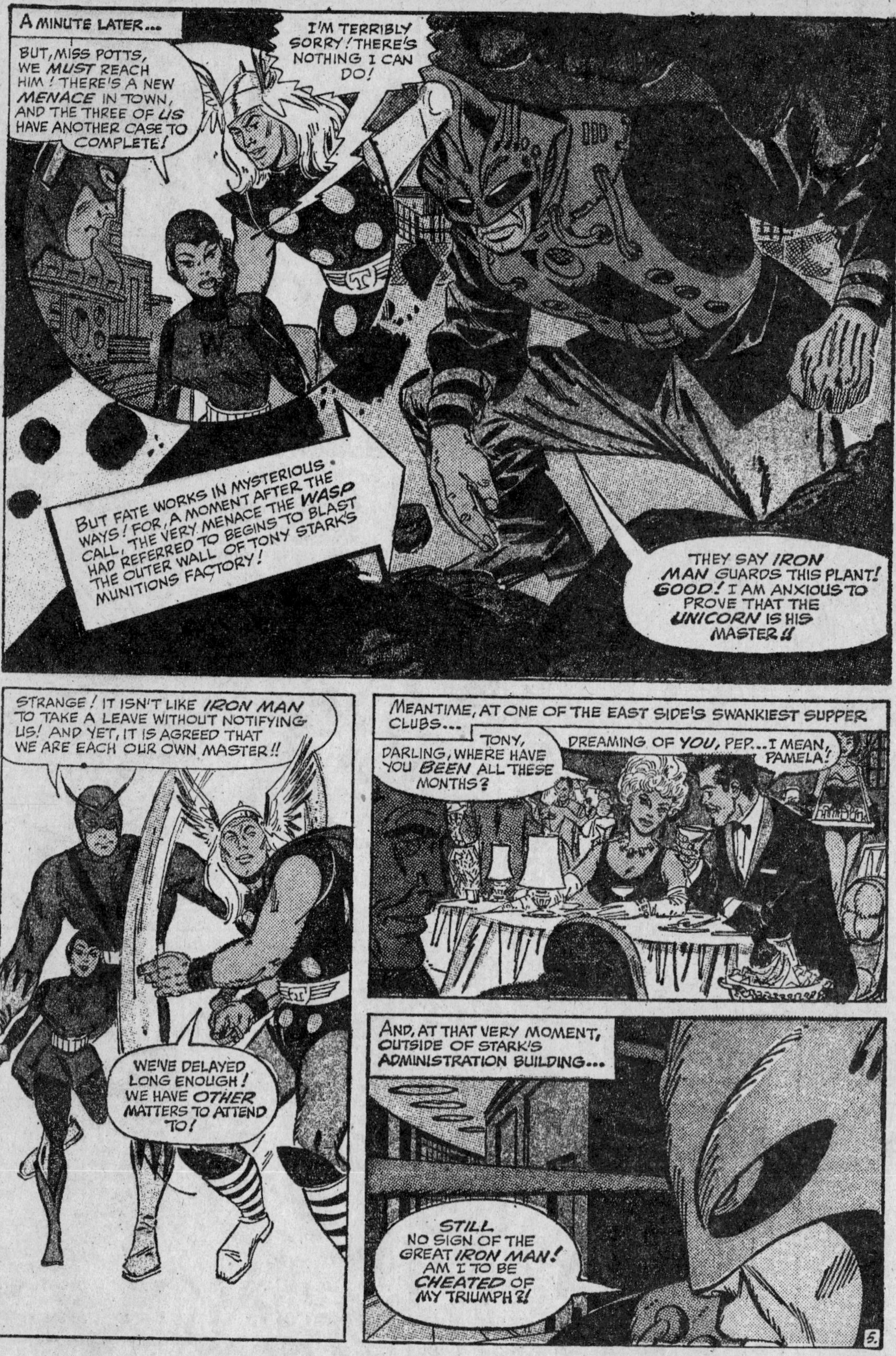

A MINUTE LATER...
BUT, MISS POTTS, WE MUST REACH HIM! THERE'S A NEW MENACE IN TOWN, AND THE THREE OF US HAVE ANOTHER CASE TO COMPLETE!
I'M TERRIBLY SORRY! THERE'S NOTHING I CAN DO!
BUT FATE WORKS IN MYSTERIOUS WAYS! FOR, A MOMENT AFTER THE CALL, THE VERY MENACE THE WASP HAD REFERRED TO BEGINS TO BLAST THE OUTER WALL OF TONY STARK'S MUNITIONS FACTORY!
THEY SAY IRON MAN GUARDS THIS PLANT! GOOD! I AM ANXIOUS TO PROVE THAT THE UNICORN IS HIS MASTER!!
STRANGE! IT ISN'T LIKE IRON MAN TO TAKE A LEAVE WITHOUT NOTIFYING US! AND YET, IT IS AGREED THAT WE ARE EACH OUR OWN MASTER!!
WE'VE DELAYED LONG ENOUGH! WE HAVE OTHER MATTERS TO ATTEND TO!
MEANTIME, AT ONE OF THE EAST SIDE'S SWANKIEST SUPPER CLUBS...
TONY, DARLING, WHERE HAVE YOU BEEN ALL THESE MONTHS?
DREAMING OF YOU, PEP...I MEAN, PAMELA!
AND, AT THAT VERY MOMENT, OUTSIDE OF STARK'S ADMINISTRATION BUILDING...
STILL NO SIGN OF THE GREAT IRON MAN! AM I TO BE CHEATED OF MY TRIUMPH?!
5.

MAC, LOOK! WHAT IN SAM HILL IS *THAT*?

SEARCH *ME*!! BUT, WHOEVER HE IS, HE'S STARTING TO TEAR THE PLACE APART!!

I CAN DELAY MY ATTACK NO LONGER! BY THE IRRESISTIBLE POWER OF MY *UNICORN HORN* I SHALL ACCOMPLISH MY MISSION--- THE SABOTAGING OF AMERICA'S MILITARY PRODUCTION!

RUN, YOU HAPLESS FOOL! FLEE BEFORE THE STAGGERING HORN OF THE *UNICORN*! TELL *IRON MAN* I AM HERE! LET HIM FACE ME...IF HE *DARES*!!

SOUNDS LIKE *BIG TROUBLE* OUTSIDE, BABY! I BETTER TAKE A LOOK-SEE!

IF ONLY *MR. STARK* WERE HERE! THE SECURITY OFFICE JUST CALLED--- THERE'S A STRANGE CHARACTER WHO CALLS HIMSELF *THE UNICORN*! HE'S CHALLENGING *IRON MAN* TO FIGHT HIM!!

LITTLE DREAMING OF THE POWER OF THE UNICORN, HAPPY HOGAN HURLS HIMSELF INTO THE ATTACK...

YOU'RE IN THE WRONG PLACE, PAL! THERE AIN'T ANY *MASQUERADE* GOIN' ON AROUND HERE!

I'M NOT EXACTLY *IRON MAN*, BUT MEBBE I'LL DO FOR A STARTER!

BUT SECONDS LATER THE ASTONISHED CHAUFFEUR GOES FLYING OVER THE UNICORN'S HEAD, TOSSED AS EASILY AS A CHILD WOULD TOSS A SMALL TOY!

HOLY COW! EVEN THAT CLOWN'S *MUSCLES* MUST HAVE MUSCLES!

6.

MISTER, I DON'T KNOW WHO YOU ARE OR WHAT YOUR GIMMICK IS, BUT YOU JUST MADE THE BIGGEST MISTAKE OF YOUR LIFE! YOU MADE FIGHTIN' HAPPY HOGAN *MAD!*

BAH! I HAVE NO DESIRE TO WASTE TIME WITH UNDER-LINGS! WHERE IS IRON MAN?!

WHAT GIVES? DOES HE OWE YOU *DOUGH* OR SOMETHING? I *TOLD* YOU HE WASN'T... OOOF!

HOLD YOUR TONGUE IN THE PRESENCE OF THE *UNICORN,* FOOL!

YEOW! WHEN AM I GONNA LEARN TO MIND MY OWN BUSINESS?!

OPERATOR! OPERATOR! GET ME THE *POLICE!* OPERATOR... WHY DON'T YOU *ANSWER??*

IT'S NO USE! THE LINE'S *DEAD!* THE UNICORN MUST HAVE RIPPED OUT THE PHONE CABLES!

YOU NO LONGER AMUSE ME! I CAN WASTE NO MORE TIME HERE!

AND SO WE SHALL END THIS LITTLE EXERCISE HERE AND NOW!

AS SOON AS I ADJUST MY *UNICORN POWER HORN,* YOU WILL LEARN *WHY* I FEAR NOTHING THAT LIVES!

7.

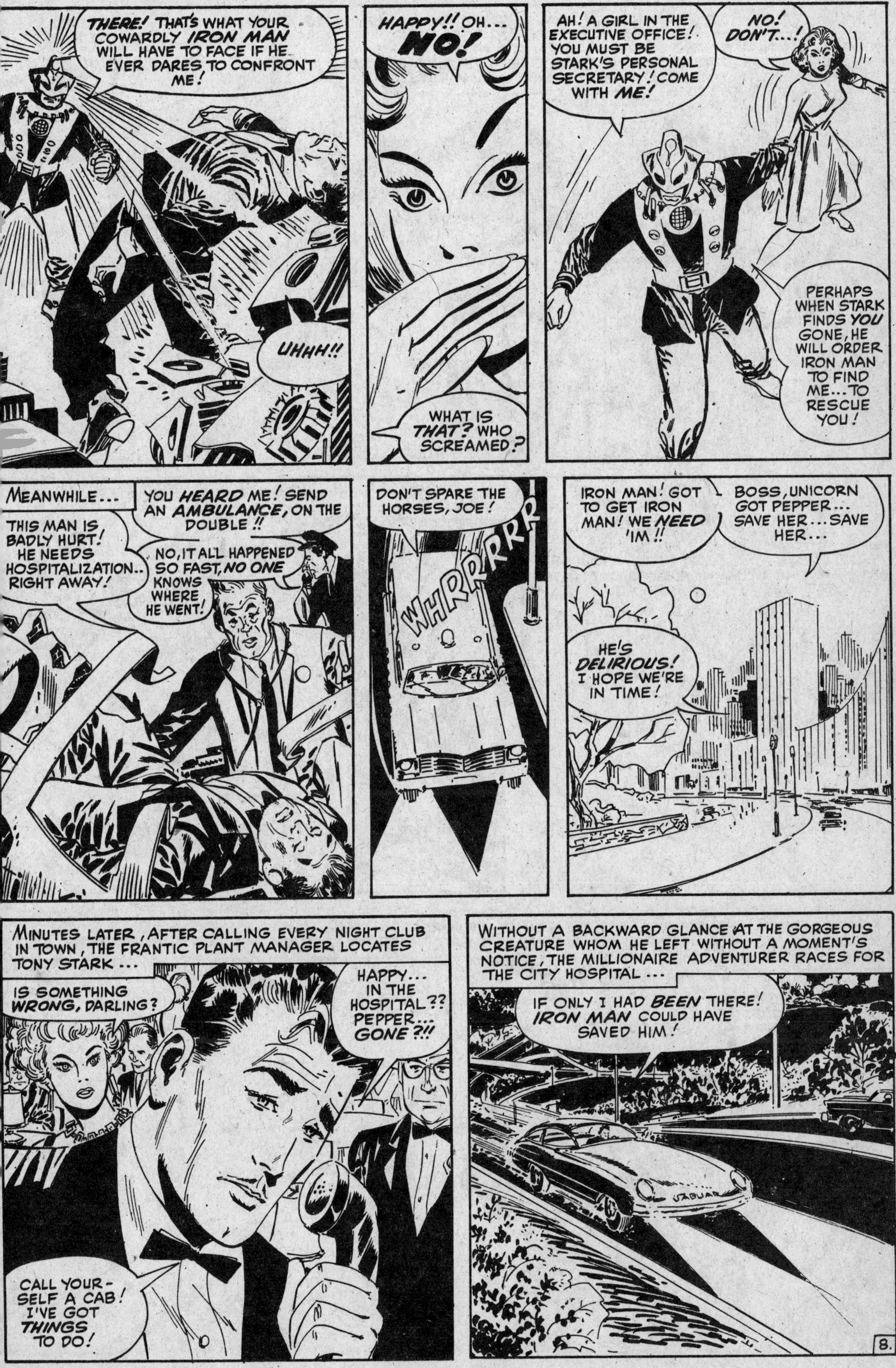
THERE! THAT'S WHAT YOUR COWARDLY IRON MAN WILL HAVE TO FACE IF HE EVER DARES TO CONFRONT ME!
UHHH!!
HAPPY!! OH... NO!
WHAT IS THAT? WHO SCREAMED?
AH! A GIRL IN THE EXECUTIVE OFFICE! YOU MUST BE STARK'S PERSONAL SECRETARY! COME WITH ME!
NO! DON'T...!
PERHAPS WHEN STARK FINDS YOU GONE, HE WILL ORDER IRON MAN TO FIND ME... TO RESCUE YOU!
MEANWHILE...
THIS MAN IS BADLY HURT! HE NEEDS HOSPITALIZATION.. RIGHT AWAY!
YOU HEARD ME! SEND AN AMBULANCE, ON THE DOUBLE!!
NO, IT ALL HAPPENED SO FAST, NO ONE KNOWS WHERE HE WENT!
DON'T SPARE THE HORSES, JOE!
WHRRRRRR
IRON MAN! GOT TO GET IRON MAN! WE NEED 'IM!!
BOSS, UNICORN GOT PEPPER... SAVE HER... SAVE HER...
HE'S DELIRIOUS! I HOPE WE'RE IN TIME!
MINUTES LATER, AFTER CALLING EVERY NIGHT CLUB IN TOWN, THE FRANTIC PLANT MANAGER LOCATES TONY STARK...
IS SOMETHING WRONG, DARLING?
HAPPY... IN THE HOSPITAL?? PEPPER... GONE?!!
CALL YOURSELF A CAB! I'VE GOT THINGS TO DO!
WITHOUT A BACKWARD GLANCE AT THE GORGEOUS CREATURE WHOM HE LEFT WITHOUT A MOMENT'S NOTICE, THE MILLIONAIRE ADVENTURER RACES FOR THE CITY HOSPITAL...
IF ONLY I HAD BEEN THERE! IRON MAN COULD HAVE SAVED HIM!
JAGUAR
8.

FINALLY, AT THE EMERGENCY WARD...

I WANT TO SEE HAPPY HOGAN! I'M HIS EMPLOYER.. ANTHONY STARK!

SORRY, SIR! NO ONE IS ALLOWED TO SEE HIM YET! BUT YOU MAY SPEAK TO HIS DOCTOR!

AH, YES, MR. STARK! WE WONDERED WHERE YOU WERE! HOGAN IS STILL TOO WEAK TO HAVE VISITORS! HE'S ON THE CRITICAL LIST, YOU KNOW!

SEE THAT HE GETS WHATEVER HE NEEDS MONEY IS NO OBJECT! HE MUST HAVE THE BEST OF EVERYTHING!!

MR. STARK, WE GIVE ALL OUR PATIENTS THE BEST CARE! EACH LIFE IS IMPORTANT TO US! YOUR MONEY CAN'T HELP HIM NOW!

I GUESS I HAD THAT COMING! I'VE BEEN SO WRAPPED UP IN MY OWN PROBLEMS, I FORGOT ABOUT EVERYONE ELSE!

AND PEPPER! WHAT OF HER? IF ANYTHING HAPPENS TO HER, I'LL NEVER FORGIVE MYSELF! I..I NEVER REALIZED HOW I FELT ABOUT THAT WONDERFUL LITTLE REDHEAD!

MEANWHILE, AT A PRIVATE ESTATE, ON THE SHORE OF LONG ISLAND...

UNICORN, YOU'RE A FOOL! WHEN MR. STARK LEARNS I'M GONE AND SENDS IRON MAN AFTER ME, THAT'LL BE THE END OF YOU!!

NOT QUITE! I AM USING YOU AS BAIT FOR MY TRAP BECAUSE I WANT IRON MAN TO COME HERE!

"I HAVE TRAINED FOR YEARS, BEHIND THE IRON CURTAIN, FOR JUST THIS MISSION! EVEN MY INGENIOUS COSTUME, WHICH IS MORE POWERFUL THAN IRON MAN'S, WAS CREATED BY THE CRIMSON DYNAMO, BEFORE HE DEFECTED TO THE WEST..."

ONCE YOU HAVE MASTERED THE MANY WEAPONS BUILT INTO THE UNIFORM YOU WEAR, YOU WILL BE MORE THAN A MATCH FOR ANY OF OUR CAPITALIST ENEMIES, UNICORN!

SEE HOW I CAN DESTROY ANY OBSTACLE WITH MY POWER HORN! I CAN'T WAIT FOR MY FIRST SABOTAGE MISSION!

9.

I CAN RAISE OBJECTS MAGNETICALLY, REGARDLESS OF THEIR WEIGHT!

MY POWER HORN MAKES ME MORE EFFECTIVE THAN AN ENTIRE BATTERY OF ANTI-TANK GUNS!!

EVEN CONCRETE FORTIFICATIONS CANNOT STAND IN THE WAY OF THE UNICORN!

AND, SHOULD I BE ATTACKED BY ROCKET-FIRING JET PLANES...

...I HAVE THE POWER TO DEFLECT AND DESTROY EACH AND EVERY MISSILE BEFORE IT CAN REACH ME! IN TRUTH, THE CRIMSON DYNAMO'S GENIUS, AND MY OWN BRILLIANT SKILL HAVE MADE THE UNICORN THE WORLD'S GREATEST LIVING FIGHTING MACHINE!

AND NOW... POSSIBLY MY GREATEST POWER...

...IS THE POWER OF MY HORN TO THROW A RADIATING ENERGY SHIELD AROUND ME, STRONG ENOUGH TO PROTECT ME FROM THE EXPLOSIVE FORCE OF A THOUSAND TONS OF T.N.T.!

SO, MY POWER IS ALMOST BEYOND DESCRIPTION! BESIDES HAVING AN UNBEATABLE OFFENSE, I ALSO POSSESS A COMPLETELY FOOL-PROOF DEFENSE!

10.

AND YOU THINK IRON MAN CAN FRIGHTEN ME! IT IS LAUGHABLE!

ALL I KNOW IS WHAT MR. STARK HAS ALWAYS SAID...HIS ENEMIES ALWAYS THINK THEY'RE SUPERIOR! BUT IRON MAN HASN'T BEEN DEFEATED YET!

EVEN AS THE LOVELY, LOYAL SECRETARY SPEAKS, THE MAN SHE IS QUOTING IS FILLED WITH NEW RESOLVE...

I'VE BEEN A SELFISH, SELF-CENTERED HEEL!

BUT PERHAPS IT'S NOT TOO LATE TO MAKE AMENDS! FOR THE SAKE OF THOSE WHO NEED ME, I PRAY THERE IS STILL TIME!

I'M GLAD I DESIGNED MY ARMOR SO THAT I CAN EXPAND IT AND PUT IT ON IN SECONDS!

THEY SAY THAT THE MAN I'M AFTER CALLS HIMSELF THE UNICORN! IF ONLY I HAD BEEN HERE!

CLICK

BUT THERE'S STILL A CHANCE OF TRACKING HIM DOWN! THE EXPERIMENTAL BLACK LIGHT TRACER WHICH I'VE DEVELOPED SHOULD DO THE TRICK!

AND NOW..LET THE UNICORN BEWARE!

I'VE STILL GOT A CHANCE IF THE MOLECULES IN THE AIR THROUGH WHICH THE UNICORN HAS PASSED HAVE NOT YET BEEN COMPLETELY BLOWN AWAY!

NO! THE TRAIL IS CRYSTAL CLEAR! ALMOST TOO CLEAR... AS THOUGH HE WANTS TO BE FOUND!

EXACTLY FIFTEEN MINUTES LATER ...

HE MUST BE IN THAT HOUSE BELOW! NOW.. IF ONLY PEPPER IS STILL SAFE...!

EVERY SECOND MAY BE VITAL! I'VE GOT TO ENTER BY THE FASTEST WAY! *THERE HE IS!!*

IRON MAN! SO I HAVE TRAPPED YOU AT LAST!

IT REMAINS TO BE *SEEN* WHO IS TRAPPED! WHERE IS THE GIRL? *TALK,* UNICORN!

SHE IS RIGHT BEHIND ME, AS YOU CAN SEE! BUT *YOU'LL* NEVER GET HER!

AND NOW, YOU ARROGANT BUFFOON, YOU WILL FEEL THE POWER OF THE *UNICORN!!*

MISTER, WHEN IT COMES TO *POWER,* YOU'RE TALKING TO THE FELLA WHO *INVENTED* THE WORD! YOU'RE IN THE *BIG LEAGUES* NOW!

BUT THE UNCANNY UNICORN RECOVERS HIMSELF INSTANTLY, AND STRIKES BACK WITH A VENGEANCE!

HERE! HAVE A TASTE OF MY SMASHING FORCE-BOLT RAY!!

UHHH! HE'S LOADED WITH BUILT-IN WEAPONS, AS *I* AM!

I'VE JUST TIME TO SLIP ON MY WRIST REVERSER-RAY, AND HURL HIS OWN FORCE-BOLT *BACK* AT HIM!

IT WORKED!!

CRASH

I DON'T KNOW WHAT HIS PURPOSE IS, BUT HE'S DANGEROUS, PEPPER! I'VE GOT TO GET *YOU* BACK WHERE YOU'LL BE SAFE!

I *KNEW* MR. STARK WOULD SEND YOU AFTER ME! BUT...WHAT ABOUT THE UNICORN?

12.

I'LL RETURN AND FINISH HIM OFF AS SOON AS I KNOW YOU'RE OUT OF HARM'S WAY!

MR. STARK OWES YOU SO MUCH! AND SO DO I, AND SO MANY PEOPLE! WHY WON'T YOU REVEAL WHO YOU *REALLY* ARE?

NO TIME FOR THAT NOW! SOME DAY I'LL EXPLAIN!

BUT, A SAFE DISTANCE BEHIND IRON MAN, WE FIND...

HE DOESN'T SUSPECT THAT I, TOO, HAVE THE POWER OF JET-ASSISTED FLIGHT! THE POWER TO *FOLLOW* HIM!

MINUTES LATER, AFTER REACHING STARK FACTORY...

STILL NO NEWS OF HAPPY! THE HOSPITAL SAYS HE HASN'T COME OUT OF HIS COMA YET!

KEEP PHONING! I WANT TO BE NOTIFIED OF ANY CHANGE IN HIS CONDITION!

AND NOW TO SETTLE ACCOUNTS WITH THE *UNICORN!*

BUT IRON MAN'S SINISTER FOE IS FAR CLOSER THAN THE GOLDEN AVENGER SUSPECTS...

MY PLAN IS SO SIMPLE! YET, SO PERFECT AND FOOL-PROOF! ALL I NEED DO IS HIDE THIS TIME-BOMB CAREFULLY...

THERE!! IT'S POWERFUL ENOUGH TO BLOW THIS ENTIRE FACTORY SKY-HIGH!

IRON MAN! WHERE *ARE* YOU?? YOU CAN'T HIDE FROM ME FOR-EVER!

THE *UNICORN!* HE DARED TO COME *HERE!*

YOU'RE *DOOMED!* I'VE HIDDEN A TIME BOMB IN YOUR FACTORY... SET TO GO OFF AT MID-NIGHT!

SO *THAT'S* WHY YOU RE-TURNED!!

SURRENDER AND LET ME TAKE YOU BEHIND THE IRON CURTAIN OR ELSE SEE YOUR LIFE'S WORK GO UP IN FLAMES!

I'VE STILL GOT 15 MINUTES!!

AND, AS IRON MAN WEIGHS HIS FATAL DECISION, THE HIDDEN LETHAL MECHANISM TICKS ON, AND ON...

TICK TICK TICK!!

13

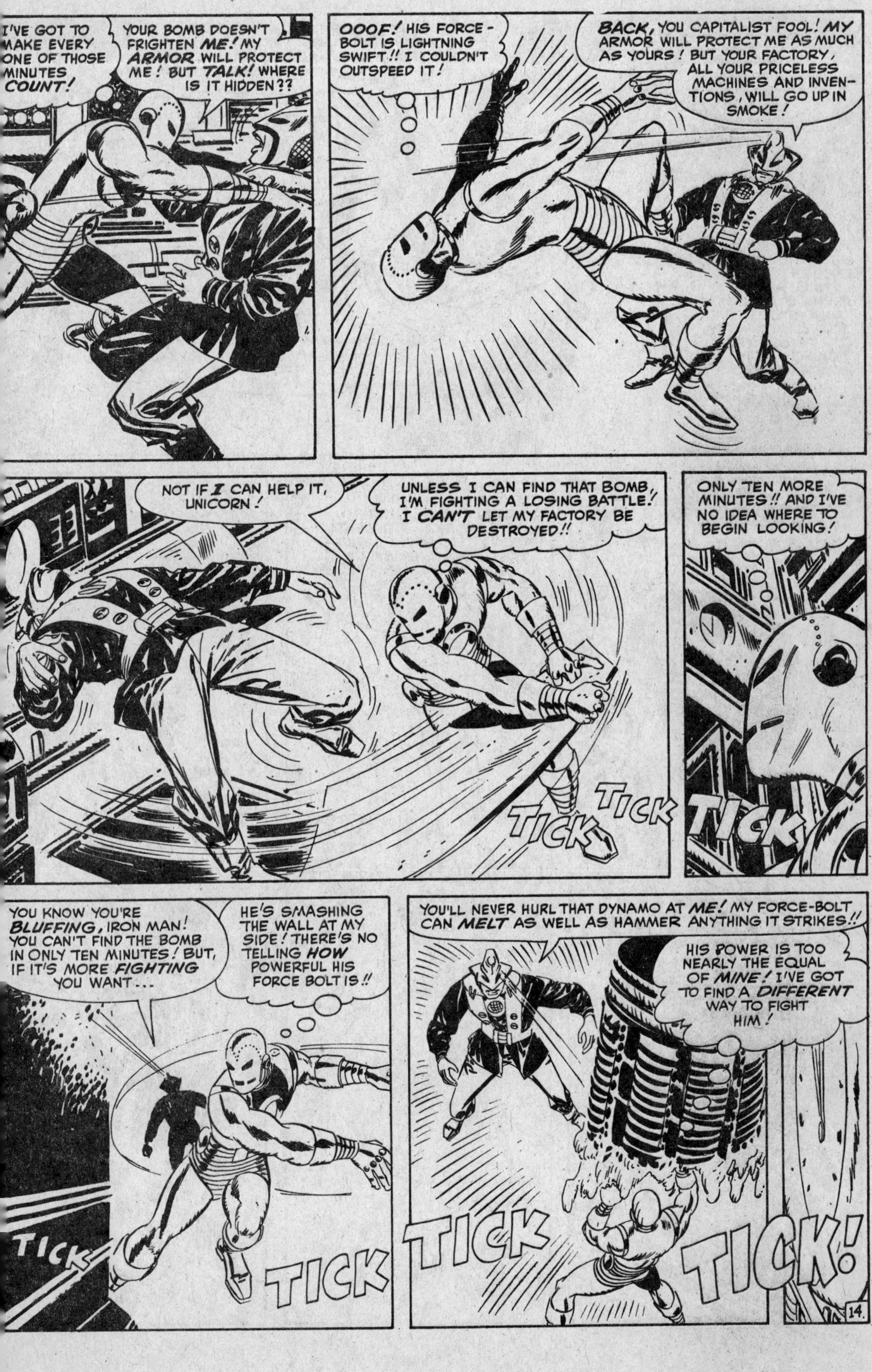
I'VE GOT TO MAKE EVERY ONE OF THOSE MINUTES COUNT!
YOUR BOMB DOESN'T FRIGHTEN ME! MY ARMOR WILL PROTECT ME! BUT TALK! WHERE IS IT HIDDEN??
OOOF! HIS FORCE-BOLT IS LIGHTNING SWIFT!! I COULDN'T OUTSPEED IT!
BACK, YOU CAPITALIST FOOL! MY ARMOR WILL PROTECT ME AS MUCH AS YOURS! BUT YOUR FACTORY, ALL YOUR PRICELESS MACHINES AND INVENTIONS, WILL GO UP IN SMOKE!
NOT IF I CAN HELP IT, UNICORN!
UNLESS I CAN FIND THAT BOMB, I'M FIGHTING A LOSING BATTLE! I CAN'T LET MY FACTORY BE DESTROYED!!
TICK TICK
ONLY TEN MORE MINUTES!! AND I'VE NO IDEA WHERE TO BEGIN LOOKING!
TICK
YOU KNOW YOU'RE BLUFFING, IRON MAN! YOU CAN'T FIND THE BOMB IN ONLY TEN MINUTES! BUT, IF IT'S MORE FIGHTING YOU WANT...
HE'S SMASHING THE WALL AT MY SIDE! THERE'S NO TELLING HOW POWERFUL HIS FORCE BOLT IS!!
TICK
TICK
YOU'LL NEVER HURL THAT DYNAMO AT ME! MY FORCE-BOLT CAN MELT AS WELL AS HAMMER ANYTHING IT STRIKES!!
HIS POWER IS TOO NEARLY THE EQUAL OF MINE! I'VE GOT TO FIND A DIFFERENT WAY TO FIGHT HIM!
TICK
TICK!
14

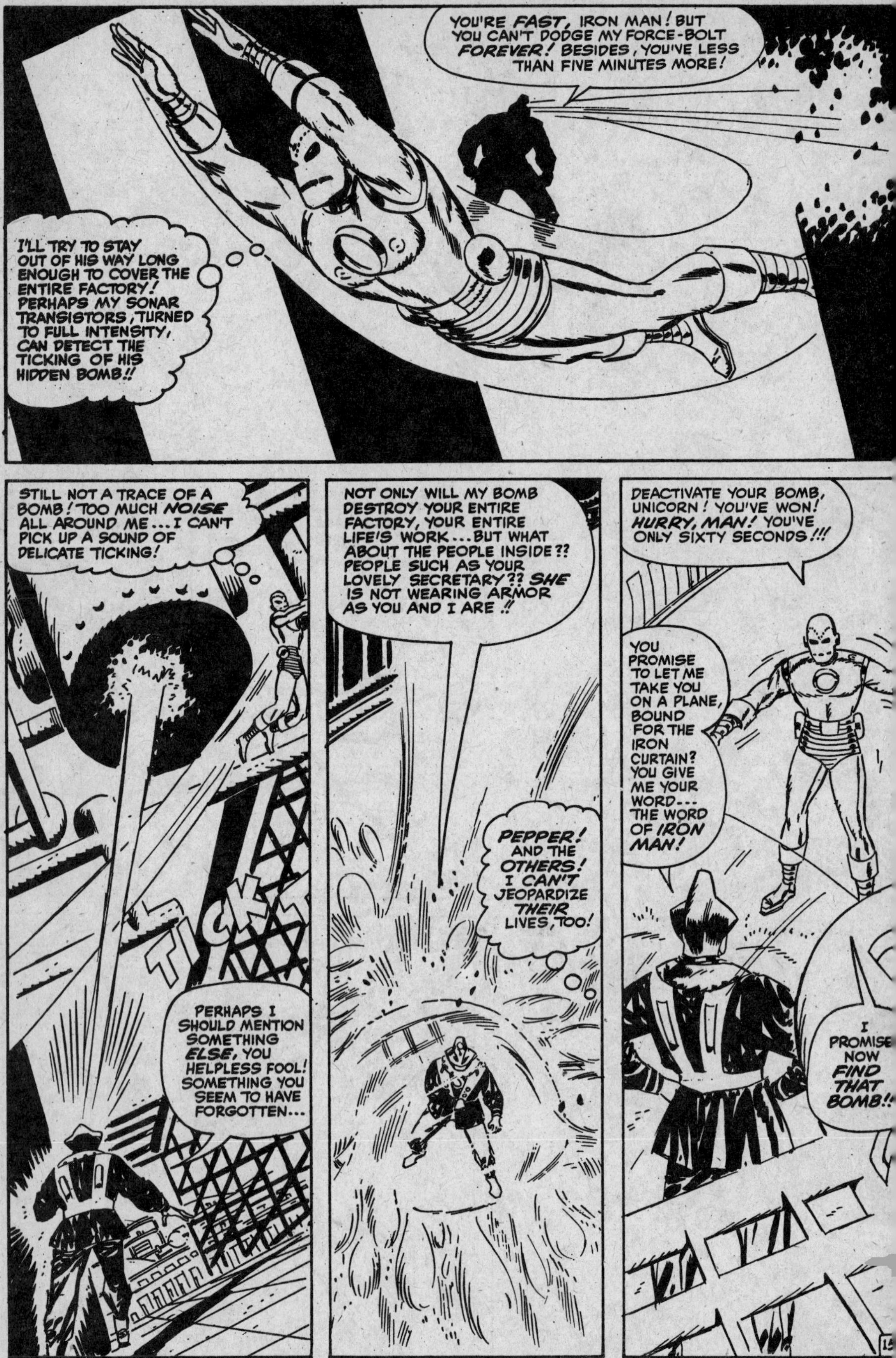
YOU'RE FAST, IRON MAN! BUT YOU CAN'T DODGE MY FORCE-BOLT FOREVER! BESIDES, YOU'VE LESS THAN FIVE MINUTES MORE!
I'LL TRY TO STAY OUT OF HIS WAY LONG ENOUGH TO COVER THE ENTIRE FACTORY! PERHAPS MY SONAR TRANSISTORS, TURNED TO FULL INTENSITY, CAN DETECT THE TICKING OF HIS HIDDEN BOMB!!
STILL NOT A TRACE OF A BOMB! TOO MUCH NOISE ALL AROUND ME... I CAN'T PICK UP A SOUND OF DELICATE TICKING!
TICK
PERHAPS I SHOULD MENTION SOMETHING ELSE, YOU HELPLESS FOOL! SOMETHING YOU SEEM TO HAVE FORGOTTEN...
NOT ONLY WILL MY BOMB DESTROY YOUR ENTIRE FACTORY, YOUR ENTIRE LIFE'S WORK... BUT WHAT ABOUT THE PEOPLE INSIDE?? PEOPLE SUCH AS YOUR LOVELY SECRETARY?? SHE IS NOT WEARING ARMOR AS YOU AND I ARE.!!
PEPPER! AND THE OTHERS! I CAN'T JEOPARDIZE THEIR LIVES, TOO!
DEACTIVATE YOUR BOMB, UNICORN! YOU'VE WON! HURRY, MAN! YOU'VE ONLY SIXTY SECONDS!!!
YOU PROMISE TO LET ME TAKE YOU ON A PLANE, BOUND FOR THE IRON CURTAIN? YOU GIVE ME YOUR WORD--- THE WORD OF IRON MAN!
I PROMISE NOW FIND THAT BOMB!!

WHAT *REWARDS* I SHALL RECEIVE WHEN I BRING THE MIGHTY *IRON MAN* BACK AS MY PRISONER! THE *UNICORN* HAS SUCCEEDED, WHERE ALL OTHERS HAVE FAILED!!

THE HIGHEST HONORS SHALL BE MINE! FOR, ALL THE SECRETS OF YOUR ARMOR, YOUR POWERFUL TRANSISTOR WEAPONS, EVERYTHING WHICH IS PART OF YOUR PROTECTIVE IRON SUIT SHALL BECOME *OURS!*

SNAP!

NOW *COME!* MY PLANE IS WAITING!

BONG! BONG!

I CAN'T *BELIEVE* IT!! THE *UNICORN* HAS DEFEATED HIM! HE'S TAKING *IRON MAN* WITH HIM... AS HIS *PRISONER!!*

OHHH, IF ONLY MR. STARK WERE HERE!!

Minutes later...

UNICORN!! YOU'VE *DONE* IT!!

OF COURSE! NOW *TAKE OFF...* WHILE WE CAN!

HOW HELPLESS YOU ARE, IRON MAN! I'VE TRAPPED YOU IN THE MOST PERFECT WAY! YOU ARE BOUND BY A *PROMISE,* WHICH YOU CANNOT BREAK!

YOU'RE *RIGHT,* UNICORN! I PROMISED THAT I'D LET YOU TAKE ME ON A PLANE, BOUND FOR YOUR HOMELAND! AND, AS YOU SEE, I'VE KEPT MY PROMISE!

BUT I DIDN'T SAY WHAT I'D DO *AFTER* I ENTERED THE PLANE!!

BAH! WHAT CAN YOU DO NOW??

THIS!!

STOP HIM!!

16.

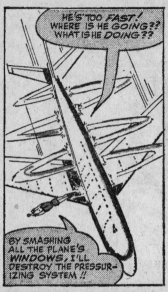

HE'S TOO *FAST!* WHERE IS HE *GOING??* WHAT IS HE *DOING??*

BY SMASHING ALL THE PLANE'S *WINDOWS,* I'LL DESTROY THE PRESSURIZING SYSTEM!!

WE CAN'T *BREATHE!* THERE'S NO *AIR* IN HERE!

QUICK!! BRING THE PLANE LOWER! BRING IT *DOWN!!*

YOU WERE ABOUT TO DESTROY MY *FACTORY,* UNICORN! LET'S SEE HOW *YOU* ENJOY HAVING THINGS TORN UP!

I GUESS IT'S THE ONE THING THEY FORGOT TO *WARN* YOU ABOUT... I NEVER *COULD* CONTROL MY SILLY OL' TEMPER!!

WAIT A MINUTE, *FELLAS!!* IT'S NOT POLITE TO RUN OUT ON A GUY WHEN HE'S STILL *TALKING* TO YOU! TSK TSK! NO MANNERS AT ALL!

HOW *ABOUT* THAT?? THEY JUST DON'T BUILD THOSE SHIPS LIKE THEY USED TO!!

STRANGE! I DIDN'T SEE THE *UNICORN* BAIL OUT! UNLESS... HE MIGHT HAVE TAKEN OFF HIS COSTUME AND BEEN DISGUISED AS ONE OF HIS CIVILIAN ASSISTANTS!

IT WAS CARELESS OF ME NOT TO PAY MORE ATTENTION TO THOSE WHO *DID* BAIL OUT!

BUT, ON THE OTHER SIDE OF THE PEAK, LEAVING THE CRASH AREA BEFORE IRON MAN CAN REACH THE SPOT...

AS LONG AS HE STILL DOESN'T SUSPECT THAT *I,* TOO, CAN FLY, I CAN STILL ESCAPE THE ACCURSED IRON AVENGER!

17.

THE NEXT DAY, AFTER THE REMAINING RED AGENTS HAVE BEEN ROUNDED UP AND IMPRISONED, ANTHONY STARK RETURNS TO HIS EXECUTIVE OFFICES!..

MORNING, PEPPER! HAVE YOU HEARD ABOUT HAP...?

OH, YOU'RE SPEAKING TO THE HOSPITAL *NOW*?

WHAT? HE *IS*?? OFF THE CRITICAL LIST? OH, HOW *WONDERFUL!* YES, I'LL TELL MR. STARK *IMMEDIATELY!*

IT'S *HAPPY*, BOSS! HE'S GOING TO BE ALL RIGHT! HE'LL PULL THROUGH!!

ISN'T IT THE MOST *THRILLING* NEWS?! OH, I COULD SHOUT FOR JOY!!

I'M SORRY I WASN'T HERE, PEPPER! BUT IRON MAN CALLED ME THIS MORNING AND BRIEFED ME!

THANK HEAVENS! GRAB YOUR COAT, GIRL! WE'RE GOING TO SEE HIM!

MINUTES LATER...

HAPPY!! WE'RE SO THRILLED FOR YOU! HOW DO YOU FEEL?

A BUSTED ARM, A FRACTURED LEG, SOME SMASHED RIBS, AND A FEW DOZEN CUTS, BUMPS AND BRUISES, AND *YOU* ASK HOW I FEEL!!

IT ONLY HURTS WHEN I *LAUGH!* AND TAKE THOSE THINGS AWAY, PEP! I'M *ALLERGIC* TO FLOWERS!!

YOU'RE IN YOUR USUAL MISERABLE, GRUMPY, SOUR UNBEARABLE MOOD!! THAT MEANS EVERYTHING IS *FINE!* NOW GET WELL SOON.. BECAUSE I *MISS* YOU, YOU BIG LUG!

I CAN NEVER BE SURE... IS PEPPER NICE TO HAPPY TO MAKE ME JEALOUS, OR... IS *HE* REALLY THE ONE??

AH-CHOO!

GESUNDHEIT!

PERHAPS IT'S BETTER THAT PEPPER *DOES* PREFER HAPPY! I REALIZE NOW I CAN *NEVER* LEAD A NORMAL LIFE... NEVER GIVE UP THE MISSION I WAS MEANT TO FULFILL! NOT WHILE MENACES SUCH AS THE *UNICORN* REMAIN TO THREATEN THE LAND I LOVE!

The End

18.

AND SPEAKING OF MENACES WHICH REMAIN...DON'T MISS THE ACTION NEXT ISH, WHEN *IRON MAN* FACES THE DEADLY THREAT OF *HAWKEYE, THE MYSTIC MARKSMAN!* IT'S GOT THE FULL-LENGTH ACTION AND DRAMA YOU LOVE, PLUS THE RETURN OF A COLORFUL GUEST VILLAIN!! STAN AND DON WENT ALL OUT ON THIS ONE! SEE YOU THEN!

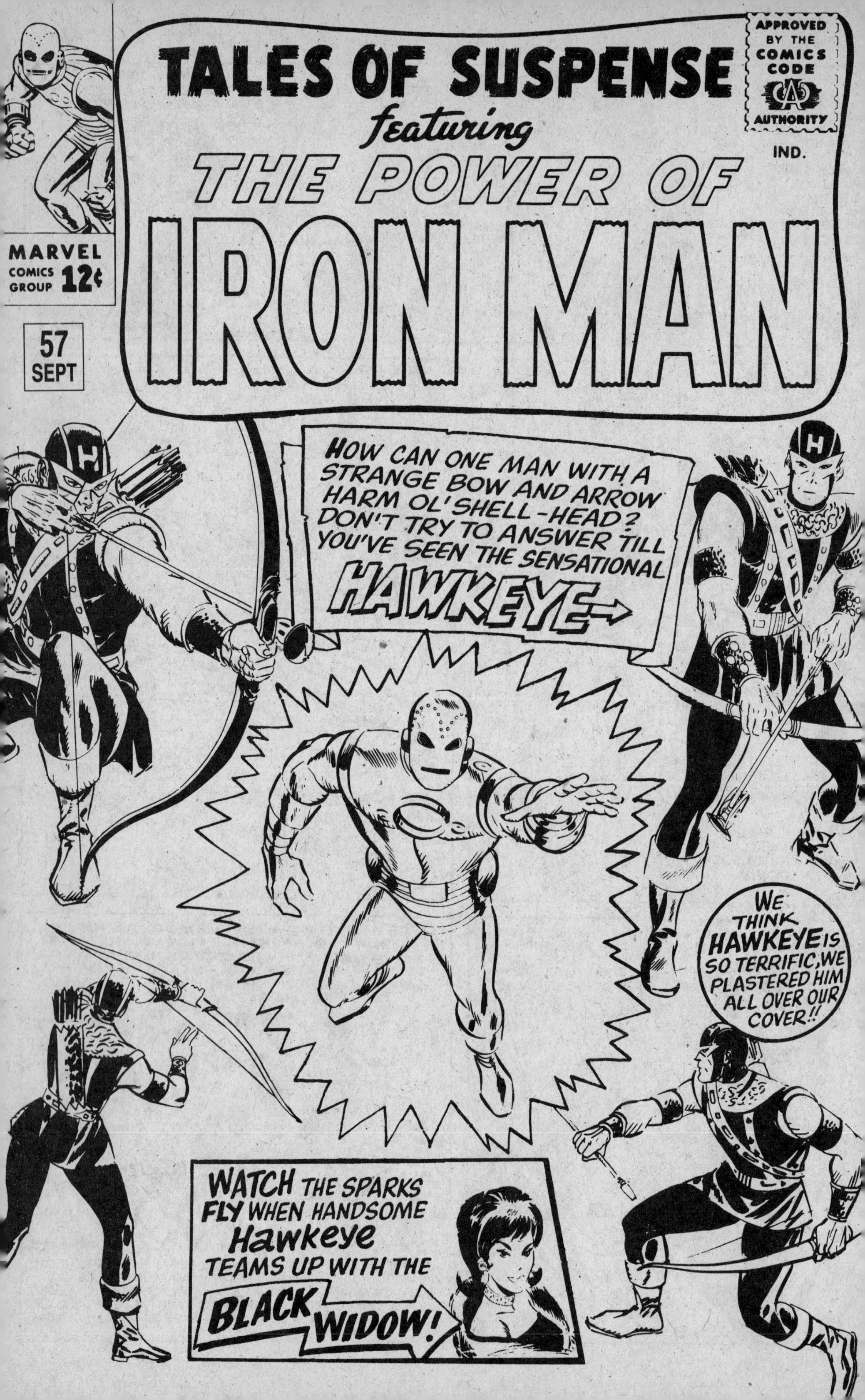

TALES OF SUSPENSE
featuring
THE POWER OF
IRON MAN
APPROVED BY THE COMICS CODE AUTHORITY
IND.
MARVEL COMICS GROUP 12¢
57 SEPT
HOW CAN ONE MAN WITH A STRANGE BOW AND ARROW HARM OL' SHELL-HEAD? DON'T TRY TO ANSWER TILL YOU'VE SEEN THE SENSATIONAL HAWKEYE
WE THINK HAWKEYE IS SO TERRIFIC, WE PLASTERED HIM ALL OVER OUR COVER!!
WATCH THE SPARKS FLY WHEN HANDSOME Hawkeye TEAMS UP WITH THE BLACK WIDOW!

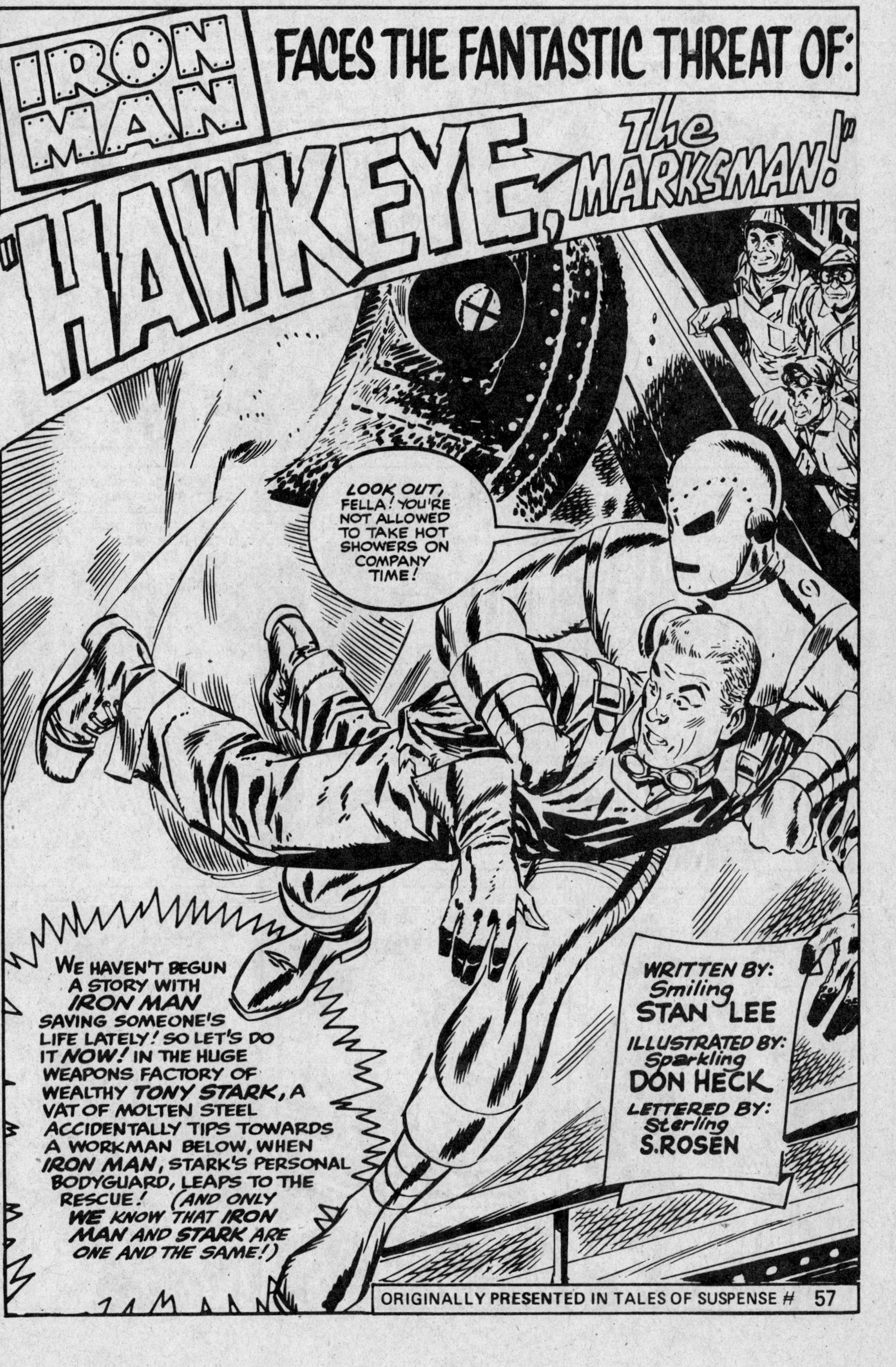
IRON MAN
FACES THE FANTASTIC THREAT OF:
"HAWKEYE, the MARKSMAN!"
LOOK OUT, FELLA! YOU'RE NOT ALLOWED TO TAKE HOT SHOWERS ON COMPANY TIME!
WE HAVEN'T BEGUN A STORY WITH IRON MAN SAVING SOMEONE'S LIFE LATELY! SO LET'S DO IT NOW! IN THE HUGE WEAPONS FACTORY OF WEALTHY TONY STARK, A VAT OF MOLTEN STEEL ACCIDENTALLY TIPS TOWARDS A WORKMAN BELOW, WHEN IRON MAN, STARK'S PERSONAL BODYGUARD, LEAPS TO THE RESCUE! (AND ONLY WE KNOW THAT IRON MAN AND STARK ARE ONE AND THE SAME!)
WRITTEN BY: Smiling STAN LEE
ILLUSTRATED BY: Sparkling DON HECK
LETTERED BY: Sterling S.ROSEN
ORIGINALLY PRESENTED IN TALES OF SUSPENSE # 57

YOU'LL BE ALL RIGHT NOW, PARKER! NEXT TIME BE CAREFUL WHERE YOU STOP TO TIE YOUR SHOE-LACE!

I SURE WILL, IRON MAN! BOY! AM I GLAD MR. STARK HAS YOU ON THE PAYROLL!

HEY, IRON MAN! GOT A MINUTE?

WHAT CAN I DO FOR YOU, HAPPY? SOMETHING WRONG IN THE FRONT OFFICE?

NAH, THIS IS PERSONAL! YOU'RE PRETTY CHUMMY WITH MR. STARK! HOW ABOUT ASKIN' HIM TO PUT IN A GOOD WORD WITH PEPPER FOR ME! SHE HASN'T GIVEN ME A DATE IN WEEKS!

LATER, IN STARK'S PRIVATE OFFICE...

WHY SHOULD I FEEL SO JEALOUS WHEN HAPPY TRIES TO DATE PEPPER?? AFTER ALL... I DON'T DARE GET SERIOUS ABOUT HER!

A MAN LIKE ME...WHOSE LIFE DEPENDS ON A TRANSISTOR-POWERED CHEST DEVICE KEEPING HIS INJURED HEART BEATING, CAN'T VERY WELL ALLOW ROMANCE TO ENTER HIS LIFE!

AND SO, TONY STARK BEGINS TO SPEAK TO HIS LOVELY SECRETARY...

PEPPER, I HAVE SOMETHING TO ASK YOU! IT'S ABOUT A DATE...

A DATE??

OH, MR. STARK! I WAS BEGINNING TO THINK YOU'D NEVER NOTICE ME! I'M SO THRILLED!

WAIT! LET ME EXPLAIN!

WHAT'S THERE TO EXPLAIN? YOU ASKED ME FOR A DATE...AND I SAY YES!! NOW LET'S SEE...WHAT WILL I WEAR...?

BUT.. I WAS SPEAKING FOR HAPPY!

'SCUSE ME, BOSS! I...DIDN'T MEAN TO...INTERRUPT!

HAPPY...!

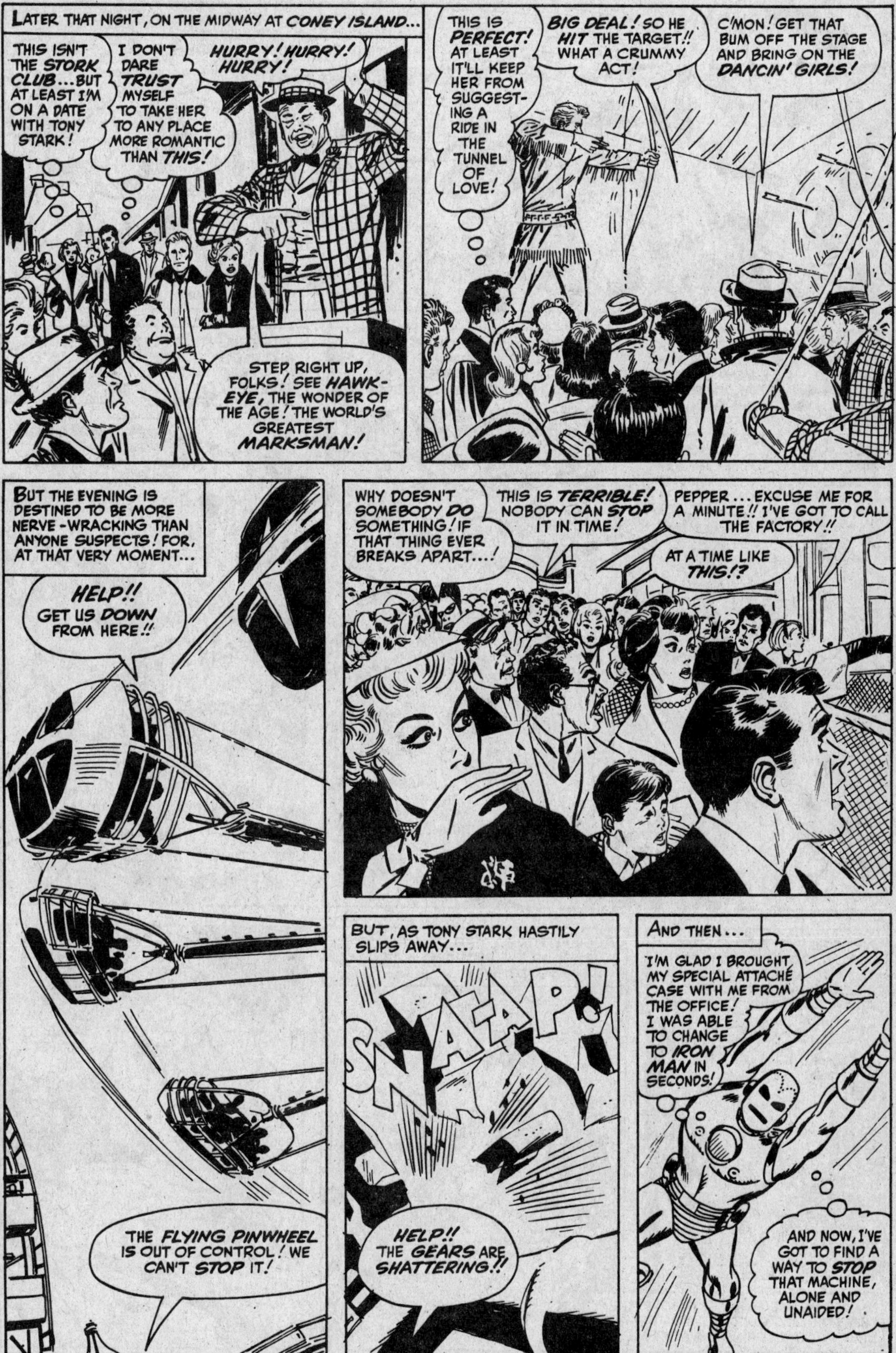
LATER THAT NIGHT, ON THE MIDWAY AT CONEY ISLAND...
THIS ISN'T THE STORK CLUB...BUT AT LEAST I'M ON A DATE WITH TONY STARK!
I DON'T DARE TRUST MYSELF TO TAKE HER TO ANY PLACE MORE ROMANTIC THAN THIS!
HURRY! HURRY! HURRY!
STEP RIGHT UP, FOLKS! SEE HAWK-EYE, THE WONDER OF THE AGE! THE WORLD'S GREATEST MARKSMAN!
THIS IS PERFECT! AT LEAST IT'LL KEEP HER FROM SUGGEST-ING A RIDE IN THE TUNNEL OF LOVE!
BIG DEAL! SO HE HIT THE TARGET!! WHAT A CRUMMY ACT!
C'MON! GET THAT BUM OFF THE STAGE AND BRING ON THE DANCIN' GIRLS!
BUT THE EVENING IS DESTINED TO BE MORE NERVE-WRACKING THAN ANYONE SUSPECTS! FOR, AT THAT VERY MOMENT...
HELP!! GET US DOWN FROM HERE!!
THE FLYING PINWHEEL IS OUT OF CONTROL! WE CAN'T STOP IT!
WHY DOESN'T SOMEBODY DO SOMETHING! IF THAT THING EVER BREAKS APART...!
THIS IS TERRIBLE! NOBODY CAN STOP IT IN TIME!
PEPPER... EXCUSE ME FOR A MINUTE!! I'VE GOT TO CALL THE FACTORY!!
AT A TIME LIKE THIS!?
BUT, AS TONY STARK HASTILY SLIPS AWAY...
SNA-A-P!
HELP!! THE GEARS ARE SHATTERING!!
AND THEN...
I'M GLAD I BROUGHT MY SPECIAL ATTACHÉ CASE WITH ME FROM THE OFFICE! I WAS ABLE TO CHANGE TO IRON MAN IN SECONDS!
AND NOW, I'VE GOT TO FIND A WAY TO STOP THAT MACHINE, ALONE AND UNAIDED!

I'LL PUT THE FULL POWER OF MY ARMORED BODY AGAINST THE FLYING PINWHEEL! =UHH!= CAN'T HOLD MUCH LONGER! THIS *HAS* TO DO IT!

FOR LONG GRUELLING SECONDS, THE MAN OF IRON HOLDS ON GRIMLY... KNOWING THAT HUMAN LIVES HANG IN THE BALANCE! AND THEN, SLOWLY, EXCRUCIATINGLY, THE GIANT MACHINE GRINDS TO A HALT...

IRON MAN *DID* IT! HE PREVENTED A DISASTER!!

BUT HOW DID HE GET HERE SO QUICKLY??

UH-OH! I'LL HAVE TO THINK OF AN ANSWER TO THAT ONE, FAST!!

I KNOW...I'LL TELL PEPPER I WENT TO FIND IRON MAN... I'LL SAY HE HAD ORDERS TO FOLLOW US TO CONEY ISLAND!

SHE'S SURE TO BELIEVE IT! MOST EVERYBODY THINKS IRON MAN ALWAYS TAGS ALONG BEHIND ME *ANYWAY!*

MEANTIME, THERE IS *ONE* OBSERVER WHO FEELS NO JOY AT WHAT HAS HAPPENED! THE ONLY EMOTION HE EXPERIENCES IS ONE OF BURNING, BLAZING *JEALOUSY!*

I'M THE GREATEST MARKSMAN THE WORLD HAS EVER KNOWN! AND YET, THEY *IGNORE* ME!!

WHY COULDN'T *I* DO ALL THE THINGS IRON MAN CAN DO?? ALL IT TAKES ARE A LOT OF MECHANICAL GIMMICKS... AND A COLORFUL COSTUME DISGUISE!

AND SO, WE ARE ABOUT TO WITNESS THE CREATION OF ONE OF THE MOST STARTLING ARCH-VILLAINS OF ALL TIME!!

A SHORT TIME LATER, IN A BASEMENT WORKSHOP, THE BROODING MARKSMAN WORKS FEVERISHLY...

I'LL MAKE MYSELF A COSTUME THAT NO ONE WILL EVER BE ABLE TO FORGET!

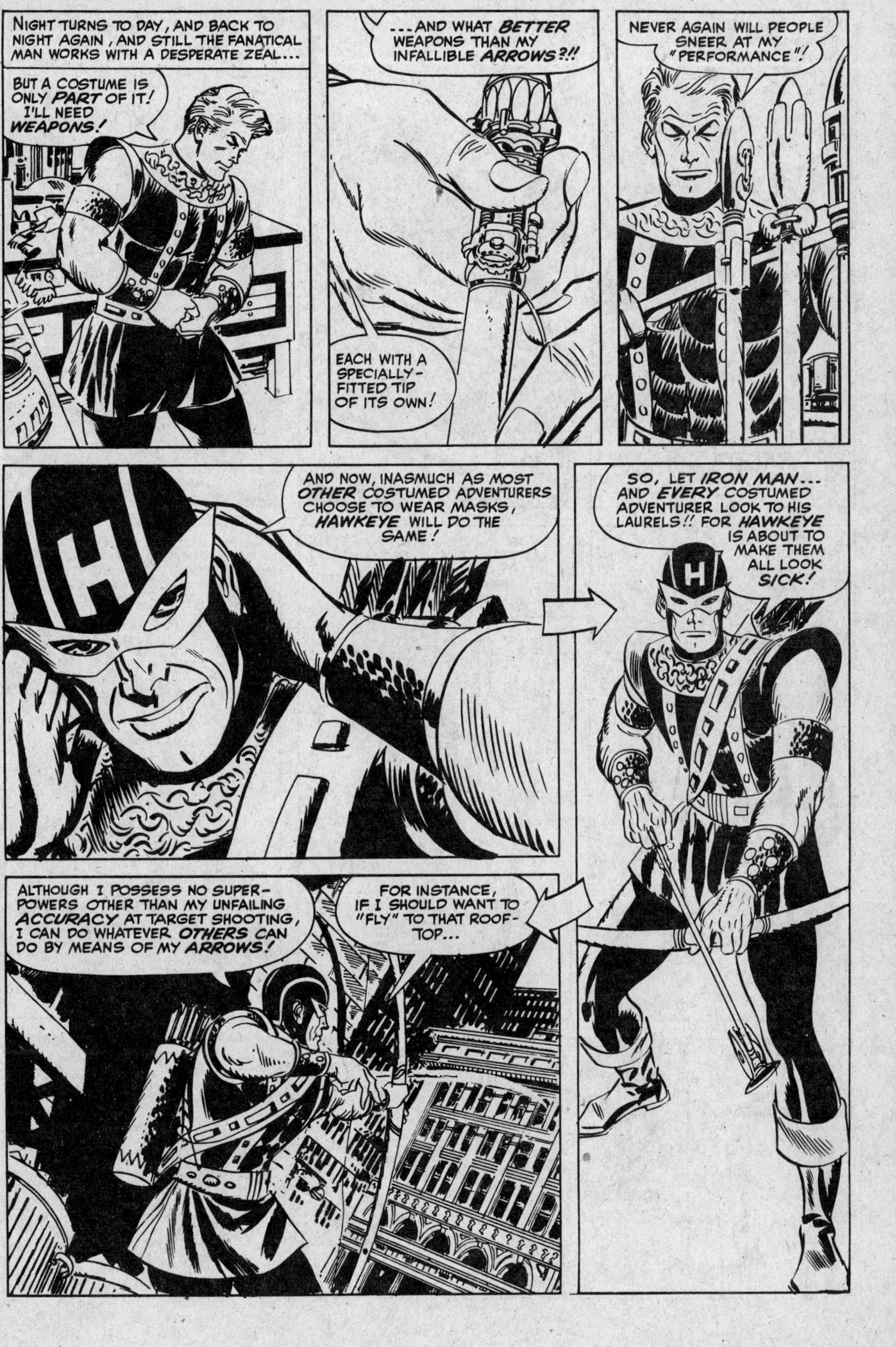

NIGHT TURNS TO DAY, AND BACK TO NIGHT AGAIN, AND STILL THE FANATICAL MAN WORKS WITH A DESPERATE ZEAL...
BUT A COSTUME IS ONLY PART OF IT! I'LL NEED WEAPONS!
...AND WHAT BETTER WEAPONS THAN MY INFALLIBLE ARROWS?!!
EACH WITH A SPECIALLY-FITTED TIP OF ITS OWN!
NEVER AGAIN WILL PEOPLE SNEER AT MY "PERFORMANCE"!
AND NOW, INASMUCH AS MOST OTHER COSTUMED ADVENTURERS CHOOSE TO WEAR MASKS, HAWKEYE WILL DO THE SAME!
SO, LET IRON MAN... AND EVERY COSTUMED ADVENTURER LOOK TO HIS LAURELS!! FOR HAWKEYE IS ABOUT TO MAKE THEM ALL LOOK SICK!
ALTHOUGH I POSSESS NO SUPER-POWERS OTHER THAN MY UNFAILING ACCURACY AT TARGET SHOOTING, I CAN DO WHATEVER OTHERS CAN DO BY MEANS OF MY ARROWS!
FOR INSTANCE, IF I SHOULD WANT TO "FLY" TO THAT ROOF-TOP...

MY SUCTION TIPPED ARROW STICKS TO THE EXACT SPOT I AIM FOR, AND THEN...

...MY SPRING PULLEY DEVICE WHISKS ME TOWARDS THE ARROW TIP IN JUST SECONDS...

WHAT A *THRILL*!! I FEEL AS THOUGH THE DESTINY OF THE ENTIRE CITY BELOW ME IS IN MY POWERFUL GLOVED HANDS!

THIS IS ALMOST TOO GOOD TO BE TRUE! RIGHT BELOW ME... THAT FLEEING FOOL JUST ROBBED A JEWELRY STORE!

I CAN STOP HIM WITH MY EYES CLOSED!!

FOR THE LUVVA PETE!!

TWANG!

A PERFECT SHOT!! AS ALWAYS!!

NOW TO MAKE THE CAPTURE AND... *WHA..?* HE'S GETTING *AWAY!*

THAT'S WHAT I GET FOR TAKING PAINS NOT TO *INJURE* HIM!!

WELL, I'LL CATCH UP WITH HIM IN A MINUTE! FIRST, I'LL JUST INSPECT WHAT HE DROPPED!

NO *WONDER* HE RAN SO FAST! THIS IS QUITE A *HAUL!* DIAMONDS... RUBIES...

JUST THEN, AN IRONIC DEVELOPMENT OCCURS! ATTRACTED BY THE NOISE, THE *POLICE* ARRIVE, AND...

DON'T MOVE!! WE CAUGHT YOUR PARTNER, AND WE'VE GOT *YOU* DEAD TO RIGHTS!

THEY THINK I HELPED ROB THE STORE!

DROPPING THE STOLEN JEWELRY, **HAWKEYE** BEGINS A MAD DASH FOR FREEDOM AS THE OFFICERS TAKE UP THE CHASE...

THEY'D NEVER BELIEVE I'M INNOCENT! I'LL HAVE TO **RUN** FOR IT!

HALT... IN THE NAME OF THE LAW!

LOOK! HE DROPPED THE LOOT! WE'D BETTER PICK IT UP BEFORE SOMEONE HELPS HIMSELF TO IT!

AND, AS HAWKEYE TAKES ADVANTAGE OF THE MOMENTARY RESPITE...

THAT MAN... RACING SO SWIFTLY! HE MIGHT BE WHAT I'M LOOKING FOR!

WHY **RUN** WHEN YOU CAN **RIDE!?** SHUT THE DOOR BEHIND YOU!

JUST WHAT I **NEED**... A LIFT! BUT, WHY DID SHE **STOP** FOR ME..??

LOOK, LADY... I... WOW!!

WHAT IS WRONG? IS SOMETHING THE **MATTER?!**

AS FATE WOULD HAVE IT, HAWKEYE SEES ONE OF THE MOST BEAUTIFUL WOMEN IN THE WORLD...

...THE DARING, DAZZLING DANGEROUS **BLACK WIDOW!!**

LADY, WHOEVER YOU ARE, DON'T PINCH ME! THIS IS **ONE** DREAM I DON'T **EVER** WANT TO WAKE UP FROM!

I ASSURE YOU, MY COSTUMED FRIEND, THIS IS NO DREAM!

IF YOU ARE AS ADVENTUROUS AND POWERFUL AS YOUR APPEARANCE WOULD INDICATE, YOU MIGHT BE THE VERY **ALLY** I'VE BEEN SEEKING!

WHATEVER YOU'RE LOOKIN' FOR, GORGEOUS, YOU CAN BET YOUR BOTTOM DOLLAR... I'M **IT!**

THUS, SMITTEN BY THE BLACK WIDOW'S FATAL BEAUTY, THE MAN CALLED **HAWKEYE** ENTERS INTO A DRAMATIC ALLIANCE WHICH IS TO CHANGE THE COURSE OF BOTH THEIR LIVES, AND **IRON MAN'S** AS WELL!

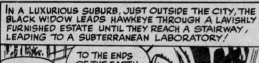

IN A LUXURIOUS SUBURB, JUST OUTSIDE THE CITY, THE BLACK WIDOW LEADS HAWKEYE THROUGH A LAVISHLY FURNISHED ESTATE UNTIL THEY REACH A STAIRWAY, LEADING TO A SUBTERRANEAN LABORATORY!

FOLLOW ME, HAWK-EYE!

TO THE ENDS OF THE EARTH, GORGEOUS!

IT IS FORTUNATE THAT HE IS TAKEN WITH MY BEAUTY! I WILL BE ABLE TO TWIST HIM AROUND MY LITTLE FINGER! BUT HE MUST NOT LEARN THAT I AM REALLY A *RED SPY!*

SAY! THIS IS SOME GREAT *LAB* YOU'VE GOT HERE! BUT YOU DON'T *LOOK* LIKE THE SCIENTIST TYPE TO ME!

I'M *NOT!* THIS EQUIPMENT BELONGS TO THE ONE I RENT THIS HOME FROM! BUT THERE ARE THINGS HERE WHICH WILL INCREASE YOUR OWN POWERS!

MY COMMUNIST MASTERS PROVIDED THIS ESTATE FOR ME! AND *NOW* THEIR INVESTMENT SHALL REALLY PAY OFF!

MM... I SEE WHAT YOU *MEAN!* SOME OF THE DEVICES DESCRIBED IN THIS BOOK WOULD MAKE GREAT WEAPONS IF FITTED ONTO MY *ARROWS!*

BUT WHAT'S THE ANGLE, BEAUTIFUL? DO YOU HAVE ANY *DRAGONS* YOU WANT SLAIN, OR WHAT??

IN A WAY, YES!! THE FAMOUS *IRON MAN* IS A MORTAL ENEMY OF MINE! ANY MAN WHO COULD *DEFEAT* HIM WOULD BE A MAN I COULD LEARN TO LOVE!

HE'S AS GOOD AS *BEATEN*, BABY!

BUT, ONE THING MORE... NO HARM MUST COME TO HIS EMPLOYER, TONY STARK!

SO! SHE'S GOT A *CRUSH* ON STARK, EH? WELL...I'LL PUT A STOP TO *THAT!!*

MEANTIME, THE MAN IN QUESTION IS NOW BACK AT HIS SPRAWLING FACTORY, LITTLE DREAMING OF THE DANGER THAT AWAITS HIM...

POOR PEPPER! I'M AFRAID I DIDN'T SHOW HER A VERY GOOD TIME LAST NIGHT!

I GUESS THE *LEAST* I CAN DO IS TAKE HER OUT AGAIN... AND *THIS* TIME GIVE HER THE TYPE OF GLAMOROUS EVENING SHE MUST HAVE EXPECTED!

I'LL *DO* IT! I'LL ASK HER RIGHT *NOW!*

IN FACT, I MIGHT AS WELL BE *HONEST* WITH MYSELF! I'M NOT DOING IT ONLY FOR HER! *I'D* LOVE TO TAKE THAT FABULOUS FEMALE TO ALL THE BEST PLACES... TO LOOK INTO THOSE GORGEOUS LIMPID EYES OF HERS...

CAREFUL, STARK, OL' BOY! YOU'RE BEGINNING TO SOUND LIKE A FELLA IN *LOVE!*

OOPS! ALMOST FORGOT! CAN'T LET HER SEE ME LIKE *THIS!*

MINUTES LATER...

HMM! LOOKS LIKE I'M A LITTLE LATE!

PEPPER, THEY'VE GOT A GREAT NEW MURDER MYSTERY AT THE DRIVE-IN TONIGHT, AND I WAS WONDERIN'...?

WHY, HAPPY HOGAN! YOU BIG SPEND-THRIFT, YOU!

OH! MR. STARK JUST CAME IN! I'LL SHOW HIM HE'S NOT THE ONLY FISH IN THE SEA! EVEN A MURDER MYSTERY WOULD BE BETTER THAN OUR DATE LAST NIGHT!

WELL, IF YOU DON'T WANNA...

WHO SAID I DIDN'T WANT TO?!

I'D BE DELIGHTED TO GO TO THE DRIVE-IN MOVIE WITH YOU TONIGHT, HAPPY! IT'S CERTAINLY MORE ROMANTIC THAN BEING WALKED ALL OVER CONEY ISLAND WITH AN ICE CREAM CONE!

GRRREAT! I KNEW YOU COULDN'T RESIST MY CHARM MUCH LONGER!

WELL, I GUESS I DESERVED THAT!

MEANWHILE, A SHORT DISTANCE AWAY FROM STARK'S FACTORY...

NOW!

BULLSEYE! MY SILENT SUCTION-TIPPED ARROW WILL GET ME INSIDE STARK'S FACTORY IN SECONDS!

THIS IS ALMOST TOO EASY FOR HAWKEYE, THE MARKSMAN!

NX8...

HI, CHARLIE! SEE THE BIG GAME ON T.V. LAST NIGHT?

YOU BET! A NO-HITTER...HOW ABOUT THAT?

LET'S GO, PETE! THEY'RE WAITING FOR THAT LOAD OF EQUIPMENT INSIDE!

THEN, ONCE THE SUPPLY TRUCK HAS PASSED THROUGH THE GUARDED ENTRANCE GATE...

SO FAR, SO GOOD! NOW I'LL START ENOUGH OF A RUCKUS TO BRING *IRON MAN* ON THE RUN!

THE DOOR TO THE MAIN PART OF THE FACTORY IS LOCKED AND BOLTED! SO I'LL JUST SHOW THEM THAT LOCKS MEAN *NOTHING* TO HAWKEYE THE *MARKSMAN!*

THWOCK!

THAT EXPLOSIVE ARROW-HEAD WHICH THE BLACK WIDOW HELPED ME RIG UP WORKS EVEN BETTER THAN WE THOUGHT!

BUT, BEFORE THE ECHO OF THE EXPLOSION HAS DIED AWAY, A JET-POWERED AVENGING *IRON MAN* STREAKS TO THE SCENE, SHOUTING A BRISK COMMAND TO THE FACTORY GUARDS WHO VAINLY TRY TO MATCH HIS BLAZING SPEED...

STAY *BEHIND* ME, MEN! IF THERE'S ANY DANGER, I'LL FACE IT FIRST!

STAY *BEHIND*?? WE COULDN'T CATCH THAT IRON WHIRL-WIND IF WE *TRIED!*

HERE HE *COMES!* THIS IS ALMOST LIKE SOME CORNY *FAIRY TALE!* ONCE I'VE POLISHED OFF THE BIG BAD IRON MAN, I'LL RETURN TO CLAIM THE FAIR DAMSEL'S HAND!

WHA...?! I'M BEING ATTACKED WITH *ARROWS*!! HOW CAN ANYONE EXPECT TO STOP *ME* WITH SOME MERE... *WAIT A MINUTE*!!

THERE'S SOME SORT OF *CHEMICAL* ON THE SUCTION TIPS!! IT HAS A *RUSTING ACTION*! MY ARMOR IS STIFFENING... IT'S GETTING HARDER TO *MOVE*!!

WHOEVER IS RESPONSIBLE HAS FOUND MY *WEAK POINT*! I CAN'T FIGHT *RUST*!

I'VE GOT TO GET AWAY... SHED MY ARMOR BEFORE IT'S TOO RUSTY TO REMOVE!

RUNNING WON'T HELP YOU, IRON MAN! I KNOW YOU'RE HERE SOMEWHERE! YOU CAN'T ESCAPE *HAWKEYE, THE MARKSMAN*!!

SO *THAT'S* MY MYSTERIOUS ATTACKER!! WELL, HE GETS THE *FIRST ROUND*, BUT THE FIGHT ISN'T OVER YET! NO ONE TAKES ME BY SURPRISE *TWICE*!

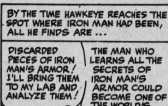

BY THE TIME HAWKEYE REACHES THE SPOT WHERE IRON MAN HAD BEEN, ALL HE FINDS ARE...

DISCARDED PIECES OF IRON MAN'S ARMOR! I'LL BRING THEM TO MY LAB AND ANALYZE THEM!

THE MAN WHO LEARNS ALL THE SECRETS OF IRON MAN'S ARMOR COULD BECOME ONE OF THE WORLD'S MOST POWERF'IL MEN!

WHILE, IN ANOTHER SECTION OF THE SPRAWLING PLANT...

THIS IS WHAT I'M AFTER!

I'M GLAD I HAD THE FORE-SIGHT TO CONCEAL DUPLI-CATE SUITS OF ARMOR FOR MYSELF IN VARIOUS PARTS OF THE FACTORY!

MOVING WITH INCREDIBLE SPEED, LIKE A MAN POSSESSED, A FIGHTING-MAD TONY STARK DONS HIS AWE-SOME ARMOR... EXCEPT FOR...

MY RIGHT BOOT ASSEMBLY! IT'S MISSING!! I'D BE TOO VULNERABLE WITHOUT IT!!

I MUST FIND IT, BEFORE HAWKEYE FINDS ME!

FRANTICALLY HE SEARCHES NEAR-BY AREAS, UNTIL HE REMEMBERS...

OF COURSE! IT NEEDED REPLATING! I LEFT IT HERE AFTER IT WAS FINISHED, WAITING TILL EVERY-ONE WAS GONE BE-FORE I'D TAKE IT!

THAT DOES IT! NOW, I'VE GOT TO GO AFTER THE MARKSMAN BEFORE HE GETS TOO BIG A HEAD START! I HEARD A CAR SPEED AWAY JUST ABOUT TWO MINUTES AGO!

I HAD WONDERED HOW I'D SPEND THE EVENING WHILE PEPPER AND HAPPY WERE AT THE MOVIES! IT LOOKS AS THOUGH FATE SOLVED THAT LITTLE PROBLEM FOR ME!

THERE'S ONLY ONE CAR ON THE ROAD AT THIS HOUR, RACING AWAY FROM MY FACTORY! THAT MUST BE *HAWKEYE*, HEADING TOWARDS LA GUARDIA AIRPORT!

WHO CAN HE *BE?* WHERE DID HE *COME* FROM?? IT SEEMS THAT EVERY MASKED, UNUSUAL CRIMINAL IN THE EAST TRIES TO ATTACK MY WEAPONS FACTORY SOONER OR LATER! EVERY TIME I TURN AROUND I'M MENACED BY SOME CRACKPOT OR SPY!

WELL, THE FIRST THING TO DO IS STOP HIS CAR!

BZZTTT!

---AND AN INTENSIFIED BLAST FROM MY *POWER RAY* IS JUST THE THING TO *DO* IT!!

CRASH!

IT'S *HIM* AGAIN! CAN THERE BE *TWO* IRON MEN??!

I'M ALL OUT OF RUSTING-FLUID! BUT I'VE PLENTY OF *OTHER* KINDS OF ARROWS FOR HIM!

BUT *THIS* TIME, IRON MAN IS *READY* FOR THE MARKSMAN'S ATTACK...

ONE OF THE HANDIEST WEAPONS OF ALL IS MY LITTLE MAGNETIC *REPULSER!*

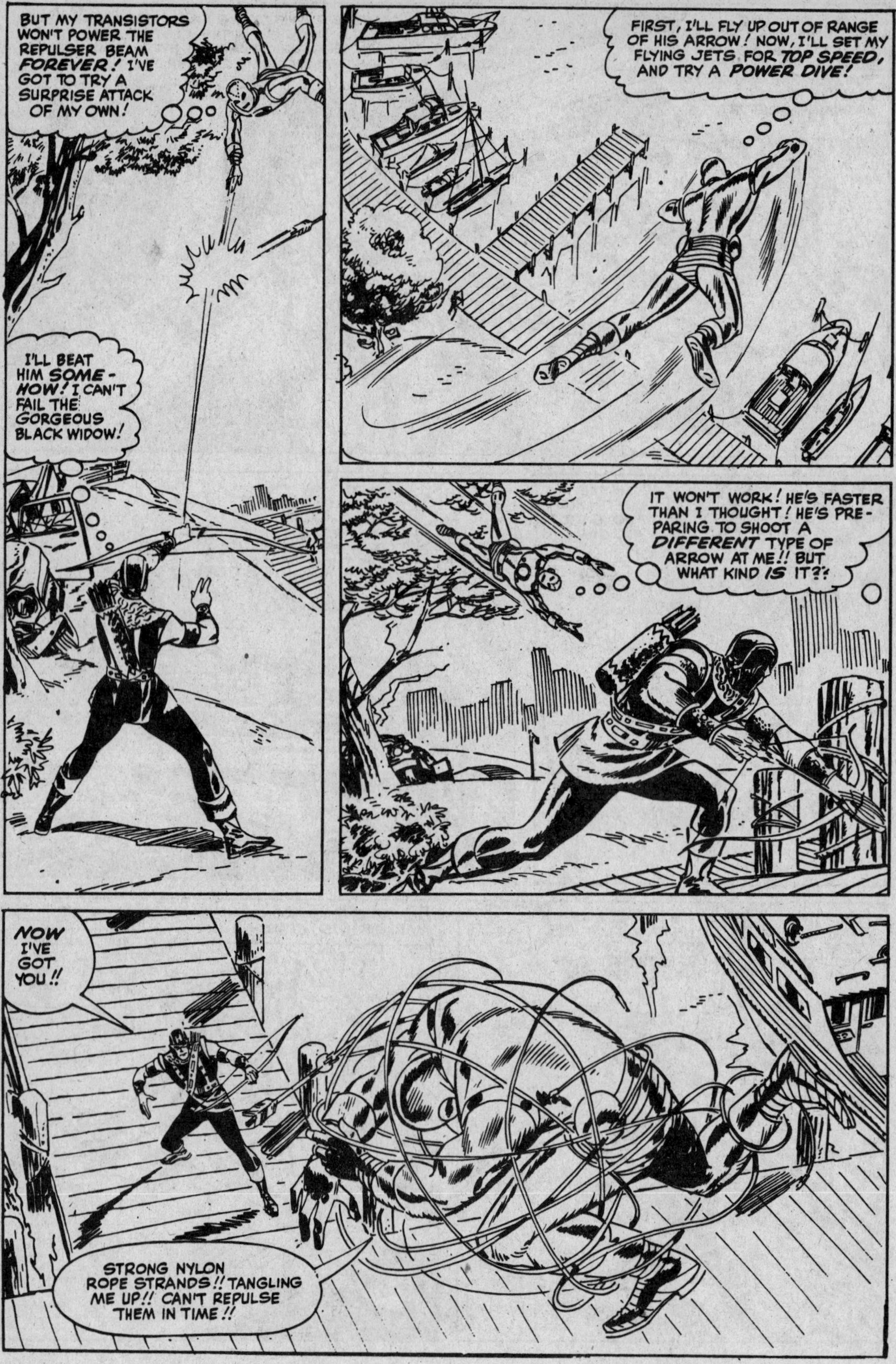
BUT MY TRANSISTORS WON'T POWER THE REPULSER BEAM FOREVER! I'VE GOT TO TRY A SURPRISE ATTACK OF MY OWN!
I'LL BEAT HIM SOME-HOW! I CAN'T FAIL THE GORGEOUS BLACK WIDOW!
FIRST, I'LL FLY UP OUT OF RANGE OF HIS ARROW! NOW, I'LL SET MY FLYING JETS FOR TOP SPEED, AND TRY A POWER DIVE!
IT WON'T WORK! HE'S FASTER THAN I THOUGHT! HE'S PRE-PARING TO SHOOT A DIFFERENT TYPE OF ARROW AT ME!! BUT WHAT KIND IS IT?!
NOW I'VE GOT YOU!!
STRONG NYLON ROPE STRANDS!! TANGLING ME UP!! CAN'T REPULSE THEM IN TIME!!

BUT, NOT FOR NOTHING IS IRON MAN'S *MIGHT* SPOKEN OF IN HUSHED TONES BY THE UNDERWORLD! WITH AN IRRESISTIBLE SURGE OF POWER, HIS TRANSISTOR-AIDED MUSCLES FLING HIS ARMS APART, THUS SNAPPING THE STRANDS BEFORE THEY CAN TIGHTEN!

HE BROKE FREE!! WHAT'S HE TRYING *NOW*??

I'VE GOT TO HIT THE PIER WITH JUST ENOUGH FORCE!

I DID IT!

WHAM!

RIP!

WHAT GOT *INTO* HIM?? HE'S LIKE AN AVENGING TORNADO!!

LOOK OUT! STOP! WHAT ARE YOU DOING?!!

JUST TRYING TO KEEP YOU FROM GETTING *BORED*, ROBIN HOOD!

TWANNG!

OH, *NO* YOU DON'T!! YOU CAN'T ESCAPE ME BY *DROWNING*! YOU'VE GOT TOO MUCH EX-PLAINING TO DO!!

BUT A PAIR OF THE MOST GLAMOROUS EYES IN THE WORLD ARE *ALSO* WATCH-ING THE GRIM TABLEAU FROM A HIDING PLACE NEARBY...

I WAS TO PICK HIM UP HERE AFTER HIS VICTORY...A VICTORY WHICH NEVER TOOK PLACE!!

BUT THEN, THINKING THE BATTLE WON, THE GOLDEN AVENGER MAKES HIS MOST SERIOUS MISTAKE... TURNING HIS BACK ON HAWKEYE...

WHILE HE'S UNCONSCIOUS, I'LL GO TO HIS CAR AND RETRIEVE THE PIECES OF MY OTHER SUIT OF ARMOR!

---AS THE MUFFLED PADDING OF IRON MAN'S HEAVY FEET FADES AWAY...

HE'S GONE!!

NOW IS MY CHANCE TO FINISH HIM OFF FOR GOOD!

NOW, WHEN HE LEAST EXPECTS IT!

I'LL USE MY MOST POTENT ARROW OF ALL...!!

...THE DEMOLITION BLAST WARHEAD WHICH THE BLACK WIDOW HELPED ME TO ASSEMBLE!!

AND NOW... FAREWELL! IRON MAN!! NOTHING CAN SAVE YOU NOW!

BUT, HAWKEYE IS *WRONG!* THERE IS ONE THING THAT *CAN* SAVE IRON MAN... AND THAT IS THE PROTECTION OF THE STRONGEST, MOST SKILLFULLY MADE FLEXIBLE IRON ARMOR IN EXISTENCE, TEMPERED TO THE HIGHEST DEGREE OF RESILIENCY EVER ATTAINED BY ANY METAL!

OHHH!

HAWKEYE!! SAVE ME!

WHOOM!

AND, ALTHOUGH THE DEMOLITION BLAST RICOCHETS HARMLESSLY OFF THE SHOULDER OF THE GOLDEN AVENGER, THE TREMENDOUS IMPACT IS HURLED AWAY IN ANOTHER DIRECTION.. RIGHT TOWARDS THE STARTLED *MADAME NATASHA*, BEFORE SHE CAN SAVE HERSELF!

YOU!! WHAT HAVE I DONE?!

IGNORING THE STUNNED IRON MAN, THE ANGUISHED MARKSMAN RACES TO THE SIDE OF THE BLACK WIDOW!

SHE'S STILL BREATHING! I CAN'T LET HER DIE!!

HER BOAT IS WAITING! IF I CAN JUST MAKE IT TO A DOCTOR WITH HER BEFORE THE FOG ROLLS IN...!

SHE HAS TO LIVE!! SHE HAS TO BE *MINE!!* SHE'S THE ONLY ONE I'VE EVER LOVED!!

THEN, BY THE TIME IRON MAN HAS FULLY RECOVERED FROM THE EFFECTS OF THE STAGGERING BLOW...

HE'S TRYING TO ESCAPE IN THE FOG!! BUT HE WON'T GET FAR! THERE'S NO PLACE HE CAN FLEE TO THAT I CAN'T FOLLOW WITH MY POWER JETS!!

IT'S HARD TO BE CERTAIN IN THE HAZE, BUT I SEEM TO SEE A *GIRL* IN THE BOAT... SHE LOOKS VAGUELY FAMILIAR... BUT IT'S SO FAR AWAY!

WELL, I'D BETTER TAKE OFF *AFTER* THEM...!!

RRRR

NO! I CAN'T! I ALMOST *FORGOT!* I'M AT THE EDGE OF LA GUARDIA AIRPORT!

WHIRRRR

I DON'T *DARE* GET AIRBORNE.. I'D BE A MENACE TO THE PLANES TAKING OFF AND LANDING!

AND SO, THE IRON CLAD AVENGER RETURNS TO HIS FACTORY ON LONG ISLAND SOUND, AND, IN THE PRIVACY OF HIS LOCKED OFFICE, PREPARES TO BECOME WEALTHY, HANDSOME TONY STARK AGAIN...NEVER SUSPECTING HOW CLOSE HE HAD BEEN TO HIS FORMER ARCH-FOE, MADAME NATASHA, BETTER KNOWN AS THE BEAUTIFUL BUT DEADLY *BLACK WIDOW!*

PEPPER AND HAPPY MUST STILL BE AT THE MOVIES! NOBODY'S HERE EXCEPT THE SKELETON NIGHT SHIFT! NOTHING MORE *I* CAN DO NOW, EXCEPT WAIT FOR MORNING!

THUS, ONE OF THE WEALTHIEST MEN IN THE WORLD SLOWLY TRUDGES THROUGH THE SAND OUTSIDE HIS WORLD-FAMOUS WEAPONS FACTORY! NOT DARING TO CONFESS HIS LOVE TO THE GIRL HE CARES FOR...NOT KNOWING WHEN THE MECHANICAL CHEST DEVICE HE WEARS WILL FAIL, ENDING HIS LIFE IN AN INSTANT...

NOR DOES HE KNOW WHEN OR WHERE HIS NEXT DEADLY THREAT WILL COME FROM! THIS IS TONY STARK, RICH, HANDSOME, SUCCESSFUL TONY STARK...ONE OF THE MOST TRAGIC HEROES THE WORLD HAS EVER KNOWN!

The End

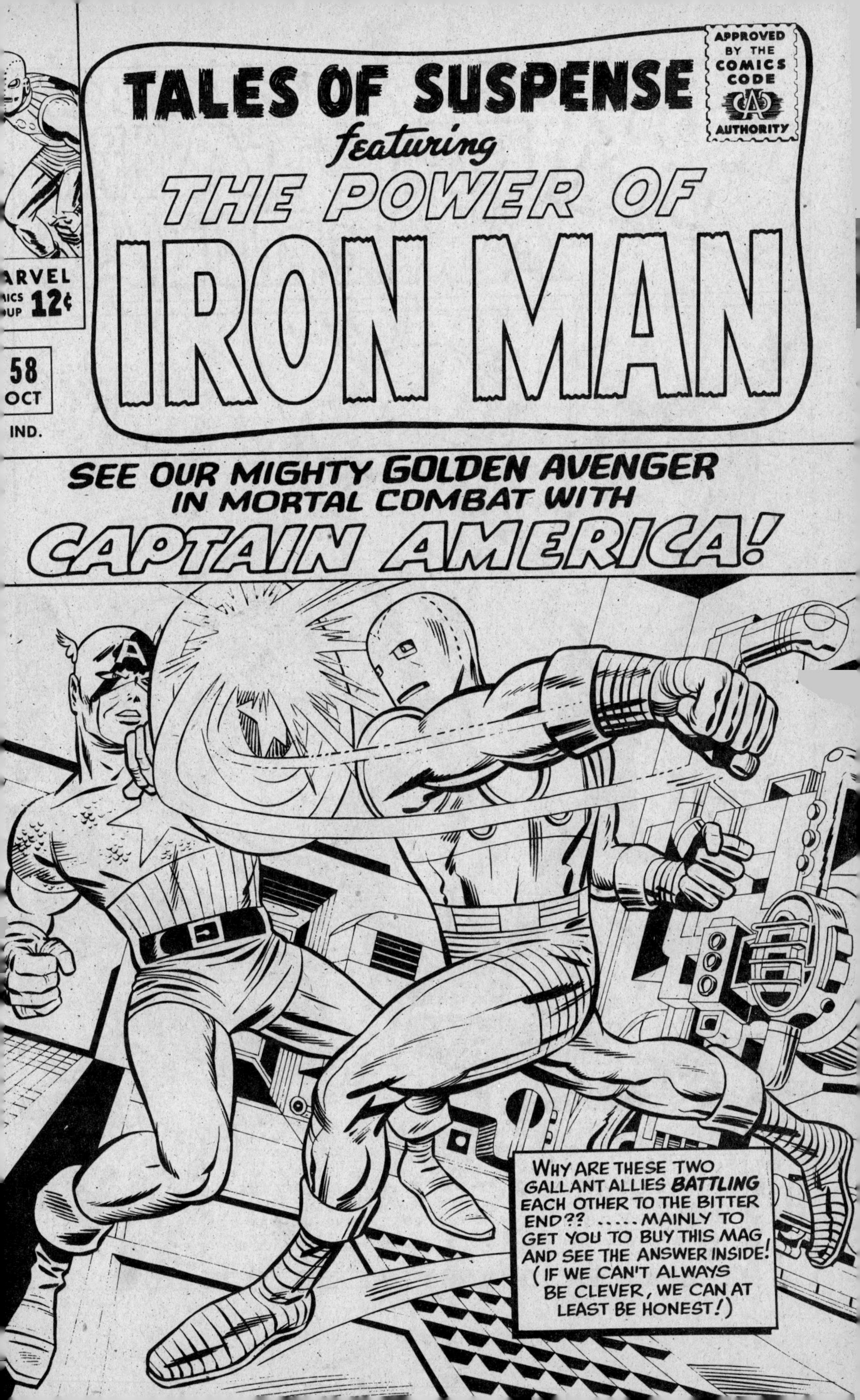
TALES OF SUSPENSE
featuring
THE POWER OF
IRON MAN
APPROVED BY THE COMICS CODE AUTHORITY
ARVEL
ICS
UP
12¢
58
OCT
IND.
SEE OUR MIGHTY GOLDEN AVENGER IN MORTAL COMBAT WITH
CAPTAIN AMERICA!
WHY ARE THESE TWO GALLANT ALLIES BATTLING EACH OTHER TO THE BITTER END?? ..... MAINLY TO GET YOU TO BUY THIS MAG AND SEE THE ANSWER INSIDE! (IF WE CAN'T ALWAYS BE CLEVER, WE CAN AT LEAST BE HONEST!)

IRON MAN "IN MORTAL COMBAT WITH CAPTAIN AMERICA!"

WHILE I'M DOWN HERE IN THE BAY TESTING MY BUILT-IN EMERGENCY UNDERWATER BREATHING APPARATUS, I MIGHT AS WELL DRIVE THIS KILLER SHARK OUT INTO THE OPEN SEA HE CAME FROM! KEEP MOVING, CUDDLES!!

ORIGINALLY PRESENTED IN TALES OF SUSPENSE # 58

EVERY WORD YOU ARE ABOUT TO READ WAS WRITTEN BY OL' FAITHFUL **STAN LEE**, ONE OF THE WORLD'S MOST PROLIFIC SCRIPT WRITERS!

EVERY DRAWING YOU ARE ABOUT TO MARVEL AT, WAS CREATED BY **DON HECK**, ONE OF AMERICA'S MOST PROMISING ILLUSTRATORS!

EVERY BIT OF INKING YOU ARE ABOUT TO SAVOR WAS DONE BY **DICK AYERS**, ONE OF THE INDUSTRY'S MOST PAINSTAKING ARTISTS!

EVERY SENTENCE YOU ARE ABOUT TO SCAN WAS HAND-PRINTED BY **SAM ROSEN**, ONE OF MARVEL'S MOST PERSPICUOUS LETTERERS!

MINUTES LATER...

THE TEST WAS A SUCCESS! I STAYED UNDER-WATER FOR ALMOST A FULL FIFTEEN MINUTES!

NOT TO MENTION THE TIME I SPENT WALTZING AROUND WITH THAT SHARK!

NOW I'D BETTER GET BACK TO THE FACTORY BEFORE EVERYONE REALIZES HOW WELL THEY CAN ALL GET ALONG WITHOUT ME!

BUT, AS THE POWERFUL GOLDEN AVENGER STREAKS TOWARDS THE WEAPONS FACTORY OF TONY STARK, HE DOESN'T SUSPECT THAT A SCENE ON THE FREIGHTER BELOW HIM WILL SOON HAVE A PROFOUND EFFECT ON HIS OWN LIFE!

FOR, ABOARD THE SILENT SHIP, AN ILLEGAL PAYOFF IS IN PROGRESS...

OKAY, THE DOUGH'S ALL HERE! LOWER THE LIFE-BOAT!!

AND THERE, IN THE GLOOM OF NIGHT, TWO MYSTERIOUS FIGURES PREPARE TO BE SMUGGLED ASHORE!

IT LOOKS LIKE WE'RE GONNA MAKE IT!!

OF COURSE WE'LL MAKE IT! WE PAID ENOUGH TO MAKE SURE THAT NOTHING GOES WRONG!

SO FAR, SO GOOD! NOW WE'LL HIDE THE BOAT! BY THE TIME IT'S FOUND, WE'LL BE SAFELY GONE!

WE'VE WAITED A LONG TIME FOR THIS MOMENT! A LONG TIME FOR OUR REVENGE!

WHEN THEY DEPORTED KRAVEN, THE HUNTER, I WARNED THEM I'D BE BACK!!

AND THE CHAMELEON, AS WELL!

NOW THAT WE'RE HERE, REMEMBER THAT *I'LL* GIVE THE ORDERS!! I'VE GOT MY PLANS ALL SET!

YOU?? THAT'S A LAUGH! AFTER THE MESS YOU MADE OF OUR FIGHT WITH SPIDER-MAN!!*

*SEE *SPIDER-MAN* #15...EDITOR.

BAH!! ONE OR TWO SMALL DEFEATS ARE MEANINGLESS! BUT ENOUGH TALK! LET'S SEE WHERE WE *ARE*!

CAREFUL, KRAVEN! THAT'S THE MUNITIONS FACTORY OF ANTHONY STARK ABOVE US! IT'S ONE OF THE MOST CAREFULLY GUARDED PLANTS IN THE WORLD!

FOLLOW ME, SPINELESS ONE! *KRAVEN* FEARS NO GUARDS THAT LIVE!

WELL, THERE'S *ONE* GUARD YOU'D BETTER *START* FEARING, MISTER!

IRON MAN!

NO MASKED INCOMPETENT IN A TIN SUIT CAN STOP *KRAVEN* THE HUNTER!! I HAVE THE STRENGTH AND SPEED OF THE JUNGLE CATS!!

GOOD FOR *YOU*, SON! YOU'RE GONNA *NEED* THEM!

OH, BY THE WAY... I DON'T LIKE BEING CALLED AN INCOMPETENT... NOT EVEN BY *YOU*!

LUCKY HE DID NOT SEE *ME* BEHIND KRAVEN IN THE SHADOWS!

AT *LAST* I'LL HAVE A CHANCE TO PROVE THAT I'M *SUPERIOR* TO KRAVEN! FOR, SOON *I*, THE CHAMELEON, SHALL DEFEAT IRON MAN!

MEANWHILE, INSIDE STARK'S FACTORY, HAPPY HOGAN COMES AS CLOSE TO A SMILE AS HE CAN...

HI, PEPPER! HOW DO YOU LIKE MY NEW SPORT JACKET?

STAND BACK!! DON'T COME ANY CLOSER!

HOLD IT RIGHT *THERE*! DON'T DARE *MOVE*!

HUH?

THAT'S IT!! STAY JUST AS YOU *ARE*!

I DON'T *GET* IT, PEP! WHAT'S IT ALL *ABOUT*?

I'LL EXPLAIN IN A MINUTE... AS SOON AS I GET MY SUNGLASSES!

THERE! THAT'S BETTER! NOW I CAN LOOK WITHOUT BEING *BLINDED*!

HEY! I'M BEGINNIN' TO THINK YOU'RE RIBBIN' ME... YOU'RE MAKIN' *FUN* OF MY JACKET!

NOBODY COULD MAKE FUN OF THAT JACKET! NO JOKE COULD DO IT JUSTICE!

COME TO THINK OF IT, THE SALESMAN AT THE CLOTHING STORE *DID* LOOK AT ME KINDA FUNNY WHEN I PICKED IT... *HEY!* WHAT GIVES?

QUICK! THERE'S NO TIME TO LOSE!! I'VE GOT TO FIND *IRON MAN!* WHERE *IS* HE??

LOOK! DON'T YOU RECOGNIZE HIM?? IT'S CAPTAIN AMERICA!

SECONDS LATER, JUST AS IRON MAN IS ABOUT TO RETURN TO HIS NORMAL IDENTITY AS TONY STARK, MILLIONAIRE MUNITIONS MANUFACTURER...

MY RED ALERT SIGNAL! I'M NEEDED! I'D BETTER RUSH TO PEPPER'S OFFICE!

SPEEDILY REACHING THE EXECUTIVE SUITE, IRON MAN FINDS...

CAP! YOU'VE BEEN HURT! QUICK...INSIDE! DON'T DISTURB US, PEPPER!

BUT WHAT SHALL I TELL MR. STARK?

DON'T WORRY ABOUT THAT! HE..WON'T BE BACK FOR A WHILE!

THEN, IN THE PRIVACY OF THE LOCKED OFFICE, CAPTAIN AMERICA TELLS AN INCREDIBLE TALE...

IT HAPPENED THIS MORNING...I WAS JUST WANDERING THROUGH TOWN WHEN I HEARD A CRY FOR HELP...!!

"RESPONDING QUICKLY AS I COULD, I FOUND..."

CAREFUL!! DON'T GO NEAR THOSE TWO MEN!! WAIT TILL I EXPLAIN...!!

WHY? WHAT'S WRONG? WHAT IS IT, OLD TIMER?

COME CLOSER.. MY VOICE.. TOO WEAK.. LISTEN...

"AND THEN, BEFORE I COULD MAKE A MOVE, HE SHOT A STRANGE CHEMICAL VAPOR AT ME, CAUSING ME TO LOSE CONSCIOUSNESS INSTANTLY!"

WHA...??

"WHEN I RECOVERED, I FOUND MYSELF A PRISONER OF THE CHAMELEON! IT WAS HE WHO HAD BEEN THE OLD MAN!"

"I WAS HELPLESSLY STRAPPED BENEATH A STRANGE ELECTRONIC THOUGHT-TRANSFERENCE MACHINE!"

"THE LAST THING I HEARD, BEFORE LAPSING INTO UNCONSCIOUSNESS AGAIN, WAS..."

NOW THAT *MY* BRAIN HOLDS ALL *YOUR* MEMORIES, I SHALL PERFORM THE MOST SUCCESSFUL IMPERSONATION OF ALL TIME!

I SHALL NOT ONLY *LOOK* LIKE CAPTAIN AMERICA... I SHALL *BE* CAPTAIN AMERICA! AND NOW... TAKE HIM AWAY!

CAPTAIN AMERICA! BIG DEAL! WHAT'S SO GREAT ABOUT *HIM*? HE'S *NUTHIN*!!

"BUT, BY THEN MY HEAD HAD CLEARED... THE VAPORS HAD WORN OFF... AND I QUICKLY MADE MY MOVE!"

NOTHIN', EH?!

URKK!

SLEEP TIGHT, BOYS!

"STILL WEAK, AS A RESULT OF THE STRANGE EXPERIMENT, I KNEW IT WOULD BE FOLLY TO REMAIN AND DO BATTLE! I DARED NOT TAKE THE CHANCE OF LOSING! MY FIRST TASK WAS TO WARN THE *AVENGERS* OF THE DANGER THAT THREATENED!"

BOSS... HE'S GETTIN' *AWAY!!* WHAT'LL WE DO ??!

NOTHING! WE'RE SIX STORIES UP! EVEN *CAPTAIN AMERICA* CANNOT *FLY* TO SAFETY!

HE'S *RIGHT!* BUT IT'S CERTAIN DEATH TO REMAIN *THERE!* I'VE GOT TO TAKE THE CHANCE!

THERE'S A DRAIN PIPE ON THE BUILDING ACROSS THE ALLEY! IF I CAN REACH IT... IT MIGHT GET ME SAFELY TO THE GROUND!

IF THE CHAMELEON SHOULD TAKE MY PLACE IN THE AVENGERS, UNSUSPECTED... *ANYTHING* CAN HAPPEN!!

UHHH! THE PIPE IS *ROTTED!* IT BROKE AWAY FROM THE WALL!!

"LUCKILY I WAS ABLE TO MANEUVER MY BODY SO THAT I FELL UPON A PILE OF SOFT RUBBLE WHICH ABSORBED MOST OF THE IMPACT! THEN, BEFORE THEY COULD CATCH UP WITH ME AGAIN, I HEADED FOR STARK'S FACTORY, HOPING YOU WERE STILL ON DUTY!"

DON'T KNOW WHERE TO REACH *THOR*... OR *GIANT-MAN*... BUT *IRON MAN* GUARDS TONY STARK'S FACTORY... I'VE GOT TO *GET* THERE!!

...AND THAT'S THE WHOLE STORY! I-I'M *STILL* GROGGY! BUT AT LEAST I MANAGED TO WARN YOU IN TIME...!!

WHAT DO YOU SUGGEST WE DO *NEXT*?

WE DON'T DO ANYTHING...*I* DO! PEPPER, CALL THE FACTORY DOCTOR! SEE THAT CAPTAIN AMERICA GETS THE BEST POSSIBLE CARE...MR. STARK WILL FOOT THE BILL!

AS FOR *ME*, I'VE GOT A LITTLE *JOB* TO TAKE CARE OF!!

BUT, AS IRON MAN STORMS OUT, A CRAFTY SMILE LIGHTS UP THE FACE OF "CAPTAIN AMERICA"...

HE *FELL* FOR IT! IT *WORKED!*

MEANWHILE, THE UNSUSPECTING IRON MAN STREAKS THROUGH THE SKY...

IF THE CHAMELEON INTENDS TO TAKE CAPTAIN AMERICA'S IDENTITY, THE MOST LOGICAL PLACE FOR HIM TO HEAD FOR IS AVENGERS' H.Q.!

REACHING THE MIDTOWN MANSION OF WEALTHY TONY STARK, WHICH SERVES AS AVENGERS' HEADQUARTERS, IRON MAN CRASHES IN, TO FIND...

SAY! WHAT'S THE HURRY, PARTNER?

I *THOUGHT* I'D FIND YOU HERE!

TAKE OFF THAT DISGUISE, CHAMELEON! I'M *WISE* TO YOU! YOUR LITTLE GAME'S A *BUST!*

WHO ARE YOU TALK-ING TO, FELLA?? THERE'S NO ONE HERE BUT *US!*

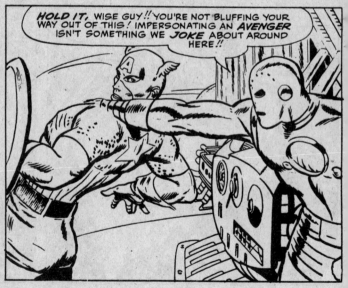

HOLD IT, WISE GUY!! YOU'RE NOT BLUFFING YOUR WAY OUT OF THIS! IMPERSONATING AN *AVENGER* ISN'T SOMETHING WE *JOKE* ABOUT AROUND HERE!!

NOW *LOOK*, FELLA...A JOKE'S A JOKE...BUT LET'S NOT CARRY IT TOO *FAR*!

UHHH!!

CLANG!

HE MUST HAVE FOUND A WAY TO ABSORB SOME OF CAP'S *PROWESS* AS WELL AS HIS MEMORY! THAT FELT LIKE THE KICK OF A *MULE*!

THIS IS NO *JOKE*, MISTER! I'M COMING *AFTER* YOU NOW... AND I'LL *GET* YOU... ONE WAY OR ANOTHER!

YOU DON'T EXPECT TO HIDE FROM *ME* ON A ROOFTOP, DO YOU??

NO! I'M JUST TRYING TO STAY OUT OF YOUR WAY TILL YOU COME TO YOUR SENSES!

I *WARNED* YOU THAT YOU CAN'T BLUFF YOUR WAY OUT OF THIS!!

AND SOME LIVE ELECTRIC BOLTS WILL MAKE THOSE WIRES TOO HOT TO HOLD YOU!

DON'T *DO* IT, IRON MAN! DON'T *FORCE* ME TO FIGHT YOU! WHATEVER IS BOTHERING YOU, LET'S TALK IT OVER!

I **TOLD** YOU YOUR MASQUERADE WON'T WORK! WE'VE **NOTHING** TO TALK ABOUT!

ALL RIGHT, THEN, IF IT'S A **FIGHT** YOU WANT...

...I SUPPOSE **I** CAN GIVE IT TO YOU AS WELL AS ANYONE ELSE!

STILL TRYING TO ACT **INNOCENT**, EH?? WHEN WILL YOU REALIZE IT WON'T **WORK**?

NOT TILL **YOU** REALIZE THAT YOU'RE BARKIN' UP THE WRONG TREE!! **STAY BACK** ... I'M **THROUGH** RUNNING!!

WHOOM!

WHAT MADE HIM BUCKLE SO QUICKLY?? HE'S RECEIVED STRONGER BLOWS THAN **THIS** IN THE PAST!!

BUT, IT IS NOT THE BLOW ALONE THAT HAS MADE IRON MAN SUDDENLY LOSE HIS EQUILIBRIUM ...

I'VE BEEN A CARELESS FOOL!! I CONDUCTED AN UNDERWATER TEST... BROUGHT KRAVEN TO THE COAST GUARD ... AND I'VE BEEN PURSUING THIS BOGUS CAPTAIN AMERICA ... ALL WITHOUT REMEMBERING TO **RECHARGE MY CHEST DEVICE!** IF I DON'T RECHARGE WITHIN MINUTES.. I'M A **GONER!!**

I'LL PLUNGE TO THE GROUND...APPLYING MY JETS AS BRAKES AT THE LAST SECOND!

HE'S GIVING UP THE FIGHT! THAT PROVES IT MUST HAVE BEEN SOME SORT OF GAG! PERHAPS THE OTHER AVENGERS WERE HIDDEN, TAKING PHOTOS OF OUR DONNYBROOK!

I'LL PROBABLY SEE THIS LATER ON CANDID CAMERA!

A FEW MINUTES LATER, AT THE FACTORY OF TONY STARK...

THE DOCTOR IS ON HIS WAY OVER, HAPPY! BETTER SEE IF CAPTAIN AMERICA IS ALL RIGHT!

OKAY, DOLL! YOU WANT ME TO HOLD HIS HAND OR TAKE HIS PULSE?

HEY! THAT'S GRATITUDE FOR YA! HE TOOK A POWDER!

BUT WHY?? HE WAS INJURED! WHERE COULD HE HAVE GONE?!

WE'VE GOT TO REACH IRON MAN! I'LL BROADCAST A RED ALERT ON HIS SPECIAL FREQUENCY!

BUT, AT THAT MOMENT, IRON MAN IS PROPPED AGAINST A WALL IN AN ALLEY...

RADIO SIGNAL... NO GOOD ...CAN'T ANSWER NOW...!

...AS HIS BUILT-IN GENERATOR, SET TO MAXIMUM POWER, RE-CHARGES HIS LIFE-SAVING CHEST DEVICE WITH SECONDS TO SPARE!

MEANTIME...

NOW WHERE ARE YOU GOIN', PEPPER? YOU DON'T EXPECT TO FIND CAPTAIN AMERICA BY YOURSELF, DO YOU??

OF COURSE NOT, HAPPY! BUT IT JUST OCCURRED TO ME THAT WE MIGHT FIND IRON MAN AT MR. STARK'S TOWN HOUSE! SO LET'S GO!

WHILE, NOT FAR AWAY, A NOW-REVITALIZED, FULLY CHARGED GOLDEN AVENGER ROCKETS INTO ACTION AGAIN!!

LOOK! IT'S IRON MAN!!

HECK! AND ME WITHOUT MY KODAK!

PERHAPS IF I'M LUCKY, THE FAKE CAPTAIN AMERICA WON'T HAVE GONE FAR!

AND, IN A BORROWED CAR OF TONY STARK'S...

LOOK!! ISN'T THIS IRON MAN'S SPECIAL *TRACER BEAM* ??

YEAH! I WONDER WHAT IT'S DOIN' IN THE BOSS'S CAR!?

LET'S FOLLOW THE DIRECTION OF THE ARROW! I HAVE A FEELING IT WILL LEAD US TO *IRON MAN!*

OKAY! MR. STARK PROBABLY KEEPS IT IN HIS CAR SO HE CAN FIND IRON MAN WHEN HE NEEDS 'IM!

AND SO, PEPPER AND HAPPY DRIVE ON, LITTLE DREAMING HOW CLOSE THEY HAVE JUST COME TO GUESSING THE SECRET IDENTITY OF THE WORLD FAMOUS GOLDEN AVENGER... WHILE A FEW BLOCKS AWAY...

I CAN'T GET IRON MAN OUT OF MY MIND! WHY *DID* HE ACT THE WAY HE DID ??! WHAT DOES IT ALL *MEAN?!*

AND, DIRECTLY OVERHEAD...

THERE HE *IS!* I'VE *FOUND* HIM!

BUT, THE BATTLE-TRAINED REFLEXES OF CAPTAIN AMERICA REACT WITH LIGHTNING RAPIDITY...

IT'S IRON MAN... DIRECTLY ABOVE ME! I'VE GOT TO *MOVE!!*

HE'S PREPARED TO *FIGHT* AGAIN... I CAN *SENSE* IT! PERHAPS I'LL BE ABLE TO LOSE HIM IN HERE FOR A WHILE!

BUT, WHEN OPERATING AT THE PEAK OF HIS POWERS, IRON MAN IS NOT SO EASILY DETERRED...

HE DUCKED INTO A CONSTRUCTION POWER STATION BELOW!

SOMEONE RUNNING IN THE DARK! A *SABOTEUR!!* STOP... OR, I'LL *SHOOT!* STOP, I SAID!

A *WATCHMAN!* HOLD YOUR FIRE, FRIEND!! I MEAN NO HARM!

THEN, AS THE STALWART SENTINEL OF LIBERTY STANDS REVEALED BY LANTERN LIGHT...

GLORY BE! IT'S CAPTAIN AMERICA... MY CHILDHOOD IDOL!!

I'M MIGHTY GLAD YOU RECOGNIZE ME!

WHAT'S *THAT* ??

JUST WHAT I'VE *FEARED!* IRON MAN HAS *FOUND* ME!

CHAMELEON.!! SURRENDER *NOW!* DON'T FORCE ME TO ATTACK YOU! I CAN'T BE RESPONSIBLE FOR WHAT MIGHT HAPPEN.!!

I DON'T UNDER- STAND! HE KEEPS USING THE NAME *CHAMELEON!* I WONDER...IS HE THE *REAL* IRON MAN ??

STAND ASIDE, OLD TIMER... THINGS MAY START GETTING *HECTIC* IN HERE SOON!

IRON MAN ...AND *CAPTAIN AMERICA*... ACTING LIKE *ENEMIES!!* IT DOESN'T SEEM *POSSIBLE!!*

AND THEN, BY AN IRONIC TWIST OF FATE, THE STAR-SPANGLED ADVENTURER BEGINS TO DOUBT THAT *IRON MAN* IS ALL THAT HE SEEMS TO BE!

WELL, CHAMELEON ?? WHAT'S YOUR *ANSWER* ?

MY ANSWER IS...

ALTHOUGH I CANNOT MATCH YOUR TRANSISTOR- POWERED *STRENGTH,* I CAN STILL FALL BACK ON MY OWN SPEED AND CUNNING...LIKE *THIS!!*

CLICK!

I DIDN'T REALIZE I WAS STANDING OVER THE LARGE TRAPDOOR THROUGH WHICH THE GRAVEL IS DROPPED!

CLANG!

THE CHAMELEON SEEMS TO THINK AS QUICKLY IN EMERGENCIES AS THE REAL CAPTAIN AMERICA DOES!

BUT THIS WON'T HELP HIM MUCH! MY ARMOR CAN PROTECT ME FROM ANYTHING I'LL ENCOUNTER IN HERE!

CLANG!
CLANG!

AND A FEW BLOCKS AWAY...

I TELL YOU I SAW THEM... IRON MAN AND CAPTAIN AMERICA... SLUGGING IT OUT IN THE CONSTRUCTION POWER BUILDING!

I'M NOT DOUBTING YOU, CHARLIE! BUT AREN'T THEY ON THE SAME TEAM?

WHILE, BACK AT THE GRAVEL PIT, WE FIND.....

ALL I CAN SAY IS, THIS IS ONE NUTTY WAY FOR A MILLIONAIRE PLAYBOY TO BE SPENDING AN IDLE AFTERNOON!

NG!
CLA
CLANG!

AND, DIRECTLY ABOVE...

HE MUST HAVE HAD ENOUGH BY NOW! I CERTAINLY DON'T WANT TO HURT HIM!

WELL, THIS FOOLISHNESS HAS GONE ON LONG ENOUGH! I'LL GIVE MY TRANSISTORS A FULL OUTPUT ADJUSTMENT, AND THEN ...

...I'LL PAY A FINAL VISIT TO THE BOGUS CAPTAIN AMERICA!! AND *THIS* TIME I WON'T HANDLE HIM WITH KID GLOVES!

WHILE, OUTSIDE THE BUILDING..

HAPPY! STOP THE CAR! WE'VE *FOUND* HIM!!

ACCORDING TO THE DIAL GAUGE, IRON MAN IS IN THE CONSTRUCTION POWER BUILDING!

WELL, WHAT ARE WE WAITIN' FOR?? MAYBE *HE* KNOWS WHERE MR. STARK'S BEEN ALL THESE DAYS!

I'M FREE OF THE *GRAVEL* ... BUT I'VE STUMBLED INTO A ROOM WITH GIANT AUTOMATIC *CEMENT MIXERS!* I'D BETTER NOT HANG AROUND *HERE* TOO LONG!

AND, AS LUCK WOULD HAVE IT, HAPPY AND PEPPER ENTER AT THAT MOMENT, BUT ARE UNSEEN BECAUSE OF THE THICK SWIRL OF THE FINE CEMENT DUST!

CAREFUL OF YOUR EYES, PEPPER! KEEP 'EM HALF CLOSED!

OHHH! YOU WON'T HAVE TO TELL ME *TWICE*, HAPPY!

WHILE, NOT MORE THAN A FEW YARDS AWAY...

THE CHAMELEON IS HERE *SOMEWHERE!* AND I WON'T REST TILL I'VE *FOUND* HIM!

SLOWLY, HIS EYES TEARING AND MOIST, HAPPY WALKS BLINDLY FORWARD THROUGH THE VAST ROOM...TOWARDS THE EDGE OF THE *GRAVEL PIT!*

FOOTSTEPS!! OFF TO MY RIGHT! CAN IT BE...??

AND JUST THEN...

HELP! I'M FALLING!

SUDDENLY, A STRONG GLOVED HAND REACHES OUT, AND STEEL-SINEWED FINGERS GRAB THE FALLING MAN'S WRIST...

GOT YOU!!

MUCH OBLIGED, CAP!...BUT I THOUGHT YOU WERE *INJURED!*

INJURED? I DON'T KNOW WHAT YOU MEAN!

I DON'T *GET* IT! WHY WOULD THE EVIL CHAMELEON BOTHER TO SAVE A TOTAL STRANGER'S LIFE?!!

WAIT! I HAVEN'T *FINISHED* WITH YOU YET!

THERE ARE STILL SOME MISSING PIECES IN THIS JIG-SAW PUZZLE OF THE *REAL* CAPTAIN AMERICA!

BUT SUDDENLY, A FEARFUL CRY RINGS OUT...

HELP!! GET ME OUT OF HERE! I STUMBLED INTO A SAND PIT! HELP!!

IT'S PEPPER! I'D KNOW HER VOICE ANYWHERE!

LET'S GO!!

DON'T WORRY, PEPPER, HONEY! WE'LL SAVE YOU!

HAPPY!! LOOK OUT... YOU'RE LEANING ON THE WATER VALVE!

WHAT DID YA SAY??

NEVER MIND!

EASY, PEPPER! YOU'RE SAFE NOW! EVERYTHING WILL BE ALL RIGHT!

IRON MAN! THANK HEAVENS YOU WERE HERE!

HERE, PEP! LET ME LEND YOU MY JACKET! YOUR CLOTHES ARE SOAKING WET!

IF THEY ARE, IT'S YOUR FAULT, YOU CLUMSY, UNOBSERVANT, EMPTY-HEADED NINCOM-POOP, YOU!!

LOOK OUT!! A STEAM SHOVEL IS ABOUT TO GRAB US!

WOTTA DAY! THIS IS WORSE THAN "THE PERILS OF PAULINE!"

DON'T PANIC, LITTLE FRIENDS! EVEN A *STEAM SHOVEL* CAN BE STOPPED BY A TRANSISTOR-POWERED FIST OF THE HARDEST IRON ALLOY KNOWN TO MAN!!

BUT STEAM SHOVELS DON'T OPERATE *THEMSELVES!* I'VE GOT TO LEARN... *WHA..??*

YOU'RE *RIGHT,* IRON MAN! STEAM SHOVELS *DON'T* OPERATE THEMSELVES! BUT THIS GUY I FOUND *DRIVING* IT, CAN BE A MIGHTY POWERFUL THREAT!!

GIANT-MAN!!

TAKE A *LOOK* AT THIS BOZO, AND SEE IF YOU NOTICE ANYTHING *FAMILIAR* ABOUT HIM!

HE'S DRESSED LIKE CAPTAIN AMERICA ...BUT WHY WOULD *HE* ATTACK ME?

LET ME *DOWN,* BLAST YOU!

SURE, LITTLE MAN... I'LL LET YOU DOWN! NO NEED TO HOLD YOU WITH *IRON MAN* NEARBY!

HE MUST BE THE CHAMELEON!! THAT MEANS I'VE BEEN FIGHTING THE *WRONG* MAN!! I'VE BEEN FIGHTING THE *REAL* CAPTAIN AMERICA!!

THAT'S WHAT WE CAME TO *TELL* YOU!

SO *THAT'S* WHY YOU'VE BEEN FIGHTING ME! YOU THOUGHT I WAS THE CHAMELEON!! COME TO THINK OF IT, THAT'S NOT VERY FLATTERING TO ME!

YOU'VE GOT *NOTHIN'* ON ME!!

HOW DID YOU HAPPEN TO *GET* HERE WHEN YOU DID?

THE *ANTS* IN THE AREA WERE WATCHING YOU FIGHT, WHILE *GIANT-MAN* HAPPENED TO BE SCANNING THE CITY WITH HIS CYBERNETIC IMPULSER, AND HE CAUGHT THEIR TONE!

"AND, AS WE APPROACHED, WE SAW SOMEONE IN A FAMILIAR UNIFORM CROUCHED ABOVE YOU..."

AREN'T YOU A LITTLE TOO *OLD* TO BE WEARING A MASQUERADE COSTUME, FELLA?!

GIANT-MAN!!

TOO BAD *THOR* IS OUT OF TOWN! WHAT WITH MOST OF THE AVENGERS HERE, THIS IS LIKE AN OLD CLASS REUNION!!

AND THEN...

SEE? I *TOLD* YOU THERE WERE COSTUMED CHARACTERS ALL *OVER* THE PLACE!

THE *POLICE!* THERE'S A WELCOME SIGHT!!

DON'T WORRY ABOUT ANY DAMAGE TO YOUR FACTORY, OLD TIMER! MR. STARK WILL PAY FOR ALL THE DAMAGES!

I WON'T GET A LONG JAIL TERM! I'LL BE OUT SOON... AND THEN I'LL TEAM UP AGAIN WITH KRAVEN... AND *NOTHING* WILL STOP US!

WHAT HAPPENED TO YOUR *HAIR,* DEAR?? IT LOOKS LIKE YOU'VE BEEN THROUGH A *WRINGER!*

MY *HAIR?!!*

WHY DIDN'T SOMEBODY TELL ME *SOONER?!*

PEPPER...!

GO *AWAY!* DON'T *STARE* AT ME NOW, YOU BRUTE!

WELL, PARTNER, I'M GLAD IT ALL CAME OUT IN THE WASH! NO HARD FEELINGS??

OF *COURSE* NOT, CAP!!

THEN, MUCH LATER THAT NIGHT...

I WAS TOO EASILY FOOLED BY THE CHAMELEON'S STORY! IT WAS UNPARDONABLY CARELESS OF ME!

SOMETIMES I GROW OVERCONFIDENT IN MY SUPER-POWERED ARMOR! I MUST ALWAYS REMEMBER PRESIDENT JOHNSON'S FAVORITE MOTTO, "LET US REASON TOGETHER"! FOR A MAN'S *BRAIN* IS STILL HIS MOST POTENT WEAPON!

The End

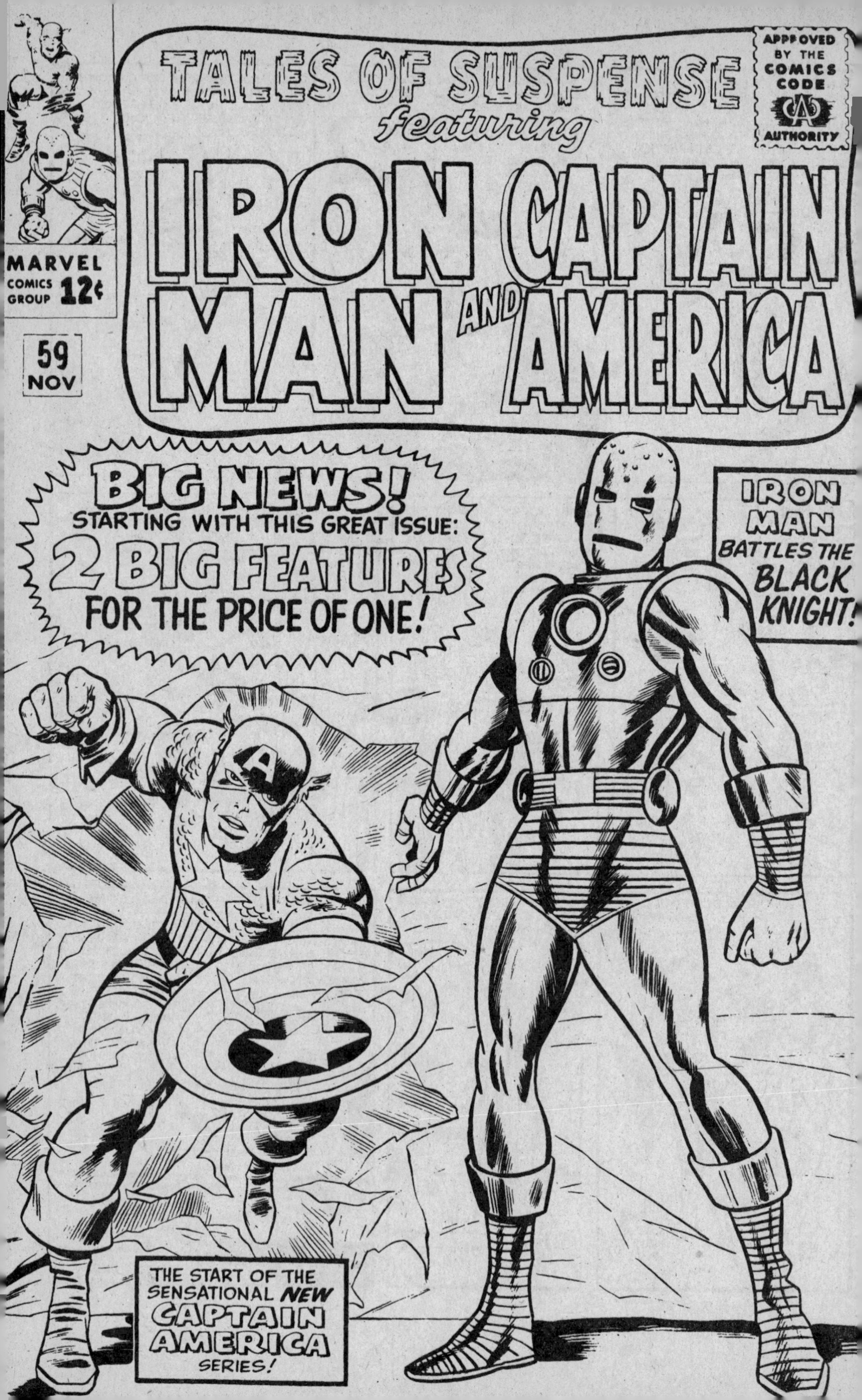

TALES OF SUSPENSE
featuring
IRON MAN AND CAPTAIN AMERICA
APPROVED BY THE COMICS CODE AUTHORITY
MARVEL COMICS GROUP 12¢
59 NOV
BIG NEWS! STARTING WITH THIS GREAT ISSUE: 2 BIG FEATURES FOR THE PRICE OF ONE!
IRON MAN BATTLES THE BLACK KNIGHT!
THE START OF THE SENSATIONAL NEW CAPTAIN AMERICA SERIES!

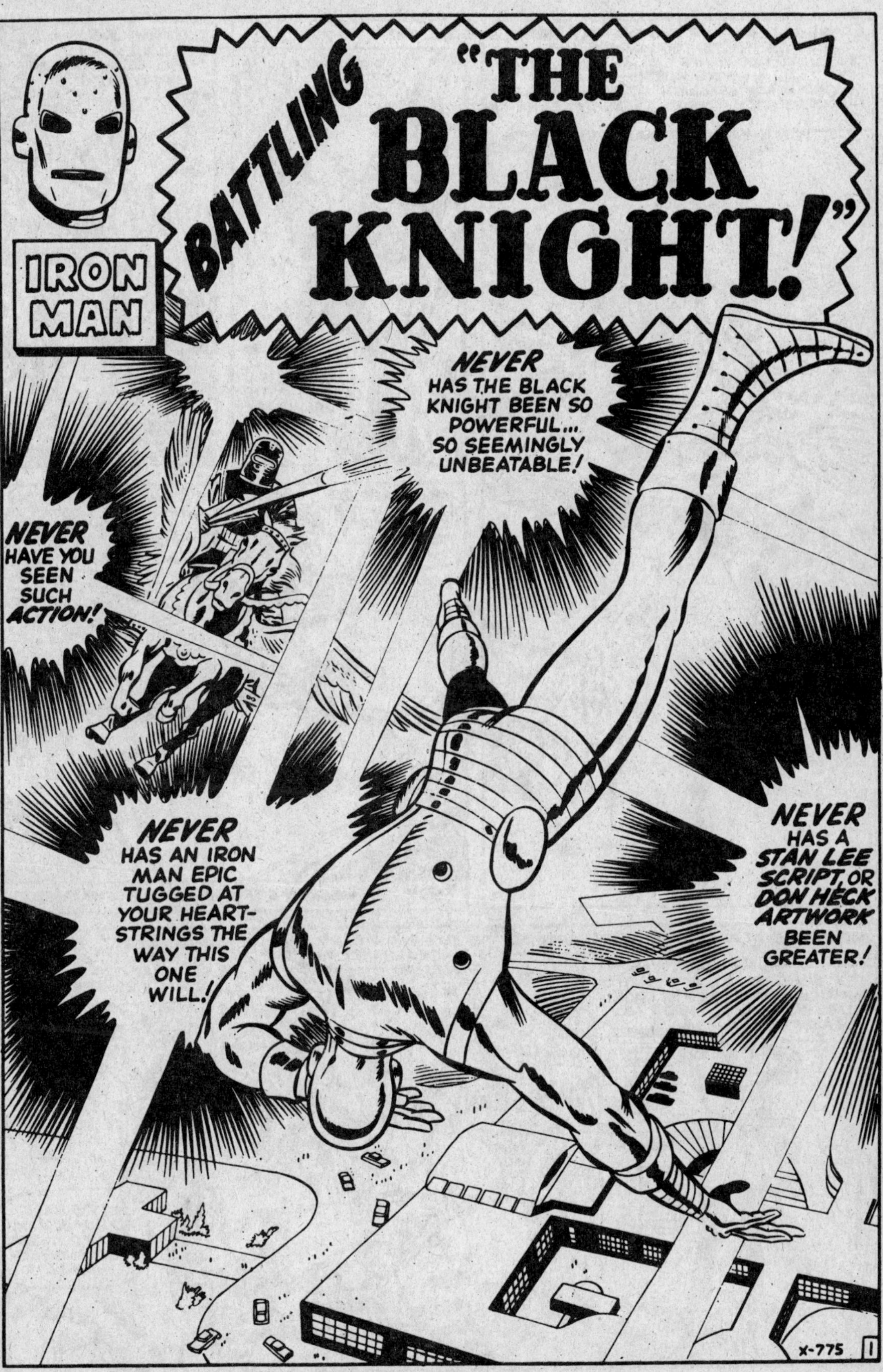
IRON MAN
BATTLING "THE BLACK KNIGHT!"
NEVER HAS THE BLACK KNIGHT BEEN SO POWERFUL... SO SEEMINGLY UNBEATABLE!
NEVER HAVE YOU SEEN SUCH ACTION!
NEVER HAS AN IRON MAN EPIC TUGGED AT YOUR HEART-STRINGS THE WAY THIS ONE WILL!
NEVER HAS A STAN LEE SCRIPT OR DON HECK ARTWORK BEEN GREATER!
X-775
1

ANYONE LOOKING UP INTO THE SKY ABOVE THE STATE PENITENTIARY MIGHT HAVE REASON TO DOUBT HIS SENSES--FOR, HE WOULD SEE A FLYING HORSE--A MIGHTY WINGED BLACK STALLION HOVERING ABOVE THE GRIM GREY PRISON, SEEKING ONE CERTAIN CELL....

AND THEN, HE *FINDS* IT!

I *KNEW* YOU WOULDN'T FAIL ME!

THE DISSOLVO-RAY IS RIGHT WHERE I LEFT IT, IN THE SADDLE BAG!

I ALWAYS *SAID* NO JAIL COULD HOLD *THE BLACK KNIGHT!*

UP, MY PROUD STALLION! THEY CAN *NEVER* RECAPTURE ME NOW!

I'VE SPENT THESE MONTHS PLANNING EVERY DETAIL OF MY *REVENGE* UPON THE UNSUSPECTING *AVENGERS!*

#SEE AVENGERS #6 "THE MASTERS OF EVIL!"--EDITOR.

MEANTIME, AT AVENGERS' HEADQUARTERS, WE FIND...

STOP BEING SO IMPATIENT, BOYS! I'LL BE WITH YOU IN A JIFFY!

SURE, WASP-- THAT'S WHAT YOU TOLD US A *HALF-HOUR* AGO!

THE TROUBLE WITH GIRLS IS-- THEY ALL ACT LIKE FEMALES!

SAY! HAVEN'T YOU *LEFT* YET?? YOU'LL BE LATE FOR THAT OUT-OF-TOWN CHARITY BENEFIT SHOW!

WE'RE READY TO GO! BUT THE *WASP* DECIDED TO CHANGE HER MAKEUP!

2

OKAY, I'M READY NOW! GOSH, LOOK AT THE *TIME!* C'MON, BOYS-- LET'S NOT BE LATE!

SEE YOU LATER, IRON MAN!

JUST LIKE A *WOMAN!* YOU MAKE IT SOUND AS THOUGH *YOU'VE* BEEN WAITING FOR *US!*

NOW, NOW, BLUE EYES! NO ARGUMENTS WHILE WE'RE SHRINKING DOWN TO ANT SIZE!

ALRIGHT, THOR! WE'RE READY WHEN *YOU* ARE!

THEN HOLD ON *TIGHT*--!

THIS MAY NOT BE AS COMFORTABLE AS A JET, BUT IT'S THE ONLY WAY TO *GET* THERE IN TIME!

MEANWHILE, AFTER THE OTHERS HAVE GONE, IRON MAN TAKES OFF HIS ARMOR...

I'D LIKE TO HAVE JOINED THEM...

BUT WE'VE DECIDED *ONE* AVENGER MUST ALWAYS REMAIN NEAR AT HAND, IN CASE OF EMERGENCIES!

MY FACTORY'S *ALARM* SIREN! SOMETHING MUST HAVE HAPPENED!

RRRRRR

HOLD IT! NO ONE GOES IN OR OUT UNLESS-- *OH!* IT'S YOU, MR. STARK! SORRY!

WHAT'S *WRONG,* BOYS?

YOU'D BETTER GO IN, CHIEF-- RIGHT AWAY!

AND SO... IT'S ALRIGHT, PEPPER! I'M HERE! FILL ME IN FAST!

BUT YOU'VE GOT TO LOCATE MR. STARK! WE *NEED* HIM--

BOSS! IT'S THE *BLACK KNIGHT!* HE'S ATTACKIN' THE FACTORY!

HE MUST HAVE BROKEN OUT OF JAIL! WE'VE GOT TO--*UHHH....*

BOSS! WHAT'S *WRONG??*

3

HE'S HAVING SOME SORT OF *ATTACK!* I-I'VE GOT TO GET A *DOCTOR!*

NO! YOU--*MUSTN'T!*

BUT, YOU'RE *SICK!* YOU NEED HELP!

I'LL BE ALRIGHT! IT'S NOTHING--BELIEVE ME!

I CAN'T TELL THEM THAT MY PROTECTIVE CHEST DEVICE ISN'T FUNCTIONING PROPERLY! THEY MIGHT GUESS I'M REALLY *IRON MAN!*

BUT, IF I DON'T RECHARGE SOON--IT'LL BE *CURTAINS!*

LOOK--JUST LEAVE ME ALONE FOR A WHILE! I-I JUST NEED SOME REST!

NOT A *CHANCE,* BOSS! WE'RE NOT DESERTIN' YOU!

HAPPY! LOOK HOW *PALE* HE'S GETTING! I'M *SCARED!*

I'VE JUST *GOT* TO CALL A DOCTOR! HE *NEEDS* ONE!

I DON'T *GET* IT, BOSS! YOU WALKED IN HERE LOOKIN' LIKE A MILLION BUCKS, AND THEN--

I--CAN'T EXPLAIN! BUT YOU--YOU'VE GOT TO--STOP PEPPER--!

DON'T LISTEN TO HIM, PEP! HE MUST BE *DELIRIOUS!*

DOCTOR--COME OVER *IMMEDIATELY!* NO, WE DON'T KNOW *WHAT'S* WRONG WITH HIM--BUT IT LOOKS *SERIOUS!*

IF HE COMES--AND FINDS MY CHEST DEVICE--MY SECRET WILL BE EXPOSED!

NO, PEPPER--*DON'T*--!

4

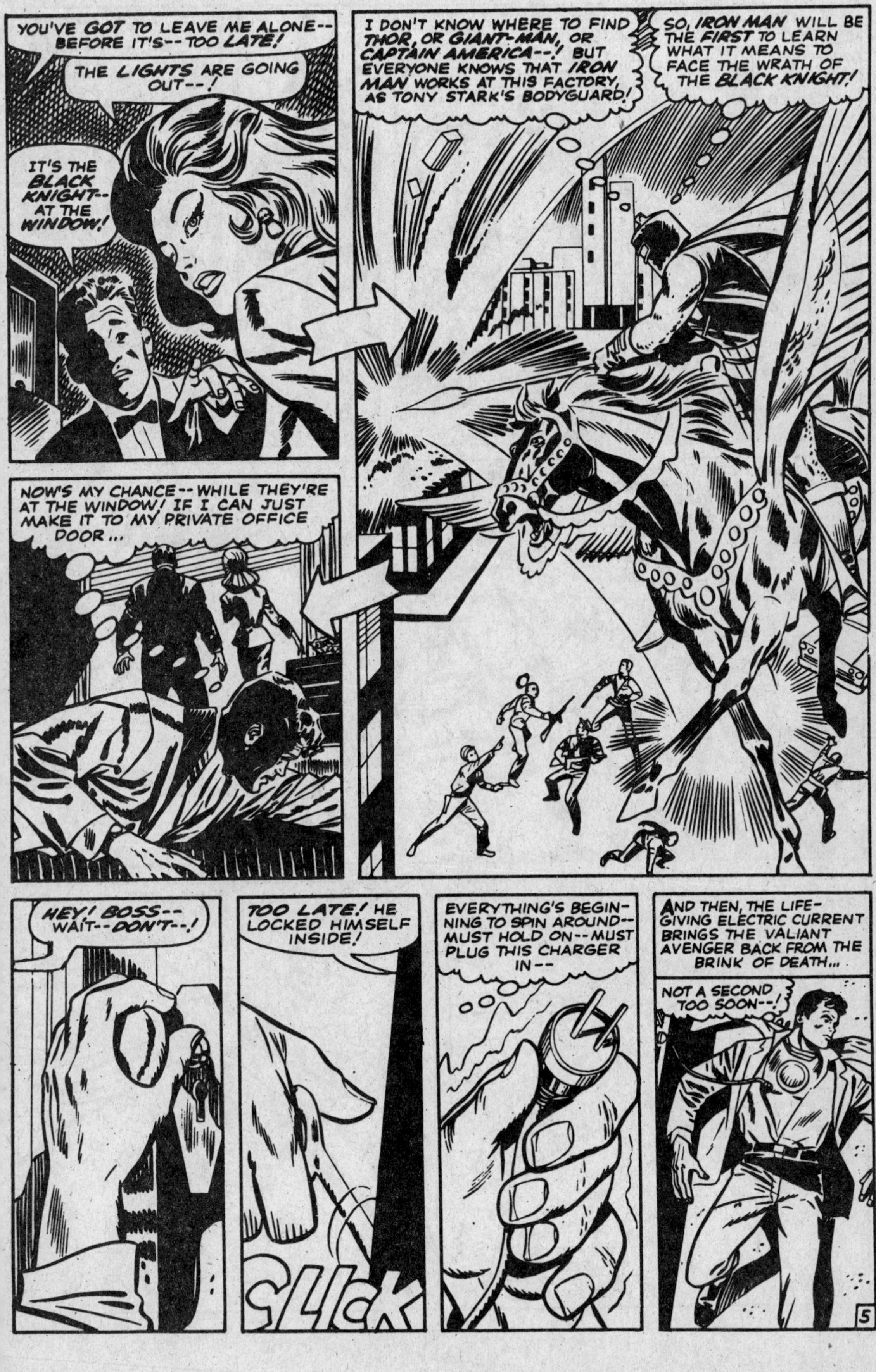
YOU'VE GOT TO LEAVE ME ALONE-- BEFORE IT'S-- TOO LATE!
THE LIGHTS ARE GOING OUT--!
IT'S THE BLACK KNIGHT-- AT THE WINDOW!
I DON'T KNOW WHERE TO FIND THOR, OR GIANT-MAN, OR CAPTAIN AMERICA--! BUT EVERYONE KNOWS THAT IRON MAN WORKS AT THIS FACTORY, AS TONY STARK'S BODYGUARD!
SO, IRON MAN WILL BE THE FIRST TO LEARN WHAT IT MEANS TO FACE THE WRATH OF THE BLACK KNIGHT!
NOW'S MY CHANCE -- WHILE THEY'RE AT THE WINDOW! IF I CAN JUST MAKE IT TO MY PRIVATE OFFICE DOOR...
HEY! BOSS-- WAIT--DON'T--!
TOO LATE! HE LOCKED HIMSELF INSIDE!
CLICK
EVERYTHING'S BEGINNING TO SPIN AROUND-- MUST HOLD ON-- MUST PLUG THIS CHARGER IN--
AND THEN, THE LIFE-GIVING ELECTRIC CURRENT BRINGS THE VALIANT AVENGER BACK FROM THE BRINK OF DEATH...
NOT A SECOND TOO SOON--!
5

BOSS! YOU'VE *GOTTA* OPEN UP! WE WANNA *HELP* YOU--!

OH, HAPPY! WHAT'S WRONG? WHAT COULD HAVE HAPPENED TO HIM?

WHILE, ON THE OTHER SIDE OF THE LOCKED DOOR, A DRAMATIC CHANGE IS BEING MADE...

I'VE GONE TOO LONG BETWEEN RE-CHARGES! I STILL FEEL WEAK!

I'LL HAVE TO IN-CREASE THE POWER OUTPUT OF MY SUIT FROM NOW ON!

FOR THAT, I'LL NEED THE EXTRA TRANSISTOR POWER OF MY BELT PODS!

NOW, BY SWINGING MY INDUCERS, I'LL SPEED THE CHARGING PROCESS...

...BECAUSE I CAN'T AFFORD TO *WAIT!* THE *BLACK KNIGHT* MUSTN'T ESCAPE ME!

IRON MAN! AT *LAST!*

YOU DON'T THINK A FEW PUNY ROCKETS CAN GET BY MY REPULSER BEAM, DO YOU??

OH, THEY'RE ONLY INTENDED AS A STARTER--TO WHET YOUR APPETITE!

BUT *HERE'S* A LITTLE PLAYTHING THAT MIGHT AMUSE YOU! I CALL IT A *WRAPPER!*

6

PERHAPS YOU CAN *GUESS* HOW IT GOT ITS NAME!

FLEXIBLE STEEL COILS--GETTING EVER TIGHTER AROUND ME!

I HATE TO WASTE SO MUCH TRANSISTOR POWER AT ONCE, BUT I'VE NO CHOICE!

I DON'T DARE WAIT TILL THEY GET *TIGHTER!*

I SEE YOUR STRENGTH IS AS PRODIGIOUS AS EVER!

BUT, IT WON'T HELP YOU AGAINST *THIS....!*

WHAT MY *STRENGTH* CAN'T DO, MY *SPEED* CAN!

WHOOM!

BUT, THOUGH MISSING IRON MAN, THE DESTRUCTIVE BLAST SHEARS OFF THE TOP OF A TALL STORAGE TOWER...

THE TOWER IS *COLLAPSING* ABOVE US!

WE HAVEN'T A *CHANCE!*

DON'T JUST STAND THERE! RUN! *RUN!*

BUT THEN, THE NEED FOR FRANTIC RUNNING *ENDS*, AS...

IRON MAN *SAVED* US!

NATCH! AS TONY STARK ALWAYS SAYS--GOOD WORKMEN ARE HARD TO FIND!

7

THEN, A FURIOUS, FIGHTING-MAD GOLDEN AVENGER RETURNS TO THE BATTLE AGAIN, LIKE SOME GREAT, IRON SKINNED LEVIATHAN!

I'M OPERATING AT PEAK FIGHTING STRENGTH AGAIN! THE BLACK KNIGHT'LL NEVER KNOW WHAT HIT HIM!

WHILE, BACK AT THE OFFICE OF ANTHONY STARK...

IF THE BOSS WON'T OPEN THE DOOR, THIS IS THE ONLY WAY!

CRASH!

HEY, LOOK AT THAT! THIS TEMPERED STEEL HATCHET CAN'T EVEN PUT A DENT IN THE DOOR!

IT SOUNDS NUTTY, BUT THE BOSS HAS BATTLE-SHIP STEEL PLATES IN THIS OFFICE DOOR OF HIS!

PRIVATE

I WONDER WHY?

IN FACT, THE WHOLE BLAMED WALL IS SOLID STEEL!

WHAT WILL WE DO??

AND, IN THE AIR ABOVE THE FACTORY...

BLAST YOU! ARE YOU INVULNERABLE TO EVERYTHING???

WELL, ONE THING'S SURE -- THESE LITTLE RED-HOT SPINNING DISCS OF YOURS CAN'T HARM IRON ARMOR LIKE MINE! I DON'T WEAR THIS SUIT FOR SHOW!

8

AND BELOW, OBLIVIOUS TO THE RAGING BATTLE...

HAPPY! DON'T LOOK DOWN!

WHO'S LOOKIN' ANYWHERE?? MY EYES ARE CLOSED!

I CAN'T STAND TO THINK OF THE BOSS, MAYBE UNCONSCIOUS IN HIS OFFICE, WITH NO ONE THERE TO HELP...!

AHHH! WHAT HAVE WE THERE?!

JUST WHAT I NEED-- A HOSTAGE!

SO I'LL JUST INSERT MY LITTLE AUTO-MATIC LASSO INTO MY LANCE'S ACCES-SORY CHAMBER...

THEN, PRESTO! I'VE CAUGHT MY HUMAN FISH!

WHA--??

DON'T STRUGGLE, HAPPY --YOU MIGHT WEAKEN THE KNOT WHICH IS HOLDING YOU!

I'LL FREE YOU SOME-HOW!

A LAUDABLE AMBITION, IRON MAN --BUT ONE YOU WILL NEVER ACHIEVE!

AND NOW, WHILE YOU WONDER WHAT TO DO NEXT, HOW ABOUT SAMPLING SOME OF MY SPECIAL LITTLE "DOUGHNUTS"!

YOU MIGHT FIND THEM RATHER AMUSING!

EACH ONE CONTAINS A SMALL ELECTRONIC POWER DRAINER-- AS YOU SHALL SEE!

9

THEY'RE HITTING ME! CLINGING TO MY ARMOR!

I CAN'T HURL THEM AT THE BLACK KNIGHT--I MIGHT HIT POOR HAPPY!

I CAN FEEL THE DISCS STARTING TO DRAIN AWAY MY TRANSISTOR POWER NOW!

THERE'S JUST ONE DESPERATE GAMBLE LEFT FOR ME TO TAKE...

IF I DIVE DOWN FAST ENOUGH, IT MAY AFFECT THEIR MECHANISMS TO MAKE THEM USELESS AGAINST ME! HERE GOES!

I'VE BEATEN HIM! HE'S PLUNGING TO THE GROUND!

NOW, I NO LONGER NEED YOU! SO YOU MAY JOIN YOUR IRON CLAD FRIEND...

AND SO, FAREWELL, FOOL!

WELL, MY LITTLE STUNT WAS DOUBLY EFFECTIVE! NOT ONLY DID I SHAKE THE BLACK KNIGHT'S DISCS OFF ME...

...BUT I ALSO TRICKED HIM INTO RELEASING YOU SO THAT I COULD CATCH YOU!

WHEW! YOU CAN PLAY ON MY BALL TEAM ANY TIME, PAL!

10

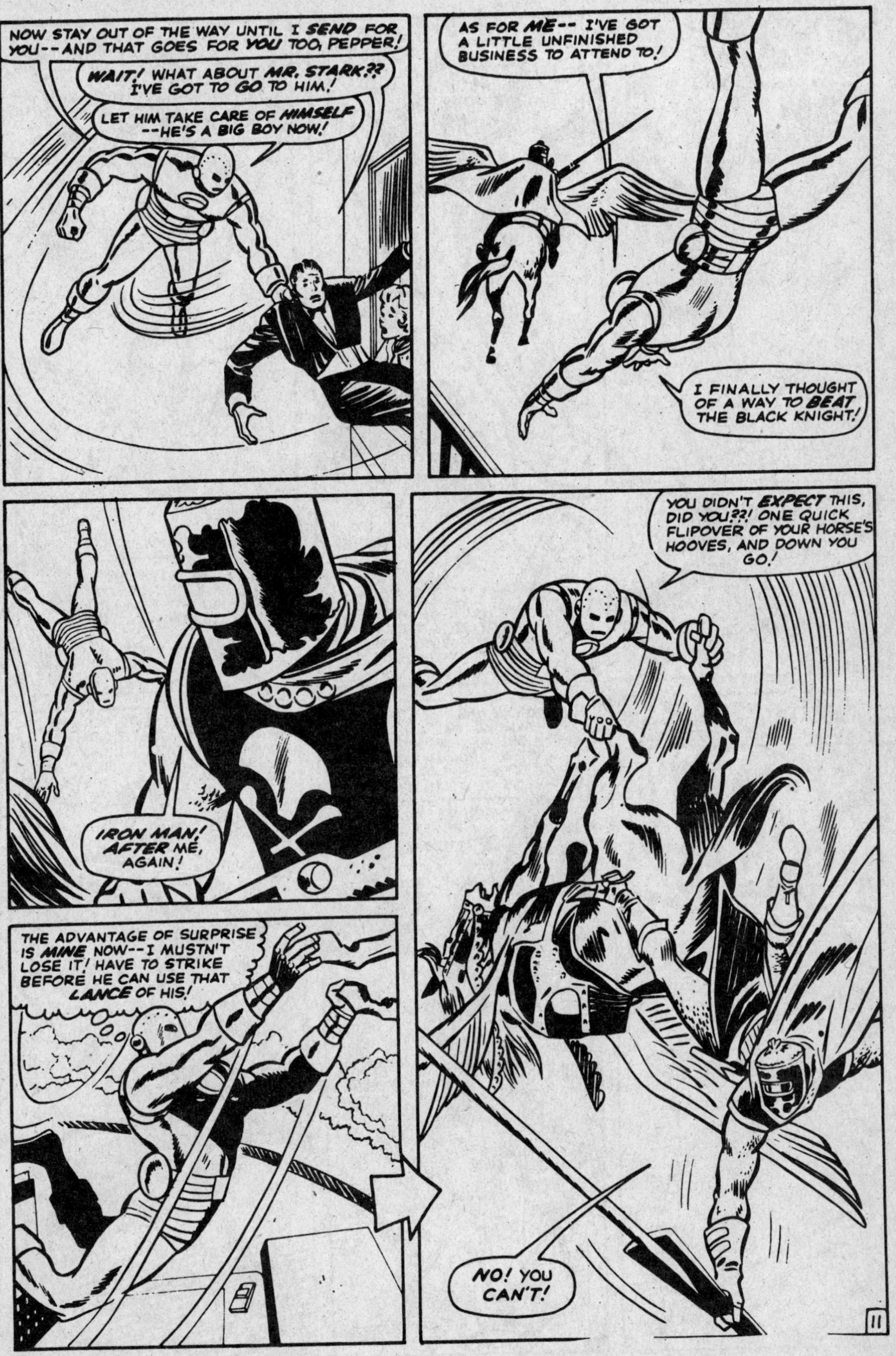

NOW STAY OUT OF THE WAY UNTIL I SEND FOR YOU--AND THAT GOES FOR YOU TOO, PEPPER!
WAIT! WHAT ABOUT MR. STARK?? I'VE GOT TO GO TO HIM!
LET HIM TAKE CARE OF HIMSELF --HE'S A BIG BOY NOW!
AS FOR ME-- I'VE GOT A LITTLE UNFINISHED BUSINESS TO ATTEND TO!
I FINALLY THOUGHT OF A WAY TO BEAT THE BLACK KNIGHT!
IRON MAN! AFTER ME, AGAIN!
YOU DIDN'T EXPECT THIS, DID YOU??! ONE QUICK FLIPOVER OF YOUR HORSE'S HOOVES, AND DOWN YOU GO!
THE ADVANTAGE OF SURPRISE IS MINE NOW--I MUSTN'T LOSE IT! HAVE TO STRIKE BEFORE HE CAN USE THAT LANCE OF HIS!
NO! YOU CAN'T!

WANT SOME COMPANY ON THE WAY DOWN?

YOU CAN'T LET ME FALL TO MY DEATH, IRON MAN! YOU CAN'T!

I WOULDN'T *BET* ON THAT, FELLA!!

WAIT! MY STALLION! HE'LL SAVE ME-- I *KNOW* IT!

NOT *NOW* HE WON'T! NOT TILL THAT COCKLE BURR I PUT UNDER HIS SADDLE FALLS OUT!

BUT, IF YOU DROP YOUR *WEAPON,* THERE MIGHT BE SOMETHING I CAN DO FOR YOU!

NO! IT'S THE SOURCE OF MOST OF MY POWER! I CAN'T *LOSE* IT!

OKAY THEN-- HAPPY LANDINGS!

BUT, AT THE LAST FEW SECONDS, THE BLACK KNIGHT'S BRAVADO VANISHES, AND SUDDENLY...

HERE! HERE IS MY LANCE! NOW SAVE ME-- *SAVE* ME!

NO SOONER HAS THE LANCE LEFT ITS OWNER'S HAND, THAN IRON MAN, AIDED BY HIS POWERFUL TRANSISTORS, PLUMMETS DOWN AND *CATCHES* HIS FALLING ARCH-FOE JUST IN TIME...!

HE'S ALL YOURS, BOYS!

THANKS, IRON MAN! ITS LIKE CHRISTMAS IN JULY!

YEAH! HE'LL MAKE A GREAT LITTLE STOCKING STUFFER!

AND NOW I'VE GOT TO RACE BACK AND BECOME TONY STARK AGAIN, TO ALLAY ANY SUSPICIONS WHICH PEPPER OR HAPPY MIGHT HAVE FORMED!

12

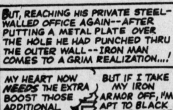

BUT, REACHING HIS PRIVATE STEEL-WALLED OFFICE AGAIN--AFTER PUTTING A METAL PLATE OVER THE HOLE HE HAD PUNCHED THRU THE OUTER WALL--IRON MAN COMES TO A GRIM REALIZATION...!

MY HEART NOW *NEEDS* THE EXTRA BOOST THOSE ADDITIONAL TRANSISTORS GAVE IT!

BUT IF I TAKE MY IRON ARMOR OFF, I'M APT TO BLACK OUT, OR WORSE, WHEN THE POWER STOPS!

BUT, I *CAN'T* KEEP MY ARMOR ON *ALL* THE TIME! AND YET-- I'M AFRAID, I *DARE NOT* TAKE IT OFF!

THE NEXT ATTACK MAY WEAKEN MY HEART SO MUCH THAT THE BLACKOUT WILL BE *PERMANENT!* I CAN'T TAKE THE CHANCE!

DOES THIS MEAN I'M DESTINED TO SPEND THE REST OF MY *LIFE* IN THIS ARMOR?? IT'S IMPOSSIBLE --INSANE--!

AND YET-- KNOCKING --AT MY DOOR!

MR. STARK! WE THOUGHT WE *HEARD* SOMEONE IN THERE! ARE YOU ALRIGHT??

KNOCK KNOCK!

I'VE GOT TO THINK OF AN EXCUSE TO GIVE THEM FOR STARK'S ABSENCE--!

MR. STARK ISN'T HERE! HE LEFT BY ANOTHER SECRET ENTRANCE!

HE'LL BE OUT OF TOWN FOR A WHILE--AND HE LEFT *ME* IN CHARGE!

YOU??!

BUT, MR. STARK WAS *ILL!* HE *COULDN'T* HAVE JUST LEFT TOWN...

IT WAS JUST A DIZZY SPELL! HE GOT OVER IT, AND THEN HE WENT OUT!

HAPPY, I DON'T *BELIEVE* IRON MAN! HE'S NOT TELLING THE TRUTH!

YOU'RE *RIGHT* --BUT HOW DO WE *PROVE* IT??

THEY'RE *SUSPICIOUS!* THEY *KNOW* I'M KEEPING SOMETHING FROM THEM! BUT I CAN NEVER *TELL* THEM! WHAT WILL HAPPEN NEXT--WHEN TONY STARK DOES NOT RETURN?

THE END

WE'LL ALL SEE *TOGETHER,* FRANTIC ONE--IN NEXT ISH'S COLLECTORS' ITEM CLASSIC!

13

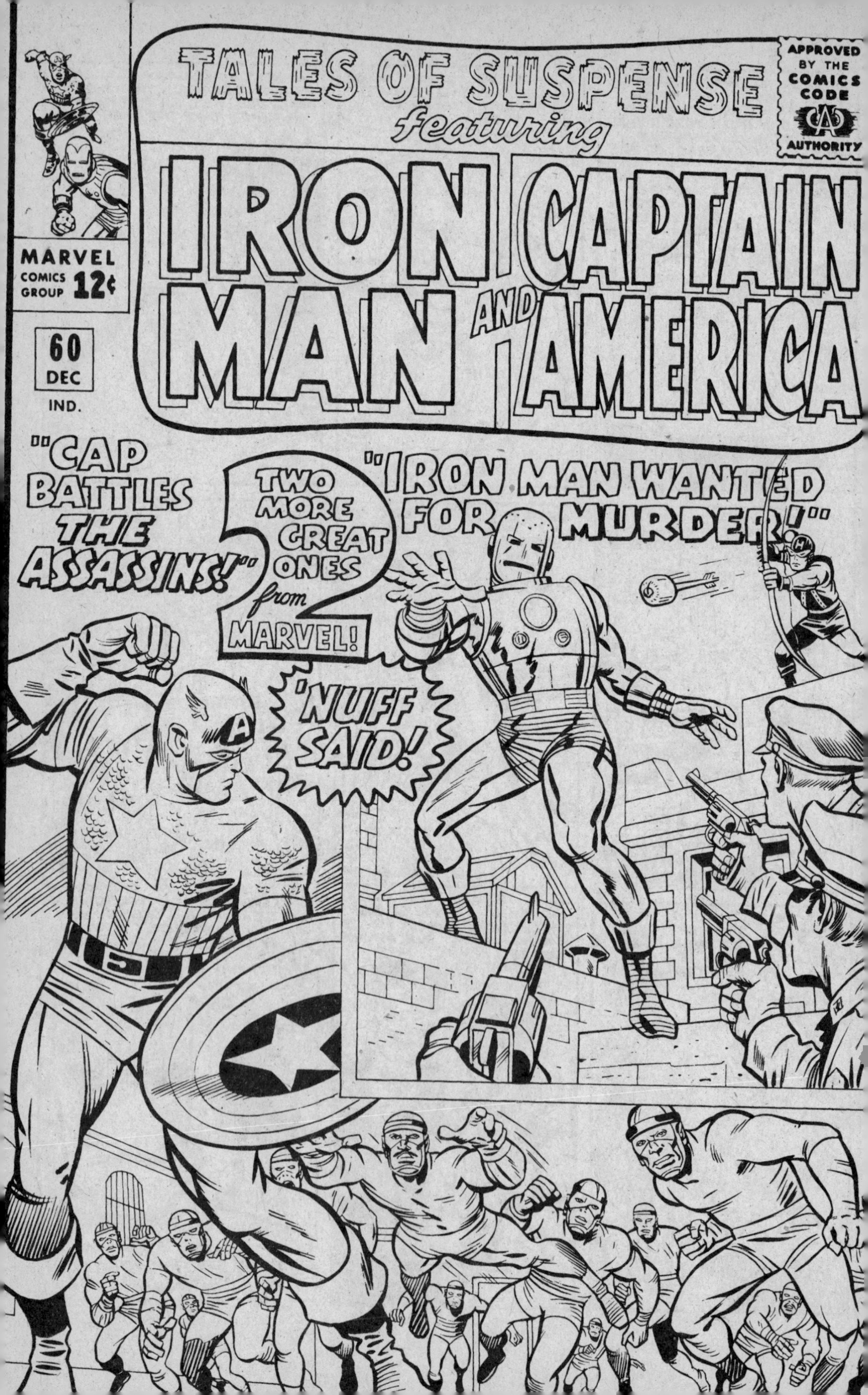
TALES OF SUSPENSE featuring
IRON MAN AND CAPTAIN AMERICA
APPROVED BY THE COMICS CODE AUTHORITY
MARVEL COMICS GROUP 12¢
60 DEC IND.
"CAP BATTLES THE ASSASSINS!"
TWO MORE GREAT ONES from MARVEL!
"IRON MAN WANTED FOR MURDER!"
'NUFF SAID!

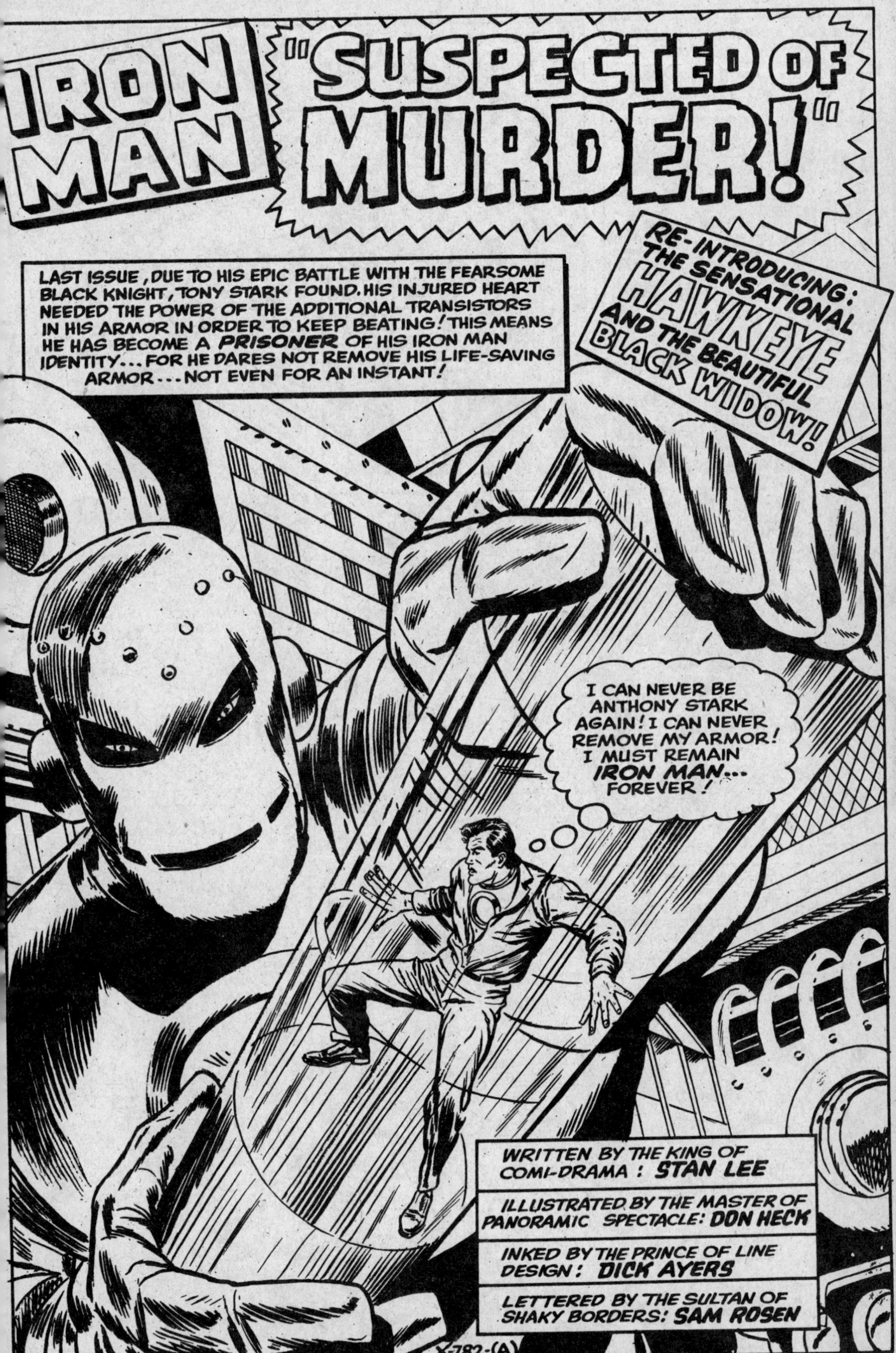
IRON MAN
"SUSPECTED OF MURDER!"
RE-INTRODUCING: THE SENSATIONAL HAWKEYE AND THE BEAUTIFUL BLACK WIDOW!
LAST ISSUE, DUE TO HIS EPIC BATTLE WITH THE FEARSOME BLACK KNIGHT, TONY STARK FOUND HIS INJURED HEART NEEDED THE POWER OF THE ADDITIONAL TRANSISTORS IN HIS ARMOR IN ORDER TO KEEP BEATING! THIS MEANS HE HAS BECOME A PRISONER OF HIS IRON MAN IDENTITY... FOR HE DARES NOT REMOVE HIS LIFE-SAVING ARMOR... NOT EVEN FOR AN INSTANT!
I CAN NEVER BE ANTHONY STARK AGAIN! I CAN NEVER REMOVE MY ARMOR! I MUST REMAIN IRON MAN... FOREVER!
WRITTEN BY THE KING OF COMI-DRAMA: STAN LEE
ILLUSTRATED BY THE MASTER OF PANORAMIC SPECTACLE: DON HECK
INKED BY THE PRINCE OF LINE DESIGN: DICK AYERS
LETTERED BY THE SULTAN OF SHAKY BORDERS: SAM ROSEN
X-782-(A)

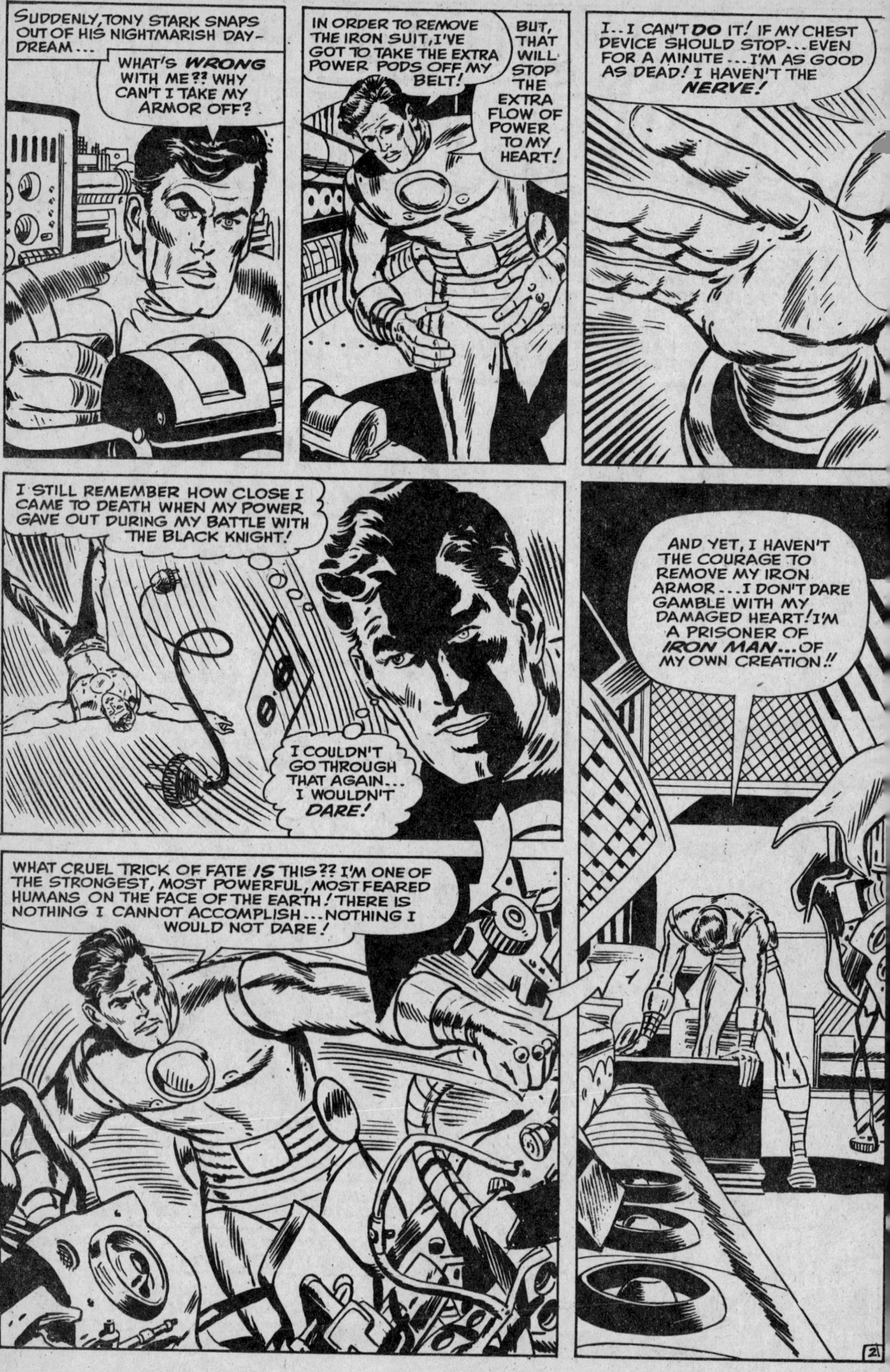
SUDDENLY, TONY STARK SNAPS OUT OF HIS NIGHTMARISH DAY-DREAM...
WHAT'S WRONG WITH ME?? WHY CAN'T I TAKE MY ARMOR OFF?
IN ORDER TO REMOVE THE IRON SUIT, I'VE GOT TO TAKE THE EXTRA POWER PODS OFF MY BELT!
BUT, THAT WILL STOP THE EXTRA FLOW OF POWER TO MY HEART!
I.. I CAN'T DO IT! IF MY CHEST DEVICE SHOULD STOP... EVEN FOR A MINUTE... I'M AS GOOD AS DEAD! I HAVEN'T THE NERVE!
I STILL REMEMBER HOW CLOSE I CAME TO DEATH WHEN MY POWER GAVE OUT DURING MY BATTLE WITH THE BLACK KNIGHT!
I COULDN'T GO THROUGH THAT AGAIN... I WOULDN'T DARE!
AND YET, I HAVEN'T THE COURAGE TO REMOVE MY IRON ARMOR... I DON'T DARE GAMBLE WITH MY DAMAGED HEART! I'M A PRISONER OF IRON MAN... OF MY OWN CREATION!!
WHAT CRUEL TRICK OF FATE IS THIS?? I'M ONE OF THE STRONGEST, MOST POWERFUL, MOST FEARED HUMANS ON THE FACE OF THE EARTH! THERE IS NOTHING I CANNOT ACCOMPLISH... NOTHING I WOULD NOT DARE!
2

MEANTIME, DESPERATELY WORRIED ABOUT THE SAFETY OF THEIR BELOVED BOSS, PEPPER AND HAPPY, USING ONE OF STARK'S OWN HIGH-POWERED CARS, SCOUR THE CITY IN A VAIN SEARCH FOR HIM...

DON'T WORRY, PEPPER! WE'LL FIND 'IM SOONER OR LATER!

I WAS A FOOL TO EVER THINK *I* COULD HAVE A CHANCE WITH PEPPER! LOOK HOW SHE'S CRYIN' OVER STARK!

WHAT A ROTTEN BREAK! THE GAL I'M HEAD OVER HEELS ABOUT ONLY HAS EYES FOR A GUY I'D GIVE MY RIGHT ARM FOR!

WE'D BETTER GET BACK TO THE FACTORY, KID! MAYBE *IRON MAN'S* HEARD SOMETHIN' ABOUT THE BOSS BY NOW!

MR. STARK HAS *NEVER* BEEN GONE THIS LONG, WITHOUT LEAVING SOME WORD! HAPPY, I'M SO..AFRAID!

BUT, UPON REACHING THE SPRAWLING MUNITIONS PLANT, THEY LEARN...

STILL NO WORD FROM HIM, EH?

NO, BUT I'M SURE HE'S ALL RIGHT!

HOW CAN YOU *SAY* THAT?? YOU'RE SUPPOSED TO BE HIS *BODYGUARD!* YOU KNOW HOW MANY *ENEMIES* HE HAS... HOW MANY *SPIES* WOULD GIVE *ANYTHING* TO CAPTURE HIM AND STEAL HIS INVENTIONS!

BUT, I WAS THE LAST TO SEE HIM! HE *TOLD* ME HE'D BE GONE FOR A WHILE!

BUT *WHERE?* WHERE DID HE SAY HE WAS *GOING??*

WHAT CAN I *TELL* HER? IF I SAY HE WENT FOR A VACATION, THEY KNOW ALL HIS HAUNTS... THEY'LL CALL EVERY PLACE FROM THE RIVIERA TO LAS VEGAS!

3.

"STARK IS TOO WELL-KNOWN, TOO FAMOUS! THEY COULD CHECK OUT ANY LIE I TELL IN MINUTES, AND KNOW THAT I'M COVERING UP! THE VACATION ANGLE IS *OUT*... I'VE GOT TO SAY SOMETHING THEY CAN'T DISPROVE!"

AND SO...

HE SAID IT WAS A SECRET BUSINESS MATTER! HE WOULDN'T TELL ME *WHERE* HE WAS GOING!

I..I SIMPLY CAN'T *BELIEVE* THAT!

HAPPY... WHAT IF IRON MAN *HIMSELF* HAS HARMED MR. STARK?? HOW WOULD WE EVER *KNOW?*

IF *ANYONE* COULD DO IT, *YOU* COULD!!

NO! YOU'RE *WRONG!*

I *SWEAR* TO YOU, I'VE DONE NOTHING TO HARM HIM! I'M AS ANXIOUS FOR HIM TO RETURN AS *YOU* ARE!

YEAH? WELL, YOU'RE NOT DOIN' MUCH TO *FIND* HIM! IF YOU EVER COME *OUT* OF THAT IRON SARDINE CAN, MISTER ...I'LL FIND A WAY TO *MAKE* YOU TALK!!

BE *CAREFUL*, HAPPY! DON'T GET HIM ANGRY! YOU KNOW HOW *DANGEROUS* HE CAN BE!!

SURE! SURE! BUT I JUST WANNA *WARN* YOU, FELLA! IF ANYTHING *HAPPENS* TO MR. STARK I'LL FIND OUT HOW, AND WHY, IF IT TAKES THE REST OF MY LIFE! DO YOU *READ* ME, TIN MAN?

IF ONLY I COULD TELL HIM THAT *I'M* STARK! IF I COULD TELL HOW TOUCHED I AM BY HIS LOYALTY!

HE'S *GONE!* OH, HAPPY... DO YOU REALLY *THINK*...?

I DON'T KNOW *WHAT* TO THINK, PEP! BUT THAT GUY'S *ALWAYS* BUGGED ME!

WHY DOES HE KEEP HIS IDENTITY A *SECRET?* WHAT'S HE *REALLY* AFTER??

...AND, WHY WOULD SOMEONE AS POWERFUL AS IRON MAN WORK FOR STARK?? THE WHOLE SETUP ALWAYS SMELLED FISHY TO ME! I NEVER DID TRUST 'IM!

AND IN STARK'S PRIVATE OFFICE...

I'VE GOT AN IDEA! I'LL WRITE A NOTE...AND SIGN STARK'S NAME! PERHAPS THAT WILL MAKE THEM STOP WORRYING!

WHAT A FANTASTIC SITUATION! I AM TONY STARK...YET, I MUST ACT AS THOUGH WE'RE TWO DIFFERENT PEOPLE!

MY FUNDS ARE LOW! I'LL TAKE SOME CASH FROM MY SAFE!

BUT, AT THAT VERY MOMENT...

PEPPER! HAPPY! WITH THE POLICE!

I WAS A FOOL NOT TO LOCK THE DOOR!

LOOK! I WAS RIGHT! THERE'S ALL THE EVIDENCE YOU NEED! HE'S ROBBIN' STARK'S SAFE!

KEEP BACK! THERE'S NO TELLING WHAT HE'LL DO WHEN HE'S CORNERED!

HE WON'T DO ANYTHING, LADY! NOT WITH US HERE!

LOOKS LIKE YOU'VE GOT SOME EXPLAINING TO DO, IRON MAN!

I'VE GOT TO THINK FAST!

YOU CAN SEE THE SAFE WASN'T FORCED! MR. STARK HAD GIVEN ME THE COMBINATION! I HAVE HIS PERMISSION TO OPEN IT WHENEVER I WISH!

AND, IT'S A GOOD THING I DID!

I FOUND THIS NOTE INSIDE! HERE, READ IT FOR YOURSELVES!

IT SAYS THAT HE'S OFF ON A SECRET GOVERNMENT MISSION AND I'M IN CHARGE TILL HE RETURNS!

LET'S HAVE A LOOK AT IT, MISTER!

5.

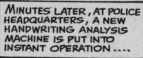

RUN THIS DOWN TO HEADQUARTERS ON THE DOUBLE, SMITH! WE'LL WAIT HERE!

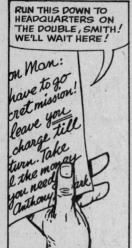

*on Man:
have to go
ret mission!
leave you
charge till
turn. Take
l the money
you need
Anthony Stark*

MINUTES LATER, AT POLICE HEADQUARTERS, A NEW HANDWRITING ANALYSIS MACHINE IS PUT INTO INSTANT OPERATION....

THEN, FINALLY...

IT'S ODD, INSPECTOR! THERE ARE NO FINGER-PRINTS ON THE NOTE.. AND THE HAND-WRITING IS STARK'S, BUT IT SEEMS ODDLY SHAKY!

I SEE...!

IF STARK REALLY WROTE THAT NOTE, WHY AREN'T HIS FINGERPRINTS ON IT?

I'M GETTING TIRED OF ALL THESE QUESTIONS! EITHER FORMALLY CHARGE ME FOR A CRIME, OR...

ANOTHER MISTAKE! I FORGOT TO REMOVE MY IRON GLOVES! THEY'RE WHAT MADE MY WRITING SEEM SHAKY, TOO!

...I'LL PUT A STOP TO THEM....MY OWN WAY!

HE'S ESCAPING!

CRASH!

HOLD IT, MEN! SMALL ARMS FIRE CAN'T AFFECT HIS ARMOR! BESIDES, WE'VE STILL GOT NO DEFINITE PROOF THAT HE'S DONE ANYTHING WRONG!

AND WE CAN'T ARREST A MAN FOR A CRIME UNTIL WE'RE SURE A CRIME HAS BEEN COMMITTED!

WHAT DO I DO NOW? I'LL REMAIN UNDER SUSPICION UNTIL STARK APPEARS! AND HE CAN'T APPEAR AS LONG AS I DARE NOT REMOVE MY ARMOR!

WHAT DOES A MIGHTY AVENGER DO WHEN FACED WITH A HOPELESS PROBLEM? THE SAME AS ANYONE ELSE...HE SEEKS SOLITUDE....A QUIET PLACE TO THINK HIS TROUBLE THOUGHTS...! AND THEN...

I JUST REMEM-BERED...A MEETING OF THE AVENGERS IS SCHEDULED FOR TONIGHT!I'LL HAVE TO CONTACT THEM!

THEN, USING HIS BUILT-IN MINIATURIZED TWO-WAY RADIO, IRON MAN CONTACTS THE AVENGER-ON-DUTY IN THE HEART OF THE CITY...

PERMISSION REQUESTED TO BE ABSENT FROM TONIGHT'S MEETING!

PER-MISSION GRANTED!

WE HAVE HEARD OF THE DISAPPEARANCE OF ANTHONY STARK! THERE IS BUT ONE QUESTION I HAVE TO ASK... HAVE *YOU* BETRAYED HIM ??

ON MY HONOR AS AN *AVENGER*, I HAVE NOT BETRAYED TONY STARK!

SO BE IT! WE EXPECT YOU TO LIFT THE CLOUD OF SUSPICION AS SOON AS POSSIBLE! OVER AND OUT!

MEANWHILE, IN A LUXURIOUS SUBURB, JUST OUTSIDE THE CITY, TWO *OTHERS* EVINCE A GREAT INTEREST IN THE AFFAIRS OF IRON MAN !

WE WILL BRING ADDITIONAL BULLETINS ABOUT ANTHONY STARK'S DISAPPEARANCE AS THEY OCCUR! NOW WE RETURN TO...

DID YOU *HEAR* THAT, HAWKEYE? THE ACCURSED *IRON MAN* IS UNDER SUSPICION IN STARK'S DISAPPEARANCE!

I HEARD, NATASHA!

WITH IRON MAN GONE, THIS IS YOUR CHANCE TO RAID STARK'S FACTORY AGAIN, AND STEAL THE PLANS FOR HIS NEWEST WEAPONS!

I HAVE AGREED TO BE YOUR ALLY, MY LOVELY BLACK WIDOW... BUT MY HEART REBELS AT THE THOUGHT OF *TREASON*!

IT WILL *NOT* BE TREASON, MY BOLD HERO! I ONLY SERVE THE CAUSE OF INTERNATIONAL *PEACE*!

HE BELIEVES ANY LIE I TELL HIM!

STRONG AS HE IS, HE IS *PUTTY* IN THE HANDS OF THE BLACK WIDOW!

VERY WELL, MY DARLING... I'LL *DO* IT!

7.

LATER...

NO protective fence can keep HAWKEYE out!

ORIGINALLY I planned to use my talents to SERVE mankind!! If only I hadn't met the BLACK WIDOW!

AND YET...WITHOUT HER, LIFE would be MEANINGLESS to ME!

BUT NOW I MUST CONCENTRATE ON THE JOB AT HAND!

SO FAR, SO GOOD! WAIT! I HEARD A FOOTSTEP BEHIND ME!

AN INTRUDER! THIS IS A CLASS "A" SECURITY SECTION! MY ORDERS ARE TO FIRE FIRST, AND ASK QUESTIONS AFTERWARDS!

I'LL GIVE HIM THE ONE NECESSARY WARNING SHOT, AND THEN, IF HE DOESN'T STOP...

I'VE BEEN SEEN!

HOLD YOUR FIRE! HE'S ENTERING MR. STARK'S PRIVATE OFFICE! HE'LL BE TRAPPED IN THERE!

BUT PEPPER POTTS IS INSIDE !!

STARK'S SECRETARY?? GOOD! SHE'LL SERVE AS A HOSTAGE FOR ME!

8

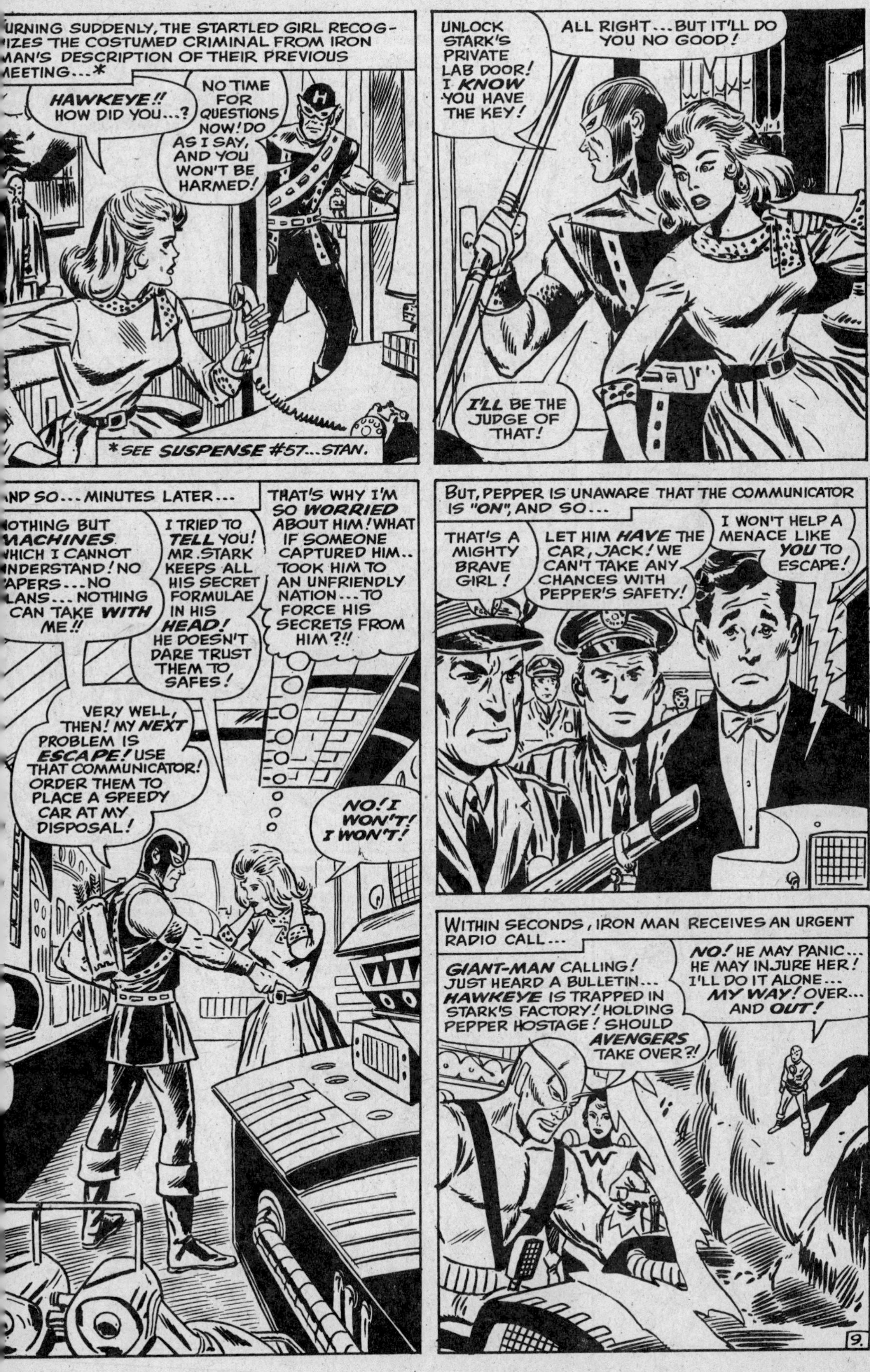
URNING SUDDENLY, THE STARTLED GIRL RECOG-
IZES THE COSTUMED CRIMINAL FROM IRON
MAN'S DESCRIPTION OF THEIR PREVIOUS
MEETING...*
HAWKEYE!! HOW DID YOU...?
NO TIME FOR QUESTIONS NOW! DO AS I SAY, AND YOU WON'T BE HARMED!
*SEE SUSPENSE #57...STAN.
UNLOCK STARK'S PRIVATE LAB DOOR! I KNOW YOU HAVE THE KEY!
ALL RIGHT...BUT IT'LL DO YOU NO GOOD!
I'LL BE THE JUDGE OF THAT!
ND SO...MINUTES LATER...
OTHING BUT MACHINES WHICH I CANNOT NDERSTAND! NO APERS...NO LANS...NOTHING CAN TAKE WITH ME!!
I TRIED TO TELL YOU! MR. STARK KEEPS ALL HIS SECRET FORMULAE IN HIS HEAD! HE DOESN'T DARE TRUST THEM TO SAFES!
THAT'S WHY I'M SO WORRIED ABOUT HIM! WHAT IF SOMEONE CAPTURED HIM.. TOOK HIM TO AN UNFRIENDLY NATION...TO FORCE HIS SECRETS FROM HIM?!!
VERY WELL, THEN! MY NEXT PROBLEM IS ESCAPE! USE THAT COMMUNICATOR! ORDER THEM TO PLACE A SPEEDY CAR AT MY DISPOSAL!
NO! I WON'T! I WON'T!
BUT, PEPPER IS UNAWARE THAT THE COMMUNICATOR IS "ON", AND SO...
THAT'S A MIGHTY BRAVE GIRL!
LET HIM HAVE THE CAR, JACK! WE CAN'T TAKE ANY CHANCES WITH PEPPER'S SAFETY!
I WON'T HELP A MENACE LIKE YOU TO ESCAPE!
WITHIN SECONDS, IRON MAN RECEIVES AN URGENT RADIO CALL...
GIANT-MAN CALLING! JUST HEARD A BULLETIN... HAWKEYE IS TRAPPED IN STARK'S FACTORY! HOLDING PEPPER HOSTAGE! SHOULD AVENGERS TAKE OVER?!
NO! HE MAY PANIC... HE MAY INJURE HER! I'LL DO IT ALONE... MY WAY! OVER... AND OUT!
9.

LIKE A GOLDEN TORNADO, THE MIGHTY AVENGER STREAKS THROUGH THE SKY, UNTIL...

EVEN THOUGH I'M UNDER SUSPICION, I CAN'T STAND IDLY BY WHILE *PEPPER* IS IN DANGER!

AND, ACROSS THE SPRAWLING CITY, *ANOTHER* OF OUR FATEFUL CAST PREPARES TO ACT...

HAWKEYE IS IN TROUBLE! PERHAPS THE *BLACK WIDOW* CAN HELP HIM!

FORGIVE US FOR SWITCHING SCENES SO SUDDENLY, BUT OUR ACTION NOW OCCURS SIMULTANEOUSLY IN TWO SEPARATE AREAS!! —STAN AND DON.

I'M IN LUCK! HE'S STILL HERE!

IRON MAN! I THOUGHT YOU WERE UNDER SUSPICION... IN HIDING SOMEWHERE!

AT THAT MOMENT, AS THE SULTRY NATASHA HEADS FOR HER CAR...

WE *HAVE* HER, SERGI!

SERGI AMKOV! HEAD OF THE IRON CURTAIN SPY SYSTEM IN NORTH AMERICA!

AT YOUR SERVICE MY DEAR! I HAVE ORDERS TO BRING YOU BACK WITH ME. *NOW*... FOR INTERROGATION!

MEANWHILE, UNAWARE THAT NATASHA IS HEADING FOR AN IRON CURTAIN SLAVE NATION...

THIS POWER-BLAST ARROW WILL STOP IRON MAN!

HAVE YOU FORGOTTEN SO SOON, HAWKEYE... HOW *FAST* MY JETS ENABLE ME TO MOVE?? AND, WHEN IT COMES TO SHEER *POWER*...

... MY TRANSISTORS AND I PRACTICALLY *INVENTED* THE WORD!!

THE FIRST THING I MUST DO IS GET *PEPPER* OUT OF DANGER... IN A WAY HE LEAST EXPECTS!

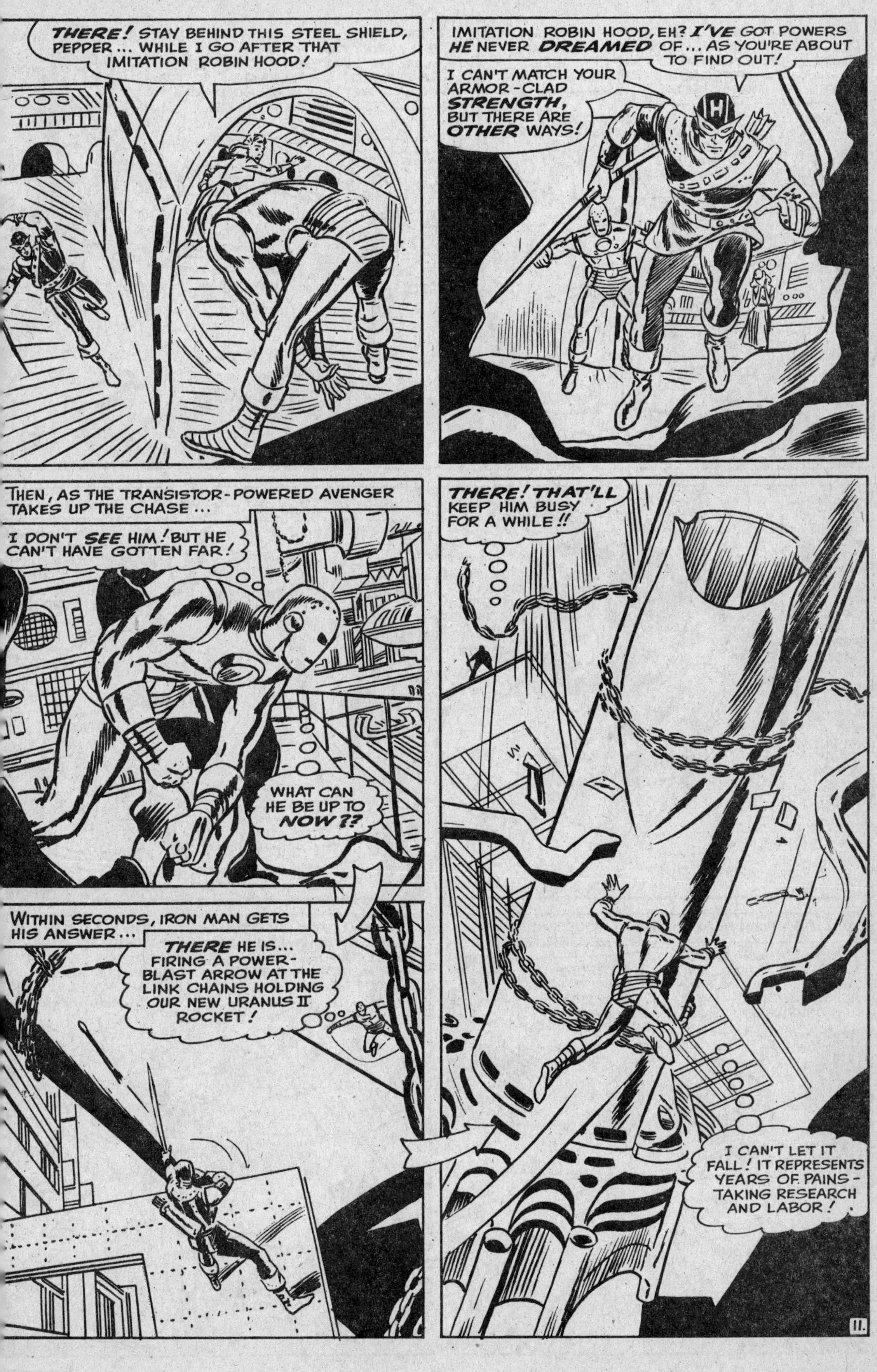

THERE! STAY BEHIND THIS STEEL SHIELD, PEPPER... WHILE I GO AFTER THAT IMITATION ROBIN HOOD!
IMITATION ROBIN HOOD, EH? I'VE GOT POWERS HE NEVER DREAMED OF... AS YOU'RE ABOUT TO FIND OUT!
I CAN'T MATCH YOUR ARMOR-CLAD STRENGTH, BUT THERE ARE OTHER WAYS!
THEN, AS THE TRANSISTOR-POWERED AVENGER TAKES UP THE CHASE...
I DON'T SEE HIM! BUT HE CAN'T HAVE GOTTEN FAR!
WHAT CAN HE BE UP TO NOW??
THERE! THAT'LL KEEP HIM BUSY FOR A WHILE!!
WITHIN SECONDS, IRON MAN GETS HIS ANSWER...
THERE HE IS... FIRING A POWER-BLAST ARROW AT THE LINK CHAINS HOLDING OUR NEW URANUS II ROCKET!
I CAN'T LET IT FALL! IT REPRESENTS YEARS OF PAINS-TAKING RESEARCH AND LABOR!
11.

THEN, SUMMONING EVERY BIT OF HIS TREMEN-DOUS TRANSISTORIZED POWER, IRON MAN GIVES A DEMONSTRATION OF DELICATELY HARNESSED STRENGTH SUCH AS FEW EYES HAVE EVER WITNESSED!...

GENTLY...GENTLY... I MUSTN'T JAR IT... EASY... I'VE GOT TO CRADLE IT WITHOUT A TREMOR! *THERE!!*

VERY IMPRESSIVE, IRON MAN! BUT THE VARIETY OF MY ARROWS IS ALMOST LIMITLESS! *HERE* IS *ANOTHER* CHALLENGE FOR YOU... AN ARROW THAT WILL BIND YOU HOPELESSLY WITH A STEEL CABLE!!

BUT AGAIN IRON MAN MOVES WITH UN-EXPECTED SPEED, CATCHING ONE END OF THE SUPER-STRONG CABLE BEFORE IT CAN ENTWINE AROUND HIM, AND GIVING IT A POWER-FUL TUG...!

I'VE GOT TO FINISH THIS QUICKLY! MY TRANSISTORS ARE STARTING TO RUN LOW!

THE SAME THOUGHT OCCURS TO HAWKEYE, AS HE QUICKLY REGAINS HIS BALANCE...

YOU'VE BEEN USING YOUR TRANSISTORS AT FULL CAPACITY, IRON MAN! THEY MUST BE STARTING TO LOSE THEIR POWER NOW!

I'VE NO INTENTION OF GIVING YOU TIME ENOUGH TO RECHARGE THEM!!

I NEVER KNOW WHAT TO EXPECT FROM HIM *NEXT!* THAT BLINDING FLASH...CAUGHT ME OFF GUARD!

IS THERE NO *LIMIT* TO THE DANGEROUS DEVICES HIS ARROWS CONTAIN??!

I *THOUGHT* MY STUN-FLASH ARROW WOULD DAZZLE HIM LONG ENOUGH FOR ME TO MAKE GOOD MY ESCAPE!!

TOO BAD I'VE NO POWER-BLAST ARROWS LEFT TO USE WHILE HE'S TEMPORARILY BLINDED!

BUT I WOULDN'T DARE ATTACK HIM WITHOUT THEM! EVEN SIGHTLESS, AND WITH HIS TRANSISTORS LOW, HE'S TOO POWERFUL FOR ANY FLESH AND BLOOD ENEMY!

THE BUILDING'S SURROUNDED! GUARDS ALL OVER! HOW WILL I... WAIT!!

THAT LOW-FLYING JET... TAKING OFF FROM LA GUARDIA FIELD! JUST WHAT I NEED...

MY SUCTION-TIPPED ARROW CAN'T MISS A TARGET THAT SIZE!!

WITH JET PLANE SPEED, IT ONLY TAKES A FEW SECONDS BEFORE...

PERFECT! IT CARRIED ME CLEAR ACROSS THE RIVER! NOW TO SLIDE OFF, BEFORE HE GAINS TOO MUCH ALTITUDE!

AND SO, HAWKEYE DISAPPEARS INTO THE NIGHT...LITTLE DREAMING THAT ABOARD THAT VERY PLANE...

HAWKEYE... MY DARLING... WILL THEY EVER LET ME SEE YOU AGAIN...?

AND, BACK AT STARK'S FACTORY...

THERE'S IRON MAN! QUICK... GET THE NEW PROTON GUN!

THE ANTI-ARMOR GUN WHICH I MYSELF INVENTED! HOW IRONIC!!

STOP!! WE HAVE NO RIGHT! HE HASN'T FORMALLY BEEN CHARGED WITH ANY CRIME!

BUT WHAT ABOUT THE BOSS'S DISAPPEARANCE?

WE CAN'T BE POSITIVE THAT IRON MAN'S RESPONSIBLE! AND BESIDES...HE DID SAVE MY LIFE!!

THANK YOU, PEPPER!

NO! DON'T THANK ME! I ONLY DID IT FOR MR. STARK! IF YOU ARE INNOCENT...YOU MAY STILL BE THE ONLY ONE WHO CAN SAVE HIM IF HE'S IN TROUBLE!

SUDDENLY...

I'VE GOT TO LEAVE! I CAN'T BEAR TO LOOK AT HER...TO BE NEAR HER...TO SEE THE ANGUISH IN HER EYES...AND NOT BE ABLE TO HELP!

I SURE HOPE YOU DID THE RIGHT THING, PEPPER!

SO DO I, HAPPY! BUT, NO MATTER HOW THE EVIDENCE POINTS AGAINST HIM, THERE'S SOMETHING ABOUT IRON MAN... SOMETHING THAT MAKES ME WANT TO TRUST HIM...SOMETHING I CAN'T EXPLAIN!

AND SO WE TAKE OUR LEAVE OF THE GOLDEN AVENGER...AS HE LABORS ALONE IN HIS LAB, DESPERATELY TRYING TO FIND A WAY TO SAFELY REMOVE THE ARMOR WHICH MAKES HIM ONE OF THE MOST POWERFUL OF HUMANS... AND ONE OF THE MOST TRAGIC!!

The End

13.

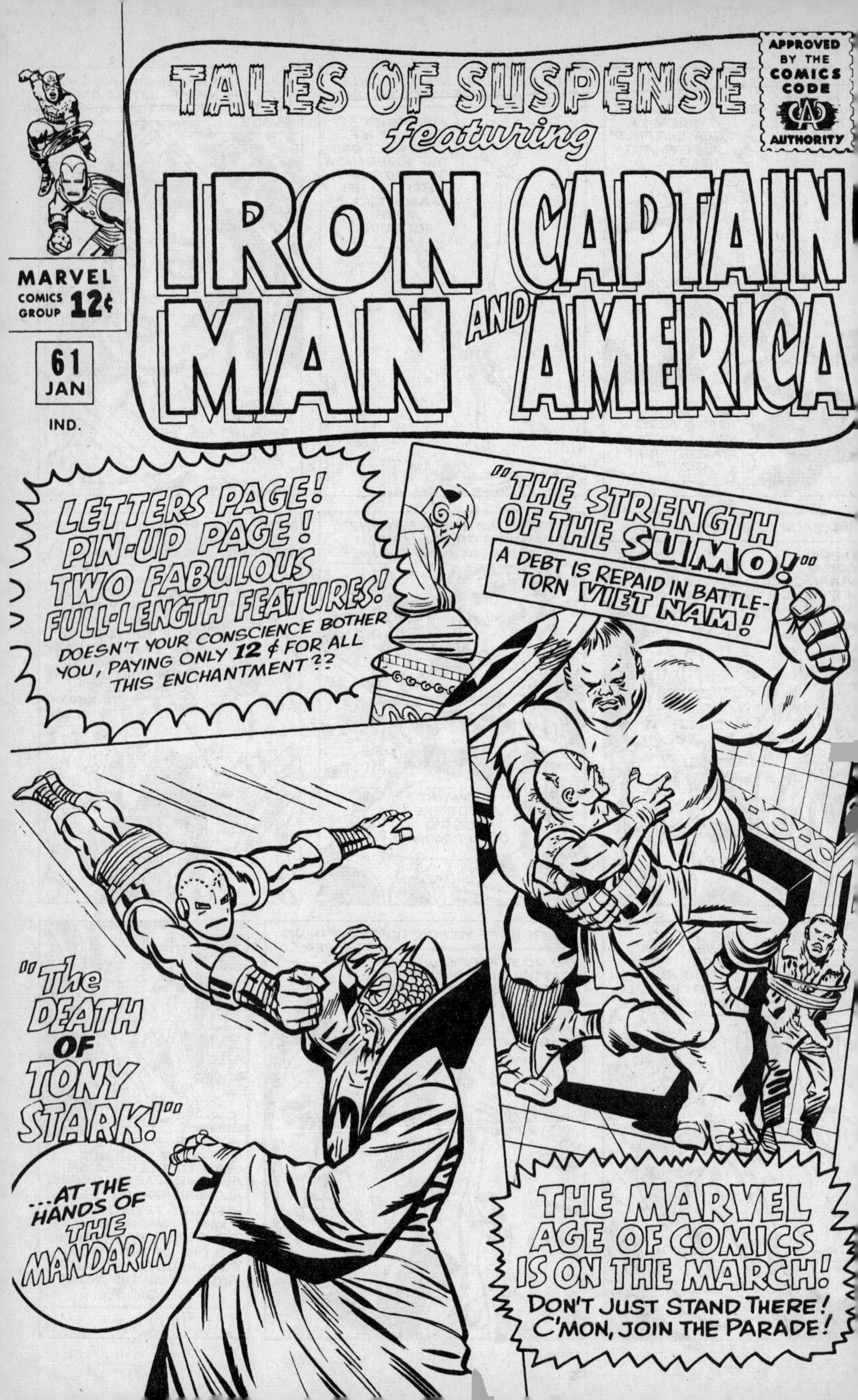

TALES OF SUSPENSE
featuring
IRON MAN AND CAPTAIN AMERICA
APPROVED BY THE COMICS CODE AUTHORITY
MARVEL COMICS GROUP 12¢
61 JAN
IND.
LETTERS PAGE! PIN-UP PAGE! TWO FABULOUS FULL-LENGTH FEATURES! DOESN'T YOUR CONSCIENCE BOTHER YOU, PAYING ONLY 12¢ FOR ALL THIS ENCHANTMENT??
"THE STRENGTH OF THE SUMO!"
A DEBT IS REPAID IN BATTLE-TORN VIET NAM!
"The DEATH OF TONY STARK!"
...AT THE HANDS OF THE MANDARIN
THE MARVEL AGE OF COMICS IS ON THE MARCH! DON'T JUST STAND THERE! C'MON, JOIN THE PARADE!

IRON MAN
"The DEATH OF TONY STARK!"
PRESENTING ONCE AGAIN BY OVERWHELMING POPULAR DEMAND...
The MANDARIN!
SITTING IN THE PLUSH PRIVATE OFFICE OF MILLIONAIRE TONY STARK... WRAPPED IN HIS OWN GLOOMY THOUGHTS... IRON MAN SUDDENLY SNAPS OUT OF HIS REVERIE AS TWO ANGRY VISITORS ENTER...
PEPPER! AND HAPPY! WHAT'S WRONG? WHY DID YOU BARGE IN THIS WAY?
TO GIVE YOU THIS LITTLE NOTE, MISTER! IT'S OUR RESIGNATION!
YEAH! WE'RE QUITTIN'!
BUT YOU CAN'T QUIT! NOT NOW!
Story by: STAN LEE BECAUSE WE WANTED THE BEST!
Art by: DON HECK BECAUSE WE WANTED THE FINEST!
Inking by: DICK AYERS BECAUSE WE WANTED THE TOPS!
Lettering by: S.ROSEN BECAUSE WE WANTED TO KEEP HIM BUSY!

TONY STARK'S BEEN MISSIN' FOR OVER A *MONTH* NOW! *YOU'VE* BEEN USIN' HIS OFFICE AND ACTIN' LIKE YOU *OWN* THE PLACE! BUT YOU'RE NOT FOOLIN' *US!*

EVEN THOUGH WE CAN'T *PROVE* IT, WE *KNOW* YOU HAD SOMETHING TO DO WITH HIS DISAPPEARANCE!

AND WE'RE GOING TO FIND *PROOF*...BUT WE CAN'T DO IT UNLESS WE QUIT OUR JOBS! COME, HAPPY!

WAIT!

IT'S NO USE! THEY'VE *GONE!* NOW...THERE IS *NO ONE* LEFT! NO ONE I CAN TURN TO...!

BUT BEFORE PEPPER AND HAPPY CAN LEAVE THE SPRAWLING PLANT...

I'VE BEEN *LOOKING* FOR YOU TWO! I'M INSPECTOR *FLINT!* I'D LIKE TO TALK TO YOU AT POLICE HEAD-QUARTERS!

NOTHING WOULD SUIT US BETTER, INSPECTOR!

AND SO... IT'S *SHOCKING* THE WAY MR. STARK HAS BEEN MISSING ALL THIS TIME AND NOTHING'S BEEN *DONE* ABOUT IT!

NOW, HOLD ON, MA'AM! WE'RE WORKING ON THE CASE! THAT'S WHY I BROUGHT YOU HERE!

I WANT YOU TO TELL ME EVERY-THING YOU KNOW ABOUT ...*IRON MAN!*

NOW WE'RE GETTIN' *SOMEWHERE!*

WOW! THE BRASS THINKS *IRON MAN* HAS SOMETHING TO DO WITH STARK'S DISAPPEARANCE! WHAT A STORY!

REMEMBER, EVEN THOUGH IRON MAN IS ONE OF THE FAMOUS *AVENGERS*, HE ISN'T ABOVE THE *LAW!* IF HE'S DONE ANYTHING *WRONG*, WE'LL *GET* HIM!

THERE MUST BE *SOME* WAY TO GET THE GOODS ON HIM! HE WAS SUP-POSED TO BE MR. STARK'S *BODY-GUARD!* HUH..WHAT A *LAUGH!*

A SHORT TIME LATER...

EXTRA! IRON MAN TOP SUSPECT IN TONY STARK'S DISAPPEARANCE!

WHERE IS TONY STARK?

WHER TONY

2

BUT, HOW SURPRISED THE WORLD WOULD BE IF IT KNEW THE *REAL* ANSWER! FOR, WHEN IRON MAN TAKES HIS HELMET OFF... *TONY STARK APPEARS* !!

I MUSTN'T GIVE UP! I MUST KEEP SEARCHING FOR A WAY TO REMOVE MY IRON ARMOR WITHOUT CAUSING MY INJURED HEART TO STOP BEATING!

FOR, SO LONG AS I MUST *WEAR* MY FIGHTING GARB, I CANNOT TAKE MY PLACE AGAIN IN PUBLIC AS TONY STARK, WITHOUT REVEALING THAT STARK AND *IRON MAN* ARE ONE AND THE SAME!

AND I CAN *NEVER* ADMIT MY TRUE IDENTITY! IF MY MANY ENEMIES EVER KNEW WHO *IRON MAN* REALLY IS, THE FACTORIES OF TONY STARK WOULD BE UNDER CONSTANT ATTACK!

THE LIVES OF MY THOUSANDS OF EMPLOYEES WOULD BE IN CONTINUAL JEOPARDY! I CAN NEVER ALLOW IT!

IT IS RELIABLY REPORTED THAT THE POLICE ARE PREPARING TO HOLD *IRON MAN* FOR A GRAND JURY INVESTIGATION INTO THE MYSTERIOUS DISAPPEARANCE OF TONY STARK! THE *AVENGERS* ARE YET TO BE HEARD FROM, BUT...

I CAN'T ALLOW THE AVENGERS TO GET MIXED UP IN MY OWN PROBLEM! SOMETIMES I THINK IT MIGHT BE BEST IF TONY STARK *WERE* GONE FOREVER... AND *IRON MAN*, AS WELL!!

BUT, THE NEXT DAY, SOMETHING HAPPENS TO *CHANGE* THE ENTIRE PICTURE! OUTSIDE THE PRIVATE ESTATE OF MULTI-MILLIONAIRE STARK, WE SEE...

MAYBE I CAN FIND A CLUE TO WHAT HAPPENED TO MR. STARK BY SEARCHING HIS HOUSE...

THE PLACE IS SURE TO BE DESERTED WHILE HE'S MISSING!

BUT HAPPY HOGAN IS *WRONG!*

SOMEONE'S *COMING!* IT'S *HAPPY!* I'M NOT WEARING MY HELMET! CAN'T LET HIM SEE ME IN MY *IRON MAN* ARMOR! NO TIME TO RUN!

THAT'S FUNNY! I COULDA *SWORN* I SAW SOMEONE *MOVIN'* IN THERE!

3.

HOLY COW! AM...AM I *SEEIN'* THINGS?? *BOSS!* IS THAT *YOU*??

I REACHED THE BED JUST IN TIME! SO LONG AS I STAY UNDER THE COVERS, HE WON'T SEE MY *ARMOR*!

OF *COURSE* IT'S ME, YOU BIG LUG! DIDN'T IRON MAN *TELL* YOU NOT TO WORRY ABOUT ME!??

YEAH...BUT WE DIDN'T *BELIEVE* HIM! WE THOUGHT...!

NEXT TIME *DON'T* THINK! *I TOLD* YOU IRON MAN CAN BE TRUSTED!

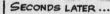

SECONDS LATER...

PEPPER! WAIT'LL YOU HEAR THE *NEWS!* MR. STARK'S *ALIVE!* HE'S HOME IN BED! HE'S GOT SOME KINDA *SICKNESS*, BUT HE'S *ALIVE!*

I'LL BE RIGHT OVER!

AND SO...

WHERE *IS* HE, HAPPY?? I'VE GOT TO *SEE* HIM! I'M SO EXCITED, I CAN'T *BEAR* IT!

EASY, PEP! HE'S RIGHT INSIDE!

THEN...

THE DOCTOR SAID I WAS RUN-DOWN... I NEEDED ABSOLUTE REST AND QUIET! I DIDN'T WANT TO *WORRY* ANYONE, SO I TOLD IRON MAN TO SAY I HAD TAKEN A TRIP!

MEANWHILE, THE NEWS THAT STARK IS ALIVE SPREADS LIKE WILDFIRE...

THIS IS TERRIBLE! I DARE NOT THROW OFF THE COVERS AND STAND REVEALED AS *IRON MAN!* BUT I CAN'T REMAIN IN *BED* FOR THE REST OF MY LIFE!!

FINALLY, AS THE CROWD CONVERGES AT STARK'S DOOR...

SORRY, NO ONE CAN GO IN NOW! THE *POLICE* ARE INSIDE, QUESTIONING HIM!

WE'LL STAY HERE TILL WE CAN SEE HIM! OUR READERS WANT TO BE SURE IT *IS* ANTHONY STARK!

4.

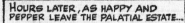

HOURS LATER, AS HAPPY AND PEPPER LEAVE THE PALATIAL ESTATE...

I HATE TO SOUND LIKE I'M LOOKIN' FOR TROUBLE, PEP... BUT I STILL FEEL THERE'S SOMETHIN' NOT KOSHER GOIN' ON IN THERE!

I KNOW WHAT YOU MEAN, HAPPY, BECAUSE I FEEL THE SAME WAY! MR. STARK DIDN'T LOOK LIKE A SICK MAN! HE JUST LOOKED WORRIED!

IN FACT, HOW DO WE KNOW HE ISN'T A PRISONER OF IRON MAN? THAT COULD BE WHY HE NEVER CALLED US OR CONTACTED US!

IRON MAN MIGHT HAVE FORCED HIM TO SAY WHAT HE DID TO US!! HE COULD HAVE BEEN HIDING BEHIND MR. STARK!

LOOK!! THERE HE IS NOW, HAPPY...ON THE TERRACE!

BUT HE'S MR. STARK'S BODYGUARD! HE SHOULD BE THERE!

THEY'VE ALL GONE! I CAN CHANGE BACK TO IRON MAN AGAIN! NOW I'LL HEAD BACK FOR THE LAB AND MORE EXPERIMENTING!

BUT, THE GOLDEN AVENGER IS NOT DESTINED TO REACH HIS LAB THAT NIGHT!...FOR, CIRCLING THE EARTH HIGH OVERHEAD, A STRANGE SATELLITE SUDDENLY COMES INTO VIEW...

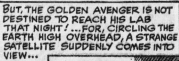

TRACKING STATIONS ALL OVER EARTH TRY TO TRACE ITS ORIGIN...

IT'S NOT ONE OF OURS! IT MUST BE A RED SPY IN THE SKY!

IT IS NOT ONE OF OURS! IT MUST BE AN AMERICAN SPY IN THE SKY!

BUT IT IS NEITHER! LET US NOW TURN TO AN IMPREGNABLE MOUNTAIN STRONGHOLD DEEP IN THE HEART OF THE ORIENT, WHERE WE FIND...THE MANDARIN!

EVERYTHING IS FUNCTIONING PERFECTLY! NOW TO GIVE MY SATELLITE ITS FINAL COMMAND!

5.

THEN, A BEAM FROM ONE OF THE MANDARIN'S MANY STRANGE FINGER RINGS SHOOTS OUT...

WITH PINPOINT ACCURACY IT STRIKES A SENSITIVE SWITCH, ACTIVATING IT!

INSTANTLY, A SERIES OF COMPLEX RELAY DEVICES GO INTO OPERATION, HARNESSING A VAST AMOUNT OF RAW POWER...

POWER ENOUGH TO SEND A LIGHTNING SWIFT LASER BEAM HALF-WAY AROUND THE EARTH!

IT IS *DONE!* NOTHING CAN STOP IT NOW!

AND, AS THE STAGGERING BEAM STRIKES THE SATELLITE WITH THE ACCURACY OF A RIFLE SHOT, THE MANDARIN GLOATS TO HIMSELF, DOWN ON EARTH...

IT TOOK ME *YEARS* TO DESIGN AND BUILD MY *KILLER SATELLITE!* IT MUST DO ITS FIRST JOB PERFECTLY! ...FOR I CAN SPEND NO MORE YEARS BUILDING ANOTHER!

ITS ONLY PURPOSE IS TO *SLAY* ANYONE I WISH... ANYWHERE ON EARTH! AND, ONE OF THOSE I HATE MOST IN THIS WORLD.. IS ANTHONY STARK!

BUT WITHIN THE ELECTRONIC RECESSES OF HIS MIGHTY ARMOR, A SENSITIZED ALARM TINGLES STEADILY... WARNING OF SOME RAPIDLY APPROACHING DANGER!

IN THE SKY... SOME SORT OF *BEAM* ...IT'S COMING RIGHT *TOWARDS* ME!

I DON'T KNOW WHAT IT IS... BUT I'M NOT HANGING AROUND TO FIND OUT!!

A LONG-DISTANCE LASER BEAM! IF I HADN'T MOVED WHEN I DID, I'D HAVE BEEN JUST ANOTHER STATISTIC!

6.

BUT, IN HOMES THROUGHOUT THE NATION, A SHOCKING BULLETIN IS BROADCAST...

TONY STARK'S HOME HAS JUST BEEN STRUCK BY A MYSTERIOUS, DEADLY RAY OF UNKNOWN ORIGIN!

FASTER, HAPPY... *FASTER!* HAVE WE JUST FOUND HIM... ONLY TO *LOSE* HIM AGAIN?!

EASY, PEPPER, HONEY! LET'S WAIT TILL WE *GET* THERE! MAYBE IT'S ALL A MISTAKE!

BUT, UPON REACHING THE SCENE, THEY REALIZE...

THE RAY HIT HIS BEDROOM WINDOW... THE ROOM HE WAS IN WHEN WE LEFT HIM!

EVERYTHING IS TOTALLY DESTROYED! WHOEVER WAS IN THAT ROOM DIDN'T HAVE A CHANCE!

OH, NO! NO!

AND AT THE CASTLE OF THE MANDARIN...

WHEN THE WITLESS AMERICAN PRESS BROADCAST THAT STARK WAS SAFE IN HIS HOME, THEY DIDN'T DREAM IT GAVE ME THE INFORMATION I NEEDED TO DESTROY HIM!

NEXT, I SHALL DEVISE A WAY TO DESTROY *IRON MAN*, AND THEN I SHALL HAVE RID MYSELF OF MY TWO GREATEST ENEMIES!

WHILE BACK IN THE STATES...

DON'T CRY, PEPPER! MAYBE...MAYBE HE WASN'T *IN* HIS ROOM WHEN THE RAY HIT!

IT'S NO USE PRETENDING! HE COULDN'T LEAVE HIS BED! HE WAS THERE! HE WAS...!!

YEAH! WE MIGHT AS WELL FACE IT... HE'S *GONE!*

YOU!! YOU CALLED YOURSELF HIS *BODY-GUARD!* HOW DID *YOU* ESCAPE??

MR. STARK HAD...EH.. SENT ME TO THE OTHER WING TO GET HIM SOME PAPERS WHEN THE RAY STRUCK! THERE WAS NOTHING I COULD DO!

7.

THEN, EARLY THE NEXT DAY...

YOU AGAIN?! LOOK, MISS POTTS, *THIS* TIME YOU'RE OUT OF LINE! IRON MAN CAN'T BE BLAMED FOR WHAT HAPPENED TO TONY STARK!

HOW DO YOU KNOW IRON MAN ISN'T *RESPONSIBLE* FOR THAT MYSTERIOUS RAY? NO ONE KNOWS WHERE IT *CAME* FROM!

I'VE *SEEN* IRON MAN IN ACTION! YOU WOULDN'T *BELIEVE* HOW STRONG HE IS---- THE FANTASTIC THINGS HE CAN DO!! WITH ALL HIS POWER, HIS ARMOR, HIS SECRET SCIENTIFIC DEVICES, WHY COULDN'T *HE* HAVE CAUSED THE DEADLY RAY TO HIT TONY STARK?!?

THAT RAY IS *MORE* THAN A ROUTINE POLICE MATTER! *WASHINGTON* IS INVESTIGATING IT NOW! UNTIL I GET WORD FROM THEM, THERE'S NOTHING I CAN DO ABOUT IRON MAN!

THE CASE IS CLOSED!

THAT NIGHT, HAPPY HOGAN STANDS AT THE LONG ISLAND SHORE WHICH TONY STARK USED TO LOVE SO WELL...

I'VE GOT TO LEARN TO ACCEPT IT! THE BOSS IS DEAD!

ACCORDING TO MR. STARK'S WILL, *IRON MAN* IS IN CHARGE! HE SAYS PEPPER AND ME CAN HAVE OUR JOBS BACK... SO I'LL BE WITH PEP WITHOUT MR. STARK CUTTIN' IN!

SO I'VE GOT NOTHIN' TO WORRY ABOUT! EVERYTHING'S GREAT! =SOB=...JUST GREAT!

MEANTIME, ALONE IN HIS LAB, A FIGHTING MAD AVENGER WORKS WITHOUT LETUP...

I'VE *GOT* TO LEARN WHERE THAT RAY CAME FROM!!

FINALLY...

BY COMPUTING THE RATE OF IMPACT, PROBABLE TRAJECTORY, AND OTHER FACTORS, I'VE NARROWED THE ANSWER TO A SMALL AREA IN THE ORIENT!!

I'VE CHECKED AND RECHECKED MY FINDINGS A DOZEN TIMES! THERE'S NO POSSIBLE CHANCE OF ERROR!

THIS IS THE SPOT!

8.

I SENSED IT...FELT IT IN MY BONES...AND NOW I'M CERTAIN!

IT CAN ONLY BE... THE MANDARIN!!

AND, EVEN AS THAT FEARSOME NAME CROSSES IRON MAN'S MIND...

SOONER OR LATER IRON MAN WILL REALIZE THAT MINE WAS THE HAND THAT GUIDED THE DEATH RAY WHICH KILLED STARK!

THEN, SURELY AS NIGHT FOLLOWS DAY, HE WILL ATTEMPT TO ATTACK ME!

IS EVERYTHING IN READINESS?

AH SO, GREAT MASTER!

THE VERY NEXT DAY, A BURLY BEARDED MAN BOARDS A PLANE FOR THE ORIENT...

I HOPE NOBODY HEARS THE CLANKING OF MY ARMOR UNDER THIS GETUP!

IT'S SO WARM IN THE PLANE AND YET THAT BEARDED MAN WON'T REMOVE HIS COAT!

OH, WELL! IT TAKES ALL KINDS, I GUESS!

LONG HOURS LATER...OVER THE ASIAN COAST...

NO, DON'T! YOU'LL BE KILLED!

STAY BACK! DO NOT TRY TO STOP ME!

HE PULLED THE EMERGENCY HANDLE...OPENED THE ESCAPE DOOR...AND THEN...HE JUMPED!!

GET HOLD OF YOURSELF, DEAR! WE'LL HAVE TO GIVE A FULL REPORT WHEN WE LAND! HE MUST HAVE BEEN MAD!!

BUT THE STARTLED HOSTESSES CANNOT REALIZE THAT, HIDDEN BENEATH THE THICK LAYER OF CLOUDS, IRON MAN IS HEADING FOR ONE OF HIS MOST DANGEROUS BATTLES...

AND NOW... FOR THE MANDARIN!

WHILE, MILES AWAY, A PAIR OF EVIL EYES WATCH HIS EVERY MOVE

JUST AS I EXPECTED! HE COMES!

9.

GUARDS! TO YOUR POSTS! MAN THE DEFENSES! PREPARE TO *DIE* IF NEED BE, FOR YOUR MASTER!

THEN, FINALLY

HIS CASTLE IS BELOW! HE PROBABLY *KNOWS* I'M HERE.. BUT THAT WON'T STOP ME!

ONCE AGAIN, THE ORIENTAL MYSTERY MAN TRAINS THE BEAM OF ONE OF HIS MANY POTENT RINGS UPON A COMPLEX CONTROL PANEL...

ZZZZ

EVERYTHING HAS NOW BEEN SET IN MOTION! THERE IS NOTHING MORE FOR *ME* TO DO BUT SIT BACK AND ENJOY IRON MAN'S HUMILIATING AND TOTAL *DEFEAT!*

A BEAM SHOT OUT FROM THE CASTLE!! I'M CAUGHT IN ITS OVERWHELMING BRILLIANCE!

IT'S PULLING ME TOWARDS THE ROCKS BELOW! THE MANDARIN MUST EXPECT THE *FALL* TO FINISH ME!

10,

BUT, AT THE LAST POSSIBLE SPLIT-SECOND, IRON MAN TURNS HIS POWERFUL REPULSORS ON, TO FULL INTENSITY...!

THEY BROKE MY FALL JUST ENOUGH! MY ARMOR WILL DO THE REST!

I DON'T *GET* IT! I SURVIVED THE IMPACT! MY ARMOR SHIELDED ME! I FEEL FINE! SO, WHY DO I SEEM TO SEE *SPOTS* BEFORE MY EYES?!

WAIT! I'M NOT JUST *IMAGINING* THEM! THEY'RE FLASHING LIGHT IMPULSES!

THEY MUST BE ANOTHER OF THE MANDARIN'S *TRAPS!* BUT... WHAT IS THEIR *PURPOSE?*

HE WONDERS WHAT MY FLASHING LIGHTS ARE! HE DOES NOT SUSPECT THEIR *HYPNO-TIC* EFFECT!

SOON, THEY WILL SAP HIS WILL... MAKE HIM FEEL TOO WEAK TO FIGHT! BUT FIRST...

KOTO! THE TIME HAS COME! ATTACK IRON MAN!

THUS, SECONDS LATER...

A GIGANTIC *ROBOT!* HOW DID HE EVER MAKE IT LOOK SO *LIFELIKE??*

I AM KOTO!

WELL, NOW THAT YOU'VE INTRODUCED YOURSELF, LET'S GET TO KNOW EACH OTHER BETTER!

BUT, FULLY UNDER THE INFLUENCE OF THE HYPNOTIC LIGHTS BY NOW, IRON MAN RECEIVES A STAGGERING SHOCK...!

HE'S *NOT* A ROBOT! HE'S *ALIVE!!* AND... HE'S BIGGER... AND STRONGER... THAN *GIANT-MAN!*

11.

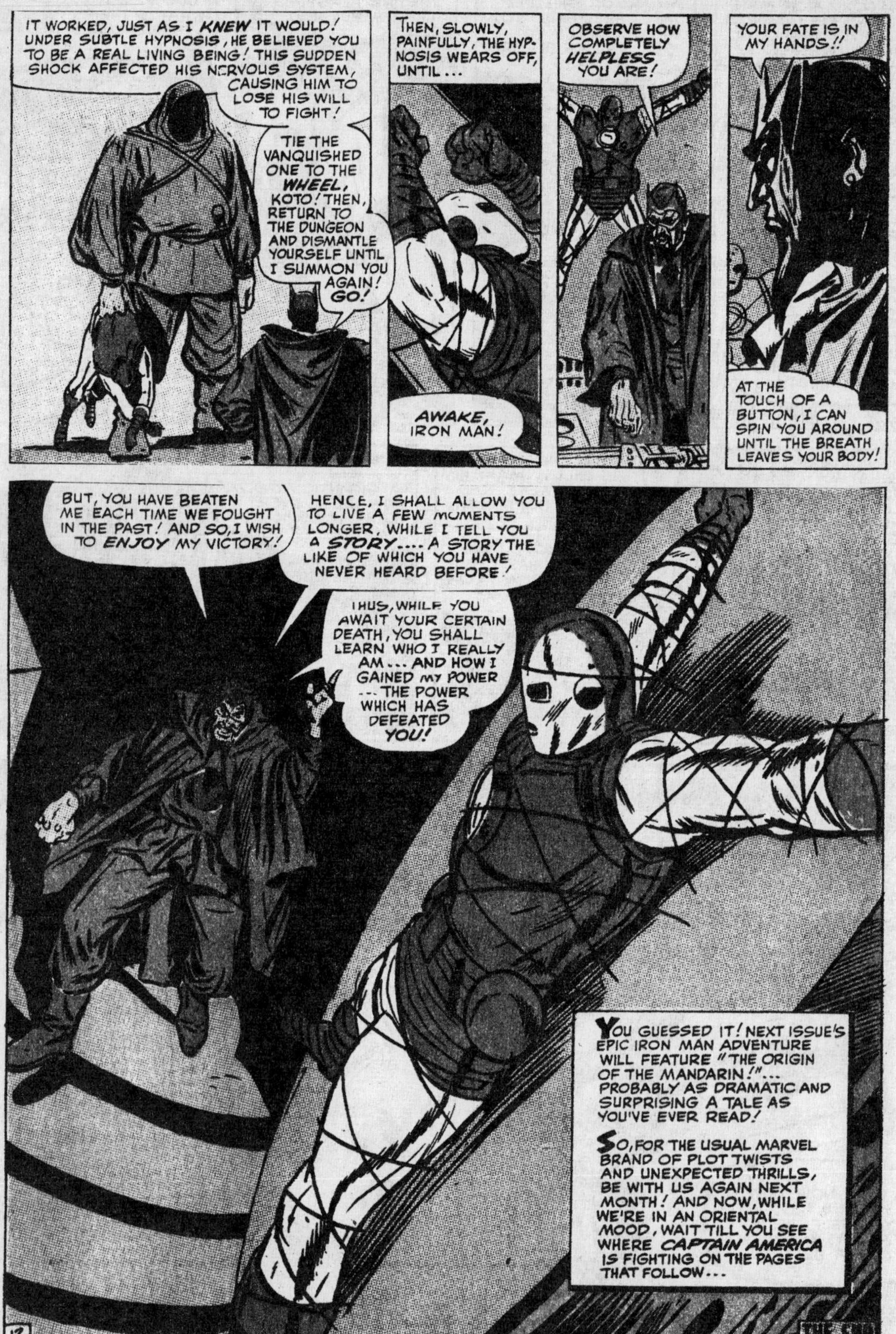
IT WORKED, JUST AS I KNEW IT WOULD! UNDER SUBTLE HYPNOSIS, HE BELIEVED YOU TO BE A REAL LIVING BEING! THIS SUDDEN SHOCK AFFECTED HIS NERVOUS SYSTEM, CAUSING HIM TO LOSE HIS WILL TO FIGHT!
TIE THE VANQUISHED ONE TO THE WHEEL, KOTO! THEN, RETURN TO THE DUNGEON AND DISMANTLE YOURSELF UNTIL I SUMMON YOU AGAIN! GO!
THEN, SLOWLY, PAINFULLY, THE HYPNOSIS WEARS OFF, UNTIL...
AWAKE, IRON MAN!
OBSERVE HOW COMPLETELY HELPLESS YOU ARE!
YOUR FATE IS IN MY HANDS!!
AT THE TOUCH OF A BUTTON, I CAN SPIN YOU AROUND UNTIL THE BREATH LEAVES YOUR BODY!
BUT, YOU HAVE BEATEN ME EACH TIME WE FOUGHT IN THE PAST! AND SO, I WISH TO ENJOY MY VICTORY!
HENCE, I SHALL ALLOW YOU TO LIVE A FEW MOMENTS LONGER, WHILE I TELL YOU A STORY.... A STORY THE LIKE OF WHICH YOU HAVE NEVER HEARD BEFORE!
THUS, WHILE YOU AWAIT YOUR CERTAIN DEATH, YOU SHALL LEARN WHO I REALLY AM... AND HOW I GAINED MY POWER ...THE POWER WHICH HAS DEFEATED YOU!
YOU GUESSED IT! NEXT ISSUE'S EPIC IRON MAN ADVENTURE WILL FEATURE "THE ORIGIN OF THE MANDARIN!"... PROBABLY AS DRAMATIC AND SURPRISING A TALE AS YOU'VE EVER READ!
SO, FOR THE USUAL MARVEL BRAND OF PLOT TWISTS AND UNEXPECTED THRILLS, BE WITH US AGAIN NEXT MONTH! AND NOW, WHILE WE'RE IN AN ORIENTAL MOOD, WAIT TILL YOU SEE WHERE CAPTAIN AMERICA IS FIGHTING ON THE PAGES THAT FOLLOW...
12.
THE END

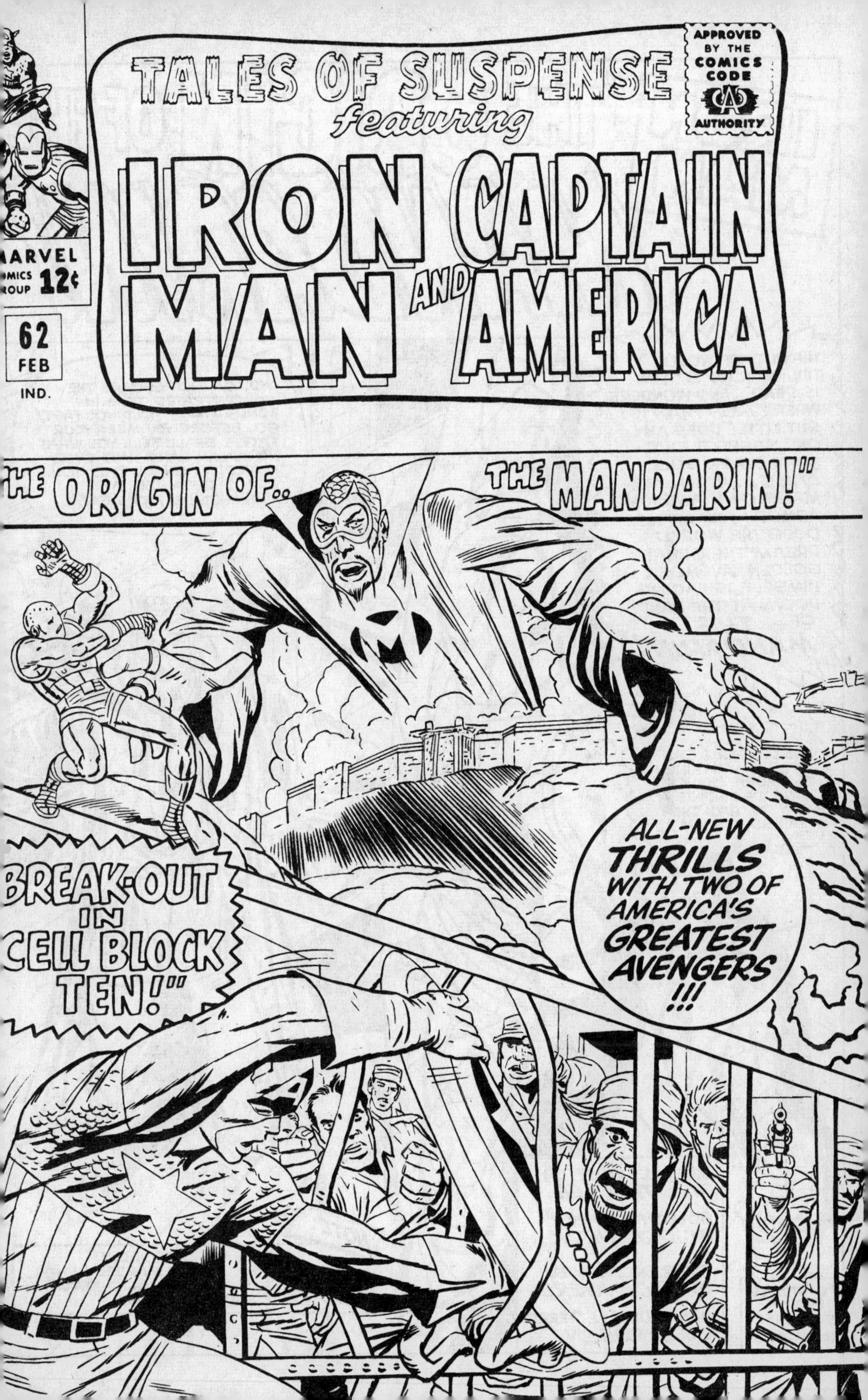
TALES OF SUSPENSE featuring
IRON MAN AND CAPTAIN AMERICA
APPROVED BY THE COMICS CODE AUTHORITY
MARVEL COMICS GROUP 12¢
62 FEB
IND.
"THE ORIGIN OF.. THE MANDARIN!"
ALL-NEW THRILLS WITH TWO OF AMERICA'S GREATEST AVENGERS !!!
BREAK-OUT IN CELL BLOCK TEN!"

IRON MAN — "THE ORIGIN OF THE MANDARIN!"

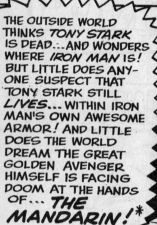

THE OUTSIDE WORLD THINKS *TONY STARK* IS DEAD... AND WONDERS WHERE *IRON MAN* IS! BUT LITTLE DOES ANYONE SUSPECT THAT *TONY STARK* STILL *LIVES*... WITHIN IRON MAN'S OWN AWESOME ARMOR! AND LITTLE DOES THE WORLD DREAM THE GREAT GOLDEN AVENGER HIMSELF IS FACING DOOM AT THE HANDS OF... *THE MANDARIN!**

YOU CANNOT ESCAPE THE CONCENTRATED TITANIUM BONDS WHICH HOLD YOU FAST! SO, BEFORE YOU MEET YOUR FATE, I SHALL TELL YOU WHAT NO HUMAN EARS HAVE EVER HEARD... I SHALL TELL YOU HOW I OBTAINED MY INVINCIBLE *POWER!*

THE LONGER I CAN KEEP HIM TALKING, THE MORE CHANCE I HAVE OF FINDING A WAY TO TURN THE TABLES ON HIM!

BRASHLY WRITTEN BY: *STAN LEE*

BOLDLY DRAWN BY: *DON HECK*

BRAZENLY INKED BY: *DICK AYERS*

BASHFULLY LETTERED BY: *S. ROSEN*

*CONTINUED FROM SUSPENSE #61--STAN

NOTE: THIS TALE WAS SPECIALLY PRODUCED BY MIGHTY MARVEL IN ANSWER TO MORE THAN 500 REQUESTS FOR MANDY'S ORIGIN!

MY **FATHER** WAS A DIRECT DESCENDANT OF **GENGHIS KHAN!** BUT HE MARRIED **BENEATH** HIM! HE WAS FOOLISH ENOUGH TO MARRY A HIGH BORN ENGLISHWOMAN!

THE GODS THEMSELVES MUST HAVE BEEN DISPLEASED, FOR WHEN I WAS BORN...

"...AN IDOL FELL UPON MY **FATHER**, KILLING HIM INSTANTLY!"

"..WHILE MY MOTHER DIED OF A BROKEN HEART UPON HEARING THE NEWS!"

"AND THUS THE GODS WERE APPEASED!'"

TRAGEDY HAS SHADOWED THE BIRTH OF THIS CHILD! IT IS AN **OMEN!**

IT IS AN **EVIL** OMEN! NEVER HAS AN IDOL TOPPLED BEFORE!

"BUT MY FAMILY HAD BEEN THE WEALTHIEST IN CHINA, AND MY FATHER'S SISTER **HATED** ME... OUR TREASURES WOULD HAVE BEEN **HERS** IF NOT FOR **ME!**"

ACCURSED CHILD! IF **YOU** HAD NOT LIVED, I WOULD BE THE RICHEST IN ALL THIS LAND! BUT... PERHAPS I MAY **STILL** BE..!

IF I WERE TO WRAP YOU AND TAKE YOU TO ANOTHER VILLAGE... NONE WOULD EVER FIND YOU AGAIN! YOU WOULD BE BROUGHT UP AS A **PEASANT!**

"BUT, AGAIN THE GODS LOOKED DOWN! THEY HAD **OTHER** PLANS FOR ME... AND GAVE MY AUNT A **SIGN!**"

ANOTHER OMEN! **AGAIN** SOMETHING **TOPPLES!**

I MUST NEVER AGAIN DARE HARM THE CHILD! THE FATES THEMSELVES PROTECT HIM! ALAS, THEY ARE SINISTER, POWERFUL FATES!

AND, WHATEVER **HIS** DESTINY MAY BE... **MINE** SHALL BE LIKEWISE! I SHALL NEVER LEAVE HIS SIDE!

I SHALL TEACH HIM TO **HATE** THE WORLD... AS **I** HATE IT! FOR I HAVE BEEN CHEATED OF MY FORTUNE... OF LOVE... OF EVERYTHING I HAVE EVER DESIRED!

2.

"AND SO I GREW! EVERY BIT OF GOLD I HAD INHERITED WAS SPENT IN TEACHING ME THE SCIENCES OF THE WORLD.. THE ARTS OF WARFARE... AND THE SUBTLE CRAFTS OF VILLAINY! BUT THEN, ONE DAY... MY WEALTH WAS GONE.."

YOU MUST *LEAVE* YOUR PALACE, AND THIS LAND! THEY BELONG TO THE GOVERNMENT, FOR YOU HAVE NOT PAID YOUR TAXES!

YOU DARE TO SPEAK SO TO A DESCENDANT OF THE *KHAN!*

SILENCE, WOMAN! IT IS BENEATH OUR DIGNITY TO SPEAK WITH SUCH RABBLE! WE SHALL DEPART!

"THE FEMALE DIED NEXT DAY, LEAVING ME COMPLETELY ALONE! BUT SUCH WAS MY TRAINING, THAT I SPENT NOT ONE SECOND MOURNING HER!"

A NOBLEMAN WITHOUT WEALTH... WITHOUT LAND! AND STILL HE WALKS PROUD!

ALMS, MASTER! ALMS FOR THE POOR!

YOU WASTE YOUR BREATH, BOY! HE HAS NOTHING!

"YES, I WALKED PROUD! FOR I WAS THE *MANDARIN!* THE BLOOD OF THE KHANS FLOWED IN MY VEINS! THE WORLD WOULD ONE DAY BE MINE!"

IF YOU WOULD EAT, YOU MUST WORK ... AS WE DO!

FOOL! YOU SPEAK TO THE *MANDARIN!* HE WOULD RATHER *STARVE!*

"BUT I KNEW I WOULD *NEVER* STARVE! FOR I HAD A *DESTINY* TO FULFILL!...!"

THE GODS HAVE PLANS FOR ME! I MUST WAIT FOR THEIR SIGN!

"AND THAT *SIGN* WAS NOT LONG IN COMING ..."

YOU MUST NOT TRAVEL YONDER ROAD, MASTER! FOR, IN TRUTH, IT LEADS TO THE DREADED *VALLEY OF SPIRITS!*

IGNORANT PEASANT! KNOW YOU THAT THE MANDARIN FEARS *NOTHING!*

"THE VALLEY OF SPIRITS! I HAD HEARD WHISPERS OF SUCH A PLACE SINCE CHILDHOOD! IT WAS A FORBIDDEN AREA, WHERE NO MAN DARED TO TREAD!"

THAT GLOW IN THE DISTANCE COMES *NOT* FROM THE SUN! I MUST LEARN THE *SECRET* OF THIS SILENT, DREADED PLACE!

3.

"TO ONE WITH THE BLOOD OF THE *KHANS* IN HIS VEINS, THERE IS NO SUCH EMOTION AS *FEAR!* CALMLY, I DESCENDED INTO THE AWESOME VALLEY..."

IT IS AS THOUGH THE GODS THEM-SELVES GUIDE MY FOOTSTEPS!

"AND THEN, I SAW A SIGHT WHICH HAD BEEN HIDDEN WITHIN THE SHADOWS OF THE SILENT CRAGS FOR COUNTLESS AGES..."

THE REMAINS OF SOME LONG-DEAD CREATURE ... A GIGANTIC *DRAGON!!*

"SO STARTLED WAS I BY THE UNEXPECTED SIGHT, THAT I LOST MY FOOTING, AND PLUNGED HEAD-LONG INTO THE VALLEY BELOW..."

LUCKILY THERE IS DENSE FOLIAGE BELOW ME! IF I CAN LAND JUST RIGHT...!

BUT, THE THICK UNDERGROWTH DID *MORE* THAN BREAK MY FALL! IT FINALLY REVEALED THE ANSWER TO THE STRANGE MYSTERY I HAD UNCOVERED!"

HIDDEN FROM SIGHT BY THIS DENSE UNDER-BRUSH ... A GLISTENING METAL SHAPE...LIKE SOMETHING NEVER BEFORE SEEN ON THE PLANET *EARTH!*

IT IS AS THOUGH IT HAS LAIN HERE ALL THESE CENTURIES... WAITING TO BE DISCOVERED BY.. THE *MANDARIN!*

"THEN, UPON ENTERING THE UNEARTHLY SHELL, I KNEW BEYOND ANY DOUBT THAT IT COULD ONLY BE *ONE THING*..."

IT IS A *VEHICLE* OF SOME SORT! A SHIP WHICH TRAVELS BETWEEN THE *PLANETS!*

4.

"TIME LOST ALL MEANING TO ME! I REMAINED WITHIN THE CHAMBER UNTIL I HAD PROBED ITS EVERY SECRET..."

WHEN I PUT THIS OBJECT OVER MY HEAD I SEEM TO HEAR *THOUGHTS!* IT IS SOME SORT OF A MENTAL-IMPULSE *LOG*... A RECORD OF THE ONE WHO FLEW THIS SHIP AGES AGO!

I AM *AXONN-KARR*, OF THE PLANET MAKLU-4! I AM EMBARKING ON A FLIGHT TO FIND NEW WORLDS! ...TO LEARN IF INTELLIGENT LIFE EXISTS IN ANY GALAXY OTHER THAN MINE!...!

"I LISTENED FOR HOURS...LEARNING OF THE WORLDS THAT AXONN-KARR HAD SEEN...SHARING HIS EVERY ADVENTURE, EVERY EXPERIENCE, THROUGH THE AGE-OLD MENTAL-IMPULSE LOG... AND THEN, HE TOLD OF FINDING... *EARTH!*"

"BUT, ONLY ON EARTH DID HE MEET DISASTER! FOR HIS FORM WAS NOT HUMAN...AND THOSE WHO SAW HIM, FEARED HIM...AND TRIED TO SLAY HIM!"

"FINALLY, THEY DROVE HIM OFF ...MORTALLY WOUNDED...TO THE HIDDEN CAVE WHEREIN HE PERISHED!"

THEN *THAT* WAS THE ORIGIN OF THE *DRAGON LEGEND* IN CHINA! THERE *WAS* SUCH A CREATURE ONCE...BUT NO ONE KNEW HE WAS AN INTELLIGENT BEING...FROM THE DISTANT STARS!

BUT NOW... ONE MORE THING REMAINS...I MUST FIND THE SOURCE OF THIS SHIP'S *POWER!*

"AND FIND IT I *DID!* A POWER SUCH AS EARTH HAS NEVER KNOWN! WITHIN TEN SMALL RINGS, WERE *GEMS* WHICH CONTAINED UNLIMITED *ENERGY!*"

THESE ARE WHAT, I SEEK!

"I TOOK THE RINGS FROM THE SLOWLY ROTTING CRAFT...KNOWING THAT THEY COULD MAKE ME THE MOST POWERFUL MAN IN ALL THE WORLD!"

THOSE TEN RINGS...HOLDING ENOUGH ENERGY TO DRIVE THAT HUGE SHIP BETWEEN GALAXIES, WILL MAKE ME MASTER OF EARTH!

5.

"I SPENT WEEKS... MONTHS... YEARS... OUTFITTING THE DESERTED CASTLE WHICH STOOD WITHIN THE VALLEY OF SPIRITS! EVERY TREASURE OF THE SPACE SHIP SOON FOUND A PLACE WITHIN THE GREAT STONE WALLS..."

NO MAN WILL INTERFERE WITH ME, FOR THIS VALLEY IS DREADED AND SHUNNED!

"HOUR AFTER HOUR I STUDIED THE ALIEN SCIENCE OF THE ONE CALLED AXONN-KARR, UNTIL I MASTERED IT!"

"AND THEN, I PUT THAT UNCANNY KNOWLEDGE TO USE...!"

AT LAST I UNDERSTAND THE TEN GEM RINGS OF MAKLU-4!

EACH ONE HAS A SEPARATE POWER WHICH I CAN NOW COMMAND! I SHALL WEAR THEM ON MY FINGERS... FOREVER!

"AGAIN IT STORMED, ON THE NIGHT I DONNED THE RINGS... JUST AS IT HAD STORMED ON THE NIGHT OF MY BIRTH!"

ANOTHER OMEN! I CANNOT FAIL!

"USING MY IRRESISTIBLE RINGS, IT WAS BUT THE WORK OF MINUTES TO COMPLETELY SUBJUGATE ENTIRE VILLAGES TO MY WILL!"

YOU WILL OBEY MY EVERY WHIM!

THE MASTER HAS SPOKEN!

ALL HAIL THE MANDARIN!

MIGHTIEST OF THE MIGHTY IS THE MANDARIN!

AND NOW, I AM READY TO EMBARK UPON MY PLAN OF WORLD CONQUEST! TONY STARK IS ALREADY SLAIN*... AND YOU, MY MOST POWERFUL FOE, SHALL LIKEWISE MEET HIS FATE!

HE'S EVEN MORE DANGEROUS ...MORE POWERFUL THAN I DREAMED! MY LIFE MEANS NOTHING... BUT HE MUST NOT BE ALLOWED TO USE HIS UNEARTHLY RINGS AGAINST MANKIND!

IF ONLY THERE WERE SOME WAY I COULD RECHARGE MY POWER TRANSISTORS!!

*SEE SUSPENSE #61..STAN.

AND NOW...FAREWELL! WHEN I MOVE THIS SWITCH, THE WHEEL YOU ARE FASTENED TO WILL BEGIN TO SPIN...FASTER AND FASTER... AND IT WILL NEVER STOP UNTIL IRON MAN BREATHES NO MORE!

ANTHONY, OLD BOY...IF YOU EVER THOUGHT FAST BEFORE... NOW'S THE TIME TO DO IT!

6.

THERE! IT IS DONE! AND, NOW THAT I HAVE ENERGIZED IT WITH MY POWER RING, NO FORCE ON EARTH CAN STOP IT!

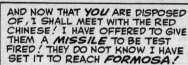

AND NOW THAT YOU ARE DISPOSED OF, I SHALL MEET WITH THE RED CHINESE! I HAVE OFFERED TO GIVE THEM A MISSILE TO BE TEST FIRED! THEY DO NOT KNOW I HAVE SET IT TO REACH FORMOSA!

WHEN IT EXPLODES THERE, IT IS SURE TO TRIGGER WORLD WAR III!

AND, AFTER BOTH THE DEMOCRACIES AND THE COMMUNISTS HAVE EXHAUSTED THEMSELVES, I SHALL STEP IN AND RULE THE EARTH!

HE MEANS IT! HE REALLY EXPECTS TO DO IT! BUT NOT WHILE IRON MAN LIVES!

APPLYING STEADY PRESSURE UPON A CONCEALED FINGER STUD, THE GOLDEN AVENGER CAUSES A DIAMOND-EDGED BLADE TO PROTRUDE FROM HIS IRON GLOVE, AND THEN...

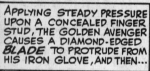

SNIP!

TITANIUM BONDS OR NOT, MY SPECIALLY-HONED DIAMOND EDGE BLADE CAN SLICE 'MOST ANYTHING! AND NOW, IF I CAN GET THE TITANIUM CORD TO TOUCH MY WRIST-POWER-PACK AT THE RIGHT SPOT....

AH, PERFECT! I MADE A SOLID ELECTRICAL CONTACT!

NOW, THE FASTER THE WHEEL TURNS, THE MORE IT WILL ENABLE ME TO RECHARGE MYSELF, JUST LIKE A TURNING BICYCLE WHEEL RECHARGES THE SMALL GENERATOR WHICH MAY BE ATTACHED!

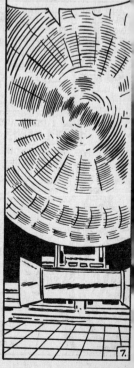

THIS SPEED WOULD HAVE FINISHED ANY ORDINARY HUMAN BEING... BUT IT IS MERELY CAUSING EVERY BIT OF TRANSISTORIZED STRENGTH TO FLOW BACK INTO MY MIGHTY IRON ARMOR! IN ANOTHER FEW SECONDS I'LL BE AT MY FIGHTING PEAK!!

7

NOW, BY APPLYING MY OWN ADDED STRENGTH, I'LL MAKE THE WHEEL TURN TOO FAST...UNTIL THE STRAIN SNAPS IT FROM ITS AXLE!

WHOOM!

NOT BAD FOR A FEW SECONDS' WORK! I DESTROYED THE WHEEL...SMASHED THROUGH THE CASTLE WALL...AND PROVED TO MYSELF THAT MY GALVANIZED ARMOR IS STILL THE GREATEST BODY-SHIELD EVER DESIGNED!

BUT, I HAVEN'T TIME TO WAIT FOR APPLAUSE RIGHT NOW!

I'VE GOT TO FIND THE MANDARIN...AND STOP HIS MISSILE FROM REACHING FORMOSA! BUT, SOMETHING TELLS ME IT ISN'T GONNA BE AS EASY AS I'M TRYING TO MAKE IT SOUND!

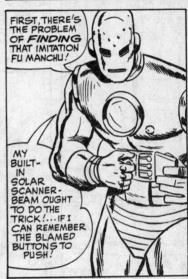

FIRST, THERE'S THE PROBLEM OF FINDING THAT IMITATION FU MANCHU!

MY BUILT-IN SOLAR SCANNER-BEAM OUGHT TO DO THE TRICK!...IF I CAN REMEMBER THE BLAMED BUTTONS TO PUSH!

THERE! THAT DID IT! NOW, ALL I'VE GOT TO DO IS FOLLOW THE SOUNDINGS OF EACH BLIP...WHICH ARE AUTOMATICALLY RECORDED AND ANALYZED BY MY MINIATURIZED PRINTED-CIRCUIT COMPUTER SYSTEM!

BOY! I'M BEGINNING TO SOUND LIKE SOME CORNY MAD SCIENTIST IN A GRADE B MOVIE!

THAT'S ONE OF THE HAZARDS OF BEING A LONE-WOLF TYPE OF ADVENTURER! AFTER A WHILE, YOU BEGIN TO TALK TO YOURSELF!

BUT, MINUTES LATER...

WELL, TALKING TIME'S OVER! THERE'S THE MISSILE...AND HERE I GO!

8.

MEANWHILE, THE MOST DANGEROUS MENACE EVER SPAWNED IN THE ORIENT WATCHES WITH GRIM SATISFACTION AS THE UNSUSPECTING RED MILITARY LEADERS PREPARE TO LAUNCH THE MANDARIN'S FATAL MISSILE...!

IF ITS PERFORMANCE PLEASES YOU, I CAN SUPPLY MANY MORE!

MAO TSE TUNG *HIMSELF* WILL PIN A MEDAL ON YOU! WITH YOUR HELP, WE SHALL CONQUER THE *WORLD*!

FOOL! THE RED CHINESE *TOO* SHALL GROVEL AT MY FEET!

FOUR SECONDS! THREE SECONDS! TWO SECONDS! ONE SECOND! *ZERO!*

IS IT NOT STRANGE THAT THE MANDARIN DOES NOT REMAIN TO OBSERVE THE FULL TEST?

NO! HE KNOWS IT WILL BE PERFECT! HE NEVER FAILS!

I MUST RETURN TO THE SAFETY OF MY CASTLE! WHEN THE MISSILE STRIKES FORMOSA, THE REDS WILL REALIZE I HAVE DECEIVED THEM! BUT THEN, THE *WAR* WILL BEGIN, AND IT WILL BE TOO LATE TO ALTER MY DESTINY!

BUT THE MANDARIN'S CONFIDENCE MIGHT BE SHAKEN A BIT, IF HE COULD SEE WHAT IS HAPPENING ABOVE...

MAKE IT! I'LL JUST HAVE TO FASTEN MY KNEE SUCTION CUPS, AND THEN...

THERE! THEY'LL HOLD ME SECURELY WHILE I ATTACH A MINIATURE *DISTORTER* TO THE MISSILE!

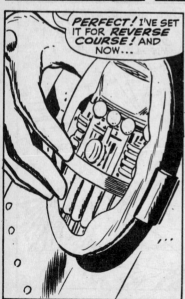

PERFECT! I'VE SET IT FOR *REVERSE COURSE!* AND NOW...

—I'LL GO AFTER THE MANDARIN WHILE MY PIGEON GOES HOME TO ROOST!

SECONDS LATER, TO THE AMAZEMENT OF ALL, THE AWESOME MISSILE RETURNS TO ITS POINT OF ORIGIN, AND...

RUN FOR YOUR LIVES!

WE'VE BEEN *BETRAYED!* THE MANDARIN IS A *TRAITOR!*

9.

THEN, AS A SILENTLY SPEEDING JET-CAR GLIDES TWO FEET OFF THE GROUND...

THERE ARE NO *TRAFFIC LIGHTS* BELOW, SO *THIS* WILL HAVE TO DO....!

THAT *BOULDER*...IT FELL IN MY PATH! CAN'T *STOP* IN TIME!

AND SO...

HOW DID IT *HAPPEN*?? WHAT MADE SO GIGANTIC AN OBJECT *FALL*??

JUST THAT LITTLE OL' IRON MAKER ...*ME*!

IRON MAN!

YOU JUST SAID THE MAGIC WORDS!

I DON'T KNOW *HOW* YOU ESCAPED MY WHEEL...BUT I'LL MAKE YOU WISH YOU *HADN'T*! MY FLAME RING WILL MELT YOU INTO MOLTEN NOTHINGNESS!

NOT A *CHANCE*, CHIN WHISKERS! IT'S GOT TO *HIT* ME FIRST... AND WITH MY TRANSISTORS WORKING AGAIN, I'M NOT EXACTLY A SITTING DUCK!

THEN, MOVING WITH SMOOTH, CALCULATED SPEED, THE GOLDEN AVENGER CLIPS A SMALL ELECTRO-BLASTER ONTO HIS MAGNETIC WRIST HOLDER...

IN CASE YOU FORGOT, MANDY... *I'VE* GOT A WEAPON OR TWO MYSELF!

BUT, THE FANTASTIC, UNEARTHLY POWER RINGS OF THE MANDARIN ARE MORE THAN EQUAL TO THEIR TASK! AT THE MERE FLICK OF A FINGER, HE LOOSES A CRACKLING, SNAPPING, THROBBING RAY WHICH MEETS IRON MAN'S ELECTRO-BLAST IN MID-AIR, NULLIFYING IT COMPLETELY!

BAH! YOU ARE FACING THE *MASTER*, NOW!

WHIZZTT!

I'VE GOT TO ADMIT IT... A PUSHOVER HE *ISN'T*!

10.

KEEP *BACK*, YOU LOW-BORN CLOD! I DO NOT DEIGN TO ENGAGE IN HAND-TO-HAND COMBAT WITH MY *INFERIORS*! THIS *POISON GAS* BLAST SHOULD SERVE TO DESTROY YOU!

NOT A CHANCE, LOUD-MOUTH! THIS IRON SUIT IS THE *DE LUXE* MODEL ...COMPLETE WITH BUILT-IN OXYGEN FILTERS! IT'S GOT EVERY-THING BUT BUCKET SEATS!

LOOKS LIKE HE'S GETTING SET TO HIT ME WITH *ANOTHER* RING! MAYBE *THIS* CAN STOP HIM IN TIME!

YOUR CRUDE DISPLAY OF TRANSISTOR-POWERED STRENGTH DOES NOT IMPRESS *ME*, IRON MAN!

NOT WHEN I CAN *BLIND* YOU WITH THE POWER OF *ONE* MERE RING!

WOW! HE'S NOT *KIDDIN'!* I CAN'T SEE A *THING!*

BUT, BLIND OR *NOT*, I CAN *STILL* TOSS THIS OVER-SIZED B-B IN THE DIRECTION YOU *HAD* BEEN IN...!

WHIZZZZZ

BAH! YOU ARE LUCKIER THAN YOU SUSPECT! I HAD PLANNED TO USE THIS *DISINTEGRATOR* RING ON *YOU*! BUT YOU FORCED ME TO WASTE IT ON THAT BOULDER! AND IT TAKES TWENTY MINUTES FOR IT TO RE-CHARGE!

THAT'S MIGHTY INTERESTING, FELLA... BUT I'VE GOT MY *OWN* TROUBLES!

YOUR FLIPPANT REMARKS WILL NOT HELP YOU *NOW*! THIS *GAS SOLIDIFIER* WILL KEEP *HARDENING* AROUND YOU UNTIL YOU ARE COMPLETELY ENCASED IN UNBREAKABLE CEMENT!

I'M *IN* FOR IT NOW! EVEN MY *REPELLOR* IS USELESS AGAINST IT!

BUT...AT THAT MOMENT...!

THERE! WE HAVE FOUND THE TRAITOR!

FIRE! LET HIM FEEL THE WRATH OF THE PEOPLE'S REPUBLIC!

BAKOOOO!

HEY! LOOKY WHO'S ARRIVING IN TIME! I'M SAVED BY YOUR OWN BUDDY BOYS!

THE FOOLS! WHY DO THEY FIRE AT ME??

I WAS HOPING YOU'D ASK! REMEMBER THAT LITTLE OL' MISSILE OF YOURS?? WELL..

...I COULDN'T BEAR TO SEE IT WASTED, SO I KINDA ARRANGED FOR IT TO GO BACK WHERE IT STARTED FROM!

I'VE UNDER-ESTIMATED YOU TOO OFTEN, IRON MAN...BUT I SHALL NEVER DO SO AGAIN!

A BEAM OF BLACK LIGHT! IT'S LIKE BEING PLUNGED INTO TOTAL DARKNESS!

THEN, BEFORE THE BLACK LIGHT CAN FADE, THE MYSTIFYING MANDARIN LEAPS UPON A LARGE FLAT ROCK, AND.. USING HIS JET RING FOR A POWER SOURCE, MAKES A VERIT-ABLE FLYING CARPET OF IT!

I MUST RETURN TO THE SAFETY OF MY CASTLE BEFORE I AM SEIZED!

THEN, BY THE TIME IRON MAN IS ABLE TO SEE AGAIN...

HE'S GONE! TOO MUCH OF A HEAD START FOR ME TO FOLLOW! I'D BETTER CUT OUT, TOO, WHILE I STILL CAN!

A FEW HOURS LATER, AS A SPEEDY MILITARY JET TRANS-PORT WINGS OVER THE PACIFIC...

NEVER EXPECTED A GUY LIKE YOU ABOARD!

GUESS YOU'RE RIGHT, DAVE! BUT I CAN'T WAIT TO GET HOME AND TELL MY SON WHO WE HAD AS A PASSENGER TODAY!

BETTER TAKE A PICTURE OF 'IM, BILL...OR THE KID'LL NEVER BELIEVE YOU!

COOL IT, BILL! LET 'IM SLEEP! HE LOOKS BUSHED!

AND, MILES AWAY, IN A LONELY CASTLE IN THE HEART OF FAR-OFF CHINA, ONE OF THE WORLD'S MOST DANGEROUS MORTALS SITS AND BROODS...

I SHALL NEVER REST UNTIL IRON MAN IS DESTROYED! I HAVE NEVER FAILED BEFORE.. I SHALL NOT FAIL NEXT TIME!

BUT, FOR NOW, WAIT TILL YOU SEE THE THRILLS AND SURPRISES AWAITING THE GOLDEN AVENGER WHEN HE RETURNS HOME! SEE YOU NEXT ISH!

The End

12.

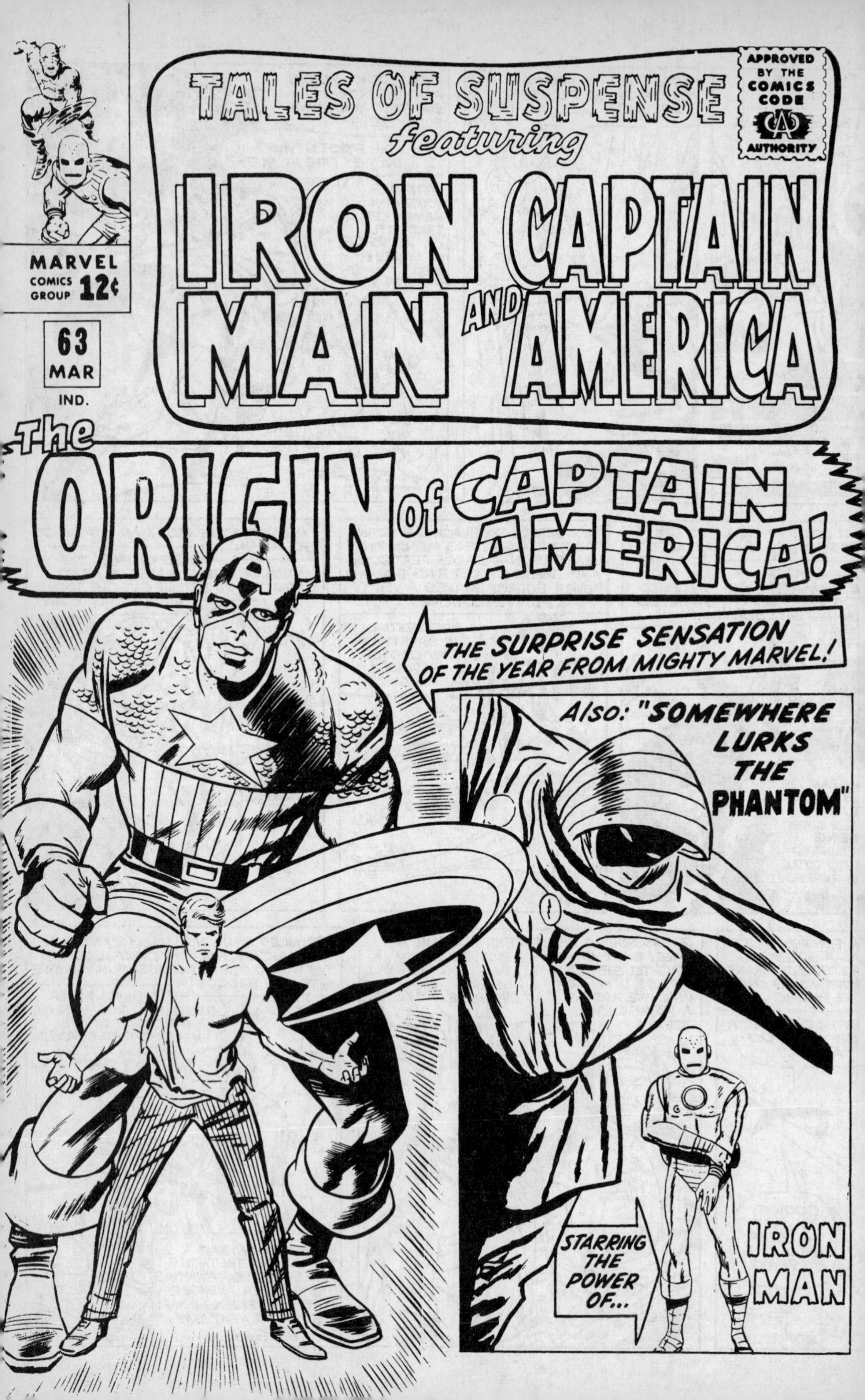

MARVEL COMICS GROUP 12¢
63 MAR
IND.
APPROVED BY THE COMICS CODE AUTHORITY
TALES OF SUSPENSE featuring
IRON MAN AND CAPTAIN AMERICA
The ORIGIN of CAPTAIN AMERICA!
THE SURPRISE SENSATION OF THE YEAR FROM MIGHTY MARVEL!
Also: "SOMEWHERE LURKS THE PHANTOM"
STARRING THE POWER OF...
IRON MAN

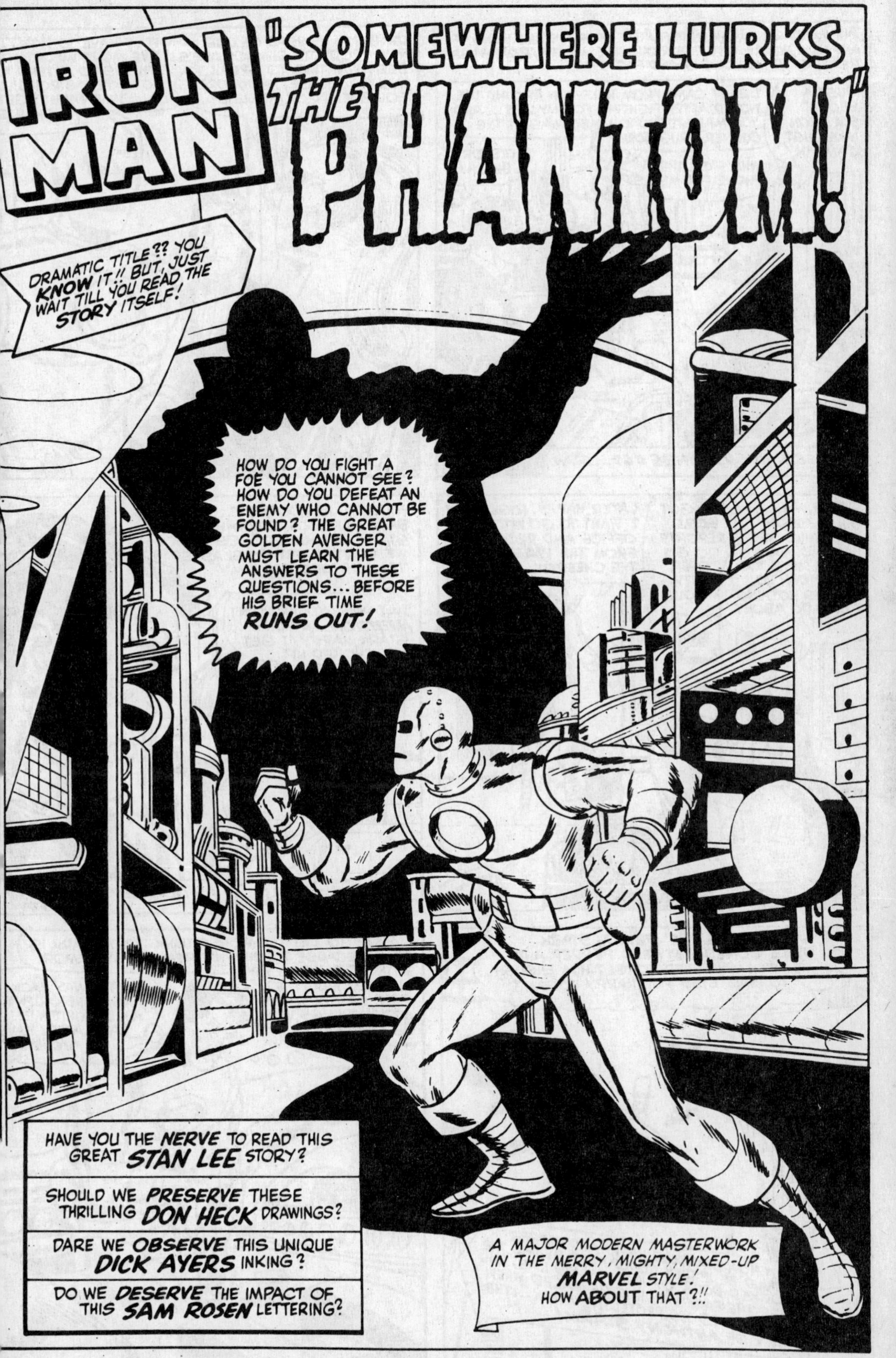
IRON MAN
"SOMEWHERE LURKS THE PHANTOM!"
DRAMATIC TITLE?? YOU KNOW IT!! BUT, JUST WAIT TILL YOU READ THE STORY ITSELF!
HOW DO YOU FIGHT A FOE YOU CANNOT SEE? HOW DO YOU DEFEAT AN ENEMY WHO CANNOT BE FOUND? THE GREAT GOLDEN AVENGER MUST LEARN THE ANSWERS TO THESE QUESTIONS... BEFORE HIS BRIEF TIME RUNS OUT!
HAVE YOU THE NERVE TO READ THIS GREAT STAN LEE STORY?
SHOULD WE PRESERVE THESE THRILLING DON HECK DRAWINGS?
DARE WE OBSERVE THIS UNIQUE DICK AYERS INKING?
DO WE DESERVE THE IMPACT OF THIS SAM ROSEN LETTERING?
A MAJOR MODERN MASTERWORK IN THE MERRY, MIGHTY, MIXED-UP MARVEL STYLE! HOW ABOUT THAT?!!

THE MANDARIN HAS BEEN DEFEATED...FOR THE TIME BEING!* AND NOW, WEARY, BUT VICTORIOUS, THE MIGHTY *IRON MAN* RETURNS TO HIS LONG ISLAND FACTORY...

JUST A SECOND, SIR! IRON MAN JUST CAME IN!

I JUST CAME FROM HALF-WAY AROUND THE WORLD, AFTER FIGHTING FOR MY LIFE...AND YOU MAKE IT SOUND LIKE I WAS AT THE CORNER DRUGSTORE!

WHO'S ON THE PHONE FOR ME?

IT'S DR. BIRCH!

* AS SEEN IN *SUSPENSE* #62...STAN.

DR. BIRCH IS HEAD OF OUR NEW PRODUCTS DIVISION! HE'S BEEN WANTING TO SPEAK TO YOU ABOUT GETTING MORE EQUIPMENT FOR HIS LAB!

IT'LL HAVE TO *WAIT!* I'VE MORE IMPORTANT THINGS TO ATTEND TO NOW! TELL BIRCH I'LL CALL HIM WHEN I GET A CHANCE!

SORRY, MR. BIRCH! IRON MAN WILL GET BACK TO YOU LATER! HE'S TOO BUSY NOW! NO, THERE'S NOTHING I CAN DO ABOUT IT!

LATER, HAPPY! RIGHT NOW I WANT TO GO INTO MY OFFICE AND RECOVER FROM THE *WARMTH* OF THE CHEERFUL WELCOME I GOT FROM YOU BOTH!

I'VE GOT SOME REPORTS TO GO OVER WITH YOU!

WHAT DID HE *EXPECT*...A BRASS BAND? AFTER THE WAY HE LET MR. STARK GET KILLED,* HE'S LUCKY WE DON'T SHORT HIS BLASTED TRANSISTORS FOR HIM!

I..I WISH YOU WOULDN'T *MENTION* ANTHONY STARK, HAPPY! I GET ALL CHOKED UP WHEN I EVEN *THINK* OF HIM!

* AS DESCRIBED IN *SUSPENSE* #61...STAN.

EVEN THOUGH HE'S *DEAD*, STARK *STILL* COMES BETWEEN PEPPER AND ME! WILL SHE EVER FORGET HIM ENOUGH TO HAVE EYES FOR HAPPY HOGAN?

BUT, HOW STARTLED HAPPY AND PEPPER WOULD BE IF THEY COULD PEER BEHIND THE LOCKED DOOR OF IRON MAN'S LAB, AND SEE THE FACE WHICH IS REVEALED WHEN HE REMOVES HIS PROTECTIVE MASK...THE FACE OF *ANTHONY STARK*!

I *HAD* TO LET THE WORLD THINK TONY STARK IS DEAD, BECAUSE I COULDN'T REMOVE MY ARMOR WITHOUT CAUSING MY INJURED HEART TO STOP BEATING! BUT *NOW*, THINGS WILL BE DIFFERENT!

ON THE WAY BACK FROM THE ORIENT, AN IDEA HIT ME! AT LAST I HAVE MY *ANSWER*!

THE ENTIRE THING HINGES UPON MY MODIFYING A MASTER TRANSISTOR, AND TRIPLING ITS POWER OUTPUT!

IF IT WORKS...AS I EXPECT IT TO...IT SHOULD ALLOW ME TO BREATHE FREELY EVEN WITHOUT THE AID OF MY IRON ARMOR!

ALL I'LL NEED TO WEAR IS MY TRANSISTORIZED CHEST DEVICE...WHICH CAN BE EASILY CONCEALED UNDER ORDINARY STREET CLOTHES!

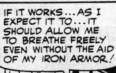

THERE! IT'S FINISHED!

AND NOW FOR THE TEST! IF IT WORKS, ANTHONY STARK WILL LIVE AGAIN!

AND, IF IT FAILS...BOTH STARK AND IRON MAN WILL HAVE BREATHED THEIR LAST!

ALL THAT REMAINS TO BE DONE IS TO REMOVE MY ARMOR...

IF..IF I FAIL...LET ME DIE WITH VALOR!

THERE'S NO TURNING BACK NOW! EVERYTHING DEPENDS UPON THE MASTER TRANSISTOR!

IT'S WORKING SO FAR! BUT... WILL IT CONTINUE TO KEEP MY HEART BEATING ??

THE FIRST FIVE MINUTES ARE CRUCIAL! IF I SURVIVE THAT LONG...I'LL HAVE SUCCEEDED!

I DID IT! I PASSED THE TIME LIMIT!

TONY STARK CAN LIVE AGAIN!

3

AND SO, A SCANT FEW MINUTES LATER...

WELL, THERE'S NO TIME LIKE THE PRESENT...!

SO! WHILE THE BOSS IS AWAY, YOU TWO JUST SIT AROUND LOAFING, EH? TSK, TSK!

MR. STARK! B-BUT YOU'RE DEAD!

IT'S HIM! BUT...IT CAN'T BE! I...I MUST BE GOING MAD! OHHH!

I DIDN'T REALIZE IT WOULD BE SUCH A SHOCK TO HER! QUICK, HAPPY... GET THE SMELLING SALTS!

YEAH, BOSS.. SURE!

THE WAY HE'S LOOKING AT HER! HE LOVES HER, TOO! I SHOULD HAVE GUESSED!

SECONDS LATER...

I'VE NO RIGHT TO STAND IN THEIR WAY! IF NOT FOR ME, PEPPER MIGHT MARRY HAPPY! I DON'T DARE MARRY... BECAUSE OF MY INJURED HEART!

PEPPER MUST NEVER KNOW THAT I LOVE HER, TOO! THE ONLY WAY I CAN PROVE MY LOVE, IS TO GIVE HER UP! TO LET HER FIND A NEW LIFE WITH HAPPY!

BOSS..WHERE DID YOU COME FROM?

THAT CAN WAIT! FIRST, I WANT TO TELL YOU...

I'M ENGAGED TO BE MARRIED!

WHAT?!!

GREAT! NOW PEP WILL HAVE TO FORGET HIM!

I WANTED TO KEEP IT SECRET! SHE'S A DEBUTANTE FROM BOSTON! THAT'S WHERE I'VE BEEN THESE WEEKS!

THAT'S WHY I DIDN'T KNOW I WAS REPORTED DEAD! WE WERE ON HER FAMILY'S YACHT... WITHOUT ANY NEWSPAPERS!

WITHIN SECONDS, THE UNEXPECTED NEWS SPREADS LIKE WILDFIRE...

ATTENTION! ATTENTION! ALL PERSONNEL! MR. STARK HAS RETURNED! HE'S ALIVE! WE REPEAT... ANTHONY STARK IS ALIVE!

HEY! DIDJA HEAR THAT? THE BOSS IS ALIVE!

IT FIGURES! HE WAS JUST TOO RICH TO DIE!

THAT'S GREAT NEWS ABOUT THE BOSS, SAM! NOW, IRON MAN WON'T BE ABLE TO ACT LIKE HE OWNS THE PLACE!

I DUNNO, PETE! STARK HIMSELF ALWAYS ACTS LIKE HE CAN'T GET ALONG WITHOUT THAT SHELL-HEADED CREEP!

4.

HELLO, BIRCH! HOW HAVE YOU BEEN?

FINE, THANKS, MR. STARK! I'VE BEEN TRYING TO DISCUSS SOME NEW EQUIPMENT WITH IRON MAN, BUT NOW THAT *YOU'RE* HERE...

SORRY, BIRCH! I'VE MORE URGENT THINGS TO DEAL WITH NOW! CHECK WITH ME NEXT WEEK!

AND SO, THE GREATEST PRODUCTION GENIUS OF HIS TIME CONDUCTS A THOROUGH TOUR OF HIS SPRAWLING MUNITIONS FACTORY, WHILE A PART OF HIS BRAIN CONCENTRATES ON STILL ANOTHER SUBJECT...

ALL OUR OPERATIONS ARE ON SCHEDULE, SIR! OUR QUOTA HAS BEEN MET PERFECTLY!

GOOD! GOOD!

I WONDER IF I'M DOING THE RIGHT THING? WHAT IF PEPPER DOESN'T REALLY *LOVE* HAPPY? WHO AM *I* TO DECIDE THEY SHOULD MARRY??

AND YET, NOW THAT SHE BELIEVES I'M ENGAGED, SHE'S BEHAVING *DIFFERENTLY* TOWARDS HAPPY! THEY *DO* SEEM IN LOVE!

OH, PEPPER... MY DARLING! IF ONLY THAT COULD BE *MY* ARM YOU'RE HOLDING!

BUT, YOU MUST NEVER KNOW HOW MUCH I TRULY LOVE YOU!

BUT NOW, BEFORE YOU START THINKING YOU BOUGHT A *LOVE* MAGAZINE BY MISTAKE, WE CHANGE OUR SCENE TO ANOTHER PART OF THE HUGE FACTORY...

HOW QUIET EVERYTHING IS! NO ONE SUSPECTS THAT WITHIN MINUTES, THE *PHANTOM* WILL STRIKE!

ALL I NEED DO IS PLANT THIS CAMOUFLAGED TIME BOMB IN THE RIGHT PLACE, AND THEN FADE BACK INTO THE SHADOWS!

THUS, LESS THAN TEN MINUTES LATER...

A FLASH FIRE... AT THE MISSILES TESTING SECTION! I'D BETTER GET RIGHT THERE... AS *IRON MAN!*

IT'S A CLEAR CASE OF *SABOTAGE!* EVERYTHING IN THIS SECTOR IS COMPLETELY FIREPROOFED! ONLY A HIGH-INTENSITY *EXPLOSIVE* COULD HAVE DONE THIS!

LOOKS LIKE A JOB CUT OUT FOR YOU, IRON MAN! A PHANTOM SABOTEUR!

5.

WHERE'S IRON MAN *GOING?* HE'LL BE ROASTED ALIVE!

YOU KIDDIN'?? THAT ARMOR OF HIS COULD PROTECT HIM AGAINST ANYTHING SHORT OF AN ATOM BOMB!

THIS IS WHAT I'M LOOKING FOR! A STILL INTACT REMNANT OF THE ORIGINAL SABOTAGE DEVICE!

IT'S ONE OF MY *OWN* COMPONENT PARTS! BUT, HOW COULD THE SABOTEUR HAVE GOTTEN HOLD OF IT, UNLESS...??

IF MY SUSPICIONS ARE CORRECT, THE PHANTOM SABOTEUR IS CERTAIN TO STRIKE *AGAIN!*...AND HE'LL USE EVERY RUSE TO PREVENT ME FROM STOPPING HIM!

AND, IT SEEMS THAT THE GOLDEN AVENGER'S SUSPICIONS *ARE* CORRECT, FOR...IN THE DAYS THAT FOLLOW...

THE FOURTH SERIOUS MISHAP IN FOUR DAYS!

I THREW THE SWITCH...AND THE CABLES BLEW! THE CIRCUIT'S BEEN *TAMPERED* WITH!

BUT, RUNNING A MUNITIONS FACTORY IS NOT A SIMPLE JOB! *MANY* PEOPLE ARE CONCERNED WITH WHAT GOES ON THERE!...PEOPLE SUCH AS *THESE*...

AS COMMANDING GENERAL OF THIS SECTOR, I'LL SEND MY *TROOPS* IN IF THE ACCIDENTS DON'T STOP!

I WON'T PERMIT MEMBERS OF MY UNION TO WORK IN A PLANT WHICH IS SO *UNSAFE!*

IF STARK CAN'T STOP THOSE OUTRAGES, CONGRESS WILL AWARD OUR DEFENSE CONTRACTS TO *ANOTHER* COMPANY!

AND, FULLY AWARE OF THE SERIOUSNESS OF THE SITUATION, ONE MAN WORKS AROUND THE CLOCK TO CATCH THE PHANTOM...

I DARE NOT REST FOR A MINUTE!

THERE'S NO TELLING WHERE OR WHEN THE PHANTOM WILL STRIKE NEXT! BUT, WHENEVER IT IS, *IRON MAN* MUST BE READY! WE CAN'T TAKE MANY MORE "ACCIDENTS"!

WAIT! WHAT'S THAT MOVING ALONG THE RAMP AHEAD? IT'S A HUMAN FORM!

AN INTRUDER! IN A COSTUME AND CAPE! IT MUST BE THE *PHANTOM!* BUT, WHY THE CORNY GET-UP?

BLAST THESE HEAVY CLANKING *BOOTS* OF MINE! HE *HEARD* ME! HE'S TURNING TAIL!

BUT, IN HIS EAGERNESS, IRON MAN HAS THROWN CAUTION TO THE WINDS, AND SO...

HE RIGGED UP A BOOBY TRAP FOR ME

...AND I BLUNDERED RIGHT INTO IT!

LUCKILY, NO SIMPLE EXPLOSIVE DEVICE CAN SERIOUSLY AFFECT MY TRANSISTOR-POWERED ARMOR...

...BUT, IN THE TIME IT TOOK ME TO REGAIN MY BALANCE AND MAKE MY WAY THROUGH THE SMOKE, THE PHANTOM HAS VANISHED!

IRON MAN! HAVE YOU SEEN MR. STARK? THERE'S A UNION DELEGATION WAITING FOR HIM!

THANKS, BILL! I'LL FIND THE BOSS AND TELL HIM!

SO...MINUTES LATER...

WHAT DO YOU WANT TO SEE ME ABOUT, ADAMS?

THESE ACCIDENTS AT YOUR FACTORY! YOU HAVEN'T BEEN ABLE TO CATCH THE PHANTOM YET!

I CAN'T ALLOW THE LIVES OF OUR UNION WORKERS TO BE ENDANGERED! EITHER YOU FIND A WAY TO CATCH THE PHANTOM AND END THESE ACCIDENTS, OR WE'LL CALL A STRIKE!

WE'LL GIVE YOU 24 HOURS... AND THAT'S ALL!

THEN, AFTER THE UNION DELEGATION HAS LEFT...

I DON'T BLAME THEM FOR THEIR CONCERN, BUT A STRIKE WOULD RUIN ME!

IT WOULD HALT MY MISSILE CONSTRUCTION, CAUSING ME TO LOSE MY DEFENSE DEPARTMENT CONTRACTS! I MUST STOP THE PHANTOM... SOMEHOW!!

7.

ONCE AGAIN, THE MIGHTY GOLDEN AVENGER PATROLS EVERY INCH OF HIS VAST, COMPLEX MUNITIONS FACTORY... THOUGH HIS LIMBS ARE ACHING FROM LACK OF REST, AND HIS HEAD IS THROBBING FROM THE OVERLONG WEARING OF HIS IRON MASK...!

IF ONLY I HAD SOME CLUE TO HIS *IDENTITY*! BUT, THE PHANTOM COULD BE ALMOST *ANYBODY*!

HAH! ANOTHER 24 HOURS AND THE *STRIKE* WILL BE CALLED! THEN, THIS WHOLE INDUSTRIAL EMPIRE WILL COLLAPSE AROUND THE EARS OF STARK AND IRON MAN, AND THE *PHANTOM* WILL HAVE *WON*!

MY BUILT-IN RADAR-TYPE DETECTOR IS BEGINNING TO TINGLE! THAT MEANS THERE IS *SOMEONE* NEAR ME... SOMEONE WHO MUST BE LURKING IN THE SHADOWS!!

THAT CAN ONLY BE... THE ONE I SEEK... THE *PHANTOM*!

UP AHEAD! I *HEARD* SOMETHING

GOT YOU!!

UHHH!

YOU'RE A PRETTY BIG MAN WHEN YOU'RE TACKLIN' AN ORDINARY JOE LIKE *ME*! TOO BAD YOU CAN'T DO AS GOOD AGAINST THE *PHANTOM*!

HAPPY! BUT... WHAT ARE *YOU* DOING, SKULKING AROUND HERE IN THE DARK? HOW DO I KNOW *YOU'RE* NOT T SABOTEUR

COOL IT, YOU WALKIN' JUNK PILE! I WAS LOOKIN' FOR THE PHANTOM.... TO HELP MR. STARK... LIKE YOU SHOULD BE DOIN'... AND THEN... HEY!! UP THERE!!

SOMEONE RUNNING ALONG THE CATWALK! IT'S HIM!

SO, YOU FOUND ME! WELL, LOOK AT ME, YOU FOOLS! THIS IS THE LAST CHANCE YOU'LL GET!!

HE'S THROWING SOMETHING!

TAKE COVER!! IF IT'S A BOMB, WE'RE COOKED!!

HOLD IT!! IT'S TOO LATE TO RUN! IF I CAN CATCH IT, I'LL SMOTHER IT WITH MY IRON GLOVE!

ALL RIGHT, HAPPY! NOW YOU CAN TAKE OFF! THIS IS JUST BETWEEN THE PHANTOM AND ME FROM HERE ON IN!

HE RACED THROUGH HERE! OUR ELECTRONIC NERVE CENTER IS BEHIND THIS DOOR! I CAN'T GIVE HIM TIME TO DAMAGE IT!

RIP!

DON'T..SQUEEZE..THAT.. TRIGGER!

YOU!!

YOU'RE TOO LATE, IRON MAN! THERE'S NO WAY YOU CAN STOP ME FROM COMPLETELY DESTROYING THIS ENTIRE CONTROL CENTER!!

9.

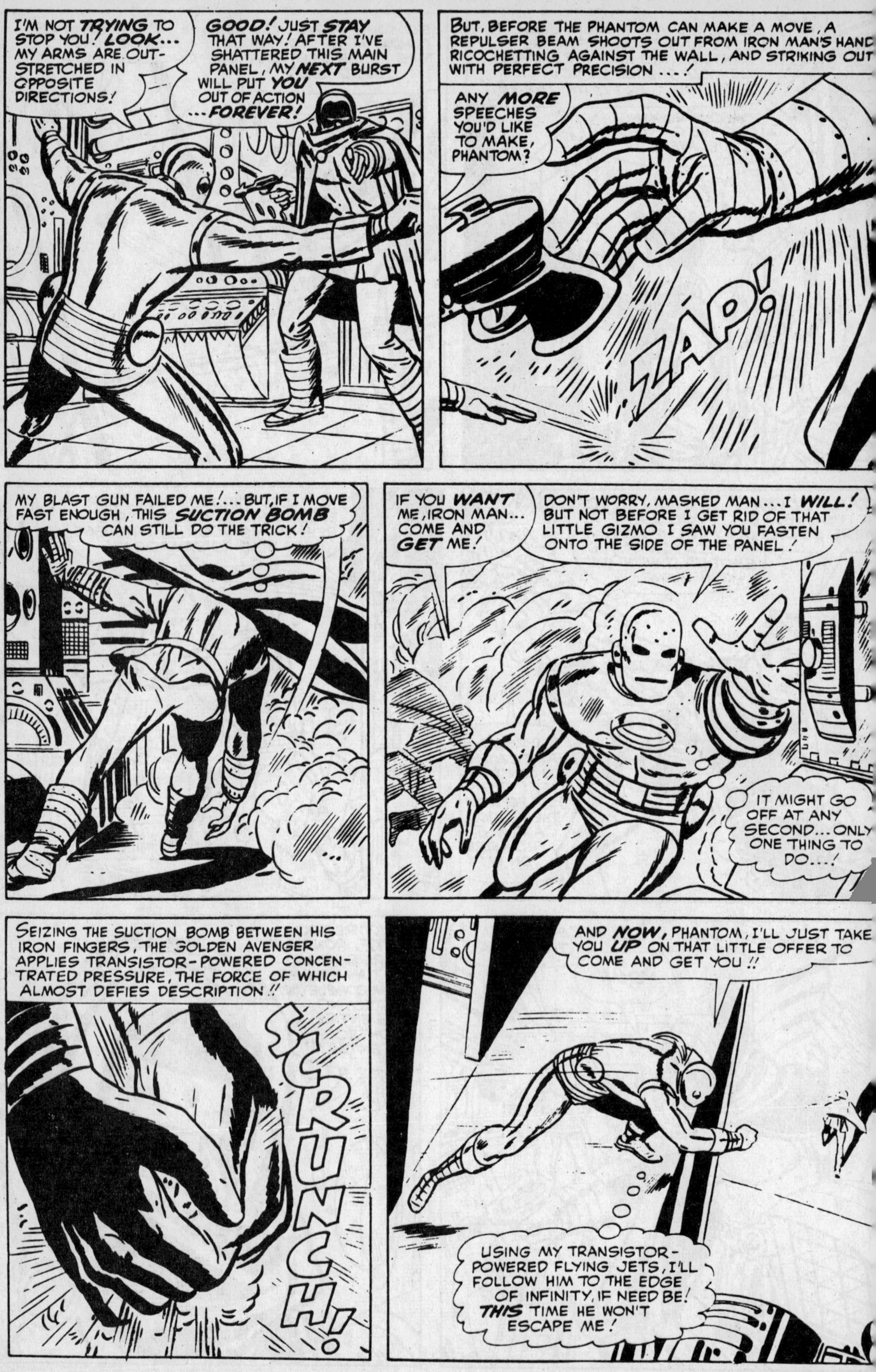
I'M NOT TRYING TO STOP YOU! LOOK... MY ARMS ARE OUT-STRETCHED IN OPPOSITE DIRECTIONS!
GOOD! JUST STAY THAT WAY! AFTER I'VE SHATTERED THIS MAIN PANEL, MY NEXT BURST WILL PUT YOU OUT OF ACTION ...FOREVER!
BUT, BEFORE THE PHANTOM CAN MAKE A MOVE, A REPULSER BEAM SHOOTS OUT FROM IRON MAN'S HAND RICOCHETTING AGAINST THE WALL, AND STRIKING OUT WITH PERFECT PRECISION ...!
ANY MORE SPEECHES YOU'D LIKE TO MAKE, PHANTOM?
ZAP!
MY BLAST GUN FAILED ME!... BUT, IF I MOVE FAST ENOUGH, THIS SUCTION BOMB CAN STILL DO THE TRICK!
IF YOU WANT ME, IRON MAN... COME AND GET ME!
DON'T WORRY, MASKED MAN... I WILL! BUT NOT BEFORE I GET RID OF THAT LITTLE GIZMO I SAW YOU FASTEN ONTO THE SIDE OF THE PANEL!
IT MIGHT GO OFF AT ANY SECOND... ONLY ONE THING TO DO...!
SEIZING THE SUCTION BOMB BETWEEN HIS IRON FINGERS, THE GOLDEN AVENGER APPLIES TRANSISTOR-POWERED CONCENTRATED PRESSURE, THE FORCE OF WHICH ALMOST DEFIES DESCRIPTION!!
SCRUNCH!
AND NOW, PHANTOM, I'LL JUST TAKE YOU UP ON THAT LITTLE OFFER TO COME AND GET YOU!!
USING MY TRANSISTOR-POWERED FLYING JETS, I'LL FOLLOW HIM TO THE EDGE OF INFINITY, IF NEED BE! THIS TIME HE WON'T ESCAPE ME!

HE'S ENTERING OUR PROTOTYPE MOON MISSILE! LOOKS AS THOUGH HE'S DETERMINED TO MAKE A FIGHT OF IT TO THE VERY END!

YOUR POWER JETS WON'T HELP YOU IN *HERE*, IRON MAN! THERE ARE TOO MANY GIRDERS AND BRACES TO ALLOW YOU TO FLY!

HE'S *RIGHT!* AND, WITH MY HEAVY ARMOR, I CAN'T CLIMB NEARLY AS FAST AS HE CAN!

ALSO, I'M TOO *HEAVY!* AS I REACH THE THINNER BRACES UP ABOVE, MY VERY WEIGHT MAY CRACK THEM, DAMAGING THE MISSILE!

ALL RIGHT, PHANTOM! YOU WIN THIS ROUND! I'M NOT CLIMBING UP ANY HIGHER!

BUT YOU CAN'T ESCAPE! I'LL BE WAITING BELOW!

GOOD! HE'S *GONE!* HE DOESN'T KNOW THAT I CAN GET AWAY IN THE *CAPSULE* ATOP THIS ROCKET... WHILE HE'S FUTILELY WAITING ON THE GROUND BELOW!

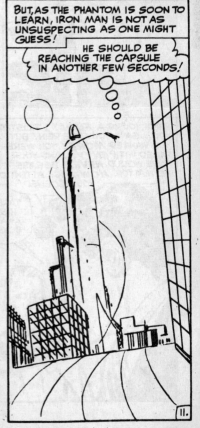

BUT, AS THE PHANTOM IS SOON TO LEARN, IRON MAN IS NOT AS UNSUSPECTING AS ONE MIGHT GUESS!

HE SHOULD BE REACHING THE CAPSULE IN ANOTHER FEW SECONDS!

11.

IT'S NOT A TRICK! HE ISN'T FOLLOWING! THAT MEANS I CAN ESCAPE *EASILY!*

THIS IS THE FIRST MISSILE IN WHICH THE CAPSULE IS ABLE TO FLY INDEPENDENTLY OF THE MAIN ROCKET...AS AN ADDED SAFETY FACTOR FOR THE PILOT!

BUT...WHAT'S *WRONG?* THE CONTROLS AREN'T RESPONDING!! THE CAPSULE IS SHAKING LOOSE! NO! *NO!*

IT'S *IRON MAN!* HE *DID* TRICK ME! HE FLEW UP HERE FROM THE *OUTSIDE!*

HE FREED THE CAPSULE! HE'S BROKEN THE CONTROL WIRES! I'M *HELPLESS!*

DON'T BE IMPATIENT! PHANTOM! YOU *WANTED* A RIDE, SO YOU'RE *GETTING* ONE!

I BELIEVE YOU BOYS HAVE BEEN *LOOKING* FOR THIS GUY! WELL, HERE HE *IS!*

THE PHANTOM!

GRAB 'IM!

NOW I'D BETTER GET THIS CAPSULE BACK AND BECOME *TONY STARK* AGAIN ON THE DOUBLE!

MINUTES LATER, A SUAVE, RELAXED ANTHONY STARK FACES THE NOW-DEFEATED PHANTOM...

BIRCH?! WHY, MAN?? WHY *YOU??*

I *HATED* YOU, STARK! YOU, AND IRON MAN! YOU TWO ARE THE GLAMOR BOYS HERE...NO ONE PAYS ANY ATTENTION TO *ME!*

I COULDN'T EVEN GET TO *SPEAK* TO YOU WHEN I WANTED TO! IT WAS ALWAYS "LATER, BIRCH!" OR "WHEN I GET THE TIME, BIRCH!" I WANTED TO BE *NOTICED!*

BIRCH, YOU'RE A *FOOL!* I TRUSTED YOU...GAVE YOU FREE REIN! BUT YOU WANTED *MORE!* YOU WERE FILLED WITH *ENVY*...AND YOUR TYPE WOULD *NEVER* BE SATISFIED, NO MATTER *HOW* MUCH ATTENTION YOU RECEIVED!

TAKE HIM AWAY, BOYS!

BOSS, IS IT OKAY IF I USE ONE OF YOUR CARS? PEPPER AND I ARE GONNA DO THE TOWN!

SURE, KIDS...HAVE A BALL! YOU DESERVE IT FOR THE WAY YOU PITCHED IN DURING MY ABSENCE!

THANK YOU, MR. STARK!

WELL, I ACCOMPLISHED WHAT I WANTED! PEPPER HAS GIVEN ME UP BECAUSE OF MY "ENGAGEMENT"! NOW, HAPPY IS FREE TO TRY TO WIN HER FOR HIMSELF! THE PHANTOM IS CAPTURED...AND EVERYTHING'S FINE!

SO, WHY IS MY HEART SO HEAVY? WHY DOES THE NIGHT SEEM SO BLEAK...AND ENDLESS..??

THUS, WE LEAVE ONE OF THE WEALTHIEST MEN IN THE WORLD...ONE OF THE MOST GLAMOROUS BACHELORS OF ALL TIME! A MAN WITH THE WORLD AT HIS FEET... AND A TRAGIC SECRET HE CAN NEVER SHARE WHICH HAUNTS HIS SOUL.!!

The End

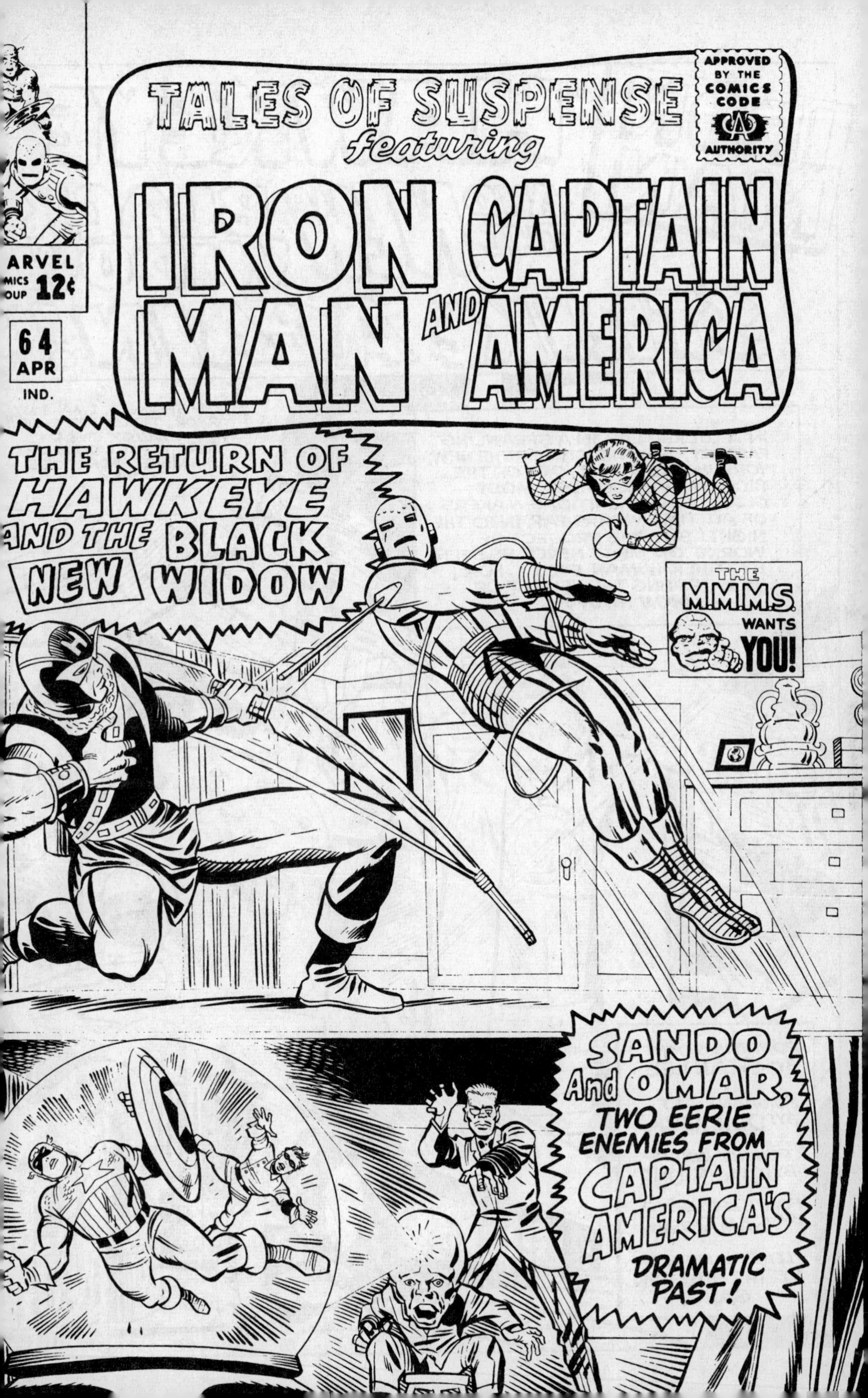

TALES OF SUSPENSE
featuring
IRON MAN AND CAPTAIN AMERICA
APPROVED BY THE COMICS CODE AUTHORITY
MARVEL COMICS GROUP 12¢
64 APR
IND.
THE RETURN OF HAWKEYE AND THE NEW BLACK WIDOW
THE M.M.M.S. WANTS YOU!
SANDO And OMAR, TWO EERIE ENEMIES FROM CAPTAIN AMERICA'S DRAMATIC PAST!

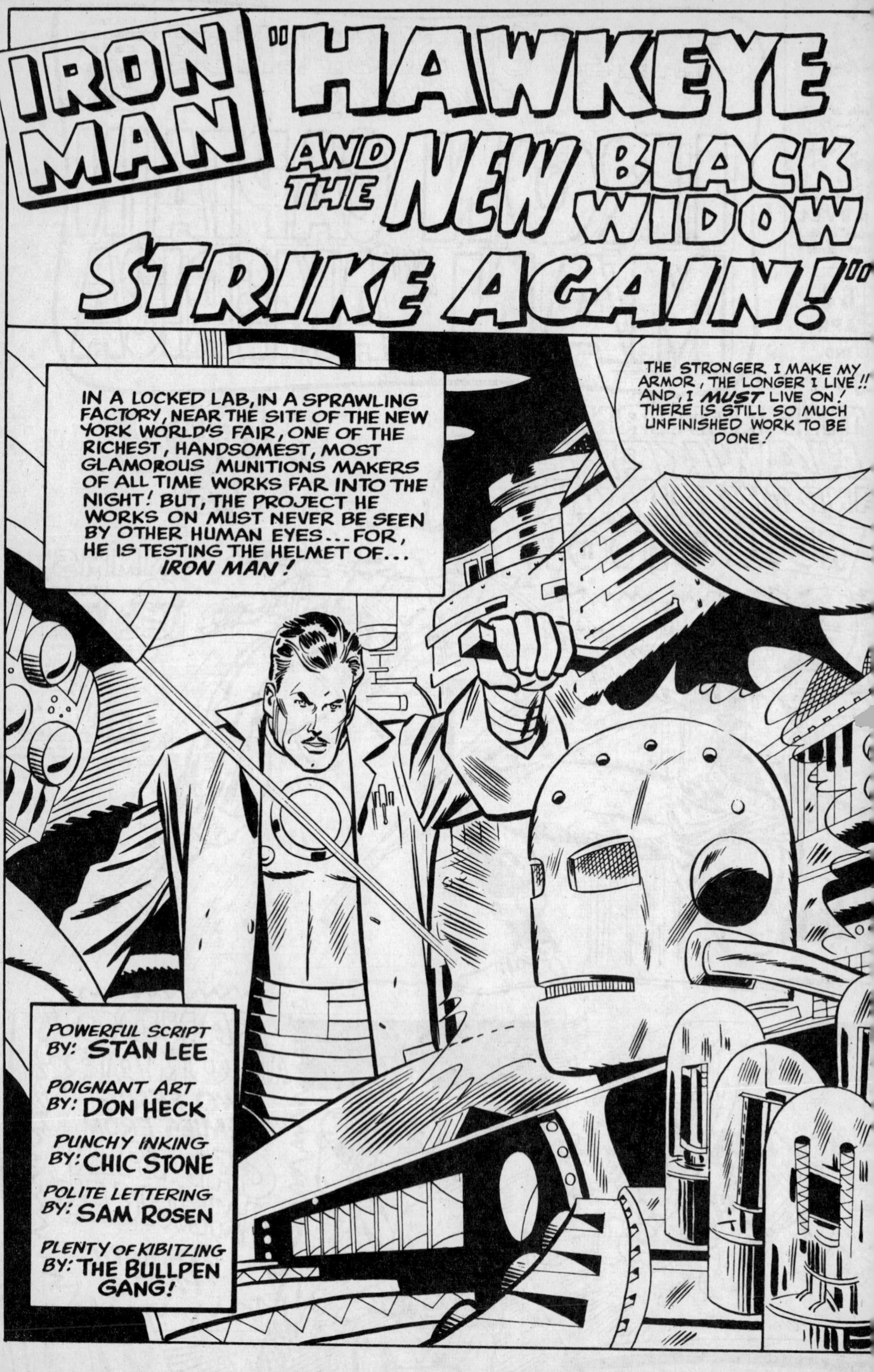
IRON MAN
"HAWKEYE AND THE NEW BLACK WIDOW STRIKE AGAIN!"
IN A LOCKED LAB, IN A SPRAWLING FACTORY, NEAR THE SITE OF THE NEW YORK WORLD'S FAIR, ONE OF THE RICHEST, HANDSOMEST, MOST GLAMOROUS MUNITIONS MAKERS OF ALL TIME WORKS FAR INTO THE NIGHT! BUT, THE PROJECT HE WORKS ON MUST NEVER BE SEEN BY OTHER HUMAN EYES... FOR, HE IS TESTING THE HELMET OF... IRON MAN!
THE STRONGER I MAKE MY ARMOR, THE LONGER I LIVE!! AND, I MUST LIVE ON! THERE IS STILL SO MUCH UNFINISHED WORK TO BE DONE!
POWERFUL SCRIPT BY: STAN LEE
POIGNANT ART BY: DON HECK
PUNCHY INKING BY: CHIC STONE
POLITE LETTERING BY: SAM ROSEN
PLENTY OF KIBITZING BY: THE BULLPEN GANG!

BUT, EVEN AS THE GOLDEN AVENGER LABORS IN HIS LAB, A STRANGELY SILENT FEMALE FORM MOVES THROUGH THE SHADOWY CITY STREETS LIKE A DARK WRAITH...

I HAVE WAITED SO LONG... SO VERY LONG... FOR THIS MOMENT!!

WITHOUT EVEN BREAKING HER STRIDE, SHE APPROACHES THE WALL OF A TOWERING APARTMENT HOUSE, AND GRACEFULLY WALKS UP THE SIDE OF THE SHEER SMOOTH SURFACE AS EASILY AS YOU MIGHT CLIMB A FLIGHT OF STAIRS!!

IT IS CERTAIN THAT NO ONE WILL NOTICE ME HERE IN THE DARK OF NIGHT!

REACHING THE ROOF, THE DRAMATIC FEMALE EJECTS A LONG, SLENDER LINE OF NYLON FROM A SPECIAL WRIST DEVICE, AND THEN...

THE POWERFUL SUCTION TIP AT THE OTHER END WILL STICK TO THAT WALL UNTIL I RELEASE IT!

BY COMBINING MY WALL-CLIMBING ABILITY WITH MY SUCTION-TIPPED NYLON LINE, THERE'S NO PLACE I CAN'T GO... NO DESTINATION I CANNOT REACH!

AND, AT THAT MOMENT, IN THE BUILDING ACROSS THE WAY, WE FIND...

TWANNNG!

THE TEST WORKED! MY NEW ACID-SPRAY ARROWHEAD BLASTED ITS WAY RIGHT THROUGH THAT THREE-INCH STEEL PIPE!

THUS, HAWKEYE HAS ANOTHER MIGHTY WEAPON TO ADD TO THE REST!

BUT THEN...

WHO'S THAT??

CRASH!

2.

DO NOT REACH FOR AN ARROW, HAWKEYE! YOU HAVE NOTHING TO FEAR FROM *ME!*

THAT *VOICE!!* CAN IT REALLY *BE??* BUT, I THOUGHT I HAD LOST YOU *FOREVER!*

WHEN YOU *LOVE* SOMEONE... CAN YOU NOT RECOGNIZE HER EVEN WHEN SHE'S MASKED?

NATASHA!! THEN IT *IS* YOU, MY DARLING! YOU'VE RETURNED TO ME AT *LAST!*

I *HAD* TO COME BACK...TO SEE YOU ONCE MORE!! TO FEEL YOUR STRONG ARMS AROUND ME!

BUT...WHY ARE YOU *MASKED,* MY DARLING?? AND HOW DID YOU GET IN THROUGH THE WINDOW?? THERE IS NO BALCONY OUTSIDE!

IT IS A LONG STORY...A FANTASTIC ONE! SO *MUCH* HAS HAPPENED SINCE LAST WE WERE TOGETHER!

TELL ME, NATASHA!

REMEMBER, HAWKEYE, WHEN *IRON MAN* LAST DEFEATED US? I WAS TAKEN BEHIND THE IRON CURTAIN, TO *PAY* FOR MY FAILURE!*

AND I THOUGH YOU HAD *DESERTED* ME!

*AS TOLD IN *SUSPENSE* #60...STAN.

NO! THEY *WANTED* YOU TO THINK SO...TO PREVENT YOU FROM FOLLOWING AFTER ME! FOR, EVEN *THEY* FEAR THE POWER OF THE MYSTERY MAN CALLED *HAWKEYE!*

I THOUGHT I WAS FLYING TO ...MY DEATH!

"BUT, INSTEAD I WAS TAKEN TO THE COMRADE *LEADER,* JUST BEFORE HIS FALL FROM POWER! HIS ANGER WAS TERRIFYING. BUT HE *STILL* HAD PLANS FOR ME!"

I CANNOT HAVE YOU SHOT! IT WOULD BE AN ADMISSION THAT MY PLAN *FAILED!* MY ENEMIES WOULD USE THAT AGAINST ME!

SO, YOU MUST ATTACK IRON MAN *AGAIN*... AND YOU *DARE NOT* FAIL!

I *WON'T!* NO MATTER *WHAT* YOU DO TO ME! I'M *THROUGH* SERVING YOUR EVIL PURPOSES!

3

I *THOUGHT* YOU MIGHT REACT THAT WAY! AND SO, I TOOK THE LIBERTY OF BRINGING YOUR *PARENTS* HERE! IF YOU HAVE NO FEAR FOR *YOURSELF,* SURELY YOU DON'T WANT THE STATE TO TREAT *THEM* AS THE PARENTS OF A...*TRAITOR!*

MOTHER! FATHER! OH, *NO!*

DO NOT FEAR FOR *US,* MY DAUGHTER! DO WHAT YOU FEEL IS *RIGHT!*

"BUT, I COULD NOT LET ANY HARM BEFALL MY PARENTS! AND SO..."

WHAT DO YOU WISH ME TO DO?

AH! *THAT* IS MORE LIKE IT! COMRADE SCIENTIST BRUSHNEV WILL EXPLAIN...

MADAM NATASHA, YOU ARE KNOWN BY THE CODE NAME *BLACK WIDOW!*

I HAVE DEVISED METHODS OF MAKING YOU *LIVE UP* TO THAT NAME! GO INTO THE NEXT ROOM!

"NEXT, I WAS GIVEN A STRANGE NEW COSTUME, WHICH I DONNED UNDER THE COLD, WATCHFUL EYE OF AN EXPRESSION-LESS MATRON..."

WHY ARE THESE *BOOTS* SO HEAVY?

THEY HAVE SPECIAL SUCTION DEVICES ON THE SOLES! YOU SHALL SEE!

"I THOUGHT I WAS HEARING THINGS WHEN SCIENTIST BRUSHNEV ORDERED ME TO WALK UP A WALL...BUT, I FOUND I COULD DO SO EASILY, WITHOUT FALLING! IN FACT..."

WITH THESE BOOTS, I CAN WALK ON *ANY* SURFACE...EVEN A ROUND, SLIPPERY PIPE!

SEE? YOU CAN EVEN HANG UPSIDE-DOWN FROM A CEILING... JUST LIKE THE SPIDER WHICH IS YOUR NAME-SAKE!

AND, TO MAKE IT POSSIBLE FOR YOU TO GO *ANYWHERE,* QUICKLY, YOU WILL ALWAYS WEAR THIS SPECIAL "BRACELET", WHICH EJECTS A SUCTION-TIPPED NYLON LINE!

CLICK!

"WITH MY HEART IN MY MOUTH, I ATTEMPTED THE FIRST TERRIFYING TEST...!"

GOOD! NOW, SWING...SWING TO THE OTHER SIDE!

IT HOLDS ME! THE THIN NYLON LINE *HOLDS* ME!

OF *COURSE!* AND, BY HAVING IT FASTENED TO YOUR WRIST, YOU CAN NEVER ACCIDENTALLY LET GO AND FALL!

EXCELLENT!! I CONGRATULATE YOU BOTH!!

4.

NOW, WITH YOUR NEW COSTUME, AND NEW POWER, YOU ARE ORDERED TO RETURN ONCE AGAIN TO AMERICA...AND *THIS* TIME IRON MAN MUST BE *DESTROYED*...BY ANY MEANS AT YOUR DISPOSAL!

YOU ARE THE CLEVEREST AGENT WE HAVE...AND NOW, YOU ARE ALSO THE MOST COLORFUL, THE MOST DANGEROUS! YOU ARE TRULY THE *BLACK WIDOW!*

ALL THAT REMAINED WAS TO DESIGN A *MASK!*...AND I MADE ONE TO RESEMBLE *YOURS*, HAWKEYE...FOR *YOU* SHALL AGAIN BE MY PARTNER!

BUT, NATASHA...NO MATTER WHAT I AM...NO MATTER WHAT I'VE DONE...I CAN'T BE A TRAITOR TO MY COUNTRY!

I ASK YOU TO BETRAY *NOTHING!* YOUR ONLY TASK IS TO HELP ME DESTROY *IRON MAN!* OR MUST I DO IT *ALONE?*

NO, MY DARLING! I CAN'T LOSE YOU AGAIN! I'LL DO IT...NO MATTER *WHAT* THE COST!

SOME TIME LATER, ON A QUIET MOONLIT LANE, OVERLOOKING THE MANHATTAN SKYLINE...

PEPPER, THERE'S SOMETHING I'VE GOTTA ASK YOU!

YES, HAPPY... WHAT IS IT?

I *KNOW* HOW YOU FEEL ABOUT TONY STARK, BUT...NOW THAT HE'S ENGAGED, I WAS WONDERIN' ABOUT YOU AND ME...ABOUT US GETTIN' *MARRIED!*

OH, I...I *DO* LIKE YOU, HAPPY...BUT..I NEED MORE TIME!

OKAY, BABY! I GUESS I SHOULDA *KNOWN* I WAS BATTIN' OUT OF MY LEAGUE!

HE'S *HURT!* AND YET, WHAT ELSE COULD I HAVE SAID? I *STILL* CAN'T FORGET TONY!

I BETTER TAKE YOU BACK NOW!

BUT, THE THOUGHTFUL COUPLE ARE NOT FATED TO REACH THEIR DESTINATION! FOR, AT THAT MOMENT...

TWANNG!

A *BLINDING FLASH* AHEAD OF US! CAN'T *SEE!* HANG ON, PEP!

HAPPY! WHAT *IS* IT?? WHAT CAN IT *MEAN??*

5

IT MEANS... YOU ARE THE PRISONERS OF HAWKEYE!

THE MAN HAS BEEN STUNNED BY THE IMPACT! IT IS BEST THAT WAY! QUICK, LET US REMOVE THEM BEFORE WE ARE DISCOVERED!

HAWKEYE! AND A GIRL... IN COSTUME!! IT MUST BE...!

OF COURSE, MY DEAR! IT IS I, MADAM NATASHA...THE BLACK WIDOW! NOW, OBEY OUR INSTRUCTIONS TO THE LETTER, AND YOU SHALL NOT BE HARMED!

THIS IS THE SAFEST WAY TO BATTLE IRON MAN! BY TAKING THESE TWO AS HOSTAGES, HE WILL NOT DARE DEFY US...NOT IF HE VALUES THEIR SAFETY!

FINALLY, IN A LONELY MANSION ON THE NORTH SHORE OF LONG ISLAND...

GUARD THE PRISONERS, HAWKEYE, WHILE I PHONE ANTHONY STARK'S FACTORY!

THIS IS THE BLACK WIDOW! CONNECT ME WITH MR. STARK! IMMEDIATELY!

AND SO... STARK? I HAVE PEPPER POTTS AND HAPPY HOGAN PRISONER! IF YOU WANT THEM, SEND IRON MAN FOR THEM!

I'LL GIVE YOU THE ADDRESS...BUT HE MUST COME ALONE!

IT'S A TRAP! HE WON'T KNOW THAT HAWKEYE IS HERE!

THEN, BEFORE ANYONE CAN STOP THE VALIANT GIRL...

MR. STARK...DON'T! THEY'LL KILL HIM! HAWKEYE IS HERE, TOO!!

THAT'S STRANGE!! WHY DON'T THEY TRY TO PULL THE PHONE AWAY FROM ME??

YOU OUT-SMARTED YOURSELF! WE WANTED YOU TO DO THAT! NOW HE'LL HAVE TO SEND IRON MAN!

DID YOU HEAR THAT? GOOD! SO YOU KNOW WE AREN'T BLUFFING!

NOW...SEND IRON MAN TO THE RAILROAD LOADING YARDS THREE MILES FROM THE BAY! YOU HAVE ONE HOUR!

6.

EXACTLY FIFTY-FIVE MINUTES LATER...

EVERYTHING IS SET! THE GUARDS ARE ALL POSTED! DO YOU HAVE ANY FINAL INSTRUCTIONS FOR US?

YES! REMEMBER THIS... *IRON MAN* OBEYS TONY STARK... AND STARK WILL ALLOW NOTHING TO HAPPEN TO OUR TWO PRISONERS! SO HE MUST HAVE ORDERED IRON MAN TO DO WHATEVER WE SAY! THEREFORE, YOU NEED NOT FEAR HIS GREAT POWER!

THANKS TO OUR HOSTAGES, THE ADVANTAGE WILL BE *OURS!*

THEN, AS THE NEXT FIVE MINUTES SLOWLY, DRAMATICALLY TICK BY...

AT *LAST!* SOMEONE IS APPROACHING!

NO! HOLD YOUR FIRE!! IT IS *NOT* IRON MAN!

STARK! WHAT ARE *YOU* DOING HERE? I ORDERED YOU TO SEND *IRON MAN!*

I *COULDN'T!* HE'S OUT OF TOWN... I COULDN'T REACH HIM! BUT I CAME *MYSELF*, TO MAKE YOU AN OFFER... TO SAVE PEPPER AND HAPPY!

I'LL TRADE YOU THESE NEW WEAPONS DESIGNS I'VE CREATED FOR BOTH OF THEIR LIVES!

VLADIMIR! YOU ARE AN ARMAMENT EXPERT! EXAMINE HIS PLANS IN THAT SHED! SEE IF THEY ARE OF ANY VALUE TO US!

JUST WHAT I *HOPED* SHE'D SAY!

BY TURNING MY BACK, THEY DIDN'T SEE ME SLIDE THIS CLIP FROM MY BELT BUCKLE....!

ONCE IT TOUCHES THE GROUND, I'LL GO INTO ACTION!

7.

IN THE NEXT SPLIT-SECOND, EVERY-THING SEEMS TO HAPPEN AT ONCE! FIRST, THE TINY CLIP EMITS A THICK CLOUD OF BILLOWING SMOKE THE INSTANT IT TOUCHES THE GROUND...!

MY EYES! I CAN'T SEE! IT'S A TRICK!

HOW DID IT HAPPEN? WHERE DID HE GO?

ALL I NEED IS ANOTHER TWO SECONDS TO OPEN MY ATTACHÉ CASE AND SLIP ON MY ARMOR!

LUCKY I'VE PRACTICED IT SO LONG THAT I CAN DO IT IN THE DARK, IN LESS TIME THAN IT TAKES TO BUTTON A SHIRT!

AND THE BATTERY-OPERATED UNITS SNAP INTO PLACE LIKE A CHARM!

ZZZTT!

FINALLY, THE STARTLED RED AGENTS ACT IN SHEER DESPERATION...

FIRE INTO THE SMOKE! HE MUST BE HERE SOMEWHERE!

SORRY, BOYS! I SENT STARK AWAY--- BUT, PERHAPS I'LL DO!!

BRAKKK!

IT'S IRON MAN!

WHY IS YOUR GUN TREMBLING SO?? DIDN'T YOU HOPE I'D APPEAR?

FIRE, YOU FOOL!! YOU HAVE ARMOR-PIERCING SHELLS!

WHY DOES HE WALK TOWARDS ME... SO UNAFRAID?

IN MY BUSINESS THERE'S NOT MUCH FUTURE FOR A MAN WHO FRIGHTENS EASILY!

AS FOR YOUR ARMOR-PIERCING SHELLS...THEY WON'T DO MUCH GOOD COMING OUT OF A BENT RIFLE BARREL!

STAND ASIDE, YOU INEPT BUNGLER! WE'LL GET HIM!

SPOKEN LIKE TRUE COMMIE TINTYPES!

BUT, NOW THAT YOU'VE GOT ME, WHAT'LL YOU DO WITH ME?

SORRY THAT I'LL HAVE TO BEAT AND RUN, GENTS! BUT, THE MAIN EVENT IS DUE TO TAKE PLACE OUTSIDE...!!

KEEP YOUR AREA CLEAN

WASTE

8.

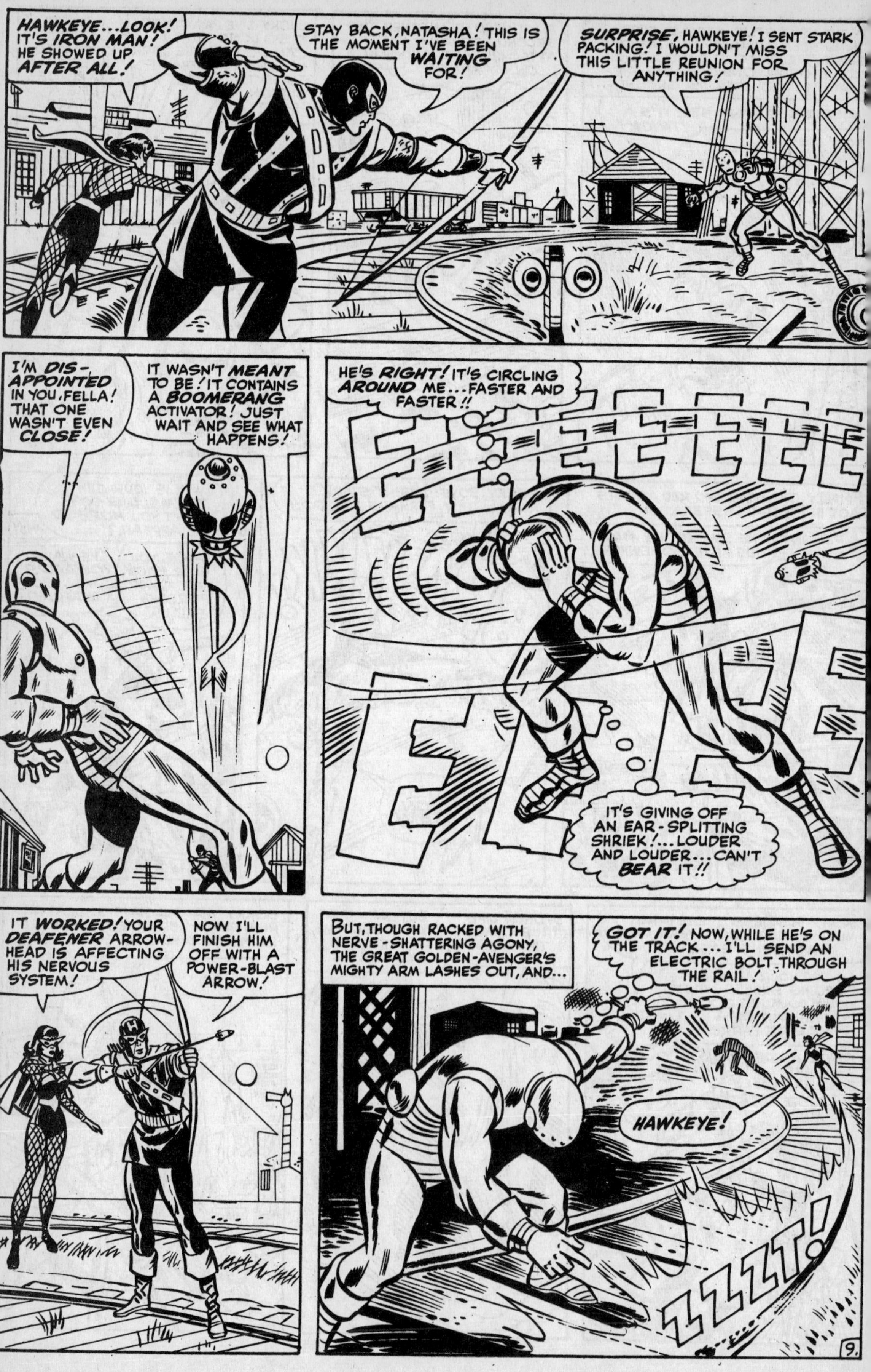
HAWKEYE...LOOK! IT'S IRON MAN! HE SHOWED UP AFTER ALL!
STAY BACK, NATASHA! THIS IS THE MOMENT I'VE BEEN WAITING FOR!
SURPRISE, HAWKEYE! I SENT STARK PACKING! I WOULDN'T MISS THIS LITTLE REUNION FOR ANYTHING!
I'M DIS-APPOINTED IN YOU, FELLA! THAT ONE WASN'T EVEN CLOSE!
IT WASN'T MEANT TO BE! IT CONTAINS A BOOMERANG ACTIVATOR! JUST WAIT AND SEE WHAT HAPPENS!
HE'S RIGHT! IT'S CIRCLING AROUND ME...FASTER AND FASTER!!
EEEEEEE
IT'S GIVING OFF AN EAR-SPLITTING SHRIEK!...LOUDER AND LOUDER...CAN'T BEAR IT!!
IT WORKED! YOUR DEAFENER ARROW-HEAD IS AFFECTING HIS NERVOUS SYSTEM!
NOW I'LL FINISH HIM OFF WITH A POWER-BLAST ARROW!
BUT, THOUGH RACKED WITH NERVE-SHATTERING AGONY, THE GREAT GOLDEN-AVENGER'S MIGHTY ARM LASHES OUT, AND...
GOT IT! NOW, WHILE HE'S ON THE TRACK... I'LL SEND AN ELECTRIC BOLT THROUGH THE RAIL!
HAWKEYE!
ZZZZT!
9.

I...I'M ALL RIGHT, NATASHA! JUST... TAKEN BY SURPRISE...STUNNED!!

GET UP...QUICKLY!! HE'S STILL DAZED HIMSELF, BECAUSE OF THE NERVOUS SHOCK HE RECEIVED!! ONE MORE ARROW WILL FINISH HIM!!

CAN'T!! EVERYTHING SPINNING AROUND!! NEED A FEW SECONDS ...TO SNAP OUT OF IT!

I CAN'T AFFORD TO WAIT! ONCE IRON MAN REGAINS HIS FULL STRENGTH, IT WILL BE TOO LATE!

WE'VE ALREADY LOST THE ADVANTAGE OF SURPRISE!

THIS WILL DO IT... BEFORE HE CAN LEAP TO SAFETY!

THERE! IT'S ROLLING AT FULL SPEED!! NOW TO SWING OFF AND LET THE IRON CAR DESTROY IRON MAN!

BUT, HEARING THE THUNDEROUS RUMBLE, IRON MAN LOOKS UP, AND THEN...

IF THAT FLATCAR HITS ME HEAD-ON, MY TRANSISTORS WILL BE SHATTERED!

AND THEN, THE GOLDEN CRUSADER NOTICES...

HAPPY AND PEPPER! DIRECTLY BEHIND ME! IF IT MISSES ME, IT'LL CRASH INTO THEM!

ONLY ONE THING TO DO... BUT, CAN I DO IT IN TIME??!

WHOOSH!

SCRUNCH!

YOU'RE SAFE NOW! I'LL HAVE YOU FREE IN SECONDS!

NO TIME FOR THAT! LOOK BEHIND YA... HAWKEYE'S LOOSING ANOTHER ARROW!

TOO LATE! HERE IT COMES!

10

Panel 1 (top left):

THANK *HEAVENS!!* IT ONLY HIT YOUR *SHOULDER!*

BUT... IT'S *DISSOLVING* MY ARMOR!

OH, *NO!!* WITHOUT YOUR ARMOR HOW CAN YOU BATTLE *HAWKEYE??*

Panel 2 (top right):

THAT'S THE *IDEA!!* MY *ACID-SPRAY* ARROWS WILL HAVE HIM *POWER-LESS* IN MINUTES!

ACID'S, EATING MY ARMOR AWAY! AND NOW, THE *BLACK WIDOW'S* SHOOTING AT ME, TOO!

CRACK!

TWANNNGG!

Panel 3 (middle):

TONY, OLD BOY, IF YOU EVER EXPECT TO GET OUT OF THIS ONE ALIVE, YOU'D BETTER MOVE *FASTER* THAN YOU'VE EVER MOVED BEFORE!

CRASH!

FIRST THING TO DO, IS PUT A BRICK WALL BETWEEN ME AND ANY MORE OF HAWKEYE'S LITTLE ARROWS!

Panel 4 (bottom left):

SO *THAT'S* WHERE THE BLACK WIDOW WAS FIRING AT ME FROM! SHE STILL DOESN'T SEEM TO KNOW WHERE I DISAPPEARED TO!

HAWKEYE! AFTER HIM! HE MUST NOT *ESCAPE!*

Panel 5 (bottom middle):

HOW CAN ANYBODY SO *BEAUTIFUL* BE SO DANGEROUSLY *BELLIGERENT*, LADY??

AND, WHILE YOU'RE THINKING UP AN ANSWER, I'LL JUST BORROW THAT POP GUN OF YOURS!

IRON MAN!!

HAWKEYE.. HURRY!! HE'S OVER HERE!!

Panel 6 (bottom right):

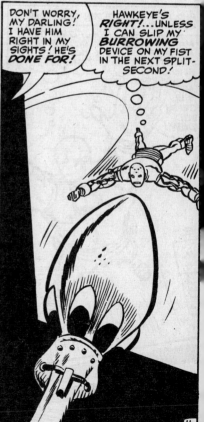

DON'T WORRY, MY DARLING! I HAVE HIM RIGHT IN MY SIGHTS! HE'S *DONE FOR!*

HAWKEYE'S *RIGHT!*...UNLESS I CAN SLIP MY *BURROWING* DEVICE ON MY FIST IN THE NEXT SPLIT-SECOND!

11.

THERE! NOW FOR AN UNEXPECTED **POWER DIVE!**

MADE IT! HE WAS SO SURE HE **HAD** ME, THAT HE AIMED TOO SLOWLY!

NOW. IT'S **MY** TURN, HAWKEYE! ENJOY IT WHILE YOU **CAN!** I'VE PLENTY MORE **ARROWS!**

CAN'T LAST MUCH LONGER... ACID IS MELTING ARMOR **FASTER** NOW!

I'LL USE **THEIR** TACTICS... STRIKE AT HIS WEAKEST LINK... THE **BLACK WIDOW!**

ONCE AGAIN, A TRANSISTOR-POWERED ELECTRICAL BOLT FINDS ITS MARK... STUNNING THE MASKED RED AGENT...!

OHHHH!

IT **WORKED!** HAWKEYE'S SHOTS ARE GOING WILD! HE'S WORRIED ABOUT THE **GIRL!**

YOU DARED ATTACK **NATASHA!!** YOU'LL PAY **DEARLY** FOR THAT ONE DAY... I **SWEAR** IT!!

THEN, TURNING FROM HIS IRON-GARBED FOE, THE FEARLESS ARCHER RACES TO THE WOMAN HE LOVES...!

NATASHA... MY DARLING! **SPEAK** TO ME!

NO! NO! GO BACK.. FINISH HIM OFF... **GO BACK!!**

NO! YOU'VE BEEN **HURT!** I CANNOT LEAVE YOU!!

YOU **FOOL!** YOU HAD YOUR CHANCE... NOW IT'S TOO **LATE!** BECAUSE OF YOUR LOVE... I'VE FAILED AGAIN!!

MEANWHILE...

YOU CAN STILL **CATCH** 'EM! THEY DROVE OFF THAT WAY!

NO! I HAVE TO REMOVE MY ARMOR! THERE'LL BE **OTHER** TIMES!

WHY IS HE SO AFRAID WE'LL LEARN, WHO HE IS IF HIS ARMOR MELTS OFF?

THEN, A FEW MINUTES LATER...

IRON MAN SENT ME TO CALL THE POLICE! THEY'LL BE HERE ANY MINUTE! BUT... WHAT **HAPPENED?**

IT'S **YOU!!** OH, THANK HEAVENS! I WAS SO AFRAID THEY HAD TAKEN YOU **WITH** THEM!

SHE **STILL** LOVES HIM! SHE'LL **ALWAYS** LOVE HIM! WHAT CHANCE CAN A NOBODY LIKE ME EVER HAVE AGAINST **TONY STARK?**

I WAS SO **WORRIED** ABOUT YOU!

PEPPER ..PEPPER! ...CAN'T YOU SEE YOU'RE BREAKING HAPPY'S HEART??

AND NOW, BEFORE YOU START THINKING THAT YOU'VE BEEN READING A ROMANCE MAG BY MISTAKE, TURN TO THE **CAPTAIN AMERICA** THRILLER WHICH FOLLOWS! WE GUARANTEE, THERE'S NOT A KISS IN A CARLOAD!

The End 12.

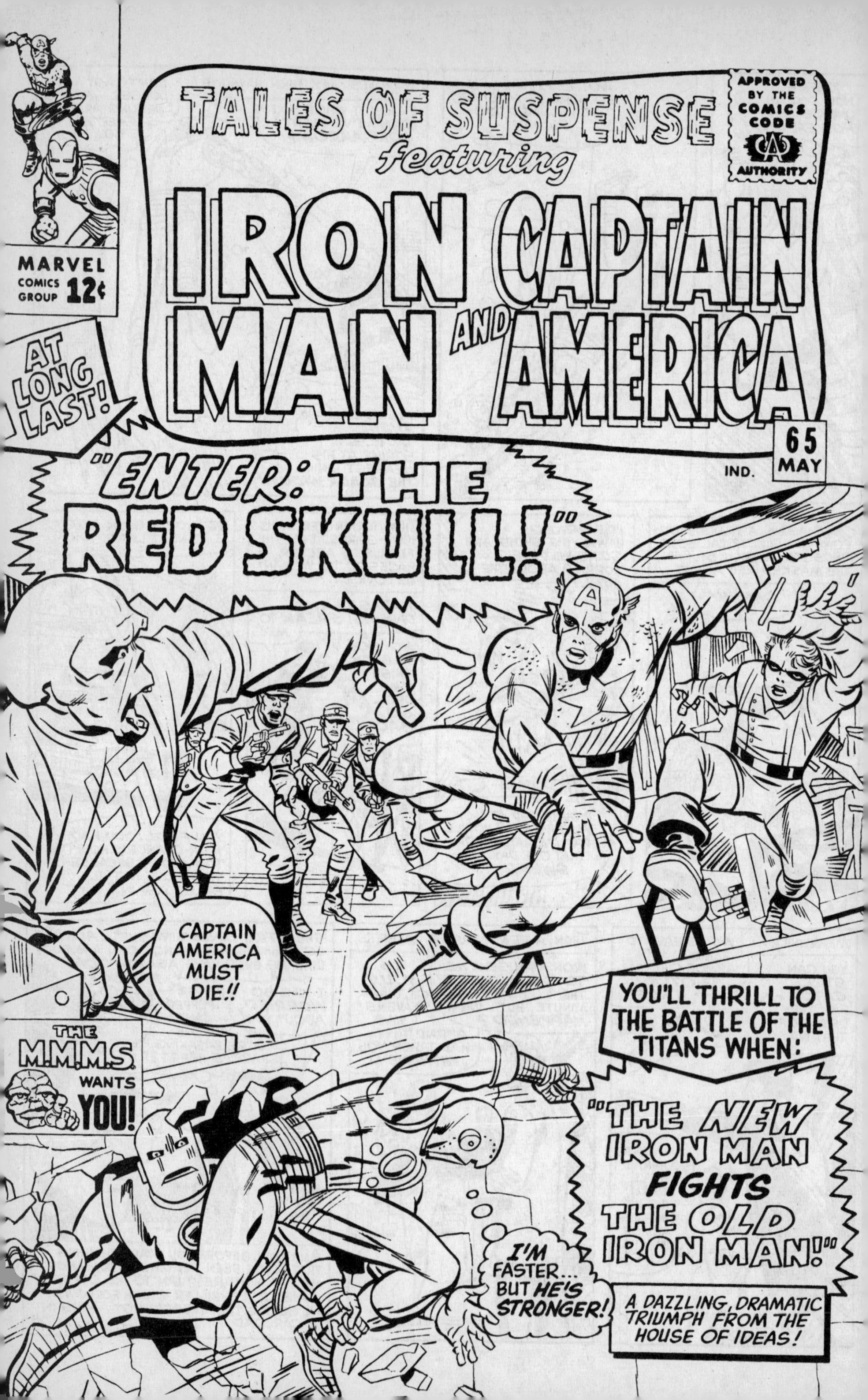
TALES OF SUSPENSE
featuring
IRON MAN AND CAPTAIN AMERICA
APPROVED BY THE COMICS CODE AUTHORITY
MARVEL COMICS GROUP 12¢
AT LONG LAST!
65 MAY
IND.
"ENTER: THE RED SKULL!"
CAPTAIN AMERICA MUST DIE!!
THE M.M.M.S. WANTS YOU!
YOU'LL THRILL TO THE BATTLE OF THE TITANS WHEN:
"THE NEW IRON MAN FIGHTS THE OLD IRON MAN!"
I'M FASTER... BUT HE'S STRONGER!
A DAZZLING, DRAMATIC TRIUMPH FROM THE HOUSE OF IDEAS!

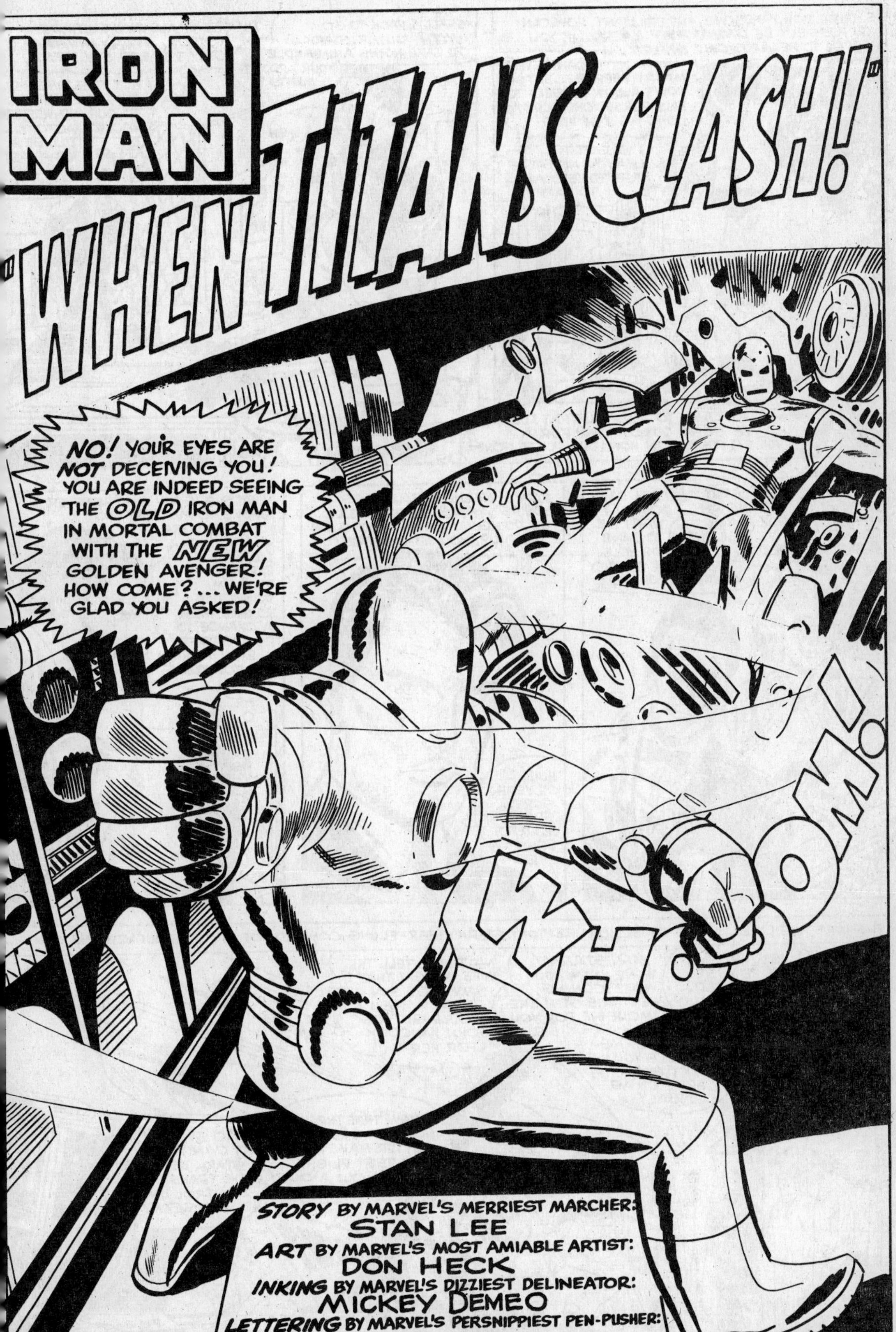
IRON MAN
"WHEN TITANS CLASH!"
NO! YOUR EYES ARE NOT DECEIVING YOU! YOU ARE INDEED SEEING THE OLD IRON MAN IN MORTAL COMBAT WITH THE NEW GOLDEN AVENGER! HOW COME?... WE'RE GLAD YOU ASKED!
WHOOOM!
STORY BY MARVEL'S MERRIEST MARCHER: STAN LEE
ART BY MARVEL'S MOST AMIABLE ARTIST: DON HECK
INKING BY MARVEL'S DIZZIEST DELINEATOR: MICKEY DEMEO
LETTERING BY MARVEL'S PERSNIPPIEST PEN-PUSHER: SAM ROSEN

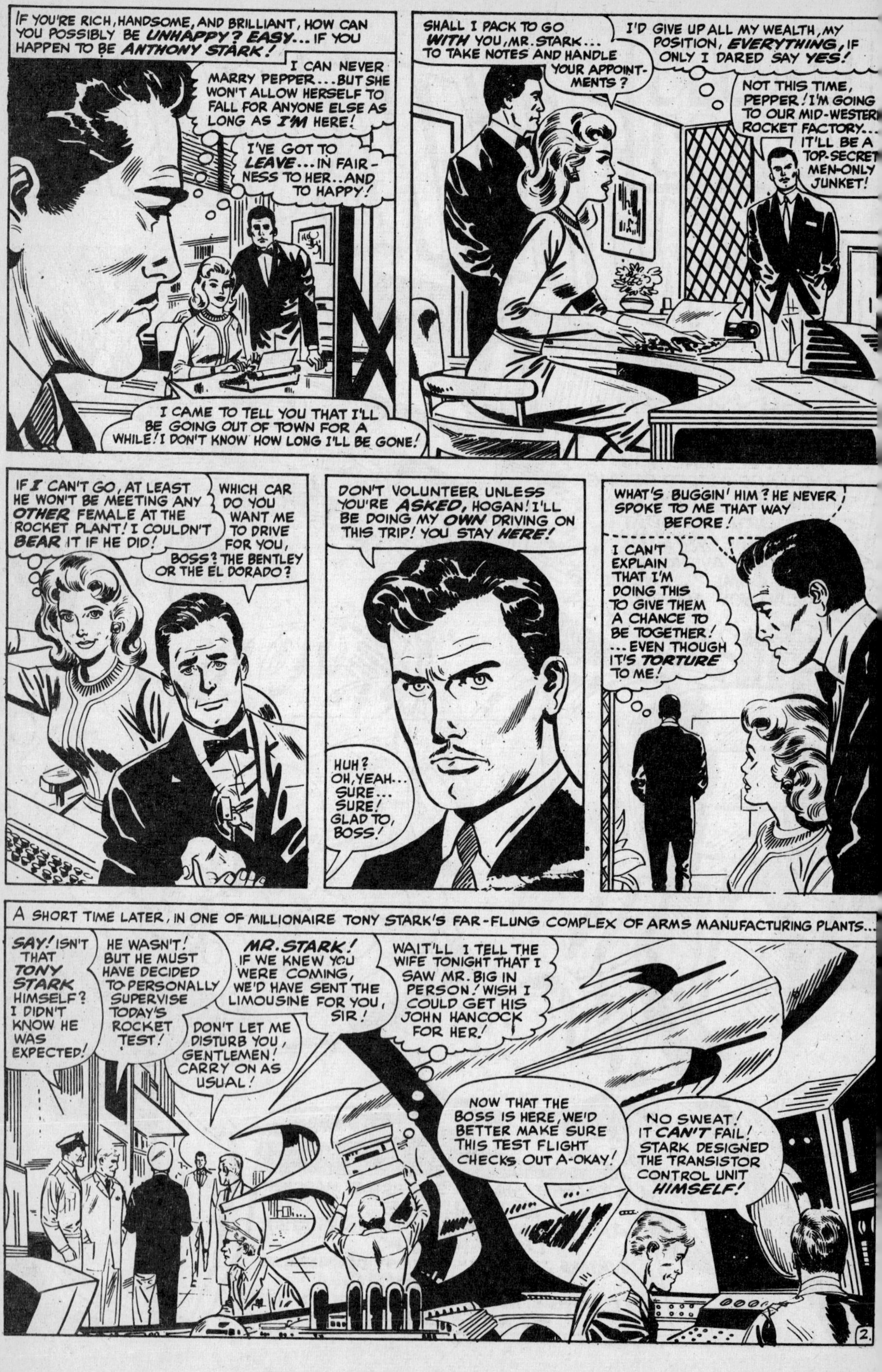
IF YOU'RE RICH, HANDSOME, AND BRILLIANT, HOW CAN YOU POSSIBLY BE UNHAPPY? EASY... IF YOU HAPPEN TO BE ANTHONY STARK!
I CAN NEVER MARRY PEPPER... BUT SHE WON'T ALLOW HERSELF TO FALL FOR ANYONE ELSE AS LONG AS I'M HERE!
I'VE GOT TO LEAVE... IN FAIRNESS TO HER.. AND TO HAPPY!
I CAME TO TELL YOU THAT I'LL BE GOING OUT OF TOWN FOR A WHILE! I DON'T KNOW HOW LONG I'LL BE GONE!
SHALL I PACK TO GO WITH YOU, MR. STARK... TO TAKE NOTES AND HANDLE YOUR APPOINTMENTS?
I'D GIVE UP ALL MY WEALTH, MY POSITION, EVERYTHING, IF ONLY I DARED SAY YES!
NOT THIS TIME, PEPPER! I'M GOING TO OUR MID-WESTER ROCKET FACTORY... IT'LL BE A TOP-SECRET MEN-ONLY JUNKET!
IF I CAN'T GO, AT LEAST HE WON'T BE MEETING ANY OTHER FEMALE AT THE ROCKET PLANT! I COULDN'T BEAR IT IF HE DID!
WHICH CAR DO YOU WANT ME TO DRIVE FOR YOU, BOSS? THE BENTLEY OR THE EL DORADO?
DON'T VOLUNTEER UNLESS YOU'RE ASKED, HOGAN! I'LL BE DOING MY OWN DRIVING ON THIS TRIP! YOU STAY HERE!
HUH? OH, YEAH... SURE... SURE! GLAD TO, BOSS!
WHAT'S BUGGIN' HIM? HE NEVER SPOKE TO ME THAT WAY BEFORE!
I CAN'T EXPLAIN THAT I'M DOING THIS TO GIVE THEM A CHANCE TO BE TOGETHER! ...EVEN THOUGH IT'S TORTURE TO ME!
A SHORT TIME LATER, IN ONE OF MILLIONAIRE TONY STARK'S FAR-FLUNG COMPLEX OF ARMS MANUFACTURING PLANTS...
SAY! ISN'T THAT TONY STARK HIMSELF? I DIDN'T KNOW HE WAS EXPECTED!
HE WASN'T! BUT HE MUST HAVE DECIDED TO PERSONALLY SUPERVISE TODAY'S ROCKET TEST!
MR. STARK! IF WE KNEW YOU WERE COMING, WE'D HAVE SENT THE LIMOUSINE FOR YOU, SIR!
DON'T LET ME DISTURB YOU, GENTLEMEN! CARRY ON AS USUAL!
WAIT'LL I TELL THE WIFE TONIGHT THAT I SAW MR. BIG IN PERSON! WISH I COULD GET HIS JOHN HANCOCK FOR HER!
NOW THAT THE BOSS IS HERE, WE'D BETTER MAKE SURE THIS TEST FLIGHT CHECKS OUT A-OKAY!
NO SWEAT! IT CAN'T FAIL! STARK DESIGNED THE TRANSISTOR CONTROL UNIT HIMSELF!
2

THEN, IN A DESPERATE EFFORT TO EASE HIS TORMENTED MIND OF THOUGHTS OF THE GIRL HE LOVES, THE INVENTIVE WIZARD THROWS HIMSELF INTO HIS WORK WITH DESPERATE PASSION...

LET ME EXAMINE THE TRANSISTOR CONTROL UNIT, GENTLEMEN! IT'S THE HEART OF THE ENTIRE SYSTEM!

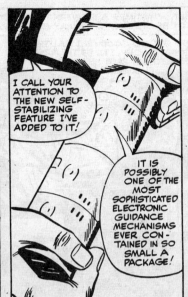

I CALL YOUR ATTENTION TO THE NEW SELF-STABILIZING FEATURE I'VE ADDED TO IT!

IT IS POSSIBLY ONE OF THE MOST SOPHISTICATED ELECTRONIC GUIDANCE MECHANISMS EVER CONTAINED IN SO SMALL A PACKAGE!

AND, ITS DELICATE TRANSISTORIZED MEMORY BANKS CONTROL EVERY OPERATION OF THE MASTER ROCKET ITSELF!

VERY WELL! BEGIN THE MISSILE TEST!

HE'S SUPERVISING IT *PERSONALLY*! WHAT AN *HONOR* FOR US!

WHOOOOOOOOSH!

BUT, SO INTENT IS TONY STARK UPON THE PROJECT AT HAND, THAT HE DOESN'T REALIZE THAT HE FORGOT *ONE THING* IN HIS HASTY DEPARTURE FROM NEW YORK...

...AND, THAT SMALL OVERSIGHT IS ABOUT TO PLUNGE HIM INTO ONE OF HIS MOST DANGEROUS, MOST UNEXPECTED LIFE-AND-DEATH BATTLES!

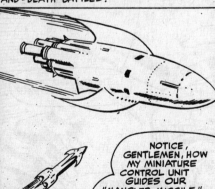

NOTICE, GENTLEMEN, HOW MY MINIATURE CONTROL UNIT GUIDES OUR "MANGLER MISSILE" UNERRINGLY TOWARDS ITS TARGET...WITH EVER-INCREASING SPEED, UNTIL...

THWUPP!

...IT FASTENS ITSELF PERMANENTLY UPON ANY ENEMY ROCKET WITHIN RANGE...

NOW, WITH OUR MANGLER MISSILE CONTROLLING THE ENEMY ROCKET, WE CAN DESTROY IT, OR NULLIFY IT, BRINGING IT SAFELY TO EARTH FOR STUDY!

3.

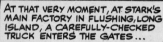

Panel 1: AT THAT VERY MOMENT, AT STARK'S MAIN FACTORY IN FLUSHING, LONG ISLAND, A CAREFULLY-CHECKED TRUCK ENTERS THE GATES...

HOW'S THE WIFE AND KIDS, CHARLIE?

JUST FINE, PETE! IT WAS TOMMY'S BIRTHDAY YESTERDAY!

CHECK POINT

Panel 2: BUT, SOMETIMES A DELIVERY TRUCK MAY NOT BE CHECKED CAREFULLY *ENOUGH!*

SO FAR, SO GOOD! IF I PULL THIS ROBBERY OFF, I'LL BE THE FIRST JOE EVER TO GET PAST STARK'S ARMY OF GUARDS!

Panel 3:

I *DID* IT! THERE MUST BE A *FORTUNE* IN WAR PLANS INSIDE!

Panel 4:

ALL I GOTTA DO IS HIDE HERE TILL THE GUARD WALKS BY, AND THEN HEAD FOR THE EXECUTIVE OFFICES SECTION!

Panel 5: SECONDS LATER, SLIPPING INTO PEPPER POTTS' OUTER OFFICE, THE BRAZEN BURGLAR FINDS THE *ONE THING* WHICH ANTHONY STARK FORGOT!

HEY! AN ATTACHE CASE... WITH THE INITIALS A.S. ON IT! IT MUST BE THE BIG MAN'S HIMSELF!

Panel 6: NOT ONLY DID THE HEARTSICK AVENGER LEAVE HIS CASE BEHIND, BUT FAR MORE SERIOUS, HE LEFT ITS PROTECTIVE DEVICE *UNSET*... THE DEVICE WHICH CAUSES IT TO *EXPLODE* IF TOUCHED BY UNAUTHORIZED HANDS!

I'LL JIMMY THIS LATCH IN A MINUTE!

I HOPE HE KEEPS SOME COLD CASH IN HERE!

Panel 7: BUT, THE CONTENTS OF TONY STARK'S ATTACHE CASE ARE FAR MORE VALUABLE THAN MERE CASH... IN FACT, THEY'RE VIRTUALLY *PRICELESS!*

IT...IT LOOKS LIKE PIECES OF *ARMOR*...THIN, FLEXIBLE *IRON* ARMOR!

Panel 8: THEN, AS THE STARTLED BURGLAR ACCIDENTALLY TOUCHES A TRANSISTOR RELEASE STUD...

SPANNNG!

THE BLAMED THING IS ALMOST *ALIVE!!*

IT...IT TELESCOPED OUT INTO AN IRON *CUFF!*

4

MINUTES LATER, THE WILY THIEF, REALIZING WHAT HE HAS FOUND, MANAGES TO SLIP INTO THE ENTIRE *IRON MAN* BODY ARMOR...

WOW! WHO'D HAVE THOUGHT IT!? TONY STARK HIMSELF MUST BE IRON MAN!

AND WEASEL WILLS IS THE ONLY GUY WHO KNOWS IT!

WELL, I MIGHT AS WELL FIND OUT WHAT ALL THESE BUTTONS ARE FOR!

IF I COULD LEARN TO USE THIS ARMOR, I'D REALLY BE IRON MAN!

BUT, NO SOONER DOES THE MAN CALLED "WEASEL" TOUCH THE JET ACTIVATOR BUTTON, THAN...

WH-UMMP!

HOLY COW! IT FLEW ME RIGHT UP TO THE CEILING!

THEN, PRESSING THE BUTTON A *SECOND* TIME, HE FINDS...

THE SECOND PRESS REVERSES THE POWER JETS! BOY! A GUY COULD DO ANYTHING IN THIS OUTFIT!

THUD!

AND THEN, FORGETTING THE MONEY, FORGETTING THE DEFENSE PLANS WHICH HE HAD HOPED TO STEAL, WEASEL WILLS WALKS OUT WITH THE BIGGEST PRIZE OF ALL...UNDER THE NOSE OF THE UNSUSPECTING GUARD...

WONDER WHERE HE'S GOIN' AT THIS HOUR?

'NITE!

ONCE I'M OUT OF SIGHT, I'LL TRY HIS FLYING POWER AGAIN!

THEN, FOR THE NEXT FEW HOURS, IN A LONELY WOODED AREA...

THIS IS TERRIFIC! I'M GETTING THE HANG OF IT, NOW! I FEEL LIKE A NEW MAN!!

...LIKE AN IRON MAN!

EVERY BUTTON I TOUCH GIVES ME NEW POWER! I COULD STAND OFF AN ARMY IN THIS OUTFIT!

FINDIN' THIS SUIT WAS THE LUCKIEST THING IN MY LIFE! STARK'LL NEVER BE ABLE TO GET IT BACK FROM ME! I'M STRONGER THAN ANYONE NOW!

FINALLY, DAYS LATER...

I CAN USE THE ARMOR AS GOOD AS STARK HIMSELF BY NOW!

SO *NOW*, HERE'S WHERE WEASEL WILLS, THE *NEW* IRON MAN, CASHES IN ON HIS LUCKY BREAK!

5

AND, CASH IN HE **DOES!** WITHIN HOURS, THE NEWS IS SPREAD THROUGHOUT THE NATION... A NEW MENACE IS AT LARGE... ONE OF THE MOST **POWERFUL** OF ALL TIME!!

IT'S NO USE! BULLETS BOUNCE RIGHT OFF HIM!

THE ONLY THING I DON'T UNDER-STAND IS... WHY DIDN'T **STARK** USE HIS ARMOR FOR **CRIME?** HE MUSTA BEEN **NUTS** TO WASTE TIME BEIN' AN **AVENGER!**

DAILY CHRONICLE
BANK FALLS EASY PREY TO IRON MAN!

IRON MAN ON CRIME SPREE!

MORNING POST
MAYOR CALLS EMERGENCY MEETING OF POLICE AND CIVIL DEFENSE!

I CAN TUNNEL MY WAY THROUGH **ANYTHING** WITH THIS TRANSISTORIZED **REPULSER RAY!**

THERE! I DUG MY **OWN** "BANK" IN THIS CAVE!

WHILE, IN THE MIDWEST, HIS MISSILE TEST SUCCESSFULLY COMPLETED, TONY STARK SCANS THE NEWSPAPERS FOR THE FIRST TIME IN DAYS...

SOMEONE MUST HAVE FOUND MY ATTACHE CASE!!

DA...
IRON ROBS

IT'S MY **FAULT!** I'VE GOT TO STOP HIM... I'M TO **BLAME!**

HOURS LATER, GRIM AND UNSMILING, STARK STORMS INTO HIS N.Y. PLANT...

WHOEVER HE IS, HE MUST KNOW WHO IRON MAN'S **OTHER** IDENTITY IS BY NOW!

BOSS..!

DON'T EVEN **TRY** TO SPEAK TO HIM, HAPPY! I'VE SEEN THAT LOOK ON HIS FACE BEFORE!

OBLIVIOUS TO EVERYTHING SAVE THE PROBLEM OF DEFEATING A NEW IRON MAN, STARK OPENS THE CABINET OF HIS PRIVATE LAB...

I NEVER THOUGHT THE DAY WOULD COME WHEN I'D RESORT TO **THIS** AGAIN... BUT THERE'S NO OTHER WAY!

IT'S LUCKY I **SAVED** IT ALL THESE MONTHS, INSTEAD OF DESTROYING IT WHEN I DESIGNED THE NEW ONE!

ONLY SOMEONE POWERFUL, AS POWERFUL AS IRON MAN CAN **DEFEAT** IRON MAN!

AND, SINCE THE OTHER **AVENGERS** ARE SCATTERED AROUND THE COUNTRY AT PRESENT, ONLY THE **OLD** IRON MAN HAS THE NECESSARY POWER!

I'VE GOT TO HOPE THE OLD COMPONENT PARTS ARE STILL IN PROPER WORKING ORDER!

6

HOW BULKY, HEAVY, AND CUMBERSOME THIS ARMOR FEELS COMPARED TO MY NEW, FLEXIBLE GARB! I HOPE MY INJURED HEART CAN WITHSTAND THE STRAIN OF THE ADDED WEIGHT!

BUT, I'VE NO OTHER CHOICE! A NEW, TERRIBLE MENACE HAS BEEN UNLEASHED BECAUSE OF MY OWN CARELESSNESS... AND I'VE GOT TO DESTROY IT... EVEN IF IT COSTS ME MY LIFE!

"MY LIFE"! WHAT A HOLLOW MOCKERY! WITH A PIECE OF SHRAPNEL FROM VIET NAM HOPELESSLY LODGED NEAR MY HEART, MY LIFE CAN END AT ANY SECOND!

BUT I'VE GOT TO FORGET ABOUT THAT NOW...

ALL MY THOUGHTS, ALL MY TALENTS, ALL MY STRENGTH MUST BE DEDICATED TO ONLY ONE AIM... THE DEFEAT OF THE ONE WHO DARES TO WEAR IRON MAN'S ARMOR!

CRASH!

IT COULD TAKE DAYS TO LOCATE THE IMPOSTOR! BUT, PERHAPS THERE'S A BETTER WAY...!

WITH LUCK, I'LL MAKE HIM COME TO ME!!

MEANWHILE, IN A HIDDEN CAVE, THE MAN WHO HAD BEEN WEASEL WILLS RELAXES AFTER HIS CRIME SPREE BY LISTENING TO THE NEWS ON HIS BUILT-IN RADIO...

SO FAR, IRON MAN HAS RESISTED EVERY EFFORT TO APPREHEND HIM! THE POLICE REPORT THAT...

THEY'LL NEVER FIND ME! AND, EVEN IF THEY DO, THEY'LL NEVER BE ABLE TO TAKE ME! I'M TOO POWERFUL NOW!

BUT SUDDENLY, A NEW VOICE BREAKS IN ON IRON MAN'S SPECIAL ULTRA-SONIC CHANNEL...

IRON MAN! I'M BROADCASTING ON A FREQUENCY WHICH ONLY YOU CAN RECEIVE! THIS IS TONY STARK! YOU'LL NEVER BE SAFE WHILE I LIVE!

STARK!!

7.

COME TO MY FACTORY IN FLUSHING TONIGHT FOR A SHOWDOWN...OR ELSE I'LL HUNT YOU DOWN AND DESTROY YOU WITHOUT MERCY!

HE'S BLUFFING! HE *MUST* BE! WHAT CAN *HE* DO TO ME NOW ??

BUT, I'LL NEVER BE ABLE TO *KNOW* UNLESS I GO THERE...!

THAT NIGHT, AFTER TONY STARK HAS ORDERED HIS ENTIRE FACTORY CLEARED OUT, A PONDEROUS, HALF-TON FIGURE SLOWLY PACES BACK AND FORTH, WAITING ...WAITING ...

WILL HE SHOW UP ?? AND, IF HE *DOES*, HOW CAN I *DEFEAT* HIM ? HE'LL HAVE THE ADVANTAGE OF SPEED, LIGHTER WEIGHT, ALL THE LATEST DEVICES I WAS ABLE TO INVENT!

BUT, STARK'S MUSINGS ARE SUDDENLY CUT SHORT, AS HE HEARS...

THE SOUND OF RIPPING METAL... THE ROOF BEING TORN APART!

IT'S *HIM*!

DROPPING THE STEEL SECTION ON ME!

SO, STARK, YOU DECIDED TO FIGHT ME IN YOUR *OLD* SUIT OF ARMOR! I SHOULD HAVE GUESSED! BUT, SURELY YOU KNOW THAT THE *IRON MAN* SUIT WHICH *I* AM WEARING IS FAR SUPERIOR!

PERHAPS IT *IS*!!

KLANNK!

BUT REMEMBER.. *I'M* THE ONE WHO DESIGNED THEM *BOTH*! I HAVE THE ADVANTAGE OF *KNOWLEDGE*!

SEE? IN YOUR EAGERNESS, YOU *MISSED* YOUR FIRST POWER BLAST AT ME! I WOULDN'T HAVE MADE SUCH A BLUNDER!

WHITTT!

KNOWLEDGE!! A FAT LOT OF GOOD *THAT'LL* DO YOU WHILE I CAN FIGHT AT *TWICE* YOUR OLD, SLOW, LUMBERING SPEED!

IF I CAN JUST KEEP HIM TALKING A FEW SECONDS LONGER ... TILL I CAN TWIST THIS IRON *CABLE* INTO POSITION...!

B

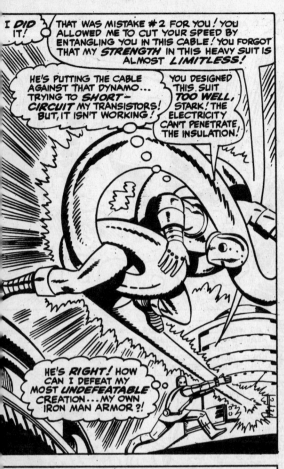

I **DID** IT! THAT WAS MISTAKE #2 FOR YOU! YOU ALLOWED ME TO CUT YOUR SPEED BY ENTANGLING YOU IN THIS CABLE! YOU FORGOT THAT MY **STRENGTH** IN THIS HEAVY SUIT IS ALMOST **LIMITLESS**!

HE'S PUTTING THE CABLE AGAINST THAT DYNAMO... TRYING TO **SHORT-CIRCUIT** MY TRANSISTORS! BUT, IT ISN'T WORKING!

YOU DESIGNED THIS SUIT **TOO WELL**, STARK! THE ELECTRICITY CAN'T PENETRATE THE INSULATION!

HE'S **RIGHT**! HOW CAN I DEFEAT MY MOST **UNDEFEATABLE** CREATION... MY OWN **IRON MAN** ARMOR?!

A SECOND LATER, WEASEL WILLS, USING HIS TRANSISTOR POWER AT FULL INTENSITY, UNTANGLES THE CONFINING CABLE, AND QUICKLY ROLLS THE IRON TUBING INTO A MAKESHIFT **BALL**....!

NO MATTER **HOW** STRONG YOUR OLD ARMOR IS, PAL, **NOTHING** CAN BE STRONGER THAN THE IRON SUIT I'M WEARING! ...AND YOU **KNOW** IT!

THEN, NONCHALANTLY CASTING THE HEAVY IRON BALL ASIDE, THE EVIL USURPER **SEIZES** A TOWERING STEEL PILLAR, AND, WITH ONE IRRESISTIBLE SWEEP...

JUST STAY WHERE YOU ARE, STARK! I'LL FINISH THIS OFF BEFORE YOU **KNOW** IT! YOU'RE TOO SLOW TO DODGE ME!

RRRAK!

AND, TRUE TO HIS WORD, WEASEL **STRIKES**... WITH DAZZLING SPEED...

THE FORGED STEEL STRAIT-JACKET WILL HOLD **YOU** A LOT EASIER THAN YOU WERE ABLE TO HOLD **ME**!

AND ONCE YOU'RE OUT OF THE WAY, I'LL POLISH OFF YOUR BUDDIES IN THE **AVENGERS**, ONE BY ONE!

HE'S GOING **MAD**! HE'S BECOMING **OBSESSED** BY HIS NEW SENSE OF POWER!

9.

THE BEAUTY OF THIS IS... I KNOW WHO *YOU* ARE, BUT YOU DON'T KNOW *ME!*

YOU'RE ABOUT TO BE *SMASHED*.. BY A NAMELESS STRANGER!

HE PLANS TO DROP THAT TEN-TON LEAD CASING ON ME! I'VE GOT TO SET MY IMPACT CONTROL SWITCH TO *TOP POWER!*

ALSO, I'VE GOT TO KEEP *NEEDLING* HIM...FIND A WAY TO MAKE HIM FLY INTO A BLIND RAGE!

I HAVE NO INTEREST IN YOUR IDENTITY! TO ME, YOU'RE A *NOBODY*...JUST A CHEAP HOOD WHO WAS LUCKY ENOUGH TO FIND MY ARMOR! YOU'RE NOT IN MY CLASS, PUNK!

AWRIGHT, YOU SWELL-HEADED SNOB...HERE'S WHERE A CRUMMY NOBODY POLISHES OFF THE GREAT TONY STARK... *FOREVER!*

WHOOOM!

BUT, AS WEASEL WILLS BENDS DOWN TO INSPECT THE DEBRIS, THE HEAVIEST, MOST INVULNERABLE SUIT OF ARMOR EVER CREATED, THUNDERS INTO GALVANIZED ACTION ONCE MORE. A LIVING, MOVING, POWER-PACKED TRIBUTE TO THE GENIUS OF TONY STARK!

THAT WAS MISTAKE #3, YOU RANK AMATEUR!! YOU UNDER-ESTIMATED THE PROTECTIVE POWER OF MY ORIGINAL SUIT OF ARMOR! THE POWER WHICH WAS ALWAYS ITS GREATEST ASSET!

KLANK!

WHAM!

BUT, ALTHOUGH STARTLED, TONY STARK'S EVIL FOE *STILL* HAS THE ADVANTAGE OF THE NEWEST, MOST POTENT ARMOR OF ALL, AND ONCE AGAIN HE LAUNCHES HIS ATTACK!

OKAY, SO I *MADE* A FEW SLIPS...SO *WHAT?* AS LONG AS I'M WEARIN' THIS IRON KIMONO OF YOURS, I CAN GOOF IT UP ALL DAY AND *STILL* BEAT YOU!

BUT *YOU* CAN'T AFFORD EVEN *ONE* MISTAKE... AND YOU *KNOW* IT!

MISTER, TONY STARK DIDN'T GET TO BE WHERE HE IS BY *MAKING* ANY MISTAKES!! GET THE PICTURE ??

BLANNG!

10.

THEN, GOADED BY STARK'S STINGING WORDS, WEASEL WILLS THROWS CAUTION TO THE WINDS AND AGAIN COMES WITHIN PUMMELING RANGE...

IT **WORKED!** I ANGERED HIM ENOUGH TO MAKE HIM FORGET ABOUT HIS ADVANTAGE OF **SPEED!** NOW HE WANTS TO SLUG IT OUT!

BUT, BY NOW, THE SOUNDS OF BATTLE HAVE AROUSED A GUARD OUTSIDE THE MAIN GATES, AND, WITHIN SECONDS...

NO! I AIN'T IMAGININ' THINGS! THERE'S **TWO** IRON MEN HERE... THEY'RE **WRECKING** THE PLACE!

AND SO... WE WERE HAVIN' ENOUGH TROUBLE WITH **ONE** IRON MAN... NOW THERE'S A **SECOND** ONE! STEP ON IT!!

AND, WITHIN THE FACTORY...

LUCKILY, MY SKILL IS ABLE TO NULLIFY HIS GREATER SPEED! BUT... FOR HOW LONG?

AND THEN... IT HAPPENS!

MY **HEART!** THAT SUDDEN **PAIN!** THE ONE THING I FEARED...!

THIS WAS THE REASON I DESIGNED THE **OTHER** ARMOR... BECAUSE **THIS ONE** IS TOO HEAVY! THE STRAIN IS TOO GREAT!

I'VE ONLY **ONE** CHANCE! IT'S A DESPERATE GAMBLE... BUT I **MUST** TAKE IT!

KA-THUNK!

YOU'RE TRYING NOT TO SHOW IT... BUT I CAN TELL... YOU'RE **WEAKENING!**

MUST HOLD ON ...JUST A LITTLE LONGER...!

OKAY, STARK! JUST HOLD THAT POSE, AND IT'LL BE OVER REAL QUICK!

I CAN'T REALLY **HURT** STARK INSIDE THAT ARMOR... BUT, IF I CAN JUST KEEP **WEAKENING** HIM, IT'LL BE JUST AS GOOD!

KLAK!

IT HAS TO HAPPEN SOON ...THE MORE HE HITS ME... THE MORE ENERGY HE USES UP!

HAH! YOU CAN HARDLY **MOVE!** NOW, ALL I GOTTA DO IS FIND YOUR **WEAKEST** SPOT, AND KEEP SMASHIN' AT IT! I **KNEW** YOU COULDN'T BEAT THE **NEW** IRON MAN!

HE'S BEGINNING TO THINK HE REALLY **IS** IRON MAN!

HOLD ON, TONY... JUST ANOTHER FEW SECONDS...!

11.

AND THEN, BEFORE WEASEL WILLS CAN BRING HIS TRANSISTOR-POWERED MIGHT DOWN ON HIS VICTIM...

I-I'M SLOWIN' DOWN...GETTIN' WEAK! WHA...WHAT'S *HAPPENING?!*

EXACTLY WHAT I *PLANNED* WOULD HAPPEN! YOUR TRANSISTORS ARE RUNNING DOWN!

HUH! BIG DEAL! ALL I NEED IS A *RE-CHARGE!*

I LEARNED HOW TO DO IT WHILE I WAS EXPERIMENTING WITH YOUR ARMOR! IT'LL ONLY TAKE A FEW MINUTES...NOT LONG ENOUGH TO DO *YOU* ANY GOOD!

HEY! TH-THERE'S NO *JUICE* GOIN' INTO THE SUIT! THE GIZMO AIN'T *CHARGING!*

NATURALLY! WHILE YOU WERE BUSY CROWING, I TOOK THE PRECAUTION OF *SHUTTING OFF* THE MAIN FACTORY POWER SWITCH!

AND, I TOOK THE PRECAUTION OF *RESTING* WHILE YOU WERE WASTING ENERGY ON YOUR USELESS BLOWS!

BY *NOW,* YOUR TRANSISTORS SHOULD BE ALMOST COMPLETELY DRAINED, SO I'LL SIMPLY *FINISH* THE JOB BY CUTTING OFF YOUR MASTER OUTPUT SWITCH

CLICK!

NO NEED FOR GUNS, GENTLEMEN! THE SITUATION IS WELL IN HAND!

YOU MUST HAVE GUESSED BY NOW THAT THE *CRIMINAL* IRON MAN WAS AN IMPOSTOR...A SHODDY CROOK WHO MANAGED TO STEAL MY ARMOR!

NO! HE'S LYING! HE'S LYING!

WELL, THAT'S THAT! I'VE ENDED THE MENACE...BUT NOW, MY *OWN* IDENTITY IS SURE TO COME OUT WHEN THIS TWO-BIT HOOD STARTS "SINGING".

IT'S *WEASEL WILLS...* A THREE-TIME LOSER! WHERE'D YOU GET THE ARMOR, WEASEL? THAT'LL TELL US WHO IRON MAN REALLY IS!

WHERE'DID *I* GET IT?

IT'S *MINE!!* I *MADE* IT! TAKE YOUR HANDS OFF ME! I'M *IRON MAN...*CAN'T YOU SEE? I'M IRON MAN!

SURE YOU ARE, FELLA! NOW COME ALONG QUIETLY!

THE STRAIN WAS TOO MUCH FOR 'IM, SAM! HE'S GONE OFF HIS ROCKER!

THEN, AT THE PLANT NEXT MORNING...

I GUESS WE'LL NEVER KNOW YOUR BODYGUARD'S *REAL* IDENTITY, MR. STARK! THAT IMPOSTOR HAS LOST HIS MIND! HE'S CONVINCED THAT *HE'S* IRON MAN!

IT'S A GOOD THING THAT IRON MAN *DIDN'T* TURN BAD! *NOBODY* WOULD EVER BE ABLE TO STOP 'IM!

BOY, WHOEVER IRON MAN REALLY IS, HE'S THE LUCKIEST GUY IN THE WORLD! HE'S GOT *EVERYTHING!*

PERHAPS! BUT SOMETIMES A PERSON CAN SEEM TO POSSESS ALL THAT ANYONE COULD EVER WANT, AND STILL HAVE...NOTHING!

NOW WHAT IN BLAZES DID HE MEAN BY *THAT*?

SO ONCE AGAIN, AMERICA'S YOUNGEST, MOST HANDSOME, WEALTHIEST TYCOON ENTERS THE SOLITUDE OF HIS PRIVATE OFFICE...WITH HIS PRIVATE SECRETS...AND HIS NEVER ENDING PRIVATE SORROW...!

THE END

TALES OF SUSPENSE
featuring
IRON CAPTAIN MAN and AMERICA

MARVEL COMICS GROUP 12¢

66 JUNE

IND.

APPROVED BY THE COMICS CODE AUTHORITY

IF ONE PICTURE IS WORTH A THOUSAND WORDS, JUST IMAGINE WHAT THESE *TWO* PICTURES ARE WORTH!

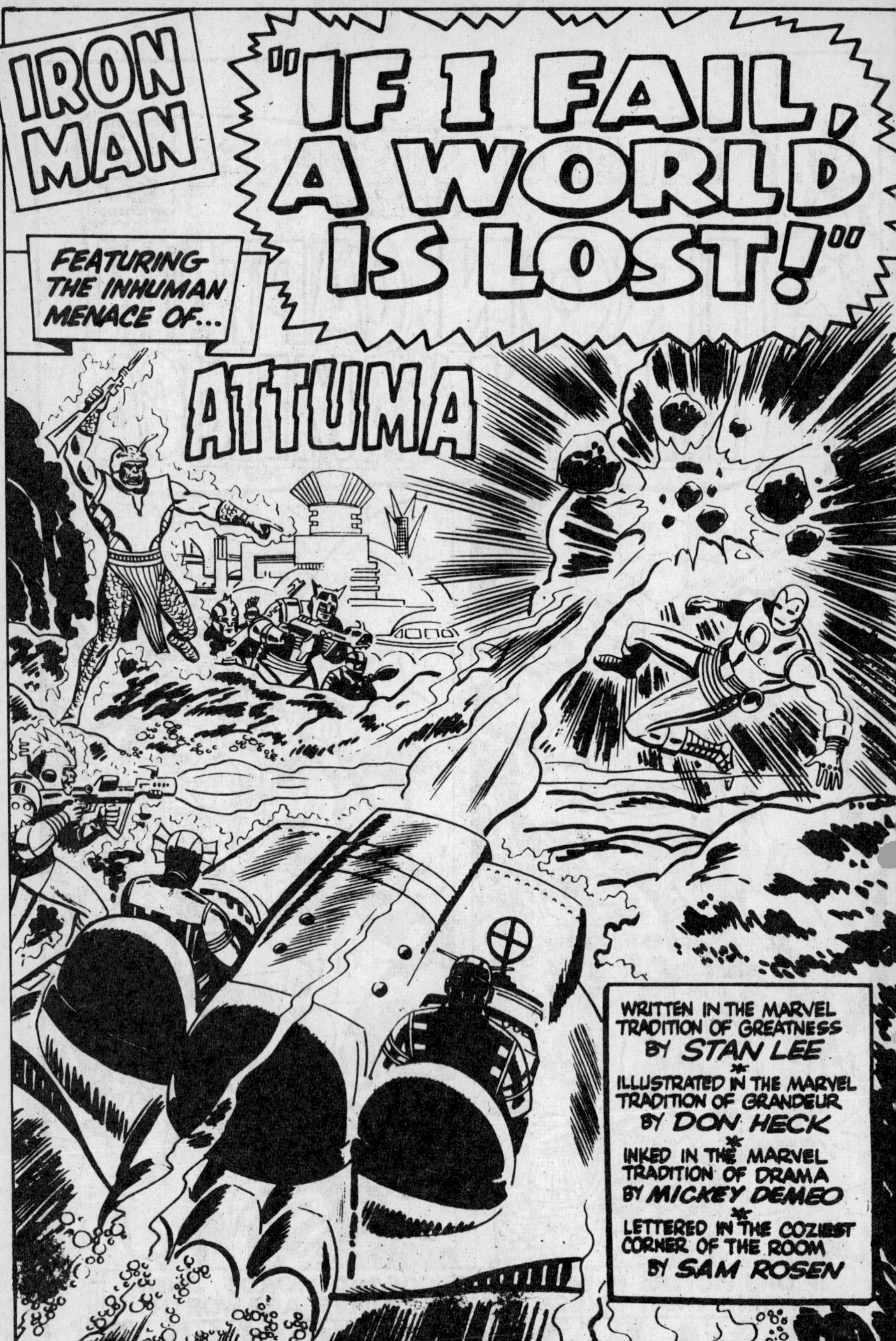
IRON MAN
"IF I FAIL, A WORLD IS LOST!"
FEATURING THE INHUMAN MENACE OF...
ATTUMA
WRITTEN IN THE MARVEL TRADITION OF GREATNESS BY STAN LEE
ILLUSTRATED IN THE MARVEL TRADITION OF GRANDEUR BY DON HECK
INKED IN THE MARVEL TRADITION OF DRAMA BY MICKEY DEMEO
LETTERED IN THE COZIEST CORNER OF THE ROOM BY SAM ROSEN

IRON MAN, ONE OF THE MOST POWERFUL MORTALS ON EARTH, IS ALSO ONE OF THE WEAKEST... UNLESS HE FAITHFULLY CHARGES THE BATTERIES OF HIS BUILT-IN CHEST DEVICE AT REGULAR INTERVALS!

MR. STARK, SENATOR BYRD IS HERE TO SEE YOU!

SENATOR BYRD? I ALMOST FORGOT OUR APPOINTMENT!

LUCKY MY CHARGING PERIOD WAS JUST ENDING!

BYRD HATES TO BE KEPT WAITING!

...ESPECIALLY BY ME! HE'S CONVINCED I'M JUST A HIGH-LIVING PLAYBOY WHO SHOULDN'T BE AWARDED VITAL U.S. GOVERNMENT DEFENSE CONTRACTS!

HE'D PUT ME OUT OF BUSINESS IN A MINUTE, IF HE COULD!

MR. STARK WILL BE RIGHT WITH YOU, SENATOR!

HE'D BETTER BE! IF HE RUNS HIS FACTORY AS CARELESSLY AS HE KEEPS TIME..

HELLO, SENATOR! SORRY TO HAVE KEPT YOU WAITING!

HRRMPH! I'LL BET YOU ARE!

I CAME TO SEE THE TESTS OF YOUR NEW, TRANSISTORIZED ONE-MAN SUBMARINE! ALTHOUGH, I THINK YOU'VE BITTEN OFF MORE THAN YOU CAN CHEW WITH THIS PROJECT, STARK!

THE TEST WILL CONVINCE YOU, SIR!

I'VE ARRANGED TO HAVE IRON MAN CONDUCT THE TEST, AND HE'LL BE READY TO BEGIN WITHIN MINUTES!

EVERY TIME PEPPER LOOKS AT STARK YOU CAN ALMOST SEE HER MELTING! IF ONLY SHE'D LOOK AT ME THAT WAY!

IF ONLY I HAD A CHANCE TO DO SOMETHING TO IMPRESS HER! WAIT! I KNOW...!

SAY, BOSS! HOW ABOUT LETTING ME TEST THAT SUB! YOU'VE OFTEN SHOWN ME HOW IT WORKS!

SORRY, HAPPY! IRON MAN'S AREADY BEEN CHECKED OUT!

2

I *FIGURED* HE'D SAY THAT! WHAT AM I HERE? JUST A DECORATION?

I NEVER EVEN *CHAUFFEUR* HIM WHEN HE'S GOT AN IMPORTANT TRIP! IT'S ALWAYS *IRON MAN!*

IF HE'S ONLY KEEPIN' ME AROUND BECAUSE I SAVED HIS LIFE ONCE * HE BETTER *FORGET* IT!

*AS SHOWN IN *SUSPENSE #45*...STAN.

LOOK, BOSS! EITHER *I* JOCKEY THE PINT-SIZED SUB, OR I *QUIT!* AND THAT'S *FINAL!*

HAPPY!

KNOCK IT OFF, HAPPY! WE'LL DISCUSS IT LATER!

THAT *DOES* IT! THERE AIN'T GONNA *BE* ANY LATER! I'VE *HAD* IT!

CAN'T EVEN MANAGE YOUR OWN EMPLOYEES, EH, STARK?

HAPPY... COME BACK! WAIT...!

MR. STARK...YOU *CAN'T* LET HIM GO!

I'VE NO OTHER CHOICE!

I *CAN'T* RISK HAPPY'S LIFE ON THIS TEST! IF SOMETHING SHOULD GO *WRONG*...!

WELL, STARK? HOW MUCH *LONGER* MUST I BE KEPT *WAITING?!!*

THERE ISN'T EVEN TIME FOR ME TO GO *AFTER* HAP—

SORRY, SENATOR!

I'LL SUMMON *IRON MAN!* THE TEST WILL BEGIN AT ONCE!

A PLAY-BOY LIKE *YOU*... CREATING WEAPONS FOR THE FREE WORLD! I JUST CAN'T *SEE* IT!

BUT, SENATOR... MANY OF MY *TRANSISTOR-POWERED* DEVICES ARE BEING SUCCESSFULLY EMPLOYED RIGHT NOW, IN EVERY CORNER OF THE GLOBE!

I KNOW! BUT I'LL NEVER BELIEVE THAT *YOU* INVENTED THEM! YOU NEVER HAD A SERIOUS THOUGHT IN YOUR HEAD, STARK! YOU PLAYBOYS ARE ALL ALIKE!

I KNOW...

PLAYBOY! CARRYING A DEADLY PIECE OF *SHRAPNEL* FROM VIET NAM LODGED IN MY HEART! RISKING MY LIFE DAILY AS IRON MAN! UNABLE TO MARRY BECAUSE EACH MOMENT MAY BE MY LAST! IF HE ONLY *KNEW*...!

MY SECRETARY WILL ESCORT YOU AND YOUR STAFF TO THE DOCK! IRON MAN WILL JOIN YOU THERE!

MINUTES LATER... DUE TO ITS EXTREME MANEUVERABILITY, OUR NEW MINI-SUB CAN OUT-RUN AND OUT-FLANK ALMOST ANY ENEMY TORPEDO! ALSO, ITS COMPACT SIZE GIVES IT GREATER STRENGTH PER CUBIC INCH, ENABLING IT TO WITHSTAND THE TREMENDOUS PRESSURE OF THE DEEP!

YES, YES! WE *KNOW* ALL THAT! JUST SKIP THE LECTURE AND GET ON WITH THE TEST!

I DON'T SEE *STARK* HERE! PROBABLY IN CONFERENCE WITH SOME FEMALE! *HRUMMPH!*

MR. STARK RARELY ATTENDS THESE TESTS, SIR! HE LEAVES THAT TO *IRON MAN!*

AND SO... THIS MINI-SUB WILL BE INVALUABLE AS A SCOUTING-ATTACK AID TO THE NAVY!

SO FAR, EVERYTHING CHECKS OUT A-OKAY!

SENATOR BYRD IS REALLY A GOOD SORT! HE'S A DEDICATED PUBLIC OFFICIAL WHO BELIEVES WHAT HE READS ABOUT ME IN THE GOSSIP COLUMNS! I CAN'T EVEN SAY I BLAME HIM!

I'VE *GOT* TO ACT THE PART OF A LIGHT-HEARTED PLAYBOY, SO THAT NO ONE WILL EVER SUSPECT MY SECRET IDENTITY! IF MY ENEMIES KNEW THAT I'M REALLY *IRON MAN,* I'D HAVE TO LIVE IN THIS ARMOR *FOREVER* TO PROTECT MYSELF FROM THEM!

UH-OH! I'VE BEEN SO WRAPPED UP IN MY OWN THOUGHTS, I ALMOST MISSED THIS SONAR-ALARM SOUNDING! THERE'S SOMETHING *AHEAD* OF ME!

THE INDICATOR IS REGISTERING WILDLY! THE SCREEN IS BRIGHT *RED!* WHAT CAN I BE HEADING *INTO?!*

AN *INTRUDER* COMES!

DESTROY HIM!

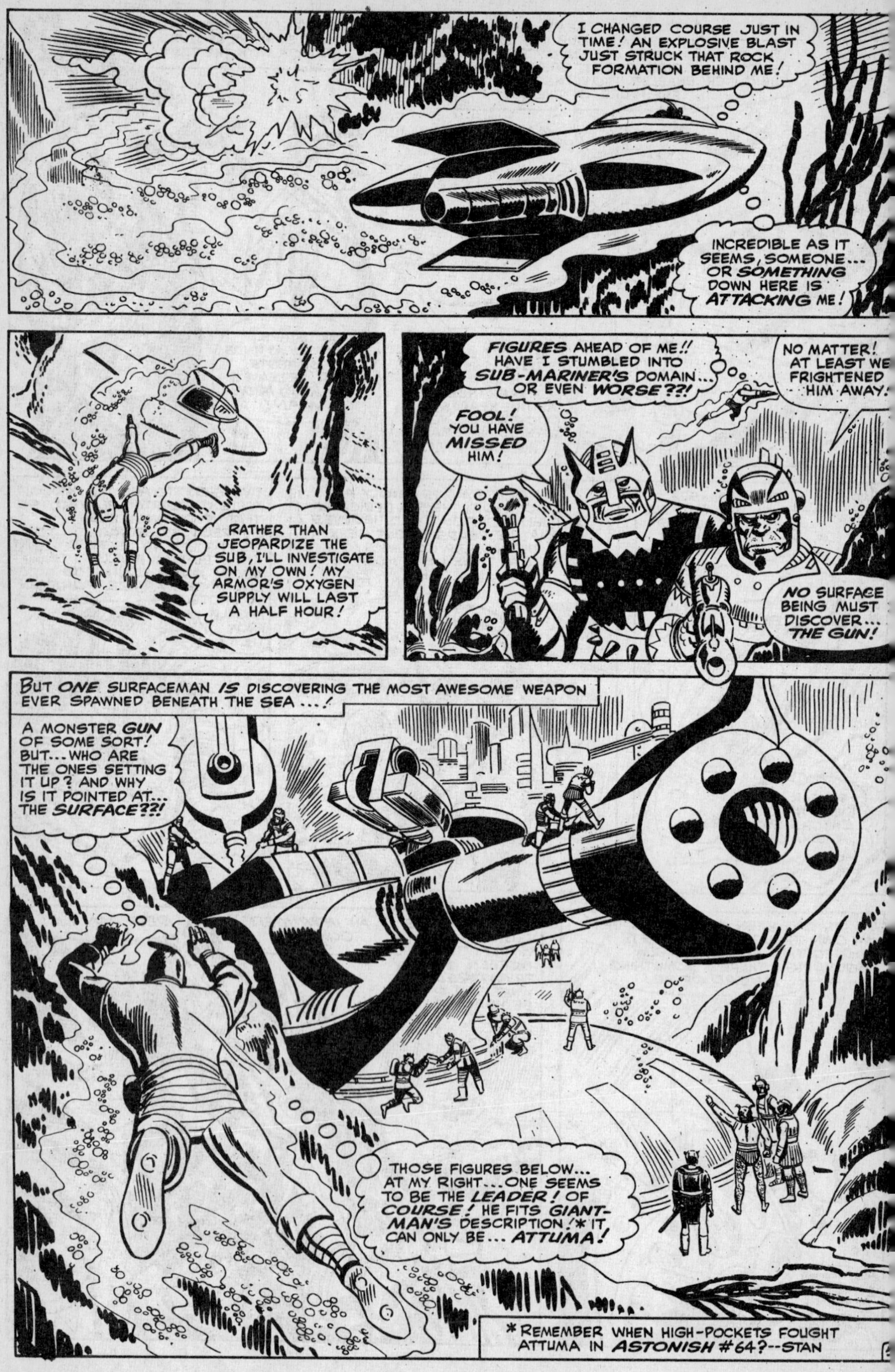
I CHANGED COURSE JUST IN TIME! AN EXPLOSIVE BLAST JUST STRUCK THAT ROCK FORMATION BEHIND ME!
INCREDIBLE AS IT SEEMS, SOMEONE... OR SOMETHING DOWN HERE IS ATTACKING ME!
RATHER THAN JEOPARDIZE THE SUB, I'LL INVESTIGATE ON MY OWN! MY ARMOR'S OXYGEN SUPPLY WILL LAST A HALF HOUR!
FIGURES AHEAD OF ME!! HAVE I STUMBLED INTO SUB-MARINER'S DOMAIN... OR EVEN WORSE??!
NO MATTER! AT LEAST WE FRIGHTENED HIM AWAY.
FOOL! YOU HAVE MISSED HIM!
NO SURFACE BEING MUST DISCOVER... THE GUN!
BUT ONE SURFACEMAN IS DISCOVERING THE MOST AWESOME WEAPON EVER SPAWNED BENEATH THE SEA...!
A MONSTER GUN OF SOME SORT! BUT... WHO ARE THE ONES SETTING IT UP? AND WHY IS IT POINTED AT... THE SURFACE??!
THOSE FIGURES BELOW... AT MY RIGHT... ONE SEEMS TO BE THE LEADER! OF COURSE! HE FITS GIANT-MAN'S DESCRIPTION!* IT CAN ONLY BE... ATTUMA!
*REMEMBER WHEN HIGH-POCKETS FOUGHT ATTUMA IN ASTONISH #64?--STAN

ATTUMA!! MERCILESS RENEGADE FROM ONCE-PROUD ATLANTIS! SWORN ENEMY OF *SUB-MARINER!* ATTUMA! HE WHO LIVES FOR CONQUEST!

HOW LONG BEFORE THE GUN CAN BE *FIRED*??

A MATTER OF *MINUTES,* MY LORD ATTUMA!

IT HAS TAKEN *MONTHS* TO BUILD SUCH A WEAPON! MY SUBJECTS HAVE COMBED THE OCEAN'S DEPTHS FOR THE RARE METAL *NAUTILIUM!*

OUR FIRST SHOT MUST *NOT* FAIL, FOR THERE IS NO NAUTILIUM LEFT WITH WHICH TO BUILD ANOTHER SHELL!

"BUT, *ONE SHOT* IS ALL WE WILL NEED! ONE SHOT, TO SEND OUR NAUTILIUM SHELL SCREAMING INTO THE UPPER ATMOSPHERE..."

"...WHERE IT WILL FUSE WITH THE OXYGEN SURFACEMEN NEED IN ORDER TO BREATHE....!"

"AND THEN, THE SURFACE WILL BE *OURS!* FOR, THE NAUTILIUM-WILL *CHANGE* THE DENSITY OF THE OXYGEN, MAKING IT MOIST... *SO MOIST,* THAT SURFACEMEN WILL HAVE DIFFICULTY BREATHING THEIR OWN AIR!"

"THUS, *WE* WILL BE ABLE TO LIVE ON EARTH'S SURFACE, PUTTING IT UNDER MY COMPLETE DOMAIN, WHILE THE FORMER RULERS OF THEIR WORLD WILL BE OUR *SLAVES* ...UNABLE TO BREATHE WITHOUT THE HELMETS WHICH *WE* SHALL SUPPLY!"

HE *MEANS* IT! HE'S MAD!

AND YET... HIS SHELL MAY *WORK!* I DARE NOT ALLOW IT TO BE *FIRED!*

6.

LOOK! A FIGURE... THE COLOR OF GOLD... LURKING NEAR THE ROCKS AHEAD!

WE MUST TAKE NO CHANCES! HE MAY BE A SPY FROM THE SURFACE! DESTROY HIM!

AN UNDERSEA SCOUT SHIP... COMING AT ME! I'VE GOT TO MOVE!

HE WAS TOO FAST! WE MISSED!

ONE ARMORED HUMAN AGAINST ATTUMA'S LEGIONS! IT SEEMS HOPELESS!... AND YET, I MUST ACCEPT THE CHALLENGE!

FIRST, I'LL DESTROY THE SCOUT SHIP, NOW... WHILE MY TRANSISTORS ARE STILL OPERATING AT PEAK EFFICIENCY!

SIRE! A STRANGER APPROACHES! HE IS ARMORED!

TAKE NO CHANCES, YOU FOOL! SEIZE HIM! HAVE THE PINCER TANK ATTACK!

THUS, AT THE COMMAND OF THEIR TYRANNICAL RULER...

OBJECTIVE WITHIN RANGE! PINCERS OPERATING AS ORDERED!

ATTUMA HAS WEAPONS WHICH SEEM TO RIVAL OUR OWN! BUT, I CAN'T LET THEM SLOW ME DOWN!

NOTHING MUST DETER ME FROM DESTROYING THAT GUN BEFORE IT CAN BE FIRED!

7.

THE TANK'S MAIN POWER SEEMS TO LIE WITHIN THESE FLEXIBLE PINCER CLAWS!

SO, IF I CAN JUST *SEIZE* THEM AND EXERT ALL MY TRANSISTORIZED POWER BEFORE THEY CAN PRY THEMSELVES LOOSE...

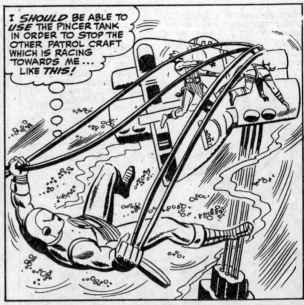

I *SHOULD* BE ABLE TO *USE* THE PINCER TANK IN ORDER TO STOP THE OTHER PATROL CRAFT WHICH IS RACING TOWARDS ME... LIKE *THIS!*

BAH! MY SHIPS ARE TOO SLOW AND CLUMSY TO COPE WITH HIM! BUT, MY PICKED CORPS OF ELITE *FOOT TROOPS* WILL DESTROY THE INTRUDER! ATTACK!

AN INFANTRY PATROL CHARGING! HOW CAN I STOP THEM *ALL* AT ONE TIME??

THEN, WITH THE SPEED OF THOUGHT, AND THE POWER OF A BEHEMOTH, THE GOLDEN AVENGER AIMS HIS REPULSOR RAY AT A MIGHTY, OVERHANGING BOULDER, AND *FIRES....FULL FORCE!*

BY THE TIME THEY CAN REGROUP, I SHOULD HAVE REACHED THE GUN!!

ENOUGH!! *BACK*, ALL OF YOU! ATTUMA HIMSELF SHALL CRUSH THAT INSOLENT INTRUDER LIKE A JELLY FISH!

8

THIS IS WHAT I *HOPED* FOR! THEY WON'T FIRE THE GUN WITHOUT ATTUMA! IF I CAN KEEP HIM OCCUPIED LONG ENOUGH...!

HE'S FIRING SOME SORT OF *HEAT RAY* AT ME!! I CAN FEEL THE BURNING SEN- SATION RIGHT THROUGH MY INVULNERABLE ARMOR!!

GETTING HOTTER ...HOTTER! CAN'T *TAKE* IT MUCH LONGER! ONLY *ONE* ANSWER!...!

I'LL PROP MYSELF AGAINST THIS OVER- HANGING LEDGE AND *REVERSE* MY FLYING POWER JETS!! IF I KEEP THE PRESSURE UP LONG ENOUGH...!

IT'S *WORKING!* THE BURNING CURRENTS ARE BEING FORCED BACK...DIRECTLY BACK WHERE THEY CAME FROM...TO *ATTUMA!*

BUT THE AWESOME ATTUMA, WHOSE STRENGTH IS RIVALLED ONLY BY THE SUB-MARINER HIMSELF, IS ABLE TO WITHSTAND THE UNEXPECTED ASSAULT... AN ASSAULT WHICH SERVES TO INCREASE HIS *RAGE!*

BY THE SEVEN SCEPTERS OF NEPTUNE, YOU SHALL PAY *DEARLY* FOR THIS!!

EVEN WITHOUT ANY *ARMOR,* HE'S AS STRONG AS IRON MAN! CAN'T AFFORD ONE SLIP-UP!

I'VE GOT TO ATTACK HIM NOW WITH ALL I'VE GOT BEFORE MY TRAN- SISTORS RUN DOWN!

HE'S GOT A *RIFLE* OF SOME SORT. I CAN'T *STOP* IN TIME! HE'S AIMING IT AT ME...!

UNABLE TO STOP HIS POWER-ASSISTED ATTACK, IRON MAN DOES THE NEXT BEST THING! USING THE ROCKET-LIKE FORCE OF HIS MINIATURE JETS, HE CAUSES HIS BODY TO DESCRIBE A LIGHTNING-SWIFT *ARC*, ARCHING AROUND THE RIFLE'S BLAST!

SO FAR, SO GOOD! BUT I CAN'T GIVE HIM A SECOND CHANCE! I MUSTN'T STOP FOR A SECOND!

THEN, WITHOUT LOSING THE MOMENTUM WHICH HIS JETS HAVE BUILT UP, THE ARMORED AVENGER WHIRLS AROUND ATTUMA, CHURNING THE WATERS WITH EVER-INCREASING PRESSURE...!

IF I DO THIS ENOUGH, IT MAY MAKE HIM SO DIZZY THAT HE'LL BLACK OUT... UNLESS *I* DO, FIRST!

NO! IT WON'T WORK! IT'S DRAINING MY TRANSISTORS TOO MUCH! I'VE *GOT* TO STOP!

I DON'T *GET* IT! WHY DID HE START *RUNNING* AS SOON AS I WITHDREW THE PRESSURE??

HE MUST *KNOW* OUR POWER IS ALMOST EQUAL! AND FROM WHAT I'VE *HEARD*, ABOUT HIM, THE ONE THING NO ONE CAN CALL HIM IS --- *COWARD!*

WELL, WHATEVER HIS REASON, I CAN'T LET HIM ESCAPE ME! THEY WON'T FIRE THAT GUN WITHOUT *ATTUMA'S* SIGNAL.... AND IT'S UP TO *ME* TO MAKE SURE HE NEVER *GIVES* THAT SIGNAL!

HE THOUGHT HE COULD LOSE ME IN THIS DARK TUNNEL! BUT, NOT WHILE I HAVE MY BUILT-IN CHEST SPOTLIGHT SET ON "AUTOMATIC"!

IT...IT'S GETTING HARDER TO *BREATHE!* I FORGOT... MY ARMOR ONLY CONTAINS A THIRTY-MINUTES' SUPPLY OF OXYGEN.... AND I'VE BEEN HERE ALMOST A HALF-HOUR *ALREADY!*

10.

I WAS A *FOOL!* HE *WASN'T* TRYING TO ESCAPE!...HE WAS SETTING A *TRAP* FOR ME! AND I BLUNDERED RIGHT *INTO* IT!

HE'S WORKING A CONTROL PANEL, CAUSING THOSE SHIMMERING BEAMS TO SEPARATE US! HE SEEMS TO *WANT* ME TO TACKLE THEM!

BUT, I *CAN'T!* MY IN-GLOVE GEIGER-COUNTER REGISTERS A HIGH DEGREE OF *RADIATION!* IT WOULD BE SUDDEN DEATH TO COME IN DIRECT CONTACT WITH THOSE BEAMS!

THEY FORM THE PERFECT *PRISON!*

BUT, THERE'S MORE THAN MY *OWN* LIFE AT STAKE! ALL *HUMANITY* MAY HANG IN THE BALANCE! I'VE *GOT* TO BREAK FREE!

...AND *SOON!* HE'S HEADING TOWARDS THE GUN... AND EACH BREATH OF MINE GROWS MORE LABORED!

WAIT! IT'S A LONG SHOT, BUT... MY *SPOT LIGHT* MAY GET ME OUT OF HERE! I'VE GOT TO ALTER THE REFRACTION ANGLE OF THE REFLECTIVE LENS!!

NOW, BY CATCHING THE GLOW OF THOSE RADIOACTIVE BEAMS AT JUST THE RIGHT ANGLE, I CAN REFLECT THEM *BACK* AGAIN... STRIKING THEM WITH THEIR *OWN* FORCE, MAGNIFIED BY MY LENS!

IT'S *WORKING!* I'M DESTROYING ATTUMA'S BEAMS WITH THEIR OWN IRRESISTIBLE POWER!

SECONDS MORE, AND I'LL BE *FREE!*

I *DID* IT! BUT...I'M *TOO LATE!* MY LUNGS FEEL LIKE THEY'RE BURSTING! MY OXYGEN IS ALL *GONE!*

NO! THERE'S *STILL* HOPE! I SEE IT UP AHEAD...!

MY *SUB!* IF I CAN JUST HOLD MY BREATH LONG ENOUGH...I'M HEADED FOR IT... POWER JETS AT TOP INTENSITY...I MUST MAKE IT...I *MUST...!*

11.

AND, MAKE IT HE *DOES!* WITHIN SECONDS, THE GOLDEN AVENGER SLIPS A NEW OXYGEN CYLINDER INTO PLACE AS THE NIMBLE MINI-SUB HURTLES FORWARD...!

THE GUN IS ELEVATING... PREPARING TO *FIRE!*

MY SUB IS *UNARMED!* I'VE NO *WEAPONS* TO ATTACK WITH!

BUT, THE GUN *MUST* BE SILENCED BEFORE IT *FIRES!* HE *SEES* ME! HE'S TRYING TO FIRE BEFORE I CAN *STOP* THEM!

BUT HE *WON'T!* I'LL STOP HIM *YET!* THERE.. I'VE LOCKED THE CONTROLS...!

AND NOW, IT'S UP TO THE *SUB!*

FIRE, YOU *DOLT!* WHAT ARE YOU *WAITING* FOR ?? ONCE THAT NAUTILIUM SHELL IS FIRED, THE WORLD WILL BE *MINE!*

BUT, *SIRE!* A VESSEL APPROACHES ---IT'S GOING TO *CRASH!!* SIRE...!

STRAIGHT AND *TRUE* THE MINI-SUB STRIKES... DIRECTLY INTO THE BARREL OF THE MONSTROUS GUN...AS ATTUMA'S DREAM OF CONQUEST IS SHATTERED WITH THE DESTRUCTION OF HIS ONLY NAUTILIUM SHELL!

IT'S *OVER!* THE SHELL WAS SMASHED! MANKIND IS *SAFE!*

MINUTES LATER...

WE *HEARD* THE EXPLOSION! YOU'RE LUCKY YOU WEREN'T KILLED! HOW DID IT HAPPEN? WHAT WENT WRONG WITH STARK'S SUBMARINE!?

I CAN'T TELL! NO ONE WOULD EVER BELIEVE!

I DON'T KNOW, SENATOR! HE'LL HAVE TO BUILD A *NEW* ONE AND TEST IT AGAIN!

THAT PLAYBOY CAN BUILD ALL HE WANTS TO...BUT NOT WITH GOVERNMENT FUNDS! *I'LL* SEE TO THAT! AND TELL STARK I *SAID* SO!

IRON MAN! HAPPY IS *GONE!* AND I CAN'T FIND MR. STARK! YOU'VE GOT TO HELP!

STARK IS *NEVER* AROUND WHEN YOU WANT HIM! HE DOESN'T *DESERVE* HIS MILITARY CONTRACTS! AND I'LL MAKE THE PENTAGON *REALIZE* IT!

THUS, THE MAN WHO HAS POSSIBLY SAVED A *WORLD*, RETURNS TO FIND HIMSELF PLAGUED BY THE SAME PROBLEMS AND VEXATIONS AS EVER! DON'T MISS THE DRAMATIC DEVELOPMENTS IN STORE NEXT ISSUE! TILL THEN, KEEP YOUR ARMOR POLISHED!

END   12.

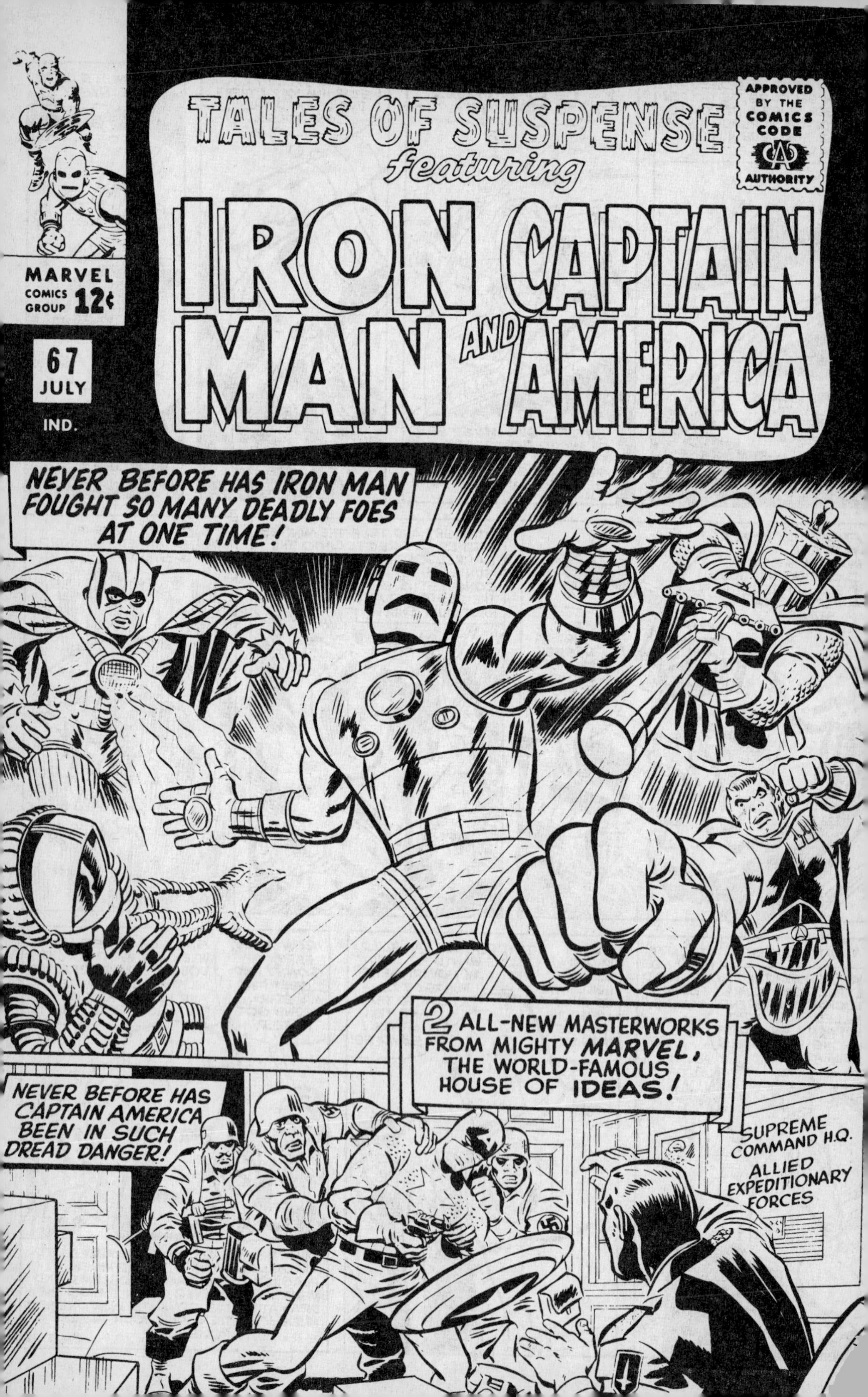

TALES OF SUSPENSE featuring
APPROVED BY THE COMICS CODE AUTHORITY
MARVEL COMICS GROUP 12¢
67 JULY
IND.
IRON MAN AND CAPTAIN AMERICA
NEVER BEFORE HAS IRON MAN FOUGHT SO MANY DEADLY FOES AT ONE TIME!
2 ALL-NEW MASTERWORKS FROM MIGHTY MARVEL, THE WORLD-FAMOUS HOUSE OF IDEAS!
NEVER BEFORE HAS CAPTAIN AMERICA BEEN IN SUCH DREAD DANGER!
SUPREME COMMAND H.Q.
ALLIED EXPEDITIONARY FORCES

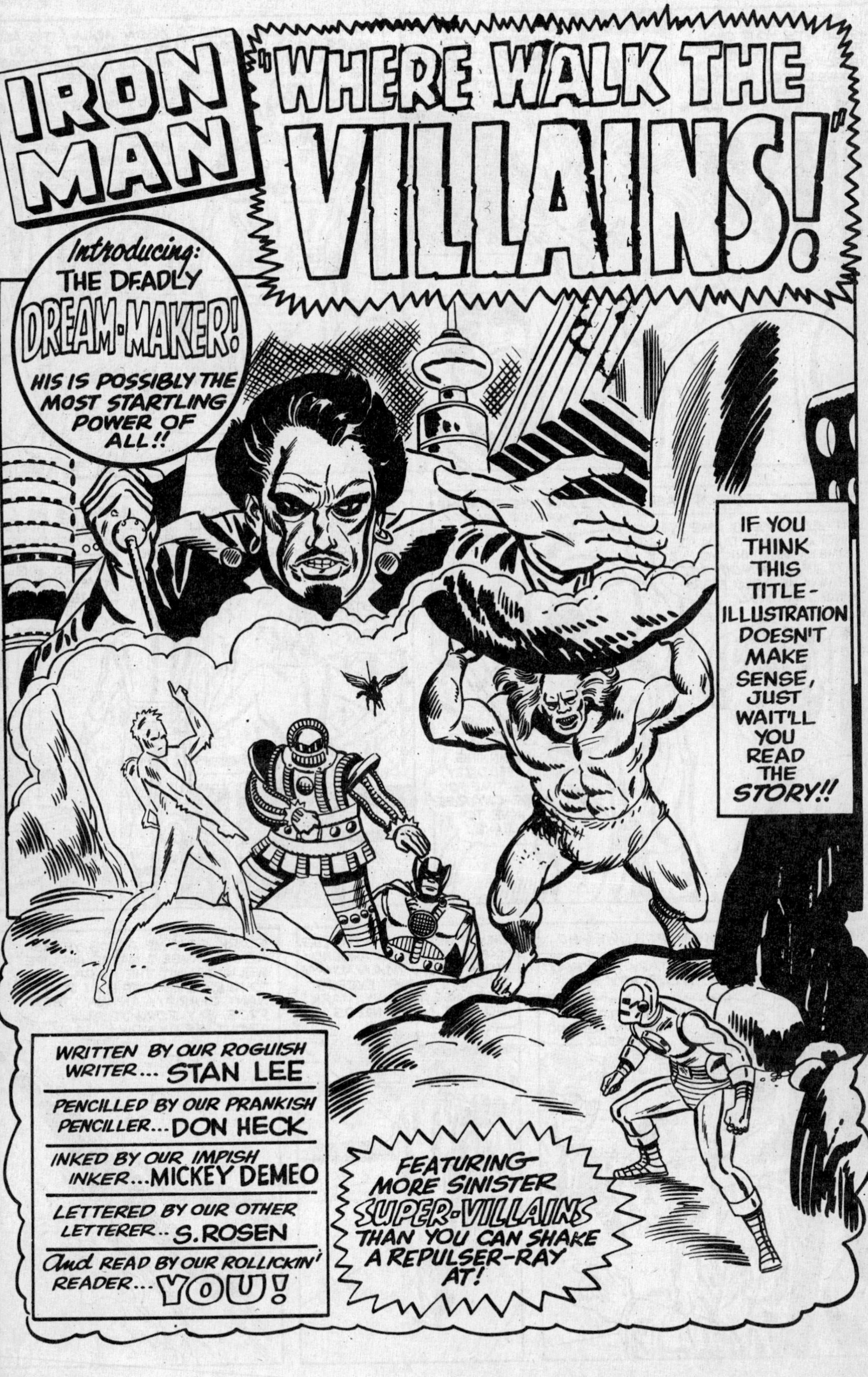
IRON MAN
"WHERE WALK THE VILLAINS!"
Introducing: THE DEADLY DREAM-MAKER! HIS IS POSSIBLY THE MOST STARTLING POWER OF ALL!!
IF YOU THINK THIS TITLE-ILLUSTRATION DOESN'T MAKE SENSE, JUST WAIT'LL YOU READ THE STORY!!
WRITTEN BY OUR ROGUISH WRITER... STAN LEE
PENCILLED BY OUR PRANKISH PENCILLER... DON HECK
INKED BY OUR IMPISH INKER... MICKEY DEMEO
LETTERED BY OUR OTHER LETTERER.. S. ROSEN
And READ BY OUR ROLLICKIN' READER... YOU!
FEATURING MORE SINISTER SUPER-VILLAINS THAN YOU CAN SHAKE A REPULSER-RAY AT!

IF YOU MISSED OUR LAST ISSUE, IT'S YOUR OWN FAULT! BUT, OUR MOTTO IS "FORGIVE AND FORGET", SO WE'LL TELL YOU THAT HAPPY HOGAN QUIT HIS JOB WITH TONY STARK IN A FIT OF ANGER...

OH, HAPPY... YOU HOT-TEMPERED FOOL! WHY DID YOU DO IT? THE PLACE ISN'T THE SAME WITHOUT YOU!

I NEVER THOUGHT YOU'D MISS HOGAN, PEPPER! YOU TWO ARGUED ALL THE TIME!

IRON MAN! IT'S ALL YOUR FAULT! IF YOU HAD LET HAPPY TEST THAT SUB, INSTEAD OF TRYING TO HOG ALL THE GLORY FOR YOURSELF, AS USUAL, HE WOULDN'T HAVE QUIT.

NO, BUT HE'D HAVE BEEN KILLED WHEN THE SUB EXPLODED! OR HAVE YOU FORGOTTEN?

BESIDES, THE DECISION WAS TONY STARK'S TO MAKE... IT WASN'T MINE!

YOU ALWAYS BLAME EVERYTHING ON MR. STARK! I SOMETIMES THINK YOU'VE GOT HIM HYPNOTIZED, THE WAY HE DOES EVERYTHING THAT YOU WANT HIM TO!

I'M BEGINNING TO FEEL DIZZY! IT'S TIME FOR A RE-CHARGE! HAVE TO LEAVE!

THAT'S JUST LIKE YOU... WALKING OUT WHENEVER SOMEONE GETS TOO CLOSE TO THE TRUTH! OH, IF ONLY I COULD CONVINCE MR. STARK TO FIRE YOU!

YOU WON'T ALWAYS BE ABLE TO HIDE BEHIND THAT UGLY IRON MASK OF YOURS, YOU... YOU RASPUTIN YOU!!

IF ONLY SHE KNEW! IF ONLY I DARED TELL HER!

MEANWHILE, AT J.F.K. AIRPORT, WE FIND...

PEPPER'S IN LOVE WITH STARK ANYWAY! SHE WON'T MISS ME! NOBODY WILL!

ONE-WAY TO SHANNON, IRELAND ...ON YOUR FIRST FLIGHT!

THEY DON'T NEED A BIG LUG LIKE ME HANGIN' AROUND! WITH IRON MAN ALWAYS THERE, I'M JUST EXCESS BAGGAGE TO TONY STARK! SO WHAT? WHO NEEDS 'IM?!

STARK GAVE ME A JOB YEARS AGO 'CAUSE I SAVED HIS LIFE! WELL, I AIN'T THE KINDA JOE TO KEEP LIVIN' OFF IT! I DON'T WANT CHARITY! ANYWAY, THEY PROBABLY FORGOT ALL ABOUT ME BY NOW!

2.

...BUT, IF HAPPY HOGAN COULD READ IRON MAN'S THOUGHTS AT THAT MOMENT, HE WOULDN'T BE SO SURE...!

IT'S BECAUSE OF *ME* THAT *HAPPY* LEFT! I'VE GOT TO FIND HIM...TO BRING HIM BACK!

BUT NOW, LET'S TURN OUR ATTENTION TO AN ABANDONED NAZI BUNKER ON A DESOLATE SECTION OF THE COAST OF NORWAY...

ALL THESE MONTHS I'VE SPENT MY VAST FORTUNE WITH ONE OBJECTIVE...TO DESTROY THE MIGHTY *AVENGERS!* AND NOW, AT LAST, I AM *READY!*

FROM THIS MOMENT FORTH, I SHALL *CEASE* BEING THE EX-LEADER OF THE *MAGGIA,* THE WORLD'S MOST NOTORIOUS INTER-NATIONAL CRIME RING! NEVER MORE SHALL I BE KNOWN AS THE MYSTERIOUS *COUNT NEFARIA!**

NOW MY MACHINE IS *COMPLETED!* NOW I SHALL BE MORE POWERFUL THAN EVER BEFORE! AND THE WORLD SHALL KNOW ME ONLY AS... THE *MASTER!* OF *DREAMS!*

*FIRST INTRODUCED TO YOU IN *AVENGERS #13.*, STAN.

HERE, HALF A WORLD AWAY, I SHALL *DESTROY* THE AVENGERS...ONE BY ONE! AND, MY *FIRST* VICTIM SHALL BE...

...*IRON MAN!* THERE HE IS NOW, FOCUSED DEAD CENTER IN MY WORLD-WIDE ELECTRO-SCANNER! HOW THE HATRED WELLS UP WITHIN ME AT THE VERY *SIGHT* OF HIM!

AFTER *HE* HAS FALLEN, THE OTHERS WILL BE NEXT! IT IS SO EASY... SO SAFE... SO SURE! I CANNOT FAIL!

AND, THE MOST MACHIAVELLIAN PART OF MY PLAN...HE WILL NEVER EVEN SUSPECT THAT *I* AM HIS DESTROYER!

"FIRST, I ARRANGE A *BATTLEGROUND*...THE TOP OF NEW YORK'S BROOKLYN BRIDGE, FOR EXAMPLE! NEXT, I BRING MY GLADIATORS TOGETHER...I'LL BEGIN WITH THE ONE KNOWN TO THE WORLD AS... THE *UNICORN!*"

PREPARE TO *DIE,* IRON MAN! YOU CANNOT ESCAPE ME *NOW!*

SECONDS AGO I WAS IN MY LAB! NOW, I'M ATOP A BRIDGE! *HOW..?*

AND...THE *UNICORN!!* HOW DID *HE* GET HERE??

YOUR FATE IS ASSURED! BEHIND YOU IS *ANOTHER* FOE...PERHAPS AS DANGEROUS AS *I!*

I HAVE *RETURNED,* IRON MAN...TO PROVE THAT *I* AM YOUR *MASTER!*

THE *CRIMSON DYNAMO!* BUT... YOU'RE *DEAD!*

3

BUT... EVEN IF YOU *ARE* ALIVE...YOU HAD BEEN MY *ALLY*!! WHY...??

THEY'RE *BLASTING* AT ME... FROM BOTH SIDES!

"I DID NOT KNOW THEY HAD BECOME *ALLIES*! MY RESEARCH WAS *FAULTY*! BUT, NO MATTER! IT'S TOO LATE TO ALTER MY *NIGHT-MARE MACHINE* NOW!"

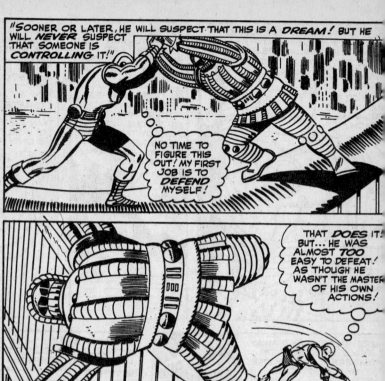

"SOONER OR LATER, HE WILL SUSPECT THAT THIS IS A *DREAM*! BUT HE WILL *NEVER* SUSPECT THAT SOMEONE IS *CONTROLLING* IT!"

NO TIME TO FIGURE THIS OUT! MY FIRST JOB IS TO *DEFEND* MYSELF!

THAT *DOES* IT! BUT... HE WAS ALMOST *TOO* EASY TO DEFEAT! AS THOUGH HE WASN'T THE MASTER OF HIS OWN ACTIONS!

THE UNICORN IS LOWERING HIS HEAD...ABOUT TO BLAST ME WITH HIS *POWER HORN*! BUT... I'VE NEVER SEEN HIM MOVE SO *SLOWLY*!

THERE! MY *REPULSER RAY* GOT HIM! BUT, IT'S ALL AS *SENSELESS* AS A *DREAM*! ...A DREAM! CAN *THAT* BE IT??

THE NEXT SPLIT-SECOND...BACK IN *IRON MAN'S* LAB...

OF *COURSE*! THAT'S WHAT IT WAS! I MUST HAVE DOZED OFF WHILE RE-CHARGING MY CHEST DEVICE!

BUT, THREE THOUSAND MILES AWAY...

THE TEST WAS A COMPLETE *SUCCESS*! HE STILL SUSPECTS *NOTHING*!

NEXT TIME HE'LL THINK IT'S *ANOTHER* DREAM...NOT REALIZING THAT WHEN *I* CONTROL THE NIGHTMARE, IF HE DIES IN HIS *DREAM*, HE WILL BE JUST AS DEAD AS IF IT HAD HAPPENED TO HIM IN *REAL LIFE*!

4

A SHORT TIME LATER, AT STARK'S OFFICE...

WHO ARE THE *FLOWERS* FROM, PEPPER?

THEY'RE FROM *HAPPY*... WITH A...A FAREWELL NOTE IN THEM... FROM HIS GRANDFATHER'S HOME IN IRELAND!

NOT THAT IT'S ANY OF *YOUR* BUSINESS, IRON MAN!

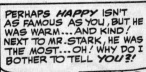

TELL ME, PEPPER... WHY DO YOU *HATE* ME SO?

BECAUSE YOU'RE SO *COLD*... SO *UNFEELING*... LIKE A HEARTLESS HUMAN MACHINE!

PERHAPS *HAPPY* ISN'T AS FAMOUS AS YOU, BUT HE WAS WARM... AND KIND! NEXT TO MR. STARK, HE WAS THE MOST... OH! WHY DO I BOTHER TO TELL *YOU*?!

THAT *DOES* IT!

SHE *DOES* CARE FOR HAPPY! AND, SINCE *I* CAN NEVER MARRY HER, I *MUST* FIND HIM AND BRING HIM BACK! ...EVEN THOUGH I MYSELF WILL LOVE HER TILL THE DAY I DIE!

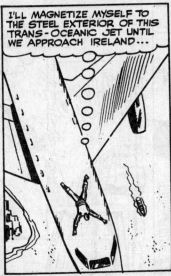

I'LL MAGNETIZE MYSELF TO THE STEEL EXTERIOR OF THIS TRANS-OCEANIC JET UNTIL WE APPROACH IRELAND...

AND NOW I'LL PROCEED UNDER MY OWN JET POWER...!

SAY, CHARLIE... WHAT'S THE NAME OF THAT *EYE DOCTOR* OF YOURS, AGAIN?

AND, FINALLY...

KLANK! KLANK!

BEGORRA, ME BOY! SURE, AND IT'S ME OWN EYES THAT ARE PLAYIN' TRICKS ON ME!

HUH? NO, GRANDFATHER, YOU'RE NOT *SEEING* THINGS!

HIS NAME IS *IRON MAN*, AND IF WE IGNORE HIM, HE'LL SOON REALIZE HE ISN'T WELCOME HERE!

HAPPY, LISTEN... I KNOW YOU'VE NO USE FOR ME, BUT THINK OF *MR. STARK*! HE WANTS YOU BACK! HE *TOLD* ME SO! AND PEPPER... SHE'S CRYING HER EYES OUT!

HUH! WHAT A LAUGH! IF SHE'S CRYING, IT'S BECAUSE *STARK* WON'T DATE HER... NOT ON ACCOUNT OF *ME!*

5.

NO, HAPPY... YOU'RE WRONG! WAIT... LISTEN TO ME...!

C'MON, GRAMPS... YOU PROMISED YOU'D SHOW ME THE FARM!

FAITH AN' BEJABBERS! I ALWAYS HEARD THE STREETS OF AMERICA WERE PAVED WITH GOLD, BUT SURE I NEVER THOUGHT I'D BE LEARNIN' THAT THE MEN ARE MADE OF IRON!

IT'S NO USE! HAPPY'S AS HARD-HEADED AS A MULE! AND YET, I'VE GOT TO GET HIM BACK TO THE STATES... IF ONLY FOR PEPPER'S SAKE! BUT... HOW? PERHAPS IF I LEAVE AND RETURN AGAIN AS TONY STARK...?

BUT, IRON MAN IS SOON TO HAVE A MUCH MORE DEADLY PROBLEM TO WRESTLE WITH...

NOW, WHILE HE LEAST SUSPECTS IT, THE DREAM MAKER SHALL STRIKE AGAIN!

AND SO...

I MUST HAVE DOZED OFF! MY EYES FEEL SO TIRED! SAY, WHAT'S THAT SOUND OUTSIDE? ALMOST LIKE SOME SORT OF OBJECT BEING THROWN AGAINST THE DOOR!

THUMP!

NOTHING OUT HERE! AND YET... I HAVE A FEELING... A DREAD SENSE OF DANGER LURKING NEARBY! WHAT CAN IT BE?

IRON MAN! I'VE BEEN WAITING FOR YOU!

THERE IS SOMEONE THERE! BUT, WHO..??

SURELY YOU DIDN'T THINK I HAD GIVEN UP THE BATTLE SO EASILY?? I MERELY WAITED FOR THE RIGHT MOMENT TO ATTACK AGAIN!

THE CRIMSON DYNAMO!! BUT THIS IS MADNESS! WHEN I SAW YOU LAST, IT WAS IN A DREAM! AND NOW... I'M WIDE AWAKE, WHILE YOU... YOU'RE DEAD! I SAW YOU DIE!*

*WE ALL SAW HIM DIE IN SUSPENSE #52... REMEMBER?... STAN.

6.

...T, IF YOU ARE SO CERTAIN ...AM DEAD, ...HEN HOW ...AN YOU BE ...URE THIS ...S NOT DREAM??

I MUST BE DREAMING! IT'S THE ONLY EXPLANATION THAT MAKES SENSE!

WHA...?!! I'M BEING COATED WITH A THICK LAYER OF FROZEN ICE! BUT... HOW??

...T'S JACK FROST... THE MENACE I FOUGHT ...YEARS AGO!*

NONE OF THIS MAKES SENSE! WHAT ARE THEY DOING HERE IN IRELAND??

I'VE GOT TO PUNCH MY WAY FREE, BEFORE THE ICE HARDENS TOO MUCH!

* IN SUSPENSE #45, TO BE EXACT!... STAN.

GIVE UP, IRON MAN! YOU HAVEN'T A CHANCE! THERE ARE TOO MANY OF US!

TOO MANY? WHO ELSE IS THERE??

WHISSST!

LOOK BEHIND YOU! LOOK AT... GARGANTUS!!

WOK!

I ALMOST DESTROYED YOU ONCE, IRON MAN...

GARGANTUS??! NO! IT CAN'T... UHHH!

THIS TIME I'LL FINISH THE JOB!

7.

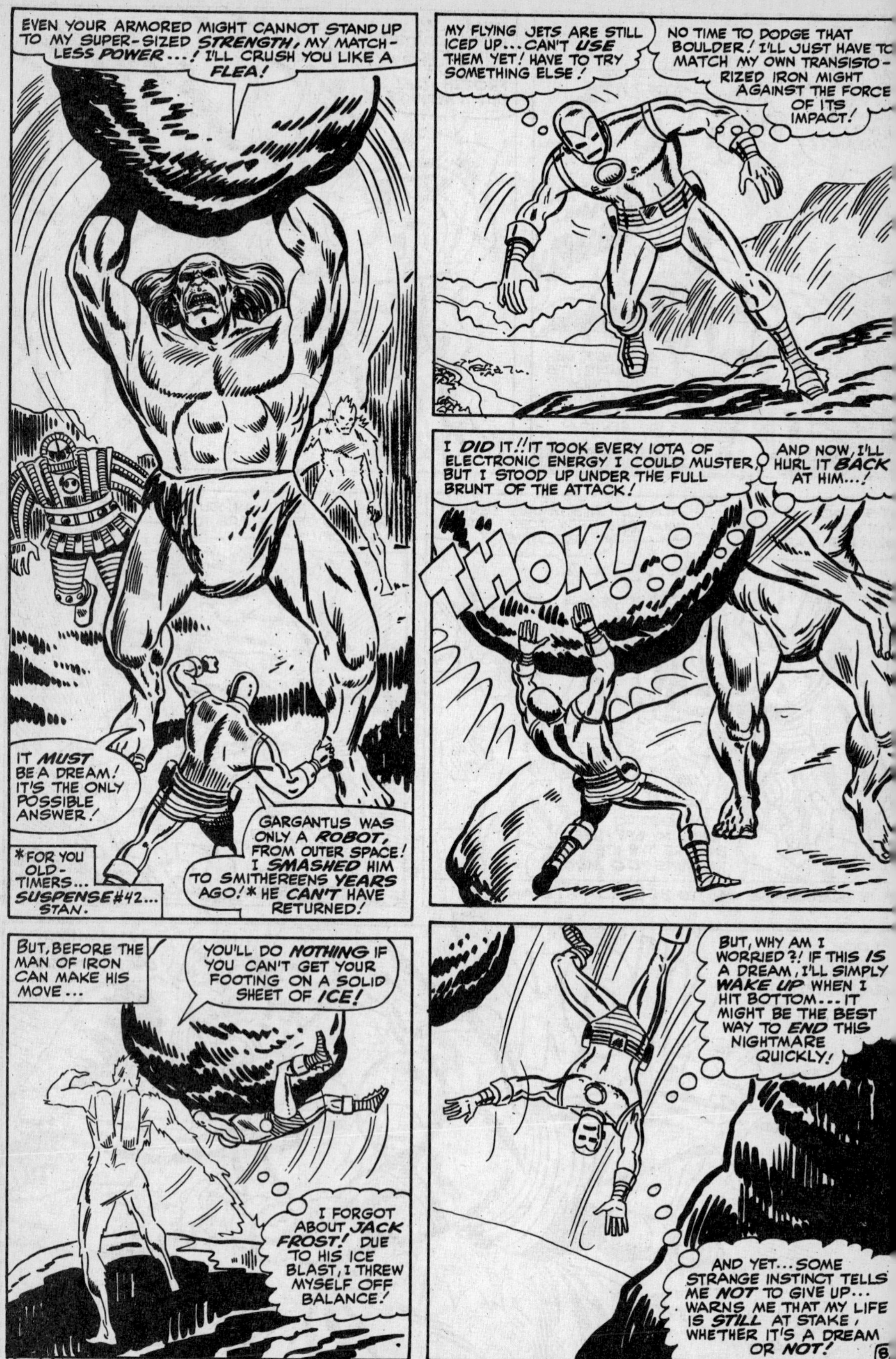
EVEN YOUR ARMORED MIGHT CANNOT STAND UP TO MY SUPER-SIZED STRENGTH, MY MATCH-LESS POWER...! I'LL CRUSH YOU LIKE A FLEA!
IT MUST BE A DREAM! IT'S THE ONLY POSSIBLE ANSWER!
GARGANTUS WAS ONLY A ROBOT, FROM OUTER SPACE! I SMASHED HIM TO SMITHEREENS YEARS AGO!* HE CAN'T HAVE RETURNED!
*FOR YOU OLD-TIMERS... SUSPENSE #42... STAN.
MY FLYING JETS ARE STILL ICED UP... CAN'T USE THEM YET! HAVE TO TRY SOMETHING ELSE!
NO TIME TO DODGE THAT BOULDER! I'LL JUST HAVE TO MATCH MY OWN TRANSISTO-RIZED IRON MIGHT AGAINST THE FORCE OF ITS IMPACT!
I DID IT!! IT TOOK EVERY IOTA OF ELECTRONIC ENERGY I COULD MUSTER, BUT I STOOD UP UNDER THE FULL BRUNT OF THE ATTACK!
AND NOW, I'LL HURL IT BACK AT HIM...!
THOK!
BUT, BEFORE THE MAN OF IRON CAN MAKE HIS MOVE...
YOU'LL DO NOTHING IF YOU CAN'T GET YOUR FOOTING ON A SOLID SHEET OF ICE!
I FORGOT ABOUT JACK FROST! DUE TO HIS ICE BLAST, I THREW MYSELF OFF BALANCE!
BUT, WHY AM I WORRIED?! IF THIS IS A DREAM, I'LL SIMPLY WAKE UP WHEN I HIT BOTTOM... IT MIGHT BE THE BEST WAY TO END THIS NIGHTMARE QUICKLY!
AND YET... SOME STRANGE INSTINCT TELLS ME NOT TO GIVE UP... WARNS ME THAT MY LIFE IS STILL AT STAKE, WHETHER IT'S A DREAM OR NOT!
8

EVEN THOUGH I CAN'T BELIEVE THIS IS ALL REALLY HAPPENING, SOMETHING INSIDE OF ME WON'T LET ME GIVE UP! I MUST FIGHT ON... FOR, IT'S MY NATURE!

AH! HOW I HAVE WAITED TO FIND YOU IN A SITUATION LIKE THIS, IRON MAN! A SITUATION JUST MADE TO ORDER FOR ME!

THE MYSTERIOUS MELTER! HOW MANY MORE OLD ENEMIES WILL I FIND HERE??

NONE, FOR I SHALL NOW MELT YOU INTO OBLIVION!

I'VE GOT TO MOVE, BEFORE HIS DEADLY BEAM TOUCHES ME!

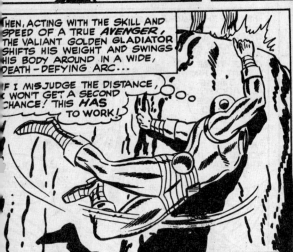

THEN, ACTING WITH THE SKILL AND SPEED OF A TRUE AVENGER, THE VALIANT GOLDEN GLADIATOR SHIFTS HIS WEIGHT AND SWINGS HIS BODY AROUND IN A WIDE, DEATH-DEFYING ARC...

IF I MISJUDGE THE DISTANCE, I WON'T GET A SECOND CHANCE! THIS HAS TO WORK!

AND, WORK IT DOES..!

WHUMP!

WHOOOF!

AT EASE, FELLA! YOU'RE LUCKY I'M NOT WEARING HOB-NAILED BOOTS!

NOW, I'LL JUST RELIEVE YOU OF YOUR MELTING RAY WHILE I SEND YOU SLEEPY-BYE WITH A KARATE LOVE TAP!

EVERYTHING IS LIKE A MAD DREAM! I HARDLY FELT IT WHEN I HIT HIM!

ZAP!

STILL ANOTHER ASSAULT! NOW, WHO CAN THIS BE? IT SEEMED TO COME FROM OUT THERE!

IT DID! IT'S... OH, NO!! IT CAN'T BE HIM!

9

THE *BLACK KNIGHT!* BUT... IT'S *IMPOSSIBLE!* I TURNED YOU OVER TO THE POLICE ONLY A FEW SHORT WEEKS AGO!*

BUT, YOU *FORGET*.. IN A *DREAM, ANYTHING* CAN HAPPEN!

THIS IS *INSANE!* WOULD A CHARACTER IN A DREAM *TELL* SOMEONE THAT HE TOO IS IN A DREAM??

*AS ANYBODY WHO READ *AVENGERS* #16 WOULD KNOW!..STAN.

I'VE JUST TIME TO OPEN MY UTILITY COMPARTMENT BEFORE HE STRIKES WITH HIS *MULTI-POWERED* LANCE!

THERE! THAT SMOKE BOMB WILL BLIND HIM LONG ENOUGH FOR ME TO PLAN MY NEXT MOVE!

THIS WON'T HELP YOU! YOU'RE *MERELY DELAY*-ING THE *INEVITABLE!*

WELL, IF IT'S ONLY A *DREAM*, WHAT HAVE I GOT TO *LOSE?*

FIRST, I'LL TURN MY *ELECTRIC HEAT APPARA*-TUS UP TO *FULL POWER*.. THE MORE *JUICE*, THE BETTER!

THERE! BY DIRECTING IT TOWARDS MY *FEET*, I CAN MELT THE REMAINING ICE RESIDUE IN A MATTER OF SECONDS!

THIS MEANS I CAN *FLY* AGAIN!

THEN, AS THE SMOKE BEGINS TO CLEAR...

OKAY, TIN MAN, YOU *HAD* YOUR FUN... AND NOW IT'S *QUIZ TIME!* I WANT TO KNOW WHAT THIS IS ALL ABOUT, AND *YOU'RE* THE BOY TO TELL ME!

NEVER! YOU'RE NOT IN THE CLEAR *YET!*

JUST LOOK *BEHIND* YOU!

HMM, I SEE WHAT YOU MEAN! LOOKS LIKE THE *GANG'S* ALL HERE, EH?

SOONER OR LATER, HE'LL COME WITHIN REACH, AND THEN I'LL *SEIZE* HIM AND SHATTER HIS ARMOR WITH THE STRENGTH OF MY BARE HANDS!

AND YOU'RE THE BOY TO *DO* IT, *GARGANTUS!* SO I'LL JUST BRING HIM CLOSER WITH A LITTLE *ICE BARRAGE!*

DON'T JUST *TALK* ABOUT IT, YOU TWO... *DO* IT! *HURRY!*

BUT, JUST AS THE FROZEN MENACE BEGINS HIS FRIGID ATTACK, THE FAST-MOVING *IRON MAN* HURLS THE *BLACK KNIGHT* INTO THE PATH OF THE STREAM OF ICE

THANKS FOR THE ASSIST, JACKIE BOY!

I WAS GETTING *BORED* WITH HIM, ANYWAY!

YOU USELESS *FOOL!* YOU FROZE *ME* INSTEAD OF *HIM!*

MEANWHILE, AT HIS VIEW-SCREEN WE FIND...

THIS ISN'T THE WAY I *PLANNED* IT! HE'S SUPPOSED TO REALIZE HE'S DREAMING AND NOT BOTHER TO FIGHT BACK!

FOR, HE DOES NOT SUSPECT THAT IF HE IS KILLED IN THE "*DREAM,*" HE WILL DIE IN *REAL LIFE* AT THAT SAME INSTANT!

HE MUST BE BEATEN! HE *MUST!*

BOK!

WELL, BIG STUFF? YOU WANTED TO REACH OUT AND GRAB ME... SO HERE'S YOUR *CHANCE!*

OF COURSE, THERE'S NO LAW THAT SAYS THE *LITTLE GUY* CAN'T LAND THE FIRST BLOW, IS THERE?

FORGIVE ME FOR NEGLECTING *YOU,* MY FROSTY FRIEND! I'VE BEEN KINDA BUSY!

BUT I'VE GOT A FEW MINUTES TO SPARE *NOW,* AND SO...

GLAD TO... AS SOON AS IT MELTS THAT ICE-MAKING EQUIPMENT OFF YOUR BACK!

IRON MAN! YOU STILL HAVEN'T BEATEN *ME!*

NO! *NO!* TURN YOUR *BEAM* OFF ME!

THE *CRIMSON DYNAMO!* I WAS CARELESS... FORGOT ABOUT HIM!

MY ELECTRICAL BLASTS WILL FINISH YOU OFF FOREVER!

THEY'LL DRAIN ALL THE REMAINING POWER FROM YOUR OWN TRANSISTORIZED CIRCUITS!

NOT IF MY *REPULSER BEAM* CAN SEND THEM RIGHT BACK TO *YOU*... LIKE *THIS!*

THAT WAS QUICK-THINKING, BUT... YOU'VE EXHAUSTED MUCH OF YOUR POWER ALREADY..

...WHILE *MY* ELECTRICAL ENERGY IS OPERATING AT THE *PEAK* OF ITS POWER! THE VICTORY *MUST* BE MINE!

HE'S *RIGHT!* MY TRANSISTORS' ENERGY *IS* RUNNING LOW!

11.

BUT MY ARMOR IS *STRONGER* THAN HIS.. AND MY REPULSERS ARE, TOO! HE ISN'T MY EQUAL IN WEAPONRY— *NOBODY* IS!

AND *THAT* IS WHAT WILL DEFEAT HIM! MY ARMOR IS SIMPLY *SUPERIOR* TO HIS OWN!

THERE ARE THOSE WHO RIDICULE AMERICA'S MANUFACTURING KNOW-HOW...THOSE WHO CLAIM THEY CAN PRODUCE GOODS CHEAPER, AND FASTER! BUT, *THERE* IS THE RESULT!

WHETHER HE'S *REAL*, OR A DREAM ...THE CRIMSON DYNAMO IS *BEATEN*!

AND, IN A FAR DISTANT LAB...

I *CAN'T* FAIL NOW! I'LL ADD MORE *POWER* TO MY MACHINE ...SEND *OTHER* FOES TO FIGHT HIM... COUNT-LESS FOES!

I AM THE *DREAM-MASTER*! I CAN DO *ANYTHING*! MORE *POWER*...!! *MORE*....!!

WHA...?? A *SHORT-CIRCUIT*! TOO MUCH STRAIN...!

I APPLIED TOO MUCH ENERGY! THE MACHINE COULDN'T *TAKE* IT! IT'S GOING TO... GOING TO...

NO! NOOOO!

WHOOOM!

AT THAT SPLIT-SECOND, IN A LITTLE COTTAGE IN IRELAND...

I WAS RIGHT! IT *WAS* JUST A DREAM! I MUST HAVE DOZED OFF AGAIN!

ALTHOUGH I NEVER *USED* TO DROP OFF THIS WAY! MAYBE I NEED VITAMIN PILLS!

THEY RETURNED WHILE I WAS SNOOZING! HAP'S ON THE PHONE!

OKAY, PEPPER, IF YOU WANT ME BAD ENOUGH TO PAY FOR A LONG DISTANCE CALL, I GUESS I *WILL* RETURN!

HOW *ABOUT* THAT! *PEPPER* DID MY JOB FOR ME WHILE I TOOK A NAP!

THIS WAS THE EASIEST ERRAND I EVER UNDER-TOOK!

WHICH JUST GOES TO SHOW THAT EVEN A SUPER-HERO CAN BE WRONG! BUT, UNLIKE YOU AND ME, IT IS DOUBTFUL THAT IRON MAN WILL EVER KNOW OF THE UNSUSPECTED BATTLE HE HAS TRULY FOUGHT...AND *WON*!

NEXT ISH: A *NEW* KIND OF DANGER AWAITS US IN: *"IF A MAN BE MAD!"* SEE YOU THEN!

12

TALES OF SUSPENSE
featuring

Iron Man and Captain America

MARVEL COMICS GROUP 12¢

68 AUG IND.

APPROVED BY THE COMICS CODE AUTHORITY

"THE SENTINEL and THE SPY!"

"IF A MAN BE MAD!"

THE GLORY OF A BYGONE AGE, CAPTURED IN THE MAGNIFICENT MARVEL MANNER!

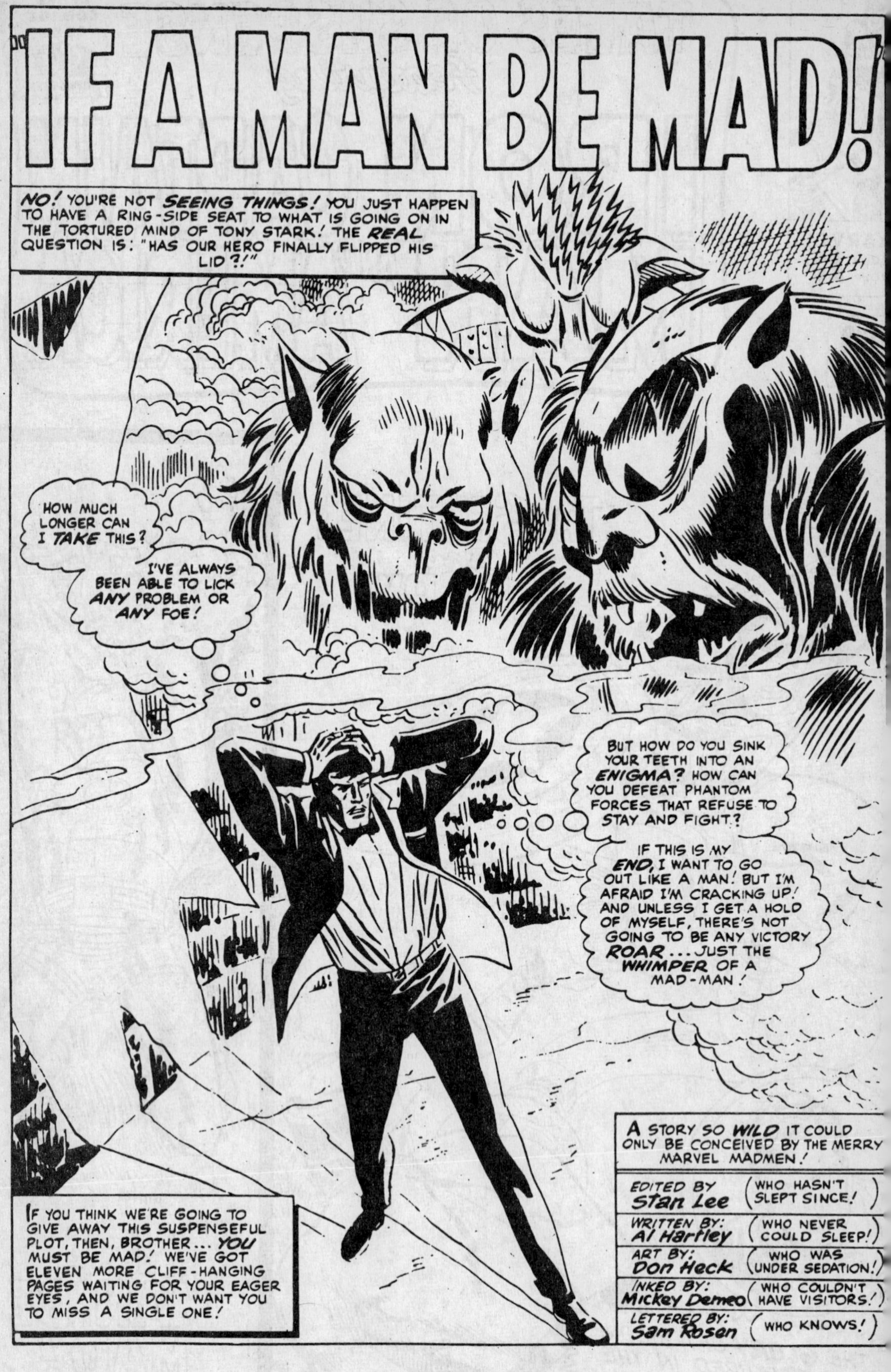
"IF A MAN BE MAD!"
NO! YOU'RE NOT SEEING THINGS! YOU JUST HAPPEN TO HAVE A RING-SIDE SEAT TO WHAT IS GOING ON IN THE TORTURED MIND OF TONY STARK! THE REAL QUESTION IS: "HAS OUR HERO FINALLY FLIPPED HIS LID?!"
HOW MUCH LONGER CAN I TAKE THIS?
I'VE ALWAYS BEEN ABLE TO LICK ANY PROBLEM OR ANY FOE!
BUT HOW DO YOU SINK YOUR TEETH INTO AN ENIGMA? HOW CAN YOU DEFEAT PHANTOM FORCES THAT REFUSE TO STAY AND FIGHT?
IF THIS IS MY END, I WANT TO GO OUT LIKE A MAN! BUT I'M AFRAID I'M CRACKING UP! AND UNLESS I GET A HOLD OF MYSELF, THERE'S NOT GOING TO BE ANY VICTORY ROAR... JUST THE WHIMPER OF A MAD-MAN!
IF YOU THINK WE'RE GOING TO GIVE AWAY THIS SUSPENSEFUL PLOT, THEN, BROTHER... YOU MUST BE MAD! WE'VE GOT ELEVEN MORE CLIFF-HANGING PAGES WAITING FOR YOUR EAGER EYES, AND WE DON'T WANT YOU TO MISS A SINGLE ONE!
A STORY SO WILD IT COULD ONLY BE CONCEIVED BY THE MERRY MARVEL MADMEN!
EDITED BY Stan Lee (WHO HASN'T SLEPT SINCE!)
WRITTEN BY: Al Hartley (WHO NEVER COULD SLEEP!)
ART BY: Don Heck (WHO WAS UNDER SEDATION!)
INKED BY: Mickey Demeo (WHO COULDN'T HAVE VISITORS!)
LETTERED BY: Sam Rosen (WHO KNOWS!)

WITHIN THE SPRAWLING, BUSINESSLIKE ARMS-MANUFACTURING COMPLEX OF STARK INDUSTRIES, THERE ARE ALSO ARMS OF COMFORT AND WARMTH!

IT'S GOOD TO HAVE YOU *BACK,* HAPPY! WE REALLY *MISSED* YOU AROUND HERE!

I'D RATHER HAVE *THAT* RECEPTION THAN MY ANNUITIES!

I NEVER WOULD HAVE *LEFT* IF SHE LOVED ME WITH THE KIND OF LOVE SHE HAS FOR *STARK!*

BUT HERE I AM... BACK AGAIN...

..JUST TO BE *NEAR* HER... HOPING THAT *SOMEDAY* THERE MAY BE A CHANCE FOR ME!

AND IN THE MEAN-TIME, I SUFFER EVERY TIME SHE EVEN *LOOKS* AT HIM!

LOOK WHO'S *BACK,* MR. STARK!

GLAD TO SEE YOU, *HAPPY!* HE'S STILL WEARING HIS HEART ON HIS SLEEVE... WHILE *MINE* MUST REMAIN ENCASED IN *IRON!*

SORRY FOR BEING SUCH A PRIMA DONNA, BOSS, BUT I COULDN'T STAY AWAY... YOU *KNOW* THAT!

WE WOULDN'T *LET* YOU, FELLA! NOW, LET'S GET TO *WORK!*

I HAVE A SPECIAL PROJECT TO WORK ON, PEPPER! ANYTHING URGENT BEFORE I STEP INTO THE LAB?

JUST THIS LETTER FROM YOUR *COUSIN,* MR. STARK!

SPECIAL DELIVERY

DRAT! EVERY TIME I HEAR FROM *MORGAN!* IT'S BAD NEWS! WHAT IS IT *THIS* TIME?!!

SECONDS LATER, TONY STARK FINISHES THE LETTER FROM HIS COUSIN!

POOR MORGAN! HE'S *STILL* THE *BLACK SHEEP* OF THE FAMILY!

BUT HE'S MY OWN FLESH AND BLOOD, MUCH AS I HATE TO ADMIT IT!

I CAN'T FAIL HIM... I JUST WISH HE'D STOP FAILING *HIM*SELF! HE'S HAD THE SAME EDUCA-TION AND THE SAME OPPORTUNI-TIES *I'VE* HAD ..HE'S JUST *WEAK!*

BUT IF I DON'T RE-CHARGE MY HEART DEVICE NOW, I WON'T BE *AROUND* TO HELP *ANYONE* MUCH LONGER!

AT THAT VERY MOMENT, IN FAR-OFF MONTE CARLO, WHERE DREAMS OF GRANDEUR FADE ON EVERY ROLL OF THE DICE, THE WHEELS OF FORTUNE SPIN DANGEROUSLY FOR TONY STARK...AS WE'RE ABOUT TO SEE...

YOU MUST GIVE ME MORE *TIME,* COUNT NEFARIA... I HAVE *WRITTEN* TO MY COUSIN!

HOW AM I TO BELIEVE THAT A MAN LIKE TONY STARK CAN HAVE A COUSIN LIKE *YOU?* IF YOU ARE ONLY *DECEIVING* ME, MORGAN, YOU WILL PAY *DEARLY* FOR YOUR DEBT!

2.

BUT ON THE *OTHER* HAND; IF THIS NE'ER-DO-WELL IS *INDEED* STARK'S COUSIN...

...THEN HE CAN DISCHARGE HIS GAMBLING DEBT TO ME IN A FAR MORE *VALUABLE* WAY!

MORGAN, I HAVE A PROPOSITION THAT SHOULD *APPEAL* TO A MAN OF YOUR PECULIAR AMBITIONS!

I'VE TRIED FOR *YEARS* TO DESTROY TONY STARK, BUT ALL MY ATTEMPTS HAVE FAILED MISERABLY! I'VE LACKED A CERTAIN FINESSE! WHICH *YOU* CAN GIVE TO MY *NEXT* PLAN!

IF YOU ARE WILLING TO HELP ME, I WILL *FORGET* YOUR GAMBLING DEBT! AND EVEN *MORE*, WILL SET YOU UP ON *EASY STREET*! YOU'LL BE ABLE TO LIVE ON A SCALE EQUAL TO YOUR *EXTRAVAGANT* TASTES!

I'VE ALWAYS *RESENTED* TONY'S SUCCESS, BUT CAN I GO *THAT FAR*?

WELL, WHY *SHOULDN'T* I? TONY'S HAD THAT SILVER SPOON LONG ENOUGH! *I'M* THE ONE WHO REALLY APPRECIATES THE FINER THINGS OF LIFE!

THIS IS THE *BIG BREAK* I'VE WANTED ALL MY LIFE!

AND IT WILL END *FOREVER* THE HUMILIATION OF ACCEPTING *HAND-OUTS* FROM TONY!

A FEW DAYS LATER, IN TONY STARK'S OFFICE....!

HAPPY, THIS IS MY COUSIN MORGAN! HE'S VISITING US FROM EUROPE AND I'D LIKE YOU TO SHOW HIM AROUND THE PLANT!

PLEASED TO MEET YOU, MORGAN! I GUESS YOU'RE MIGHTY *PROUD* OF THE BOSS!

BUT, SOON, THE TABLES WILL BE TURNED! I WILL BE GIVING THE ORDERS!

HE'S JUST AS I PICTURED HIM FROM HIS LETTERS!

I'LL BET HE'S WASTED AWAY HIS *INHERITANCE* AND PROBABLY HASN'T WORKED A DAY IN HIS LIFE!

EXACTLY ONE DAY LATER, THE DYNAMIC TONY STARK IS DRIVING HOME AFTER WORKING LATE AT HIS OFFICE....!

WHOA, THERE, TONY BOY!

I MAY BE LATE FOR MY DINNER DATE! IF THAT'S WHAT I *THINK* IT IS UP AHEAD!

IT *IS*!

I DON'T KNOW WHY SOMETHING LIKE *THIS* HAS TO POP UP WHEN I'VE GOT A BLONDE COVER GIRL WAITING FOR ME!

AND I MUST HAVE ROCKS IN MY HEAD TO GAPE AT ROCKETS, INSTEAD OF WOMEN!

BUT THERE'S SOMETHING FISHY ABOUT THAT BIRD! IT'S NOT ONE OF *OURS* AND I KNOW ENOUGH ABOUT THE *CAVIAR CROWD* TO KNOW IT'S NOT *THEIRS*!

WELL, BLONDIE, I GUESS YOU'LL HAVE TO WAIT A LITTLE *LONGER*! IF I DON'T ALERT THE *C.I.A.* TO THIS, I'LL NEVER FORGIVE MYSELF IN THE MORNING!

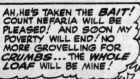

AH, HE'S TAKEN THE *BAIT!* COUNT NEFARIA WILL BE *PLEASED!* AND *SOON* MY *POVERTY* WILL END! NO MORE GROVELLING FOR *CRUMBS...* THE *WHOLE LOAF* WILL BE MINE!

BUT, WHILE DRIVING TO A PHONE BOOTH, THE SELF-RELIANCE AND INITIATIVE THAT *MADE* TONY STARK AN INTERNATIONAL CELEBRITY, CHANGE HIS PLANS!

WAIT A MINUTE! THERE MAY NOT BE TIME FOR THE C.I.A. TO GET THEIR PEOPLE OUT HERE! I'D BETTER SNOOP AROUND MYSELF!

OR BETTER YET, I'LL INVESTIGATE AS *IRON-MAN!* WHO KNOWS WHAT EVIL LURKS WITHIN THOSE HOLLOW ROCKET WALLS! BUT THE BIGGEST QUESTION OF THE EVENING IS...

WHAT AM I GOING TO TELL THAT BLEACHED BEAUTY WHO'S WAITING FOR ME?

SHE'LL NEVER SWALLOW A STORY LIKE THIS! I'LL HAVE TO THINK OF SOMETHING CLEVER ----- IKE, I HAD A *FLAT TIRE!*

NOW *THERE'S* A DEVELOPMENT TO MAKE MY EVENING *BRIGHTER!* THE DARNED THING IS EMITTING AN OMINOUS GLOW!

I'D BETTER SWITCH ON MY GEIGER COUNTER!

BLAST IT! STARK'S CALLED *IRON-MAN* INTO THE ACT! I DIDN'T COUNT ON *THIS!*

I'M GETTING A NEGATIVE READING! WHATEVER IS CAUSING THE GLOW IS *NOT* RADIO-ACTIVE!

THEN WHAT IN THE NAME OF A TWISTED TRANSISTOR CAN IT *BE?*

GUESS I MIGHT AS WELL GO IN AND SEE IF ANYONE'S HOME!

NO SIGNS OF ANY FACILITIES FOR *FLY-BOYS...* IT MUST BE REMOTE CONTROLLED!

HMM...THAT GIZMO IN THE CENTER HAS ALL THE EARMARKS OF A THERMONUCLEAR DEVICE!

AND IT'S TICKING AWAY AS NICE AS BIG BEN!

HOLY HANNAH! IT COULD GO *OFF* ANY SECOND! I'D BETTER ALERT THE *BOMB SQUAD!*...IF I GET *OUT* OF HERE IN TIME!

CLICK! CLICK CLICK CLICK

4.

WITHIN FIFTEEN MINUTES, IRON-MAN HAS CHANGED BACK TO TONY STARK... AND RETURNS TO THE SCENE, ONLY TO FIND...

BUT I'M TELLING YOU IT WAS STANDING RIGHT *THERE!* I *TOUCHED* IT! I WAS *IN* IT!

MR. STARK, ARE YOU SURE YOU'RE NOT PUTTING US ON?

THERE'S NOT A *SIGN* THAT ANYTHING'S BEEN HERE!

I KNOW THIS LOOKS LIKE A WILD GOOSE CHASE, BUT THERE'S GOT TO BE SOME EVIDENCE *SOMEWHERE!*

MR. STARK, WHY DON'T YOU STICK TO HIGH FINANCE AND LEAVE DETECTIVE WORK TO JOES LIKE *US!?*

NEXT TIME YOU GET A BRIGHT IDEA FOR A GAG, TELL IT TO THE JET-SET, WILL YOU?

INSPECTOR... *WAIT!* LOOK BEHIND YOU! THERE'S A *SPACE-MAN!*

ONE HOUR LATER...

YOU'RE A REAL *CUTIE*, STARK! WE'VE BEEN TRAMPING THROUGH THESE WOODS LOOKING FOR YOUR SPACE-MAN AND WE CAN'T EVEN FIND A *BUNNY-RABBIT!*

I'LL NEVER CONVINCE HIM I REALLY *SAW* THOSE THINGS! BUT THEY *WERE* HERE! I *KNOW* IT!

MEANWHILE, JUST ONE HUNDRED YARDS AWAY...

COUNT NEFARIA'S VISIO-PROJECTOR IS A REMARKABLE INSTRUMENT! IT SHOULD SOON HAVE COUSIN TONY DOUBTING HIS *SANITY!*

FAR INTO THE NIGHT, TONY STARK SEARCHES FOR SOME EXPLANATION TO THE BAFFLING EVENTS OF THE EVENING...

MAYBE SOMETHING'S GONE WRONG WITH ALL THIS ELECTRONIC JAZZ I'M WEARING! IT'S JUST POSSIBLE SOME FAULTY CIRCUIT COULD HAVE CAUSED A VIDEO EFFECT!

BUT, NO... *THAT'S NOT* THE ANSWER! EVERYTHING CHECKS OUT OKAY!

AND FINALLY, BY EARLY MORNING...!

WHAT A WAY TO SPEND THE NIGHT! I'VE GONE OVER THE *ENTIRE* AREA AND THERE'S NOT A *SINGLE* CLUE!

I MIGHT AS WELL GET TO THE OFFICE! AT LEAST I CAN ACCOMPLISH SOMETHING *THERE!*

AND I GUESS THE *FIRST* THING I'D BETTER DO IS TAKE THAT BLONDE'S NUMBER OUT OF MY LITTLE BLACK BOOK! I DIDN'T GET THE *CHANCE* TO CALL HER LAST NIGHT...AND I DON'T DARE EVER TRY *AGAIN!*

AND, THUS, WITHOUT ANY SLEEP, TONY STARK ENTERS IS OFFICE...HIS STEEL-TRAP MIND AS ALERT AS VER... EVEN IF *OTHERS* DON'T SEEM TO SHARE OUR OPINION...

HERE HE COMES NOW, HAPPY...BE DISCREET!

ALL RIGHT, YOU TWO...WHAT *IS* IT? I CAN TELL YOU HAVE SOMETHING *SERIOUS* ON YOUR MINDS!

WELL, WE WERE JUST THINKING THAT A *VACATION* MIGHT BE *GOOD* FOR YOU, BOSS! YOU'VE BEEN UNDER A PRETTY HEAVY *STRAIN* LATELY!

OKAY! OKAY! YOU HEARD ABOUT LAST NIGHT AND YOU THINK I'M CRACKING UP, IS *THAT* IT?

OH, *TONY!* I LOVE YOU AND I *BELIEVE* IN YOU! BUT *NO ONE* CAN WORK AS HARD AS YOU DO WITHOUT *PAYING* FOR IT...*SOMEHOW!*

TER THAT MORNING....!

E WANT TO EE MR. TARK! WE EAR HE'S OT A GREAT TORY TO TELL!

I'M SORRY, GENTLEMEN! THE BOSS ISN'T SPEAKING TO THE PRESS TODAY!

AT THAT VERY INSTANT!

HAPPY! COME IN HERE RIGHT AWAY!

AND BRING THE BOYS FROM THE PRESS *WITH* YOU!

CLICK!

I'M SORRY...YOU GOT IN HERE TOO *LATE!* THERE WAS A *GIANT SPACE-SHIP* SUSPENDED IN FLIGHT RIGHT OUTSIDE MY WINDOW...BUT IT'S *GONE!* AND IT DIDN'T *FLY AWAY*...IT JUST *VANISHED!*

DON'T SAY ANY *MORE*, BOSS! THE NEWS-HOUNDS WILL MAKE YOU LOOK *CRAZY* IN PRINT!

BOY! AND *HE'S* RESPONSIBLE FOR THE WEAPONS TO PROTECT US FROM ALL THE *OTHER* NUTS IN THE WORLD!

GUESS YOU'VE OT TO BE A LITTLE HACKY TO DREAM P ALL THOSE NEW-ANGLED ADGETS!

WILL YOU EX-CUSE ME NOW, GENTLEMEN? I HAVE WORK TO DO!

I'VE ALWAYS WANTED A CHANCE WITH PEPPER...BUT NOT *THIS* WAY!

THERE MUST BE *SOME* SANE ANSWER TO ALL THIS! I *CAN'T* BE CRACKING UP! AND YET, THERE JUST DOESN'T SEEM TO BE ANY OTHER EXPLANATION!

MAYBE PEPPER AND HAPPY ARE *RIGHT!* MAYBE I *HAVE* BEEN WORKING TOO HARD!

AND ON THE ROOF OF THE OFFICE BUILDING...

BRO-*THER!* WAIT TILL *THIS* NEWS REACHES OUR WASHINGTON BUREAU!

SPLENDID! THE COUNT'S VISIO-PROJECTOR CONTINUES TO FUNCTION *PERFECTLY!* THAT SPACE-SHIP IMAGE I PROJECTED CAUGHT TONY'S EYE ...AND HIS *IMAGINATION* AS WELL!

STARK'S WORLD IS *FALLING APART*...AND *MINE* IS JUST *BEGINNING!*

6.

WITHIN MINUTES, THE HOTTEST NEWS ITEM OF THE DAY HAS SPREAD THROUGHOUT THE NATION'S CAPITAL!

ATTENTION! ALL MEMBERS OF THE ARMED SERVICES COMMITTEE...

...PLEASE REPORT TO THE OFFICE OF SENATOR BYRD!

GENTLEMEN, THIS NEWS ITEM PROVES I'VE BEEN RIGHT ALL ALONG ABOUT TONY STARK! HE'S UNSTABLE!

AND HE HAS NO BUSINESS HANDLING TOP SECRET PROJECTS!

MARTIANS LAND SPACESHIP OR IS

The Washington

STARK C...

I WANT YOUR UNANIMOUS AND IMMEDIATE SUPPORT FOR A RESOLUTION I INTEND TO INTRODUCE ON THE FLOOR OF THE SENATE TODAY! I WILL DEMAND THAT TONY STARK BE STRIPPED OF ALL DEFENSE CONTRACTS AFFECTING OUR NATIONAL SECURITY!

MEANWHILE, TONY STARK, WHO NEVER BELIEVES EVERYTHING HE READS IN THE PAPERS, ENLISTS THE AID OF IRON MAN TO VINDICATE HIMSELF!

THERE MUST BE SOME SMALL DETAIL I'VE OVERLOOKED! ...SOMETHING THAT WILL MAKE SENSE OUT OF ALL THIS! I'LL TAKE AN ELECTRO-PROBE OUT TO THE SCENE!

I KNOW I HAVEN'T BEEN SEEING THINGS! I KNOW THERE'S GOT TO BE AN ANSWER SOMEWHERE! AND THIS TIME I'LL GO OVER EVERYTHING WITH A FINE-TOOTH COMB!

I ANTICIPATED THAT MY DESPERATE COUSIN MIGHT CALL ON IRON MAN! WHAT A FEATHER IN MY CAP IF I CAN DESTROY HIS REPUTATION AS WELL!

THIS IONOSPHERE ECHO RAY SHOULD SEND HIM A BAFFLING MESSAGE!

I HAVEN'T TURNED THE SET ON YET... AND MAYBE I WON'T HAVE TO! THERE'S SOMETHING NEW UP THERE! MAYBE THAT WILL GIVE ME A CLUE

STRANGE! I FIRED ONLY ONCE, BUT THERE ARE TWO SIGNALS IN THE SKY!! COULD IT BE AN ECHO FROM THE IONOSPHERE OR... SOMETHING ELSE?!!

SPECIAL BULLPEN BULLETIN... THIS YARN REALLY GETS CRITICAL NOW, SO FACE FRONT... GET A GRIP ON YOURSELF... TURN THE PAGE SLOWLY...

See what we mean?

I DEFY anybody to tell me I'm seeing things NOW! I can feel the heat of those RETRO-ROCKETS right THROUGH my BERRYLIUM UNDERWEAR!

DISPATCH a message back to the moon... advise them that we have LANDED and are proceeding AS PLANNED!

And NO-BODY could DREAM UP characters like THAT!

HOLD! There is an EARTHMAN! ELIMINATE him!

AFFIRMATIVE, GOUDA!

BLAT!

BZZZZZT

WOW! That SETTLES it! Those boys are really playing for KEEPS!

YOU HAD BETTER improve your AIM, EDAM!

My AIM is FAULTLESS, GOUDA! But my TARGET moves with the speed of MOONBEAMS!

IF he ESCAPES, we will return to the moon in DISGRACE! GET him!

I DON'T mind tackling these boys ALONE...

..but if I don't GET some WITNESSES to this brawl, NO ONE is going to BELIEVE it!

FINISH him! We must get on with our MISSION!

The EARTH PEOPLE are preparing to launch still ANOTHER rocket towards our BELOVED moon!

IT MUST BE DESTROYED!

I'LL TRY to sucker them over a NIKE BASE! The defense command will have a FIELD DAY!

And they can CONFIRM that I HAVEN'T been having PIPE DREAMS!

BUZZ!

IT MAY NOT BE EASY! The EARTH-PEOPLE can fire ELECTRIC BOLTS from their FINGERS!

8.

ATTACK! WE OUT-NUMBER HIM!

WE'VE SCORED A NEAR-*MISS*! ENOUGH TO AFFECT HIS *PROPULSION UNIT*!

THEY'RE *GAINING* ON ME! I'LL NEVER REACH THE NIKE BASE IN *TIME*! I'M GOING TO HAVE TO FIGHT *EVERY* ONE OF THEM!

WE *HAVE* HIM! NOW... *CLOSE*!

UNGPH HE HAS MUSCLES OF IRON!

IF I CAN KEEP THEM AT *CLOSE QUARTERS*, THEY WON'T BE ABLE TO USE THEIR *GUNS*!

HE MOVES WITH THE SPEED OF SHOOTING STARS!

AND HIS FISTS STRIKE LIKE PLUNGING METEORS

THAT'S IT! HOLD HIM! I CAN FINISH HIM AND... *BEHOLD*! LOOK WHAT HE HAS DONE TO MY *SPEAR*!

I'VE GOT ALL *SORTS* OF SURPRISES FOR YOU, MOON BOY!

I *SHOULD* BE ABLE TO CRUSH HIM WITH *EASE*, BUT MY STRENGTH IS OF NO AVAIL!

WE WILL NEVER TAKE HIM *THIS* WAY! EMPLOY YOUR *BLAST GUNS*!

IT NEVER *FAILS*! EVERY TIME I HAVE MY SUIT *SIMONIZED*, SOME JOKER TRIES TO *SPOIL THE FINISH*!

WELL, I'M NOT ABOUT TO GIVE THEM AN EASY TARGET!

I'M GLAD I ORDERED ALL THE *EXTRAS* ON THIS 1965 MODEL!

THIS SUPER-DELUXE *VAPOR EJECTOR* BEATS THE *STANDARD* EXHAUST PIPE EVERY TIME!

HERE YOU GO, FELLAS! WATCH MY *SMOKE!*

ZAP!

IN FACT, IF *THEY* WON'T GET LOST, I WILL!

⁚HUMPH⁚ AFTER SEEING THROUGH *MOON DUST,* THIS FLIMSY FOG IS *CHILD'S PLAY!*

NOW, *THIS* WOULD BE A *GREAT* TIME AND PLACE FOR AN *AVENGERS'* CONVENTION!

IT WOULD BE *EASIER* TO TAKE THOSE MOON-GOONS IF WE COULD CHOOSE UP SIDES!

BUT I'VE GOT TO DO IT *ALONE!* AND I'M RUNNING OUT OF *JUICE!*

HE'S MOVING *OUT!* CONCENTRATE YOUR *FIRE!*

UNABLE TO MANEUVER AT MAXIMUM SPEED, THE GOLDEN GLADIATOR IS SUDDENLY CAUGHT BY THE ALIEN GUNS! AND THE AIR EXPLODES WITH THE SOUND OF A THOUSAND SONIC BOOMS!

BAROOOOM!

HE FOUGHT WITH NOBLE *VALOR!* OUR VICTORY IS A CREDIT ONLY TO OUR *NUMBERS!*

IF *ALL* EARTHMEN FIGHT AS HE, I FEAR OUR MISSION IS IN *JEOPARDY!*

TAKE HIM TO OUR SPACE-CRAFT!

HOLD IT, SWEETIES! IT'S FORTUNATE YOU DON'T HAVE ANY *POSSUMS* ON THE MOON, OR YOU MIGHT HAVE RECOGNIZED THE *GAME* I WAS PLAYING!

THAT LITTLE TIME-OUT GAVE MY TRANSISTORS TIME TO RE-CHARGE!

WHA...! THE CREATURE IS *AMAZING!* HOW COULD HE SURVIVE OUR *FIRE?!!*

ONE LOVE-PAT FROM THE *HULK* WOULD SHAKE ME UP MORE THAN *THOSE* POP-GUNS!

10.

AS THE MOON-MEN ARE CAUGHT OFF-BALANCE, IRON MAN SWIFTLY REACHES TO HIS CHEST AND TRIGGERS HIS AWESOME ULTRA-BEACON!

ST. ELMO'S FIRE! WHAT SORCERY IS *THIS*?!!

...AND, IN THE NEXT INSTANT, THE SEARING INTENSITY OF THE BURNING SUN IS RIVALED BY HIS BLAZING CHEST PLATE!

I HAD TO *LURE* THEM INTO CLOSE CONTACT SO THAT I COULD GAIN THE FULL SHOCK VALUE OF MY TRANSISTORIZED *LIGHT BEAM!*

I'M *BLINDED!*

THERE IS NO *END* TO HIS EARTHLY RESOURCE-FULLNESS!

ABANDON THE *MISSION!* REPAIR TO OUR CRAFT!

MEANWHILE, COUSIN MORGAN, WHO IS BY NOW SORRY HE EVER GOT MIXED *UP* IN THIS PLOT, *REALLY* PUTS HIS FOOT INTO IT!

GREAT *SCOTT!* I'M *SLIPPING!*

BEHOLD! HERE IS *ANOTHER* SPECIES OF EARTHMAN! PERHAPS *HE* WILL PROVIDE US WITH A MEAGER TROPHY FOR THIS EXPEDITION!

BUT, BEFORE THE MOON-MAN CAN SQUEE HIS TRIGGER, IRON FINGERS ADJUST TH PRISMS OF THE ULTRA-BEACON, DIRECTING... BETWEEN COUSIN MORGA AND HIS ATTACKERS...AN INVISIBLE SHIELD SIMILAR TO THE KIND YOU HAV SEEN ON THOSE T.V. TOOTHPAST COMMERCIALS!

DON'T *PANIC*, MORGAN! SHOW THEM YOUR *TEETH!*

MAKE *HASTE!* PRESS THE BLAST-OFF BUTTON!

WE CANNOT DESTROY THE EARTH ROCKETS!

WHAT CON-FOUNDED *LUCK!* ALL MY HOPES HAVE GONE UP IN SMOKE!

DO SOME-THING, IRON MAN! THEY'RE *FIRING* AT US!

WE MUST EVACUATE OUR MOON COLONY AND FIND *ANOTHER* PLANET!

GET ON YOUR FEET AND STOP SNIVELIN LIKE A *COWARD* THEY'RE JUST TRYIN TO GET *OUT* OF HERE AS FAST AS THEY *CAN!*

...L SEND THE [AU]THORITIES OUT [H]ERE! THERE'S [AM]PLE EVIDENCE [N]OW THAT TONY [S]TARK IS *SANE!* [W]AIT HERE, MORGAN, [A]ND TELL THEM [W]HAT YOU'VE [B]EEN!

WHAT *CHOICE* DO I HAVE? THIS IS THE STORY OF MY *LIFE!* ALWAYS FOILED BY FATE... ALWAYS *FAILING!*

BY THE WAY... WHAT WERE *YOU* DOING OUT HERE?

I..EH..I *NATURALLY* HAVE AN INTEREST IN MY COUSIN'S *FATE!* I THOUGHT I COULD *DO* SOMETHING!

WELL, YOU'VE GOT YOUR CHANCE *NOW!*

YOU'LL BE ABLE TO TELL WHAT YOU *SAW!*

MINUTES LATER...!

THERE'S *NO QUESTION* ABOUT IT! THIS CRATER VERIFIES YOUR STORY, MORGAN!

YOUR COUSIN IS GOING TO BE MIGHTY *PROUD!*

YOU'VE CLEARED HIS NAME!

THIS WILL CERTAINLY DEFEAT YOUR AMENDMENT, SENATOR BYRD!

BAH!

THE SENATE WILL *NEVER* VOTE TO CENSOR TONY STARK *NOW!*

[L]ATER... AT TEMPESTUOUS TONY'S OFFICE...

STARK! YOU LEAD A *CHARMED* LIFE! I *KNOW* [Y]OU'RE NOTHING BUT A PLAY-[B]OY AND HAVE NO BUSINESS [B]EING A VITAL DEFENSE CONTRACTOR...

...AND YET EVERY TIME HE'S READY TO LOWER THE BOOM ON YOU, YOU MANAGE TO EMERGE LILY-WHITE!

THE SENATOR'S A DEDICATED MAN... DOING HIS *JOB* AS HE *SEES* IT! I JUST WISH I COULD LET HIM IN ON MY DUAL IDENTITY... THEN HE WOULD UNDER-STAND WHY I ACT AS I *DO!*

ALL I CAN SAY, STARK, IS... YOU'RE LUCKY YOUR COUSIN SUBSTANTIATED YOUR STORY! YOU OWE HIM A *LOT!*

I *AM* GRATEFUL TO MORGAN, MR. SENATOR! AND I FULLY INTEND TO *SHOW* MY APPRECIATION!

[Y]ES, INDEED! I'M SENDING [HI]M BACK TO MONTE CARLO [I]N MY COMPANY PLANE!

IF I COULD *JOIN* HIM, I WOULD, BUT I INTEND TO SEE THAT HE RECEIVES *EVERYTHING* HE DESERVES!

AND TWO MEMBERS OF MY STAFF WILL ESCORT HIM IN *STYLE!*

IS IT ANY WONDER I *LOVE* HIM SO?

TWO DAYS LATER... AT THE CASINO OF COUNT NEFARIA...!

THE COUNT HAS BEEN *WAITING* FOR YOU AND HE IS *VERY DISTURBED* THAT YOU HAD TO BE *BROUGHT* HERE!

HE IS NOT ACCUSTOMED TO DEALING WITH *FAILURES!*

COME IN, MORGAN... *COME IN!*

I WISH I WERE *DEAD!*

WELL, IT'S ALL OVER! I JUST WISH *ALL* OF MY TROUBLES COULD HAVE VANISHED WITH THE MOON MEN!

BUT ALAS, THE TROUBLES OF THE WORLD'S MOST *TRAGIC* MILLIONAIRE HAVE HARDLY *BEGUN!* NEXT ISSUE HE MEETS HIS GREATEST CHALLENGE AS HE FACES *TITANIUM MAN!* BE SURE TO BRING YOUR GREASE GUNS! SEE YA THEN!

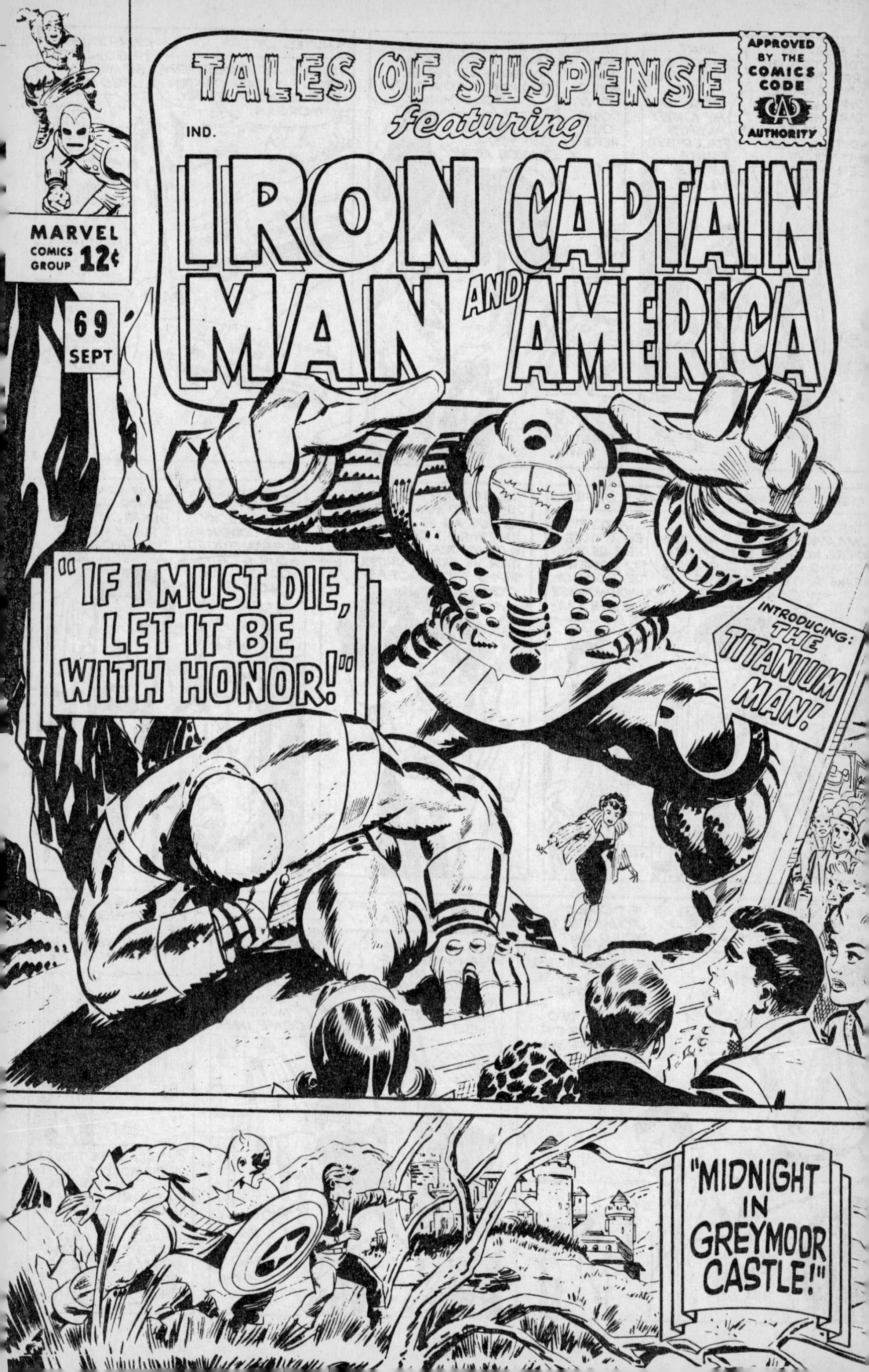

TALES OF SUSPENSE
featuring
IND.
APPROVED BY THE COMICS CODE AUTHORITY
IRON MAN AND CAPTAIN AMERICA
MARVEL COMICS GROUP 12¢
69 SEPT
"IF I MUST DIE, LET IT BE WITH HONOR!"
INTRODUCING: THE TITANIUM MAN!
"MIDNIGHT IN GREYMOOR CASTLE!"

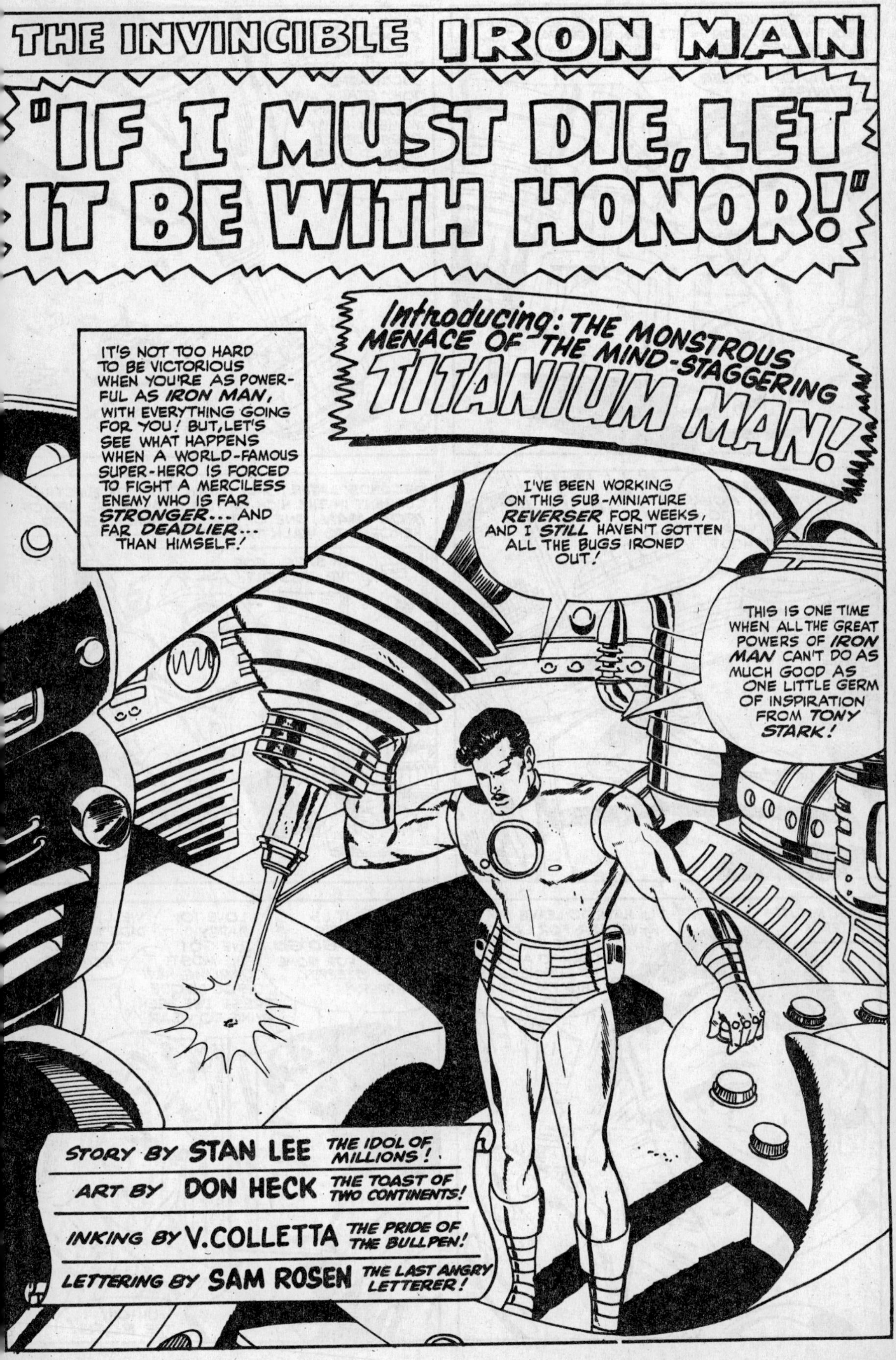

THE INVINCIBLE IRON MAN
"IF I MUST DIE, LET IT BE WITH HONOR!"
Introducing: THE MONSTROUS MENACE OF THE MIND-STAGGERING TITANIUM MAN!
IT'S NOT TOO HARD TO BE VICTORIOUS WHEN YOU'RE AS POWERFUL AS IRON MAN, WITH EVERYTHING GOING FOR YOU! BUT, LET'S SEE WHAT HAPPENS WHEN A WORLD-FAMOUS SUPER-HERO IS FORCED TO FIGHT A MERCILESS ENEMY WHO IS FAR STRONGER... AND FAR DEADLIER... THAN HIMSELF!
I'VE BEEN WORKING ON THIS SUB-MINIATURE REVERSER FOR WEEKS, AND I STILL HAVEN'T GOTTEN ALL THE BUGS IRONED OUT!
THIS IS ONE TIME WHEN ALL THE GREAT POWERS OF IRON MAN CAN'T DO AS MUCH GOOD AS ONE LITTLE GERM OF INSPIRATION FROM TONY STARK!
STORY BY STAN LEE THE IDOL OF MILLIONS!
ART BY DON HECK THE TOAST OF TWO CONTINENTS!
INKING BY V. COLLETTA THE PRIDE OF THE BULLPEN!
LETTERING BY SAM ROSEN THE LAST ANGRY LETTERER!

ONE GOOD THING ABOUT WORKING ON ALMOST IMPOSSIBLE PROBLEMS...IT TAKES MY MIND OFF *OTHER THINGS!*

...SUCH AS THE FACT THAT I CAN NEVER DARE TELL PEPPER HOW MUCH I REALLY LOVE HER!

BECAUSE ONLY *I* KNOW THAT THE *HEART* OF RICH, GLAMOROUS, SUCCESSFUL TONY STARK MAY *STOP* AT ANY MOMENT, IF MY CHEST DEVICE SHOULD EVER FAIL!

IN FACT...IT NEEDS RE-CHARGING *NOW!* I--I'VE GROWN TOO CARELESS...WORKED TOO LONG WITHOUT A REST...!

SECONDS LATER, ONLY A THIN FLOW OF ELECTRIC CURRENT IN THE NICK OF TIME, SAVES THE LIFE OF *IRON MAN*, ONE OF THE STRONGEST SUPER-HEROES TO WALK THE EARTH!

I'M SAFE...FOR THE PRESENT!

BUT, IF EVER I'M *UNABLE* TO RE-CHARGE ...IT WILL BE... THE END!

THEN, MINUTES LATER...

I'LL HAVE TO LEAVE MY REVERSER FOR LATER! IT'S TIME FOR TONY STARK TO ATTEND TO BUSINESS IN HIS FACTORY NOW!

HOW ABOUT US GOING TO THE *FRUG A-GO GO* TONIGHT FOR SOME FANCY STEPPIN', PEPPER?

LOVE TO, HAPPY! I'VE GOT THE MOST DARLING NEW DISCOTHEQUE DRESS I'VE BEEN DYING TO WEAR!

WELL, WELL! I DIDN'T KNOW TODAY WAS A *HOLIDAY!*

UH-OH! THE *BOSS!*

2

LOOK, KIDS, I'LL TELL YOU WHAT! IF YOU DO A LITTLE WORK FOR THE REST OF THE DAY, YOU CAN USE MY LIMOUSINE WHEN YOU GO OUT TONIGHT!

WOULD YOU LIKE TO JOIN US, MR. STARK?

SORRY, I HAVE.. EH... OTHER THINGS TO DO!

WHY'D SHE HAVE TO ASK HIM? CAN'T SHE EVER GET OVER HER CRUSH ON STARK?

BUT NOW, LET US TURN OUR ATTENTION THOUSANDS OF MILES AWAY, TO A COMMUNIST WORK CAMP NOT FAR FROM BARREN SIBERIA...

THE NEW CAMP COMMISSAR HAS JUST ARRIVED!

IT IS THE ONE WE DREADED... THE FEARFUL COMRADE BULLSKI!

BULLSKI THE MERCILESS! HE WAS TRANSFERRED HERE BECAUSE EVEN THE PREMIER FEARS HIM!

QUIET! HE IS ENTERING NOW!

THIS IS OUR MAIN LABORATORY, COMRADE BULLSKI! IT IS HERE OUR CAPTIVE SCIENTISTS WORK!

YOU ARE TOO EASY ON THEM! THEY DO NOT WORK FAST ENOUGH! FROM NOW ON THEY WILL LABOR THREE HOURS MORE EACH DAY!

AND, IF ANYONE SLOWS DOWN, HE'LL ANSWER TO ME FOR IT!

I'LL CRUSH THE SPIRIT OF RESISTANCE OR REBELLION JUST AS EASILY AS I CRUSH THIS IRON PIPE! NEVER FORGET THAT!

MOMENTS LATER...

YOU SEEM TO BE DISTURBED, COMRADE...!

DISTURBED?? OF COURSE I'M DISTURBED! WHY SHOULD I, THE GREAT BORIS BULLSKI, BE STUCK IN THIS FORSAKEN CAMP IN THE MIDDLE OF NOWHERE?? I WAS MEANT FOR BIGGER THINGS!

BUT, THEY CAN'T KEEP BULLSKI HERE! I'LL MAKE THEM TRANSFER ME!

I'LL SCORE SUCH A VICTORY THAT THEY'LL MAKE ME DICTATOR! AND I KNOW JUST HOW TO DO IT!

SINGLE-HANDED, I WILL DEFEAT ONE OF COMMUNISM'S GREATEST ENEMIES! I KNOW HOW TO DESTROY IRON MAN HIMSELF!

3.

THE MAN KNOWN AS BULLSKI SPENDS THE NEXT HOUR CHECKING THE RECORD OF EVERY CAPTIVE SCIENTIST AT THE CAMP, AND THEN, WHEN HE IS DONE...

I KNOW THE ONES I NEED! ORDER THE FOLLOWING PRISONERS TO REPORT TO THE YARD...!

AND SO...

IT IS WITHIN MY POWER TO SET YOU *FREE*! DO AS I COMMAND, AND I SHALL *DO* SO! DISOBEY ME, AND YOU'LL REMAIN IN THIS PLACE AS LONG AS YOU LIVE! WHAT IS YOUR ANSWER?

A CHANCE FOR *FREEDOM*? WE WILL DO *ANYTHING*, COMRADE!

DA! NOW PAY ATTENTION! YOU ARE THE GREATEST SCIENTIFIC BRAINS IN THE CAMP! I WANT YOU TO BEGIN WORK ON A NEW PROJECT... *IMMEDIATELY*!

YOU WILL CREATE A *SUIT* FOR ME...A SUIT MADE OF *TITANIUM*! IT MUST BE THE GREATEST SUIT OF ARMOR THE WORLD HAS EVER KNOWN!

TITANIUM! IT WILL BE STRONGER THAN *IRON*!

WE WILL *DO* IT, COMRADE!

WE WILL NOT FAIL!

THIS IS THE LABORATORY WHICH THE *CRIMSON DYNAMO* USED TO DESIGN *HIS* ARMOR... BEFORE HE DEFECTED TO THE WEST!

YOU MUST BUILD A SUIT EVEN STRONGER THAN *HIS*...ONE WHICH CAN DESTROY *IRON MAN*!

BUT WE CANNOT MAKE IT AS *SMALL* AS IRON MAN'S! WE HAVE NOT HIS UNEQUALLED KNOWLEDGE OF MINIATURE TRANSISTORS!

NO MATTER! I AM POWERFUL ENOUGH TO WEAR A LARGER, HEAVIER SUIT! NOW, *BEGIN*!

IN THE DAYS THAT FOLLOW, BULLSKI STUDIES EVERY AVAILABLE FILM RECORD OF AMERICA'S GREAT GOLDEN CHAMPION...

BAH! I AM ALMOST *TWICE* HIS SIZE!

...INCLUDING NEWSREEL CLIPS OF SOME OF IRON MAN'S GREATEST BATTLES...

I COULD ALMOST DEFEAT SUCH FOES *WITHOUT* ANY ARMOR!

IF *THAT* IS THE BEST HE CAN DO, HE WON'T STAND A *CHANCE* AGAINST BULLSKI!

BAH! THESE PICTURES BEGIN TO *BORE* ME!

WITHIN A FEW MORE DAYS, IRON MAN SHALL EXIST *NO LONGER*!

4

AND, AS THE CONFIDENT BULLSKI IMPATIENTLY COUNTS THE HOURS...

IT IS TIME FOR THE FINAL STAGE! LET US BEGIN TO POUR THE TITANIUM ORE!

WHILE OUR TRANSISTORS ARE NOT AS SOPHISTICATED AS IRON MAN'S, THEY ARE THE MOST POWERFUL WE CAN PRODUCE!

BUT, WE HAVE ADVANTAGES IRON MAN DOES NOT!

SUCH AS THE FACT THAT BULLSKI'S TITANIUM ARMOR WILL BE LARGE ENOUGH TO ACCOMODATE THIS DEADLY DISINTEGRATOR RAY!

SEND FOR THE COMMISSAR! WE ARE READY!

IT IS SO ENORMOUS, COMRADE! WILL YOU BE ABLE TO SUPPORT ITS WEIGHT... TO MOVE FREELY WITHIN IT?

OF COURSE! I HAVE THE STRENGTH OF A GIANT! I MUST PUT IT ON AT ONCE!

AND SO...

THEY HAVE DONE AS YOU WISHED, COMRADE BULLSKI! SHALL I ORDER THEIR RELEASE NOW?

OF COURSE NOT! THEY WERE FOOLS TO BELIEVE ME! SEND THEM TO ANOTHER CAMP, WITH NO LABORATORY, SO THEY CAN NEVER MAKE AN EQUALLY POWERFUL SUIT FOR ANYONE ELSE!

BUT SAY NOTHING UNTIL I HAVE COMPLETELY TESTED THE ARMOR!

INCREDIBLE, COMRADE! YOU WEAR IT AS IF IT IS *WEIGHTLESS!*

IT IS AS IT *SHOULD* BE! AM I NOT THE MOST POWERFUL ONE OF ALL ??

THE POWER-ASSISTED CONTROLS WITHIN THE ARMOR WILL GIVE YOU GREATER EASE OF MOVEMENT, COMMISSAR!

I DON'T EVEN *NEED* THEM! WITH MY GREAT STRENGTH, I CAN MOVE AS EASILY AS IF I'M WEARING AN ORDINARY *OVERCOAT!*

IT'S UNBELIEVABLE! *IRON MAN* WILL HAVE NO CHANCE AGAINST HIM!

NOW, ALL THAT REMAINS TO DO IS ISSUE MY *CHALLENGE* TO IRON MAN!

FIRST, I WILL LET HIM SEE HOW *USELESS* HIS WEAPONS ARE AGAINST MY TITANIUM ARMOR!

"AND THEN, WHEN HE HAS EXHAUSTED EVERY TYPE OF DEVICE HE CAN THROW AGAINST ME...WHEN HE REALIZES HE CANNOT HARM ME...THE *TITANIUM MAN* SHALL STRIKE BACK...."

"FOR, MY ARMOR WAS CREATED WITH BUT ONE THOUGHT IN MIND...TO BE ABLE TO SMASH *IRON MAN!*"

"AND, ONCE THE WORLD KNOWS THAT *I* HAVE DEFEATED DEMOCRACY'S GREATEST FIGHTER, I SHALL BE UNDISPUTED *MASTER* OF THE COMMUNIST WORLD!"

6.

...AND NOW TO *FORCE* IRON MAN TO MEET ME IN MORTAL COMBAT!

THUS, A FEW HOURS LATER, IN AMERICA...

A *TELEGRAM* FOR YOU, MR. STARK... FROM BEHIND THE IRON CURTAIN!

FROM COMMIELAND? SOUNDS LIKE *TROUBLE,* PEPPER!

OPEN IT...AND READ IT!

IT'S NOT REALLY FOR *YOU,* BOSS! IT'S FOR *IRON MAN!*

IT'S FROM SOMEONE WHO CALLS HIMSELF *TITANIUM MAN,* CHALLENGING IRON MAN TO *FIGHT* HIM AT SOME NEUTRAL BATTLEGROUND!

AND HE SAYS HE'S SENT A *COPY* OF THIS CHALLENGE TO ALL THE WORLD'S *NEWSPAPERS!*

HOW CAN I ACCEPT? MY LIFE-SAVING CHEST DEVICE HAS BEEN GIVING ME CONSTANT TROUBLE LATELY! IT'S ONE OF THE REASONS I FELT COMPELLED TO LEAVE THE *AVENGERS!*

IRON MAN WILL *HAVE* TO FIGHT HIM, BOSS....OR AMERICA MIGHT LOSE FACE IN THE EYES OF THE WORLD!

I KNOW...BUT THIS DECISION CAN ONLY BE MADE BY *IRON MAN!*

HE SOUNDS SO *STRANGE*...SO WORRIED!

I NEVER SAW HIM LOOK SO UPSET! LIKE HE DIDN'T *WANT* TO TELL IRON MAN!

LATER, IN WASHINGTON, D.C....

YOU MEAN IRON MAN HASN'T *ACCEPTED* THAT COMMUNIST'S CHALLENGE YET ??

THAT'S RIGHT, SENATOR BYRD!

IT'S PROBABLY THAT CONCEITED PLAYBOY, TONY STARK'S DOING! HE DOESN'T WANT TO *LOSE* HIS PERSONAL BODY-GUARD!

BUT, IRON MAN *MUST* ACCEPT THE CHALLENGE! IT'S A MATTER OF NATIONAL PRIDE...OF PRESTIGE!

TAKE A LETTER, MISS SMITH...TO TONY STARK...!

BUT WHAT IF IRON MAN SHOULD BE *DEFEATED,* SIR ?

THAT'S A CHANCE WE'LL HAVE TO TAKE!

7

AFTER RECEIVING THE SENATOR'S WIRE, A TORTURED TONY STARK GRIMLY SEEKS THE RIGHT DECISION...

DO I *DARE* FIGHT A POWERFUL FOE WHILE MY CHEST DEVICE IS FAULTY?

YET, WOULD IT BE BETTER TO FIGHT AND *LOSE*...THAN TO STAND BRANDED AS A *COWARD?*

I'VE GOT TO FIND A WAY TO STRENGTHEN MY CHEST DEVICE... LONG ENOUGH FOR ONE BATTLE! I'VE *GOT* TO...!

THUS, THROUGH THE LONG NIGHT, THE WORLD'S HANDSOMEST, WEALTHIEST "PLAYBOY" BACHELOR WORKS HARDER THAN MOST MEN WILL EVER WORK IN A LIFETIME!

WHILE, THROUGHOUT THE WORLD, THE BIG QUESTION ON EVERYONE'S LIPS IS...

DAILY GLOBE

WILL IRON MAN ACCEPT CHALLENGE?

CONGRESS PRESSING FOR SHOWDOWN ON RED BID!

IF IRON MAN CHICKENS OUT, I'LL MAKE STARK *REGRET* IT!

I DON'T FEAR DEATH FOR MYSELF...I LIVE IN THE SHADOW OF IT EACH MOMENT ANYWAY! BUT, I DON'T WANT TO *FAIL*...NOT WHEN I'M NEEDED!

IF ONLY I COULD FIND A WAY TO BRING MYSELF UP TO MY PEAK FIGHTING STRENGTH...!

AND THEN, AS THE FIRST FAINT FLICKER OF DAWN APPEARS IN THE SKY...

I'VE *GOT* IT! IT'S A LONG SHOT...BUT IT JUST MIGHT WORK!

ALL AROUND THE CLOCK WORKS THE BRILLIANT INDUSTRIAL DESIGNER, USING EVERY BIT OF KNOWLEDGE HE POSSESSES...UNTIL...

THIS WON'T BE A *PERMANENT* CURE-ALL, BUT IT SHOULD REINFORCE MY CHEST DEVICE LONG ENOUGH TO DO WHAT MUST BE DONE!

NOW TO *TEST* IT...

IT *WORKS!* I CAN FEEL THE POWER SURGING THROUGH ME!

THE *TITANIUM MAN* WILL *GET* THE FIGHT HE WANTS!

AND SO, THE IMPATIENT BULLSKI FINALLY RECEIVES HIS ANSWER...

PREPARE THE COMBAT AREA! IRON MAN HAS SNAPPED AT THE *BAIT!*

SEE TO IT THAT ALL THE *TRAPS* ARE POSITIONED AND READY!

EVERYTHING IS READY, COMRADE! IRON MAN IS *DOOMED!*

8

NEXT MORNING, PEPPER AND HAPPY RECEIVE A SURPRISE...

I WANT YOU BOTH TO ACCOMPANY ME TO EUROPE TO WATCH IRON MAN'S BATTLE!

I MAY *NEED* SOMEONE I CAN TRUST COMPLETELY!

BOSS... THAT'S *WONDERFUL!*

I WONDER WHY THE *BOSS* IS GOING? WITH ALL THE WORK GOIN' ON HERE, YOU'D THINK HE'D STAY BEHIND TO LOOK AFTER BUSINESS!

MAYBE HE JUST WANTS TO BE NEAR *PEPPER*...AND I GUESS I CAN'T *BLAME 'IM!*

AND SO, THE GREAT MISSION BEGINS...!

THE BATTLE WILL BE HELD IN ALBERIA, SUPERVISED BY AN INTERNATIONAL COMMITTEE...!

AND, IN THE TINY, NEUTRAL NATION OF ALBERIA, A CARNIVAL ATMOSPHERE FILLS THE LAND AS ONE OF THE GREATEST FEATS OF COMBAT OF ALL TIME IS ABOUT TO BEGIN...!

TOURISTS FROM EVERY NATION IN THE WORLD HAVE FLOCKED TO ALBERIA TO WITNESS THE FORTHCOMING FIGHT!

LUCKY IT'S GOING TO BE *TELEVISED* ON PUBLIC TV SCREENS! *NOBODY* WILL MISS A MINUTE OF IT!

IRON MAN VS.

WHILE, HIGH OVERHEAD, A SPECIAL TELSTAR SATELLITE HANGS IN ORBIT, TO BEAM THE BATTLE THROUGHOUT THE WORLD!

AS FOR THE CHOSEN ARENA ITSELF, IT CONSISTS OF A LONG-DESERTED BATTLEFIELD FROM WORLD WAR TWO... STILL LITTERED WITH THE DEBRIS AND THE SCARS OF COUNTLESS ENGAGEMENTS WHICH HAVE FOUND THEIR PLACE IN HISTORY...

9

MEANWHILE, AT ALBERIA'S INTERNATIONAL HOTEL...

LOOK, HAPPY! ISN'T THAT THE COUNTESS DE LA SPIROZA?

BEATS ME, DOLL! NEVER HEARD OF HER!

WHO'S THE COUNTESS WHATCHAMACALLIT, ANYWAY?

SHE HAPPENS TO BE AN OLD FLAME OF MR. STARK'S!

I SHOULDA KNOWN THAT WAS IT! I CAN HEAR THE JEALOUSY IN PEPPER'S VOICE FROM HERE!

MINUTES LATER...

TONY STARK! I NEVER EXPECTED TO FIND YOU IN THIS LITTLE FLYSPECK ON THE MAP!

COUNTESS! YOU'RE LOVELIER THAN EVER, STEPHANIE! HAVE YOU COME TO SEE THE BIG BATTLE?

OF COURSE! THINGS WERE SO BORING AT THE RIVIERA.. TILL NOW!

I CAN'T IMAGINE THINGS EVER BEING BORING WHEN YOU'RE THERE, MY DEAR!

WELL! IT DIDN'T TAKE HER LONG TO GET HER CLAWS BACK IN TONY STARK!

GOSH, PEPPER, WHY SHOULD YOU CARE?

AND THAT'S THE DUMBEST QUESTION OF THE CENTURY!

GIVE ME JUST A MINUTE, TONY DEAR, AND I'LL CHANGE AND JOIN YOU FOR A NIGHTCAP DOWNSTAIRS!

SORRY, COUNTESS! I'VE GOT TO GET TO SLEEP EARLY TONIGHT! PERHAPS SOME OTHER TIME!

WELL, MR. STARK, IF YOUR BEAUTY SLEEP MEANS MORE TO YOU THAN I...!

I CAN HARDLY TELL HER THAT I HAVE TO SPEND THE EVENING CHECKING MY IRON MAN EQUIPMENT!

YOU JILTED ME ONCE, TONY STARK, AND I'VE NEVER FORGIVEN YOU FOR IT! NOW THAT WE'VE MET AGAIN, I'LL MAKE YOU PAY FOR IT SOMEHOW...I PROMISE YOU THAT!

10.

FINALLY, WITH THE COMING DAWN, THE FATEFUL MOMENT ARRIVES. IN THE CENTER OF THE BARREN EX-BATTLE AREA, THE BURGOMASTER OF ALBERIA REVIEWS THE AGREED-UPON RULES OF COMBAT...

SO *THAT'S* TITANIUM MAN! JUDGING BY THE SIZE OF HIS ARMORED SUIT, HE MUST BE A VERITABLE *GIANT* HIMSELF!

YOU BOTH AGREE TO ABIDE BY THE INTERNATIONAL RULES AND COVENANT AS SET FORTH AND SIGNED BY REPRESENTATIVES OF EACH OF YOUR NATIONS!

WE ALL *KNOW* THE RULES! DO NOT WASTE ANY FURTHER TIME! I AM EAGER FOR THE *BATTLE* TO BEGIN!

LOOK AT THE DIFFERENCE IN THEIR SIZES! IRON MAN WILL BE HOPELESSLY OUTCLASSED!

THIS SHALL BE A PROPAGANDA VICTORY FROM WHICH AMERICA WILL *NEVER* RECOVER!

AT LAST, THE FIELD IS CLEARED, AND THE TWO COMBATANTS FACE EACH OTHER...

I HAVE WAITED A *LONG TIME* FOR THIS MOMENT... BUT, IT SHALL BE *WORTH* IT!

I *HOPE* SO, SWEETIE! I SURE WOULDN'T WANT YOU TO GO AWAY DISAPPOINTED!

ONE BLAST IS ALL IT WILL TAKE TO... *WHA*...? WHERE DID YOU...??

YOU DIDN'T EXPECT ME TO JUST *STAND* THERE, DID YOU?

ZAT!

HEADS UP, BIG MAN! LET'S SEE WHAT A REPULSER-RAY BLAST CAN DO AGAINST *YOU!*

WHOOOM!

11.

I DON'T *LIKE* IT! HE'S AS STRONG AS HE *LOOKS*! I'M NOT *HARMING* HIM A BIT!

WOK!

NOW IT'S *MY* TURN...!

UHHH! HE PULLED ME TO HIM, BY MAGNETIC ATTRACTION!

THIS SHALL BE MY MOMENT OF TRIUMPH...WITH REMOTE-CONTROL TV CAMERAS RECORDING EVERY DETAIL!

SEE HOW POWERLESS YOU ARE AGAINST MY SUPERIOR SIZE AND STRENGTH!

HE'S NOT JUST WHISTLIN' DIXIE!

BUT, THEN, IN A DESPERATE MANEUVER, IRON MAN *REVERSES* HIS JETS, AND...

TTTT!

HAPPY LANDINGS, PLAYMATE! BETTER LUCK *NEXT* TIME!

WHY DOES HE WASTE TIME FIRING THOSE BLASTS AT ME? HE *KNOWS* I CAN OUTRUN THEM!

HE MUST HAVE A REASON... BUT *WHAT??*

THAT'S *IT*, YOU FOOL! RUN...KEEP *RUNNING*..!

YOU'RE ALMOST MAKING IT *TOO EASY* FOR ME! YOU'RE RUNNING RIGHT TO YOUR *DOOM*...

...IN THE *MINE FIELD* WHICH WE HAD SECRETLY PREPARED!

I WAS *CARELESS!* I SHOULD HAVE *EXPECTED* TREACHERY FROM... *UHHHH!*

BAROOM!

AND, IN ONE OF THE MANY PUBLIC TV RECEIVERS PROVIDED BY THE ALBERIAN GOVERNMENT, PEPPER AND HAPPY WATCH THE FATAL-SEEMING EXPLOSION...

HE *TRICKED* IRON MAN! I NEVER THOUGHT...*OHH!*

WHAT HAPPENED TO THE *BOSS?* WHY ISN'T *HE* HERE?

DOESN'T HE *CARE* WHAT HAPPENS TO IRON MAN??

THOSE OF YOU WHO HAVE BEEN MARVELITES FOR LONG KNOW THAT THE ACTION AND SUSPENSE IS JUST *BEGINNING!* NEXT ISH WILL BRING YOU COUNTLESS UNEXPECTED DEVELOPMENTS, PLUS ALL THE DRAMA AND FANTASY YOU EXPECT FROM A MARVEL MASTERWORK! SO, BE WITH US FOR *SUSPENSE #70*, WHEN IRON MAN FIGHTS THE MOST DESPERATE FIGHT OF HIS LIFE! TILL THEN, KEEP YOUR TRANSISTORS DRY AND *FACE FRONT!*

12

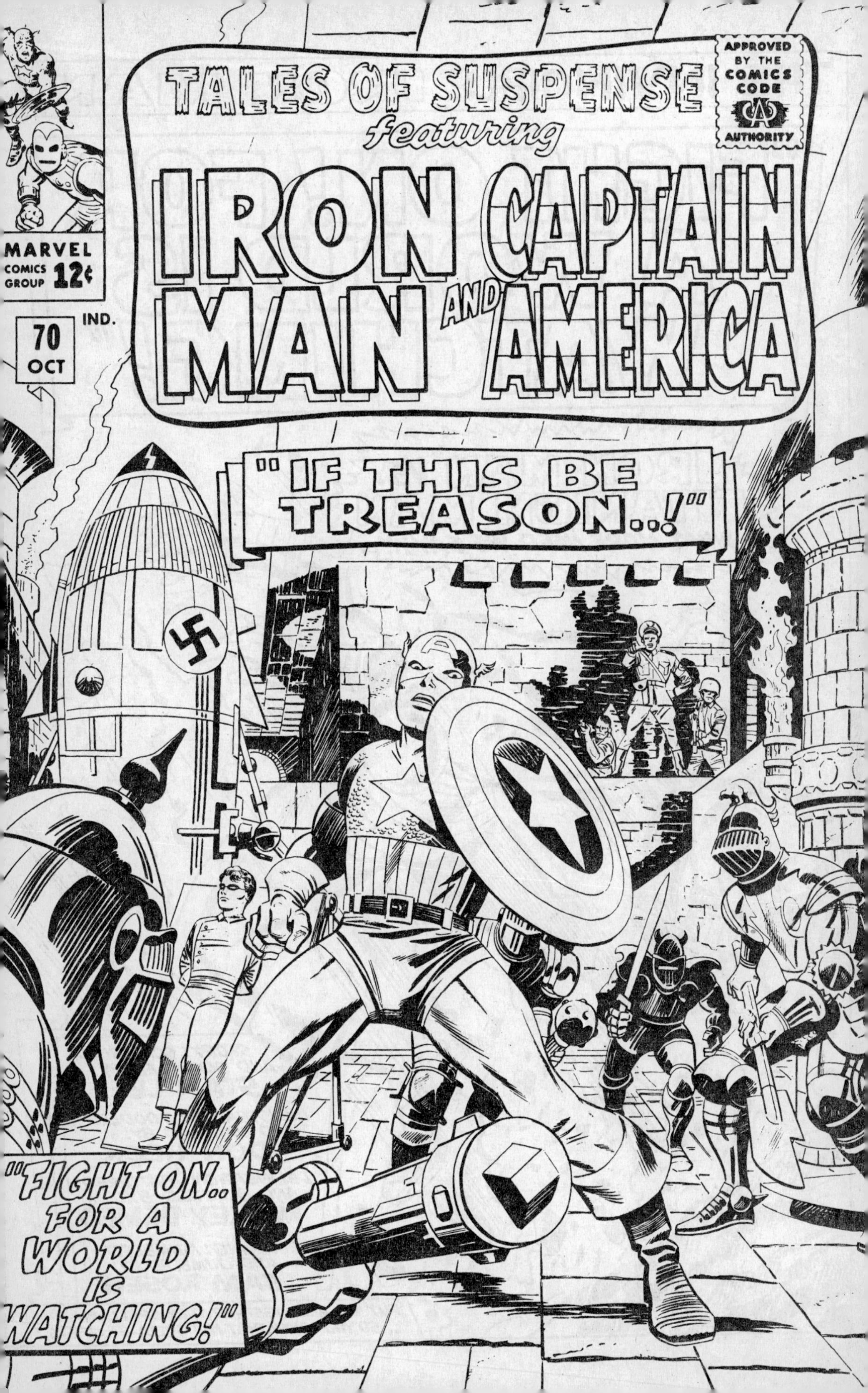
TALES OF SUSPENSE
featuring
IRON MAN AND CAPTAIN AMERICA
APPROVED BY THE COMICS CODE AUTHORITY
MARVEL COMICS GROUP 12¢
IND.
70 OCT
"IF THIS BE TREASON..!"
"FIGHT ON.. FOR A WORLD IS WATCHING!"

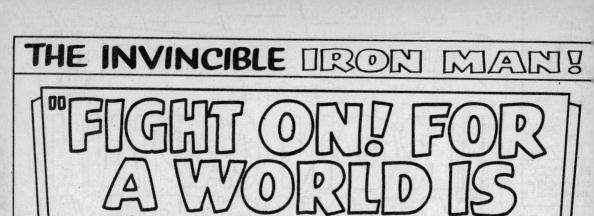

THE INVINCIBLE IRON MAN!

"FIGHT ON! FOR A WORLD IS WATCHING!"

IRON MAN VS. TITANIUM MAN
WHAT MORE NEED WE SAY?!!

STORY: SCRIBBLED AND SCRAWLED BY: **STAN LEE**

ILLUSTRATION: DOODLED AND DAWDLED BY: **DON HECK**

DELINEATION: BATTERED AND BLOTTED BY: **MICKEY DEMEO**

LETTERING: MUMBLED AND JUMBLED BY: **SAM ROSEN**

PUT 'EM ALL TOGETHER, THEY SPELL MARVEL ...SO YOU KNOW THAT IT'S GOTTA BE GREAT!

JUDGING BY OUR PHENOMENAL SALES FIGURES, THERE MUST BE ONLY ONE PERSON IN THE FREE WORLD WHO SOMEHOW MISSED OUR LAST GREAT ISH OF *SUSPENSE!* BUT, IF *YOU* ARE THAT LUCKLESS SOUL, WE'LL QUICKLY BRING YOU UP TO DATE! IN AN IRON CURTAIN COUNTRY, COMMISSAR *BULLSKI* HAS A POWERFUL TITANIUM SUIT DESIGNED FOR HIMSELF, WITH ONLY *ONE* PURPOSE IN MIND...

HE WHO WEARS THAT SUIT WILL BE IRON MAN'S *MASTER!*

ONLY SOMEONE AS HUGE, AS MIGHTY AS COMMISSAR BULLSKI COULD HAVE THE STRENGTH TO WEAR AND OPERATE SO CUMBERSOME A COMPLEX OF ARMOR! BUT TO *HIM*, IT IS LIKE WEARING AN OVERCOAT!

NOW, FOR THE GREATER GLORY OF COMMUNISM, THE *TITANIUM MAN* SHALL CHALLENGE... AND *DESTROY* IRON MAN!

AND, IN THE TINY, NEUTRAL NATION OF ALBERIA, A CARNIVAL ATMOSPHERE FILLS THE LAND AS ONE OF THE GREATEST FEATS OF COMBAT OF ALL TIME IS ABOUT TO BEGIN...!

TOURISTS FROM EVERY NATION IN THE WORLD HAVE FLOCKED TO ALBERIA TO WITNESS THE FORTHCOMING FIGHT!

LUCKY IT'S GOING TO BE *TELEVISED* ON PUBLIC TV SCREENS! *NOBODY* WILL MISS A MINUTE OF IT!

IRON MAN VS.

IF THE PANELS ON THIS PAGE LOOK SOMEWHAT FAMILIAR, IT'S BECAUSE SNEAKY STAN BORROWED THEM FROM OUR LAST ISH, IN ORDER TO ACCURATELY BRING YOU UP TO DATE...

FINALLY, WE MET THE STUNNING, SULTRY *COUNTESS STEPHANIE DE LA SPIROSA*, A MYSTERIOUS CHARMER FROM TONY STARK'S PAST... WHO SEEMS TO HAVE DESIGNS ON HIS *FUTURE*, AS WELL!

YOU JILTED ME *ONCE*, TONY STARK, AND I'VE NEVER FORGIVEN YOU FOR IT! NOW THAT WE'VE MET AGAIN, I'LL MAKE YOU *PAY* FOR IT SOMEHOW... I *PROMISE* YOU THAT!

FINALLY, OUR PREVIOUS INSTALLMENT ENDED WITH THE TITANIUM MAN TRICKING THE GALLANT GOLDEN GLADIATOR INTO RUNNING THROUGH A SECRET *MINE FIELD!* AND NOW... ON WITH OUR SUPER-SPECTACLE...!

MY ARMOR WILL PROTECT ME FROM *THIS* BLAST... BUT, I WOULDN'T WANT TO FACE MANY *MORE* OF THEM!

BAROOOM!

2

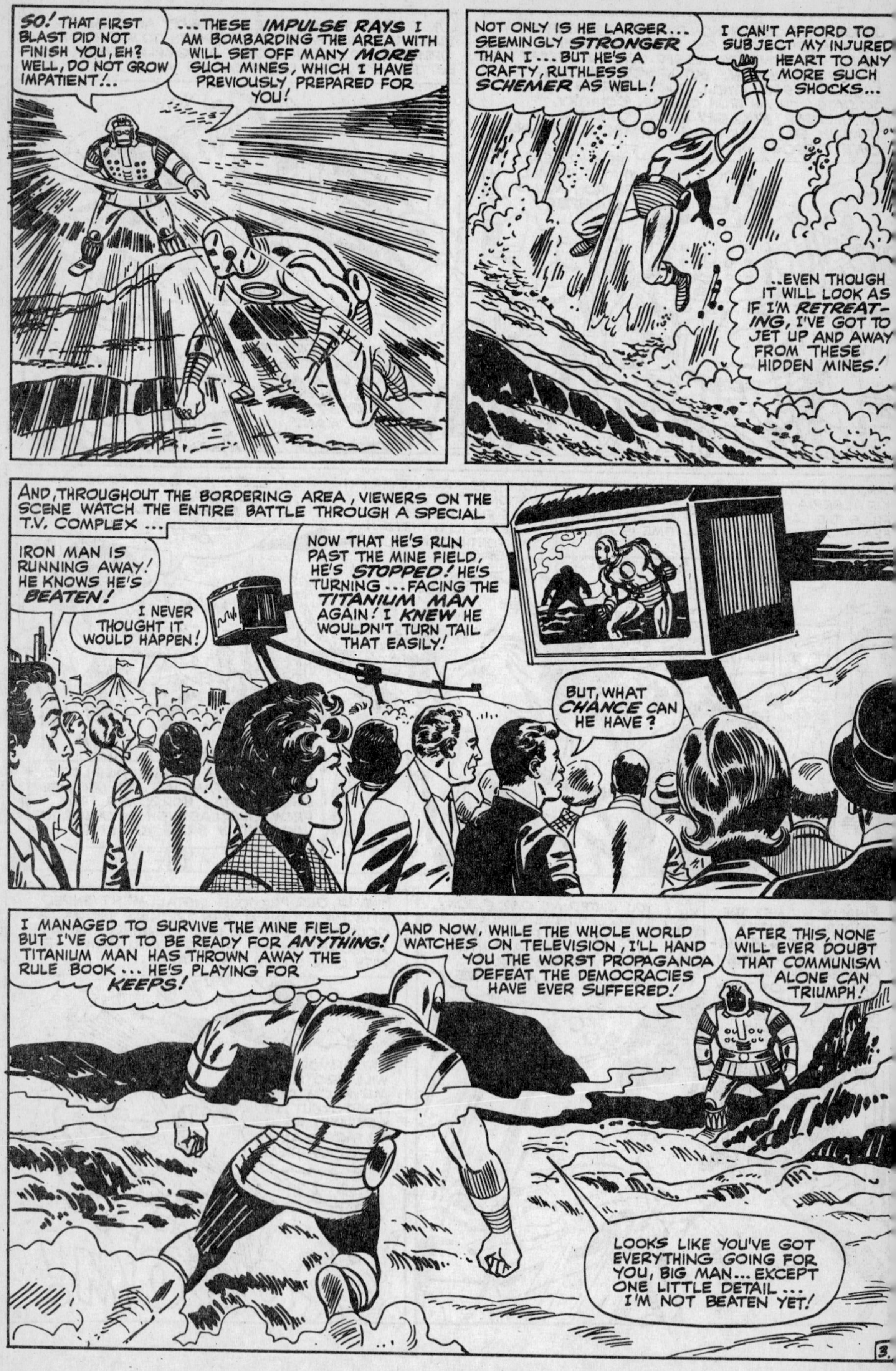

SO! THAT FIRST BLAST DID NOT FINISH YOU, EH? WELL, DO NOT GROW IMPATIENT!..
...THESE IMPULSE RAYS I AM BOMBARDING THE AREA WITH WILL SET OFF MANY MORE SUCH MINES, WHICH I HAVE PREVIOUSLY PREPARED FOR YOU!
NOT ONLY IS HE LARGER... SEEMINGLY STRONGER THAN I... BUT HE'S A CRAFTY, RUTHLESS SCHEMER AS WELL!
I CAN'T AFFORD TO SUBJECT MY INJURED HEART TO ANY MORE SUCH SHOCKS...
..EVEN THOUGH IT WILL LOOK AS IF I'M RETREATING, I'VE GOT TO JET UP AND AWAY FROM THESE HIDDEN MINES!
AND, THROUGHOUT THE BORDERING AREA, VIEWERS ON THE SCENE WATCH THE ENTIRE BATTLE THROUGH A SPECIAL T.V. COMPLEX...
IRON MAN IS RUNNING AWAY! HE KNOWS HE'S BEATEN!
I NEVER THOUGHT IT WOULD HAPPEN!
NOW THAT HE'S RUN PAST THE MINE FIELD, HE'S STOPPED! HE'S TURNING... FACING THE TITANIUM MAN AGAIN! I KNEW HE WOULDN'T TURN TAIL THAT EASILY!
BUT, WHAT CHANCE CAN HE HAVE?
I MANAGED TO SURVIVE THE MINE FIELD, BUT I'VE GOT TO BE READY FOR ANYTHING! TITANIUM MAN HAS THROWN AWAY THE RULE BOOK... HE'S PLAYING FOR KEEPS!
AND NOW, WHILE THE WHOLE WORLD WATCHES ON TELEVISION, I'LL HAND YOU THE WORST PROPAGANDA DEFEAT THE DEMOCRACIES HAVE EVER SUFFERED!
AFTER THIS, NONE WILL EVER DOUBT THAT COMMUNISM ALONE CAN TRIUMPH!
LOOKS LIKE YOU'VE GOT EVERYTHING GOING FOR YOU, BIG MAN... EXCEPT ONE LITTLE DETAIL... I'M NOT BEATEN YET!
3

HE'S ALMOST *TWICE* MY SIZE, AND LOADED WITH WEAPONS! UNTIL I CAN DISCOVER SOME WEAKNESSES, I'D BETTER MOVE FAST! I'LL TRY A *DIVE BOMB* ATTACK, AND...

MY JETS... THEY'RE NOT *LIFTING* ME FAST ENOUGH!!

MY LEFT BOOT! IT WAS DAMAGED IN THE MINE FIELD!!

AND, THE SHARP-EYED *TITANIUM MAN* IS QUICK TO NOTICE HIS SMALLER FOES NEW HANDICAP...!

SO! ONE OF YOUR POWER JETS DOES NOT FUNCTION! WHAT A *PITY*... FOR *YOU*, IRON MAN!

NORMALLY, I COULD FLY *RINGS* AROUND HIM, BUT NOW... HE'S GAINING FAST!

YOUR PITIFUL FLIGHT IS *USELESS!* YOU CANNOT ESCAPE MY RADAR RINGS!

RADAR RINGS??

ALL I NEED DO IS POINT AT MY VICTIM... PRESS A CONTROL STUD... AND THE RINGS ON MY ARM SHOOT OUT...!

...GROWING *LARGER* BY THE SECOND...!

TRY THOUGH HE MAY TO OUT-MANEUVER THE FLYING RINGS, THEIR BUILT-IN RADAR IS TOO SENSITIVE... AND SO...

THEY'RE *ENCIRCLING* ME! HE OPERATES THEM BY REMOTE CONTROL! WHAT HAPPENS *NEXT?*

A SPLIT-SECOND LATER, IRON MAN *GETS HIS* ANSWER...

THEY'RE *SHRINKING!* ...BECOMING SO TIGHT I CAN'T *MOVE!*

4.

THEY'RE FORCING ME DOWN... TOWARDS THE GROUND!

TONY BOY...YOU SHOULD HAVE STUCK TO WINE WOMEN AND SONG! WHO NEEDED *THIS*?!!

MEANWHILE, UNNOTICED IN THE TENSE CROWD OF SPECTATORS, COUNTESS DE LA SPIROSA SEARCHES FOR ONE MAN...

I HAVE SEEN NO TRACE OF TONY STARK!

AH, THERE IS ONE *WHO WORKS* FOR HIM! PERHAPS *HE* KNOWS WHERE I MIGHT FIND TONY!

NO, *I* HAVEN'T SEEN 'IM, COUNTESS! I THOUGHT HE MIGHTA BEEN WITH *YOU*!

IS THE *BOSS* ALL SHE CAN THINK OF AT A TIME LIKE *THIS*?

THANK YOU! I SHALL LOOK ELSEWHERE!

WOTTA COLD TOMATO! SHE SHOULD WORRY IF IRON MAN'S TAKING THE BEATING OF HIS LIFE!

BUT, COME TO THINK OF IT, HAPPY... WHERE *IS* MR. STARK? WHY ISN'T HE *HERE* AT A TIME LIKE THIS?

OW! LOOK AT THE T.V. SCREEN...!!

NOW THAT I'VE BROUGHT YOU BACK TO EARTH, THIS *POWER-SAPPER* BEAM WILL MAKE YOU WEAKER BY THE MINUTE...!

LET THE WORLD SEE HOW HELP-LESS YOU ARE BEFORE ME!

I'VE GOT TO *FREE* MYSELF! I'LL APPLY FULL PRESSURE AT EVERY STRESS POINT, NO MATTER HOW IT DRAINS MY POWER..!

IT'S *WORKING!* I CAN FEEL THEM BEGINNING TO GIVE...!

I *DID* IT! I FORCED THEM TO *EXPAND* AGAIN!

I'M *FREE!*

BUT MY POWER PACK IS RUNNING LOW! I'VE GOT TO STALL FOR *TIME*.....TIME TO RECHARGE!

BACK *UP*! BROTHER! THIS *CHEMICAL BATH* OUGHT TO SLOW YOU DOWN!

MEANWHILE, AT TONY STARK'S HOTEL LAB...

TONY, ARE YOU *HERE?* I WAS PASSING BY, AND SAW THAT YOUR DOOR WAS OPEN!

AGAIN I WASTED MY TIME! HE'S *GONE*... AND WITHOUT A WORD TO ME!

BUT I WON'T GIVE UP!

THERE JUST HAS TO BE *SOME* WAY I CAN MAKE *HIM* RUN AFTER *ME!*

IRON MAN TO TAKE ON TITANIUM MAN

WHAT IS THAT ON THE TABLE!?

IT MUST BE SOME *SILLY* NEW TRANSISTOR DEVICE HE'S BEEN WORKING ON!

AND, WHEN HE RETURNS TO FIND IT *MISSING*, HE'LL MOST CERTAINLY WANT IT *BACK!*

I'LL FIND *SOME* WAY TO LET HIM KNOW *I* HAVE IT!

AND THEN, WHEN HE COMES BEGGING FOR IT, IT SHALL BE *MY* TURN TO PLAY HARD-TO-GET!

BUT, ALAS, THE COUNTESS DOESN'T REALIZE HOW VITALLY *IMPORTANT* THAT DEVICE REALLY IS!

6.

BUT, UNAWARE OF WHAT HAS HAPPENED TO HIS NEWEST TRANSISTORIZED WEAPON, IRON MAN CONTINUES HIS DESPERATE BATTLE TO GAIN TIME...

THERE! THE PROPER COMBINATION OF CHEMICALS WILL MAKE IT SO HOT INSIDE HIS SUIT THAT TITANIUM MAN WILL FORGET ABOUT *ME* FOR A FEW MINUTES!

WHIST!

IT *WORKED!* HE'S ROLLING AROUND, RUBBING THE CHEMICAL OFF IN THE DIRT... GIVING ME THE TIME I NEED!

BY SETTING MY CONTROLS TO *QUICK RECHARGE*, I CAN FEEL THE STRENGTH RETURNING TO ME BY THE SECOND!

HE'S BEEN ROLLING THAT WAY LONGER THAN I *EXPECTED!* PERHAPS THE CHEMICALS WERE *TOO* POTENT! THEY MAY PROVE *FATAL!*

SETTING CAUTION ASIDE FOR A MOMENT... CONSCIOUS ONLY OF COMING TO THE AID OF ANOTHER... IRON MAN APPROACHES HIS FOE... WHEN SUDDENLY...

FOOL! I RELIED UPON YOUR WEAK AMERICAN *COMPASSION* TO BRING YOU WITHIN *STRIKING* RANGE!

BLANG!

UNHHH..!

HERE, AT CLOSE RANGE, MY SUPERIOR SIZE AND STRENGTH GIVE ME EVERY ADVANTAGE!

REMEMBER, MY ARMOR WAS CREATED FOR JUST *ONE* PURPOSE.... TO BE SUPERIOR TO *YOURS!* I *KNEW* THAT ONCE I GOT MY TITANIUM-SHOD HANDS ON YOU, THE BATTLE WOULD BE *WON!*

7

AND, AMONG THE COUNTLESS OBSERVERS OF THE EPIC BATTLE, WE FIND U.S. SENATOR HARRINGTON BYRD... A LONG-TIME FOE OF ANTHONY STARK...

IT LOOKS BAD FOR IRON MAN!

IF THAT TITANIUM GIANT *BEATS* HIM, I'LL HOLD *TONY STARK* PERSONALLY RESPONSIBLE FOR THE DEFEAT!

BUT *WHY,* SIR!

STARK IS SUPPOSED TO BE OUR WEAPONS GENIUS! HE SHOULD HAVE MADE IRON MAN'S ARMOR *STRONGER!* THIS PROVES WHAT I'VE ALWAYS SAID... STARK IS A *PHONY!*

THE EYES OF THE WORLD ARE ON US... AND WE'RE *LOSING!*

INDEED, AT THAT VERY MOMENT, NOT MANY VIEWERS WOULD *ARGUE* THE SENATOR'S POINT...

ALTHOUGH LIGHTER IN WEIGHT, AND SMALLER... MY ARMOR IS MORE SOPHISTICATED THAN HIS!

I CAN EASILY WITHSTAND TITANIUM MAN'S BLOWS!

THUD!

BUT, THE STRAIN ON MY INJURED *HEART* IS ANOTHER MATTER! HOW MUCH LONGER CAN I *TAKE* IT??

ACCORDING TO THE RULES, THERE'LL BE A *REST PERIOD* AFTER FIFTEEN MINUTES OF FIGHTING... BUT, CAN I *HOLD OUT* UNTIL THE END OF THIS ROUND??

I'VE GOT TO RESORT TO MY OWN ACE-IN-THE-HOLE... THE NEW SUB-MINIATURE DEVICE I WAS WORKING ON BEFORE I LEFT AMERICA!

IT'S STILL *UNTESTED...* BUT IT MIGHT BE THE ONLY THING TO TURN THE TIDE OF BATTLE!

IF I MOVE FAST, I CAN SLIP IT INTO PLACE AND... OH *NO!*

IT'S *GONE!* I MUST HAVE LEFT IT AT THE HOTEL LAB!

NOW I'VE *GOT* TO HOLD OUT TILL THE END OF THE ROUND...

BUT, UNKNOWN TO IRON MAN, HIS TOWERING FOE HAS THE VERY *SAME* IDEA....!

I'VE HIT HIM WITH ALMOST EVERYTHING... AND STILL HE SURVIVES! HE'S MIGHTIER THAN I *THOUGHT!* I'VE GOT TO STALL UNTIL THE ROUND ENDS, SO I CAN PLAN A NEW STRATEGY!

I CAN'T LET HIM SUSPECT THE PAIN IN MY CHEST! I MUST KEEP ACTING *CONFIDENT!*

THUS, LIKE TWO SUPER-POWERED HEAVYWEIGHTS IN THE PRIZE RING, THE ARMORED POWERHOUSES PARRY AND THRUST... ATTEMPTING TO CONSERVE THEIR REMAINING ELECTRONIC ENERGY SOURCES UNTIL THE NEXT ROUND...!

HE'S STALLING, TOO! THAT MEANS MY BATTLE TACTICS... MY SURVIVAL ABILITY, HAVE HIM CONFUSED!

DESPITE HIS GREATER BULK... HIS LARGER WEAPONS... HE'S BEGINNING TO FEEL UNCERTAINTY... PERHAPS EVEN FEAR!

NOW I KNOW WHY YOUR NAME IS WHISPERED WITH AWE BY ALL WHO HAVE EVER FACED YOU!

BUT HAVING SAMPLED THE EXTENT OF YOUR TRUE POWER, MY EVENTUAL VICTORY WILL BE ALL THE GREATER!

THE WARNING SIREN! THE ROUND IS OVER AT LAST!

WHEEEEEEEEEEE

WEARILY, EACH COMBATANT LEAVES THE BATTLE SITE TO PARTAKE OF THE TEN-MINUTE REST PERIOD...!

YOU WERE SUPERB, COMRADE! YOU TOYED WITH HIM MAGNIFICENTLY!

FOOL! HIS POWER EQUALS MY OWN! I MUST PLAN A NEW, DEADLY ASSAULT!

TITANIUM

THERE'S SENATOR BYRD, PEPPER, AND HAPPY BELOW ME! BUT I CAN'T STOP NOW!

I'VE GOT TO GET MY NEW WEAPON FROM THE LAB BEFORE ROUND 2 BEGINS!

HE'S FLYING OFF.. HEADING FOR TOWN! IF HE'S DESERTING THE BATTLE, IT'LL GIVE US THE WORST PROPAGANDA DEFEAT WE'VE EVER SUFFERED!

I DON'T GET IT! WHERE'S HE GOING AND WHERE IN BLAZE IS TONY STARK?

I CAN'T BELIEVE HE'D RUN OUT... I JUST CAN'T!

IRON MAN, OF COURSE, HAS NOT DESERTED... BUT THE SHOCK THAT AWAITS HIM AT THE HOTEL LAB MIGHT ALMOST MAKE HIM WISH HE HAD--!

IT'S GONE! THE ONE THING THAT MIGHT BRING VICTORY... IT'S BEEN STOLEN!

BUT, WAIT! WHAT'S THIS ??

STEPHANIE'S HANDKERCHIEF... IT WAS SHE WHO TOOK IT!!

THE LITTLE FOOL... SHE'S PLAYING A GAME... TO BRING TONY STARK TO HER!

I CAN'T DELAY ANY LONGER! ONLY MINUTES LEFT! LUCKY I BROUGHT AN EXTRA PAIR OF JET BOOTS!

NOW, IF I CAN JUST FIND HAPPY IN TIME!

FOR ONCE LUCK IS WITH ME!

QUICKLY...I'VE GOT TO SPEAK TO YOU!

IRON MAN! THEN...YOU DIDN'T RUN OUT ON US!

LISTEN! I'VE NO TIME TO REPEAT THIS! COUNTESS DE LA SPIROSA HAS A TRANSISTOR DEVICE WHICH SHE TOOK FROM STARK'S ROOM! YOU MUST GET IT FOR ME... EVERYTHING DEPENDS ON IT!

OKAY! OKAY! LEGGO MY SHOULDERS!

THOSE IRON MITTS OF YOURS AINT EXACTLY FEATHERS! I'LL GO AFTER HER RIGHT NOW!

BRIEF MINUTES LATER...

THIS IS YOUR LAST CHANCE, CHUM! YOU MUSTA SEEN WHICH DIRECTION SHE DROVE OFF IN! NOW TALK!

VERY WELL! I..I WILL TELL YOU!

SHE DIDN'T HAVE TOO MUCH OF A START! I CAN CATCH ANYBODY IN THIS FOUR-WHEELED TORPEDO OF STARK'S!

I'M GETTIN' WHY STARK IS NEVER AROUND WHEN IRON MAN'S ON THE SCENE! IT'S NUTTY...BUT IT MUST BE THE ANSWER!

THERE'S HER CAR AHEAD OF ME! IT WON'T TAKE LONG NOW!

SCREEETCH!

OKAY, BABY! END OF THE LINE!

I HAD TAKEN THAT SILLY THING TO MAKE TONY STARK FOLLOW ME... NOT SOME UNCOUTH UNDERLING!

SURE, LADY... SURE! IF I KNEW YOU FELT THAT WAY, I'DA TAKEN SOME COUTH LESSONS BEFORE I CAME AFTER YA!

WHERE'S IRON MAN? DID THE SECOND ROUND BEGIN YET?

IT JUST STARTED! WHAT ARE YOU DOING WITH THE COUNTESS, HAPPY?

I CAN'T STOP TO EXPLAIN NOW, DOLL! I'VE GOTTA GIVE SOMETHIN' TO IRON MAN RIGHT AWAY!

BUT, THAT'S IMPOSSIBLE! YOU CAN'T ENTER THE BATTLE AREA!

I SURE CAN'T WAIT'LL THE END OF THE ROUND, EITHER!

HAPPY! COME BACK! YOU'LL BE KILLED! HAPPY...PLEASE... DON'T DO IT... DON'T!!

I'VE GOT TO, HONEY! I'M NOT THE ONLY JOE RISKIN' HIS LIFE OUT HERE!

THAT TONE IN HER VOICE... I NEVER HEARD IT BEFORE!! IT'S LIKE SHE REALLY CARES!

NO MATTER WHAT HAPPENS TO ME NOW... THAT MAKES IT ALL WORTH IT!

10.

WHILE, ON THE FIELD OF BATTLE, *TITANIUM MAN* AGAIN TRIES TO DEFEAT THE GOLDEN AVENGER BY CONSTANT *ATTACK*, HOPING TO EXHAUST HIS SMALLER, LIGHTER OPPONENT!

THIS *MOLECULE SCRAMBLER RAY* WILL DISINTEGRATE YOUR ARMOR WITH *ONE* BLOW! YOU CAN'T KEEP DODGING IT FOREVER!

HE'S RIGHT! ALTHOUGH I'M FULLY CHARGED AGAIN, THE PAIN IN MY CHEST IS ALMOST UNBEARABLE!

IF ONLY *HAPPY* HADN'T FAILED ME!

MY PROTON GUN HAS ONLY A, SINGLE BLAST! IF *THIS* DOESN'T STOP HIM...!

IT'S NO GOOD! I DAMAGED HIS ARMOR, BUT NOT ENOUGH TO STOP HIS DEADLY ATTACK!

B.WATT!

BUT, SUDDENLY AN URGENT CRY RINGS OUT...!

IRON MAN! I GOT IT! I GOT THAT GIZMO YOU WANTED!

HAPPY! GO BACK! IT'S TOO LATE! YOU'RE *UNARMED!!* YOU CAN'T LAST A *MINUTE* OUT HER

THAT DOESN'T MATTER IF YOU NEED THIS AS MUCH AS YOU SAID YOU DID!

THIS IS MY CHANCE...NOW, WHILE HE'S TURNED AWAY FROM ME! I'LL UNLEASH ALL MY MOLECULE SCRAMBLER RAYS AT *ONCE!*

HE MUST HAVE EYES IN BACK OF HIS HEAD... HE *STILL* DODGED IN TIME!!

≥UNNNH.!.!

DUCK, HAPPY... GET DOWN... *DOWN..!!*

TOO LATE..! IT--IT RICOCHETED INTO ME..! BUT QUICK...TAKE THIS...HERE..!

HAPPY!

C'MON... DON'T WORRY ABOUT *ME*... TAKE IT!

PERHAPS....IF I COULD GET YOU TO A *DOCTOR* IN TIME....

ARE YOU SOME KINDA *NUT* OR SOMETHIN'? I'VE *HAD* IT! BUT...I DON'T MIND...IT WAS *WORTH* IT!

WORT IT!

SURE! I KNOW AT LAST.. IT'S *ME..* WHO PEPPER LOVES!

HAPPY...HANG ON! I'LL FIND SOME WAY TO...!

FORGET IT, BOSS! JUST GIVE THAT COMMIE CREEP ONE FOR...OL' HAP...!

AND, FROM AMONG THE COUNTLESS VIEWERS, GLUED TO THEIR T.V. SCREEN, ONE ANGUISHED SCREAM CUTS THROUGH THE SILENCE LIKE A KNIFE...!

HAPPY!

SHE *FAINTED!* STAND BACK THERE! GIVE HER AIR! GIVE HER ROOM!

THE *TITANIUM MAN* COULDN'T STRIKE WHILE IRON MAN'S BACK WAS TURNED, BUT NOW...THEY'RE STARTING TO *FACE* EACH OTHER! LET'S GET BACK TO THOSE SCREENS!

I'M *GLAD* FOR THE BRIEF RESPITE! IT GIVES ME TIME TO ASSEMBLE ONE OF MY MOST POTENT WEAPONS! IRON MAN SHALL SOON *JOIN* HIS WITLESS FRIEND!

HE..HE CALLED ME *BOSS!* HE *KNEW!* AND STILL HE HELPED ME...EVEN THOUGH I'VE ALWAYS STOOD BETWEEN HIM AND PEPPER...!

BUT NOW...I'VE GOT TO MAKE SURE HE DIDN'T SACRIFICE HIS LIFE IN *VAIN*...!

WHILE A BREATH STILL REMAINS WITHIN ME, I'LL FIGHT...I'LL MAKE THIS MOMENT MEANINGFUL, OLD FRIEND... I SWEAR IT!

SLOWLY, THE VENGEFUL GOLDEN GLADIATOR APPROACHES HIS GLOATING, GARGANTUAN FOE...AS A STORM OF RAGE WELLS WITHIN HIS BREAST! FORGOTTEN IS THE PAIN WHICH RACKS HIS TORTURED BODY... FORGOTTEN IS THE DANGER...THE MENACE! ALL THAT MATTERS IS THE BATTLE THAT AWAITS HIM...THE BATTLE THAT MUST BE WON!

WHEREVER YOU ARE, HAPPY...I PRAY THAT YOU KNOW...THIS IS FOR *YOU!*

NEXT ISSUE: "WHAT PRICE VICTORY?"

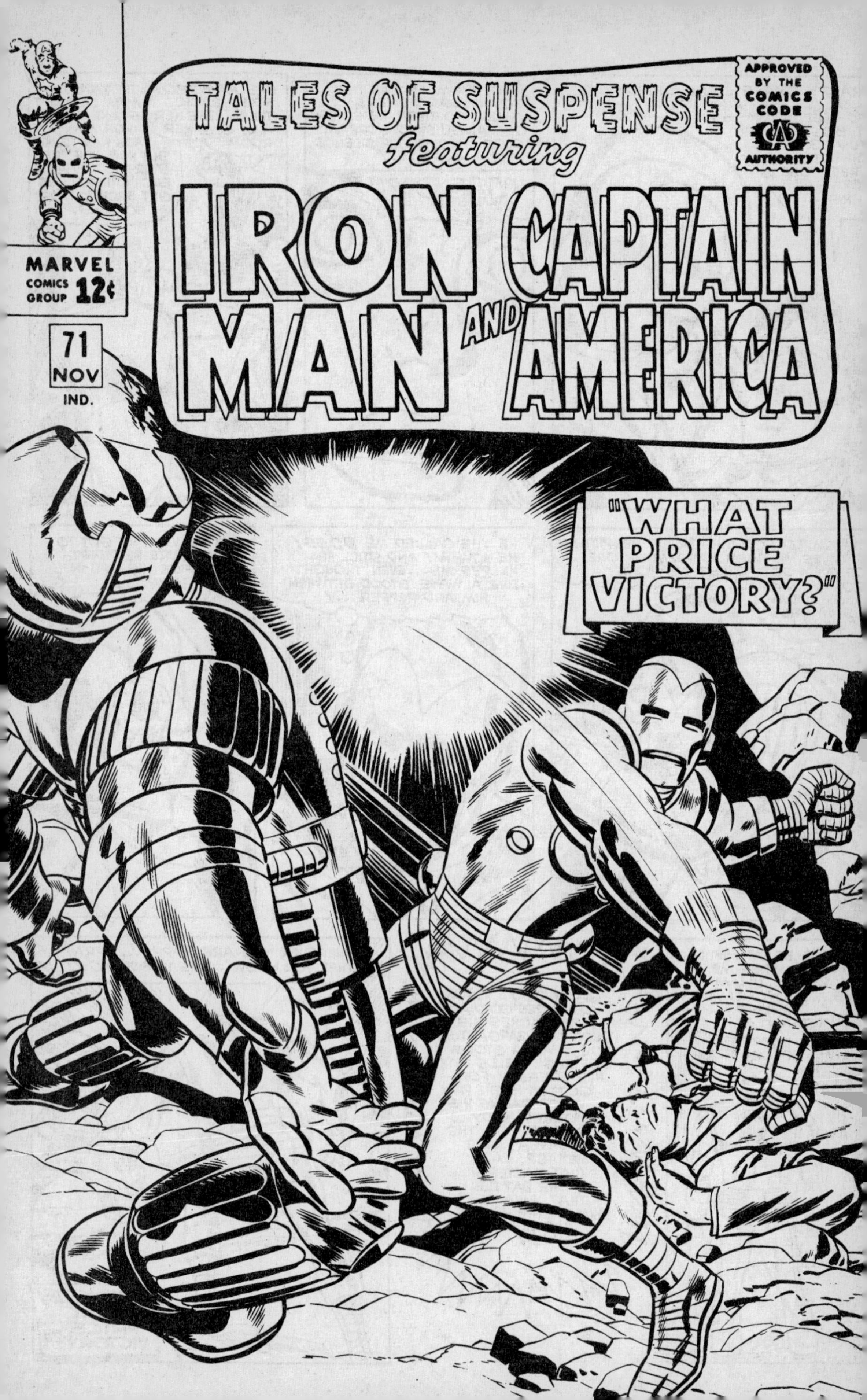
TALES OF SUSPENSE
featuring
IRON MAN AND CAPTAIN AMERICA
APPROVED BY THE COMICS CODE AUTHORITY
MARVEL COMICS GROUP 12¢
71
NOV
IND.
"WHAT PRICE VICTORY?"

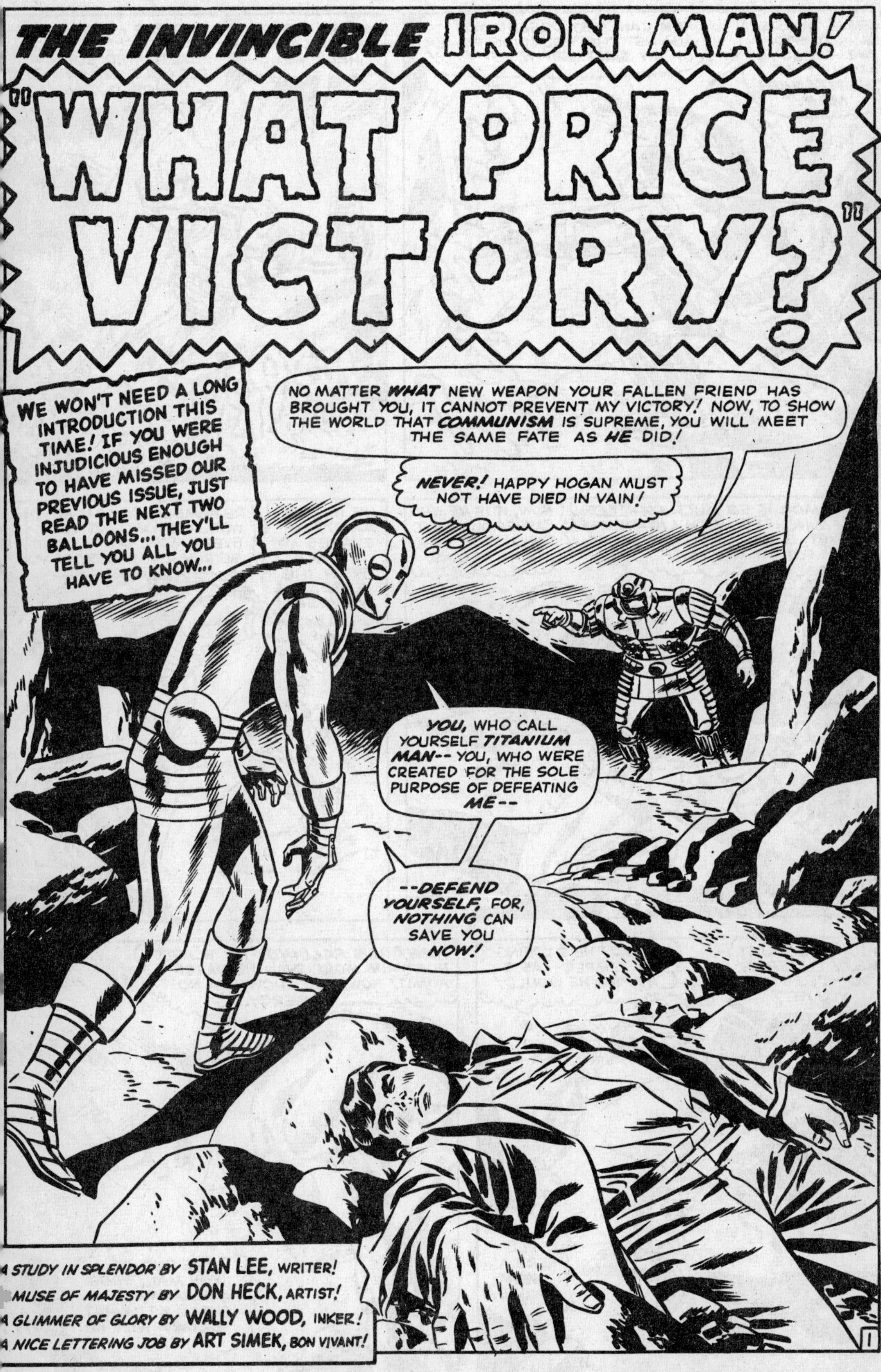
THE INVINCIBLE IRON MAN!
"WHAT PRICE VICTORY?"
WE WON'T NEED A LONG INTRODUCTION THIS TIME! IF YOU WERE INJUDICIOUS ENOUGH TO HAVE MISSED OUR PREVIOUS ISSUE, JUST READ THE NEXT TWO BALLOONS... THEY'LL TELL YOU ALL YOU HAVE TO KNOW...
NO MATTER WHAT NEW WEAPON YOUR FALLEN FRIEND HAS BROUGHT YOU, IT CANNOT PREVENT MY VICTORY! NOW, TO SHOW THE WORLD THAT COMMUNISM IS SUPREME, YOU WILL MEET THE SAME FATE AS HE DID!
NEVER! HAPPY HOGAN MUST NOT HAVE DIED IN VAIN!
YOU, WHO CALL YOURSELF TITANIUM MAN-- YOU, WHO WERE CREATED FOR THE SOLE PURPOSE OF DEFEATING ME--
--DEFEND YOURSELF, FOR, NOTHING CAN SAVE YOU NOW!
A STUDY IN SPLENDOR BY STAN LEE, WRITER!
A MUSE OF MAJESTY BY DON HECK, ARTIST!
A GLIMMER OF GLORY BY WALLY WOOD, INKER!
A NICE LETTERING JOB BY ART SIMEK, BON VIVANT!
1

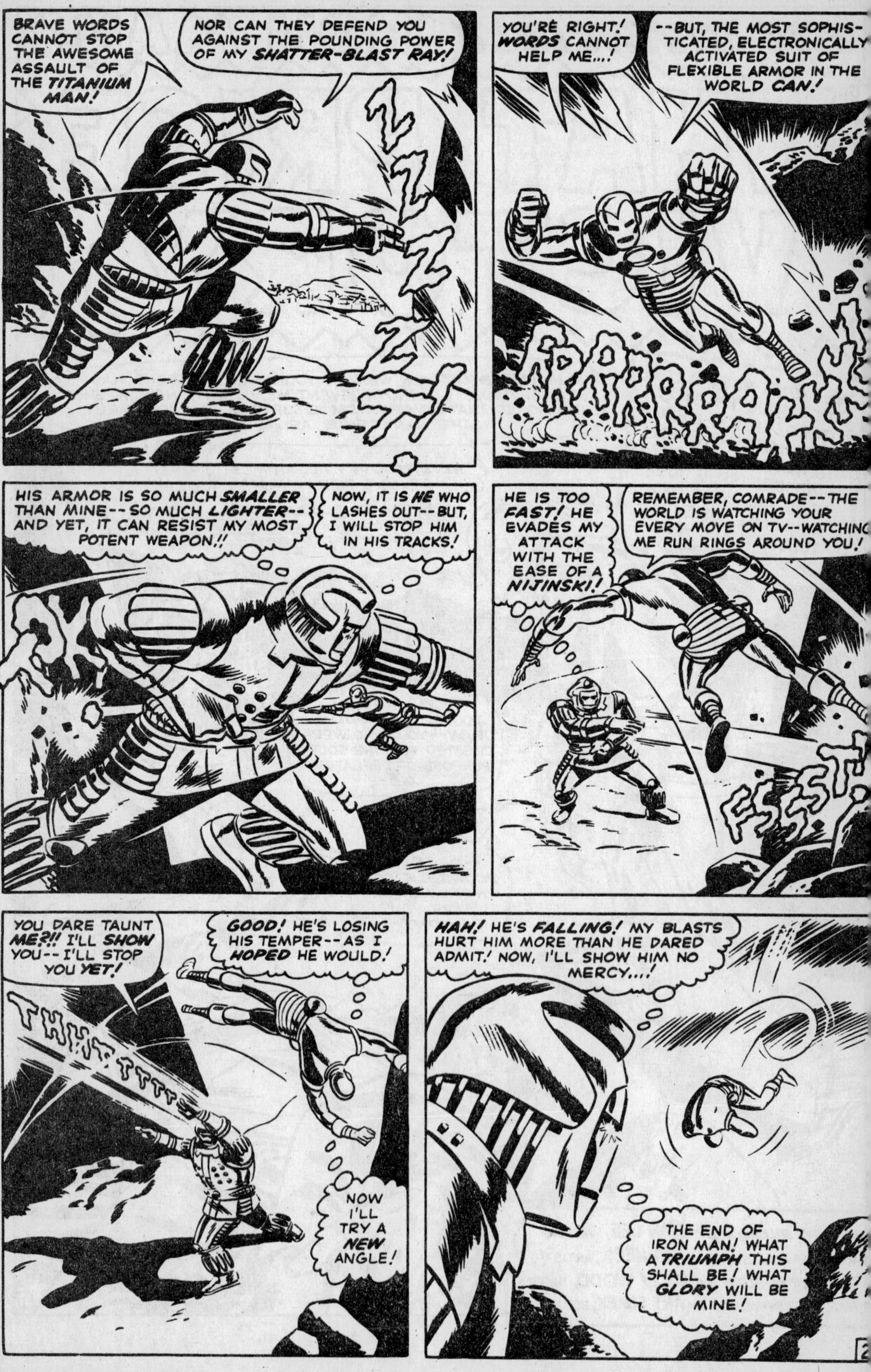
BRAVE WORDS CANNOT STOP THE AWESOME ASSAULT OF THE TITANIUM MAN!
NOR CAN THEY DEFEND YOU AGAINST THE POUNDING POWER OF MY SHATTER-BLAST RAY!
YOU'RE RIGHT! WORDS CANNOT HELP ME...!
--BUT, THE MOST SOPHISTICATED, ELECTRONICALLY ACTIVATED SUIT OF FLEXIBLE ARMOR IN THE WORLD CAN!
HIS ARMOR IS SO MUCH SMALLER THAN MINE--SO MUCH LIGHTER--AND YET, IT CAN RESIST MY MOST POTENT WEAPON!!
NOW, IT IS HE WHO LASHES OUT--BUT, I WILL STOP HIM IN HIS TRACKS!
HE IS TOO FAST! HE EVADES MY ATTACK WITH THE EASE OF A NIJINSKI!
REMEMBER, COMRADE--THE WORLD IS WATCHING YOUR EVERY MOVE ON TV--WATCHING ME RUN RINGS AROUND YOU!
YOU DARE TAUNT ME?!! I'LL SHOW YOU--I'LL STOP YOU YET!
GOOD! HE'S LOSING HIS TEMPER--AS I HOPED HE WOULD!
NOW I'LL TRY A NEW ANGLE!
HAH! HE'S FALLING! MY BLASTS HURT HIM MORE THAN HE DARED ADMIT! NOW, I'LL SHOW HIM NO MERCY...!
THE END OF IRON MAN! WHAT A TRIUMPH THIS SHALL BE! WHAT GLORY WILL BE MINE!

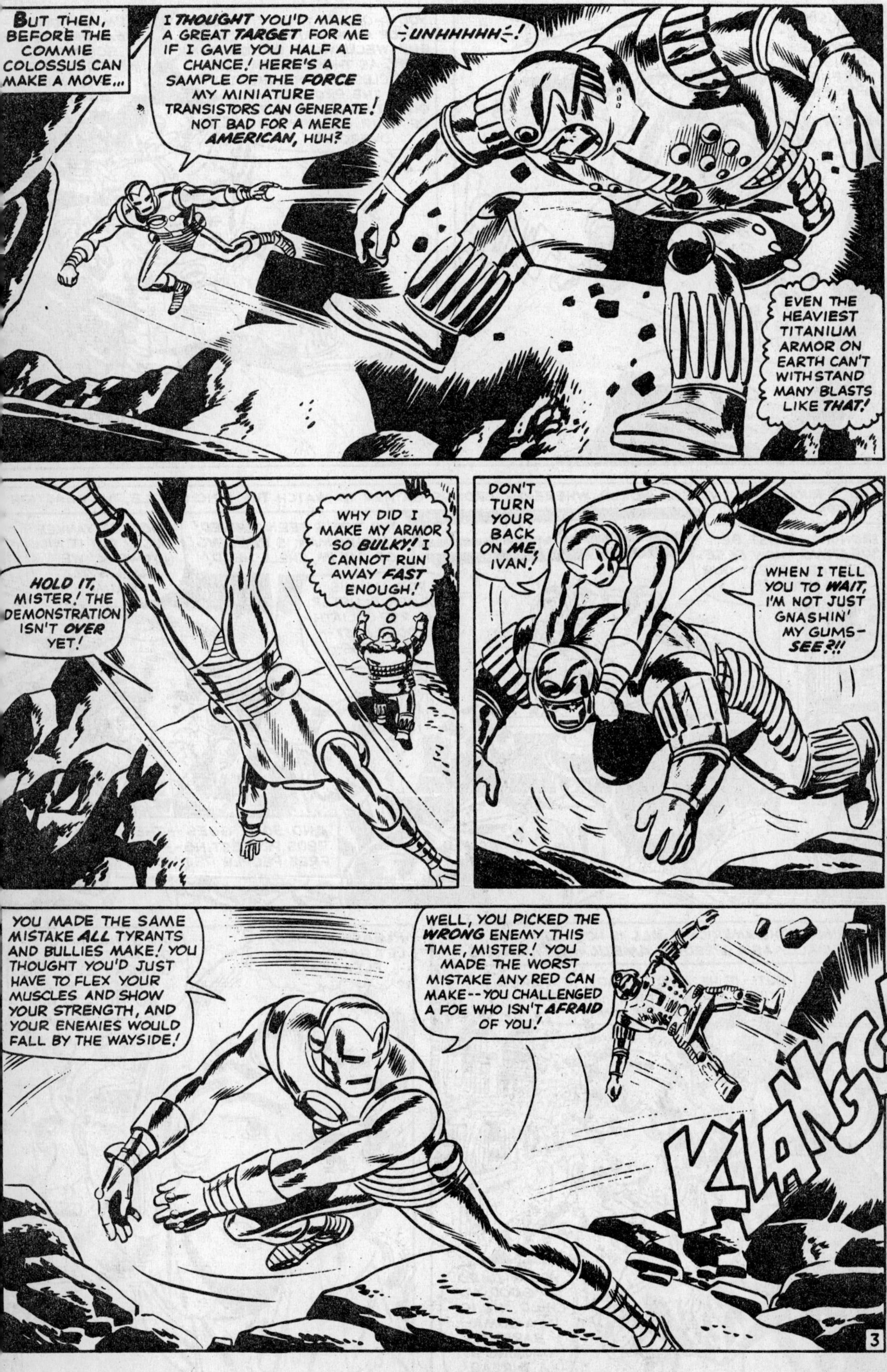

BUT THEN, BEFORE THE COMMIE COLOSSUS CAN MAKE A MOVE...
I THOUGHT YOU'D MAKE A GREAT TARGET FOR ME IF I GAVE YOU HALF A CHANCE! HERE'S A SAMPLE OF THE FORCE MY MINIATURE TRANSISTORS CAN GENERATE! NOT BAD FOR A MERE AMERICAN, HUH?
UNHHHHH--!
EVEN THE HEAVIEST TITANIUM ARMOR ON EARTH CAN'T WITHSTAND MANY BLASTS LIKE THAT!
HOLD IT, MISTER! THE DEMONSTRATION ISN'T OVER YET!
WHY DID I MAKE MY ARMOR SO BULKY! I CANNOT RUN AWAY FAST ENOUGH!
DON'T TURN YOUR BACK ON ME, IVAN!
WHEN I TELL YOU TO WAIT, I'M NOT JUST GNASHIN' MY GUMS- SEE?!!
YOU MADE THE SAME MISTAKE ALL TYRANTS AND BULLIES MAKE! YOU THOUGHT YOU'D JUST HAVE TO FLEX YOUR MUSCLES AND SHOW YOUR STRENGTH, AND YOUR ENEMIES WOULD FALL BY THE WAYSIDE!
WELL, YOU PICKED THE WRONG ENEMY THIS TIME, MISTER! YOU MADE THE WORST MISTAKE ANY RED CAN MAKE--YOU CHALLENGED A FOE WHO ISN'T AFRAID OF YOU!
KLANGG!

I'M USING UP MY LIFE-SAVING TRANSISTOR STRENGTH RECKLESSLY--BUT IT'S WORTH IT!

THP!

IF ONLY HAPPY COULD BE HERE TO SEE THIS!

YOU THOUGHT YOUR TITANIUM ARMOR MADE YOU INVULNERABLE, EH? WELL, WHAT DO YOU THINK NOW, AS THESE NEGATIVE PARTICLES OF IONIC ENERGY DRAIN THE PROTECTIVE QUALITIES RIGHT OUT OF YOUR CLUMSY TIN OVERCOAT!

I'M GETTING WEAKER! HE HAS SCIENTIFIC WEAPONS I NEVER DREAMED EXISTED!

AND THRUOUT THE CIVILIZED WORLD, WHEREVER CROWDS GATHER TO WATCH THE EPIC BATTLE, THE REACTION KEEPS SWELLING...

IRON-MAN MUST BE CHEATING! HOW ELSE COULD HE DEFEAT OUR CHAMPION?!!

THE TIDE'S BEEN TURNED! TITANIUM MAN IS REELING! GO GIT IM, SHELL HEAD!

ANOTHER YANKEE TRICK! BUT IT WILL NOT WORK! WE SHALL STILL TRIUMPH!

FOR ALL HIS FORMER BLUSTER, THE RED GOLIATH LOOKS LOST-- HELPLESS--!

AND SO IT GOES -- THE REDS PROTESTING-- THE FREE PEOPLE REJOICING!

BUT, AMONG THE AMERICANS, ALL IS NOT REJOICING! ESPECIALLY AS A SPEEDING AMBULANCE DEPARTS...

BUT--IF HE ISN'T DEAD--IF THERE'S STILL A SPARK OF LIFE--WHY CAN'T I GO WITH HIM?

YOU WILL DO NO GOOD, MY CHILD! HE IS IN A COMA--BARELY HANGING BY A THREAD!

PLEASE--LORD! LET HAPPY LIVE-- PLEASE--!

AND STILL NO SIGN OF THAT PLAYBOY, STARK! EVEN HIS FRIEND MEANS NOTHING TO HIM!

YOU MAY HAVE THE USE OF *MY CAR* TO TAKE YOU TO THE HOSPITAL, MISS POTTS.!

THANK YOU, *SENATOR BYRD!* IT'S VERY KIND OF YOU!

MEANWHILE, *I'LL* WAIT HERE, IN CASE *TONY STARK* RETURNS! I'VE A FEW THINGS TO SAY TO *HIM!*

BUT, HIS VERY SOUL ANGRILY RAGING BENEATH HIS MIGHTY *IRON MAN* ARMOR, TONY STARK IS IN NO MOOD FOR *ANYTHING*, SAVE THE BUSINESS AT HAND...

YOU CAN'T ESCAPE ME BY TRYING TO HIDE AMONG THOSE BOULDERS! I'LL FIND YOU *ANYWHERE!*

THIS IS THE *PAY-OFF*, COMRADE! THERE'S NO WAY YOU CAN ESCAPE IT! MY ONLY REGRET IS THAT IT DIDN'T HAPPEN *SOONER*--

IN TIME TO SAVE POOR *HAPPY!*

...AH! ONCE *AGAIN* YOUR DECADENT CAPITALISTIC *INNOCENCE* HAS BETRAYED YOU!

THE BOULDER WAS CONCEALING A MODIFIED *ROCKET LAUNCHER*-- AIMED AT *ME!*

THEN, A FATAL MICRO-SECOND LATER...

FOOOM

HE HAD IT WAITING IN RESERVE-- IN CASE THE BATTLE WAS LOST!

IT'S ZEROED-IN ON ME! I CAN'T EVADE IT! HAVE TO MOVE *FAST*--!

DESPERATELY, THE GOLDEN AVENGER ACTIVATES THE DEVICE WHICH HAPPY HOGAN HAD RISKED ALL TO DELIVER...

I HAD INTENDED TO USE MY *REVERSER* AGAINST *TITANIUM MAN* HIMSELF, BUT *YOU'LL* DO FOR A STARTER!

5

IT *WORKED!* IT TOOK ALL THE *PAZAZZZ* OUT OF THAT METAL MOSQUITO!

HEAR *THAT,* COMRADE?

THAT'S JUST TO KEEP YOU *AWAKE* UNTIL I GET BACK TO YOU!

AH, *THERE* YOU ARE, YOU ELUSIVE PIMPERNEL!

I'VE TRIED *EVERYTHING!* I HAVE NO MORE *TRAPS* LEFT-- NO MORE WEAPONS--!

AT THIS VERY MOMENT, IF WE COULD PEER BENEATH HIS MASSIVE TITANIUM MASK, WE WOULD SEE-- THE FACE OF *FEAR!*

I'VE NO PLACE LEFT TO RUN--!

WHEN HE *CATCHES* ME --WITH THOSE TRANSISTORIZED *POWERS* OF HIS --WHAT WILL HE *DO??*

IN CASE YOU'VE BEEN *WONDERING,* BIG MAN, THIS IS CALLED A *REVERSER RAY!* IT REVERSES THE ENERGY OUTPUT OF ANYTHING MECHANICAL--LIKE THAT TITANIUM KIMONO OF YOURS!

AND, AFTER THAT, THE POWER APPARATUS GOES COMPLETELY OUT OF CONTROL -- JUST AS YOUR *ARMOR* IS NOW IMMOBILE AND *USELESS* TO YOU!

NO *WONDER* THE OTHER AMERICAN SACRIFICED HIMSELF TO DELIVER SUCH A WEAPON! I AM COMPLETELY *POWERLESS!*

6

OKAY, HOLD ON, IVAN-- WE'RE GOING TO GIVE A LITTLE DEMONSTRATION NOW--

IT'S FOR THE BENEFIT OF OUR TV AUDIENCE-- SO THEY WON'T GET BORED!

WHRRRRRRP

SMILE FOR THE CAMERAS! IT MAY WIN YOU A TRY-OUT ON ED SULLIVAN'S HOUR!

AWWW, I GUESS YOU WERE RIGHT ABOUT US AMERICANS BEING CARELESS! LOOK HOW I LET YOU SLIP THRU MY FINGERS!

KRAK

=WUPFF=

NOW, NOW! WE DON'T WANT YOU TO GET A TUMMY-ACHE, DO WE? HERE, LET ME BURP YOU!

HOLD STILL, COMRADE! DON'T MAKE ME LET GO OF YOU AGAIN!

WOOM!

MAYBE A LITTLE ALTITUDE WILL CLEAR YOUR HEAD!

ALTHOUGH, IT WOULD BE REAL EMBARRASSING IF I DROPPED YOU, WOULDN'T IT?

SAY! I'VE A PEACHY IDEA! WHY DON'T YOU SAY THAT YOU SURRENDER-- AND THEN I'LL CARRY YOU DOWN TO EARTH AGAIN!

YOU'VE MADE MY SUIT INOPERATIVE! A FALL WOULD FINISH ME! I'LL SAY ANYTHING! I SURRENDER-- I SURRENDER!

7

SOMEHOW I *THOUGHT* YOU'D SAY THAT! AND YOU'LL BE HAPPY TO KNOW THAT YOUR BRAVE WORDS WERE REBROADCAST ALL OVER EARTH VIA MY BUILT-IN RADIO CIRCUITRY!

NOW, JUST MAKE YOUR-SELF COMFORTABLE FOR A MINUTE OR TWO...

WHA--WHAT WILL YOU DO *NOW*?

DON'T WORRY! LUCKY FOR *YOU*, I'M NOT A *RED*! I CAN'T CONTINUE TO ATTACK A HELPLESS ENEMY!

SO, I'LL *LEAVE* YOU HERE TILL YOUR FELLOW BULLY-BOYS COME FOR YOU! MEANTIME, I'LL JUST TAKE A LITTLE SOUVENIR BACK WITH ME!

NO! YOU'VE *DISGRACED* ME! YOU'VE MADE ME *LOSE FACE!* DO YOU KNOW WHAT THEY'LL *DO* TO ME?

WHO? THE LEADERS OF THE PEOPLES' REPUBLIC? THE FRIENDS OF THE MASSES? YOU CAN'T BE AFRAID OF *THEM*?!!

THIS WAS FOR *YOU*, HAPPY! IT WAS THE *LEAST* I COULD DO!

FINALLY...

CONGRATULATIONS, IRON MAN! THE ENTIRE FREE WORLD IS PROUD OF YOU!

THANK YOU, SENATOR! BUT NOW, IF YOU DON'T MIND, I'D LIKE TO KNOW WHERE --THEY'VE TAKEN HAPPY HOGAN'S BODY?

OH, YOU HAVEN'T *HEARD*? HE WAS STILL *ALIVE*--ALTHOUGH HE WAS SINKING FAST! THEY TOOK HIM TO THE INTERPOL HOSPITAL!

HAPPY?? STILL *ALIVE*?!!

THEN, I'VE GOT TO *GO* TO HIM! I'VE GOT TO *BE* THERE IN CASE I'M *NEEDED*,...!

WAIT! WHAT ABOUT THE *PARADE* IN YOUR HONOR?

I'VE NO TIME! *YOU* HANDLE IT, SENATOR! HAPPY WAS-- MY *FRIEND*!

WHY COULDN'T A REAL *MAN* LIKE HIM BE HEAD OF STARK INDUSTRIES, INSTEAD OF THAT HEARTLESS, MOUSTACHED PLAYBOY, *TONY STARK*!??

8

WHILE, AT THE HOSPITAL... THE COUNTESS DE LA SPIROSA HAS BEEN HERE ALL THE TIME --WAITING TO SEE TONY STARK WHEN HE ARRIVES!

LADIES, THERE IS NOTHING MORE WE CAN DO FOR MR. HOGAN! I HAVE JUST SENT FOR A *SPECIALIST* FROM VIENNA!

BUT, WHERE *IS* HE?? HIS BEST FRIEND IS ON THE CRITICAL LIST, AND HE DOESN'T EVEN CARE ENOUGH TO SHOW UP!

HE HAS NOT RESPONDED TO ANY TREATMENT! I HOPE HE CAN LAST UNTIL THE SPECIALIST ARRIVES!

THEN--ALL WE CAN DO IS-- *PRAY!*

IF ONLY *YOU* HADN'T TAKEN THAT DEVICE FROM MISTER STARK'S ROOM--THEN *IRON MAN* WOULDN'T HAVE HAD TO SEND HAPPY FOR IT--!*

DON'T TRY TO PUT THE BLAME ON *ME*, YOUNG LADY! THE ONE WHO'S *REALLY* RESPONSIBLE IS THAT TWO-TIMING, HEARTLESS, SELFISH PLAYBOY--YOUR BOSS--*TONY STARK!*

*REMEMBER THE INCIDENT IN LAST MONTH'S *SUSPENSE?*--STAN.

I NEVER THOUGHT I'D LET ANYONE TALK ABOUT MISTER STARK THAT WAY-- BUT THE COUNTESS IS *RIGHT!* SHE *MUST* BE RIGHT!

ANY MAN WHO WOULDN'T COME TO SEE A DYING FRIEND--IS JUST *NO GOOD!*

BUT, PERHAPS A FEW OPINIONS WOULD BE *CHANGED,* IF CERTAIN PARTIES COULD SEE "HEARTLESS, SELFISH" TONY STARK *NOW...*

EVEN THOUGH I *WON,* THE FIGHT ALMOST FINISHED ME! IF I HAD REACHED MY RECHARGER A FEW SECONDS LATER, IT WOULD HAVE BEEN THE *END!*

9

BUT, THE END FOR ME WOULD HAVE COME MUCH *SOONER* IF NOT FOR *HAPPY*-- BRAVE, LOYAL, WONDERFUL HAPPY!

I'VE GOT TO *GO* TO HIM....!

I CAN'T WAIT ANY LONGER! EVERY SECOND MAY COUNT....!

MEANWHILE, THE CRAFTY REDS DESPERATELY ATTEMPT TO MAKE POLITICAL CAPITAL OUT OF THE DEFEAT OF TITANIUM MAN...

WE CLAIM THAT YOU AMERICANS VIOLATED THE RULES OF THE BATTLE IN ORDER TO WIN YOUR ILL-GOTTEN VICTORY!

DON'T TELL *ME*, GENERAL! I'M NOT *BUYING*!

WE REJECT YOUR PROTEST, AMBASSADOR! THE CONTEST IS *OVER*, AND IRON MAN HAS *WON*! NOTHING CAN CHANGE THAT!

BUT, THAT OTHER AMERICAN ENTERED THE FIELD OF BATTLE, BRINGING YOUR CHAMPION A *WEAPON*! EVERYONE *SAW* THAT!

AH SO! WE WILL NOT TAKE THIS LYING DOWN!

YOU *WON'T*, WON'T YOU?

HAVE YOU *FORGOTTEN* ABOUT ALL THE *ILLEGAL TRAPS* YOUR TITANIUM MAN SET FOR OUR BOY? REMEMBER-- MILLIONS OF PEOPLE *SAW* THEM ON THEIR OWN TV SCREENS!

I,--EH--WILL DISCUSS IT NO LONGER! YOU AMERICAN USE *ANY* MEANS TO GAIN YOUR OWN ENDS!

BLAMED *RIGHT* WE DO! AND *ONE* OF THOSE MEANS WHICH YOU OBJECT TO IS A LITTLE THING CALLED THE *TRUTH*!

OUR COMRADES IN PEKING WILL NEVER LET US HEAR THE *END* OF THIS!

NOR WILL OUR SUPERIORS IN THE *KREMLIN*!

PERHAPS WE SHOULD TAKE A LONG *JOURNEY*!

AND, AT THE INTERNATIONAL HOTEL...

I'LL USE MY *PORTABLE* CHARGING UNIT TO FINISH THE JOB WHILE I RUSH TO THE HOSPITAL!

IF--IF ONLY I'M NOT--TOO LATE!

10

THUS, MINUTES LATER...

PEPPER! WHERE IS HAPPY? HOW IS HE? IS HE-- IS HE STILL--?

YES, HE'S STILL ALIVE! BUT THE DOCTOR DOESN'T SEEM TO HOLD MUCH HOPE FOR HIM! NO ONE IS ALLOWED TO SEE HIM!

TONY! SO THERE YOU ARE!

IF-- IF ANYTHING HAPPENS TO HAPPY-- I JUST COULDN'T BEAR IT--!

IS THIS HER NATURAL CONCERN FOR A FRIEND? OR, IS IT SOMETHING MORE?

TONY STARK! I WAS SPEAKING TO YOU! OR IS THAT REDHEADED PEASANT MORE IMPORTANT?

SHUT UP, COUNTESS!! A MAN IS DYING IN THERE! PEPPER, DID YOU TELL THE DOCTOR TO SPARE NO EXPENSE...?

OF COURSE I DID! BUT IT WILL TAKE MORE THAN MONEY TO HELP HAPPY NOW!

YOU'LL REGRET SPEAKING TO THE COUNTESS DE LA SPIROSA THAT WAY!

SLAM!

AND, JUST A FEW DOORS AWAY...

HIS PULSE HAS GROWN WEAKER, DOCTOR!

HE CAN'T HOLD OUT MUCH LONGER WITHOUT SURGERY!

WHILE, IN THE WAITING ROOM, PEPPER ASKS TONY STARK A QUESTION WHICH HE CANNOT-- HE DARES NOT ANSWER!

WHERE WERE YOU DURING THE BATTLE, MR. STARK?

HOW CAN I TELL HER? WHAT CAN I SAY?

I, ¿EH? HAD SOME BUSINESS TO ATTEND TO! AS A MATTER OF FACT, IT WAS A MOST IMPORTANT DEAL....!

WHILE IRON MAN WAS FIGHTING FOR HIS LIFE, AND HAPPY WAS SACRIFICING HIS??

SHE'S NEVER USED THAT TONE TO ME BEFORE! A TONE OF-- SHEER LOATHING!

11

HOW COULD I HAVE *EVER* THOUGHT I LOVED SUCH A MAN? I MUST HAVE BEEN *BLIND!*

BUT THEN, BEFORE ANOTHER WORD CAN BE SAID...

I'M DOCTOR SCHILLER! WHERE IS THE PATIENT?

HE IS UPSTAIRS -- IN SURGERY, DOCTOR! THANK HEAVEN YOU ARE HERE IN TIME!

PLEASE HURRY, SIR! HE IS SINKING FAST!

THE OPERATION STARTS IMMEDIATELY, AND CONTINUES THRUOUT THE NIGHT...

SCALPEL....!

UNTIL, AT DAWN...

DOCTOR! HOW *IS* HE? DID HE -- *MAKE* IT?

THEY LOOK SO *GRIM!*

HE IS STILL ALIVE -- BUT DANGEROUSLY WEAK! I CAN DO NO MORE! ONLY HIS WILL TO LIVE IS KEEPING HIM GOING!

GO HOME! WE WILL NOTIFY YOU OF -- ANY CHANGE!

I'LL LEAVE *NOW!* I--I COULDN'T EVEN BEAR THE THOUGHT OF WALKING THRU THE STREET WITH -- *HIM!*

SHE BLAMES *ME* FOR ALL THIS -- I *KNOW* IT!

IT'S WHAT I THOUGHT I ALWAYS *WANTED!* SHE HATES *ME!*

YET, *IS* IT WHAT I WANT? THE GIRL I LOVE -- DESPISING ME!

BUT, I'VE NO RIGHT TO THINK OF *MY* PROBLEMS WHILE *HAPPY* LIES DYING!

MY HEART MUST REMAIN AS COLD AS THE ARMOR I WEAR -- FOREVER!

The END

STARTLING NEW DEVELOPMENTS WILL OCCUR NEXT ISSUE! LET'S SHARE THEM TOGETHER WITH *IRON MAN*, JUST AS WE'VE ALWAYS DONE! WE'LL BE LOOKING FOR YOU!

12

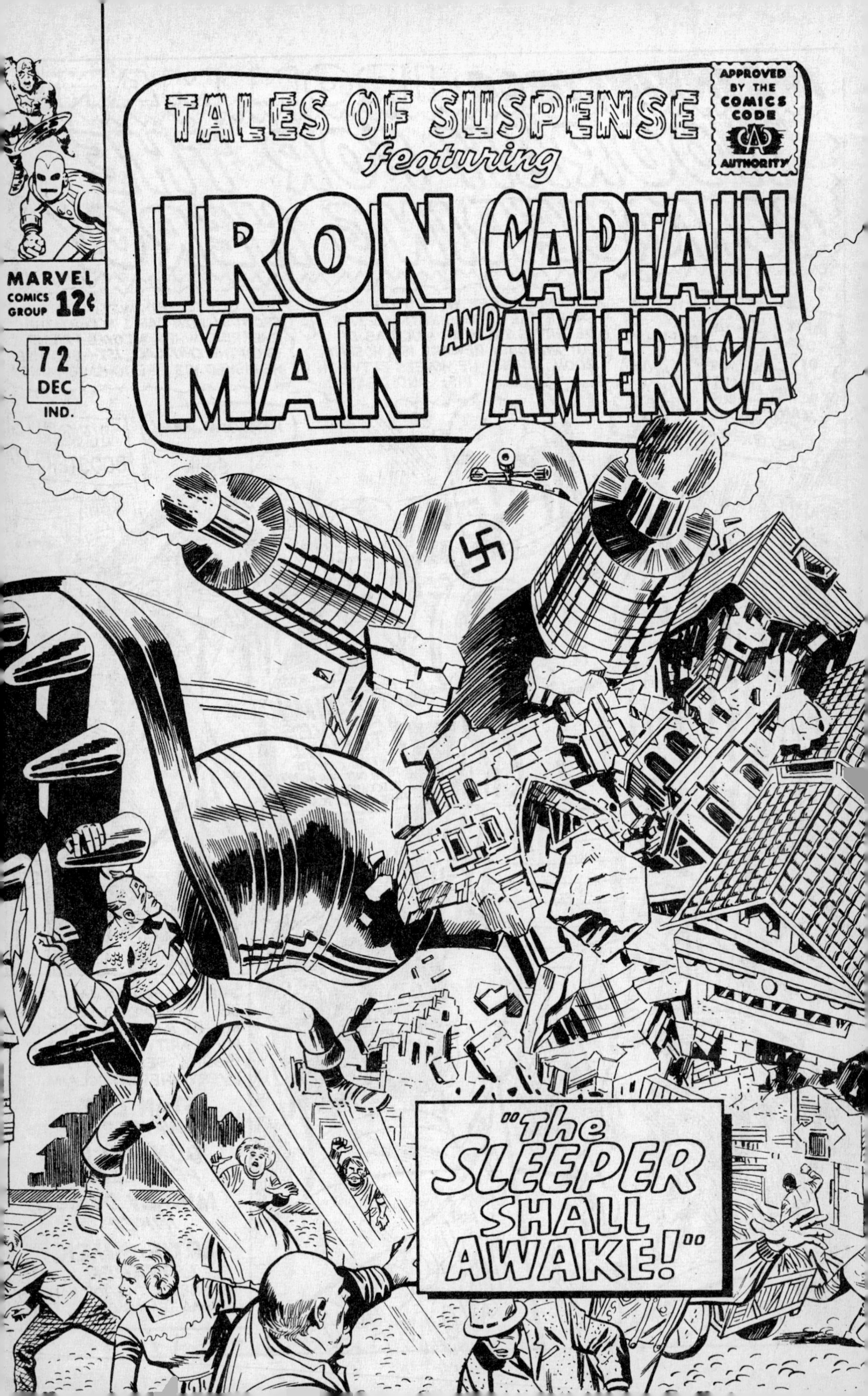
TALES OF SUSPENSE
featuring
IRON MAN AND CAPTAIN AMERICA
APPROVED BY THE COMICS CODE AUTHORITY
MARVEL COMICS GROUP 12¢
72
DEC
IND.
"The SLEEPER SHALL AWAKE!"

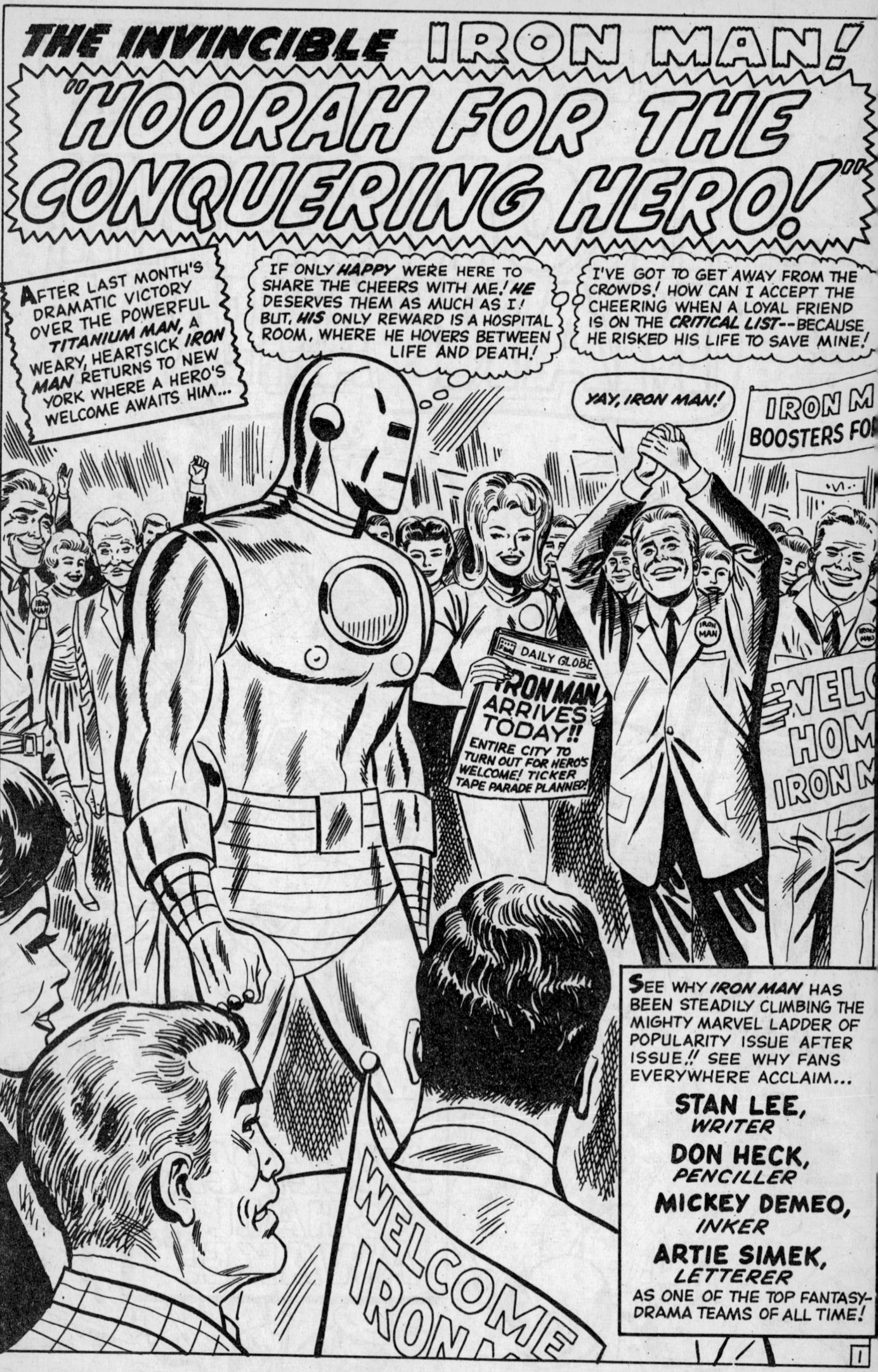
THE INVINCIBLE IRON MAN!
"HOORAH FOR THE CONQUERING HERO!"
AFTER LAST MONTH'S DRAMATIC VICTORY OVER THE POWERFUL TITANIUM MAN, A WEARY, HEARTSICK IRON MAN RETURNS TO NEW YORK WHERE A HERO'S WELCOME AWAITS HIM...
IF ONLY HAPPY WERE HERE TO SHARE THE CHEERS WITH ME! HE DESERVES THEM AS MUCH AS I! BUT, HIS ONLY REWARD IS A HOSPITAL ROOM, WHERE HE HOVERS BETWEEN LIFE AND DEATH!
I'VE GOT TO GET AWAY FROM THE CROWDS! HOW CAN I ACCEPT THE CHEERING WHEN A LOYAL FRIEND IS ON THE CRITICAL LIST--BECAUSE HE RISKED HIS LIFE TO SAVE MINE!
YAY, IRON MAN!
IRON M
BOOSTERS FO
DAILY GLOBE
IRON MAN ARRIVES TODAY!! ENTIRE CITY TO TURN OUT FOR HERO'S WELCOME! TICKER TAPE PARADE PLANNED!
WELC HOM IRON M
WELCOME IRON M
SEE WHY IRON MAN HAS BEEN STEADILY CLIMBING THE MIGHTY MARVEL LADDER OF POPULARITY ISSUE AFTER ISSUE!! SEE WHY FANS EVERYWHERE ACCLAIM...
STAN LEE, WRITER
DON HECK, PENCILLER
MICKEY DEMEO, INKER
ARTIE SIMEK, LETTERER
AS ONE OF THE TOP FANTASY-DRAMA TEAMS OF ALL TIME!
1

EXACTLY ONE HOUR LATER... I DON'T CARE *WHAT* THE MAYOR SAYS! I'M IN NO MOOD FOR A CELEBRATION, PEPPER!

I UNDERSTAND! I'LL MAKE YOUR EXCUSES FOR YOU!

--ALTHOUGH OUR COLD-HEARTED BOSS, *TONY STARK*, WILL PROBABLY OFFER TO GO IN YOUR PLACE!

HAPPY'S INJURY WON'T STOP *HIM* FROM HAVING A GOOD TIME!

CLICK!

YOU *LOVED* TONY STARK *ONCE*, PEPPER! BUT NOW, YOU'VE ONLY *CONTEMPT* FOR HIM!

IT'S WHAT I'VE ALWAYS *WANTED*! TONY STARK LOVES YOU TOO MUCH TO WANT YOU TO *RETURN THAT LOVE*!

FOR, A MAN WHO LIVES IN THE SHADOW OF *DEATH* CAN NEVER DARE TAKE A BRIDE!

AND YET, ONCE *AGAIN* FATE HAS FOUND A WAY TO FRUSTRATE AND DISAPPOINT ME...

EVEN THOUGH SHE HAS LOST HER LOVE FOR TONY STARK--

--THE LOVE HE VALUED MORE THAN ANYTHING ELSE IN THE WORLD--

SHE'S REPLACED IT WITH A NEW FONDNESS-- A NEW HERO WORSHIP FOR *IRON MAN*!

HOW *DESTINY* MUST BE LAUGHING IN THE SHADOWS OF LIMBO--

LAUGHING AT THE FACT THAT *STARK* AND *IRON MAN* ARE ONE AND THE *SAME*!

2

MEANWHILE, IN NEWSROOMS THRUOUT THE NATION, REPORTERS EVERYWHERE ASK THE SAME BURNING QUESTION IN THEIR COLUMNS...

"THE NATION ASKS-- NO, IT *DEMANDS* TO KNOW THE TRUE IDENTITY OF ONE OF ITS GREATEST HEROES! WE *MUST* LEARN-- WHO IS IRON MAN??!"

ANY LATE SCOOP ON THE IRON MAN IDENTITY STORY, BILL?

CLAKITTY CLAK CLAK

AND, IN A LUXURIOUS PARK AVENUE SUITE, THE GLAMOROUS *COUNTESS DE LA SPIROZA* STILL FUMES OVER BEING "STOOD UP" BY TONY STARK LAST MONTH...

AND SO, AN ENTIRE NATION ASKS THE QUESTION-- WHO IS IRON MAN???

I'LL SHOW TONY HE CAN'T TOSS *ME* ASIDE LIKE AN OLD SHOE AND GET AWAY WITH IT!

IF ONLY THERE WAS SOME WAY TO--WAIT! IRON MAN! THAT'S THE *ANSWER!*

IRON MAN *WORKS* FOR STARK! HE'D DO *ANYTHING* TO KEEP HIS IDENTITY A SECRET!

IF I COULD LEARN WHO HE REALLY *IS*, I'D HAVE TONY AT MY BECK AND CALL!

THAT VERY EVENING...

ALL IT TOOK WAS SOME DISCREET PHONE CALLS AND A FEW BRIBES-- AND I'VE LEARNED THE *ONE MAN* WHO CAN FIND OUT WHAT I WANT TO KNOW!

IT COST ME A *THOUSAND DOLLARS* TO GET THE ADDRESS OF HIS HIDEOUT...

BUT, IF HE CAN PROVIDE ME WITH THE SECRET OF IRON MAN'S REAL IDENTITY, IT WILL BE WORTH A *HUNDRED* TIMES AS MUCH TO ME!

THE DOOR IS UNLOCKED! *ENTER!* I'VE BEEN *EXPECTING* YOU!

EXPECTING ME? BUT-- *HOW?*

I TOLD *NO ONE* I WAS COMING HERE!

DO NOT BE ALARMED! MERELY WALK TO THE ROOM IN FRONT OF YOU!

TO A MAN WHO CAN LIVE IN A PLACE LIKE *THIS*-- MONEY ALONE MUST BE MEANINGLESS!

QUITE RIGHT, MY DEAR! MONEY *IS* ALMOST MEANINGLESS TO *ME!*

OH, *NO!* YOU-- YOU'RE ACTUALLY A *MIND READER!!*

NOT AT ALL! NOTHING QUITE SO *COMMON-PLACE!*

3

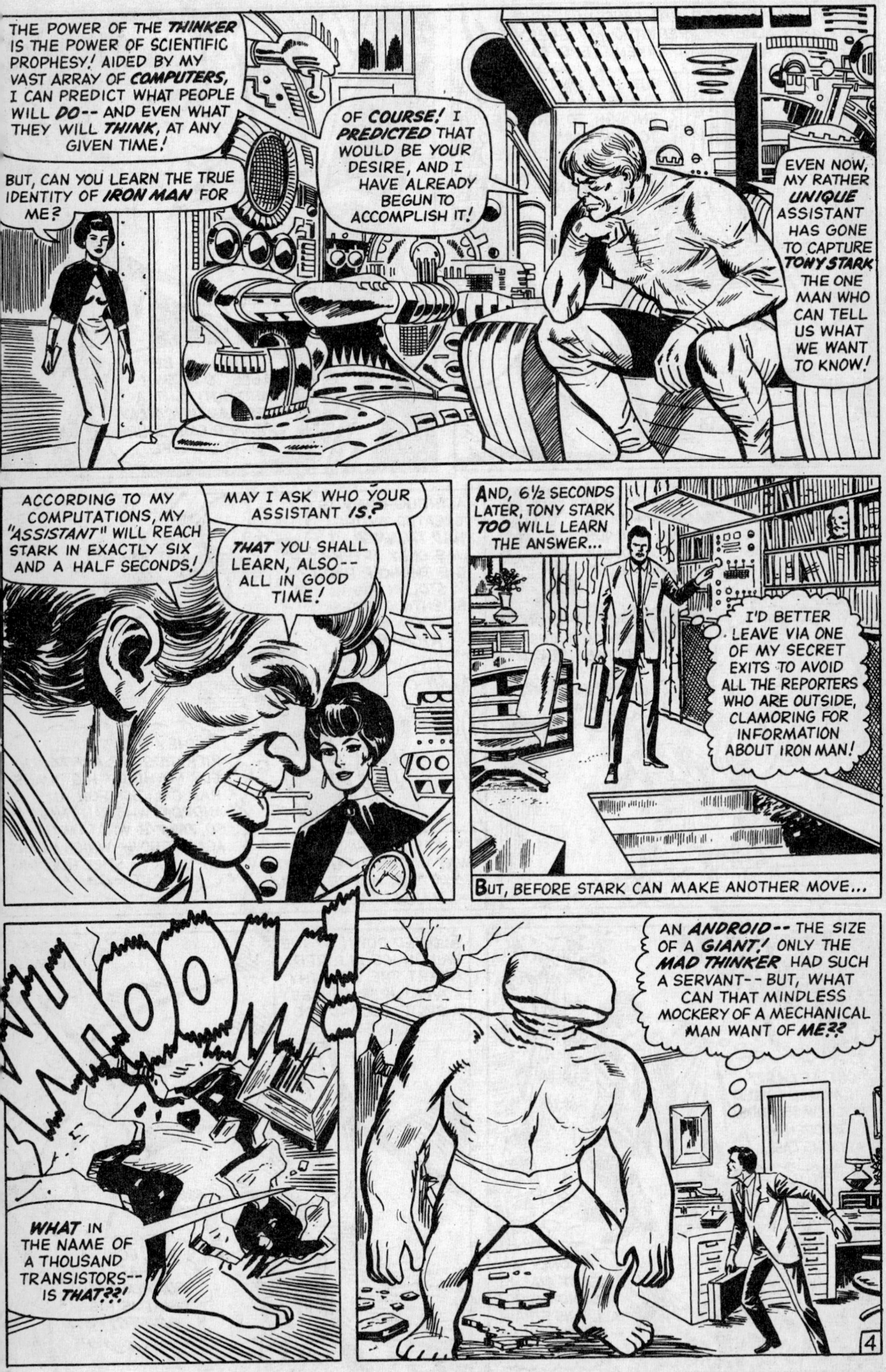
THE POWER OF THE THINKER IS THE POWER OF SCIENTIFIC PROPHESY! AIDED BY MY VAST ARRAY OF COMPUTERS, I CAN PREDICT WHAT PEOPLE WILL DO-- AND EVEN WHAT THEY WILL THINK, AT ANY GIVEN TIME!
BUT, CAN YOU LEARN THE TRUE IDENTITY OF IRON MAN FOR ME?
OF COURSE! I PREDICTED THAT WOULD BE YOUR DESIRE, AND I HAVE ALREADY BEGUN TO ACCOMPLISH IT!
EVEN NOW, MY RATHER UNIQUE ASSISTANT HAS GONE TO CAPTURE TONY STARK THE ONE MAN WHO CAN TELL US WHAT WE WANT TO KNOW!
ACCORDING TO MY COMPUTATIONS, MY "ASSISTANT" WILL REACH STARK IN EXACTLY SIX AND A HALF SECONDS!
MAY I ASK WHO YOUR ASSISTANT IS?
THAT YOU SHALL LEARN, ALSO-- ALL IN GOOD TIME!
AND, 6½ SECONDS LATER, TONY STARK TOO WILL LEARN THE ANSWER...
I'D BETTER LEAVE VIA ONE OF MY SECRET EXITS TO AVOID ALL THE REPORTERS WHO ARE OUTSIDE, CLAMORING FOR INFORMATION ABOUT IRON MAN!
BUT, BEFORE STARK CAN MAKE ANOTHER MOVE...
WHOOM!
WHAT IN THE NAME OF A THOUSAND TRANSISTORS-- IS THAT??!
AN ANDROID-- THE SIZE OF A GIANT! ONLY THE MAD THINKER HAD SUCH A SERVANT-- BUT, WHAT CAN THAT MINDLESS MOCKERY OF A MECHANICAL MAN WANT OF ME??
4

IF THE MAD THINKER *DID* SEND HIM, HE'S PROBABLY ALREADY PREDICTED MY EVERY DEFENSIVE ACTION, AND TAKEN STEPS TO *TRAP* ME!

BUT, IF I CAN JUST EVADE HIM LONG ENOUGH TO CHANGE TO *IRON MAN*, AT LEAST I'LL HAVE A FIGHTING CHANCE!

I SHOULD BE ABLE TO OUTWIT AND OUTFIGHT A MERE *ARTIFICIALLY-CREATED* CARICATURE OF REAL LIFE!

BUT, IT'S *INCREDIBLE!* THE THINKER MUST HAVE *PROGRAMMED* HIM TO EXPECT ME TO FLEE DOWN AN UNDERGROUND PASSAGE--HE'S FOLLOWING AS EASILY AS IF HE IS CAPABLE OF INDEPENDENT THOUGHT!

WAIT!! I JUST *REMEMBERED* SOMETHING! I'VE *UNDERESTIMATED* HIM!

ALTHOUGH HE WAS CREATED BY THE *MAD THINKER*, IT WAS ONLY AFTER THE THINKER HAD STOLEN HIS SCIENTIFIC NOTES FROM *REED RICHARDS!* *

*IF YOU CAN REMEMBER 'WAY BACK TO *FANTASTIC FOUR #15*, YOU'RE A *REAL* MARVELITE!--STAN.

THEY DON'T CALL RICHARDS *MR. FANTASTIC* FOR NOTHING! HIS PLANS HAD CALLED FOR AN ANDROID WHO CAN *THINK!* SO, *THAT'S* WHAT I'M UP AGAINST NOW--WHICH MEANS MY LUCK IS STILL HOLDING OUT--*BAD!*

OUT AT *LAST!* NOW, ALL I NEED IS A FEW SECONDS TO OPEN MY ATTACHE CASE...

IF ONLY MY *HEART* WASN'T POUNDING SO! ALL THIS STRAIN -- IT'S BEGINNING TO TELL--!

SLOWED DOWN BY THE PAIN IN HIS INJURED HEART, THE WEALTHY ADVENTURER PAUSES A SPLIT-SECOND TOO LONG...

MY *LEG!* HE *HAS* ME!

BUT, FOR WHAT *PURPOSE??* WHAT IS HIS *OBJECT??*

5

MEANWHILE, MISS *PEPPER POTTS*, WHO HAD FAINTED UPON SEEING THE AWESOME *ANDROID*, NOW RECOVERS CONSCIOUSNESS, STARING AT THE SHATTERED WALL WITH DAZED ASTONISHMENT...

THEN I *WASN'T* IMAGINING THINGS! I-I REALLY *SAW* IT! IT BROKE THRU THE *WALL!*

GUARDS! GUARDS! WHERE *ARE* YOU?? COME *QUICK!!!*

WHAT *HAPPENED,* MISS POTTS? WHY ALL THE SCREAM-- *HOLY SMOKE!*

LOOK AT THAT *WALL!* IT WOULD HAVE TAKEN A *BULLDOZER* TO SMASH IT LIKE THAT!

A BULLDOZER, OR--A GIGANTIC *ANDROID!!*

WE DON'T KNOW ANYTHIN' ABOUT ANY *ANDROIDS,* LADY--BUT THERE'S NOTHING HERE *NOW!* HE COULDN'T HAVE VANISHED INTO THIN AIR!

MR. STARK HAS MANY SECRET EXITS FROM THE PLANT, FOR SECURITY! ANY *ONE* OF THEM COULD HAVE BEEN USED!

IF ONLY *IRON MAN* WERE HERE! *HE'D* KNOW WHAT TO DO! WE'VE GOT TO *GET* HIM!

STARK MISSING! IRON MAN MISSING! YOU TALKIN' ABOUT SOME KINDA GIANT *ANDROID!* WHAT'S GOIN' *ON* HERE, ANYWAY???!

LATER, AT THE WASHINGTON OFFICE OF *SENATOR HARRINGTON BYRD...*

URGENT AND CONFIDENTIAL

ANTHONY STARK MISSING! C.I.A. ALERTED! WAS WORKING ON NEW WEAPONS! U.S. DEFENSE POSTURE IN JEOPARDY!

THIS JUST CAME IN VIA YOUR PRIVATE LINE, SENATOR!

SINCE YOU'RE ON THE NATIONAL DEFENSE BOARD, YOU WERE INFORMED IMMEDIATELY, SIR!

BAH! HE'S PROBABLY JUST IN *HIDING!* HE MUST HAVE LEARNED I PLAN TO SUMMON HIM TO WASHINGTON, TO *ORDER* THAT HE TELL US WHO IRON MAN REALLY *IS!*

AFTER ALL, IRON MAN IS TOO *POWERFUL* TO BE SERVING TONY STARK *ALONE!* HE MUST BE *UNMASKED,* SO OUR MILITARY ESTABLISHMENT CAN STUDY HIS ARMOR!

WELL, DON'T JUST *STAND* THERE, MAN! *FIND TONY STARK!!*

BUT, IN ORDER TO FIND TONY STARK, ONE WOULD HAVE TO SEARCH THE MOST UNLIKELY PLACE OF ALL-- THE MYSTERIOUS SANCTUM OF THE *MAD THINKER*....!

WHY HAVE YOU *BROUGHT* ME HERE? I *DEMAND* TO KNOW!

SURELY YOU REALIZE THAT YOU ARE IN NO POSITION TO DEMAND *ANYTHING,* TONY STARK!

I'M NOT JUST A *NOBODY!* THERE'LL BE A *NATIONWIDE MAN HUNT* FOR ME!

AND, ACCORDING TO MY *INFALLIBLE* COMPUTATIONS, I SHALL HAVE *FINISHED* WITH YOU LONG BEFORE YOU CAN BE *FOUND!*

NOW THEN, YOU CAN SAVE US *BOTH* A LOT OF TROUBLE BY REVEALING *IRON MAN'S* REAL IDENTITY TO ME!

NOT A *CHANCE!* TRY ONE OF YOUR "CALCULATIONS"!

I *WARN* YOU! IT IS *DEADLY DANGEROUS* TO DEFY THE *THINKER!*

YOU DON'T SCARE *ME!* OTHERS HAVE BEATEN YOU IN THE PAST!

TRUE-- BUT ONLY BECAUSE OF THE *FAILINGS* OF MY *ALLIES!* THIS TIME I HAVE *NO* ALLY-- ONLY MY BLINDLY OBEDIENT *ANDROID!*

I *TOLD* YOU I WOULD CAPTURE HIM WITH EASE, COUNTESS!

COUNTESS--?!!

FANCY MEETING *YOU* HERE, TONY!

YOU LITTLE *FOOL!* HOW DID YOU GET MIXED UP WITH A MENACE LIKE *HIM?!*

LET HER *GO,* THINKER! I'LL MAKE IT WORTH YOUR WHILE!

HOW *GALLANT* OF YOU, TONY! BUT, I AM NOT HIS *PRISONER!* I AM HIS *EMPLOYER!*

HOLD IT! PUT DOWN THAT *ATTACHE CASE!!!*

CERTAINLY, MR. STARK-- AFTER I'VE OPENED IT AND EXAMINED ITS CONTENTS!

NO! STOP! YOU *MUSTN'T!* WAIT--DON'T *TOUCH* THAT--!

SNAP!

EVEN *YOU* COULD HAVE PREDICTED THAT THE MORE YOU *PROTEST,* THE MORE ANXIOUS I SHALL BE TO LEARN WHAT IS INSIDE!

7

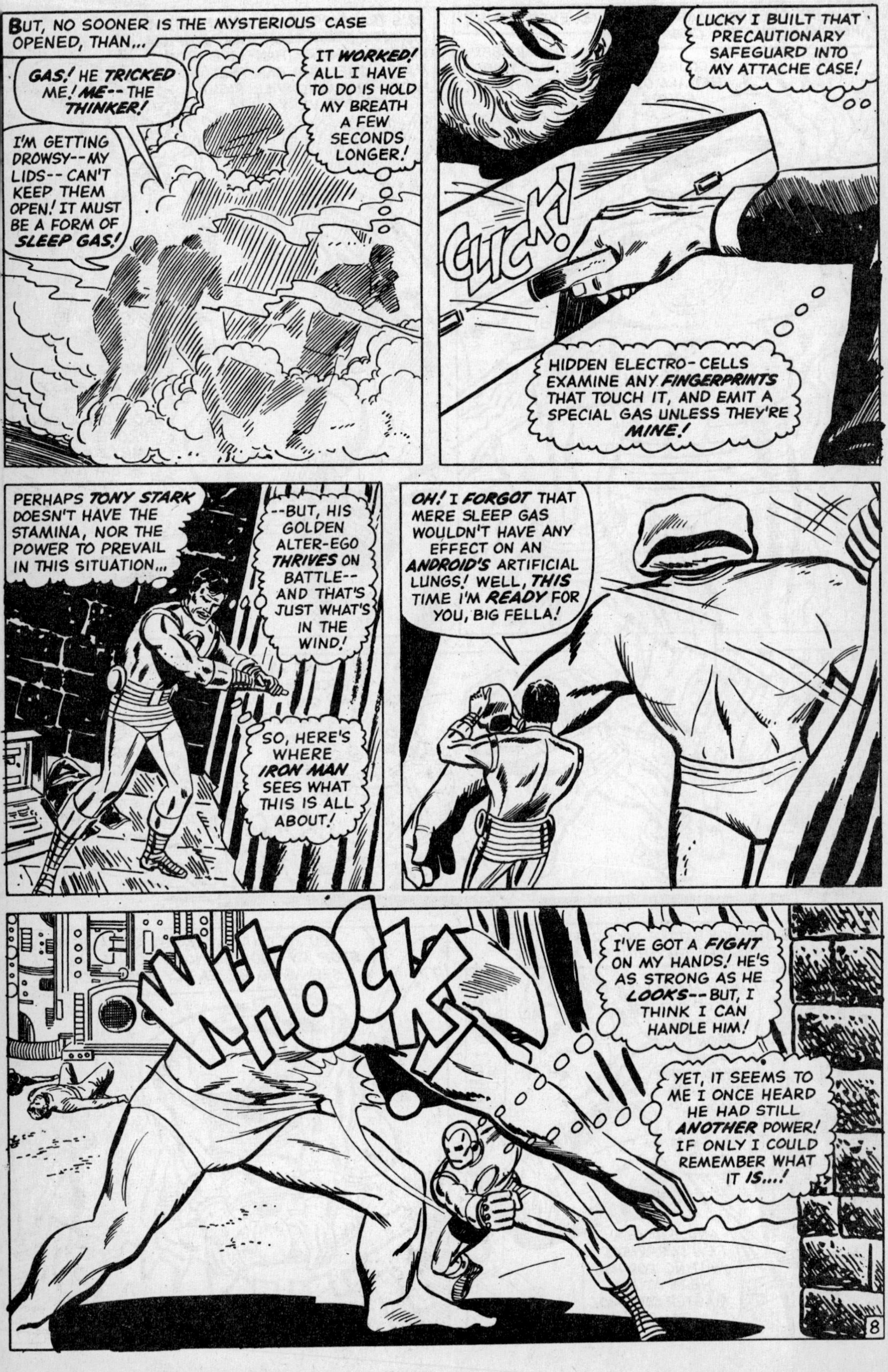
BUT, NO SOONER IS THE MYSTERIOUS CASE OPENED, THAN...
GAS! HE TRICKED ME! ME-- THE THINKER!
I'M GETTING DROWSY--MY LIDS-- CAN'T KEEP THEM OPEN! IT MUST BE A FORM OF SLEEP GAS!
IT WORKED! ALL I HAVE TO DO IS HOLD MY BREATH A FEW SECONDS LONGER!
LUCKY I BUILT THAT PRECAUTIONARY SAFEGUARD INTO MY ATTACHE CASE!
CLICK!
HIDDEN ELECTRO-CELLS EXAMINE ANY FINGERPRINTS THAT TOUCH IT, AND EMIT A SPECIAL GAS UNLESS THEY'RE MINE!
PERHAPS TONY STARK DOESN'T HAVE THE STAMINA, NOR THE POWER TO PREVAIL IN THIS SITUATION...
--BUT, HIS GOLDEN ALTER-EGO THRIVES ON BATTLE-- AND THAT'S JUST WHAT'S IN THE WIND!
SO, HERE'S WHERE IRON MAN SEES WHAT THIS IS ALL ABOUT!
OH! I FORGOT THAT MERE SLEEP GAS WOULDN'T HAVE ANY EFFECT ON AN ANDROID'S ARTIFICIAL LUNGS! WELL, THIS TIME I'M READY FOR YOU, BIG FELLA!
WHOCK!
I'VE GOT A FIGHT ON MY HANDS! HE'S AS STRONG AS HE LOOKS--BUT, I THINK I CAN HANDLE HIM!
YET, IT SEEMS TO ME I ONCE HEARD HE HAD STILL ANOTHER POWER! IF ONLY I COULD REMEMBER WHAT IT IS...!
8

THEN, BEFORE IRON MAN'S STARTLED EYES -- THE ANDROID BEGINS TO -- *CHANGE* --!

NOW I REMEMBER! OF COURSE -- IT'S THE ONE THING THAT ALMOST BEAT THE *FANTASTIC FOUR!*

HIS MOST DANGEROUS POWER IS -- HE HAS THE ABILITY TO *MIMIC* ANY ENEMY -- SUCH AS HE'S DOING *NOW!*

HE'S TRANSFORMED HIMSELF INTO A GIGANTIC *IRON MAN* -- AN ARTIFICIAL, DEADLY, BIGGER-THAN-LIFE IRON MAN -- ONE WHO CAN FEEL NO PAIN -- ONE WHO WILL FIGHT TO THE VERY END!

BOY! IF THERE ARE ANY *EASY* MENACES AROUND, YOU CAN'T PROVE IT BY ME! *I* NEVER SEEM TO GET THEM!

WHONK!

THONK!

I CAN'T *HURT* HIM! HIS BODY HAS BECOME A VIRTUAL *DUPLICATE* OF MY OWN ARMOR -- BUT MANY TIMES LARGER, AND EVEN *STRONGER!*

YET, HIS *OWN* BLOWS ARE SLOWING ME DOWN, AND EVEN WORSE -- THEY'RE STARTING TO DENT *MY ARMOR!*

THEN, AS THE STRANGE BATTLE PROGRESSES, THE SLEEP GAS WEARS OFF THE THINKER AND THE COUNTESS, AND...

IRON MAN! WHERE DID *HE* COME FROM??

I *PREDICTED* THAT HE'D SHOW UP WITHIN THE FIRST HOUR!

AND, I HAVE A FEW *SURPRISES* WAITING FOR HIM HERE AT MY *MASTER CONTROL PANEL!*

BUT YET, IT IS ALMOST A SHAME TO *STOP* MY ANDROID NOW -- SINCE HE SEEMS TO BE EASILY *WINNING!*

THUMP!

9

THINKER! YOU'VE GOT TO STOP THEM! YOUR ANDROID MAY KILL IRON MAN!

SILENCE, YOU FEMALE FOOL!

HOW DARE YOU SPEAK TO ME THAT WAY--AFTER WHAT I'M PAYING YOU!!!

DID YOU THINK YOU COULD GIVE ORDERS TO THE THINKER.??!

I MERELY TOLERATED YOU, COUNTESS! WITH MY BRAINS, I CAN MAKE MORE MONEY IN AN HOUR THAN YOU HAVE EVER SEEN IN A LIFETIME!

BUT, YOU MUST EXCUSE ME NOW! I SEE THAT IRON MAN HAS BROKEN FREE AGAIN! MY ANDROID MAY NEED MY GUIDANCE!

LUCKILY, I CAN MOVE MUCH FASTER THAN MY KING-SIZED SPARRING PARTNER... BUT EACH NEW MANEUVER SHORTENS THE LIFE OF MY POWER TRANSISTORS!

UNHHH! POWER-SAPPING RAYS, SLAMMING ME FROM ABOVE! THIS IS THE WORK OF THE MAD THINKER!

HE MUST HAVE HAD THEM PREVIOUSLY PREPARED--EXPECTING ME TO COME!

YOU DIDN'T THINK I WOULD LET THE OUTCOME OF THIS ENCOUNTER HINGE UPON A BRAINLESS ANDROID ALONE, DID YOU?

ACCORDING TO MY CALCULATIONS, THOSE RAYS WILL HAVE YOU AT MY MERCY IN EXACTLY 35 MORE SECONDS! AND THEN, THE SECRET OF YOUR TRUE IDENTITY WILL BE MINE!

NOT IF I CAN HELP IT!

LET'S SEE IF YOUR COMPUTERS PREDICTED THIS LITTLE GIZMO!

WHAT CAN THAT PUNY DEVICE DO AGAINST MY ALL-POWERFUL RAYS.??

IT CAN EMIT A LITTLE VAPOR, THINKER--A VAPOR OF MY OWN DESIGN!

IT'S CALLED REFLECTING MIST-- AND, YOU'LL SEE WHY IN A FEW SECONDS!

WHOOSH

10

BEFORE THE MAD THINKER CAN MAKE A MOVE, THE REFLECTING MIST DIRECTS THE BEAM OF HIS POWER-SAPPING RAY BACK TO HIS OWN *ANDROID*...

THANKS FOR THE ASSIST, THINKER! I MIGHT NOT HAVE BEEN ABLE TO FINISH HIM OFF SO QUICKLY WITHOUT YOUR RAY! MUCH OBLIGED!

YOU'RE RESOURCEFUL, IRON MAN-- BUT MY COMPUTER PREDICTED A .003 POSSIBILITY OF THIS HAPPENING, AND I'VE SET *OTHER* TRAPS FOR YOU-- AS YOU SHALL *SEE!*

I CANNOT BE DEFEATED AGAIN! I JUST *CANNOT!* EVERYTHING DEPENDS UPON MY REACHING MY MASTER CONTROL PANEL IN *TIME---!*

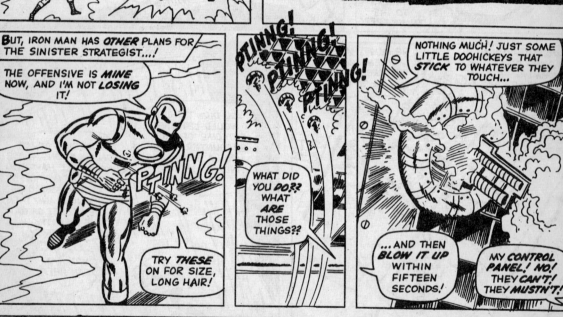

BUT, IRON MAN HAS *OTHER* PLANS FOR THE SINISTER STRATEGIST...!

THE OFFENSIVE IS *MINE* NOW, AND I'M NOT *LOSING* IT!

PT-INNG!

TRY *THESE* ON FOR SIZE, LONG HAIR!

PTINNG! PTINNG! PTINNG!

WHAT DID YOU *DO?? WHAT ARE* THOSE THINGS??

NOTHING MUCH! JUST SOME LITTLE DOOHICKEYS THAT *STICK* TO WHATEVER THEY TOUCH...

...AND THEN *BLOW IT UP* WITHIN FIFTEEN SECONDS!

MY *CONTROL PANEL!* NO! THEY *CAN'T!* THEY *MUSTN'T!*

THWOOM

TSK TSK! A *PITY!* THEY MUST NOT HAVE *HEARD* YOU!

WHAT'S YOUR *NEXT* PREDICTION, THINKER?

OR, WOULD YOU LIKE *ME* TO MAKE IT FOR YOU? THIS WHOLE *PLACE* WILL BLOW SKY HIGH WITHIN A COUPLE OF MINUTES! HOW'S *THAT??!*

YOU'RE *RIGHT!* YOUR EXPLOSION CAUSED A *CHAIN REACTION!* WE'LL ALL BE *KILLED!*

11

HEN IT COMES TO PREDICTIONS, UR BATTING AVERAGE IS ETTING LOWER AND LOWER, STER! BUT, I WON'T OLD IT AGAINST YOU!

LET ME GO! I'VE GOT TO RUN--RUN!

IF YOU DO, IT'LL BE YOUR LAST GALLOP! I'VE GOT A BETTER IDEA!

WAIT! MY ANDROID!! WE CAN'T LEAVE MY ANDROID!!!

SURE, WE CAN! JUST WAVE BYE-BYE LIKE A GOOD FELLA!

BUT, WHERE IS TONY STARK??

I WAS AFRAID SHE'D ASK THAT!

I HELPED STARK ESCAPE WHILE YOU WERE BOTH ASLEEP FROM THE GAS! HE'S PROBABLY BACK JUGGLING HIS MONEY-BAGS BY NOW!

THEN, THIS WHOLE PLOT-- IT WAS ALL FOR NOTHING!

NOT EXACTLY! LOOK AT THE GREAT FIREWORKS DISPLAY YOU GOT OUT OF IT!

BAROOM!

SHORT TIME LATER... STOP SCOWLING, PAL! IF YOU LIKE TO THINK SO MUCH, THIS IS THE BEST PLACE TO DO IT!

AND THERE'S NO RUSH! YOU'LL HAVE MONTHS TO THINK THINGS OUT!

NOT QUITE! I'VE ALREADY COMPUTED A MEANS OF ESCAPE!

YEAH? IN A PIG'S EYE!

AND, IN A LAVISH PENTHOUSE SUITE, WE FIND...

I WISH HE HAD TAKEN ME TO JAIL WITH THE THINKER, INSTEAD OF MAKING ME WALK ALL THOSE MILES HOME!

MEN! I'M BEGINNING TO HATE THEM ALL!

WHILE TONY STARK RETURNS TO HIS FACTORY, ONLY TO FACE A BARRAGE OF NEWSMEN...

SORRY, GENTLEMEN! I CAN TELL YOU NOTHING ABOUT IRON MAN!

HAVE YOU HEARD THAT SENATOR BYRD WILL DEMAND HIS IDENTITY FROM YOU?

I'LL CROSS THAT BRIDGE WHEN I COME TO IT!

BYRD WILL BREAK YOU YET! WAIT AND SEE!

T TOOK ME A ALF HOUR TO SHAKE THOSE REPORTERS, EPPER! WHY WERE THEY LLOWED ON THE PREM-SES?

I'M SORRY, MR. STARK! I WAS BUSY PHONING THE HOSPITAL-- I DIDN'T THINK...

PHONING THE HOSPITAL? WHY?

IT'S HAPPY, BOSS! SOMETHING'S HAPPENED-- AND THEY WON'T TELL ME WHAT IT IS!

NONSENSE! YOU MUST BE IMAGINING THINGS--JUST LIKE YOU IMAGINED THAT ANDROID CREATURE! NOW GET BACK TO WORK!

I WAS RIGHT! HE IS HEARTLESS! HE'S MORE OF A MACHINE THAN A MAN!

HOW COULD I HAVE EVER THOUGHT I-- LOVED HIM--??!

BUT, SECONDS LATER, ALONE IN HIS STUDY...

MY CHEST IS PAIN-ING ME AGAIN! I NEED REST-- QUIET--!

BUT IF SOMETHING IS WRONG WITH HAPPY--I'VE GOT TO GO TO HIM --AS IRON MAN!

AS FOR PEPPER, IT'S BEST THAT SHE DESPISES ME...

...THOUGH IT TEARS MY HEART IN TWO!

AND SO WE LEAVE ONE OF THE WORLD'S WEALTHIEST, HANDSOMEST, MOST ENVIED MEN! HOW LITTLE THE WORLD REALLY KNOWS! AND, HOW LITTLE WE CAN EVEN SUSPECT OF THE STARTLING SURPRISES THAT AWAIT US NEXT ISSUE! SEE YOU THEN!

THE END

The cover is the most important part of any magazine-- the part that makes it more or less likely to sell to a potential reader. As such, editor Stan Lee and publisher Martin Goodman paid particular attention to what went on the covers of the early Marvel titles, often completely scrapping a finished piece in favor of a more compelling image. Once in a while, this would lead to a conundrum.

The cover below, discovered in the Marvel archives, was originally commissioned for TALES OF SUSPENSE #41, featuring Iron Man's battle with the nefarious Dr. Strange. For whatever reason, a different cover image was used on the actual issue-- but this piece resurfaced a month later, slightly revised (to turn Dr. Strange into the Red Barbarian, as seen at right) as the cover to issue #42.

The question remains: why reject a cover only to turn around and print it a month later?

Were two pieces accidentally commissioned, and the second one used later because it had been paid for? Or was this a simple mistake where some-body pasted up the masthead and cover copy for #41 on artwork commissioned for #42, and it was photographed and archived that way?

Or is there another explanation entirely?

We may never know for sure.

MARVEL COMICS

Similarly, a glance at the archived cover to TALES OF SUSPENSE #48 depicted below reveals a different original name for that month's villain. In the published book, he was Mister Doll, but on this initial cover he's referred to as Mister Pain.

Why the change?

We suspect it was at the insistence of the then-more-strident Comics Code Authority, who may have considered "Mister Pain" too violent-sounding in the aftermath of the crackdown on comics in the mid-1950s.

A close examination of the lettering in the story shows that the name was relettered as Mister Doll throughout the issue, certainly after the final artwork had been completed.

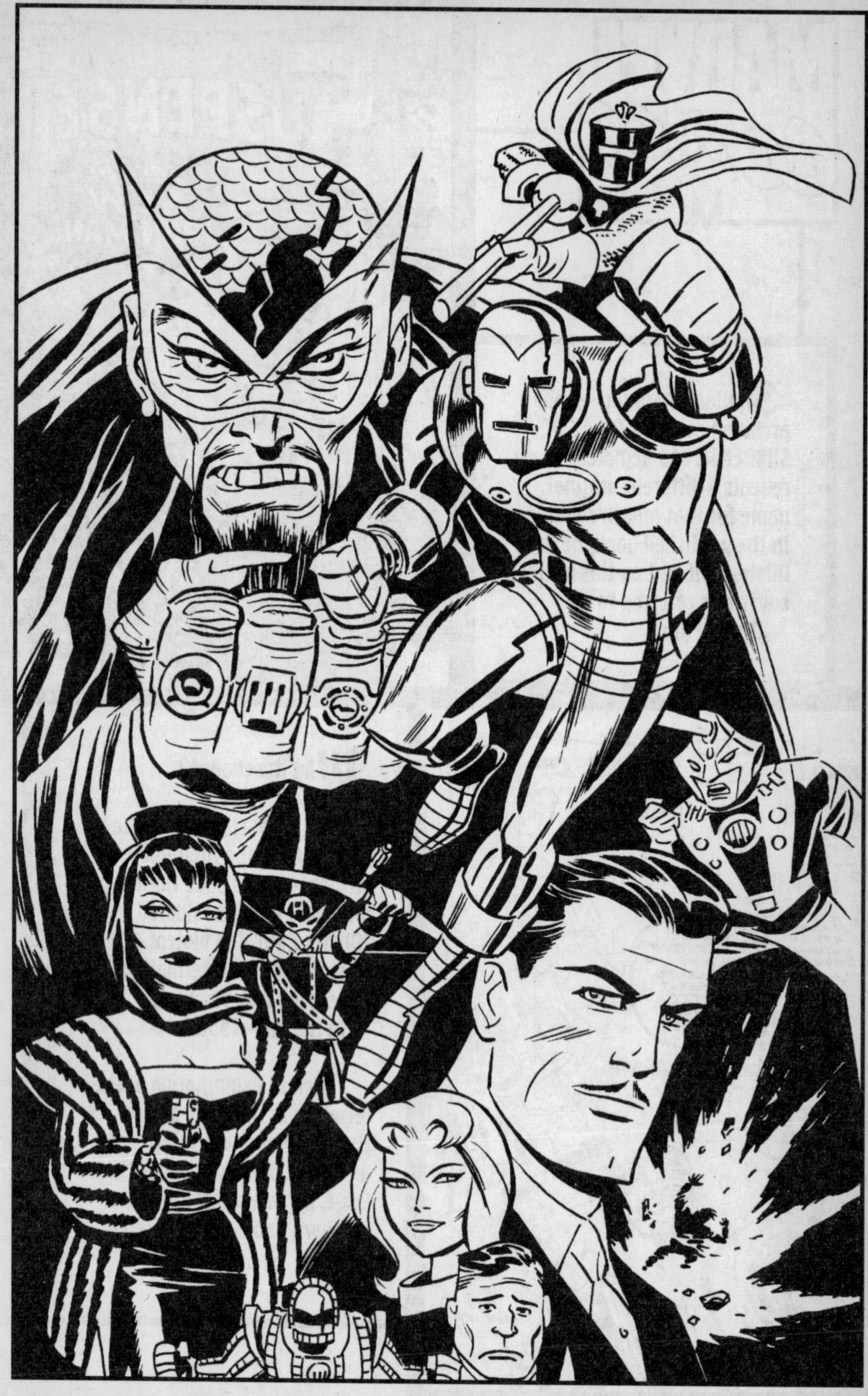